Present value of $1 at the end of period *n* at discount rate *k (concluded)*

Period (n)	Discount Rate (k) 11%	12%	13%	14%	15%	16%	17%	18%	19%	20%
1	0.90090	0.89286	0.88496	0.87719	0.86957	0.86207	0.85470	0.84746	0.84034	0.83333
2	0.81162	0.79719	0.78315	0.76947	0.75614	0.74316	0.73051	0.71818	0.70616	0.69444
3	0.73119	0.71178	0.69305	0.67497	0.65752	0.64066	0.62437	0.60863	0.59342	0.57870
4	0.65873	0.63552	0.61332	0.59208	0.57175	0.55229	0.53365	0.51579	0.49867	0.48225
5	0.59345	0.56743	0.54276	0.51937	0.49718	0.47611	0.45611	0.43711	0.41905	0.40188
6	0.53464	0.50663	0.48032	0.45559	0.43233	0.41044	0.38984	0.37043	0.35214	0.33490
7	0.48166	0.45235	0.42506	0.39964	0.37594	0.35383	0.33320	0.31393	0.29592	0.27908
8	0.43393	0.40388	0.37616	0.35056	0.32690	0.30503	0.28478	0.26604	0.24867	0.23257
9	0.39092	0.36061	0.33288	0.30751	0.28426	0.26295	0.24340	0.22546	0.20897	0.19381
10	0.35218	0.32197	0.29459	0.26974	0.24718	0.22668	0.20804	0.19106	0.17560	0.16151
11	0.31728	0.28748	0.26070	0.23662	0.21494	0.19542	0.17781	0.16192	0.14757	0.13459
12	0.28584	0.25668	0.23071	0.20756	0.18691	0.16846	0.15197	0.13722	0.12400	0.11216
13	0.25751	0.22917	0.20416	0.18207	0.16253	0.14523	0.12989	0.11629	0.10421	0.09346
14	0.23199	0.20462	0.18068	0.15971	0.14133	0.12520	0.11102	0.09855	0.08757	0.07789
15	0.20900	0.18270	0.15989	0.14010	0.12289	0.10793	0.09489	0.08352	0.07359	0.06491
16	0.18829	0.16312	0.14150	0.12289	0.10686	0.09304	0.08110	0.07078	0.06184	0.05409
17	0.16963	0.14564	0.12522	0.10780	0.09293	0.08021	0.06932	0.05998	0.05196	0.04507
18	0.15282	0.13004	0.11081	0.09456	0.08081	0.06914	0.05925	0.05083	0.04367	0.03756
19	0.13768	0.11611	0.09806	0.08295	0.07027	0.05961	0.05064	0.04308	0.03670	0.03130
20	0.12403	0.10367	0.08678	0.07276	0.06110	0.05139	0.04328	0.03651	0.03084	0.02608

Finance For Executives

Managing for Value Creation

FINANCE FOR EXECUTIVES

Managing for Value Creation

FOURTH EDITION

Gabriel Hawawini
INSEAD

Claude Viallet
INSEAD

SOUTH-WESTERN
CENGAGE Learning™

Australia • Brazil • Canada • Mexico • Singapore • Spain
United Kingdom • United States

SOUTH-WESTERN
CENGAGE Learning™

Finance for Executives: Managing for Value Creation, Fourth Edition

Gabriel Hawawini and Claude Viallet

Vice President of Editorial, Business: Jack W. Calhoun

Publisher: Joe Sabatino

Executive Editor: Mike Reynolds

Supervising Developmental Editor: Jennifer Thomas

Sr. Editorial Assistant: Adele Scholtz

Marketing Manager: Nathan Anderson

Marketing Coordinator: Suellen Ruttkay

Sr. Content Project Manager: Diane Bowdler

Sr. Media Editor: Scott Fidler

First Print Buyer: Kevin Kluck

Production Service: KnowledgeWorks Global Ltd.

Production Technology Analyst: Emily Gross

Sr. Art Director: Michelle Kunkler

Internal Designer: Juli Cook/Plan-It-Publishing

Cover Designer: Rokusek Design

Cover Image: © Andrey Yurlov/Shutterstock

Sr. Rights Acquisitions Specialist—Image: Deanna Ettinger

Sr. Rights Acquisitions Specialist—Text: Mardell Glinski Schultz

Library of Congress Control Number: 2010928370

ISBN-13: 978-0-538-75134-6
ISBN-10: 0-538-75134-7

South-Western Cengage Learning
5191 Natorp Boulevard
Mason, OH 45040
USA

Cengage Learning products are represented in Canada by Nelson Education, Ltd.

For your course and learning solutions, visit www.cengage.com
Purchase any of our products at your local college store or at our preferred online store **www.CengageBrain.com**

Printed in the United States of America
1 2 3 4 5 6 7 14 13 12 11 10

To our spouses and children, with love and gratitude.

GH *and* CV

Brief Contents

CONTENTS

PREFACE

Finance is an essential and exciting area of management that many executives want to learn about or explore in more depth. Most finance textbooks, however, are either too advanced or too simplistic for many nonfinancial managers. Our challenge was to write an introductory text that is specifically addressed to executives, and that is both practical and rigorous.

The target audience includes executives directly and indirectly involved with financial matters and financial management—that is, just about every executive. Over the past few years, several thousand managers around the world have used most of the material in this book. The text works well in executive-development programs—including executive masters of business administration (MBA) programs—and corporate finance courses for an undergraduate or MBA audience either as a core text, where a more practical and applied emphasis is desired, or as a companion to a theoretical text to translate theory to practice.

Finance for Executives has a number of important features:

- **It is based on the principle that managers should manage their firm's resources with the objective of increasing their firm's value.**

Managers must make decisions that are expected to raise their firm's market value. This fundamental principle underlies our approach to management. This book is designed to improve managers' ability to make decisions that create value, including decisions to restructure existing operations, launch new products, buy new assets, acquire other companies, and finance the firm's investments.

- **It fills the gap between introductory accounting and finance manuals for nonfinancial managers and advanced texts in corporate finance.**

Finance for Executives is based on modern finance principles. It emphasizes rigorous analysis but avoids formulas that have no direct application to decision making. Whenever a formula is used in the text, the logic behind it is explained and numerical examples are provided. Mathematical derivations of the formulas are given in the appendices that follow the chapter in which they first appear. Recognizing that executives often approach financial problems from a financial accounting perspective, we begin with a solid review of the financial accounting system. We then show how this framework can be extended and used to make sound financial decisions that enhance the firm's value.

- **Most chapters are self-contained.**

Most chapters can be read without prior reading of the others. When knowledge of a previous chapter would enhance comprehension of a specific section, we direct the reader to that previously developed material. Further advice on this score is provided in the section titled "How to Read This Book."

- **It can be read in its entirety or used as a reference.**

The book can be used as a quick reference whenever readers need to brush up on a specific topic or close a gap in their financial management knowledge. A comprehensive glossary and the index at the end of the book help the reader determine which chapters deal with the desired issue or topic. Most financial terms are explained when first introduced in the text; they appear in boldface type and are defined in the glossary.

- **Data from the same companies are used throughout the book to illustrate diagnostic techniques and valuation methods.**

We focus on the same set of firms to illustrate most of the topics covered in this book. This approach provides a common thread that reinforces understanding.

- **Spreadsheet solutions and formulas are included in the text.**

Recognizing that spreadsheets have become part of most executives' tool kit, the text shows the spreadsheet solutions to all the examples, cases, and self-test problems, when applicable. Formulas used in the spreadsheets are shown at the bottom of the tables for an immediate understanding of the solutions and for reproduction of the spreadsheets for personal use.

- **Each chapter is followed by self-test and review problems.**

The self-test problems that appear at the end of each chapter allow the readers to assess their knowledge of the subject. Most of the questions require the use of a financial calculator or a spreadsheet. Detailed, step-by-step solutions to the self-test problems can be found at the end of the book.

The review problems, which follow the self-test problems at the end of each chapter, provide the readers with the opportunity to challenge their knowledge of the subject and give the instructors relevant material to test the student's grasp of the concepts and techniques presented in the chapter. Solutions to review problems are available online only to instructors.

WHAT IS IN THIS BOOK?

Although the book consists of self-contained chapters, those chapters follow a logical sequence built around the idea of value creation. The overall structure of the book is summarized in the following diagram, which illustrates the value-based business model. Managers must raise cash (the right side) to finance investments (the left side) that are expected to increase the firm's value and the wealth of the firm's owners.

WHAT IS IN THIS BOOK?

PART I: INTRODUCTION

Chapter 1:
What does managing for value creation mean?

Chapter 2:
How are balance sheets and income statements constructed?

PART II: FINANCIAL DIAGNOSIS AND MANAGEMENT

Chapters 3 to 5:
How do financial structure and operational efficiency affect a firm's liquidity (Chapter 3), its ability to generate cash (Chapter 4) and its profitability, risk, and capacity to grow (Chapter 5)?

PART III: INVESTMENT DECISIONS

Chapters 6 to 8:
How should firms evaluate investment proposals and select value-creating projects?

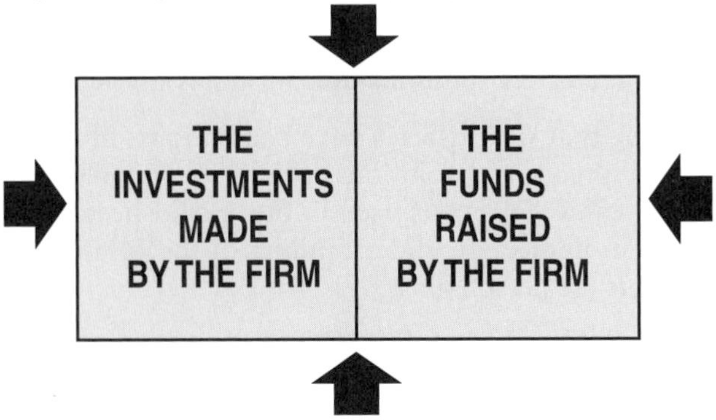

PART IV: FINANCING DECISIONS

Chapter 9:
How do firms raise the funds needed to finance their investments?

Chapter 10:
What is the cost of these funds?

Chapter 11:
What is the best mix of owners' funds and borrowed funds?

PART V: BUSINESS DECISIONS

Chapter 12:
How is a firm valued?

Chapter 13:
How risky is the firm?

Chapter 14:
How do international activities affect the firm's value?

Chapter 15:
Is the firm using its resources to create value?

Part I, Introduction, begins with a chapter that surveys the principles and tools executives need to know to manage for value creation. Chapter 2 explains and illustrates how balance sheets and income statements are constructed and interpreted. As an application, the appendix includes the financial statements of The Home Depot.

Part II, Financial Diagnosis and Management, reviews the techniques that executives should use to assess a firm's financial health, evaluate and plan its future development, and make decisions that enhance its chances of survival and success. The chapters in this part examine in detail a number of financial diagnostics and managerial tools that were introduced in Chapter 1. Chapter 3 shows how to evaluate a firm's liquidity position and operational efficiency. Chapter 4 shows how to assess the firm's ability to generate and control its cash flow. Chapter 5 identifies the factors that drive a firm's profitability, analyzes the extent of its exposure to business and financial risks, and evaluates its capacity to finance its activities and achieve sustainable growth. The financial analysis tools presented in these chapters are applied to The Home Depot, whose statements are included in the Chapter 2 appendix. The analyses appear in the appendices to Chapters 2 through 5.

Part III, Investment Decisions, demonstrates how managers should make investment decisions that maximize the firm's value. Chapter 6 examines the net present value (NPV) rule in detail and shows how to apply this rule to make value-creating investment decisions. Chapter 7 reviews a number of alternative approaches to the NPV rule, including the internal-rate-of-return (IRR) and the payback period rules, and compares them with the NPV rule. Chapter 8 shows how to identify and estimate the cash flows generated by an investment proposal and assess the proposal's capacity to create value.

Part IV, Financing Decisions, explains how managers should make financing decisions that maximize value. Chapter 9 looks at the function of financial markets as a source of cash and examines the role markets play in the process of value creation. Chapter 10 shows how to estimate the cost of capital for a project and for the entire firm. Chapter 11 explains how a firm can make value-creating financing decisions by designing a capital structure (the mix of owners' funds and borrowed funds) that maximizes its market value and minimizes its cost of capital.

Part V, Business Decisions, concludes with four chapters on making value-creating business decisions. Chapter 12 reviews various models and techniques used to value firms, particularly in the context of an acquisition. Chapter 13 provides a comprehensive framework to identify, measure, and manage the risks a firm faces. Chapter 14 looks at financial management and value creation in an international environment where currency and country risks must be taken into account. Chapter 15 summarizes the analytical framework underlying the process of value creation and examines some of the related empirical evidence.

HOW TO READ THIS BOOK

Depending on your background and your needs, you may want to use this book in different ways. Here are a few guidelines.

- If you are unfamiliar with financial management and financial accounting, you may want to begin by reading Chapter 1. It provides an overview of these subjects and will help you understand the fundamental objective of modern corporate finance and the logical relationships among the various issues and topics that make up that field. Although reading the first chapter will facilitate the understanding of those that follow it, it is not necessary to read it to comprehend the rest of the book—the chapters are self-contained.

- If you are not familiar with financial statements, it would be helpful, but not essential, to read Chapter 2 before you continue with the chapters in Part II. Chapter 2 explains balance sheets and income statements.
- If you are not familiar with the techniques of discounted cash flows, you should read Chapter 6 before going through the rest of Part III. Chapter 6 reviews the foundations of discounted cash-flow techniques.
- If you are unfamiliar with the functioning of financial markets, you should read Chapter 9 before you continue with the rest of Part IV. Chapter 9 provides an overview of the structure, organization, and role of financial markets.
- Last, if you have a basic knowledge of accounting and finance, you can go directly to the chapter dealing with the issue you wish to explore. Because the chapters are self-contained, you will not have to review the preceding chapters to fully understand your chosen chapter.

MAJOR CHANGES IN THE FOURTH EDITION

As was the case with the third edition of *Finance for Executives*, we have incorporated in the fourth edition recommendations received from our colleagues at INSEAD and other schools and from a large number of students and executives who have attended courses and seminars in which the book was assigned. Here are the major changes from the last edition:

- All chapters have been updated with the latest available financial information.
- We use a new set of companies, The Home Depot Inc. and Lowe's Companies Inc., to illustrate how to perform a financial analysis using the concepts and techniques presented in Chapters 2 through 5.
- Chapter 12, which covers company valuation, has been revised completely using the concept of "enterprise value," which is now popular with financial analysts.
- We have written a new chapter, Chapter 13, entitled "Managing Risk," that presents a comprehensive framework for managing corporate risk with the objective of creating value, which is the same objective that underlies all the book chapters.
- We have prepared a new set of professionally designed PowerPoint slides to accompany the book.

About the Authors

Gabriel Hawawini (Ph.D., New York University) is the Henry Grunfeld Chaired Professor of Investment Banking at INSEAD, where he served as dean. He taught finance at INSEAD, New York University, Columbia University, and the Wharton School of the University of Pennsylvania, where he received the Helen Kardon Moss Anvil Award for Excellence in Teaching.

Professor Hawawini is the author of ten books and more than seventy research papers on financial markets and corporate finance. He teaches value-based management seminars around the world and sits on the board of several companies.

Claude Viallet (Ph.D., Northwestern University) is emeritus professor of finance at INSEAD. He was visiting professor of finance at Kellogg School of Management, Northwestern University. Before joining INSEAD, he worked as a project manager at a major oil company and as chief financial officer of a service company in Paris.

Professor Viallet has been president of the European Finance Association and has published widely in leading academic and professional journals. He also organizes, directs, and teaches management-development programs in Europe, the United States, Asia, and Latin America and provides consulting services to companies around the world.

Acknowledgments

A number of colleagues and friends have been most generous with the time they spent reading parts of the manuscript for the previous editions and providing specific comments and suggestions. We also have received many useful comments from students and executives to whom the book was assigned.

We want to thank in particular our colleague Professor Pierre Michel, who read the entire manuscript for the fourth edition and made numerous comments that improved the final version, as well as our colleague Professor Lee Remmers, who reviewed the first draft of many chapters. We would also like to express our gratitude to Mrs. Chittima Silberzahn, who assisted us in the preparation of the fourth edition, and Mr. Bennett Stewart of EVA Dimensions LLC, who kindly provided us with the data in Chapter 15.

Below is the list of the individuals who made comments and suggestions to some of the chapters in the current and previous editions of the book. We thank them all for their comments and suggestions.

Soren Bjerne-Nielsen *(Danisco A/S)*
John Boquist *(Indiana University)*
David Borst *(Concordia University)*
Jay T. Brandi *(University of Louisville)*
Dave Brunn *(Carthage College)*
Bruno Chaintron *(La Poste)*
David Champion *(Harvard Business Review)*
Sudip Datta *(Wayne State University)*
Jean Dermine *(INSEAD)*
Hélène Doré *(Deloitte)*
Theodoros Evgeniou *(INSEAD)*
Paolo Fulghieri *(University of North Carolina)*
Dwight Grant *(University of New Mexico)*
George Hachey *(Bentley College)*
Alfred Hawawini *(Carrefour)*
Pekka Hietala *(INSEAD)*
A. Can Inci *(Bryant University)*
Laurent Jacque *(Tufts University)*
Paul Kleindorfer *(The Wharton School)*
Pascal Maenhout *(INSEAD)*
Kenneth J. Martin *(New Mexico State University)*
Roger Mesznik *(Columbia University)*
Pierre Michel *(Universities of Liège and Luxembourg)*
John Muth *(Regis University)*
Jerome Osteryoung *(Florida State University)*
Urs Peyer *(INSEAD)*
Art Raviv *(Northwestern University)*
Lee Remmers *(INSEAD)*
Maryanne Rouse *(University of South Florida)*
Antonio Sanvicente *(IBEC São Paulo)*
Ravi Shukla *(Syracuse University)*
K. P. Sridharan *(Delta State University)*
Aris Stouraitis *(City University of Hong Kong)*
John Strong *(College of William & Mary)*
Matti Suominen *(Aalto University School of Economics)*
Lucie Tepla *(INSEAD)*
Andy Terry *(University of Arkansas at Little Rock)*
Nikhil P. Varaiya *(San Diego State University)*
Maria Vassalou *(Columbia University)*
Theo Vermaelen *(INSEAD)*
Ingo Walter *(New York University)*
David Young *(INSEAD)*

Finally, we thank Devanand Srinivasan, senior project manager at Knowledge-Works Global, and the staff at South-Western Cengage Learning for their help and support in all the phases of development and production. We would like to especially thank Jennifer Thomas, supervising developmental editor; Diane Bowdler, senior content project manager; Nathan Anderson, marketing manager; and Mike Reynolds, executive editor.

Gabriel Hawawini
Claude Viallet
July 2010

Financial Management and Value Creation: An Overview

CHAPTER 1

An executive cannot be an effective manager without a clear understanding of the principles and practices of modern finance. The good news is that these principles and practices can be communicated simply, without sacrificing thoroughness or rigor. Indeed, you will discover that most of the concepts and methods underlying modern corporate finance are based on business common sense. But translating business common sense into an effective management system can be a real challenge. It requires, in addition to a solid understanding of fundamental principles, the determination and the discipline to manage a business according to the precepts of modern finance. Consider, for example, one of financial management's most useful guiding principles:

> **Managers should manage their firm's resources with the objective of increasing the firm's value.**

This may seem to be an obvious statement. But you probably know a number of companies that are not managed to their full potential value. You may even know well-intentioned managers who are value destroyers. Their misguided actions, or lack of actions, actually reduce the value of their firms.

How do you manage for value creation? This book should help you find the answer. Our main objective is to present and explain the methods and tools that will help you determine whether the firm's current investments are creating value and, if they are not, what remedial actions should be taken to improve operations. We also show you how to determine whether a business proposal—such as the decision to buy a piece of equipment, launch a new product, acquire another firm, or restructure existing operations—has the potential to raise the firm's value. Finally, we show you that managing with the goal of raising the firm's value provides the basis for an integrated financial management system that helps you not only evaluate actual business performance and make sound business decisions but also design effective management compensation packages—compensation packages that align the interests of the firm's managers with those of the firm's owners.

This introductory chapter reviews some of the most challenging issues and questions raised by modern corporate finance and gives a general but comprehensive overview. Although the topics of this chapter are examined in detail in later chapters, many of the important terms and concepts are introduced and defined here. After reading this chapter, you should have a broad and clear understanding of the following:

- The meaning of managing a business for value creation
- How to measure the value that may be created by a business proposal, such as an investment project, a change in the firm's financial structure, a business acquisition, or the decision to invest in a foreign country
- The significance of the firm's cost of capital and how it is measured
- The function of financial markets as a source of corporate funds and the role they play in the value-creation process
- A firm's business cycle and how it determines the firm's capacity to grow
- The basic structure and the logic behind a firm's balance sheet, income statement, and cash-flow statement
- Risk, how to define it, and how it affects the firm's cost of capital
- How to measure a firm's profitability
- How to determine if a firm is creating value

THE KEY QUESTION: WILL YOUR DECISION CREATE VALUE?

Suppose you have identified a need in the marketplace for a new product. You believe the product can be manufactured cheaply and rapidly. You are even confident it can be sold for a tidy profit. Should you go ahead? Before you make this decision, you should check the project's *long-term financial viability*. How will your firm finance the project? Where will the money come from? Will the project be sufficiently profitable to cover the cost of the funds required to finance it? More to the point, will the firm be more valuable *with* the project than *without* it? You should answer these questions before making a final decision.

The proposed venture will be financed by the firm's owners, its **shareholders** (you may be one of them), and by those who lend money to the firm, the **debt holders** (a bank, for example). Cash contributed by shareholders is called **equity capital**; cash contributed by lenders is **debt capital**. As with any other resource, capital is not free. It has a cost. Let's assume that the firm's annual **cost of capital** is 12 percent of the total amount of **capital employed**, the sum of equity and debt capital. The firm's owners will find the venture attractive only if its **operating profitability** *exceeds* 12 percent, that is, only if its profitability *before financing it* is higher than the cost of capital of 12 percent. Why? Because a project whose operating profitability *exceeds* its cost of capital should generate *more* cash than is required to pay for the cost of capital. It is that excess cash that makes the firm more valuable. (We will explain this in more detail throughout the book.) In other words, before deciding to go ahead with a business proposal, you should ask yourself the Key Question:

Will the proposal create value?

If, in light of existing information and proper analysis, you can confidently answer yes, then go ahead with the project. Otherwise, you should abandon it.

The Key Question applies not only to a business proposal but also to current operations. If some existing investments are destroying rather than creating value, you should take immediate corrective actions. If these actions fail to improve performance, you should seriously consider selling those investments.

THE IMPORTANCE OF MANAGING FOR VALUE CREATION

We realize, of course, that the Key Question is much easier asked than answered. The next section describes how to apply the **fundamental finance principle** to help you answer the Key Question. Before introducing that principle, we want to explain why management's paramount objective should be the creation of value for the firm's owners. This objective makes business common sense if you think about a firm that fails to create value for its owners: it will be unable to attract the equity capital it needs to fund its activities. And without equity capital, no firm can survive.

You may rightly ask whether we are forgetting the contributions of employees, customers, and suppliers. No firm can succeed without them. Great companies have not only satisfied owners, but also loyal customers, motivated employees, and reliable suppliers. The point, of course, is not to neglect customers, squeeze suppliers, or ignore the interest of employees for the benefit of owners: more value for shareholders does not mean less value for employees, customers, or suppliers. On the contrary, firms managed with a focus on creating value for their owners are among those that have built durable and valuable relationships with their customers, employees, and suppliers. They know that dealing successfully with employees, customers, and suppliers is an important element in achieving their ultimate objective of creating value for their owners.

Indeed, evidence supports the fact that firms that take care of their customers and employees also deliver value to their owners. Consider the results of an annual survey that asked executives, outside directors, and financial analysts to rate the ten largest U.S. companies in their industry according to the following eight criteria: (1) quality of management; (2) quality of products or services; (3) ability to attract, develop, and keep talented people; (4) company's value as a long-term investment; (5) use of corporate assets; (6) financial soundness; (7) capacity to innovate; and (8) community and environmental responsibilities.[1] The twenty companies with the *highest* scores across all industries significantly outperformed the Standard & Poor's market index (an average of 500 companies) during the ten-year period that preceded the ranking. What was the stock market performance of the twenty companies with the *lowest* scores? They were value destroyers. They delivered a *negative* return to their shareholders during the ten-year period that preceded the ranking. An analysis based on only the three criteria that relate to the way companies treat their customers (the second criterion), their employees (the third criterion), and their community (the last criterion) showed similar results.[2]

These results clearly indicate that *the ability of firms to create value for their shareholders is related to the way they treat their customers, employees, and community.* But you should not conclude that the guaranteed recipe for value creation consists of delighting customers, establishing durable relations with suppliers, and motivating employees. Some firms that deal successfully with their customers, employees, and

[1] *Fortune.com*: America's Most Admired Company Ranking.

[2] See Alex Edmans (2008).

suppliers are unable to translate this goodwill into a higher firm value. What should the firm's managers do in this case? They must revise the firm's current business strategy because their shareholders will eventually question the relevance of a strategy that does not allow the firm to produce a satisfactory return on the equity capital they have invested in it. Dissatisfied shareholders, particularly those holding a significant portion of the firm's equity capital, may try to force the firm's management to change course or may try to oust the existing management team. Or, they may simply withdraw their support by selling their holdings to others who might force changes.

Whether shareholders will be successful in getting management to change its strategy, or even be replaced, depends on a number of factors, including the institutional and legal frameworks that govern the relationship between management and shareholders, and the structure and organization of the country's equity markets in which the firm's shares are listed and traded. We simply suggest that *no firm can afford to have delighted customers, motivated employees, and devoted suppliers for too long if it does not also have satisfied shareholders.*

When asked in whose interest corporations are run, Mr. Jack Welch, the former chief executive officer of General Electric, replied, "A proper balance between shareholders, employees, and communities is what we all try to achieve. But it is a tough balancing act because, in the end, if you don't satisfy shareholders, you don't have the flexibility to do the things you have to do to take care of employees or communities. In our society, whether we like it or not, we have to satisfy shareholders."[3]

THE SATURN STORY

In the early 1980s, General Motors (GM), then the world's largest vehicle manufacturer, faced strong competition from foreign producers of small, efficient, reliable, and inexpensive cars. In response to this challenge, GM set up in 1985 a separate company to build an entirely new car, the Saturn. The car was designed, produced, and sold according to the best practices available at the time. Workers were highly motivated, car dealers could not keep up with demand, and customers were extremely satisfied with their cars. According to these criteria, Saturn was an undeniable success story.

The first car rolled off the assembly line in 1990. The project, however, never delivered the rise in the value of GM's shares that management had hoped would occur.[4] Why?

According to knowledgeable consultants, the $6 billion spent to develop, manufacture, and market the Saturn line of models was already so high that for GM to earn an acceptable return for its shareholders it would have had "to operate existing facilities at full capacity forever, earn more than double standard profit margins, and keep 40 percent of the dealers' sticker price as net cash flow."[5]

At the time of this writing, GM announced that it would stop producing its current line of Saturn cars in 2010 after acknowledging that it lost about $20 billion on the project.[6]

---

[3] *Fortune*, May 29, 1995, p. 75.

[4] *Fortune*, December 13, 2004, "GM's Saturn Problem," pp. 199–127.

[5] McTaggart, Kontes, and Mankins (1994), p. 16.

[6] See the *New York Times*, October 1, 2009, "GM to Close Saturn After Deal Fails."

Our question is: how long should a firm fund a project that delights its customers, pleases its distributors, and satisfies its employees but fails to deliver value to its shareholders? Obviously, not very long if it wishes to survive. So what can we conclude about the ultimate purpose of a business enterprise? Is it exclusively about shareholder wealth creation, or is it about a "**stakeholders approach**" that tries to balance the interests of all the parties associated with the firm (its customers, employees, suppliers, and owners)? We believe that this is a false debate. The focus should be on making decisions that raise the value of the firm, *and in doing so, the firm ultimately creates value for its stakeholders and society as a whole.*[7]

THE FUNDAMENTAL FINANCE PRINCIPLE

Recall the Key Question you should ask before making a business decision: will the decision create value? The Key Question can be answered with the help of the fundamental finance principle:

A business proposal—such as a new investment, the acquisition of another company, or a restructuring plan—will create value only if the present value of the future stream of net cash benefits the proposal is expected to generate exceeds the initial cash outlay required to carry out the proposal.

The **present value** of the future stream of expected net cash benefits is the amount of dollars that makes the firm's owners *indifferent* to whether they receive that sum today or get the expected future cash-flow stream. For example, if the firm's owners are indifferent to whether they receive a cash dividend of $100,000 today or get an expected cash dividend of $110,000 next year, then $100,000 is the present value of $110,000 expected next year.

MEASURING VALUE CREATION WITH NET PRESENT VALUE

The difference between a proposal's present value and the initial cash outlay required to implement the proposal is the proposal's **net present value** or **NPV**:

Net present value = –Initial cash outlay + Present value of future net cash benefits

For example, if a firm's owners are indifferent between $100,000 today and $110,000 in one year, then a project that requires $105,000 today to buy a machine that is expected to generate next year a net cash flow of $110,000, has a *negative* NPV of $5,000 because next year's cash flow is worth $100,000 today, which is $5,000 less than the initial cash outlay:

$$\text{NPV} = -\$105{,}000 + \$100{,}000 = -\$5{,}000$$

If the project is undertaken, it would reduce the value of the firm by $5,000.

We can use the NPV concept to restate the fundamental finance principle more succinctly:

A business proposal creates value if its NPV is positive, and destroys value if its NPV is negative.

---

[7]For a discussion on whether creating value for owners also creates value for all the firm's stakeholders, see John Martin, William Petty, and James Wallace (2009).

The proposal's NPV goes to the investors who *own* the project—in other words, to the shareholders of the firm that undertakes the project. This means that the shareholders should be able to sell their equity stake in the company that announced the project for more than they could sell it for if the project were not undertaken, and the difference should be equal to the project's NPV.

The firm's ability to identify the project, and the market expectation that the firm will carry out the project successfully, create an increase in the firm's value and in the wealth of its owners. More precisely, if the shares of the firm are listed and traded on a stock exchange, the market value of the firm (the share price multiplied by the number of shares outstanding) should rise by an amount equal to the project's NPV on the day the project is announced, assuming the announcement is unanticipated and the market agrees with the firm's analysis of the project's profitability. We return to this point later in the chapter when we examine the role played by financial markets in the process of value creation.

ONLY CASH MATTERS

The fundamental finance principle requires that the initial investment needed to undertake a proposal, as well as the stream of net future benefits it is expected to generate, be measured in cash. As Exhibit 1.1 shows, the investors who are financing the proposal—the firm's shareholders and debt holders—have invested *cash* in the firm and thus are interested only in *cash* returns. Note that the cash benefits of a project must not be confused with the increase in the firm's net profit expected from the project, because profits are accounting measures of benefits, not of cash returns.

Chapter 4 identifies the differences between a firm's cash flows, its revenues, its expenses, and its net profit, and Chapter 8 shows how to estimate the cash flows that are relevant to an investment decision.

DISCOUNT RATES

Consider an investment proposal that requires a firm to invest \$100,000 today in order to generate an expected \$110,000 of cash at the end of the year. Suppose that the present value of the \$110,000 is \$100,000. Recall that the present value is the value that makes the firm's owners indifferent to whether they receive \$100,000 today or receive the expected \$110,000 in one year. This is the same as

EXHIBIT 1.1 ONLY CASH MATTERS TO INVESTORS.

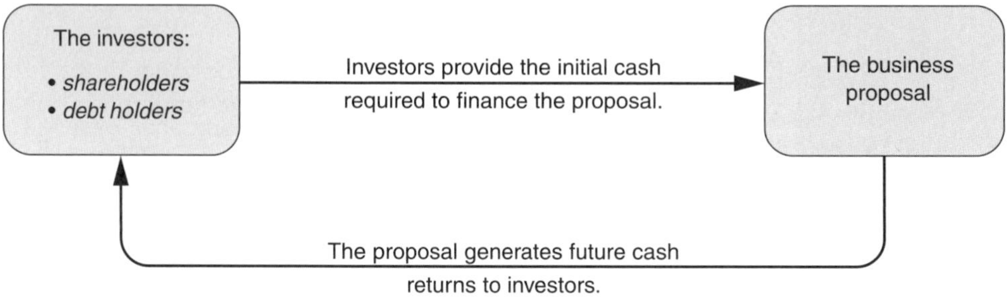
The investors:
• shareholders
• debt holders
Investors provide the initial cash required to finance the proposal.
The business proposal
The proposal generates future cash returns to investors.

saying that the firm's owners expect to receive a return of 10 percent from the project because $100,000 invested at 10 percent will yield $110,000 in one year. The 10 percent is called the **discount rate**: it is the rate at which the future cash flow must be *discounted* to find its present value. In other words, $100,000 is the *discounted value* at 10 percent of $110,000 to be received in one year.

If we want to estimate the NPV of a proposal, we must first discount its future cash-flow stream to find its present value and then deduct from that present value the initial cash outlay required to carry out the proposal. Chapter 6 examines the **discounting** mechanism in detail and explains how to calculate present values and how to estimate a project's NPV when the project has an expected cash-flow stream that is longer than one year.

In our example, we know the discount rate (10 percent) because we already know the expected future cash flow ($110,000) and its present value ($100,000). However, this is not usually the case. In general, a proposal's future cash flow must be estimated and the discount rate must be determined. But what discount rate should be used? *A proposal's appropriate discount rate is the cost of financing the proposal.*

In the example, the return expected from the project must be at least 10 percent to induce shareholders to invest in the project. In other words, because 10 percent is the rate of return required by shareholders to fund the project, it is also the project's **cost of equity** capital. It represents the cost of using shareholders' cash to finance the investment proposal.

A PROPOSAL'S COST OF CAPITAL

Firms typically finance their investment proposals with a combination of equity capital and debt capital, and both shareholders and debt holders require a return from their contribution to the financing of the proposal. When a project is funded with both equity and debt capital, the cost of capital is no longer equal to just the cost of equity. It is the weighted average of the project's cost of equity and its **after-tax cost of debt**,[8] where the weights are the proportions of equity and debt financing in the total capital used to fund the project.

To illustrate, suppose a project will be financed 50 percent with equity and 50 percent with debt. Also, assume the project has an estimated after-tax cost of debt of 4 percent and a cost of equity of 12 percent. Then, the project's **weighted average cost of capital** or **WACC** is equal to 8 percent:

$$\begin{aligned}\text{Project cost of capital (WACC)} &= [4\% \times 50\%] + [12\% \times 50\%] \\ &= 2\% + 6\% \\ &= 8\%\end{aligned}$$

In other words, the contribution of debt financing to the project's cost of capital is 2 percent (50 percent of 4 percent) and that of equity financing is 6 percent (50 percent of 12 percent) as shown in Exhibit 1.2.[9]

If the proportions of equity and debt financing are modified, the WACC will be affected, not only because the financing proportions have changed but also because

---

[8] We explain in Chapter 10 why the cost of debt must be taken after tax.

[9] Note that the cost of debt is measured after tax, that is, if the pre-tax cost of debt is 8 percent and the tax rate is 50 percent, then the after-tax cost of debt is 4 percent. We explain this in Chapter 10.

EXHIBIT 1.2 THE COST OF FINANCING A BUSINESS PROPOSAL IS ITS WEIGHTED AVERAGE COST OF CAPITAL.

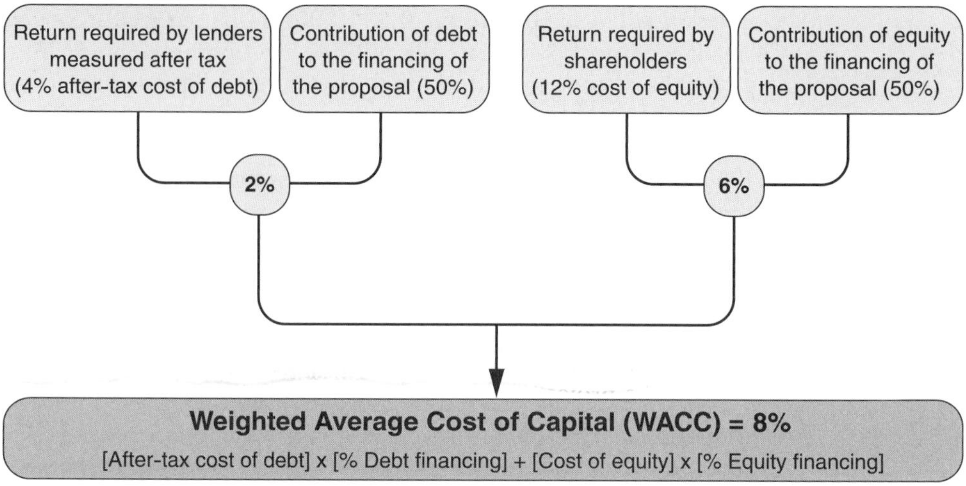

the cost of debt and the cost of equity change when the financing proportions are altered. Chapter 10 shows how to estimate a project's cost of debt as well as its cost of equity and WACC. Chapter 11 demonstrates how the WACC is affected when the financing proportions change.

APPLYING THE FUNDAMENTAL FINANCE PRINCIPLE

The fundamental finance principle has widespread applications in major areas of corporate decision making. In this book, we address the capital budgeting decision (whether an investment project should be accepted or rejected), the capital structure decision (how much of the firm's assets should be financed with equity and how much with debt), the business acquisition decision (how much should be paid to acquire another company), and the foreign investment decision (how to account for multiple-currency cash flows and for the different **risks** of operating in a foreign country). The capital budgeting decision is covered in Chapters 6 through 8, the capital structure decision in Chapter 11, the acquisition decision in Chapter 12, and the management of cross-border operations in Chapter 14. This section provides an overview of these corporate decisions.

THE CAPITAL BUDGETING DECISION

The **capital budgeting decision**, also called the **capital expenditure decision**, is primarily concerned with the acquisition of fixed assets, such as plants and equipment. This is a major corporate decision because it typically affects the firm's business performance for a long period of time. The decision criteria used in capital budgeting, such as the NPV rule and the **internal rate of return (IRR) rule**, are direct applications of the fundamental finance principle.

THE NET PRESENT VALUE RULE

According to the NPV rule, an investment project with a positive NPV should be undertaken and one with a negative NPV should be rejected:

A project should be undertaken if its NPV is positive, and should be rejected if its NPV is negative.

The NPV rule is a direct application of the fundamental finance principle because it says that a project should be undertaken only if it creates value. If the project has a positive NPV, it creates value because the present value of its expected future cash benefits is *greater* than the initial cash outlay required to launch the project. If the proposal has a negative NPV, it destroys value because the present value of its expected future cash benefits is *less* than the initial cash outlay required to launch the project. If a business proposal has a zero NPV, the firm breaks even in the sense that the proposal neither creates nor destroys value: the present value of its expected future cash benefits is equal to the initial cash outlay required to undertake the project.

THE INTERNAL RATE OF RETURN RULE

One of the most commonly used alternatives to the NPV rule, especially in the analysis of capital expenditures, is the IRR rule. A project's IRR is its rate of return *before* taking into account the cost of financing the project. Chapter 7 shows how to calculate a project's IRR.

To use the IRR rule to determine whether a project creates value, we must compare the project's IRR with its WACC. Suppose a project has an IRR of 15 percent, meaning that it is expected to produce a return of 15 percent *before* taking into account the cost of financing the project. The project can be financed at an estimated WACC of 9 percent. Would you invest in this project? The answer is yes because its operating profitability, measured by its IRR, *exceeds* the cost of financing the project, measured by its estimated WACC, and thus the project creates value. If the project's IRR is *lower* than its WACC, the project cannot be financed profitably and should be rejected. In general,

A project should be undertaken if its IRR is higher than its cost of capital, and should be rejected if its IRR is lower than its cost of capital.

Chapter 7 examines the properties of the IRR rule and other capital budgeting rules, and compares them with the NPV criterion.

SOURCES OF VALUE CREATION IN A BUSINESS PROPOSAL

We have seen that firms with positive NPV proposals are expected to generate excess cash profits—that is, cash profits above the level required to remunerate the firm's shareholders. However, there is nothing more powerful than excess cash profits to attract a horde of eager competitors into a new market. Clearly, the challenge for firms with *recurrent* positive NPV businesses is to keep competitors at bay and prevent them from entering their markets. They must erect **entry barriers** that are costly enough to discourage potential competitors. Entry barriers must be costly enough to make the NPV of their competitors' proposals to enter the market negative, but not so costly as to wipe out their own positive NPV.

What are these entry barriers? Some of the most effective barriers are patents or trademarks on products that competitors are legally prevented from copying or imitating. For example, the pharmaceutical companies that own the patent for some of the world's best-selling drugs create considerable value for their owners during the period of time competitors are legally prohibited to produce the same medicine. But legal protection is not the only type of entry barrier. Some companies are able to create value for their shareholders without patent protection. Examples include companies, such as Coca-Cola, that use their superior marketing and advertising expertise to build a powerful brand name that is the source of value creation, or companies, such as Apple, that produce innovative and attractively designed products that cannot be easily imitated by competitors and that lead to strong sales at premium prices. Entry barriers also can be erected by creating a unique distribution channel. For example, Dell Computers has thrived for many years by selling directly to customers, over the phone and via the Internet, computers that are practically manufactured to order and delivered by mail.

Some firms also create value for their owners even without the benefit of a powerful brand name, an innovative and attractive product, or a unique distribution channel. These firms are able to erect entry barriers around markets for standard products that, in principle, could be reproduced easily and legally. How do they do it? They have simply managed to become their market's lowest-cost producer or service provider. Their market is protected because no one else is capable of producing the goods or services as cheaply as they can.

The point we want to make is that positive NPV businesses are not easily created, discovered, or protected. Firms that have developed or found positive NPV businesses have to prevent competitors from entering their markets and reducing their excess profit to zero. This is the essence of strategic management.

THE CAPITAL STRUCTURE DECISION

Why would a firm want to modify its capital structure? We show in Chapter 11 that a firm's capital structure usually affects its value. And there is a particular capital structure for which the firm's value is the highest. The fundamental finance principle can help you determine the **optimal capital structure**, the one that maximizes the firm's value.

Contrary to an investment decision, the decision to change the firm's capital structure is not accompanied by an initial cash outlay. For example, if a firm decides to replace $100 million of equity with $100 million of debt, the net effect on the firm's cash position will be zero. (We ignore the transaction costs required to carry out this capital restructuring, also called **recapitalization**.) Thus, to apply the fundamental finance principle to the capital structure decision, we need to find out whether the value of the firm will increase or decrease as a result of the decision to change the structure of the capital used to finance the firm's assets.

To illustrate, suppose $100 million is borrowed at 5 percent and the corporate tax rate is 40 percent. Interest expenses are $5 million (5 percent of $100 million), and the firm's *taxable* profits are reduced by that amount because interest expenses are tax deductible. The $5 million reduction in taxable profits will save the firm's owners $2 million in taxes *every year* (40 percent of $5 million). Conclusion: *Everything else remaining the same*, the new capital structure should raise the value of the firm to reflect all the tax savings the firm is expected to receive in the future.

Unfortunately for shareholders, other things usually do not remain the same. As the firm replaces increasing amounts of equity with borrowed funds, the *risk* that it may be unable to service its debt (pay interest and repay the loan in full and on time) will rise. This risk, called **financial distress risk**, will reduce the firm's value, thus offsetting the value created by the tax benefits of debt financing. Examples of these costs include the loss of sales caused by customers' reluctance to buy products from a firm that soon may experience financial difficulties, and the inability to obtain supplies from companies that are reluctant to provide goods and services to a firm that may be unable to pay for them. Clearly, *as long as the present value of the expected tax savings from debt financing is higher than the present value of the expected costs of financial distress, additional borrowing will increase the firm's value*. When the present value of the expected tax advantage of debt financing is exactly offset by the present value of the expected costs of financial distress, the firm has reached its optimal capital structure. This **trade-off model of capital structure** is examined in detail in Chapter 11 along with a review of a number of other factors managers must consider when they establish their firm's capital structure.

THE BUSINESS ACQUISITION DECISION

The acquisition of a company is just another type of investment, often a large one. It will create value for the shareholders of the acquiring firm only if the present value of the future net cash flows, that the combined assets of the merged firms are expected to generate after the acquisition, *exceeds* the price paid to acquire the target company's assets (which is the same as the initial cash outlay). Applying the fundamental finance principle, we can write the following:

NPV (acquisition) = – Price paid to acquire the target company's assets
+ Present value of the post-acquisition net cash flows from the merged assets

If this NPV is positive, the acquisition is a value-creating investment. If it is negative, the acquisition is a value-destroying investment. Chapter 12 shows how the post-acquisition cash flows can be estimated, depending on the type of acquisition envisioned. For a pure **conglomerate merger**, one in which the business to be acquired is unrelated to the business of the acquiring firm, the relevant cash flows are those generated by the assets of the target company as "**stand alone**" assets or "**as is.**"

Sometimes, an acquisition is expected to generate **synergies** that will raise sales or reduce costs *beyond the sum of the two companies' pre-acquisition sales and costs*. In this case, we have to estimate the amounts by which the cash flows of the combined assets are expected to increase when the acquisition is achieved, taking into account any synergistic effects. The discount rate that should be used to estimate the present value of these cash flows, and the various steps required to determine whether an acquisition proposal will create value, are the subjects of Chapter 12.

THE FOREIGN INVESTMENT DECISION

As with any other type of investment, investing abroad requires spending cash now with the expectation that the present value of the future net cash flows generated by the investment will be higher than the amount poured into the investment.

Again, the fundamental finance principle is applicable to that situation. The implementation of the principle is somewhat more complicated than for a domestic investment, however, because the cash flows from a cross-border investment are usually denominated in a different currency from the home currency and are exposed to additional risks, such as **currency risk** and **country risk**.

"Currency risk" refers to the risk associated with *unanticipated changes* in the value of the currency in which the investment cash flows are denominated; "country risk" refers to the risk associated with *unexpected events*, such as expropriation and exchange controls, that may adversely affect the project's future cash-flow stream. Chapters 13 and 14 examine these risks in detail and show how they should be taken into account when analyzing a cross-border investment project.

After an investment project is undertaken, currency and political risks must be managed on a day-to-day basis. Chapters 13 and 14 describe how managers can reduce their firm's exposure to these risks. In particular, Chapter 13 explains how managers can use foreign exchange instruments, such as forward, futures, and options contracts, as well as currency swaps, to reduce the effect of currency movements on the cash flows generated by a foreign project.

THE ROLE OF FINANCIAL MARKETS

Financial markets play a key role in the process of business growth and value creation by performing two fundamental functions (see Exhibit 1.3). As **primary markets**, they provide the financing required to fund new business ventures and sustain business growth. They perform this function by acting as intermediaries between individuals and institutions that have a cash surplus they wish to invest and companies that have a cash deficit they wish to eliminate by raising new capital through the issuance of **securities** (certificates that recognize the rights of the holder). As **secondary markets**, they provide an efficient mechanism for trading

EXHIBIT 1.3 THE DUAL FUNCTION OF FINANCIAL MARKETS.

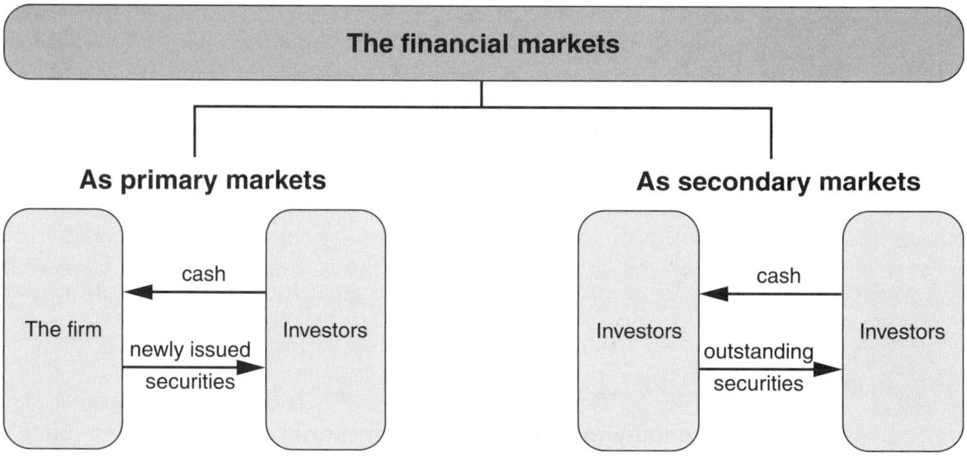

outstanding (already issued) **securities** and translating the value-creating (or value-destroying) decisions of firms into increases (or decreases) in shareholders' wealth via higher (or lower) security prices.

These two functions are not independent of each other. The price of securities in the secondary markets is determined by the buying and selling carried out by traders in these markets. The price observed in the secondary market is then used by **investment bankers** as a benchmark against which they can set the price of newly issued securities in the primary market. (Investment bankers are financial intermediaries who help companies issue securities in financial markets to raise funds. See Chapter 9.) Thus, a well-functioning secondary market facilitates the pricing of new securities issued in the primary market. As a consequence, the two markets are closely related. The structure and organization of financial markets, the role played by investment bankers, and the determination of the price of the securities traded in these markets are examined in detail in Chapter 9. This section provides an overview of the role of financial markets in value creation and as a source of capital.

THE EQUITY MARKET

In an **efficient equity market**, the share price of firms adjusts instantly to new and relevant information as soon as it becomes available to market participants. Relevant information is any piece of news that is expected to affect a firm's future cash-flow stream. In an efficient equity market, stock prices should rise instantly on favorable news and drop instantly on unfavorable news (assuming, of course, that the piece of news was unanticipated). You can see why efficient equity markets play a key role in the process of value creation. As soon as a company announces a business decision that market participants interpret as having a positive NPV, the company's market value should increase by an amount equal to the market's estimation of that decision's positive NPV. Shareholders who wish to cash in do not have to wait for the firm to actually carry out its business decision. All they have to do is sell their shares to immediately receive their part of the value created by the firm's positive announcement. The opposite is also true. If market participants believe the decision has a negative NPV, the company's aggregate market value should fall by an amount equal to the market's estimation of that decision's negative NPV, and shareholders will suffer an immediate loss.

Are equity markets efficient processors of information? And do they actually provide an efficient mechanism to determine reliable stock prices? The evidence indicates that, *on average*, most *well-developed* stock markets around the world can be described as sufficiently efficient to be relied on to provide unbiased estimates of share prices. This is not to say that equity markets are *always* efficient: the Internet stock bubble of 1999–2002 and the financial crisis of 2007–2009 are reminders that, at times, stock prices can significantly move away from their underlying, fundamental value. The story that follows illustrates how the stock markets react to firms' announcements that could affect their future cash-flow streams.

THE VIOXX RECALL

Early in the morning on September 30, 2004, the pharmaceutical company Merck & Co. announced that it would withdraw, and stop selling, its blockbuster arthritis drug Vioxx because of an increased risk of heart attack and stroke. By 10 o'clock that morning, Merck shares were down 24.5 percent from the close of September 29, from $45.07 to $34.02, although the broad stock market index (the Standard & Poor's 500 index) did not change significantly. This $11.05 decrease in share price applied to the 2.22 billion of Merck's outstanding shares represented $24.5 billion of value destruction ($11.05 times 2.22 billion). In other words, at that time, the market anticipated a decrease of $24.5 billion in the present value of Merck's expected future net cash flows, following the decision to retire Vioxx.[10]

It could have been expected that the withdrawal of Vioxx would benefit Pfizer Inc., which makes Celebrex, another arthritis drug belonging to the same class as Vioxx called COX-2 drugs. More precisely, it would have made sense that patients using Vioxx would now use Celebrex, thus increasing the future cash flows of Pfizer by an amount of the same order of magnitude as the decrease in Merck's cash flows. Indeed, by the time Merck's stock price was down to $34.02, shares of Pfizer were trading at $31.50, or $1.32 above the close on September 29. With 7.55 billion shares outstanding, this represents a $9.97 billion ($1.32 times 7.55 billion) increase in the **market capitalization** of Pfizer compared with the $24.5 billion decrease in that of Merck.

At that point, we could conclude that the market was not that efficient, because Pfizer's share price increase was far from reflecting the expected transfer of cash flows from Merck. However, the withdrawal of Vioxx immediately raised questions about the safety of COX-2 drugs. For example, less than a couple of hours after the Vioxx recall, the U.S. Food and Drug Administration issued a public health advisory hinting that the agency would require longer-term studies for COX-2 drugs. The lower-than-expected increase in Pfizer's market capitalization, relative to the decrease in that of Merck's, reflected the market expectation that many patients using Vioxx would be reluctant to switch to Celebrex.

Late on October 6, 2004, the *New England Journal of Medicine* published two reports from researchers who suggested that the side effects that caused the withdrawal of Vioxx were likely to affect all drugs belonging to the same COX-2 class. From the close of October 5 to the close of October 7, 2004, shares of Pfizer went down from $31.29 to $29.99, a decrease of $1.30, or 4.2 percent, while the Standard & Poor's index decreased insignificantly. This represents a decrease of $9.82 billion in the market capitalization of Pfizer.

The Vioxx recall illustrates the role played by the stock markets as instant processors of news, and as translators of relevant information about companies, into value creation when the news is favorable and value destruction when it is unfavorable.

EXTERNAL VERSUS INTERNAL FINANCING

We now consider how financial markets function as primary markets. In this role, they act as a source of external financing to companies. Firms can raise equity capital by issuing shares of common stock in the equity market, or they can borrow by issuing debt securities in the debt markets. As mentioned earlier, to carry out this fund-raising task, they use the services of investment bankers (as opposed

[10]Merck's shareholders sued in 2004 and the company agreed in 2007 to a $4.85 billion settlement in the United States. And the court ordered Merck to appoint a chief medical officer to monitor product marketing and safety, which it did in December 2009. See the *New York Times*, April 4, 2010.

to **commercial bankers**, who extend loans). Short-term funds can be raised by issuing **commercial paper** in the **money market**, and long-term funds can be raised by issuing **bonds** in the corporate bond market. These markets, and the securities that are traded in them, are described in Chapter 9.

Debt financing is necessarily external. Firms either borrow from financial institutions, such as banks and insurance companies, or issue debt securities, such as commercial paper and corporate bonds, in debt markets. Equity financing, however, can be either external (in the form of a new equity issue) or internal. **Internal equity financing** refers to **retained earnings**, the part of a firm's profits that the firm's owners have decided to invest back into their company instead of withdrawing it in the form of a **cash dividend**. The percentage of profit retained within the firm is called the **profit retention rate**. The percentage paid out in the form of a cash dividend is known as the **dividend payout ratio**.

Companies retain part (and sometimes all) of their profit because, for most firms, *regular* access to external equity financing is often unavailable and, when it is available, is relatively expensive. For example, fees must be paid to investment bankers and numerous costs are incurred to comply with the rules and regulations that govern external **equity funding**. Hence, calling on existing and new shareholders to raise external equity through a new share issue is usually an infrequent event in the life of a company. Most firms rely primarily on internal equity financing, through profit retention, to build up their equity capital. *Profit retention is the fuel of sustainable business expansion.* No business can travel the road of long-term growth without retaining some of its profit on a continual basis.

THE BUSINESS CYCLE

Suppose you decide to start a firm that you will call New Manufacturing Company (NMC), and you want to understand the financial implications of this decision. The following dialogue explains the system that ties the various drivers of your new business to the financial implications of your decision.

- "Why does NMC need capital (cash)?"
- "It has to purchase assets. Without the cash provided by investors in the form of equity and debt capital, NMC would not be able to buy assets."
- "Of course, but why does NMC need assets?"
- "It has to generate sales. Without productive assets, such as plants and equipment, NMC would not be able to manufacture goods for sale."
- "Surely, but then why does NMC need sales?"
- "It has to make profits. Without sales revenues, how could NMC generate any profits?"
- "True, but then why does NMC need profits?"
- "It must reward its owners (you and your partners in the business) in the form of dividend payments and must build up its capital base. By retaining part of its profits, NMC will be able to increase its equity capital, which, in turn, will allow it to increase the amount of cash it can borrow from **creditors**. For example, with a **debt-to-equity ratio** equal to one, NMC needs one dollar of additional equity to be able to borrow one extra dollar."

- "I understand. One last question: why does NMC need more capital?"
- "To purchase more assets, to generate more sales, to produce higher profits, to pay dividends, to increase retained earnings, to build up equity capital, to raise new debt, and to grow the business."

This sequence of events is called the firm's **business cycle** and is illustrated in Exhibit 1.4. With an initial capital, made of equity and debt, NMC can finance an equal amount of assets. These assets will be used by NMC to generate sales. The amount of sales will depend on the efficiency with which NMC manages its assets. Efficient asset management means that NMC is able to produce a planned amount of sales using the *least* amount of assets.

Sales eventually will generate a profit. What will NMC do with that profit? Part will be reinvested in the business in the form of retained earnings, and the rest will be distributed to shareholders in the form of dividends. With additional equity capital (in the form of retained earnings), NMC will be able to borrow an amount that will depend on the firm's debt-to-equity ratio. With this added capital, NMC will start a new cycle with more capital to fund more assets, which will produce more sales. The rate at which a company's sales can grow under those circumstances, that is, without issuing new equity capital, is called the **self-sustainable growth rate (SGR)**.

The SGR is an important indicator of business performance and an important component of a firm's financial strategy. Chapter 5 shows how a firm can increase its SGR, and Chapter 15 shows how the SGR concept can be used to formulate an optimal financial strategy.

EXHIBIT 1.4 THE BUSINESS CYCLE.

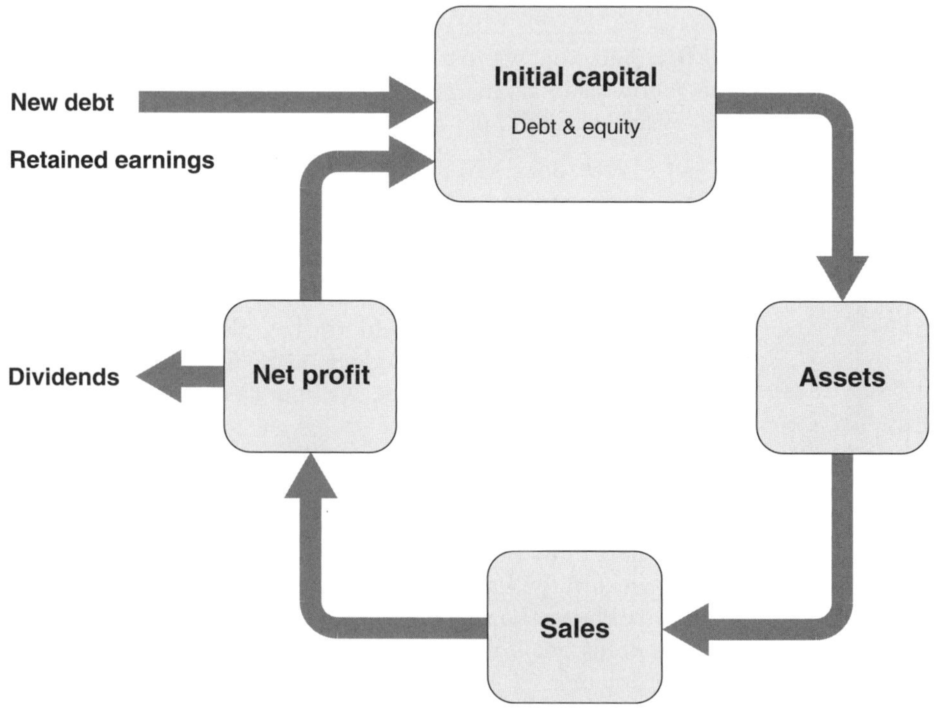

HLC'S FINANCIAL STATEMENTS

Financial statements, such as **balance sheets** and **income statements**, are the products of the financial accounting process. This process, shown in Exhibit 1.5, records financial transactions between the firm and the rest of the world.

THE BALANCE SHEET

The balance sheet is a statement that shows what a firm's shareholders own, called **assets** (such as cash, inventories, and buildings), and what they owe, called **liabilities** (such as money owed to banks and suppliers), at a specific date (usually at the end of a year or a quarter). The difference between a firm's assets and its liabilities is an accounting estimate of the equity shareholders have invested in their firm, called **owners' equity** or **book value of equity**.

As an introduction to the balance sheet, which is analyzed in detail in Chapter 2, we show in Exhibit 1.6 a simplified version of the balance sheet of the Hologram Lighting Company (HLC)—a fictitious firm—on December 31, 2009, and December 31, 2010.

EXHIBIT 1.5 A SIMPLIFIED VIEW OF THE FINANCIAL ACCOUNTING PROCESS.

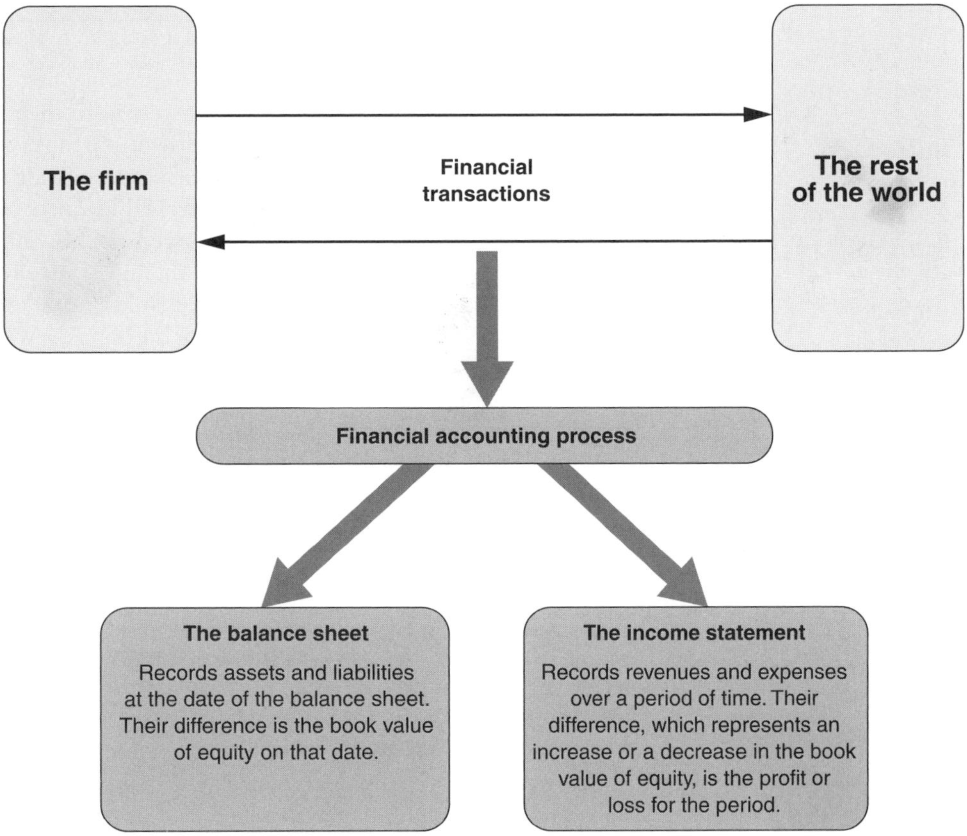

EXHIBIT 1.6 HLC'S BALANCE SHEETS.

FIGURES IN MILLIONS

	December 31, 2009	December 31, 2010
Assets		
• Cash	$ 100	$ 110
• Accounts receivable	150	165
• Inventories	250	275
• Net fixed assets[1]	600	660
Total assets	**$1,100**	**$1,210**
Liabilities and owners' equity		
• Short-term debt	$ 200	$ 220
• Accounts payable	100	110
• Long-term debt	300	330
• Owners' equity	500	550
Total liabilities and owners' equity	**$1,100**	**$1,210**

[1]During 2010, HLC acquired new assets worth $120 million and depreciated its fixed assets by $60 million. Thus, net fixed assets at the end of 2010 were $600 million plus $120 million of new assets less $60 million of depreciation, which equals $660 million.

The upper part of the exhibit lists the firm's assets with their corresponding accounting values at the date of the statement. The lower part lists the firm's liabilities and shareholders' equity with their corresponding accounting values at the same date.

The assets include (1) **cash**; (2) **accounts receivable** (also called **trade receivables** or **trade debtors**), which represent cash owed to HLC by customers who bought goods from HLC but did not yet pay for them; (3) **inventories** (raw materials, work-in-process, and finished goods not yet sold); and (4) **net fixed assets** (long-term assets such as plants, equipment, and buildings). When estimating the net value of fixed assets, an accountant deducts from the purchase price of the assets the **accumulated depreciation expense** to account for the loss in value caused by the wear and tear of the assets or their obsolescence.

How were these assets financed? According to the lower part of the balance sheet, they were financed with (1) short-term borrowing from banks; (2) **accounts payable** (also called **trade payables** or **trade creditors**, accounts representing cash HLC owes its suppliers for purchases made on credit and not yet paid); (3) long-term debt; and (4) equity capital.

A VARIANT OF THE STANDARD BALANCE SHEET: THE MANAGERIAL BALANCE SHEET

Note that HLC's balance sheet shows accounts receivable and inventories as assets, and accounts payable as liabilities. Although this presentation makes sense from an accounting point of view, it does not fit well with the traditional organization of a business for which these three accounts are managed together by operating managers. For this reason, we often will work with a variant of the traditional balance sheet, which we call the **managerial balance sheet**.

THE NET INVESTMENT REQUIRED TO OPERATE A FIRM'S FIXED ASSETS

HLC must hold both trade receivables and inventories, because sales are not paid immediately by customers, and goods must be manufactured and stored before they can be sold. Without inventories and receivables, HLC would be unable to produce goods and sell them. However, these accounts represent required investments that HLC must finance. This financing is partly provided by trade payables because HLC does not have to pay its suppliers immediately. As a result, the *net* investment that HLC must make to support its production and sales activities is equal to the sum of its trade receivables and inventories *less* its trade payables. This net investment in operations, which is required to generate sales and profits from the firm's fixed assets, is called **operating working capital** or **working capital requirement** (**WCR**).

HLC's WCR on December 31, 2009, was equal to $300 million ($150 million of receivables plus $250 million of inventories less $100 million of payables). The optimal management of a firm's WCR, which is one of the most effective ways to create value through improved efficiency, is a major topic of Chapter 3.

HLC'S MANAGERIAL BALANCE SHEET

Exhibit 1.7 shows HLC's managerial balance sheets on December 31, 2009, and December 31, 2010. The upper part of the managerial balance sheet lists the firm's **invested capital**: cash, WCR, and net fixed assets. Note that it is invested capital, not the assets in the standard balance sheet, that must be financed by debt and equity capital. To finance its invested capital, HLC uses the capital listed on the lower part of the managerial balance sheet: short-term debt, long-term debt, and equity capital. Note also that HLC's invested capital is lower than its total assets ($1,000 million versus $1,100 million in 2009 and $1,100 million versus $1,210 million in 2010).

EXHIBIT 1.7 HLC'S MANAGERIAL BALANCE SHEETS.

ALL DATA FROM THE BALANCE SHEETS IN EXHIBIT 1.6. FIGURES IN MILLIONS

	December 31, 2009	December 31, 2010
Invested capital		
• Cash	$ 100	$ 110
• Working capital requirement (WCR)[1]	300	330
• Net fixed assets	600	660
Total invested capital	**$1,000**	**$1,100**
Capital employed		
• Short-term debt	$ 200	$ 220
• Long-term debt	300	330
• Owners' equity	500	550
Total capital employed	**$1,000**	**$1,100**

[1]WCR = (Accounts receivable + Inventories) − Accounts payable. These are given in Exhibit 1.6.

The difference ($100 million in 2009 and $110 million in 2010) is the amount of accounts payable, which, in the managerial balance sheet, is recognized as a source of financing generated by the firm's operations and is accounted for in the WCR.

The managerial balance sheet gives a clearer picture than a standard balance sheet of the structure of the firm's investments and the capital it uses to finance them. Capital invested in cash, operations, and fixed assets is reported under the heading "invested capital." And the sources of capital used to fund these investments are reported under the heading "capital employed." Chapter 3 shows why the managerial balance sheet is a better starting point for analyzing, interpreting, and evaluating the firm's investing, operating, and financing strategies.

HCL's debt-to-equity ratio is equal to one at the end of year 2010 ($550 million of total debt divided by $550 million of owners' equity). Is this capital structure the right one for HCL? How a firm should establish an optimal capital structure is the topic of Chapter 11. At the end of 2010, HCL had $220 million of short-term debt and $330 million of long-term debt. Is this the best combination of short-term and long-term debt for HCL? This question is addressed in Chapter 3.

THE INCOME STATEMENT

The purpose of the income statement, also called the **profit-and-loss (P&L) statement,** is to determine the amount of **net profit** (or **net loss**) the firm has generated during the accounting period. It is the difference between the firm's **revenues** and its **expenses** during that period.

A detailed analysis of a firm's income statement is presented in Chapter 2. In this section, we present a simplified version of HLC's income statement for 2010, shown in Exhibit 1.8, and use it to show how this statement can provide valuable information about a firm's financial performance.

EXHIBIT 1.8 HLC's 2010 INCOME STATEMENT.

FIGURES IN MILLIONS

	Year 2010
Sales	**$1,000**
less operating expenses (including $60 of depreciation expense)[1]	(760)
Earnings before interest and tax (EBIT)	$ 240
less interest expense	(40)
Earnings before tax (EBT)	$ 200
less tax expense[2]	(100)
Earnings after tax (EAT)	$ 100
less dividend payment	(50)
Addition to retained earnings	$ 50

[1]See footnote 1 at the bottom of Exhibit 1.6.

[2]The corporate tax rate is 50 percent of pre-tax profit.

To generate sales revenue, HLC had to incur several types of expenses: first are **operating expenses** (such as the cost of raw material used in the manufacturing of the firm's products, and production costs, including depreciation expense); second is interest expense (the amount of interest HLC must pay to its debt holders); and third is the tax expense the firm must pay on its pre-tax profits.

The difference between sales and operating expenses is called **earnings before interest and tax** or **EBIT** (also called **pre-tax operating profit** or **trading profit**). What is left of EBIT after interest expenses are paid is called **earnings before tax** or **EBT**. After accounting further for tax expense, the remaining profit, which belongs to the firm's shareholders, is referred to as **earnings after tax** or **EAT** (also called net profit). Finally, a portion of EAT is paid as dividends to the firm's shareholders, with the remaining reinvested in the business as retained earnings.

Think of EBIT as profit from HLC's operations that will be shared by three categories of claimants in accordance with a legally established order: first come the debt holders, then the tax authorities, and finally the owners. Debt holders, the first claimants, are entitled to interest payments. They are followed by the tax authorities that are entitled to a tax payment. Finally, the owners or shareholders are entitled to whatever is left. They, in effect, have a *residual ownership* of the firm's pre-tax operating profit.

HOW PROFITABLE IS THE FIRM?

Information provided in a firm's balance sheets and income statements can be combined to evaluate its financial performance, in particular the profitability of its equity capital and the profitability of its invested capital.

THE PROFITABILITY OF EQUITY CAPITAL

How profitable is a firm to its owners? The amount of the investment made by shareholders in the firm is reported as owners' equity on the firm's balance sheet (see Exhibit 1.7) and is also called equity capital. Because earnings after tax represents the shareholders' claim on the firm's profit, the return on their equity investment is equal to earnings after tax divided by owners' equity. This return is called **return on equity (ROE)**:

$$\text{Return on equity (ROE)} = \frac{\text{Earnings after tax (EAT)}}{\text{Owners' equity}}$$

In the case of HLC, EAT is \$100 million in 2010 (see Exhibit 1.8). Dividing this figure by \$550 million of owners' equity at the end of that year (see Exhibit 1.7) gives an ROE of 18.2 percent.[11]

[11] If we divide EAT by owners' equity at the end of 2009 (\$500 million), we get an ROE of 20 percent. Because the amount of equity that generates the year's profit is closer to the average amount of owners' equity (\$525 million), the least distorted measure of ROE is EAT divided by average owners' equity, that is, 19.1 percent (\$100 million divided by \$525 million).

THE PROFITABILITY OF INVESTED CAPITAL

To measure the after-tax profitability of HLC's invested capital, we must use the after-tax profits generated by that investment. This is the firm's *after-tax operating profit,* which is equal to EBIT (1 – Tax rate). The tax rate is applied *before* interest expense is deducted from earnings because we want to measure the profitability of the firm's *total* capital, which is provided by both shareholders and debt holders. We thus need a measure of earnings *before* payments are made to debt holders and shareholders but after tax. This is after-tax operating profit. Dividing the after-tax operating profit by the amount of capital that was used to generate that profit gives a measure of the firm's **return on invested capital (ROIC)**.

$$\text{Return on invested capital (ROIC)} = \frac{\text{After-tax operating profit}}{\text{Invested capital}}$$

ROIC is the same as **return on capital employed (ROCE)**, because invested capital is equal to capital employed, as indicated in the managerial balance sheet shown in Exhibit 1.7. What is ROIC for HLC? After-tax EBIT is $120 million (50 percent of $240 million; see Exhibit 1.8) and year-end invested capital is $1,100 million. HLC's ROIC is thus 10.9 percent ($120 million divided by $1,100 million).[12]

Chapter 5 examines the relationship between a firm's ROE and its ROIC and analyzes in detail how managerial decisions can improve these two measures of profitability.

HOW MUCH CASH HAS THE FIRM GENERATED?

The cash flows expected from a business proposal are a key factor in deciding whether the proposal will create or destroy value. Measuring the cash flows generated by the firm's activities on a continuous basis is essential to verify that these activities indeed create value. We now show how to estimate the amount of cash a firm's activities generate using information in the firm's balance sheets and income statement. Chapter 4 answers this question in detail and examines the managerial implications of running a business with a focus on generating cash and creating value. In this section, we provide some insights on the issue of estimating cash flows from financial statements.

Note that profits generated by a firm such as EBIT, or EAT, do not represent cash. To illustrate this point, consider an increase in sales. Both EBIT and EAT will increase immediately, but the firm's cash holdings will not increase until the customers pay for what they bought. We want to know how much *cash* there is behind EBIT and EAT during the year in which these profits are recorded.

SOURCES AND USES OF CASH

A firm gets cash from three sources: (1) from its operations when customers pay the invoices that were sent to them; (2) from selling assets (an investment decision, or, more precisely, a divestment or asset disposal decision); and (3) from borrowing

[12]If we take initial invested capital, ROIC is 12 percent ($120 million divided by $1,000 million). If we take average invested capital, ROIC is 11.43 percent ($120 million divided by $1,050 million).

or issuing new shares (a financing decision). A firm also spends cash on operating, investing, and financing activities: (1) on operating activities when it pays its suppliers, its employees, and the tax authorities; (2) on investing activities when it makes **capital expenditures**, such as investments in new equipment; and finally (3) on financing activities when it makes interest payments, reimburses debt, and pays dividends. We show in Chapter 4 how data from balance sheets and income statements can be used to measure the respective contributions of operating, investing, and financing activities to the firm's total net cash flow. Of particular interest is the cash flow from operating activities, because operations are at the heart of the business. *A firm that does not generate sufficient cash from its operations over a period of time may destroy value and be headed for trouble.* It can buy time by borrowing or selling assets, but these sources of cash will eventually dry up.

THE STATEMENT OF CASH FLOWS

A firm's cash transactions over the reporting period can be summarized in a statement of cash flows. As an example, we show in Exhibit 1.9 a cash-flow statement for HLC in 2010.

EXHIBIT 1.9 HLC'S 2010 STATEMENT OF CASH FLOWS.

BASED ON THE INCOME STATEMENT IN EXHIBIT 1.8 AND THE BALANCE SHEETS IN EXHIBIT 1.7. FIGURES IN MILLIONS

		Year 2010
Cash flows from operating activities		
Sales	$1,000	
less operating expenses (which include $60 of depreciation expense)	(760)	
less tax expense	(100)	
plus depreciation expense	60	
less cash used to finance the growth of working capital requirement[1]	(30)	
A. Net operating cash flow (NOCF)		**$170**
Cash flows from investing activities		
Capital expenditures and acquisitions	(120)	
B. Net cash flow from investing activities		**($120)**
Cash flows from financing activities		
New borrowings	50	
less interest payments	(40)	
less dividend payments	(50)	
C. Net cash flow from financing activities		**($ 40)**
D. Total net cash flow (A + B + C)		**$ 10**
E. Opening cash		**$100**
F. Closing cash (E + D)		**$110**

[1]This is the difference between the working capital requirement at the end of 2010 and at the end of 2009.

Note that the statement breaks down the firm's total net cash flows into the three main corporate activities we mentioned earlier: operating, investing, and financing activities. HLC has generated a positive net cash inflow from operations of $170 million. Investing activities generated a negative net cash outflow of $120 million (see Note 1 in Exhibit 1.6) and financing activities produced a negative net cash outflow of $40 million. Total net cash flow is thus $10 million ($170 million less $120 million less $40 million) and HLC, which began the year with $100 million of cash, ended the year with $110 million ($100 million plus $10 million) as indicated in the balance sheets in Exhibit 1.7.

Like balance sheets and income statements, statements of cash flow are integral parts of annual reports. There are alternative ways to present the statement of cash flows. Most of them are presented in Chapter 4.

HOW RISKY IS THE FIRM?

A firm does not know for certain whether its projected sales figures will actually be achieved. The firm may sell more or less than what it expected to sell. This is risk. It originates from uncertain sales figures and works itself through the firm's income statement until it finally hits the **bottom line**, that is, the firm's net profits.

How risk is transmitted from sales to profits is illustrated in Exhibit 1.10. First, sales fluctuate because of the uncertain economic, political, social, and competitive environments in which firms operate. These fluctuations are then transmitted to EBIT. This is **business risk**. Business risk is further magnified by the presence of fixed interest expenses that create a **financial risk**. The cumulative effect of business risk and financial risk is transmitted to the firm's earnings after tax, whose resulting fluctuations reflect the total risk. We will discuss risk in several chapters. How a firm should measure and manage the risks it faces is covered in Chapter 13.

Total risk is borne by the firm's *owners*. Owners have a claim on the firm's residual gains (the firm's net profits), but they must bear any residual losses. Whereas the remuneration of HLC's lenders is fixed, the remuneration of HLC's owners is

EXHIBIT 1.10 SOURCES OF RISK THAT AFFECT PROFIT VOLATILITY.

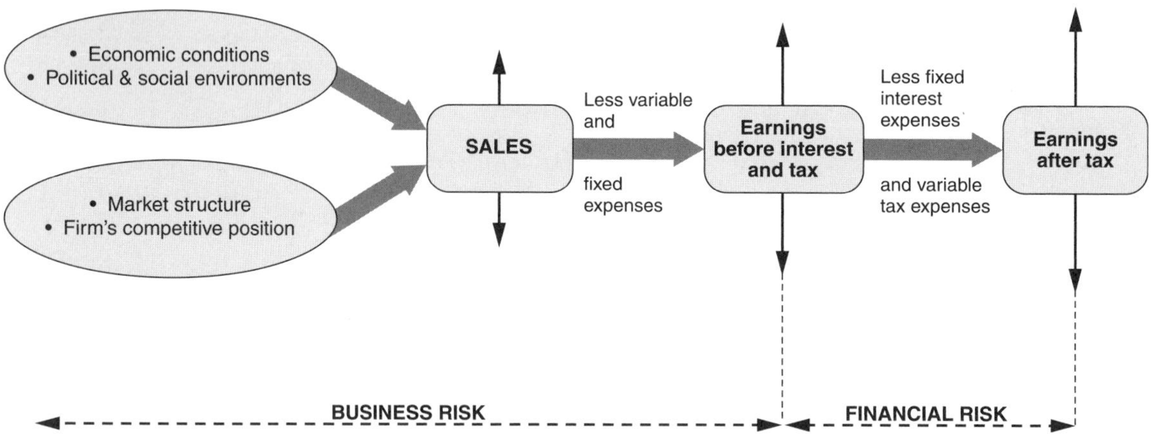

the [illegible]
than deb[illegible]ertain profits. Thus, equity capital, the owners' investment, is riskier
higher rate o[illegible] the lenders' investment. For this reason, HLC's owners require a
lenders. Most sh[illegible]n their equity investment than the return required by HLC's
higher rate of return to[illegible]rs dislike risk—they are **risk averse**—and they require a
uity capital. The effect of [illegible]ensate them for the higher level of risk attached to eq-
Chapter 5. The relationship be[illegible] the firm's profitability is examined in detail in
suppliers of capital is explored in C[illegible] risk and the rate of return required by the
[illegible]rs 10 and 11.

HAS THE FIRM CREATED VALUE?

The ultimate success of a firm is not measured by its ca[illegible]city to grow its sales or produce profits. In the final analysis, what really matters is [illegible]hether the firm's activities are making the firm more valuable. How can we find out [illegible]hether a firm is creating value?

Consider the case of HLC. Has it created value in 2010? We can ans[illegible]er that question by comparing the return it earned on its invested capital that year ($ROIC_{2010}$) and compare it to the cost of that capital (which is HLC's $WACC_{2010}$, its weighted average cost of capital). If $ROIC_{2010}$ is *higher* than $WACC_{2010}$, then we can conclude that HLC has *created* value *that year* because the return on capital *exceeds* its cost. If $ROIC_{2010}$ is *lower* than $WACC_{2010}$, then we can conclude that HLC has *destroyed* value *that year* because the return on capital is *lower* than its cost. We can write the following:

If $ROIC_{2010} > WACC_{2010}$, there is value creation that year

If $ROIC_{2010} < WACC_{2010}$, there is value destruction that year

We have seen earlier that HLC's ROIC is 10.9 percent in 2010. Assume that in 2010 its WACC is 7 percent. Has HLC created or destroyed value that year? Given that its ROIC of 10.9 percent exceeded its WACC of 7 percent, we can conclude that HLC has created value in 2010. Chapter 15 examines in detail how value creation should be measured and how managers should manage their firm with the objective to create value.

SUMMARY

The objective of financial management is value creation. This simply means that before making a business decision, managers should always ask themselves the Key Question: *will the decision create value?* If, in light of existing information and proper analysis, they can confidently answer yes, then they should go ahead with the project.

The Key Question can be answered with the help of the fundamental finance principle. This principle says that a business proposal, such as a new investment, the acquisition of another company, or a restructuring plan, will create value only if the present value of its expected future cash benefits exceeds the initial cash outlay required to undertake the proposal. In other words, a business proposal creates value only if its net present value (NPV) is positive.

...porate decisions,
The fundamental finance principle can be appli... to m...ny the firm's capital such as whether or not to invest in a new ...oject, ...ad. The implementation of structure, to acquire another company, or to inves... ...ture cash-flow stream the decision the principle requires the estimation of (1) ... financing the proposal. In general, is expected to generate and (2) the ...al chapters in this book are devoted to the neither input is easy to determine... estimated, because they lie at the heart of all issue of how these two inputs ...tems. sound financial managem...

Financial markets ...t only a source of capital to finance corporate growth but also a process ... information and an indicator of value creation. Firms, however, do not g... the financial markets to raise fresh equity every time they need additional ...uity capital to finance their growth. They can retain a portion of their profits ...nd use it to meet their funding needs. Profit retention is necessary for a fir... to sustain long-term growth.

Despite the fact that a firm's financial statements are prepared according to accounting conventions that generally do not reflect market values, these statements are often a useful source of information when evaluating a firm's financial performance. The example of Hologram Lighting Company (HLC) provides preliminary answers to the following six questions:

1. How fast can a firm grow without raising new equity? Look at the self-sustainable growth rate (SGR) (more on this in Chapter 5).
2. How profitable is the firm? Look at return on equity (ROE) and return on invested capital (ROIC) (more on this in Chapter 5).
3. How much cash is the firm generating? Look at net operating cash flow (more on this in Chapter 4).
4. How risky is the firm? Look at business and financial risks (more on this in Chapter 3 and Chapter 13).
5. What is the firm's cost of capital? Look at the weighted average cost of capital (WACC) (more on this in Chapter 10).
6. Has the firm created value during the year? Check whether ROIC exceeds the WACC (more on this in Chapter 15).

Managers should be able to answer other important questions: how should they manage their firm's assets? (more on this in Chapter 3); how should they make value-creating investment decisions? (see Chapters 6 to 8 as well as Chapter 14 for decisions in an international context); how should they finance their firm's investments? (see Chapter 9 and Chapter 11); how should they value their firm? (see Chapter 12). Chapter 15 shows that these various issues, together with the fundamental finance principle, form the basis of a comprehensive **value-based management system.**

FURTHER READING

1. Brealey, Richard, Stewart Myers, and Franklin Allen. *Principles of Corporate Finance,* 9th ed. McGraw-Hill, 2008. See Chapter 1.
2. Edmans, Alex. "Does the Stock Market Fully Value Intangibles? Employee Satisfaction and Equity Prices." Working Paper, Wharton School of the University of Pennsylvania, December 30, 2008.

3. Martin, John, William Petty, and James Wallace. "Shareholder Value Maximization—Is There a Role for Corporate Social Responsibility?" *Journal of Applied Corporate Finance* 21 (Spring 2009).
4. McTaggart, James, Peter Kontes, and Micheal Mankins. *The Value Imperative*. The Free Press, 1994. See Chapters 2, 3, and 4.
5. Jensen, Michael C. "Value Maximization and the Corporate Objective Function." In *Unfolding Stakeholder Thinking*, edited by Joerg Andriof, Sandra Waddock, Sandra Rahman, and Bryan Husted. Greenleaf Publishing, 2002.
6. Rappaport, Alfred. *Creating Shareholder Value*. The Free Press, 1998. See Chapter 1.
7. Ross, Stephen, Randolph Westerfield, and Jeffrey Jaffe. *Corporate Finance*, 8th ed. McGraw-Hill Irwin, 2008. See Chapter 1.
8. Stuart, Bennett. *The Quest for Value*. HarperCollins, 1991. See Chapters 1, 2, and 3.

Understanding Balance Sheets and Income Statements

CHAPTER 2

Firms are required by regulatory authorities and the stock markets in which their shares are traded—if they are listed on a stock exchange—to provide financial information about their business transactions. The purpose of financial accounting is to systematically collect, organize, and present financial information according to standard rules known as *accounting principles* or *accounting standards.* The formal outputs of the financial accounting process are the financial statements.

This chapter presents an overview of the two most important financial statements: the balance sheet and the income statement, also called the profit-and-loss statement (P&L statement) or the statement of income. The chapter defines the words and expressions that are commonly used in financial accounting and explains the logic of—as well as the relationship between—the firm's balance sheet and its income statement. After reading this chapter, you should understand the following:

- The terminology generally used in financial accounting
- How balance sheets and income statements are prepared and how they are interrelated
- The most important accounting principles used to prepare financial statements
- How business and financial decisions affect the balance sheet and income statement

FINANCIAL ACCOUNTING STATEMENTS

Financial statements are formal documents issued by firms to provide financial information about their business and financial transactions. Firms must regularly issue at least three primary statements: a **balance sheet**, an **income statement**, and a **statement of cash flows**. Those statements can be found in the **annual report** that firms publish every year.[1] This chapter examines the balance sheet and income statement, leaving the analysis of cash flows to Chapter 4.

The fundamental objective of the balance sheet is to determine the value of the net investment made by the firm's owners (the **shareholders**) in their firm at a specific date. The principal objective of the income statement is to measure the net profit (or loss) generated by the firm's activities during a period of time referred to as the **accounting period** (usually a year). Net profit (or loss) is a measure of the *change* in the value of the owners' investment in their firm during that period. In other words, a profit increases the value of the owners' investment reported in the balance sheet, whereas a loss reduces it.

The balance sheet has information about what shareholders collectively own and what they owe at the date of the statement. The income statement has information about the firm's activities that resulted in increases and decreases in the value of the owners' investment in the firm during a period of time. In addition, notes are usually added to the financial statements. They provide more information about the statements' accounts, such as their nature and how they have been valued.

Financial statements are prepared according to **accounting standards** and **principles**. Accountants follow two prevailing systems of accounting standards: the U.S. standards known as **Generally Accepted Accounting Principles**, or U.S. GAAP, and the international standards known as **International Financial Reporting Standards**, or IFRS.[2] Accountants have some leeway in implementing these standards, mostly in the valuation of some items in the balance sheet and income statement. Thus, to make meaningful comparisons between financial statements over time and across firms, it is necessary to check that the standards used and their implementation are identical from one period to another and from one firm to another. If they are not, adjustments need to be made.

To illustrate how business transactions are recorded in balance sheets and income statements and to facilitate the understanding of the logic behind these statements, we use the fictitious company called Office Supplies (OS) Distributors. OS Distributors is a nationwide distributor of office equipment and supplies. Exhibit 2.1 presents OS Distributors' balance sheets at year-ends 2008, 2009, and 2010. Notes at the bottom of the balance sheets provide detailed information about some of the statements' accounts. Exhibit 2.2 shows the company's income statements for the years 2008, 2009, and 2010. Each income statement spans a full year—in this case, from January 1 to December 31. Two balance sheets flank an income statement: an *opening*, or *beginning*, balance sheet on December 31 of the *previous* year and a

---

[1] In many countries, *publicly* held companies are required to provide additional information and reports. For example, in the United States, publicly held companies are required to provide another report, called the 10-K, to shareholders who request it. The 10-K is a detailed version of the statements appearing in the annual report.

[2] Since 2005, all listed European companies are required to prepare their consolidated financial statements according to IFRS. More than 100 countries around the world (including India, Japan, South Korea, and Canada) have adopted IFRS accounting standards, and U.S. companies are expected to switch to IFRS in 2014. The world's two most influential accounting standard-setting bodies, the U.S. **Financial Accounting Standards Board (FASB)** and the **International Accounting Standards Board (IASB)**, are currently working on reducing the differences between U.S. GAAP and IFRS. A summary of the key differences between the two standards can be found in Jacob Cohen and David Young (2005).

EXHIBIT 2.1 OS DISTRIBUTORS' BALANCE SHEETS.

FIGURES IN MILLIONS

	December 31, 2008		December 31, 2009		December 31, 2010	
Assets						
• **Current assets**						
Cash[1]		$ 6.0		$ 12.0		$ 8.0
Accounts receivable		44.0		48.0		56.0
Inventories		52.0		57.0		72.0
Prepaid expenses[2]		2.0		2.0		1.0
Total current assets		104.0		119.0		137.0
• **Noncurrent assets**						
Financial assets and intangibles		0.0		0.0		0.0
Property, plant, and equipment						
Gross value[3]	$90.0		$90.0		$93.0	
less accumulated depreciation	(34.0)	56.0	(39.0)	51.0	(40.0)	53.0
Total noncurrent assets		56.0		51.0		53.0
Total assets		$160.0		$170.0		$190.0
Liabilities and owners' equity						
• **Current liabilities**						
Short-term debt		$ 15.0		$ 22.0		$ 23.0
Owed to banks	$ 7.0		$14.0		$15.0	
Current portion of long-term debt	8.0		8.0		8.0	
Accounts payable		37.0		40.0		48.0
Accrued expenses[4]		2.0		4.0		4.0
Total current liabilities		54.0		66.0		75.0
• **Noncurrent liabilities**						
Long-term debt[5]		42.0		34.0		38.0
Total noncurrent liabilities		42.0		34.0		38.0
• **Owners' equity**[6]		64.0		70.0		77.0
Total liabilities and owners' equity		$160.0		$170.0		$190.0

[1]Consists of cash in hand and checking accounts held to facilitate operating activities on which the firm earns no interest.
[2]Prepaid expenses is rent paid in advance (when recognized in the income statement, rent is included in selling, general, and administrative expenses).
[3]In 2009, there was no disposal of existing fixed assets or acquisition of new fixed assets. However, during 2010, a warehouse was enlarged at a cost of $12 million and existing fixed assets, bought for $9 million in the past, were sold at their net book value of $2 million.
[4]Accrued expenses consist of wages and taxes payable.
[5]Long-term debt is repaid at the rate of $8 million per year. No new long-term debt was incurred during 2009, but during 2010, a mortgage loan was obtained from the bank to finance the extension of a warehouse (see Note 3).
[6]During the three years, no new shares were issued and none were repurchased.

EXHIBIT 2.2 OS DISTRIBUTORS' INCOME STATEMENTS.

FIGURES IN MILLIONS

	2008		2009		2010	
• **Net sales**	$390.0	*100.0%*	$420.0	*100.0%*	$480.0	*100.0%*
Cost of goods sold	328.0		353.0		400.0	
• **Gross profit**	**62.0**	*15.9%*	**67.0**	*16.0%*	**80.0**	*16.7%*
Selling, general, and administrative expenses	39.8		43.7		48.0	
Depreciation expense	5.0		5.0		8.0	
• **Operating profit**	**17.2**	*4.4%*	**18.3**	*4.4%*	**24.0**	*5.0%*
Special items	0.0		0.0		0.0	
• **Earnings before interest and tax (EBIT)**	**17.2**	*4.4%*	**18.3**	*4.4%*	**24.0**	*5.0%*
Net interest expense[1]	5.5		5.0		7.0	
• **Earnings before tax (EBT)**	**11.7**	*3.0%*	**13.3**	*3.2%*	**17.0**	*3.5%*
Income tax expense	4.7		5.3		6.8	
• **Earnings after tax (EAT)**	**$ 7.0**	*1.8%*	**$ 8.0**	*1.9%*	**$ 10.2**	*2.1%*
Dividends	$ 2.0		$ 2.0		$ 3.2	
Addition to retained earnings	$ 5.0		$ 6.0		$ 7.0	

[1]There is no interest income, so net interest expense is equal to interest expense.

closing, or *ending,* balance sheet on December 31 of the *same* year.[3] We have a complete set of statements for OS Distributors only for the years 2009 and 2010 (the opening and closing balance sheets as well as the in-between income statement).

THE BALANCE SHEET

The main purpose of the balance sheet is to provide an estimate of the cumulative investment made by the firm's owners at a given point in time, generally at the end of the accounting period. This investment is known as **owners' equity**. It is the difference, at a particular date, between what a firm's equity holders collectively own, called **assets** (such as cash, inventories, equipment, and buildings), and what they collectively owe, called **liabilities** (such as debts owed to banks and suppliers):

$$\textbf{Owners' equity} = \textbf{Assets} - \textbf{Liabilities} \qquad (2.1)$$

Many other terms are used to refer to owners' equity, including **shareholders' equity, shareholders' funds, book value of equity, net worth,** and **net asset value.**

OS Distributors' balance sheet in Exhibit 2.1 does not follow the format shown by equation 2.1. In the exhibit, assets are listed in one section and liabilities and

[3]Note that the closing balance sheet at the end of a given year is the same as the opening balance sheet at the beginning of the following year.

owners' equity are listed in a different section. The dollar value of assets, however, is equal to the sum of the dollar value of liabilities and owners' equity because equation 2.1 can also be written as follows:

$$\textbf{Assets} = \textbf{Liabilities} + \textbf{Owners' equity} \tag{2.2}$$

According to equation 2.2, a firm's total assets must have the same value as the sum of its liabilities and owners' equity. In general, balance sheets follow the format of Exhibit 2.1 and equation 2.2.

For companies following U.S. GAAP accounting rules, assets are usually listed on the balance sheet in *decreasing* order of **liquidity**, where liquidity is a measure of the speed with which assets can be converted into cash. Cash, the most liquid of all assets,[4] is listed first, and land, the least liquid of all assets, is shown last. Assets are divided into two categories: **current assets** and **noncurrent** (or **fixed**) **assets**. Current assets are assets that are expected to be converted into cash within one year, whereas fixed assets have a life that is longer than one year.

Liabilities are listed in *increasing* order of **maturity**. **Current** or **short-term liabilities**, which are obligations that must be paid within one year, are listed first. **Noncurrent** or **long-term liabilities**, which are not due until after one year, are shown last. Liabilities are followed by owners' equity, which does not have to be repaid because it represents the owners' investment in their firm.

Assets and liabilities are usually recorded according to the **conservatism principle**. According to this principle, when in doubt, assets and liabilities should be reported at a value that would be *least* likely to overstate assets or to understate liabilities.

OS Distributors' owners' equity was $64 million, $70 million, and $77 million at the end of 2008, 2009, and 2010, respectively. At each of these dates, owners' equity was equal to the difference between the firm's total assets and its total liabilities. For example, on December 31, 2009, owners' equity was equal to the difference between total assets of $170 million and total liabilities of $100 million ($66 million of current liabilities plus $34 million of long-term debt). Note that owners' equity is a **residual value**. It is equal to whatever dollar amount is left after deducting all the firm's liabilities from the total amount of its assets. If total liabilities *exceed* total assets, owners' equity is *negative* and the firm is technically bankrupt. The following sections present a detailed analysis of the balance sheet structure.

Current or Short-Term Assets

Current assets include cash and cash equivalents, accounts receivable, inventories, and prepaid expenses.

Cash and Cash Equivalents

Cash and cash equivalents include cash in hand and on deposit with banks and short-term investments with a maturity not exceeding one year. These short-term investments are usually referred to as **marketable securities**. They carry little risk and are highly liquid, meaning that they can be easily sold (converted into cash) with minimal change in value, that is, with relatively small capital gain or loss.

[4] Cash serves also as a basis for measuring the value of all assets and liabilities.

Examples of marketable securities are **certificates of deposit** issued by banks, shares in **money market funds**, short-term **government bills**, and **commercial paper** issued by corporations with good credit ratings. These securities are described in Chapter 9.

OS Distributors held $6 million in cash at the end of 2008. This amount rose to $12 million at the end of 2009 and then fell to $8 million at the end of 2010 (see Exhibit 2.1). Chapter 4 examines in detail why OS Distributors experienced these particular movements in its cash holdings. Note that OS Distributors did not hold any marketable securities at the dates of the balance sheets.

ACCOUNTS RECEIVABLE

Most firms do not receive immediate cash payments for the goods or services they sell. They usually let their customers pay their invoices at a later date. The invoices that have not yet been paid by customers at the date of the balance sheet are recorded as **accounts receivable**, also called **trade receivables** or, simply, **receivables.** Accounts receivable are debts owed to the firm by its customers and, for this reason, are also known as **trade debtors.** These assets will be converted into cash when customers pay their bills. The amount is usually reported *net* of **allowances for doubtful accounts.** Doubtful accounts arise when management expects that some customers will not meet their payment obligations.

OS Distributors' receivables have grown steadily during the three-year period, rising from $44 million at the end of 2008 to $56 million at the end of 2010 (see Exhibit 2.1). Chapter 3 examines whether this phenomenon should be cause for concern or is justified by the firm's activity.

INVENTORIES

Inventories are goods held by the firm for future sales (finished goods) or for use in the manufacturing of goods to be sold at a later date (raw materials and work in process). Thus, a manufacturing firm normally has three inventory accounts: one for raw materials, a second for work in process, and a third for finished goods. Inventories are reported in the balance sheet at cost unless their market value has fallen below their cost. If, for example, some inventories have become obsolete and have an estimated liquidation value lower than their cost, then the firm should report them at their (lower) estimated value. This method, called the **lower-of-cost-or-market,** is an example of the conservatism principle mentioned earlier.

The cost assigned to materials that have not yet entered the production process at the date of the balance sheet is reported as **raw materials inventory.** In addition, some of the units in production may not yet have been completed. The cost of the raw materials that were used in the production of these units plus the labor and other costs applicable to these unfinished units make up the **work in process inventory.** Finally, the cost of completed units not yet sold at the date of the balance sheet constitutes the **finished goods inventory.**

Inventories for OS Distributors consist of goods purchased from manufacturers and stored in its warehouses until sold to retail stores. Like receivables, inventories have grown during the period 2008 to 2010, rising from $52 million at the end of 2008 to $72 million at the end of 2010. Again, Chapter 3 examines whether this growth should be worrisome or is justified by the firm's operations.

The growth in inventories could be caused by an increase in the price of the items purchased by OS Distributors from its suppliers for resale to its customers. Suppose it paid $100 for an item purchased two weeks ago, $101 for the same item purchased last week, and $102 for the same item purchased this week. OS Distributors holds three identical items in its inventory but paid a different price for each of them. When it sells one of these items to a customer, a question arises: Which one has it sold? The first ($100), the second ($101), or the third ($102)?

If OS Distributors uses the **first-in, first-out** (or **FIFO**) **method** to measure the cost of its inventories, it will assume that it sold the first item it acquired ($100). If it uses the **last-in, first-out** (or **LIFO**) **method**, it will assume it sold the last item it acquired ($102). Alternatively, OS Distributors could use the **average cost method**. In this case, it will assume it sold an item at the average of the three prices ($101). The implication is clear: the firm's financial statements will be different, depending on which of the three valuation methods is adopted. After the sale of one item, two are left in inventories. With FIFO, the reported value of the remaining two items is $203 ($101 plus $102); with LIFO, the value is $201 ($100 plus $101); and with averaging, the value is $202 ($101 plus $101). Furthermore, if we assume that the item was sold to a customer for $110, the reported gross profit will be $10 with FIFO ($110 less $100), $8 with LIFO ($110 less $102), and $9 with the average cost method ($110 less $101). Compared with LIFO, FIFO *overstates* both the value of inventories ($203 instead of $201) and reported gross profit ($10 instead of $8) when prices are rising.

PREPAID EXPENSES

Prepaid expenses recorded on a balance sheet are payments made by the firm for goods or services it will receive *after* the date of the balance sheet. A typical example is the payment for an insurance policy that will provide protection for a period of time that extends beyond the date of the balance sheet. It is recorded as a prepaid expense because the payment is made before the firm can benefit from the insurance coverage. Other common prepaid expenses include prepaid rent and leases. OS Distributors' balance sheets in Exhibit 2.1 indicate that the firm had $2 million of prepaid expenses at the end of 2008 and 2009 and $1 million at the end of 2010.

The way prepaid expenses are accounted for illustrates a key accounting principle, known as the **matching principle**. This principle says that expenses are recognized (in the income statement) not when they are paid but during the period when they effectively contribute to the firm's revenues. Expenses *prepaid* by the firm must be carried in its balance sheet as an asset until they become a recognized expense in its (future) income statement.

Suppose, for example, that on January 1, 2007, OS Distributors paid rent for three years, including rent for 2007. The rent for the first year (2007) would be recorded as an expense in the 2007 income statement. The remaining two-thirds of the total rent paid on January 1, 2007, and not "consumed" during the year 2007, would be reported as prepaid expenses in the balance sheet at the end of 2007. In the balance sheet at the end of 2008, prepaid rent would represent only one-third of the total rent payment. On December 31, 2009, the total rent payment would be completely "consumed" and no prepaid rent would appear in the balance sheet on that date assuming the firm had not entered into a new rental agreement for 2010 and beyond.

NCURRENT OR FIXED ASSETS

Noncurrent assets, also called fixed or **capital assets**, are assets that are expected to produce economic benefits for more than one year. These assets are of two types: tangible and intangible. **Tangible assets** are items such as land, buildings, machines, and furniture, collectively called **property, plant, and equipment**. They also include long-term financial assets, such as shares in other companies and loans extended to other firms. **Intangible assets** are items such as patents, trademarks, copyrights, and goodwill.

TANGIBLE ASSETS

Nonfinancial tangible assets are generally reported at their **historical cost**, which is the price the firm paid for them. As time passes, the value of these assets is expected to decrease. To account for this loss of value, their purchase price, reported in the balance sheet as the **gross value** of fixed assets, is systematically reduced (or written down) over their expected useful life.[5] This periodic and systematic value-reduction process is called **depreciation**. If depreciation is done on a yearly basis, the dollar amount by which the gross value of fixed assets is reduced every year is called an annual **depreciation charge** or **expense**. This dollar amount is determined by the length of the period over which the asset is depreciated and the speed with which depreciation takes place.

Several methods are used to determine the annual depreciation charge. The most commonly used is the **straight-line depreciation method**. When this method is used, the firm's assets are depreciated by an equal amount each year. According to the less frequently used **accelerated depreciation method**, the depreciation charge is higher in the early years of the asset's life and lower in the later years. The *total* amount that is depreciated is the same regardless of the depreciation method used; it is equal to the acquisition cost of the asset, assuming that the asset will be worthless at the end of the period over which it is depreciated.

To illustrate the effect of different depreciation methods, consider a firm that paid $300,000 at the beginning of the year for a machine that will be fully depreciated over a period of three years. Although the $300,000 was paid during the year the asset was bought, this amount is not recognized as an expense for that year. If a straight-line depreciation schedule is applied, one-third of the equipment cost is depreciated every year, and the annual depreciation charge is equal to one-third of $300,000, that is, $100,000. An accelerated depreciation schedule would call for half the cost of the equipment to be depreciated the first year, one-third the second year, and one-sixth the third year. The annual depreciation charges would then be $150,000 the first year (one-half of $300,000), $100,000 the second year (one-third of $300,000), and $50,000 the third year (one-sixth of $300,000).

The value at which a fixed asset is reported in the balance sheet is its **net book value**. If the firm applies the **historical** or **acquisition cost principle** to value its fixed assets, then the net book value of a fixed asset is equal to its acquisition price less the accumulated depreciation since that asset was bought. In the above example,

---

[5]Note that plant and equipment are systematically depreciated, but not land. It is assumed that the value of land does not decline with the passage of time.

EXHIBIT 2.3 COMPUTATION OF NET BOOK VALUE FOR TWO DEPRECIATION METHODS.

FIGURES IN MILLIONS

	Straight-Line Method			Accelerated Method		
	Year 1	Year 2	Year 3	Year 1	Year 2	Year 3
Gross value (acquisition cost)	$300	$300	$300	$300	$300	$300
Annual depreciation charge	($100)	($100)	($100)	($150)	($100)	($50)
Accumulated depreciation	(100)	(200)	(300)	(150)	(250)	(300)
Net book value	$200	$100	$ 0	$150	$ 50	$ 0

the net book value of the equipment at the end of each year after the asset was bought is computed as shown in Exhibit 2.3 for the two depreciation methods.

This example clearly illustrates that fixed asset values reported in the balance sheet can differ considerably, depending on the depreciation method applied. It is therefore important to keep this in mind before comparing the financial performance of different firms on the basis of their financial statements.

INTANGIBLE ASSETS

Intangible assets include patents, copyrights, trademarks, property rights, franchises, licenses, and goodwill. When one firm acquires the assets of another for a price higher than the net book value in the acquired firm's balance sheet, this difference is **goodwill**. For example, suppose Firm A pays $10 million for the assets of Firm B, and the net book value of those assets on Firm B's balance sheet is $7 million. This transaction creates $3 million of goodwill on the balance sheet of Firm A.

Intangible assets are recorded at cost. As in the case of tangible assets, their value is usually gradually reduced as time passes. This cost-reduction process, called **amortization**, follows the same principles as depreciation for tangible assets. An exception is goodwill, which does not have to be amortized. Instead, firms must conduct an annual **impairment test**. If the net book value of the acquired assets, including goodwill, falls below their estimated **fair market value**,[6] goodwill must be reduced by the amount of the difference, called an **impairment loss**. That impairment loss is then reported in the firm's income statement as a reduction in revenues. In the previous example, if Firm A estimates two years after the acquisition of Firm B's assets that the fair market value of these assets is $9 million, it will have to recognize an impairment loss of $1 million by reducing goodwill from $3 million to $2 million ($3 million less $1 million).

OS DISTRIBUTORS' NONCURRENT ASSETS

We can now examine the structure of OS Distributors' fixed assets, as reported in Exhibit 2.1. They include only property, plant, and equipment. Their net book value was $56 million at the end of 2008, $51 million at the end of 2009, and $53 million

[6]Fair market value is usually estimated using a discounted cash-flow technique, explained in Chapter 12.

at the end of 2010. Annual depreciation charges, recorded as expenses in OS Distributors' income statements in Exhibit 2.2, were $5 million, $5 million, and $8 million, respectively.

At the end of 2008, the **book value** of OS Distributors' fixed assets before depreciation (their gross value) was $90 million. This was the price paid when these assets were acquired. Accumulated depreciation was $34 million, so the net book value of the firm's fixed assets was $56 million, which was the difference between their gross value ($90 million) and accumulated depreciation ($34 million).

During 2009, fixed assets did not change, so their gross value remained at $90 million. (See Note 3 in Exhibit 2.1.) **Net fixed assets**, however, dropped to $51 million because accumulated depreciation increased to $39 million, the sum of accumulated depreciation at the end of 2008 ($34 million) and the additional depreciation charge in 2009 ($5 million).

During 2010, OS Distributors enlarged its warehouse at a cost of $12 million. That same year, the firm sold a piece of equipment it no longer needed at its net book value of $2 million. (The equipment was bought some time ago for $9 million and had been depreciated by $7 million.) What was the effect of these two transactions on the value of net fixed assets at the end of 2010? The gross value of the fixed assets increased by $12 million when the warehouse was enlarged and decreased by $9 million when the equipment no longer needed was sold. Together, these two transactions increased the gross value of the fixed assets from $90 million at the end of 2009 to $93 million at the end of 2010 ($90 million plus $12 million less $9 million), as shown in Exhibit 2.1. At the same time, accumulated depreciation increased by $8 million (the 2010 depreciation charge) and decreased by $7 million (the recorded accumulated depreciation of the piece of equipment that was sold the same year). Thus, accumulated depreciation increased to $40 million ($39 million of initial accumulated depreciation plus $8 million less $7 million). Consequently, the net book value of OS Distributors' fixed assets at the end of 2010 was equal to $53 million ($93 million less $40 million).

You could have obtained the same net book value of $53 million in a different way: start with the $51 million of net fixed assets at the end of 2009, add the $12 million cost of the warehouse extension, and subtract both the net book value of the piece of equipment that was sold ($2 million) and the 2010 depreciation charge of $8 million ($51 million plus $12 million less $2 million less $8 million equals $53 million). More generally:

Net fixed assets at the end of a period =
Net fixed assets at the beginning of the period
+ Gross value of fixed assets acquired during the period
– Net book value of fixed assets sold during the period
– Depreciation charges for the period (2.3)

CURRENT OR SHORT-TERM LIABILITIES

Current liabilities include short-term debt, accounts payable, and accrued expenses.

SHORT-TERM DEBT

Short-term debt includes **notes payable**, bank **overdrafts**, **drawings** on **lines of credit**, and short-term **promissory notes**. The portion of any long-term debt due within a year is also a short-term obligation and is recorded in the balance sheet as a short-term borrowing.

OS Distributors' short-term borrowings consist of debt owed to banks and the portion of long-term debt being repaid by the firm at the rate of $8 million per year from 2008 to 2010. In total, short-term borrowing grew from $15 million at the end of 2008 to $23 million at the end of 2010.

ACCOUNTS PAYABLE

Accounts payable, also called **trade payables** or, simply, **payables**, are liabilities to the firm's suppliers of goods and services. Payables arise because the firm does not usually pay its suppliers immediately for the goods and services received from them. As a result, there is a time lag between the receipt of goods or services and payment for them. Until payment is made, the firm must recognize in its balance sheet the credit extended by its suppliers. (For this reason, payables are also known as **trade creditors**.) Accounts payable are equal to the dollar value of the invoices the firm has received from its suppliers but has not yet paid at the date of the balance sheet.

The balance sheets in Exhibit 2.1 show that OS Distributors' payables have increased from $37 million at the end of 2008 to $48 million at the end of 2010. Is that increase justified? This question is examined in the next chapter.

ACCRUED EXPENSES

Accrued expenses are liabilities other than short-term debt and accounts payable that are associated with the firm's operations. They arise from the lag between the date at which these expenses have been incurred and the date at which they are paid. Examples are wages and payroll taxes that are due but have not yet been paid on the date of the balance sheet. Note that the allocation of expenses to the accrued expenses account in the balance sheet is another application of the matching principle.

OS Distributors' accrued expenses were $2 million at year-end 2008 and $4 million at year-ends 2009 and 2010. They consist of wages and taxes payable. **Wages payable** represent compensation for vacation days owed to OS Distributors' employees that had not yet been taken at the date of the balance sheets. OS Distributors must recognize its "debt" to its employees as wages payable in its balance sheet. Similarly, **taxes payable** are the amount of taxes owed at the date of the balance sheets. They are a debt to the tax collection agency and are recognized as taxes payable in the balance sheet until the firm pays its tax bill.

NONCURRENT LIABILITIES

Long-term liabilities reported on the balance sheet are liabilities with a maturity longer than one year at the date of the balance sheet. Examples of long-term liabilities are **long-term debt** owed to lenders, **pension liabilities** owed to employees (to be paid to them when they retire), and **deferred taxes** owed to the government's tax collection agency.

Deferred taxes originate from the difference between the amount of tax due on the firm's reported pre-tax profit and the amount of tax claimed by the tax authorities. These two measures of tax due may differ because firms usually depreciate their fixed assets on a straight-line basis in their financial statements but the tax authorities usually apply accelerated depreciation schedules to the same assets to determine the amount of taxes the firm must pay. Depreciation is a tax-deductible expense, so the two approaches can produce different taxable income and, thus, different tax expenses.

Consider a firm with $1,000,000 of revenues and $700,000 of expenses *before* depreciation charges are deducted. If depreciation charges are $100,000 on the basis of a straight-line depreciation schedule and $150,000 on the basis of an accelerated depreciation schedule, then profit before tax is $200,000 in the first case ($1,000,000 less $700,000 less $100,000) and $150,000 in the second ($1,000,000 less $700,000 less $150,000). If the tax rate is 40 percent, the amount of tax is $80,000 (40 percent of $200,000) when straight-line depreciation is used and $60,000 (40 percent of $150,000) when accelerated depreciation is used. In other words, the firm reports a tax expense of $80,000 in its income statement but actually owes only $60,000 in taxes. The difference of $20,000 between the two tax estimates represents a *postponement,* not an *elimination* of the tax owed to the collecting agency. The amount that is depreciated (the asset acquisition price) and the total amount that is deductible are the same in both cases; hence, the $20,000 must be recognized as a liability in the firm's balance sheet.[7]

OS Distributors had an outstanding (not yet repaid) long-term debt of $50 million at the end of 2008. However, the firm repays $8 million of this debt every year, and this amount is recorded as a short-term borrowing (current portion of long-term debt). As a result, the long-term debt in the 2008 balance sheet was equal to only $42 million ($50 million less $8 million due within a year). At the end of 2009, the firm had repaid $8 million of its outstanding debt, but it still owed $42 million, $8 million of which was due in 2010. Consequently, its long-term debt at that date was $34 million ($42 million less $8 million) and the current portion of its long-term debt was $8 million.

In 2010, the firm borrowed $12 million to finance the extension of its warehouse. (See Note 5 in Exhibit 2.1.) As a consequence, long-term debt increased by $12 million in 2010, while still decreasing by the annual repayment of $8 million. Therefore, the long-term debt at the end of 2010 was equal to $38 million (the initial $34 million less $8 million due within a year plus $12 million of new debt). In general:

Long-term debt at the end of a period =
Long-term debt at the beginning of the period
– Portion of long-term debt due during the period
+ New long-term debt issued during the period (2.4)

OWNERS' EQUITY

As shown in equation 2.1, owners' equity at the date of the balance sheet is simply the difference between the book value of the firm's assets and liabilities at that same

[7]Compared with the straight-line depreciation method, accelerated depreciation schedules overestimate depreciation expenses (underestimate profit before tax) during the beginning of the life of an asset, and likewise underestimate depreciation expenses (overestimate profit before tax) toward the end of the asset's life. Accordingly, the firm pays less taxes during the early years, and more taxes during the later years, of the asset's life.

date. The book value of the investment made in the firm by OS Distributors' owners is reported at the bottom of the balance sheets in Exhibit 2.1. Owners' equity has grown from $64 million at the end of 2008 to $77 million at the end of 2010.

In most balance sheets, the owners' equity account shows several components, each representing a source of equity. Because one of these sources is the firm's reinvested profit, we postpone the presentation of the components of owners' equity (and the reason for the growth of OS Distributors' equity) until after the firm's income statement is discussed.

THE INCOME STATEMENT

The purpose of the income statement, also called the **profit-and-loss** or **P&L statement**, is to present a summary of the operating and financial transactions that have contributed to the change in the firm's owners' equity during the accounting period.[8] The accounting period is usually one year, but limited versions of the income statement can be produced more frequently, as often as quarterly.

We define **revenues** as the transactions that increase owners' equity and **expenses** as the transactions that decrease owners' equity during the accounting period. It follows that the net change in owners' equity during that period, known as **net income**, **net profit**, or, as shown in Exhibit 2.2, **earnings after tax** (EAT), is simply

$$\textbf{Earnings after tax} = \textbf{Revenues} - \textbf{Expenses} \tag{2.5}$$

This relationship is the model used to construct a firm's income statement. The firm's revenues are recorded first. They originate from many sources, including the sales of goods and services and the collection of fees and rental income. Then the firm's expenses are listed. They include material costs, depreciation charges, salaries, wages, administrative and marketing expenses, and interest and tax expenses. Expenses are deducted from revenues in a multiple-step procedure to measure the contribution of different activities to the firm's earnings after tax (see Exhibit 2.2). The revenues and expenses related to the firm's operating activities are shown first followed by those related to nonoperating activities, that is, financing activities. Finally, the tax expense is reported. A detailed explanation of the structure of a firm's income statement is given in the following sections.

Among the many accounting principles used to construct financial statements, two are of particular importance in understanding the income statement. First is the **realization principle**, which says that revenue is recognized during the period in which the transaction generating the revenue takes place, *not when the cash from the transaction is received*. In other words, the firm's revenues increase when a product it sells or a service it renders is invoiced or sent to the customer, not when the cash payment takes place. Revenues are unaffected when payment is made. When the payment is received, the firm adjusts its balance sheet accordingly: cash rises by the amount received, and accounts receivable decrease by the same amount.

The second principle is the matching principle, which was explained in the discussion of the valuation of prepaid expenses. According to this principle, expenses

[8]There is one exception to these definitions. The issuance of new shares increases owners' equity, and the repurchase of outstanding shares decreases it. These transactions, however, are not recorded in the firm's income statement as revenue or expense.

associated with a product or service are recognized when the product is sold or the service rendered, *not when the expense is actually paid.* For example, consider a distribution company that purchases an item from a wholesaler, stocks it, and then sells it. Expenses will increase during the period when the item is sold, not when it was purchased and not when the company paid for it.

The realization and matching principles form the basis of what is known as **accrual accounting.** A consequence of accrual accounting is that a firm's earnings after tax is *not* equal to the difference between the firm's cash inflows and outflows that occurred during the accounting period (the firm's **net cash flow**). For example, the fact that OS Distributors realized a net profit of $10.2 million in 2010 does not mean that the firm has generated $10.2 million of cash during that year. A detailed analysis of the relationship between a firm's profits and its cash flows is presented in Chapter 4.

NET SALES

For most firms, sales are the main source of revenues. The revenues of the accounting period, net of any discounts and allowances for defective merchandise, make up the **net sales** account. OS Distributors' sales grew 7.7 percent during 2009, from $390 million in 2008 to $420 million in 2009. Sales rose to $480 million in 2010. Thus, the growth rate in 2010 was 14.3 percent, almost double the 2009 growth rate. The next chapter examines the consequences of this acceleration in the growth rate in sales on the firm's income statement and balance sheet.

COST OF GOODS SOLD

The **cost of goods sold** (COGS), sometimes called **cost of sales**, represents the cost of the goods the firm has sold during the accounting period. For a distribution company, such as OS Distributors, the cost of goods sold is the acquisition price of the items sold from inventory plus any direct costs related to these items. In a manufacturing firm, goods incur various costs in the process of transformation from raw material to finished product, such as labor and other direct manufacturing costs. These costs make up the value of the finished goods inventory. They become cost of goods sold when the goods are released from inventory for sale. Depreciation expense on plant and equipment is often included in the cost of goods sold, although some firms report depreciation as a separate account in their income statement.

OS Distributors' cost of goods sold consists of goods purchased from manufacturers for resale to retailers. (Depreciation expense on the firm's warehouses is shown separately.) Cost of goods sold rose from $328 million in 2008 to $400 million in 2010.

GROSS PROFIT

Gross profit is the first and broadest measure of the firm's profit shown in its income statement. It is the difference between the firm's net sales and its cost of goods sold. OS Distributors' gross profit was $62 million in 2008, $67 million in 2009, and $80 million in 2010. Gross profit rose from 15.9 percent of sales in 2008 to 16.7 percent of sales in 2010 because the firm's cost of goods sold grew at a slightly slower rate than sales.

SELLING, GENERAL, AND ADMINISTRATIVE EXPENSES

Selling, general, and administrative expenses (SG&As), sometimes referred to as **overhead expenses** or simply **overhead,** are the expenses incurred by the firm that relate to the sale of its products and the running of its operations during the accounting period. Expenses related to the training of salespeople are an example of overhead. For OS Distributors, SG&As amounted to $39.8 million in 2008, $43.7 million in 2009, and $48 million in 2010.

DEPRECIATION EXPENSE

Depreciation expense is the depreciation charge defined in the discussion of the balance sheet. It represents the portion of the cost of fixed assets that is expensed during the accounting period. When a fixed asset is purchased, the firm incurs a cost equal to the purchase price. This cost is recorded in the balance sheet as the gross value of the fixed asset. It is then charged or "expensed" (according to a depreciation schedule) over the years during which the asset is expected to generate some benefits. The amount expensed during each accounting period is recorded in the income statement in the depreciation expense account.[9]

If the firm expensed the full cost of a fixed asset the same year it acquired it, the matching principle would be violated. A fixed asset, by definition, generates benefits beyond the year in which it was purchased. Thus, allocating its full cost to the purchase year would cause a mismatch between expenses and revenues for a number of years.

OPERATING PROFIT

Operating profit is a measure of the firm's profit from continuing operations that takes into account all of the firm's recorded expenses related to its operating activities: its cost of goods sold, its SG&As, and its depreciation expense. It is the difference between the firm's gross profit and the sum of the SG&As and depreciation expense. It measures the profit generated by the firm's normal and recurrent business activities before interest expense, nonrecurrent gains and losses, and taxes. OS Distributors generated an operating profit of $17.2 million in 2008, $18.3 million in 2009, and $24 million in 2010. Operating profit, measured as a percentage of sales, rose from 4.4 percent of sales in 2008 to 5 percent of sales in 2010.

SPECIAL ITEMS

We have grouped under this heading a number of special items such as (1) extraordinary and exceptional losses and gains, (2) nonrecurring items, (3) losses and gains related to discontinued operations, and (4) impairment losses resulting from a reduction in the value of goodwill. Extraordinary losses and gains are *unusual* and *infrequent* items such as a loss from the destruction of assets caused by fire or a gain from the restructuring of troubled debt. They are reported net of tax. Nonrecurring items are items that are *either* unusual in nature *or* infrequent in occurrence

[9]Note that a "cost" can be either "capitalized" (meaning that it is recorded in the balance sheet) or "expensed" (meaning that it is recorded in the income statement).

such as gains or losses on the sale of fixed assets. OS Distributors had no special items to report in its income statements.

EARNINGS BEFORE INTEREST AND TAX (EBIT)

Earnings before interest and tax, or **EBIT,** is the firm's operating profit less any special items such as earnings, capital gains, or losses from businesses or other investments that were sold during the accounting period. Because OS Distributors has not reported any special items in 2008, 2009, and 2010 (see the company's income statements in Exhibit 2.2), its earnings before interest and tax in each of these three years is the same as its operating profits. Chapter 5 shows that EBIT plays an important role in the analysis of a firm's profitability because it enables the comparison of profitability for firms with different debt policies and tax obligations.

NET INTEREST EXPENSE

Net interest expense is the interest expense incurred by the firm on its borrowings less any income it received from its financial investments during the accounting period. OS Distributors has no interest income (see Note 1 of the company's income statements); hence, the firm's net interest expense is equal to its total interest expense.

EARNINGS BEFORE TAX (EBT)

Earnings before tax, or **EBT,** is the difference between the firm's EBIT and its net interest expense. It is a measure of a firm's profits before taking taxation into account. OS Distributors' EBT was $11.7 million in 2008, $13.3 million in 2009, and $17 million in 2010. Expressed as a percentage of sales, EBT grew from 3 percent of sales in 2008 to 3.5 percent of sales in 2010. This improvement in the firm's pre-tax profits in comparison to its sales is analyzed in detail in Chapter 5.

INCOME TAX EXPENSE

The income tax expense account is a tax provision computed in accordance with the firm's accounting rules. As mentioned earlier, this tax provision frequently differs from the actual income tax that the firm must pay. The difference is accounted for in the deferred tax account in the balance sheet. OS Distributors has no deferred taxes. Tax expense is thus equal to 40 percent of the firm's pre-tax profits.

EARNINGS AFTER TAX (EAT)

Earnings after tax, or **EAT,** are obtained by deducting the firm's income tax expense from its reported pre-tax profits, or EBT. It is also called the firm's **net earnings, net profit,** or **net income,** and often is referred to as the firm's **bottom line.** When earnings after tax are positive, the firm has generated a profit and is said to be **in the black.** When its earnings after tax are negative, the firm has generated a loss and is said to be **in the red.** More precisely, earnings after tax are a measure of the net change in owners' equity resulting from the transactions recorded in the income statement during the accounting period.

OS Distributors' earnings after tax were $7 million in 2008, $8 million in 2009, and $10.2 million in 2010. As a percentage of sales, they grew from 1.8 percent in 2008 to 2.1 percent in 2010. Are the levels and growth rates of OS Distributors' earnings after tax adequate? The answer to this important question is the topic of Chapter 5.

RECONCILING BALANCE SHEETS AND INCOME STATEMENTS

Transactions other than those recorded in the income statement can also affect owners' equity. For example, when a firm declares a **cash dividend** to be paid to its owners, the book value of owners' equity in the firm's balance sheet decreases by the amount of the declared **dividend**. Thus, the *net* increase in owners' equity is the difference between net earnings and dividends. This difference is called *addition to retained earnings*. When a firm sells (issues) new shares during the accounting period, the amount raised, less issuance costs, increases the firm's owners' equity. Conversely, when a firm repurchases some of its own shares, the amount paid to the shareholders who tender their shares, less transaction costs, decreases the firm's owners' equity. In general,

Net change in owners' equity = Earnings after tax
− Dividends
+ Amount raised by new share issuance
− Amount paid for share repurchase (2.6)

OS Distributors did not issue or repurchase shares during the three-year period from 2008 to 2010. (See Note 6 in Exhibit 2.1.) As a result, each year's change in owners' equity was exactly equal to the addition to retained earnings from that year. Additions to retained earnings are reported at the bottom of Exhibit 2.2. OS Distributors retained $5 million of its net earnings at the end of 2008, $6 million at the end of 2009, and $7 million at the end of 2010. Therefore, owners' equity at the end of 2009 was equal to $70 million, the sum of owners' equity at the end of 2008 ($64 million) and earnings retained in 2009 ($6 million). At the end of 2010, owners' equity had grown to $77 million, the sum of owners' equity at the end of 2009 ($70 million) and earnings retained in 2010 ($7 million).

The link between a firm's balance sheets and its income statements is illustrated in Exhibit 2.4 for OS Distributors. On the left side of this exhibit is OS Distributors' balance sheet drawn up on December 31, 2009, and on the right side is its balance sheet drawn up on December 31, 2010. Between the two balance sheets is the income statement for 2010. The balance-sheet identity, expressed in equation 2.2, is illustrated by showing the book value of the firm's assets on the left side and the sum of its liabilities and owners' equity on the other side. The income statement identity, expressed in equation 2.5, is illustrated by showing the firm's revenues on the left side and the sum of its expenses and its reported profits on the right side.

OS Distributors generated $480 million of sales revenues during 2010. To get those sales, it used $170 million of assets (as indicated on the balance sheet at the end of 2009). After deducting $469.8 million of total expenses from its sales, OS Distributors reported a net profit of $10.2 million in 2010. It declared a dividend of $3.2 million and retained the rest ($7 million). Because it had not raised new equity in 2010, the firm's owners' equity increased at the end of 2010 to $77 million,

EXHIBIT 2.4 OS DISTRIBUTORS: THE LINK BETWEEN THE BALANCE SHEETS AND THE INCOME STATEMENT.

DATA FROM EXHIBIT 2.1 AND EXHIBIT 2.2. FIGURES IN MILLIONS

Balance Sheet December 31, 2009	Income Statement Year 2010	Balance Sheet December 31, 2010

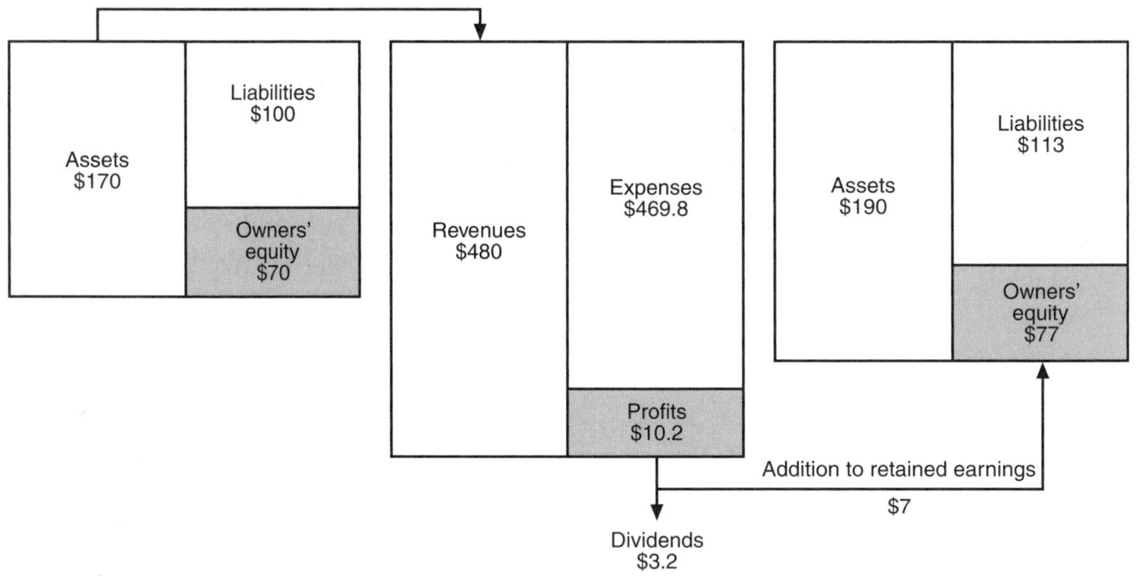

the sum of its original owners' equity of $70 million at year-end 2009 and the retained earnings of $7 million.

Firms usually report changes in owners' equity, such as cash dividends, and stock issued and repurchased, in the **statement of shareholders' equity**.

THE STRUCTURE OF THE OWNERS' EQUITY ACCOUNT

Our analysis of owners' equity has shown that the *changes* in owners' equity come from earnings that are retained, net of any new issues of equity or any share repurchases that occurred during the accounting period. The owners' equity account in the balance sheet represents the accumulated contribution of these changes over many accounting periods, from the date at which the firm was created until the date of the balance sheet. To clarify the origin of their equity, most firms provide a breakdown of their owners' equity into separate accounts that identify the different sources of equity. The most common items making up the owners' equity account are shown in Exhibit 2.5, which presents a detailed account of OS Distributors' owners' equity at year-end 2010.

The first source of equity shown is **common stock**. The dollar amount is the number of shares the firm has issued since its creation multiplied by the **par value**,

EXHIBIT 2.5 OS DISTRIBUTORS: OWNERS' EQUITY ON DECEMBER 31, 2010.

FIGURES IN MILLIONS

	December 31, 2010	
Common stock	$10	
10,000,000 shares at par value of $1		
Paid-in capital in excess of par	20	
Retained earnings	47	
(Treasury stocks)	(0)	
Owners' equity		$77

or **stated value**, of the shares. The par value of a common stock is an *arbitrary* fixed value assigned to each share of stock that is unrelated to its *market* price. The par value was set by those who created the firm and is stated in the firm's charter. It represents the maximum liability of the owner of the share in the event of the firm's dissolution. OS Distributors had 10 million shares outstanding at the end of 2010, and each of the firm's shares has a par value of $1. Thus, the firm's common stock was recorded at $10 million at the end of 2010.

The second source of equity shown is **paid-in capital in excess of par.** This is the difference between the cumulative amount of cash that the firm received from shares issued up to the date of the balance sheet and the cash it would have received if those shares had been issued at par value. The paid-in capital of OS Distributors was $20 million at the end of 2010, indicating that the firm issued shares in the past that were sold for more than $1. Suppose, for example, that one million shares were sold five years ago for $5 each. That year, OS Distributors' paid-in capital in excess of par increased by $4 million, one million shares multiplied by the difference between $5 and a par value of $1.

The third source of equity, **retained earnings** or **reserves,** is the total amount of retained earnings since the creation of the firm. For OS Distributors, this "earned" capital amounted to $47 million at the end of 2010.

The last account, **treasury stock**, is subtracted from the previous accounts. It represents the amount the firm spent to repurchase its shares up to the date of the balance sheet. OS Distributors has not repurchased any of its shares, so this account remains equal to zero.

SUMMARY

This chapter explains how a firm's balance sheet and income statement are prepared, what type of information they provide, and how they are related to each other. The next three chapters show how this information is used to assess firms' business and financial performances.

The usefulness of financial statements, however, is often limited by the relative quality of the information they contain. Financial statements are prepared according to principles and rules that are not necessarily applied in the same fashion and with the same rigor by all firms. Furthermore, despite the nearly universal adoption of the International Financial Reporting Standards (IFRS), accounting rules may differ between some countries and even between industries within the same country. Thus, to make meaningful comparisons between financial statements over time and between firms, it is necessary to check that the standards that are used and the way they are implemented are identical from one period to another and from one firm to another. If they are not, adjustments need to be made.

For these reasons, a firm's financial statements should be interpreted with a critical eye. You should never take for granted a firm's reported profit figures or asset values. Always ask yourself how they were generated and which rules were used to estimate them. This point is clearly illustrated in Exhibit 2.6 with the case of the Singer Company.

EXHIBIT 2.6 How to Spot the Seams at Singer Co.[1]

Investors love a good story, and Singer Co. has all the makings of a bestseller: a strong brand name, operating in exploding consumer markets such as China and India and plenty of fans on Wall Street. Singer, which is synonymous with sewing machines, also uses its name to sell televisions, refrigerators and washing machines in more than 100 countries.

Analysts rave about the company's consistent earnings, which have risen for 23 consecutive quarters. James G. Ting, 44, the Chinese-Canadian businessman who took over Singer in 1989, wants people to consider the stock as much a blue-chip as Du Pont Co. or Coca-Cola Co.

Singer, however, is not the real thing. Without doing anything illegal, and with the blessing of auditors at Ernst & Young, the company employs a myriad of tactics to brighten its profit picture. Nearly one-fifth of the $98.5 million that the company earned last year [1994] came from sources other than basic operations: asset sales, one-time investment gains and interest income and fees from affiliated companies.

Singer's story provides clear examples of reasons that investors need to look at more than just the bottom line to determine the quality of a company's earnings.

The basic lessons:

- **Profits can be too predictable.**
  Wall Street hates to be surprised, and Singer has a history of meeting analysts' earnings-per-share expectations quarter after quarter almost to the penny.

  Only the devaluation of the Mexican peso caused the company to miss the mark by 9 cents when it reported fourth-quarter 1994 results—the first time Singer's earnings had significantly trailed expectations since it went public in 1991.

---

[1]This article was written by Reed Abelson. It appeared in *The New York Times* dated May 15, 1995. Copyright © 1995 The New York Times Co. Reprinted by permission.

EXHIBIT 2.6 HOW TO SPOT THE SEAMS AT SINGER CO. (*CONTINUED*)

Whenever a company's profit projections are so completely on target, however, investors should wonder how it is pulling off the feat—especially when it is subject to wildly fluctuating currencies.

- **Family ties can be too close.**
Investors should also look out when much of a company's business involves dealings with related businesses. Singer has close ties to a Canadian holding company, Semi-Tech Corp., and Mr. Ting is chairman of both companies.
Semi-Tech Global Ltd., a Hong Kong–based company also headed by Mr. Ting, bought Singer in 1989 from a group including Paul A. Bilzerian, the former Singer chairman who was convicted that year of securities fraud and sentenced to four years in prison. Semi-Tech later sold a majority of Singer's shares to the public. Almost half of Singer's stock is still owned by Semi-Tech, however, and only two of its eight directors are not linked to Semi-Tech. "It's very incestuous," said Howard Schilit, who heads the Center for Financial Research and Analysis in Rockville, Maryland.
Singer seems to use these relationships to particular advantage. For instance, Semi-Tech Global, a company in which Semi-Tech Corp. has a big stake, owns a group of lackluster businesses that used to be owned by Singer. If the businesses turn around, Singer has the right to buy them at low prices—indeed, it has already bought back 7 of the original 12.

- **The best profits are the year-in, year-out kind.**
Of the $98.5 million profit that Singer reported for last year, a high 18 percent came from one-time gains: a $4.7 million profit on investments, foreign-exchange gains of $600,000, asset sales totaling $4.8 million, $5.3 million in interest income and $2 million in consulting fees.

- **Cash is more important than earnings.**
At healthy companies, cash flow—which excludes noncash items such as depreciation—roughly approximates net income over time.
In Singer's annual report, Mr. Ting says that its cash flow "remained strong" as $46 million more cash flowed into the company's coffers than flowed out last year.
That claim would be beyond question if all the incoming cash came from operations. But at least $132 million came from a rise in borrowings. Looking just at operations, Singer's cash flow has significantly trailed its reported earnings.

- **Cash beats credit any day.**
Whenever a company allows consumers to buy its wares on generous terms, investors should look for signs that customers are not paying their bills.

In Singer's case, half of its sales come from Asia and Latin America, and much of its success results from making it easy for people of limited means to buy items such as refrigerators on credit.

Specimen Financial Statements

Appendix 2.1

THE HOME DEPOT'S BALANCE SHEETS AND INCOME STATEMENTS

The balance sheets and income statements that we have presented so far—those of Office Supplies (OS) Distributors, a fictitious firm—have purposely been reduced to their simplest form to make it easier to grasp financial accounting's basic principles and terminology. The financial statements published by companies are more complex and more difficult to read than those of OS Distributors, even with the help of the notes that often accompany them. The purpose of this appendix is to help you decipher actual financial statements by going through the balance sheets and income statements taken from the annual reports of The Home Depot, Inc., the world's largest home improvement retailer. The company stores sell a wide assortment of building materials, products for home improvement as well as lawn and garden products; they also provide a number of services. Exhibit A2.1.1 presents the firm's balance sheets and Exhibit A2.1.2 shows its income statements taken from the firm's annual reports for fiscal year 2006 (ending January 28, 2007) to fiscal year 2008 (ending February 1, 2009). To avoid duplication, we review only the few accounts in both statements that have not already been discussed in the body of the chapter. An analysis of The Home Depot's financial statements is presented in the appendices of the next three chapters to complement the analysis made in these chapters on OS Distributors.

THE HOME DEPOT'S BALANCE SHEETS

A number of new accounts appear on both sides of The Home Depot's balance sheets. They are examined in the following sections.

Short-Term Investments

The Home Depot distinguishes between cash equivalents and short-term investments. The former includes all highly liquid investments with original maturities of three months or less, while the latter records remaining investments with maturities of less than a year available for sale. Both types of investments are recorded at market values.

Other Current Assets

This account consists mainly of prepaid taxes and rents.

EXHIBIT A2.1.1 THE HOME DEPOT, INC.'S CONSOLIDATED BALANCE SHEETS.

FROM THE COMPANY ANNUAL REPORTS FOR FISCAL YEARS 2007 (ENDING FEBRUARY 3, 2008) AND 2008 (ENDING FEBRUARY 1, 2009). FIGURES IN MILLIONS

	January 28, 2007	February 3, 2008	February 1, 2009
Assets			
• Current assets			
Cash and cash equivalents	$ 600	$ 445	$ 519
Short-term investments	14	12	6
Accounts receivable, net	3,223	1,259	972
Merchandise inventories	12,822	11,731	10,673
Other current assets	1,341	1,227	1,192
Total current assets	18,000	14,674	13,362
• Property and equipment, at cost			
Land	8,355	8,398	8,301
Buildings	15,215	16,642	16,961
Furniture, fixtures and equipment	7,799	8,050	8,741
Leasehold improvements	1,391	1,390	1,359
Construction in progress	1,123	1,435	625
Capital leases	475	497	490
	34,358	36,412	36,477
Less accumulated depreciation and amortization	7,753	8,936	10,243
Net property and equipment	26,605	27,476	26,234
• Notes receivable	343	342	36
• Goodwill	6,314	1,209	1,134
• Other assets	1,001	623	398
Total assets	**$52,263**	**$44,324**	**$41,164**
Liabilities and stockholders' equity			
• Current liabilities			
Short-term debt	$ –	$ 1,747	$ –
Accounts payable	7,356	5,732	4,822
Accrued salaries and related expenses	1,307	1,094	1,129
Sales taxes payable	475	445	337
Deferred revenue	1,634	1,474	1,165
Income taxes payable	217	60	289
Current installments of long-term debt	18	300	1,767
Other accrued expenses	1,924	1,854	1,644
Total current liabilities	12,931	12,706	11,153
• Long-term debt, excluding current installments	11,643	11,383	9,667
• Other long-term liabilities	1,243	1,833	2,198
• Deferred income taxes	1,416	688	369
Total liabilities	27,233	26,610	23,387

(Continued)

EXHIBIT A2.1.1 THE HOME DEPOT, INC.'S CONSOLIDATED BALANCE SHEETS. (CONTINUED)

	January 28, 2007	February 3, 2008	February 1, 2009
• Stockholders' equity			
Common stock	121	85	85
Paid-in capital	7,930	5,800	6,048
Retained earnings	33,052	11,388	12,093
Accumulated other comprehensive income (loss)	310	755	–77
Treasury stock	–16,383	–314	–372
	25,030	17,714	17,777
Total liabilities and stockholders' equity	**$52,263**	**$44,324**	**$41,164**

EXHIBIT A2.1.2 THE HOME DEPOT, INC.'S CONSOLIDATED STATEMENTS OF INCOME.

FROM THE COMPANY ANNUAL REPORT FOR FISCAL YEAR 2008 (ENDING FEBRUARY 1, 2009). FIGURES IN MILLIONS

	Fiscal Year Ended[1]		
	January 28, 2007	February 3, 2008	February 1, 2009
Net sales	$79,022	$77,349	$71,288
Cost of sales	52,476	51,352	47,298
Gross profit	26,546	25,997	23,990
Operating expenses:			
Selling, general, and administrative expenses	16,106	17,053	17,846
Depreciation and amortization	1,574	1,702	1,785
Total operating expenses	17,680	18,755	19,631
Operating income	8,866	7,242	4,359
Interest and other (income) expense:			
Interest and investment income	–27	–74	–18
Interest expense	391	696	624
Other			163
Interest and other, net	364	622	769
Earnings from continuing operations before provision for income tax	8,502	6,620	3,590
Provision for income taxes	3,236	2,410	1,278
Earnings from continuing operations	5,266	4,210	2,312
Earnings (loss) from discontinued operations, net of tax	495	185	–52
Net earnings	$ 5,761	$ 4,395	$ 2,260

[1]Fiscal years ended February 1, 2009 and January 28, 2007 include 52 weeks. Fiscal year ended February 3, 2008 includes 53 weeks.

Capital Leases

The Home Depot leases some retail locations, office space, warehouse, equipment, and vehicles. Accountants classify leases as either operating leases or capital leases (see Chapter 9). An operating lease is not recorded in the balance sheet because the payments to the leasing company are expensed in the income statement as incurred. On the other hand, a capital lease is recorded both as an asset (for example, a leased retail location) and a liability (debt owed to the leasing company), typically at the present value of the lease payments. The Financial Accounting Standards Board (FASB) provides criteria for when a lease should be considered a capital lease. In the case of The Home Depot, most leases are operating leases.

Notes Receivable and Other Assets

These accounts include items such as long-term prepaid expenses and intangible assets.

Sales Taxes Payable and Income Taxes Payable

In OS Distributors' balance sheet, sales and taxes payable are included in the company's accrued expenses. In the case of The Home Depot, they are shown separately.

Deferred Revenue

The Home Depot recognizes revenue at the time the customer takes possession of the merchandise or receives services. When the firm receives payments from customers before they take possession of the merchandise or before the service has been rendered, the amount received is recorded as deferred revenue in the balance sheet until the sale or service is completed. An example is the sale of gift cards, the revenue of which is recognized in the income statement only upon the redemption of the cards.

Other Accrued Expenses

These expenses include mainly accrued property taxes and accrued insurance.

Other Long-Term Liabilities

These long-term liabilities represent provisions for unforeseen events related to workers' compensation and other general reserves.

Accumulated Other Comprehensive Income (Loss)

This account shows the accumulated amount of transactions that affected the company's equity over time, up to the date of the balance sheet, and that are not included in reported profit. Comprehensive income includes adjustments related to previous periods, such as corrections of errors.

THE HOME DEPOT'S INCOME STATEMENTS

The Home Depot's income statements presentation in the company annual report does not differ much from that of OS Distributors. The Home Depot has two additional sources of revenues or expenses: one account entitled "Other" and another account entitled "Earnings (loss) from discontinued operations, net of tax."

OTHER

The $163 million expense during fiscal year 2008 is a write-down on a company activity, which was disposed of during that year.

EARNINGS (LOSS) FROM DISCONTINUED OPERATIONS (NET OF TAX)

Over the three fiscal years, 2006 to 2008, The Home Depot has disposed of some of its operations. The contribution of these discontinued operations to the company's Net Earnings in each of these years is reported in the account entitled "Earnings (Loss) from Discontinued Operations, net of tax."

Finally, note that the income tax expense is reported as "Provision for Income Tax." The terminology is (slightly) different, but the meaning is the same.

FURTHER READING

1. Cohen, Jacob, and David Young. *The Convergence of Global Accounting Standards,* Working Paper, INSEAD, 2005.
2. Kieso, Donald, Jerry Weygandt, and Terry Warfield. *Intermediate Accounting*, 13th ed. John Wiley & Sons, 2010. See Chapters 1 to 5.
3. Stickney, Clyde, Roman Weil, Katherine Schipper, and Jennifer Francis. *Financial Accounting,* 13th ed. South-Western, 2010. See Chapters 2, 3, and 4.

SELF-TEST PROBLEMS

2.1 CONSTRUCTING INCOME STATEMENTS AND BALANCE SHEETS.

Based on the information provided below, prepare the following financial statements for CompuStores, a company that assembles and distributes personal computers:

a. An income statement for the calendar year 2010
b. A balance sheet on December 31, 2009
c. A balance sheet on December 31, 2010

1. Accounts receivable increased by $6,400,000 in 2010
2. Profits in 2010 were taxed at 40 percent
3. At the end of 2010, inventories equaled 10 percent of the year's sales
4. The net book value of fixed assets at the end of 2009 was $76 million
5. Cost of goods sold, other than the direct labor expenses related to the assembling of computers, equaled 70 percent of sales in 2010
6. The average interest rate on short- and long-term borrowing in 2010 was 10 percent of the amount of funds borrowed at the *beginning* of the year

7. Accounts receivable at the end of 2010 equaled 12 percent of sales
8. Accounts payable at the end of 2009 equaled $30 million
9. Depreciation expense was $9 million in 2010
10. The company owed its employees $4 million at the end of 2009; a year later, it owed them $1,810,000
11. Material purchased in 2010 amounted to $228 million
12. Selling, general, and administrative expenses for 2010 were $18 million
13. Fees related to a technical license amount to $4 million per year
14. Taxes payable in 2009 equaled $6 million, and the company paid in advance the same amount on December 15, 2009
15. The balance of long-term debt was $27 million at the end of 2009, of which $4 million was due at year-end
16. Shares of common stocks were not issued and outstanding shares were not repurchased in 2010
17. Direct labor expenses equaled 11.25 percent of sales
18. Repayment of long-term debt is $4 million per year
19. Inventories rose from $28 million at the end of 2009 to $32 million at the end of 2010
20. In 2010, one of the company's warehouses was enlarged at a cost of $14 million, which was partly financed with a $6 million long-term loan
21. Dividend payments for 2010 were $9,360,000
22. Accounts payable at the end of 2010 equaled 1.85 of a month of purchases
23. Equity capital at the end of 2009 was $81 million
24. At the end of 2009, the company had enough cash that it could have immediately paid one-fourth of its accounts payable; at the end of 2010, it could have paid only one-tenth
25. The company paid in advance $9,600,000 of taxes on December 15, 2010
26. The company's line of credit was $3 million at the end of 2009. A year later it increased by two-thirds
27. In 2010, the company had a $2 million nonrecurrent loss related to the discontinuation of an old product line
28. The company prepaid $1,500,000 on rent and insurance in 2009, and $2,085,000 a year later

2.2 FORECASTING INCOME STATEMENTS AND BALANCE SHEETS.

Having prepared CompuStores' financial statements for the year 2010, the company's financial manager wishes to *forecast* next year's income statement and balance sheet (called projected or **pro forma statements**). Prepare these projected statements using the following assumptions and the 2010 statements in the previous problem:

1. Sales are expected to grow by 10 percent
2. Gross profit and the components of the cost of goods sold, expressed as a percentage of sales, should be the same as in 2010

3. Selling, general, and administrative expenses will rise by $4,280,000
4. The licensing fee, depreciation expense, interest payments, and corporate tax rate are not expected to change next year
5. Collection of receivables, payment of payables, and inventory management should be at the same level of efficiency as the previous year. Thus, accounts receivable should be collected at the same speed as in 2010 and will remain at 12 percent of the year's sales. Accounts payable should still be equal to 1.85 month of purchases, and inventories should stay at 10 percent of sales
6. Prepaid and accrued expenses are not expected to change
7. The company should upgrade one of its assembly lines at a cost equal to the year's depreciation
8. The company will not borrow or issue new shares of common stocks
9. The company wishes to hold as much cash in 2011 as it did in 2010 and will pay a dividend that will allow it to achieve this objective

REVIEW PROBLEMS

1. **Accounting allocation of transactions.**
Indicate the components of the balance sheet and income statement that will change as a consequence of the following transactions:

	CA	NCA	CL	NCL	OE	REV	EXP	RE
1. Factory equipment purchased for cash								
2. Goodwill impairment loss								
3. Interest income received								
4. Dividend declared								
5. Shares repurchased								
6. Sell merchandise on account								
7. Pay two months' rent in advance								
8. Purchase raw material on account								
9. Receive cash advance from customer								
10. Recognize salaries earned by employees								

CA: Current Assets — NCA: Noncurrent Assets — CL: Current Liabilities
NCL: Noncurrent Liabilities — OE: Owners' Equity — REV: Revenues
EXP: Expenses — RE: Retained Earnings

2. **Missing accounts.**
Find the missing values for the following three firms. Show your computations.

	Firm 1	Firm 2	Firm 3
Assets, beginning of period	$1,000		
Assets, end of period	1,100	$500	
Owners' equity, beginning of period	500	200	
Owners' equity, end of period			$1,000
Liabilities, beginning of period		200	600
Liabilities, end of period			500
Revenues of the period	2,000		600
Expenses of the period	1,800	180	
Earnings after tax of the period		20	100
Dividends (from earnings of the period)	100	10	0
Shares issued ($ amount) during the period	0	50	0

3. **Balance sheet changes.**
Below are incomplete balance sheets of ABC Corporation (figures in millions).

End-of-year for balance sheet items	Year 1	Year 2	Year 3	Year 4
Current assets	$16,870	$18,732	$19,950	$19,976
Noncurrent assets			29,920	
Total assets		48,050		
Current liabilities	13,466	15,284	16,574	16,080
Noncurrent liabilities	11,998		18,414	
Paid-in capital		2,298		2,798
Retained earnings	13,438	15,844		
Earnings (loss) after tax	2,014		(1,312)	5,048
Dividends	1,580	2,040	2,234	2,480
Owners' equity				
Total liabilities and owners' equity	40,936			51,070

a. Compute the missing amounts, and show the balance sheet at year-end 1, 2, 3, and 4. Show your computations.
b. What transactions might explain the change in total assets between years 1 and 2?
c. What transactions might explain the change in retained earnings between years 2 and 3?
d. What transactions might explain the change in total liabilities plus owners' equity between years 3 and 4?

4. **Balance sheet changes.**
Below are incomplete balance sheets of XYZ Corporation (figures in millions).

End-of-year for balance sheet items	Year 1	Year 2	Year 3	Year 4
Current assets	$25,305		$29,925	$29,964
Noncurrent assets			44,880	
Total assets		$72,075		
Current liabilities	20,199	22,926	24,861	
Current assets—current liabilities		5,712		5,844
Noncurrent liabilities	17,997		27,621	
Paid-in capital		3,447		4,197
Retained earnings	20,157	23,766		
Earnings (loss) after tax	n.a.	n.a.	(1,968)	7,572
Dividends	n.a.	n.a.	3,351	3,720
Total liabilities and owners' equity	61,404			76,605

a. Compute the missing amounts, and show the balance sheet at year-end 1, 2, 3, and 4. Show your computations.
b. What transactions might explain the change in total assets between years 1 and 2?

5. **Balance sheet changes.**
Below are incomplete balance sheets of OPQ Corporation (figures in millions).

End-of-year for balance sheet items	Year 1	Year 2	Year 3	Year 4
Current assets	**$ 3,092**		**$ 2,932**	
Noncurrent assets		$18,160	17,996	$20,286
Total assets	21,094			
Current assets/current liabilities			1.023	1.04
Current liabilities	2,978			3,002
Noncurrent liabilities	9,286	9,830		
Owners' equity		8,868	8,058	8,084
Total liabilities and owners' equity		21,182		

a. Compute the missing amounts, and show the balance sheet at year-ends 1, 2, 3, and 4. Show your computations
b. Comment on the asset and liability structure of the firm

6. **Reconstructing an income statement.**
Below is some income statement information on company DEF. Prepare an income statement for each of the three years. Show your computations.

	Year 1	Year 2	Year 3
Sales	$21,184		$49,308
Interest income	24	$ 132	208
Cost of goods sold	16,916	24,372	
Administrative and selling expenses	2,380	3,304	4,808
Research and development expenses	380	504	816
Income tax expense	444	864	1,696
Earnings after tax		2,124	3,776

7. **Reconstructing an income statement.**
Below is some income statement information on company ABD. Prepare an income statement for each of the three years. Show your computations.

	Year 1	Year 2	Year 3
Sales	$21,087		$26,613
Interest expense	75	$ 90	81
Cost of goods sold	16,182	17,709	
Administrative and selling expenses	3,966	4,533	5,547
Income tax expense	324	252	192
Earnings after tax		408	312

8. **Reconstructing a balance sheet.**
From the following data, reconstruct the balance sheet at the end of the year.

1. Earnings after tax	$ 300	At beginning of year:	
2. Increase in depreciation expense	200	13. Cash	$ 450
3. Sales of common stock	1,000	14. Accounts receivable	250
4. Acquisition of equipment	1,000	15. Inventories	300
5. Annual long-term debt reimbursement	100	16. Plant and equipment, net	2,000
6. Dividends	100	17. Accumulated depreciation	1,000
7. Increase in cash	50	18. Short-term debt	400
8. Increase in receivables	200	19. Accrued expenses	100
9. Increase in inventories	100	20. Long-term debt	500
10. Increase in payables	100	21. Common stock	600
11. Increase in wages payable	100	22. Retained earnings	1,100
12. Increase in taxes payable	100		

9. Constructing income statements and balance sheets.
Based on the information provided below, prepare the following financial statements for VideoStores:

a. An income statement for the calendar year 2010
b. A balance sheet on December 31, 2009
c. A balance sheet on December 31, 2010

1. Accounts receivable increased by $6,400,000 in 2010
2. Profits in 2010 were taxed at 36 percent
3. At the end of 2010, inventories equaled 10 percent of the year's sales
4. The net book value of fixed assets at the end of 2009 was $76 million
5. Cost of goods sold, other than the direct labor expenses related to the assembling of computers, equaled 70 percent of sales in 2010
6. The average interest rate on short- and long-term borrowing in 2010 was 10 percent of the amount borrowed at the *beginning* of the year
7. Accounts receivable at the end of 2010 equaled 12 percent of sales
8. Accounts payable at the end of 2009 equaled $30 million
9. Depreciation expense was $9 million in 2010
10. The company owed its employees $4 million at the end of 2009; a year later it owed them $2 million
11. Material purchased in 2010 amounted to $228 million
12. Selling, general, and administrative expenses for 2010 were $18 million
13. Taxes payable in 2009 equaled $6 million, and the company paid in advance the same amount on December 15, 2009
14. The balance of long-term debt was $27 million at the beginning of 2009, of which $4 million was due at year-end
15. The company did not issue shares of common stocks or repurchase outstanding shares in 2010
16. Direct labor expenses equaled 11.25 percent of 2010 sales
17. Repayment of long-term debt is $4 million per year
18. Inventories rose from $28 million at the end of 2009 to $32 million at the end of 2010
19. In 2010, one of the company's warehouses was enlarged at a cost of $14 million, which was partly financed with a $6 million long-term loan
20. In 2010, dividends were $9,200,000
21. Accounts payable at the end of 2010 equaled two months of purchases
22. Equity capital at the end of 2009 was $81 million
23. At the end of 2009, the company had enough cash to pay a quarter of its accounts payable; at the end of 2010, to pay 30 percent
24. The company paid in advance $10,800,000 of taxes on December 15, 2010
25. The company borrowed $3 million short-term at the end of 2009. A year later, it borrowed $5 million short-term
26. The company's prepaid expenses were $1,500,000 (prepaid rent and insurance premium) in 2009, and $2,200,000 a year later

10. **Forecasting financing needs.**

Ambex Inc. expects sales to increase to \$36 million next year, from \$27 million this year. Its current assets are \$9 million, accounts payable is \$2.7 million, fixed assets are \$9 million, long-term debt is \$3.6 million, owners' equity is \$11 million, and earnings after tax-to-sales ratio is 5 percent. Current assets and accounts payable can be assumed to increase in the same proportion as sales. Other current liabilities are expected to stay at the same level. Net fixed assets will increase by \$1 million, and the firm plans to pay \$800,000 as dividends.

a. What are Ambex's total financing needs for next year?

b. How much money would Ambex have to borrow to finance its needs?

ASSESSING LIQUIDITY AND OPERATIONAL EFFICIENCY

CHAPTER 3

A firm that can no longer pay its creditors—its bankers and suppliers—is illiquid and technically bankrupt, a situation that no manager wishes to face. Managers must make decisions that do not endanger their firm's liquidity—a term that refers to the firm's ability to meet its *recurrent* cash obligations toward various creditors. A firm's liquidity is driven by the structure of its balance sheet, namely, by the nature and composition of its assets and the way they are financed.

It is easier to understand and measure a firm's liquidity if its standard balance sheet is restructured to emphasize the concerns of its operating and financial managers rather than those of its accountant and auditors. In this restructured balance sheet, called the *managerial balance sheet*, the firm's investments are classified into three categories: (1) cash and cash-equivalent assets; (2) assets required to support the firm's *operating* activities, such as inventories and trade receivables, less the firm's operating liabilities, such as trade payables; and (3) fixed assets, such as property, plant, and equipment.

To finance these investments, the firm uses a combination of short-term and long-term sources of funds. One way a firm can manage its balance sheet and enhance its liquidity is by using the *matching strategy*. This strategy requires that long-term investments be financed with long-term funds and short-term investments with short-term funds. We show in this chapter that the matching principle helps explain how a firm's liquidity should be measured and how liquidity is affected by managerial decisions.

New concepts and terms, such as *working capital requirement*, *net short-term financing*, and *net long-term financing*, are introduced. We then show how they can be combined to construct a reliable measure of a firm's liquidity. Other, more traditional indicators of liquidity, such as the *current ratio* and the *acid test ratio*, also are presented and compared with our suggested measure. To illustrate these concepts, we use Office Supplies (OS) Distributors, the company whose balance sheets and income statements for the years 2008 to 2010 are described in Chapter 2. After reading this chapter, you should understand the following:

- How to restructure a standard balance sheet into a managerial balance sheet
- The meaning of working capital requirement, net long-term financing, net short-term financing, net working capital, current ratio, acid test ratio, and other ratios used to measure, analyze, and manage liquidity
- How to measure a firm's investment in its operating activities using information drawn from its balance sheet
- The meaning of financial cost risk and refinancing risk
- How a firm's operating decisions affect its liquidity
- How to improve a firm's liquidity through better management of the firm's operating cycle

THE MANAGERIAL BALANCE SHEET

Recall that the purpose of the firm's balance sheet is to determine the investment made by the firm's owners—its shareholders—in their firm at a specific date. The investment, called owners' equity, is the difference between the firm's assets and liabilities, where assets are items owned by shareholders, and liabilities are debts owed to creditors, suppliers, employees, and other entities. This type of balance sheet, shown in Exhibit 3.1 for OS Distributors, emphasizes the accounting view in determining the owners' investment in the firm.

For managers of a firm's operating activities, the standard balance sheet may not be the most appropriate tool for assessing their contribution to the firm's financial performance. To illustrate this point, consider trade payables. They are correctly recorded in the balance sheet as a liability because they represent cash owed to suppliers. Most operating managers, however, would consider trade payables an account under their full responsibility, much like trade receivables (cash owed to the firm by its customers) and inventories, both of which are recorded on the asset side of the balance sheet. It makes more *managerial* sense to associate trade payables with trade receivables and inventories than to combine them with other liabilities—such as short-term borrowings and long-term debt—that are primarily the responsibility of the financial manager.

In the following sections, we show how to restructure the standard balance sheet into the **managerial balance sheet**, and explain why it is a more appropriate tool to identify the links between managerial decisions and financial performance. The managerial balance sheet is shown in Exhibit 3.2 and contrasted with the standard balance sheet.

On the left side of the managerial balance sheet, three items are grouped under the heading **invested capital**. These are cash and cash-equivalent holdings, **working capital requirement** (**WCR**) (the difference between the firm's **operating assets** and its **operating liabilities**), and net fixed assets:

Invested capital = Cash + Working capital requirement + Net fixed assets (3.1)

On the right side of the managerial balance sheet, two items are grouped under the heading **capital employed**. These are short-term debt and long-term financing,

EXHIBIT 3.1 OS DISTRIBUTORS' BALANCE SHEETS.

FIGURES IN MILLIONS

	December 31, 2008		December 31, 2009		December 31, 2010	
Assets						
• **Current assets**						
Cash[1]		$ 6.0		$ 12.0		$ 8.0
Accounts receivable		44.0		48.0		56.0
Inventories		52.0		57.0		72.0
Prepaid expenses[2]		2.0		2.0		1.0
Total current assets		104.0		119.0		137.0
• **Noncurrent assets**						
Financial assets and intangibles		0.0		0.0		0.0
Property, plant, and equipment						
Gross value[3]	$90.0		$90.0		$93.0	
less accumulated depreciation	(34.0)	56.0	(39.0)	51.0	(40.0)	53.0
Total noncurrent assets		56.0		51.0		53.0
Total assets		$160.0		$170.0		$190.0
Liabilities and owners' equity						
• **Current liabilities**						
Short-term debt		$ 15.0		$ 22.0		$ 23.0
Owed to banks	$ 7.0		$14.0		$15.0	
Current portion of long-term debt	8.0		8.0		8.0	
Accounts payable		37.0		40.0		48.0
Accrued expenses[4]		2.0		4.0		4.0
Total current liabilities		54.0		66.0		75.0
• **Noncurrent liabilities**						
Long-term debt[5]		42.0		34.0		38.0
Total noncurrent liabilities		42.0		34.0		38.0
• **Owners' equity**[6]		64.0		70.0		77.0
Total liabilities and owners' equity		$160.0		$170.0		$190.0

[1]Consists of cash in hand and checking accounts held to facilitate operating activities on which the firm earns no interest.

[2]Prepaid expenses is rent paid in advance (when recognized in the income statement, rent is included in selling, general, and administrative expenses).

[3]In 2009, there was no disposal of existing fixed assets or acquisition of new fixed assets. However, during 2010, a warehouse was enlarged at a cost of $12 million and existing fixed assets, bought for $9 million in the past, were sold at their net book value of $2 million.

[4]Accrued expenses consist of wages and taxes payable.

[5]Long-term debt is repaid at the rate of $8 million per year. No new long-term debt was incurred during 2009, but during 2010, a mortgage loan was obtained from the bank to finance the extension of a warehouse (see Note 3).

[6]During the three years, no new shares were issued and none were repurchased.

EXHIBIT 3.2 THE MANAGERIAL BALANCE SHEET VERSUS THE STANDARD BALANCE SHEET.

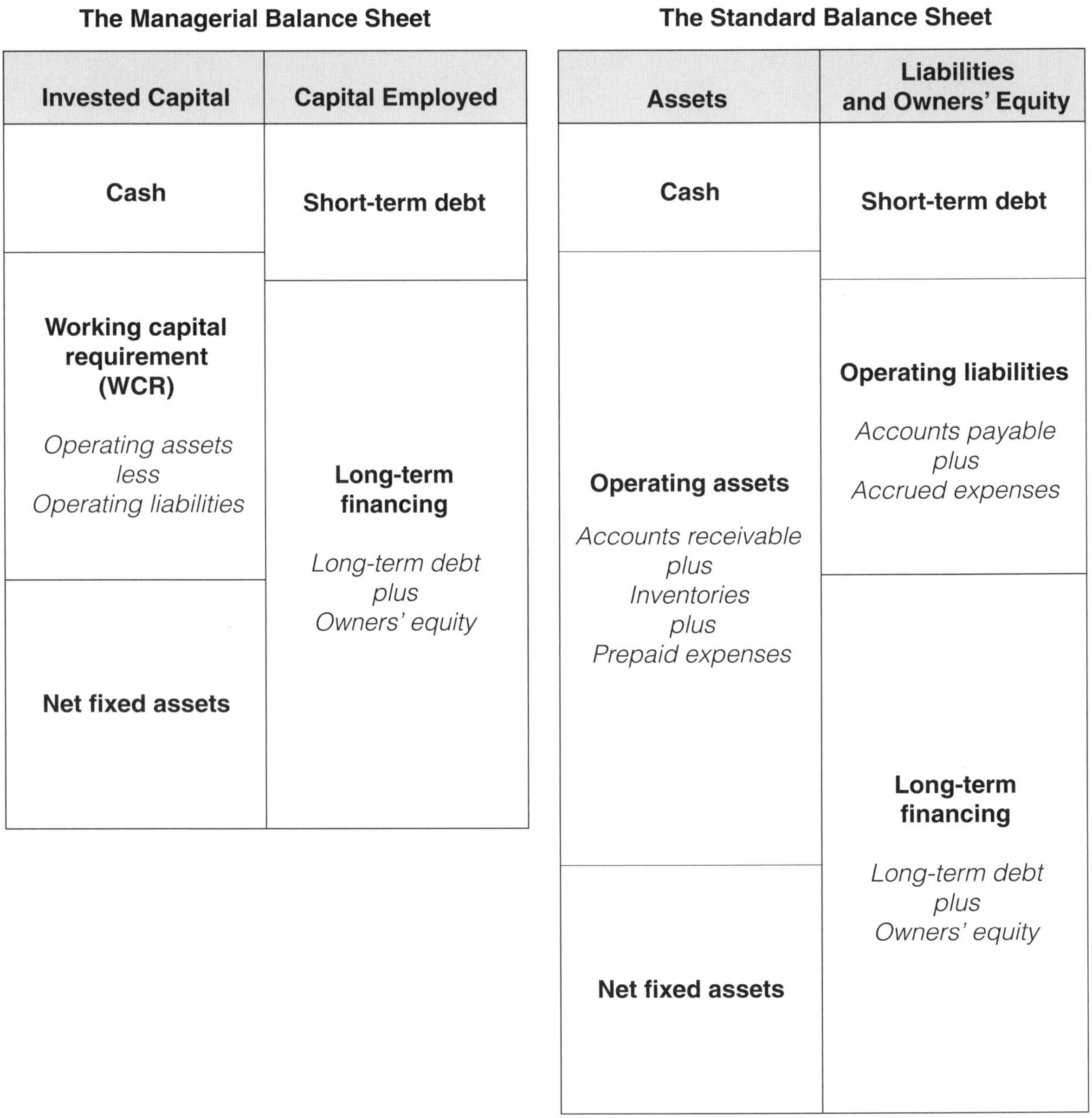
The Managerial Balance Sheet
Invested Capital
Capital Employed
Cash
Short-term debt
Working capital requirement (WCR)
Operating assets less Operating liabilities
Long-term financing
Long-term debt plus Owners' equity
Net fixed assets
The Standard Balance Sheet
Assets
Liabilities and Owners' Equity
Cash
Short-term debt
Operating liabilities
Accounts payable plus Accrued expenses
Operating assets
Accounts receivable plus Inventories plus Prepaid expenses
Long-term financing
Long-term debt plus Owners' equity
Net fixed assets

the latter consisting of long-term debt and owners' equity (as in previous chapters, we use the terms *financing, funding*, and *capital* interchangeably):[1]

Capital employed = Short-term debt + Long-term debt + Owners' equity (3.2)

The managerial balance sheet provides a snapshot of the total capital the firm has available at a point in time (the capital employed shown on the right side) and the way that capital is invested in the firm's net assets (the invested capital shown on the left side). The following sections examine the structure of the managerial balance sheet and its relevance to the measurement of the **firm's liquidity**.

THE THREE COMPONENTS OF A FIRM'S INVESTED CAPITAL

A firm's capital is used to finance investments in (1) cash and cash-equivalent assets; (2) working capital requirement (WCR); and (3) fixed assets, such as property, plant, and equipment. We begin with a brief review of cash and fixed assets and then analyze WCR in more detail.

CASH AND CASH-EQUIVALENT ASSETS

Firms hold **cash and cash-equivalent** assets (also called **liquid assets**) for at least two reasons: (1) as a precautionary measure and (2) to build up cash balances for future uses. Some customers may not pay the invoices sent to them exactly at the agreed-upon date. In between, the firm may find itself not being able to pay its suppliers or pay its employees' salaries on time. To avoid being caught in a cash squeeze, most firms hold cash balances as a precautionary measure, referred to as **operating cash.**[2] On top of cash balances needed to support operating activities, firms also may hold temporary amounts of cash, or **excess cash**, for future uses, such as the payment of cash dividends, the repurchase of shares, or the acquisition of new businesses. Also, firms sometimes hold cash because banks require their corporate clients to maintain some **compensating balances** for services they provide to the firm. We use the generic word *cash* to refer not only to cash in hand but also to any cash-equivalent assets.

To have access to more cash, some firms, particularly large ones, can negotiate **credit lines** with their banks. This is an agreement in which the bank, for a fee, extends a specific amount of credit for a short period of time at the discretion of the firm. Information about the agreement is usually found in the notes to the firm's balance sheet.

---

[1]In practice, many companies and financial analysts define capital employed as the amount of capital used to finance a firm's core activities. Because many firms, especially large ones, hold cash far in excess from what is needed to run the cash transactions associated with their fundamental activities, capital employed is then defined as the sum of equity capital and debt (short term and long term) *minus* the amount of cash held by the firm. Some analysts and companies go as far as excluding non-interest-bearing debt, such as pension fund liabilities, from capital employed, on the basis that no (accounting) costs are associated with their use in financing the firm's activities.

[2]The amount of cash that a company should hold as a precautionary measure is not well documented. One source indicates that it should be between 0.5 percent and 2 percent of annual sales. See Koller, Goedhart, and Wessels (2005). When the information is available, daily changes in the firm's cash account can be used to estimate the minimum amount of cash balance needed to support the firm's recurrent activities. See also Chapter 10 in Damodaran (2006).

As indicated in Note 1 of Exhibit 3.1, below OS Distributors' balance sheets, the firm does not hold any cash-equivalent assets, such as marketable securities (securities that can be sold rapidly without a significant loss of value). It held $6 million in cash at the end of 2008, $12 million at the end of 2009, and $8 million at the end of 2010. The changes in the firm's cash position between 2008 and 2010 are explained in the next chapter.

INVESTMENT IN FIXED ASSETS

Investments in fixed assets include items such as property, plant, and equipment. Their book value is recorded in the balance sheet as net fixed assets, which is their purchase price less accumulated depreciation. Exhibit 3.1 indicates that the book value of OS Distributors' fixed assets was $56 million in 2008, $51 million in 2009, and $53 million in 2010. Decisions about the acquisition and disposal of long-term assets are part of the firm's strategic activities, which are analyzed in detail in Chapters 6 through 8. In this and the following two chapters, we focus on the firm's operating activities.

WORKING CAPITAL REQUIREMENT OR OPERATING WORKING CAPITAL

Fixed assets alone cannot generate sales and profits. The managerial activities required to operate these assets in order to generate sales and profit are referred to as the firm's **operating activities**. These activities require investments in the form of inventories and trade receivables as shown in the firm's **operating cycle**, described in Exhibit 3.3 for a manufacturing company.

The cycle starts on the right side with *procurement*, the act of acquiring raw materials. It is followed by *production*, during which the raw materials are transformed into finished goods. The cycle continues with the *sales* of these goods, ending when *cash* is collected from customers. The cycle repeats itself as long as the firm's production activity continues.

Each stage in the operating cycle affects the firm's balance sheet. Exhibit 3.3 shows the balance sheet accounts that change at each stage of the cycle. For example, when the firm buys raw materials (procurement), both inventories and accounts payable increase by the same amount—the former to reflect the purchase of the raw materials and the latter to acknowledge a debt to the firm's suppliers.

An alternative way to describe the operating cycle is shown in Exhibit 3.4. In this case, the firm pays its suppliers *before* receiving cash from its customers because it holds inventories (of raw materials, work in process, and finished goods) and accounts receivable over a period of time that is *longer* than its payment period. The period between the date the firm pays its suppliers and the date it collects its invoices is called the **cash-to-cash period** (or **cycle**) or the **cash conversion period** (or **cycle**).

What is the *net* investment (at the date of the balance sheet) that the firm must make to support its operating cycle? It is simply the sum of its inventories and accounts receivable less its accounts payable. If prepaid expenses are included in the firm's operating assets and accrued expenses are included in its operating liabilities, then the firm's net investment in its operating cycle is measured (at the date of the balance sheet) by the difference between its operating assets and operating liabilities.

Exhibit 3.3 The Firm's Operating Cycle and Its Effect on the Firm's Balance Sheet.

Δ = CHANGE IN THE BALANCE SHEET ACCOUNT

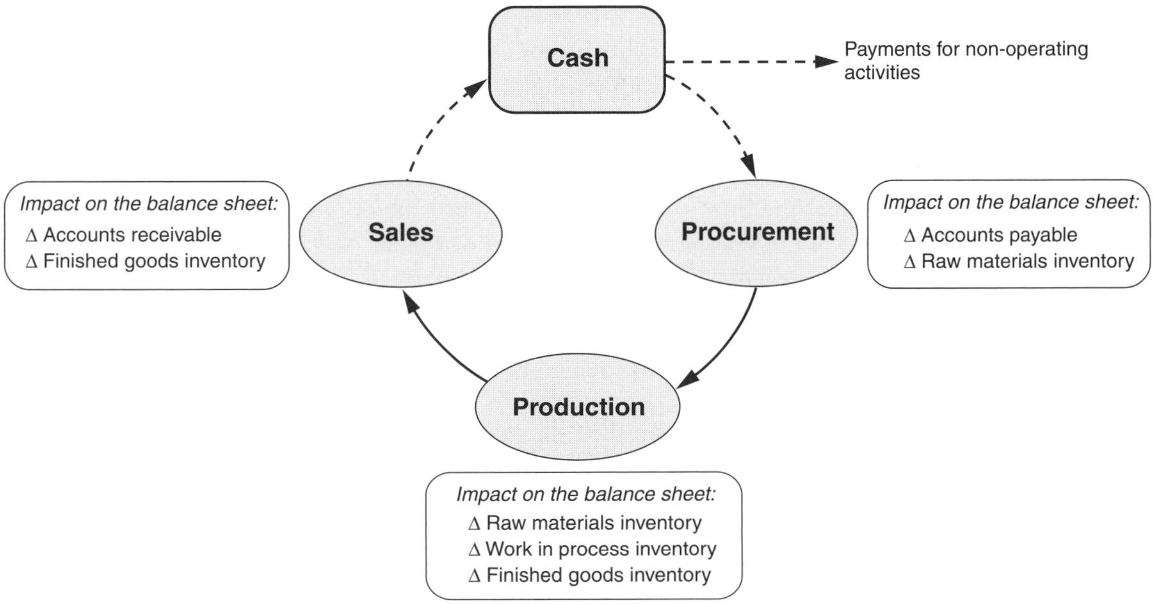

This difference is called the firm's working capital requirement (WCR) or **operating working capital:**

$$\begin{gathered}\textbf{Working capital requirement (WCR)}\\=\\ [\textbf{Operating assets}] - [\textbf{Operating liabilities}]\\=\\ [\textbf{Accounts receivable + Inventories + Prepaid expenses}]\\ -[\textbf{Accounts payable + Accrued expenses}]\end{gathered} \tag{3.3}$$

Exhibit 3.4 The Firm's Operating Cycle, Showing the Cash-to-Cash Period.

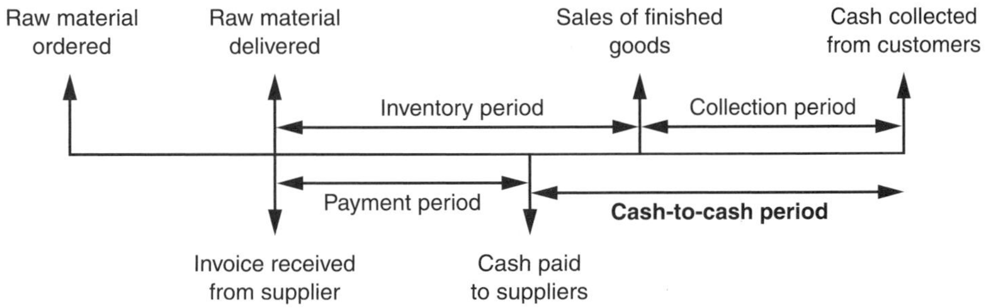

WCR does not include the firm's cash holdings. There are two reasons for this. First, a company holds cash not only to support its operating activities but also to meet future cash expenses that are not related to its operations, such as the payment of dividends and the purchase of fixed assets. Second, operating cash is a separate investment held for precautionary reasons to meet payment obligations resulting from unexpected short-term changes in components of the WCR. Finally, WCR does not include the firm's short-term debt. Short-term debt is used to *finance* the firm's investments, including its WCR. It may contribute to the financing of the firm's operating cycle, but it is not a component of it.

For most firms, operating assets exceed operating liabilities and WCR is *positive*, meaning that the firm has to finance it. When the opposite occurs, WCR is *negative* and the firm's operating cycle becomes a *source of cash* rather than a use of funds. Firms with a negative WCR are found in the retail and service sectors of the economy. Such firms collect cash from their customers before they pay their suppliers and carry small inventories relative to their sales. Large supermarkets are a typical example. They sell mostly for cash and, thus, have few receivables. And because their inventories move rapidly, they are usually low relative to the sales they generate. The amount of money they owe their suppliers, however, can be very large because big supermarket chains often manage to extract generous credit terms from their suppliers. Few receivables, low inventories, and large amounts of payables is the perfect recipe for turning the firm's operating cycle into a source of cash.

For example, consider Carrefour, one of the world's biggest chains of very large supermarkets. Exhibit 3.5 shows some figures taken from the company's 2006, 2007, and 2008 balance sheets. The firm has practically no prepaid expenses, so its WCR is equal to the sum of the company's receivables and inventories less its payables and accrued expenses. Note the negative sign and magnitude of WCR. At the end of 2008, Carrefour owed its suppliers €17.3 billion and its WCR was a negative €12.6 billion. This negative WCR is a major *source of cash* to the company. Other firms with a negative working capital requirement are in industries such as publishing (customers pay for their subscription before they receive their magazine) and air transportation (customers pay for their trip before their departure).

EXHIBIT 3.5 EXTRACTS FROM CARREFOUR'S BALANCE SHEETS AND INCOME STATEMENTS.

FIGURES IN MILLIONS

Year	Accounts Receivable	Inventories	Accounts Payable	Accrued Expenses	WCR[1]	Cash
2006	€955	€6,051	€16,449	€2,639	–€12,082	€3,697
2007	863	6,867	17,077	2,848	–12,195	4,164
2008	779	6,891	17,276	2,947	–12,553	5,317

[1]WCR = Working capital requirement = Receivables + Inventories – Payables – Accrued expenses

Source: Company's Annual Reports.

EXHIBIT 3.6 OS DISTRIBUTORS' MANAGERIAL BALANCE SHEETS.

ALL DATA FROM THE BALANCE SHEETS IN EXHIBIT 3.1. FIGURES IN MILLIONS

	December 31, 2008			December 31, 2009			December 31, 2010		
Invested capital									
• Cash		$ 6.0	*5%*		$ 12.0	*10%*		$ 8.0	*6%*
• Working capital requirement (WCR)[1]		59.0	*49%*		63.0	*50%*		77.0	*56%*
• Net fixed assets		56.0	*46%*		51.0	*40%*		53.0	*38%*
Total invested capital		**$121.0**	***100%***		**$126.0**	***100%***		**$138.0**	***100%***
Capital employed									
• Short-term debt		$ 15.0	*12%*		$ 22.0	*17%*		$ 23.0	*17%*
• Long-term financing									
Long-term debt	$42.0			$34.0			$38.0		
Owners' equity	64.0	106.0	*88%*	70.0	104.0	*83%*	77.0	115.0	*83%*
Total capital employed		**$121.0**	***100%***		**$126.0**	***100%***		**$138.0**	***100%***

[1]WCR = (Accounts receivable + Inventories + Prepaid expenses) – (Accounts payable + Accrued expenses).

With the information in the balance sheets in Exhibit 3.1, we can calculate OS Distributors' working capital requirement on December 31, 2008, 2009, and 2010, using equation 3.3:

$$WCR_{12/31/08} = \$44 \text{ million} + \$52 \text{ million} + \$2 \text{ million} - \$37 \text{ million} - \$2 \text{ million} = \$59 \text{ million}$$

$$WCR_{12/31/09} = \$48 \text{ million} + \$57 \text{ million} + \$2 \text{ million} - \$40 \text{ million} - \$4 \text{ million} = \$63 \text{ million}$$

$$WCR_{12/31/10} = \$56 \text{ million} + \$72 \text{ million} + \$1 \text{ million} - \$48 \text{ million} - \$4 \text{ million} = \$77 \text{ million}$$

These are the figures reported in OS Distributors' managerial balance sheets shown in Exhibit 3.6. OS Distributors' WCR has risen from $59 million in 2008 to $77 million in 2010. How can we explain this growth? We examine this issue later in the chapter.

THE TWO COMPONENTS OF A FIRM'S CAPITAL EMPLOYED

How should the firm's invested capital be financed? Two primary sources of capital are available to firms: (1) the **equity capital** provided by owners and (2) the debt capital provided by debt holders. Debt can be *short term* (due to be repaid within one year) or *long term* (due to be repaid after one year).[3] Thus, a firm's total capital employed can be classified either as equity and debt capital or as **long-term financing** (equity plus long-term debt) and **short-term financing** (short-term debt). The first approach distinguishes the *nature* of the firm's capital employed whereas the second distinguishes its *duration*.

Given these alternative sources of capital, the firm's managers must answer two questions when deciding which strategy should be adopted to fund the firm's investments:

1. What is the best combination of equity capital and debt capital?
2. What proportion of borrowed funds should be in the form of long-term debt and what proportion in the form of short-term debt?

The answer to the first question affects the firm's profitability and financial risk. It is examined in detail in Chapters 5 and 11. The answer to the second question affects primarily the firm's liquidity.[4] It is examined later in this chapter.

THE STRUCTURE OF THE MANAGERIAL BALANCE SHEET

Exhibit 3.2 compares the structure of the standard balance sheet with that of the managerial balance sheet. The two statements differ in the way operating assets and operating liabilities are handled. In the standard balance sheet, operating liabilities are part of the firm's total liabilities. In the managerial balance sheet, operating liabilities are deducted from operating assets to determine the net investment required to support the firm's operations, in other words, its WCR. Adding the cash and net fixed assets to WCR gives the firm's invested capital. What remains on the liability side of the balance sheet, after the operating liabilities are removed, are the sources of funds needed to finance the firm's investments: short-term debt, long-term debt, and owners' equity. The sum of these sources of funds is the total capital employed.

Now consider Exhibit 3.6, which shows OS Distributors' managerial balance sheets. At the end of 2010, the firm's invested capital of $138 million was funded with $23 million of short-term debt and $115 million of long-term financing ($38 million of long-term debt plus $77 million of owners' equity). The managerial balance sheets show that the proportion of cash held by the firm fluctuated between 5 and 10 percent of total invested capital. The proportion of WCR fluctuated between 49 and 56 percent, and that of net fixed assets fluctuated between 38 and 46 percent. The relatively large amount of WCR is not surprising, given that OS Distributors is a wholesale distribution company. Compared with typical manufacturing companies, firms in the wholesale distribution business have a significant amount of capital invested in their operating cycle. Turning to the structure of capital employed, notice that 83 to 88 percent of OS Distributors' investments were financed with long-term funds compared with 12 to 17 percent with short-term debt.

---

[3]This distinction is somewhat arbitrary, but it is the one used in standard accounting models. In practice, there is a gray area of medium-term debt, due to be repaid after one year but less than, say, three years.

[4]A distinction needs to be made between liquidity and **solvency**. Liquidity refers to the firm's ability to meet its cash obligations in the short term, whereas solvency refers to the same concept but from a long-term perspective. In the case of solvency, the issue is whether the firm can raise the funds required to sustain its long-term growth, service its long-term debt, and distribute a regular stream of dividends to its shareholders. The issue of solvency is dealt with in Chapter 5 in conjunction with the analysis of profitability.

THE MATCHING STRATEGY

In deciding how much of the firm's investments should be financed with long-term funds and how much with short-term debt, most firms try to apply the **matching strategy**. According to this strategy, *long-term investments should be financed with long-term funds and short-term investments should be financed with short-term funds.* By matching the life of an asset and the duration of its financing source, a firm can minimize the risk of *not* being able to finance the asset over its entire useful life.

Consider a piece of equipment with a useful life of five years. Its purchase price can be financed either with a five-year loan (a matched financing strategy) or with a one-year renewable loan (a mismatched financing strategy), both at the same interest rate. Which of the two strategies is riskier?

The mismatched strategy is riskier for two reasons. First, the interest rate, and thus the cost of financing the equipment, may change during the following four years. Second, the lender may be unwilling to renew the one-year loan, thus forcing the firm to repay its loan after one year. This situation may require the sale of the equipment and the early termination of the investment. These two types of risk, called **financial cost risk** and **refinancing risk**, respectively, are clearly much lower under the matching strategy.

However, matching the maturity structure of the firm's sources of financing with the maturity of its assets is not necessarily the *optimal* financing strategy for every firm at all times. Some firms, at times, may be willing to carry some financial cost and refinancing risks if they expect short-term interest rates to go down.[5] On the other hand, firms that are more risk averse may choose to carry more long-term funds than necessary under the matching strategy. Appendix 3.1 provides an illustration of matched and mismatched financing strategies for firms with growing and seasonal sales.

We can use the managerial balance sheets in Exhibit 3.6 to find out whether OS Distributors has been applying the matching strategy during the period 2008 to 2010. We examine each of the three investments and their financing. Cash, a short-term asset, has been fully funded with short-term debt at the end of each year and was thus matched. Similarly, net fixed assets, which are long-term investments, have been fully funded with long-term financing and also were thus matched. The matching strategy applied in both cases. Does it also apply to WCR?

Before we can answer this question, we need to know if WCR is a short-term or a long-term investment. At first glance, it may seem that WCR is a short-term investment because it is made up of current assets, which will become cash within a year, and current liabilities, which will decrease the firm's cash holdings within a year. But the answer is not that simple. Although these assets and liabilities are classified as current, or short-term, they will be replaced by *new* current assets and *new* current liabilities as the operating cycle repeats itself. So, as long as the firm stays in business, WCR will remain in its (managerial) balance sheet and, hence, is more *permanent* than transient in nature. In other words, WCR is essentially a long-term investment. Under a matching strategy, it should be financed with long-term funds. Exhibit 3.6 indicates that a small proportion of OS Distributors' WCR was

[5] If the short-term interest rate is expected to go down, then a short-term loan that is renewable over the life of the asset would be cheaper than a long-term loan that matches the life of the asset.

EXHIBIT 3.7 THE BEHAVIOR OF WORKING CAPITAL REQUIREMENT (WCR) OVER TIME FOR A FIRM WITH SEASONAL SALES.

WCR IS ASSUMED TO BE SET AT 25 PERCENT OF SALES

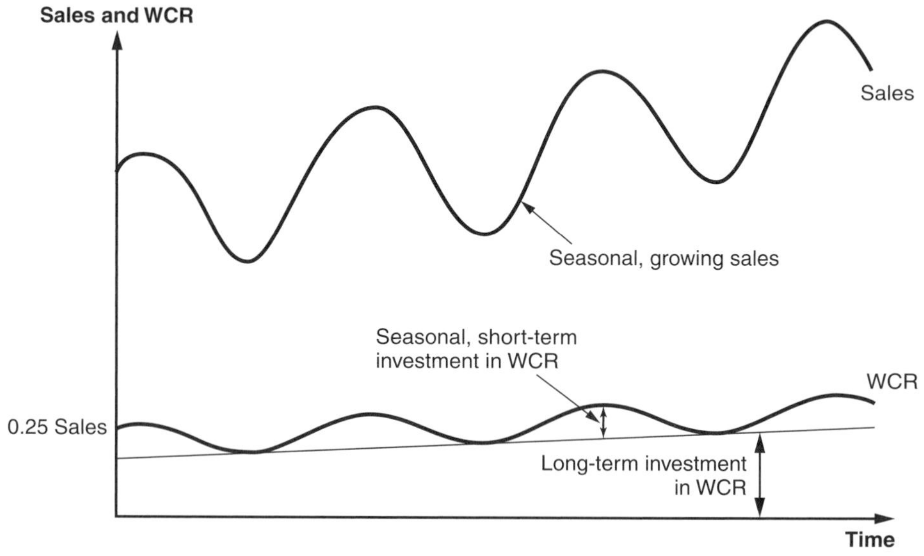

financed with short-term funds, implying that the firm did not adhere strictly to the matching strategy.[6] Let's examine this point further.

Some firms can adhere to the matching strategy without entirely financing their WCR with long-term funds. Consider a firm that has growing but *seasonal* sales. If the firm maintains a constant ratio of WCR to sales over time, then its working capital requirement will display a seasonal growth behavior. Exhibit 3.7 illustrates this situation for WCR equal to 25 percent of sales. In this case, WCR has a *long-term growth* component (called *permanent* WCR) and a *short-term seasonal* component (called *seasonal* WCR). According to the matching strategy, the long-term growth component should be financed with long-term funds and the seasonal component with short-term funds. Applying this funding strategy should reduce both financial cost and refinancing risks.

A MEASURE OF LIQUIDITY BASED ON THE FUNDING STRUCTURE OF WORKING CAPITAL REQUIREMENT

For most firms that adopt it, the matching strategy is an objective rather than a day-to-day reality. The goal of management is for long-term funds to match the firm's long-term investments (net fixed assets and permanent WCR) and for short-term funds to match the firm's short-term investments (cash, marketable securities, and seasonal working capital requirement) *over time*. This objective may not be

[6]The firm had more short-term debt than cash in 2008, 2009, and 2010. The difference went to finance part of its investment in working capital.

easily achieved in practice, and at times, the firm may find itself in a mismatched situation in which a *significant* portion of its permanent working capital is funded with short-term debt. This situation can create a liquidity problem. This section presents a measure of liquidity that managers can use to monitor their firm's liquidity position. The measure is based on the funding structure of WCR—more precisely, on the portion of WCR that is funded with long-term financing.

How much long-term financing is available to fund the firm's WCR? Because net fixed assets are funded with long-term financing, any long-term financing in *excess* of net fixed assets can be used to fund WCR. These excess long-term funds are called **net long-term financing** (NLF):

$$\textbf{Net long-term financing} = \textbf{Long-term financing} - \textbf{Net fixed assets} \qquad (3.4)$$

NLF is the portion of the firm's long-term financing available to finance the firm's other two fundamental investments, its WCR and cash. Exhibit 3.8 shows that OS Distributors' NLF at the end of 2010 was \$62 million. It is equal to the firm's \$115 million of long-term financing (\$38 million of long-term debt plus \$77 million of equity) less the \$53 million of net fixed assets.

How much short-term financing is used to fund the firm's WCR? It is simply the amount of short-term debt that is not used to finance the firm's cash. The amount of short-term debt in excess of cash is called **net short-term financing** (NSF):

$$\textbf{Net short-term financing} = \textbf{Short-term debt} - \textbf{Cash} \qquad (3.5)$$

As shown at the bottom of Exhibit 3.8, OS Distributors' WCR of \$77 million at the end of 2010 was financed with \$62 million of long-term funds (NLF \$62 million) and \$15 million of short-term funds (NSF \$15 million). Thus, in 2010, 80.5 percent of WCR was funded with long-term financing and 19.5 percent with short-term debt. We call the ratio of NLF to WCR the firm's **liquidity ratio** and use it to measure the firm's liquidity position:

$$\textbf{Liquidity ratio} = \frac{\textbf{Long-term financing} - \textbf{Net fixed assets}}{\textbf{Working capital requirement}}$$

$$= \frac{\textbf{Net long-term financing}}{\textbf{Working capital requirement}} \qquad (3.6)$$

OS Distributors' liquidity ratio dropped from 84.7 percent in 2008 to 80.5 percent in 2010, indicating a slight deterioration in the firm's liquidity position. In general, all else the same, *the higher the proportion of WCR financed with long-term funds, the more liquid the firm.* This is because working capital is essentially a long-term investment; financing it with higher proportions of short-term funds creates a mismatch between investment and funding durations that could lead to a liquidity problem. In other words, *the higher the liquidity ratio, the more liquid the firm.*

If we deduct NLF from working capital requirement, we get the portion of WCR that is financed with short-term funds, in other words, NSF:

$$\text{Working capital requirement} - \text{Net long-term financing} = \text{Net short-term financing}$$

This equation clearly shows that a firm's *net* short-term financing depends on the relative amounts of working capital and *net* long-term financing on its balance

EXHIBIT 3.8 OS DISTRIBUTORS' NET INVESTMENTS IN ITS OPERATING CYCLE AND ITS FINANCING.

ALL DATA FROM THE BALANCE SHEETS IN EXHIBIT 3.1. FIGURES IN MILLIONS

December 31, 2008	December 31, 2009	December 31, 2010
Net Investment in the Operating Cycle or Working Capital Requirement (WCR)		
WCR = [Accounts receivable + Inventories + Prepaid expenses] – [Accounts payable + Accrued expenses]		
[\$44 + \$52 + \$2] – [\$37 + \$2] = **\$59**	[\$48 + \$57 + \$2] – [\$40 + \$4] = **\$63**	[\$56 + \$72 + \$1] – [\$48 + \$4] = **\$77**
The Financing of the Operating Cycle		
Net long-term financing (NLF) = Long-term debt + Owners' equity – Net fixed assets		
\$42 + \$64 – \$56 = **\$50**	\$34 + \$70 – \$51 = **\$53**	\$38 + \$77 – \$53 = **\$62**
Net short-term financing (NSF) = Short-term debt – Cash		
\$15 – \$6 = **\$9**	\$22 – \$12 = **\$10**	\$23 – \$8 = **\$15**
Net long-term financing / Working capital requirement Percentage of working capital requirement financed with long-term funds		
\$50 / \$59 = **84.7%**	\$53 / \$63 = **84.1%**	\$62 / \$77 = **80.5%**
Net short-term financing / Working capital requirement Percentage of working capital requirement financed with short-term funds		
\$9 / \$59 = **15.3%**	\$10 / \$63 = **15.9%**	\$15 / \$77 = **19.5%**

Working Capital Requirement and Its Financing

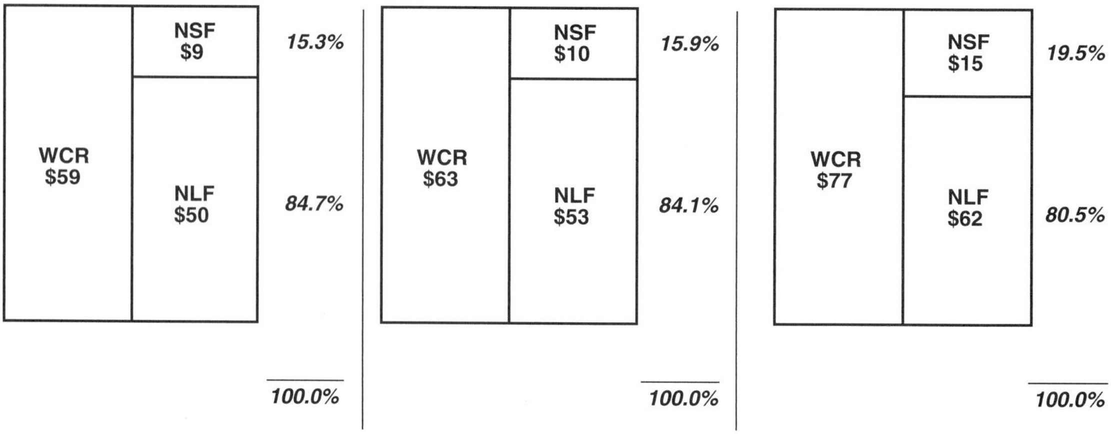

sheet. As the amount of long-term funds used to finance WCR (NLF) increases, the firm's liquidity ratio rises (see equation 3.6). Simultaneously, the amount of short-term funds used to finance WCR (NSF) decreases. In other words, when the firm increases its liquidity ratio, it is also reducing its NSF.

IMPROVING LIQUIDITY THROUGH BETTER MANAGEMENT OF THE OPERATING CYCLE

What drives a firm's liquidity? The answer to this question is given by the liquidity ratio in equation 3.6: a firm's liquidity position is the consequence of decisions that affect its NLF (the numerator of the liquidity ratio) and its WCR (the denominator of the liquidity ratio). A firm's liquidity position will improve if its liquidity ratio rises. According to equation 3.6, this will happen under the following circumstances:

1. Long-term financing increases, and/or
2. Net fixed assets decrease, and/or
3. WCR decreases

Decisions related to the management of long-term financing and net fixed assets are *strategic* in nature. Long-term financing will increase if the firm (1) issues long-term debt, (2) raises new equity capital (issues new shares), or (3) increases retained earnings by reducing dividend payments. Net fixed assets will decrease if the firm sells property and other fixed assets. Generally, these decisions are infrequent and involve large amounts of cash. They are also prepared well in advance so that the firm's financial manager, who actively participates in this decision-making process, can easily forecast their effect on the firm's liquidity.

Decisions affecting the firm's working capital requirement are related to the management of the firm's *operating* cycle. They determine the amount of receivables, inventories, prepaid expenses, payables, and accrued expenses in the firm's balance sheet. Contrary to strategic decisions, operating decisions are made frequently (a company receives payments from its customers many times a day), they involve relatively small amounts of cash, and, often, they do *not* directly involve the firm's financial manager. They affect the firm's liquidity continually and are difficult to forecast in the aggregate. Through these operating decisions, a firm's *operating* managers influence the firm's liquidity. *The lower the firm's investment in its operating cycle, the lower its WCR and the higher the firm's liquidity.* Furthermore, the lower the frequency of unexpected changes in the firm's WCR, the less volatile the firm's liquidity position and the easier it is to manage. Clearly, *control of the amount and fluctuations of a firm's WCR is the key to the sound management of the firm's liquidity.*

Controlling WCR requires identifying and understanding the factors that affect its size. Five items make up a firm's WCR: receivables, inventories, prepaid expenses, payables, and accrued expenses. The size of these five items depends on the following three basic factors:

1. The nature of the *economic sector* in which the firm operates,
2. The *degree of efficiency* with which the firm manages its operating cycle, and
3. The *level and growth of sales*

The Effect of the Firm's Economic Sector on Its Working Capital Requirement

The nature of a firm's business, the technology it uses, and the economic sector in which it operates affect the amount of WCR it needs to support a given level of sales. For example, an aircraft manufacturer needs more working capital than a department store to support the *same* level of sales. The business system underlying a department store allows it to operate with significantly lower amounts of receivables and inventories than those of an aircraft company with the same amount of sales. As mentioned earlier, some firms, such as large supermarket chains, may even have a *negative* WCR; in this case, the firm's operating cycle is a source of cash rather than a use of capital.

The sector effect on WCR can be measured by calculating the ratio of WCR to sales for a sample of firms in the same sector. Exhibit 3.9 reports this ratio for a number of industries in the United States. Firms in sectors with higher ratios require larger investments in their operating cycles to generate a dollar of sales. This indicates a longer operating cycle for firms in those industries. For example, in 2008, a typical firm in the machinery and equipment manufacturing industry needed, on average, to invest in its operating cycle an amount of capital equal to 19 percent of its sales, whereas a grocery store had, on average, *no* net investment in its operating cycle because the average WCR-to-sales ratio for the sector was

Exhibit 3.9 Some Benchmark Ratios of Working Capital Requirement to Sales for a Sample of U.S. Economic Sectors in 2008[1]

Working Capital Requirement as Percentage of Sales			
Sector		Sector	
Aircraft manufacturing	22%	Beverage manufacturing	10%
Textile mills	21%	Soap & cleaning compound manufacturing	10%
Leather & allied product manufacturing	20%	Petrochemical manufacturing	9%
Apparel manufacturing	19%	Paper manufacturing	9%
Iron & steel mills	19%	Computer & equipment manufacturing	9%
Machinery & equipment manufacturing	19%	Wholesalers: Nondurable goods	8%
Electrical contractors	15%	Wood product manufacturing	8%
Motor vehicle manufacturing	15%	Natural gas distribution	8%
Plastics & rubber products manufacturing	13%	Drilling oil & gas wells	7%
Wholesalers: Durable goods	13%	Publishing industries (except Internet)	6%
Clothing & clothing accessories stores	11%	Electric power generation	5%
Food manufacturing	11%	Grocery stores	0%
Department stores	10%	Air transport	–3%
Printing & related support activites	10%	Warehousing & storage	–6%
Average all sectors: 11%			

[1]Source: Calculated by the authors using *Compustat* data.

zero in 2008. This difference simply reflects the fact that the operating cycle of a typical company making machinery and equipment is significantly longer than that of a typical grocery store. Note that very few sectors have an average WCR-to-sales ratio exceeding 25 percent and that the average ratio across all sectors is 11 percent.

Exhibit 3.10 shows that OS Distributors' ratio of WCR to sales rose from 15 percent in 2008 to 16 percent in 2010, indicating a slight deterioration in the management of its operating cycle during that period. Note also that OS Distributors' WCR-to-sales ratio is higher than its sector average of 13 percent reported in Exhibit 3.9 (wholesalers of durable goods), indicating a less efficient use of working capital than the average U.S. wholesaler.

EXHIBIT 3.10 OS DISTRIBUTORS' MANAGEMENT OF ITS OPERATING CYCLE.

ALL DATA FROM THE BALANCE SHEETS IN EXHIBIT 3.1 AND THE INCOME STATEMENTS IN EXHIBIT 2.2. FIGURES IN MILLIONS

Ratio	Objective	December 31, 2008	December 31, 2009	December 31, 2010
Working capital requirement (WCR)[1] / Sales	To evaluate the overall efficiency with which the firm's operating cycle is managed	$\frac{\$59}{\$390} = 15\%$	$\frac{\$63}{\$420} = 15\%$	$\frac{\$77}{\$480} = 16\%$
Cost of goods sold (COGS) / Inventories	To evaluate the efficiency with which inventories are managed	$\frac{\$328}{\$52} = 6.3$ times	$\frac{\$353}{\$57} = 6.2$ times	$\frac{\$400}{\$72} = 5.6$ times
Accounts receivable / Average daily sales[2]	To evaluate the efficiency with which accounts receivable are managed	$\frac{\$44}{\$390/365} = 41$ days	$\frac{\$48}{\$420/365} = 42$ days	$\frac{\$56}{\$480/365} = 43$ days
Accounts payable / Average daily purchases[2,3]	To evaluate the efficiency with which accounts payable are managed	$\frac{\$37}{\$332/365} = 41$ days	$\frac{\$40}{\$358/365} = 41$ days	$\frac{\$48}{\$415/365} = 42$ days

[1]WCR is found in Exhibit 3.6.

[2]We assume the year has 365 days.

[3]Purchases are equal to COGS plus the change in inventories (see equation 3.11). In 2007, inventories were $48, thus purchases (2008) = $328 + ($52 – $48) = $332. Purchases (2009) = $353 + ($57 – $52) = $358; and purchases (2010) = $400 + ($72 – $57) = $415.

The Effect of Managerial Efficiency on Working Capital Requirement

Firms in the same sector do not necessarily have the same ratio of WCR to sales. Even though they face similar constraints, some are able to manage their working capital better than others. For example, if a firm does not control its inventories and receivables as well as its sector's average, its WCR-to-sales ratio will be higher than that of its sector.

Several ratios can be used to estimate the efficiency with which a firm manages the components of its WCR. They have the advantages of being simple and of requiring data readily available in balance sheets and income statements. These ratios, discussed in the following sections, provide managers and analysts with good signals regarding both changes in a firms' managerial efficiency over time and differences across firms in the same sector.

Inventory Turnover

A firm's **inventory turnover**, or **inventory turns**, is generally defined as the ratio of its cost of goods sold (COGS) to its end-of-period inventories:

$$\textbf{Inventory turnover} = \frac{\textbf{Cost of goods sold}}{\textbf{Ending inventories}} \tag{3.7}$$

For a distribution company, an inventory turnover of, say, six means that items in inventory turn over, on average, six times per year. Or, to put it another way, an item stays in the firm's warehouse for two months, on average. The *higher* the inventory turnover, the *lower* the firm's investment in inventories and the *higher* the efficiency with which the firm manages its inventories.

When COGS is not available, the level of sales is often used as a substitute to compute inventory turnover. Sometimes, inventories at the end of the period are replaced by average inventories during the period. Strictly speaking, the definition of inventory turnover given in equation 3.7 applies only to finished goods. To obtain the turnover for raw material inventory, the COGS in equation 3.7 is replaced by the amount of purchases.

The ratios reported in Exhibit 3.10 indicate that OS Distributors' inventory turnover deteriorated slightly, dropping from 6.3 times at the end of 2008 to 5.6 times at the end of 2010.

Average Collection Period

Also called the **average age of accounts receivable**, or **days of sales outstanding (DSO)**, the **average collection period**, expressed in days, is defined as accounts receivable at the end of the period divided by the average *daily* sales during that period:

$$\textbf{Average collection period} = \frac{\textbf{Accounts receivable}_{\textbf{end}}}{\textbf{Average daily sales}} \tag{3.8}$$

The average collection period is the number of days' worth of sales *that have not yet been collected at the date of the balance sheet.* It is an estimate of the *average* number of days the firm must wait from the time it ships its goods or delivers its services until its customers pay their bills. The faster the bills are collected, the *lower* the firm's receivables, the *higher* the efficiency with which the firm manages its receivables, and the *lower* its WCR.

This ratio is just an average; it does not represent the actual number of days a firm must wait between the time a sale is made and payment for it is collected. Not all customers settle their invoices after the same number of days. Some pay earlier than the average collection period and others pay later. If a certain group of customers is often late paying its bills, the firm should monitor that group separately.

OS Distributors' average collection periods, reported in Exhibit 3.10, indicate a slight lengthening of its collection period from forty-one days at the end of 2008 to forty-three days at the end of 2010.

AVERAGE PAYMENT PERIOD

The **average payment period** is to *purchases* what the average collection period is to sales. It is defined as the ratio of accounts payable at the end of the period to the average daily purchases during that period:

$$\textbf{Average payment period} = \frac{\textbf{Accounts payable}_{\textbf{end}}}{\textbf{Average daily purchases}} \tag{3.9}$$

The average payment period is the number of days' worth of purchases that have not yet been paid at the date of the balance sheet. The *longer* the average payment period, the *higher* the firm's payables and the *lower* its WCR.

To compute the average daily purchases, you need to know the amount of purchases made during the accounting period ending at the date of the balance sheet. Although this information is not directly reported in the firm's financial statements, purchases made during the accounting period can be obtained indirectly from data provided in balance sheets and income statements.

First, we consider a manufacturing firm. The cost of the goods manufactured during the accounting period equals the cost of purchases plus the cost of production. We add this sum to the beginning of the period's inventories account (raw material, work in process, and finished goods inventories). As the firm sells its finished goods, inventories decrease by the COGS. The net effect of these transactions is the ending inventories:

$$\text{Beginning inventories} + \text{Purchases} + \text{Production costs} - \text{COGS} = \text{Ending inventories}$$

We can rearrange the terms in the above equation to calculate the firm's purchases during the accounting period as a function of COGS, production costs, and the change in inventories:

$$\textbf{Purchases} = \textbf{COGS} + \textbf{Change in inventories} - \textbf{Production costs} \tag{3.10}$$

where the change in inventories equals the firm's ending inventories less its beginning inventories during the accounting period.

For a trading firm with no production costs, such as OS Distributors, equation 3.10 simplifies to this:

$$\textbf{Purchases} = \textbf{COGS} + \textbf{Change in inventories} \tag{3.11}$$

Equation 3.11 could have been obtained directly because, for a distributor, if the amount of goods purchased during the accounting period exceeds the amount of goods sold during that period, the inventories account will increase by the difference.

If a distributor sells more goods than it buys during the accounting period, the inventories account will decrease by the difference.

The purchases of OS Distributors reported in Exhibit 3.10 are computed according to equation 3.11. These purchases are divided by 365 to obtain the average daily purchases for each year. Notice that the average payment period rose slightly from forty-one to forty-two days.

THE EFFECT OF SALES GROWTH ON WORKING CAPITAL REQUIREMENT

Suppose a firm's sales are expected to grow by 10 percent next year. How would the firm's WCR be affected if there is *no change in the efficiency* with which its operating cycle is managed (same inventory turnover and same collection and payment periods)? Even though efficiency remains the same, higher sales will require additional investments in the firm's operating cycle because the firm will need more receivables, more inventories, and more payables to support its additional sales. As a consequence, the firm's WCR will increase. As a first approximation, you can expect *WCR to grow at the same rate as sales*, that is, at 10 percent.

Consider the case of OS Distributors. At the end of 2010, its WCR was equal to $77 million. If sales are expected to grow by 10 percent in 2011 and the WCR-to-sales ratio is expected to remain the same as in 2010, then we can expect OS Distributors' working capital requirement also to grow by 10 percent, or $7.7 million, in 2011. Thus, OS Distributors will need $7.7 million of cash to finance the anticipated growth of its WCR. If OS Distributors does not have or cannot obtain $7.7 million of cash, it may face a liquidity problem. If management is able to improve the efficiency of the firm's operating cycle (through a combination of higher inventory turnover and faster collection of receivables), then OS Distributors will need less than $7.7 million of cash in 2011.

As this example illustrates, *an unplanned or unexpected growth in sales may create liquidity problems*. These problems can be alleviated if management maintains tight control over the firm's operating cycle and anticipates the funding needs that will result from future changes in the firm's WCR. How far can managers improve the efficiency of their firm's WCR to release the cash tied up by the firm's operating cycle? An increasing number of *manufacturing firms* have set themselves the ambitious goal of operating with close to *zero* WCR. The article reproduced in Exhibit 3.11 explains how this can be achieved.

Inflation also puts pressure on the firm's WCR. When the price level rises, the nominal value of the firm's sales will rise even though the number of units sold may not change. Inflated sales figures require higher levels of receivables; thus, the firm's investment in its operating cycle will increase unless management becomes more efficient.

TRADITIONAL MEASURES OF LIQUIDITY

Some of the traditional measures of a firm's liquidity are reviewed in this section. We also explain why these measures are often *not* reliable indicators of the firm's liquidity.

EXHIBIT 3.11 RAIDING A COMPANY'S HIDDEN CASH.[1]

Reducing working capital yields two powerful benefits. First, every dollar freed from inventories or receivables rings up a one-time $1 contribution to cash flow. Second, the quest for zero working capital permanently raises earnings. Like all capital, working capital costs money, so reducing it yields savings. In addition, cutting working capital forces companies to produce and deliver faster than the competition, enabling them to win new business and charge premium prices for filling rush orders. As inventories evaporate, warehouses disappear. Companies no longer need forklift drivers or schedulers to plan production months in advance.

Over the 12 months that ended May 1996, Campbell Soup pared working capital by $80 million. It used the cash to develop new products and buy companies in Britain, Australia, and other countries. But Campbell also expects to harvest an *extra* $50 million in profits over the next few years by lowering overtime, storage costs, and other expenses—savings that will persist year after year.

The most important discipline that zero working capital necessitates is speed. Many companies today produce elaborate long-term forecasts of orders. They then manufacture their products weeks or months in advance, creating big inventories; eventually they fill orders from the bulging stocks.

Minimizing working capital forces organizations to demolish that system. Scrapping forecasts, companies manufacture goods as they are ordered. The best companies start producing an auto braking system or cereal flavor after receiving an order and yet still manage to deliver just when the customer needs it.

The system, known as demand flow or demand-based management, builds on the familiar idea of just-in-time inventories but is far broader. Most companies achieve just-in-time in one or two areas. They demand daily shipments from suppliers, for example, or dispatch finished products the hour the customer wants them. But just-in-time deliveries don't guarantee efficiency. To meet the rapid schedule, many companies simply ship from huge inventories. They still manufacture weeks or months in advance.

Achieving zero working capital requires that every order and part move at maximum pace, never stopping. Orders streak from the processing department to the plant. Flexible factories manufacture each product every day. Finished goods flow from the assembly line onto waiting trucks. Manufacturers press suppliers to cut inventories as well, since minimal stocks translate into lower raw materials prices to the manufacturer. Instead of cluttering plants or warehouses, parts and products hurtle through the pipeline. As velocity rises, inventory—working capital—dwindles. That's why working capital levels are such a useful yardstick for efficiency and why manufacturers with the least working capital per dollar of sales will reign as the world's best-run companies.

[1] "Raiding a Company's Hidden Cash" by Shawn Tully and Robert A. Miller from *Fortune*, August 22, 1994. Copyright © 1994. Reprinted by permission of *Fortune*.

NET WORKING CAPITAL

The traditional definition of a firm's **net working capital** is the difference between its current assets and its current liabilities. The rationale for this definition is that the higher the firm's net working capital, the easier it would be in the case of default to meet the firm's current liabilities by selling its current assets. However, we are interested in estimating a company's ability to meet its cash obligations on a *continual* basis as opposed to its ability to meet the same obligations only in the case of default. Thus, this definition of net working capital is of limited value.

There is an alternative, and in our opinion superior, way to interpret net working capital. We write the balance sheet identity as follows:

Current assets + Net fixed assets = Current liabilities + Long-term financing

Rearranging the terms in this equation, we get the following:

Current assets – Current liabilities = Long-term financing – Net fixed assets

which, using the definition of net working capital, can be written as:

Net working capital = Long-term financing – Net fixed assets (3.12)

Now compare equation 3.12 with equation 3.4, which measures the net long-term funds available to finance WCR. *Net working capital* given by equation 3.12 and *net long-term financing* given by equation 3.4 are the same. In other words, net working capital can be interpreted in the same way as NLF. The definition of net working capital as the difference between long-term financing and net fixed assets has a clear economic meaning. It says that *net working capital is the amount of long-term financing available to fund the firm's operating cycle after the firm has funded its long-term strategic investment in fixed assets*. This definition of net working capital is more useful than the traditional definition, which has no particular managerial meaning. Furthermore, using the traditional definition of net working capital may lead to the conclusion that net working capital is determined by the firm's short-term operating decisions, which we know is not the case.

Exhibit 3.12 reports OS Distributors' net working capital at the end of 2008, 2009, and 2010, using the two definitions presented above. Net working

EXHIBIT 3.12 OS DISTRIBUTORS' NET WORKING CAPITAL AND CURRENT AND QUICK RATIOS.

ALL DATA FROM THE BALANCE SHEETS IN EXHIBIT 3.1. FIGURES IN MILLIONS

	December 31, 2008	December 31, 2009	December 31, 2010
• **Net working capital** = [Current assets – Current liabilities][1]	\$104 – \$54 = **\$50**	\$119 – \$66 = **\$53**	\$137 – \$75 = **\$62**
• **Net working capital** = [Long-term financing[2] – Net fixed assets][3]	(\$42 + \$64) – \$56 = **\$50**	(\$34 + \$70) – \$51 = **\$53**	(\$38 + \$77) – \$53 = **\$62**
• **Current ratio** = $\frac{\text{Current assets}}{\text{Current liabilities}}$	$\frac{\$104}{\$54} = 1.93$	$\frac{\$119}{\$66} = 1.80$	$\frac{\$137}{\$75} = 1.83$
• **Quick ratio** = $\frac{\text{Cash + Accounts receivable}}{\text{Current liabilities}}$	$\frac{\$6 + \$44}{\$54} = 0.93$	$\frac{\$12 + \$48}{\$66} = 0.91$	$\frac{\$8 + \$56}{\$75} = 0.85$

[1]This is the traditional definition of net working capital.
[2]Long-term financing = Long-term debt + Owners' equity.
[3]According to this definition, net working capital is the same as net long-term financing (see equation 3.4).

capital grew from $50 million at the end of 2008 to $62 million at the end of 2010, meaning that OS Distributors had, in 2010, an additional $12 million of long-term financing to fund its operating cycle compared with what it had in 2008.

THE CURRENT RATIO

The **current ratio** is obtained by dividing the firm's current assets by its current liabilities:

$$\textbf{Current ratio} = \frac{\textbf{Current assets}}{\textbf{Current liabilities}} \tag{3.13}$$

It is often said that the larger the current ratio, the more liquid the firm and that the current ratio should be at least greater than one and preferably close to two. This reasoning, similar to the one used for the traditional definition of net working capital, is based on the notion that the higher the current ratio, the easier it would be for the firm to repay its short-term liabilities with the cash raised from the sale of its short-term assets. For this to be possible, the firm's current assets should be at least equal to its current liabilities. In other words, its current ratio should be at least equal to one.

But if liquidity increases when the current ratio increases, why not have clients pay as late as possible to increase the firm's accounts receivable, why not keep as many goods as possible in stock, and why not pay the firm's suppliers as soon as possible? The first two decisions will significantly increase the firm's current assets, and the third decision will substantially reduce its current liabilities. As a result, the firm's current ratio will go sky-high. But has the firm's liquidity increased? Certainly not. The current ratio is definitely not a reliable measure of the firm's liquidity.

The value of OS Distributors' current ratio at the end of 2008, 2009, and 2010 is given in Exhibit 3.12. It varied from a low of 1.80 in 2009 to a high of 1.93 in 2008.

THE ACID TEST OR QUICK RATIO

Sometimes, analysts modify the current ratio by eliminating the relatively illiquid inventories and prepaid expenses from the firm's current assets. What remains is simply the sum of cash and receivables, the two most liquid current assets, also called **quick assets**. The result is called the **acid test** or **quick ratio**:

$$\textbf{Acid test or quick ratio} = \frac{\textbf{Cash + Accounts receivable}}{\textbf{Current liabilities}} \tag{3.14}$$

The quick ratio is an improvement over the current ratio, but it still emphasizes a *liquidation view* of the firm as opposed to a *going-concern approach* to liquidity analysis. Furthermore, a firm's inventories are not always less liquid than its accounts receivable.

The value of OS Distributors' quick ratio is reported in Exhibit 3.12. It varied from a low of 0.85 in 2010 to a high of 0.93 in 2008. Creditors usually prefer a ratio close to one for most manufacturing firms.

SUMMARY

A firm's liquidity is driven by the structure of its balance sheet, that is, by the nature and composition of its assets and the way they are financed. Liquidity is easier to analyze if the standard balance sheet is restructured into the managerial balance sheet. This alternative presentation identifies the three components of the firm's invested capital: (1) cash and cash-equivalent assets; (2) working capital requirement (WCR); and (3) net fixed assets. It also identifies the three sources of capital employed to finance invested capital: (1) short-term debt; (2) long-term debt; and (3) equity capital. WCR, which measures the firm's investment in its operating cycle, is equal to the difference between operating assets (accounts receivable, inventories, and prepaid expenses) and operating liabilities (accounts payable and accrued expenses).

A firm's liquidity, which refers to its ability to meet its recurrent cash obligations, should be measured by the ratio of its net long-term financing (NLF) to WCR, where NLF is the sum of equity capital and long-term debt minus net fixed assets. The higher that ratio, the higher the proportion of working capital that is financed with long-term funds and the higher the firm's liquidity.

The portion of working capital that is not financed with long-term funds is obviously financed with short-term debt. These short-term borrowings in *excess* of cash are called net short-term financing (NSF). To minimize the effect of both financial cost risk (unexpected changes in short-term interest rates) and refinancing risk (unexpected cuts in the availability of short-term debt), most firms should limit the short-term financing of their working capital to its seasonal short-term component while financing the permanent long-term component with long-term funds. This approach to funding is known as the matching strategy.

The key to good liquidity management is good management of the firm's working capital cycle; a *liquidity crisis is often the symptom of a mismanaged working capital cycle*. If a firm's working capital requirement grows out of control and is not properly financed, liquidity problems appear immediately. Broadly speaking, good management of the working capital cycle means two things. First, accounts receivable and inventories, the two major components of working capital, must be held at their *minimum* levels relative to sales. This will allow the firm to save the cash it would have needed to fund a larger amount of receivables and inventories. Second, because WCR is essentially a long-term investment, a firm's liquidity will rise as higher proportions of its working capital are financed with long-term funds.

Finally, the ratio of NLF to WCR is a better indicator of a firm's liquidity position than the traditional benchmarks of net working capital, current ratio, or quick ratio. These last two ratios may be good indicators of a firm's ability to rapidly repay its current liabilities with the cash raised from the sale of its current assets, but they are not reliable measures of a firm's capacity to meet its cash obligations on a *recurrent* basis.

FINANCING STRATEGIES

APPENDIX **3.1**

Firms may choose different financial strategies regarding the maturity structure of the funds used to finance their invested capital. The matching strategy, examined in this chapter, is the most common one and calls for matching the duration of the sources of funds with that of the investments. Some firms, however, may adopt other financing strategies, depending on the level of risk they are willing to take. They can adopt a **conservative strategy** if they want less risk or an **aggressive strategy** if they are prepared to accept more risk. This appendix examines the three strategies for a firm with seasonal and growing sales. The three strategies are illustrated in Exhibits A3.1.1, A3.1.2, and A3.1.3

A firm with seasonal sales experiences changes in its working capital requirement (WCR) during the seasonal cycle. WCR increases as sales increase and decreases as sales decrease. This is shown in Exhibit 3.7, where the behavior of WCR is decomposed into a long-term permanent component and a short-term seasonal component. This short-term component of WCR is usually the only component of

EXHIBIT A3.1.1 FINANCING INVESTMENTS USING A MATCHING STRATEGY.

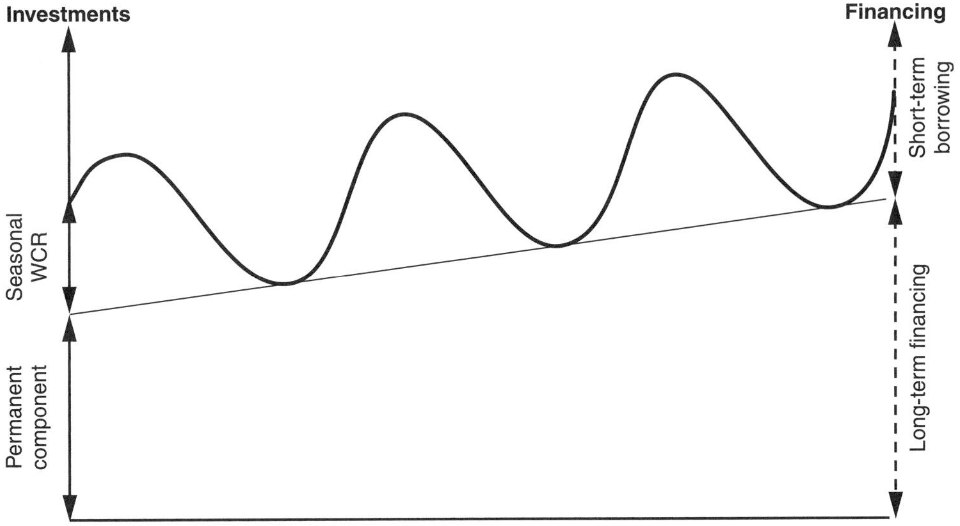

EXHIBIT A3.1.2 FINANCING INVESTMENTS USING A CONSERVATIVE STRATEGY.

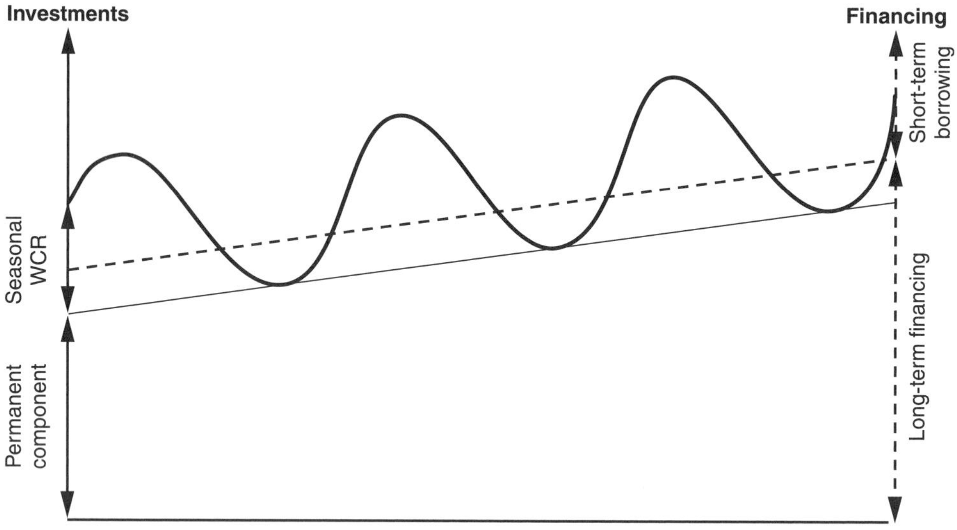

the firm's three fundamental investments that is directly linked to changes in sales during the seasonal cycle. The sum of cash, net fixed assets, and the long-term component of WCR makes up the firm's *permanent* investments. These investments are not significantly affected by seasonality in sales. Seasonal and permanent components of the firm's investments are shown on the left side of Exhibits A3.1.1 to A3.1.3. The right side shows the two components of the financing policy: long-term financing (owners' equity plus long-term debt) and short-term borrowing.

EXHIBIT A3.1.3 FINANCING INVESTMENTS USING AN AGGRESSIVE STRATEGY.

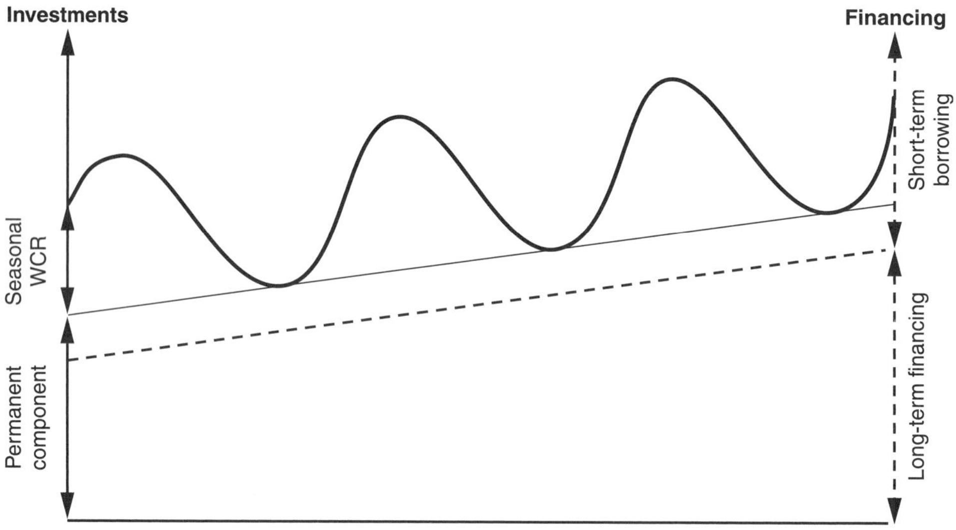

Exhibit A3.1.1 illustrates the matching strategy. *Permanent investment is financed with long-term funds and seasonal investment with short-term funds.* The objective of this strategy is to minimize (but not completely eliminate) the risk resulting from having a mismatched balance sheet.

Exhibit A3.1.2 shows the effect of adopting a conservative strategy. *Permanent needs and some seasonal needs are financed with long-term funds.* In this case, short-term borrowing covers only a portion of the firm's seasonal needs. At times, near the cyclical trough, the firm would have some excess cash (negative short-term financing). This "margin of safety" can be used to meet unforeseen cash needs that would have to be financed by an increase in short-term borrowing under the matching strategy.

The aggressive strategy, illustrated in Exhibit A3.1.3, implies that *the firm uses short-term funds to finance a portion of the permanent component of its investments.* This strategy is riskier than either of the other two strategies because the firm would bear greater financial cost and refinancing risks. The financial cost risk originates from possible variations in the cost of debt during the useful life of the investments; the refinancing risk refers to the possibility that the firm may not be able to renew the short-term loans needed to finance a portion of the permanent component of the firm's investments.

A firm may choose to bear more financial cost and refinancing risks if it expects the short-term interest rate to decrease and, on average, to be lower than the current long-term rate over the useful life of the investment. In some instances, a firm may be forced to adopt an aggressive strategy. This situation happens when firms have limited access to long-term funds and must rely heavily on short-term financing.

THE HOME DEPOT'S LIQUIDITY AND OPERATIONAL EFFICIENCY

APPENDIX 3.2

To analyze The Home Depot's liquidity, we first restructure the company's balance sheets, which were presented in Appendix 2.1 to Chapter 2, into managerial balance sheets. The balance sheets cover the three-year period from 2006 to 2008.[7] We then apply the approach taken in the chapter to examine the company's liquidity and the management of its operating cycle. For comparison purposes, we also show the results of the same analysis applied to Lowe's Companies, Inc., the world's second-largest home improvement retailer, and a major competitor to The Home Depot.[8]

THE HOME DEPOT'S MANAGERIAL BALANCE SHEETS

Exhibit A3.2.1 presents The Home Depot's balance sheets at the end of the fiscal years 2006, 2007, and 2008 taken from the firm's annual reports, and Exhibit A3.2.2 shows how we allocated the accounts from the balance sheets to the "invested capital" and "capital employed" accounts in the firm's managerial balance sheets. Generally, this allocation is rather straightforward.

When in doubt, refer to the notes accompanying the financial statements to identify the transactions recorded in the particular account that has no obvious allocation. With this information, you should be able to assign the account to the relevant component of the managerial balance sheet.

For example, note that we have allocated the firm's receivables to the cash account. We did this because, in a note to the balance sheet, The Home Depot indicates that customers' payments by credit cards (or payments by a third party that extends credit to other customers) need one or two days to clear. For all practical purpose, these receivables are another form of cash equivalent and must be considered as cash in the managerial balance sheet.

---

[7]The Home Depot's fiscal year 2006 ends on January 28, 2007, fiscal year 2007 ends on February 3, 2008, and fiscal year 2008 ends on February 1, 2009. We refer to the fiscal years simply as 2006, 2007, and 2008, respectively.

[8]Lowe's fiscal year 2006 ends on February 2, 2007, fiscal year 2007 ends on February 1, 2008, and fiscal year 2008 ends on January 2, 2009. We also refer to the fiscal years as 2006, 2007, and 2008, respectively.

Exhibit A3.2.1 The Home Depot, Inc.'s Consolidated Balance Sheets.

From the company annual reports for fiscal year 2007 and 2008. Figures in millions

Fiscal Year	2006	2007	2008
Assets			
• Current assets			
Cash and cash equivalents	$ 600	$ 445	$ 519
Short-term investments	14	12	6
Accounts receivable, net	3,223	1,259	972
Merchandise inventories	12,822	11,731	10,673
Other current assets	1,341	1,227	1,192
Total current assets	18,000	14,674	13,362
• Property and equipment, at cost			
Land	8,355	8,398	8,301
Buildings	15,215	16,642	16,961
Furniture, fixtures and equipment	7,799	8,050	8,741
Leasehold improvements	1,391	1,390	1,359
Construction in progress	1,123	1,435	625
Capital leases	475	497	490
	34,358	36,412	36,477
Less accumulated depreciation and amortization	7,753	8,936	10,243
Net property and equipment	26,605	27,476	26,234
• Notes receivable	343	342	36
• Goodwill	6,314	1,209	1,134
• Other assets	1,001	623	398
Total assets	**$52,263**	**$44,324**	**$41,164**
Liabilities and stockholders' equity			
• Current liabilities			
Short-term debt	$ –	$ 1,747	$ –
Accounts payable	7,356	5,732	4,822
Accrued salaries and related expenses	1,307	1,094	1,129
Sales taxes payable	475	445	337
Deferred revenue	1,634	1,474	1,165
Income taxes payable	217	60	289
Current installments of long-term debt	18	300	1,767
Other accrued expenses	1,924	1,854	1,644
Total current liabilities	12,931	12,706	11,153

(Continued)

EXHIBIT A3.2.1 THE HOME DEPOT, INC.'S CONSOLIDATED BALANCE SHEETS. *(CONTINUED)*

Fiscal Year	2006	2007	2008
• Long-term liabilities			
Long-term debt, excluding current installments	$11,643	$11,383	$9,667
Other long-term liabilities	1,243	1,833	2,198
Deferred income taxes	1,416	688	369
Total liabilities	27,233	26,610	23,387
• Stockholders' equity			
Common stock	121	85	85
Paid-in capital	7,930	5,800	6,048
Retained earnings	33,052	11,388	12,093
Accumulated other comprehensive income (loss)	310	755	−77
Treasury stock	−16,383	−314	−372
	25,030	17,714	17,777
Total liabilities and stockholders' equity	**$52,263**	**$44,324**	**$41,164**

THE HOME DEPOT'S LIQUIDITY POSITION

Four observations can be made from examining The Home Depot's managerial balance sheets in Exhibit A3.2.3.

First, the size of the balance sheets decreased significantly over the three-year period, from $52,263 million at year-end 2006 to $41,164 million at year-end 2008. The decrease was most significant in 2007 during which time owners' equity went down from $25,030 million to $17,714 million. In its 2007 annual report, the company indicates that it spent $10,815 million to repurchase shares with the proceeds from the sale of one of its largest operations and from excess cash. Note that the amount of cash the company held at year-end 2006 decreased by more than half, from $3,837 million to $1,716 million during 2007. Given the prevailing market conditions, the company suspended its stock repurchase program in 2008. The decrease in fixed assets contributed also to the reduction in size of the balance sheet. According to the company's annual report, the disposition of some businesses, the decision to discontinue some operations, and the impairment of some assets, particularly in 2008, contributed to lower fixed assets.

Second, the proportion of capital invested in the operating cycle nearly tripled over the three-year period, going from 3 percent to 8 percent with most of the increase occurring in 2007.

Third, as The Home Depot invested capital decreased, so did its capital employed due mainly to share repurchases in 2007. Note that the company total debt

Exhibit A3.2.2 From the Actual to the Managerial Balance Sheets of The Home Depot, Inc.

Actual Balance Sheet	Managerial Balance Sheet
Assets	
Cash and cash equivalents	Cash
Short-term investments	Cash
Accounts receivable, net	Cash
Merchandise inventories	Working capital requirement
Other current assets	Working capital requirement
Net property and equipment	Net fixed assets
Notes receivable	Net fixed assets
Goodwill	Net fixed assets
Other assets	Net fixed assets
Liabilities and stockholders' equity	
Short-term debt	Short-term debt
Accounts payable	Working capital requirement
Accrued salaries and related expenses	Working capital requirement
Sales taxes payable	Working capital requirement
Deferred revenue	Working capital requirement
Income taxes payable	Working capital requirement
Current installments of long-term debt	Short-term debt
Other accrued expenses	Working capital requirement
Long-term debt, excluding current installments	Long-term financing
Other long-term liabilities	Long-term financing
Deferred income taxes	Long-term financing
Common stock	Owners' equity
Paid-in capital	Owners' equity
Retained earnings	Owners' equity
Accumulated other comprehensive income (loss)	Owners' equity
Treasury stock	Owners' equity

(short-term plus long-term) did not change much over the three-year period. Indeed, the amount of debt at year-end 2008 ($11,434 million, the sum of $1,767 million and $9,667 million) is practically the same as that at year-end 2006 ($11,661 million, the sum of $18 million and $11,643 million).

Finally, notice that the liquidity ratio (net long-term financing divided by working capital requirement [WCR]) dropped drastically from a high of 4.06 at year-end

EXHIBIT A3.2.3 THE HOME DEPOT'S MANAGERIAL BALANCE SHEETS.

ALL DATA FROM THE BALANCE SHEETS IN EXHIBIT A3.2.1. FIGURES IN MILLIONS

Fiscal Year		2006			2007			2008	
Invested capital									
• Cash		$3,837	*10%*		$1,716	*5%*		$1,497	*5%*
• Working capital requirement		1,250	*3%*		2,299	*7%*		2,479	*8%*
• Net fixed assets		34,263	*87%*		29,650	*88%*		27,802	*87%*
Total invested capital		$39,350	*100%*		$33,665	*100%*		$31,778	*100%*
Capital employed									
• Short-term debt		$18	*0%*		$2,047	*6%*		$1,767	*6%*
• Long-term financing		39,332	*100%*		31,618	*94%*		30,011	*100%*
Long-term debt	$11,643			$11,383			$9,667		
Other long-term liabilities	2,659			2,521			2,567		
Owners' equity	25,030			17,714			17,777		
Total capital employed		$39,350	*100%*		$33,665	*100%*		$31,778	*100%*
Net long-term financing[1]		$5,069			$1,968			$2,209	
Net long-term financing[2] / Working capital requirement		4.06	*406%*		0.86	*86%*		0.89	*89%*

[1]Long-term financing minus net fixed assets.
[2]The liquidity ratios of Lowe's were 1.63, 0.62, and 0.77 in fiscal year-end 2006, 2007 and 2008, respectively.

2006 to a low of 0.86 at year-end 2007. It then rose slightly to 0.89 at year-end 2008, indicating a deterioration of the firm's liquidity position, as reported in the bottom line of Exhibit A3.2.3. The company had a very conservative financing strategy during 2006 (all its WCR was financed with *long-term* funding), but following the sharp reduction in owners' equity due to share repurchases in 2007, the strategy became more aggressive with 14 percent of the company's WCR financed *short term* at year-end 2007 (100 percent minus 86 percent) and 11 percent at year-end 2008 (100 percent minus 89 percent).[9]

[9]The liquidity position of The Home Depot is not as risky as it appears just by looking at its liquidity ratio. In a note to its 2008 annual report, the company mentions it has a credit facility of $3.25 billion expiring December 2010. However, such facilities contain certain restrictive covenants such as the requirement to maintain a debt ratio under a certain level. The Home Depot indicates it was in compliance with these covenants at the end of fiscal year 2008.

It is also interesting to note that Lowe's liquidity ratio (see Note 2 in Exhibit A3.2.3), which was much higher than one at year-end 2006, also decreased over the following two years, dropping to 0.77 (meaning that 23 percent of the firm's WCR was financed with short-term debt) at year-end 2008. In other words, Lowe's liquidity position at year-end 2008 was more aggressive than that of The Home Depot.

THE HOME DEPOT'S MANAGEMENT OF THE OPERATING CYCLE

Exhibit A3.2.4 reports three ratios related to the management of the operating cycle of The Home Depot and Lowe's, at year-ends 2006, 2007, and 2008. Note that the exhibit does not provide any information about the management of receivables. As mentioned above, The Home Depot receivables are cash equivalents because they represent payments in the process of being cleared by credit institutions. This is also the case for Lowe's.

The Home Depot's ratio of WCR-to-net sales more than doubled between year-end 2006 and year-end 2008, rising from 1.6 percent to 3.5 percent, indicating that the company needed to invest more than twice as much in the operating cycle to generate one dollar of sale. Over the two-year period, the company's WCR increases from $1,250 million to $2,479 million (see Exhibit A3.2.3) while its sales went down from $79,022 million to $71,288 million (see Exhibit A2.1.2 in Chapter 2).

Lowe's ratio of WCR-to-net sales followed the same pattern as that of The Home Depot, rising from 2.3 percent at year-end 2006 to 3.3 percent at year-end 2008. At that date, the company investment in its operating cycle per dollar of sale was lower than that of The Home Depot, although the difference was not significant (3.3 percent versus 3.5 percent).

As Exhibit A3.2.4 shows, the inventory turnover ratio of The Home Depot improved during the two-year period, rising from 4.1 to 4.4. In its annual reports, the company attributes the improvement to constant upgrading of its logistic programs, including faster delivery from its distribution centers and transit facilities. During the same two-year period, Lowe's inventory turnover ratio declined from 4.3 to 3.9. In its 2008 annual report, the company recognizes that the management of its inventory is not very satisfactory and announced merchandise processing improvements for the following year.

The average payment period to suppliers of The Home Depot decreased drastically from 49.8 days to 36.4 days during the two-year period. The difference of 13.4 days represents approximately $1,700 million of "lost" suppliers' credit, and, subsequently, an increase of the company's WCR of the same amount. Part of this amount can be attributed to the disposal of HD Supply, one of its major business units. The balance, as suggested in the company's 2008 annual report, is the effect on payment terms of new strategic alliances and exclusive relationships with selected suppliers. Contrary to The Home Depot, Lowe's average payment period to suppliers increased from 41.2 to 46.4 days. Given the size of suppliers' credit in the retail business the ten-day difference in the average payment period between

EXHIBIT A3.2.4 THE HOME DEPOT AND LOWE'S OPERATING CYCLE MANAGEMENT.

DATA FROM THE FIRMS' INCOME STATEMENTS AND MANAGERIAL BALANCE SHEETS

	The Home Depot			Lowe's		
Fiscal Year	**2006**	**2007**	**2008**	**2006**	**2007**	**2008**
$\frac{\text{Working capital requirement}}{\text{Net revenues}}$	1.6%	3.0%	3.5%	2.3%	3.1%	3.3%
$\frac{\text{Cost of goods sold}}{\text{Inventories}}$	4.1 times	4.4 times	4.4 times	4.3 times	4.1 times	3.9 times
$\frac{\text{Accounts payable}^{1,2}}{\text{Average daily purchases}}$	49.8 days	39.9 days	36.4 days	41.2 days	43.6 days	46.4 days

[1]Daily averages are computed on the basis of 365 days a year.
[2]Purchases are computed as the sum of cost of goods sold plus change in inventories.

the two companies at year-end 2008 explains why Lowe's ratio of WCR-to-net-sales is lower than that of The Home Depot, despite a lower inventory turnover ratio.

FURTHER READING

1. Brealey, Richard, Stewart Myers, and Franklin Allen. *Principles of Corporate Finance*, 9th ed. McGraw-Hill, 2008. See Chapters 29 to 31.
2. Damodaran, Aswath. *Corporate Finance: Theory and Practice*, 2nd ed. John Wiley & Sons, 2001. See Chapter 13.
3. Damodaran, Aswath. *Damodaran on Valuation*, 2nd ed. John Wiley & Sons, 2006. See Chapter 10.
4. Koller, Tim, Marc Goedhart, and David Wessels. *Valuation: Measuring and Managing the Value of Companies*, 4th ed. John Wiley & Sons, 2005.
5. Ross, Stephen, Randolph Westerfield, and Jeffrey Jaffe. *Corporate Finance*, 8th ed. McGraw Hill Irwin, 2008. See Chapters 26 to 28.

SELF-TEST PROBLEMS

3.1 EVALUATING MANAGERIAL PERFORMANCE.

Allied & Consolidated Clothier (ACC), a clothing manufacturer, launched an aggressive marketing program aimed at raising the *growth rate* in sales in 2010 by at least 50 percent compared with the *growth rate* achieved in 2009. The company's financial statements from 2008 to 2010 are shown below and on the following page. The income statements span a calendar year and balance sheets are dated December 31. All figures are in millions of dollars.

a. Has ACC achieved its marketing objective?
b. Restate ACC's balance sheets in their managerial form. What does working capital requirement (WCR) measure? Is it a long-term or a short-term investment?
c. Examine the structures of invested capital and capital used in the managerial balance sheets prepared in the previous question (state each component as a percentage of the total). What do you observe?
d. Compare the 2008 balance sheet with the 2010 balance sheet. Are these balance sheets matched or unmatched?
e. Analyze ACC's operational efficiency from 2008 to 2010. Calculate and compare the following efficiency ratios for the three-year period. What can you conclude?

    1. WCR-to-sales ratio
    2. Average collection period
    3. Inventory turnover
    4. Average payment period (use cost of goods sold)

f. Analyze ACC's liquidity position from 2008 to 2010. Calculate and compare the following liquidity ratios over the three-year period. What can you conclude?

    1. The liquidity ratio (net long-term financing to WCR)
    2. The current ratio
    3. The quick ratio

g. What general conclusion can you draw from your analysis?

Balance Sheets (in millions)

Year end	2008	2009	2010		2008	2009	2010
Cash	$100	$ 90	$ 50	Short-term debt	$ 80	$ 90	$ 135
Trade receivables	200	230	290	Trade payables	170	180	220
Inventories	160	170	300	Accrued expenses	40	45	50
Prepaid expenses	30	30	35	Long-term debt	140	120	100
Net fixed assets	390	390	365	Owners' equity	450	475	535
Total assets	**$880**	**$910**	**$1,040**	**Total liabilities & owners' equity**	**$880**	**$910**	**$1,040**

Income Statements (in millions)			
	2008	2009	2010
Net sales	**$1,200**	**$1,350**	**$1,600**
Cost of goods sold	860	970	1,160
Selling, general, and administrative expenses	150	165	200
Depreciation expense	40	50	55
Earnings before interest and tax (EBIT)	**150**	**165**	**185**
Net interest expense	20	20	25
Earnings before tax (EBT)	**130**	**145**	**160**
Income tax expense	40	45	50
Earnings after tax (EAT)	**$ 90**	**$ 100**	**$ 110**
Dividends	$ 75	$ 75	$ 50

3.2 WORKING CAPITAL MANAGEMENT FOR A RETAILER.

The consolidated financial statements of Carrefour, the French retailer, for the years 2007 and 2008, are shown below and on the following page.

a. Calculate working capital requirement at year-ends 2007 and 2008. Interpret your results.
b. Calculate the ratio of working capital requirement to sales. What is the effect of faster growth on Carrefour's liquidity position?
c. What were Carrefour's average collection periods, inventory turnover, and average payment periods (based on cost of sales) in 2007 and 2008? What can you conclude about the effect of these parameters on the magnitude of Carrefour's working capital requirement?
d. Calculate Carrefour's current ratios and quick ratios. What can you conclude about the reliability of these liquidity ratios for the case of retailers such as Carrefour?

Income Statements (in millions)		
	2007	2008
Net sales	**€82,149**	**€86,967**
Cost of goods sold	64,609	68,709
Selling, general, and administrative expenses	12,526	13,096
Depreciation, amortization, and provisions	1,723	1,816
Financial income, net of expenses	526	562
Net profit of affiliated companies	2,765	2,738
Income tax expense	807	743
Net income[1]	**€ 1,958**	**€ 1,995**

[1] Excluding nonrecurring income, nonrecurring expenses, and discontinued operations.

Balance Sheets (in millions)					
Year end	**2007**	**2008**		**2007**	**2008**
Current assets			**Liabilities**		
Cash and securities	€ 4,164	€ 5,317	Short-term borrowings	€ 3,247	€ 2,709
Trade receivables[2]	863	779	Accounts payable	17,077	17,276
Inventories	6,867	6,891	Accrued expenses	2,848	2,947
Other current assets[3]	6,231	6,190	Other current liabilities[4]	4,866	4,800
			Long-term borrowings	11,542	12,725
Long-term assets	33,224	32,232	**Stockholders' equity**	11,770	10,952
Total assets	**€ 51,349**	**€ 51,409**	**Total liabilities and owners' equity**	**€ 51,349**	**€ 51,409**

[2]Mainly from the group's franchisees.
[3]Receivables from suppliers for rebates and commercial incentives plus short-term consumer credit.
[4]Mainly short-term consumer credit refinancing.

REVIEW PROBLEMS

1. **Transactions.**
Indicate the effects of the following transactions on *net long-term financing (NLF), working capital requirement (WCR), net short-term financing (NSF),* and *net profit.* Use + to indicate an increase, – to indicate a decrease, and 0 to indicate no effect.

	NLF	WCR	NSF	NET PROFIT
Shares are issued for cash				
Goods from inventory are sold for cash				
Goods from inventory are sold on account				
A fixed asset is sold for cash for less than book value				
A fixed asset is sold for cash for more than book value				
Corporate income tax is paid				
Payment is made to trade creditors				
Cash is obtained through a short-term bank loan				
Cash is obtained through a long-term bank loan				
A cash dividend is declared and paid				
Accounts receivable are collected				
Merchandise is purchased on account				
Cash advances are made to employees				
Minority interest in a firm is acquired for cash				
Equipment is acquired for cash				

2. Constructing a managerial balance sheet.
Prepare the managerial balance sheet of Lowe's from the following company consolidated balance sheet:

In millions	Fiscal year-end 2008
Assets	
Current assets	
Cash and cash equivalents	$ 245
Short-term investments	416
Merchandise inventories	8,209
Deferred income taxes	166
Other current assets	215
Total current assets	9,251
Property, less accumulated depreciation	22,722
Long-term investments	253
Other assets	460
Total assets	**$32,686**
Liabilities and shareholders' equity	
Current liabilities	
Short-term borrowings	$ 987
Current portion of long-term debt	34
Accounts payable	4,109
Accrued compensation and employees benefits	434
Self-insurance liabilities	751
Deferred revenue	674
Other current liabilities	1,033
Total current liabilities	8,022
Long-term debt	5,039
Deferred income taxes, net	660
Other liabilities	910
Total liabilities	14,631
Shareholders' equity	
Common stock	735
Capital-in-excess of par value	277
Retained earnings	17,049
Accumulated other comprehensive income (loss)	(6)
Total shareholders' equity	18,055
Total liabilities and shareholders' equity	**$32,686**

3. **Reconstructing a balance sheet.**
Use the following information to complete the balance sheet below.

a. Collection period: forty days
b. Inventory turnover: six times sales
c. Working capital requirement/sales: 20 percent
d. Liabilities/total assets: 60 percent
e. Cash in days of sales: twenty days
f. Short-term debt: 10 percent of total financial debt

Assume a 360-day year.

Balance Sheet			
Cash	$ 400,000	Short-term debt	
Accounts receivable		Accounts payable	
Inventory			
Total current assets		**Total current liabilities**	
Net fixed assets		Long-term debt	
		Owners' equity	
Total assets	$5,000,000	**Total liabilities and owners' equity**	

4. **Effect of transactions on working capital requirement.**
Indicate the effect of the following transactions on the working capital requirement:

a. More customers pay with cash instead of credit
b. More of raw material is paid for with cash
c. More discounts are offered to customers
d. More finished goods are produced for order

5. **Managing liquidity.**
Indicate which of the following four statements are right or wrong:

a. Because working capital requirement (WCR) = net long-term financing (NLF) + net short-term financing (NSF), I can reduce my investment in the operating cycle by either reducing my long-term financing through the repurchase of shares or by borrowing less on short-term basis
b. The lower my WCR, the more liquid my business unit is. One way to reduce WCR is to reduce inventories. I can do that by writing down some of my obsolete inventories
c. Although I can improve my liquidity or acid test ratios by letting my customer pay later, the result would be a decrease in the liquidity of my business unit
d. If I decrease my WCR, I will increase my cash holdings and be able to borrow less from my bank. But my bank, which makes money by lending funds, will be unhappy

6. The cash-to-cash conversion period.
The income statement and end-of-year balance sheet of Altar Inc., a distribution company, are as follows:

Income Statement	
Net sales	**$2,000,000**
Cost of goods sold	1,300,000
Selling, general, and administrative expenses	300,000
Depreciation expense	100,000
Earnings before interest and tax	**300,000**
Net interest expense	20,000
Earnings before tax	**280,000**
Income tax expense	50,000
Earnings after tax	**$ 230,000**

Balance Sheet	
Cash	$ 100,000
Accounts receivable	500,000
Inventories[1]	400,000
Other current assets	300,000
Noncurrent assets	500,000
Total assets	**$1,800,000**
Short-term debt	$ 100,000
Accounts payable	600,000
Accrued expenses	400,000
Long-term debt	300,000
Owners' equity	400,000
Total liabilities and owners' equity	**$1,800,000**

[1]The amount of inventories at the beginning of the year was equal to $350,000.

What is the cash-to-cash conversion period of Altar Inc. at the end of the year?

7. **Industry effect on the working capital requirement.**
Below are selected accounting data of four U.S. firms:

(in millions)	Firm 1	Firm 2	Firm 3	Firm 4
Revenue	$428	$3,498	$21,870	$166,809
Accounts receivable	78	63	5,385	1,341
Inventories	299	84	3,463	19,793
Prepaid expenses	4	100	–	1,366
Other current assets	–	–	108	–
Accounts payable	25	196	2,272	13,105
Accrued expenses	7	262	1,905	7,290
Other current liabilities	14	741	2,037	–

a. For each one of the firms, compute the following: working capital requirement (WCR), WCR-to-revenue ratio, collection period in days (using 365 days per year), and inventory turnover (using revenue rather than cost of goods sold)
b. The four firms and their industry are

Firm	Wal-Mart Stores, Inc.	The Robert Mondavi Corp.	Dow Chemical Company	Carnival Corp.
Industry	Retail (Nongrocery)	Beverages (Alcoholic)	Chemical Manufacturing	Recreational Activities (Cruises)

Which company is Firm 1, Firm 2, Firm 3, and Firm 4? Explain your choice.

8. **Financing strategies.**
Which of the following three companies has a matching, a conservative, and an aggressive financing strategy? Explain why.

	Firm A	Firm B	Firm C
Cash	$ 0	$ 10	$ 0
Accounts receivable	25	20	25
Inventories	25	20	25
Net fixed assets	50	50	50
Total assets	$ 100	$ 100	$ 100
Short-term debt	$ 0	$ 0	$ 10
Accounts payable	25	25	25
Long-term debt	25	25	15
Owners' equity	50	50	50
Total liabilities and owners' equity	$ 100	$ 100	$100

9. **The financial effect of the management of the operating cycle.**
Below are financial statements for Sentec Inc., a distributor of electrical fixtures, for 2008, 2009, and 2010.

Income Statements (in thousands)			
	2008	2009	2010
Net sales	$ 22,100	$24,300	$31,600
Cost of goods sold	17,600	19,300	25,100
Selling, general, and administrative expenses	3,750	4,000	5,000
Depreciation expense	100	100	150
Earnings before interest and tax	650	900	1,350
Net interest expense	110	130	260
Earnings before tax	540	770	1,090
Income tax expense	220	310	430
Earnings after tax	$ 320	$ 460	$ 660
Dividends	$ 180	$ 200	$ 200

Balance Sheets (in thousands)			
	December 31, 2008	December 31, 2009	December 31, 2010
Cash	$ 600	$ 350	$ 300
Accounts receivable	2,730	3,100	4,200
Inventories	2,800	3,200	4,300
Prepaid expenses	0	0	0
Net fixed assets	1,200	1,300	1,450
Total assets	$ 7,330	$7,950	$10,250
Short-term debt	$ 300	$ 500	$ 1,900
Accounts payable	1,400	1,600	2,050
Accrued expenses	200	260	350
Long-term debt	1,300	1,200	1,100
Owners' equity	4,130	4,390	4,850
Total liabilities and owners' equity	$ 7,330	$7,950	$10,250

a. Compute Sentec Inc.'s working capital requirement (WCR) on December 31, 2008, 2009, and 2010.
b. Prepare Sentec Inc.'s managerial balance sheets on December 31, 2008, 2009, and 2010.
c. Compute Sentec Inc.'s net long-term financing (NLF) and net short-term financing (NSF) on December 31, 2008, 2009, and 2010. Comment on the change in Sentec Inc.'s financing policy. Has it become more conservative? Aggressive? What caused this change?

d. In 2010, firms in the same business sector as Sentec Inc. had an average collection period of thirty days, average payment period of thirty-three days, and inventory turnover of eight days. Suppose that Sentec Inc. had managed its operating cycle like the average firm in the sector. On December 31, 2010, what would its WCR have been? Its managerial balance sheet, NLF, and NSF? What would have been the effect on its financing strategy?

10. **Seasonal business.**
Mars Electronics is a distributor for the Global Electric Company (GEC), a large manufacturer of electrical and electronics products for consumer and institutional markets. Below are the semiannual financial statements of the company for the last year and a half.

Income Statements (in thousands)	Six Months to June 30, 2009	Six Months to December 31, 2009	Six Months to June 30, 2010
Net sales	$ 10,655	$ 13,851	$ 11,720
Cost of goods sold	8,940	11,671	9,834
Selling, general, and administrative expenses	1,554	1,925	1,677
Depreciation expense	44	55	76
Interest expense	62	90	70
Income tax expense	23	44	26
Earnings after tax	$ 32	$ 66	$ 37
Dividends	$ 5	$ 44	$ 1

Balance Sheets (in thousands)	June 30, 2009	December 31, 2009	June 30, 2010
Cash	$ 160	$ 60	$ 70
Accounts receivable	1,953	2,616	2,100
Inventories	1,986	2,694	2,085
Prepaid expenses	80	42	25
Net fixed assets	733	818	830
Total assets	$ 4,912	$ 6,230	$ 5,110
Short-term debt	$ 50	$ 880	$ 50
Accounts payable	1,450	1,950	1,650
Accrued expenses	98	114	138
Long-term debt	800	750	700
Owners' equity	2,514	2,536	2,572
Total liabilities and owners' equity	$ 4,912	$ 6,230	$ 5,110

a. Compute Mars Electronics' working capital requirement on June 30, 2009, December 31, 2009, and June 30, 2010. Also, compute the collection period, inventory turnover, and payment period at the same dates. (The average payment period on June 30, 2009, was twenty-nine days.)
b. Prepare Mars Electronics' managerial balance sheet on June 30, 2009, December 31, 2009, and June 30, 2010.
c. Compute Mars Electronics' net long-term financing and net short-term financing on June 30, 2009, December 31, 2009, and June 30, 2010. Comment on Mars Electronics' financing strategy. Is it a conservative one? Aggressive? Matching one?

Measuring Cash Flows

CHAPTER 4

If a firm keeps spending more cash than it generates, it will eventually run into trouble. Your ability to make decisions that generate cash over time is essential to your firm's long-term survival. Making profits will help, but only if those profits can be quickly converted into cash. The firm's suppliers, its bankers, and the tax authorities require payment in cash, not accounting profits. The road to business success is cluttered with bankrupt firms that were actually showing a profit in their last published income statement. Statistics for most developed countries indicate that almost four out of five firms that went bankrupt were actually profitable; they died from a lack of cash, not from meager profits.

There are two categories of cash flow: cash inflows, which are the number of dollars that come into the firm, and cash outflows, which are the number of dollars that go out of the firm. A successful value-creating manager must have a clear understanding of where these cash flows originate, how they are measured, and how they should be managed.

This chapter presents a general framework for analyzing cash flows and their relation to business decisions. We first construct a preliminary cash-flow statement based on the firm's three fundamental activities: operating, investing, and financing activities. Next, we show how to use the firm's balance sheets and income statements to measure the cash flows generated by each of these activities during the accounting period. We then put all the information together in a detailed cash-flow statement. Finally, we present alternative methods for calculating cash flows that are often used by firms in presenting their cash-flow statements. As in Chapter 3, Office Supplies (OS) Distributors' financial statements for the years 2008, 2009, and 2010 are used to illustrate the analysis. After reading this chapter, you should understand the following:

- The relationship between cash and cash flows
- The relationship between profit and cash flows
- How business decisions affect cash flows

- How to use a firm's balance sheets and income statements to calculate the cash flows generated by the firm's operating, investing, and financing activities
- How to prepare and interpret a cash-flow statement

CASH FLOWS AND THEIR SOURCES

The amount of cash held by a firm at a particular time is found on the asset side of its balance sheet. OS Distributors' balance sheets in Exhibit 4.1 show the firm had \$6 million in cash at the end of 2008, \$12 million at the end of 2009, and \$8 million at the end of 2010. Define **total net cash flow** as the difference between the total amount of dollars received (**cash inflows**) and the total amount of dollars paid out (**cash outflows**) over a period of time. With the information in Exhibit 4.1, you can easily find OS Distributors' total net cash flow in 2009 and 2010. Each time OS Distributors received a dollar, its cash account increased by a dollar; each time it spent a dollar, its cash account decreased by a dollar. The amount of cash held by OS Distributors increased from \$6 million to \$12 million between December 31, 2008, and December 31, 2009. Therefore, during 2009, its activities must have generated a *positive* total net cash flow of \$6 million, the difference between \$12 million and \$6 million. During 2010, the firm generated a *negative* total net cash flow of \$4 million, because cash decreased from \$12 million to \$8 million during that year. Thus, a firm's total net cash flow is equal to the *change* in the firm's cash position during a period of time.

Total net cash flow, which accounts for *all* the transactions the firm undertakes during a period of time, is, unfortunately, too broad a measure of a firm's net cash flow to be a useful indicator of the firm's ability to generate a surplus of cash over time. We want to know the *specific* activities that have contributed to an improvement and those that have contributed to a deterioration in the firm's cash position during a given period of time. For example, we want to identify activities associated with the following transactions: the firm receives cash from a customer (a cash *inflow* resulting from an operating activity); the firm purchases some new equipment (a cash *outflow* resulting from an investment decision); or the firm borrows from its bank (a cash *inflow* resulting from a financing decision). Each of these transactions will cause a change in the firm's cash position.

In general, a firm's cash position will change as a result of decisions related to three separate types of activities: (1) operating activities; (2) investing activities; and (3) financing activities. These activities are usually both a source of cash inflows and a source of cash outflows. Exhibit 4.2 shows typical transactions associated with each of these activities. The upper part of the exhibit presents the sources of cash inflow, and the lower part presents the sources of cash outflow from these transactions. Each type of activity generates a net cash flow. The net cash flow from operating activities is called **net operating cash flow** (**NOCF**); in the case of investing activities, it is called **net cash flow from investing activities**; and in the case of financing activities, it is called **net cash flow from financing activities**. We explain how to calculate the cash-flow amounts shown in Exhibit 4.2 in the next sections.

EXHIBIT 4.1 OS DISTRIBUTORS' BALANCE SHEETS.

FIGURES IN MILLIONS

	December 31, 2008		December 31, 2009		December 31, 2010	
Assets						
• **Current assets**						
Cash[1]		$ 6.0		$ 12.0		$ 8.0
Accounts receivable		44.0		48.0		56.0
Inventories		52.0		57.0		72.0
Prepaid expenses[2]		2.0		2.0		1.0
Total current assets		**104.0**		**119.0**		**137.0**
• **Noncurrent assets**						
Financial assets and intangibles		0.0		0.0		0.0
Property, plant, and equipment						
Gross value[3]	$90.0		$90.0		$93.0	
less accumulated depreciation	(34.0)	56.0	(39.0)	51.0	(40.0)	53.0
Total noncurrent assets		56.0		51.0		53.0
Total assets		**$160.0**		**$170.0**		**$190.0**
Liabilities and owners' equity						
• **Current liabilities**						
Short-term debt		$ 15.0		$ 22.0		$ 23.0
Owed to banks	$7.0		$14.0		$15.0	
Current portion of long-term debt	8.0		8.0		8.0	
Accounts payable		37.0		40.0		48.0
Accrued expenses[4]		2.0		4.0		4.0
Total current liabilities		54.0		66.0		75.0
• **Noncurrent liabilities**						
Long-term debt[5]		$ 42.0		34.0		38.0
Total noncurrent liabilities		42.0		34.0		38.0
• **Owners' equity**[6]		64.0		70.0		77.0
Total liabilities and owners' equity		**$160.0**		**$170.0**		**$190.0**

[1]Consists of cash in hand and checking accounts held to facilitate operating activities on which the firm earns no interest.
[2]Prepaid expenses is rent paid in advance (when recognized in the income statement, rent is included in selling, general, and administrative expenses).
[3]In 2009, there was no disposal of existing fixed assets or acquisition of new fixed assets. However, during 2010, a warehouse was enlarged at a cost of $12 million, and existing fixed assets, bought for $9 million in the past, were sold at their net book value of $2 million.
[4]Accrued expenses consist of wages and taxes payable.
[5]Long-term debt is repaid at the rate of $8 million per year. No new long-term debt was incurred during 2009, but during 2010, a mortgage loan was obtained from the bank to finance the extension of a warehouse (see Note 3).
[6]During the three years, no new shares were issued and none were repurchased.

Exhibit 4.2 Sources of Cash Inflow and Cash Outflow.

Amounts are OS Distributors' cash flows in 2010. Figures in millions

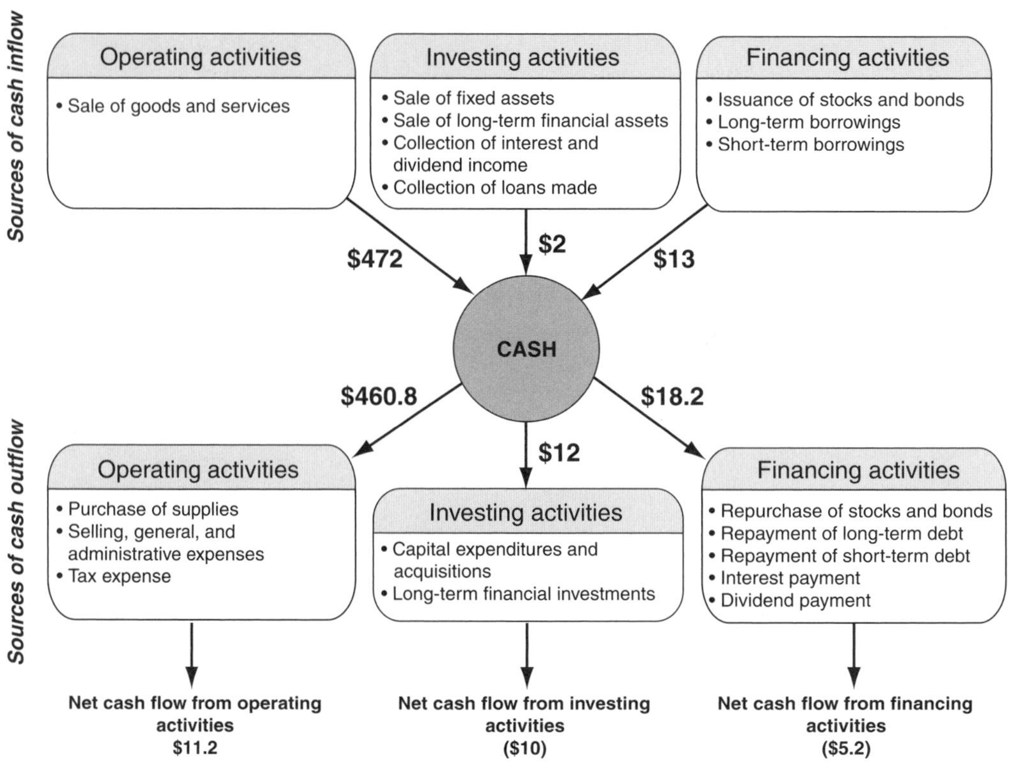

Exhibit 4.3 shows a preliminary cash-flow statement for OS Distributors for 2010, using the information in Exhibit 4.2. The statement breaks down the change in the firm's cash position according to its operating, investing, and financing activities. The firm began the year with $12 million in cash (see Exhibit 4.1). As shown in Exhibit 4.2, its operations generated a cash inflow of $472 million and a cash

Exhibit 4.3 OS Distributors' Preliminary Cash-Flow Statement for 2010.

Figures in millions

• **Cash on January 1, 2010**[1]		**$12**
Net operating cash flow (NOCF)	$11.2	
+ Net cash flow from investing activities	($10.0)	
+ Net cash flow from financing activities	($5.2)	
Total net cash flow for year 2010		**($4)**
• **Cash on December 31, 2010**		**$8**

[1]Cash on January 1, 2010, is the same as cash on December 31, 2009. See balance sheets in Exhibit 4.1.

EXHIBIT 4.4 OS DISTRIBUTORS' INCOME STATEMENTS.

FIGURES IN MILLIONS

	2008	2009	2010
• **Net sales**	**$390.0**	**$420.0**	**$480.0**
Cost of goods sold	328.0	353.0	400.0
• **Gross profit**	**62.0**	**67.0**	**80.0**
Selling, general, and administrative expenses	39.8	43.7	48.0
Depreciation expense	5.0	5.0	8.0
• **Operating profit**	**17.2**	**18.3**	**24.0**
Special items	0.0	0.0	0.0
• **Earnings before interest and tax (EBIT)**	**17.2**	**18.3**	**24.0**
Net interest expense[1]	5.5	5.0	7.0
• **Earnings before tax (EBT)**	**11.7**	**13.3**	**17.0**
Income tax expense	4.7	5.3	6.8
• **Earnings after tax (EAT)**	**$ 7.0**	**$ 8.0**	**$ 10.2**
Dividends	$ 2.0	$ 2.0	$ 3.2
Addition to retained earnings	$ 5.0	$ 6.0	$ 7.0

[1]There is no interest income, so net interest expense is equal to interest expense.

outflow of $460.8 million. Hence, net cash flow from operating activities, that is, NOCF, is equal to $11.2 million ($472 million less $460.8 million). Net cash flow from investing activities is a net outflow of $10 million ($2 million less $12 million) and net cash outflow from financing activities is a net outflow of $5.2 million ($13 million less $18.2 million). These transactions left OS Distributors with a cash deficit of $4 million for the year ($11.2 million less $10 million less $5.2 million). This deficit was financed by taking $4 million from OS Distributors' cash account, leaving the firm with $8 million in cash at the end of 2010 (see Exhibit 4.1).

No obvious relationship is evident between total net cash flow and net profit (earnings after tax) of the same year. In 2010, OS Distributors "lost" $4 million in cash but generated $10.2 million in net profit (see OS Distributors' income statements in Exhibit 4.4).

PREPARING A DETAILED CASH-FLOW STATEMENT

Detailed cash-flow statements for OS Distributors for the two years ending December 31, 2009, and December 31, 2010, are shown in Exhibit 4.5. The sources of cash inflow and outflow are those identified in Exhibit 4.2, and the amounts of the three components of OS Distributors total net cash flow—operating, investing, and financing cash flows—are derived from the firm's balance sheets at year-end 2008, 2009, and 2010 and its income statements for the years 2009 and 2010. The next sections explain how these cash flows are calculated.

EXHIBIT 4.5 OS DISTRIBUTORS' CASH-FLOW STATEMENTS.

FIGURES IN MILLIONS

	2009		2010	
• **Cash flows from operating activities**				
(+) Net sales	$420.0		$480.0	
(–) Cost of goods sold	(353.0)		(400.0)	
(–) Selling, general, and administrative expenses[1]	(43.7)		(48.0)	
(–) Tax expense	(5.3)		(6.8)	
(–) Change in working capital requirement	(4.0)		(14.0)	
A. Net operating cash flow (NOCF)		**$14.0**		**$11.2**
• **Cash flows from investing activities**				
(+) Sale of fixed assets	0.0		2.0	
(–) Capital expenditures and acquisitions	0.0		(12.0)	
B. Net cash flow from investing activities		**$0.0**		**($10.0)**
• **Cash flows from financing activities**				
(+) Increase in long-term borrowings	0.0		12.0	
(+) Increase in short-term borrowings	7.0		1.0	
(–) Long-term debt repaid	(8.0)		(8.0)	
(–) Interest payments	(5.0)		(7.0)	
(–) Dividend payments	(2.0)		(3.2)	
C. Net cash flow from financing activities		**($8.0)**		**($5.2)**
D. Total net cash flow (A + B + C)		**$6.0**		**($4.0)**
E. Opening cash		**$6.0**		**$12.0**
F. Closing cash (E + D)		**$12.0**		**$8.0**

[1]Excluding depreciation expense.

If you want to prepare a cash-flow statement for a given year, you need an income statement for that year and two balance sheets, one at the beginning of the year (which is the same as the one at the end of the previous year) and the other at the end of the year. For example, to prepare a cash-flow statement for 2009, you need the income statement for 2009, the balance sheet at the end of 2008, and the balance sheet at the end of 2009. Note that because the balance sheet at the end of 2007 is not available, you cannot prepare a cash-flow statement for OS Distributors for 2008.

NET CASH FLOW FROM OPERATING ACTIVITIES

Net cash flow from operating activities, or NOCF, is simply the net cash flow originating from the firm's operating activities during the period under consideration:

$$\text{Net operating cash flow (NOCF)} = \text{Cash inflow from operations} - \text{Cash outflow from operations}$$

The sources of operating cash flows are the operating revenues and expenses in the income statement (see Exhibit 4.4). Operating revenues are net sales, and operating expenses are the sum of cost of goods sold (COGS); selling, general, and administrative (SG&A) expenses; and depreciation and tax expenses. However, not all these revenues or expenses generate or consume cash. A typical example is depreciation. There is no one to whom the firm pays depreciation.[1] Consequently, depreciation is excluded from the calculation of NOCF. Furthermore, even though revenues and expenses eventually end up as cash inflows or outflows, they are not recorded as such in the income statement. As discussed in Chapter 2, revenues are shown in the income statement only when recognized, that is, when customers are invoiced, not when cash changes hands. Thus, an increase in revenues does not necessarily imply a corresponding cash inflow. Similarly, some expenses are *not* recorded in the income statement when payment is made, but only when they generate revenue. For example, expenses related to the purchase of merchandise by a distributor are recorded in the income statement as cost of goods sold only when merchandise is sold, not when payment is made.[2] Thus, an increase in expenses related to sales does not necessarily imply a corresponding cash outflow. How then can we measure the cash flows from operating revenues and operating expenses?

We first consider the cash inflows from operations that originate from the sale of goods and services. Each time a customer is invoiced, the firm's accountant records the sale by increasing both the firm's net sales account and its accounts receivable by the amount of the sale. Cash comes in later when the customer pays. At that time, the accountant records the transaction by increasing the firm's cash account and decreasing its accounts receivable by the amount paid. Therefore, by following what happens to receivables over a period of time, we can estimate the cash inflow from sales during that period. Starting at the beginning of the period, receivables increase each time a sale is made and decrease each time a bill is paid. We can write the following:

$$\text{Accounts receivable}_{\text{end}} = \text{Accounts receivable}_{\text{beginning}} + \text{Sales} - \text{Cash inflow from sales}$$

Rearranging the terms of the above equation gives us this:

$$\text{Cash inflow from sales} = \text{Sales} - [\text{Accounts receivable}_{\text{end}} - \text{Accounts receivable}_{\text{beginning}}]$$

This equation can be written as follows:

$$\text{Cash inflow from sales} = \text{Sales} - \Delta\text{Accounts receivable}$$

where ΔAccounts receivable is the change in receivables during the estimation period.

When accounts receivable *increase* during a period of time (ΔAccounts receivable *positive*), the cash inflow from sales is *less* than the sales revenue during that

---

[1]When a fixed asset is acquired, the cash outflow is equal to the acquisition price of the asset. When that asset is subsequently depreciated over a period of time, the firm no longer experiences any cash movements related to the purchase of the asset.

[2]This is an application of the realization and matching principles, which are discussed in Chapter 2.

period of time. When they *decrease* (ΔAccounts receivable *negative*), the corresponding cash inflow from sales is *more* than the sales revenue during that period of time. Hence, *given a target level of sales, the key to higher cash inflow from sales is a faster collection of accounts receivable.*

The procedure for estimating the cash inflow from sales can be applied to all the operating expenses that involve cash transactions. As shown in Appendix 4.1, the related cash outflow is obtained by adjusting the dollar amount of an income statement account with the change in the corresponding balance sheet account during the period. But the balance sheet accounts used for the adjustments are exclusively those related to the firm's operating cycle, which, by definition, are the accounts that make up its working capital requirement (see Chapter 3). The result, shown in Appendix 4.1, is a simple formula for obtaining the NOCF from balance sheet and income statement accounts:

$$\textbf{NOCF = Sales – COGS – SG\&A expenses – Tax expense – }\Delta\textbf{WCR} \quad (4.1)$$

where NOCF is net operating cash flow; COGS is cost of goods sold; SG&A expense is selling, general, and administrative expenses; and ΔWCR is the change in working capital requirement.

Here is an intuitive interpretation of equation 4.1. The firm's operations generate revenues and expenses that are recorded in the income statement and captured by the first four terms on the right side of the equation. These activities require an investment in the firm's operating cycle that is recorded in the balance sheet and that is measured by the change in working capital requirement (ΔWCR) during the period. Working capital requirement changes with the change in the amount of cash due to the firm by its customers, the change in the amount of cash paid for inventories, and the change in the amount of cash the firm owes its suppliers and other creditors. That is, the increase in ΔWCR represents the amount of cash the firm has used to finance the growth of its investment in operations. Because this cash is unavailable to the firm, it reduces its operating cash flow.

Using the data in Exhibit 4.6, which reproduce the managerial balance sheets of OS Distributors presented in Chapter 3, we can compute the change in OS Distributors' working capital requirement in 2009 and 2010 as follows:

$$\Delta WCR_{2009} = WCR_{12/31/09} - WCR_{12/31/08} = \$63 \text{ million} - \$59 \text{ million} = \$4 \text{ million}$$

$$\Delta WCR_{2010} = WCR_{12/31/10} - WCR_{12/31/09} = \$77 \text{ million} - \$63 \text{ million} = \$14 \text{ million}$$

Using equation 4.1 and the data in the income statements in Exhibit 4.4, we can now calculate the firm's NOCF in 2009 and 2010:

$$NOCF_{2009} = [\$420 \text{ million} - \$353 \text{ million} - \$43.7 \text{ million} - \$5.3 \text{ million} - \$4 \text{ million}] = \$14.0 \text{ million}$$

$$NOCF_{2010} = [\$480 \text{ million} - \$400 \text{ million} - \$48 \text{ million} - \$6.8 \text{ million} - \$14 \text{ million}] = \$11.2 \text{ million}$$

The upper part of Exhibit 4.5 presents OS Distributors' NOCF for 2009 and 2010, calculated using equation 4.1. Notice the contribution of the change in WCR to

EXHIBIT 4.6 OS DISTRIBUTORS' MANAGERIAL BALANCE SHEETS.

ALL DATA FROM THE BALANCE SHEETS IN EXHIBIT 4.1. FIGURES IN MILLIONS

		December 31, 2008		December 31, 2009		December 31, 2010
Invested capital						
• Cash		$ 6.0		$ 12.0		$ 8.0
• Working capital requirement (WCR)[1]		59.0		63.0		77.0
• Net fixed assets		56.0		51.0		53.0
Total invested capital		**$121.0**		**$126.0**		**$138.0**
Capital employed						
• Short-term debt		$ 15.0		$ 22.0		$ 23.0
• Long-term financing						
Long-term debt	$42.0		$34.0		$38.0	
Owners' equity	64.0	106.0	70.0	104.0	77.0	115.0
Total capital employed		**$121.0**		**$126.0**		**$138.0**

[1]WCR = (Accounts receivable + Inventories + Prepaid expenses) – (Accounts payable + Accrued expenses).

NOCF in the two years. In 2009, the $4 million increase in WCR represents less than 30 percent of NOCF; in 2010, the $14 million increase in WCR represents more than 120 percent of NOCF. In other words, the decrease in NOCF that OS Distributors experienced in 2010 compared with 2009 was mostly caused by the growth of its investment in operations (ΔWCR) that was required to support growing sales.

NOCF can also be computed using a different approach. Because earnings before interest and tax (EBIT) are equal to sales less the sum of COGS, SG&A expenses, and depreciation expense (see Exhibit 4.4), we can write the following:

$$\textbf{EBIT + Depreciation expense = Sales – COGS – SG\&A expenses} \qquad (4.2)$$

Replacing the "Sales – COGS – SG&A expenses" in equation 4.1 with "EBIT plus depreciation expense," we get this:

$$\textbf{NOCF = EBIT + Depreciation expense – Tax expense –} \,\boldsymbol{\Delta}\textbf{WCR} \qquad (4.3)$$

Note that in equation 4.1 as well as in equation 4.3, tax expense is taken directly from the income tax account in the firm's income statement, and thus is affected by all the taxable transactions incurred by the firm, not just those related to its operations. For example, because interest payments are tax deductible, the tax expense in these two equations is affected by the firm's decision to borrow. More precisely, the more debt the firm carries, the more interest payments it will have to make, and the lower its tax bill will be. In other words, NOCF is indirectly affected by the firm's *financing* decisions. A more precise measure of the cash flow generated by a firm's *operating* activities would ignore the tax effect of financing decisions. Such an adjustment is made in the definition of another well-known measure of cash flow, the free cash flow (FCF), which we examine later. However, most analysts and corporate finance managers still use NOCF as defined in equation 4.1 or equation 4.3 when analyzing a firm's operating cash flows.

For OS Distributors, we have the following:

$$NOCF_{2009} = \$18.3 \text{ million} + \$5 \text{ million} - \$5.3 \text{ million} - \$4 \text{ million} = \$14.0 \text{ million}$$

$$NOCF_{2010} = \$24 \text{ million} + \$8 \text{ million} - \$6.8 \text{ million} - \$14 \text{ million} = \$11.2 \text{ million}$$

A compact version of equation 4.3 can be obtained by noting that "EBIT plus depreciation" in equation 4.2 is equal to **earnings before interest, tax, depreciation, and amortization**, known as **EBITDA**. Replacing EBIT plus depreciation by EBITDA in equation 4.3 we get this:

$$NOCF = EBITDA - \text{Tax expense} - \Delta WCR$$

For OS Distributors, EBITDA is equal to \$23.3 million in 2009 (\$18.3 million plus \$5 million) and \$32 million in 2010 (\$24 million plus \$8 million).

NET CASH FLOW FROM INVESTING ACTIVITIES

The firm's investments during the accounting period are not directly reported in its balance sheet or income statement. The balance sheet reports only the net book value of all the firm's fixed assets, and the income statement reports only the depreciation expense for the accounting period. Fortunately, firms usually provide supplementary information in the form of notes to their financial statements from which it is possible to estimate the cash flows related to the firm's investing activities during the accounting period.

For example, Note 3 at the bottom of OS Distributor's balance sheets in Exhibit 4.1 explains that the firm did not sell or acquire fixed assets during 2009. However, during 2010, a warehouse was enlarged at a cost of \$12 million and existing assets were sold at their book value of \$2 million. Because OS Distributors does not hold any long-term financial assets, the cash flows from its investing activities are related only to the acquisition and disposal of fixed assets. They are shown in the second part of the cash-flow statement in Exhibit 4.5. The net effect of the firm's investment decisions is a net cash flow of zero in 2009 and a net outflow of \$10 million in 2010.

You can check that the net fixed assets accounts in the balance sheets are consistent with this information. Note that over a period of time these accounts increase when the firm acquires fixed assets and decrease when the firm deducts depreciation expense and sells fixed assets. Thus,

$$\begin{aligned}\textbf{Net fixed assets}_{\textbf{end}} = \textbf{Net fixed assets}_{\textbf{beginning}} + \textbf{Fixed assets acquisitions} \\ - \textbf{Depreciation expense} - \textbf{Fixed assets disposals}\end{aligned} \quad (4.4)$$

OS Distributors had no fixed assets acquisitions or disposals during 2009. The 2009 income statement shows depreciation expense of \$5 million, and the 2008 balance sheet indicates \$56 million of net fixed assets at the end of 2008. As a result,

$$\text{Net fixed assets}_{12/31/09} = \$56 \text{ million} + \$0 - \$5 \text{ million} - \$0 = \$51 \text{ million}$$

This is the same amount of net fixed assets reported in the balance sheet at the end of 2009. In 2010, OS Distributors acquired \$12 million of new assets, sold

$2 million of old assets, and had depreciation expense of $8 million. Given that net fixed assets at the end of 2009 were $51 million, we have the following:

$$\text{Net fixed assets}_{12/31/10} = \$51 \text{ million} + \$12 \text{ million} - \$8 \text{ million} - \$2 \text{ million} = \$53 \text{ million}$$ [3]

NET CASH FLOW FROM FINANCING ACTIVITIES

Most firms carry out a large number of financing transactions over the accounting period. Some add cash to the firm, while others absorb cash. The most frequently reported financial transactions are shown in Exhibit 4.2. They are also reported in the third part of the detailed cash-flow statement for OS Distributors shown in Exhibit 4.5. Using data from OS Distributors' balance sheets in Exhibit 4.1 and income statements in Exhibit 4.4, you can identify and calculate the cash flows related to its financing decisions in 2009 and 2010.

A look at the balance sheets in Exhibit 4.1 indicates that in 2009 the firm increased its short-term borrowings by $7 million, as shown by the increase in its short-term bank debt from $7 million to $14 million during that year. During the same period, it repaid $8 million of its long-term debt (see Note 5 in Exhibit 4.1). The 2009 income statement shows that the firm paid $5 million in interest and $2 million in dividends. In 2010, short-term borrowings increased by $1 million, from $14 million to $15 million. The firm's long-term debt increased by the $12 million borrowed to finance the extension of its warehouse (see Note 5), and the firm continued to repay $8 million of its existing long-term debt (see Note 5). Interest payments were $7 million, and dividend payments amounted to $3.2 million.[4] In total, net cash flow from financing activities was a negative $8 million in 2009 and a negative $5.2 million in 2010, as shown in line C in Exhibit 4.5.

THE CASH-FLOW STATEMENT

The firm's total net cash flow is the balance of the firm's cash flows related to its operating, investing, and financing activities during a period of time. Recall that this net cash flow must be equal to the firm's change in its cash position during the period. We can now reconcile the cash flows from OS Distributors' activities in 2009 and 2010 with the changes in its cash position during these two years.

The firm's cash position at the beginning of 2009 was $6 million, as shown in line E of the cash-flow statement in Exhibit 4.5. This is the amount of cash shown in the firm's balance sheet at year-end 2008 in Exhibit 4.1. During 2009, operations generated an NOCF of $14 million (line A). The firm made no investments in 2009 (line B), and its financing activities absorbed $8 million of cash (line C).

---

[3] The value of disposed assets in equation 4.4 is the net book value of the assets. If the sale price is different, the difference is either an extraordinary gain (the sale price is higher than the net book value) or an extraordinary loss (the asset is sold at a lower price than the net book value). These gains or losses are accounted for in the income statement and affect the firm's earnings after tax.

[4] Interest and dividend payments are equal to the figures shown in the income statements because OS Distributors does not have any accrued interest payable or accrued dividend payable. At the end of both years (2009 and 2010), the firm paid its interest expense and its dividends for the year.

Hence, its total net cash flow was $6 million, the difference between $14 million and $8 million (line D). Its cash position was $6 million at the beginning of the year, so its cash position at the end of 2009 was $12 million, the sum of the initial $6 million and the additional $6 million generated during the year (line F). This is the amount shown in the firm's balance sheet at the same date.

During 2010, the total net cash outflow was $4 million (operations generated $11.2 million, investing activities absorbed $10 million, and financing activities absorbed $5.2 million). OS Distributors began the year with $12 million in cash, so it ended the year with $8 million (the initial $12 million less the $4 million consumed during the year).

We have pointed out that OS Distributors' cash-flow statements are not needed to learn that the firm generated $6 million in cash in 2009 and consumed $4 million in 2010. This information is available in the balance sheets given in Exhibit 4.1. OS Distributors' cash position was $6 million at the end of 2008, $12 million at the end of 2009, and $8 million at the end of 2010. Hence, total net cash flow is $6 million in 2009 ($12 million less $6 million) and a negative $4 million in 2010 ($8 million less $12 million). If this information is readily available, what is the usefulness of a cash-flow statement?

The cash-flow statement tells you *how* and *why* the firm's cash position has changed during a particular period of time. It tells you *which* of the firm's decisions have generated cash and *which* have absorbed cash. A sequence of historical cash-flow statements indicates whether and how a firm's cash flow is improving or deteriorating over time and thus, whether the firm is in a sound financial position or heading toward troubled times.

THE STATEMENT OF CASH FLOWS ACCORDING TO THE FINANCIAL ACCOUNTING STANDARDS BOARD

Firms are required by regulatory authorities to provide a **statement of cash flows** that classifies the firm's cash flows differently from the cash-flow statement we have presented in Exhibit 4.5. The **Financial Accounting Standards Board (FASB)**, one of the major U.S. organizations in charge of developing accounting standards, issued *Standard No. 95* in November 1987 titled "statement of cash flows." Like the cash-flow statement presented in Exhibit 4.5, the statement of cash flows provides information on cash flows related to operating, investing, and financing activities, in that order. However, the way these cash flows are calculated and the allocation of cash flows to these three activities are somewhat different, as can be seen by comparing Exhibit 4.7, which presents OS Distributors' statement of cash flows, with the cash-flow statements in Exhibit 4.5.

CASH FLOWS FROM OPERATING ACTIVITIES

The net cash flow provided by operating activities in the statement of cash flows reported in Exhibit 4.7 differs from the NOCF in Exhibit 4.5 in two ways. First, it is estimated according to the **indirect method**.[5] This method starts with earnings af-

[5]Under the alternative or **direct method**, which was used in the cash-flow statements in Exhibit 4.5, cash receipts and cash disbursements related to operating activities are reported directly and separately.

EXHIBIT 4.7 OS DISTRIBUTORS' CASH-FLOW STATEMENTS: FINANCIAL ACCOUNTING STANDARDS BOARD (FASB) *STANDARDS NO. 95.*

FIGURES IN MILLIONS

	2009		2010	
• **Cash flows from operating activities**				
(+) Earnings after tax	$8.0		$10.2	
(+) Depreciation expense	5.0		8.0	
(−) Change in working capital requirement	(4.0)		(14.0)	
A. Net cash flow provided by operating activities		**$9.0**		**$4.2**
• **Cash flows from investing activities**				
(+) Sale of fixed assets	0.0		2.0	
(−) Capital expenditures and acquisitions	0.0		(12.0)	
B. Net cash flow from investing activities		**$0.0**		**($10.0)**
• **Cash flows from financing activities**				
(+) Increase in long-term borrowings	0.0		12.0	
(+) Increase in short-term borrowings	7.0		1.0	
(−) Long-term debt repaid	(8.0)		(8.0)	
(−) Dividend payments	(2.0)		(3.2)	
C. Net cash flow from financing activities		**($3.0)**		**$1.8**
D. Total net cash flow (A + B + C)		**$6.0**		**($4.0)**
E. Opening cash		**$6.0**		**$12.0**
F. Closing cash (E + D)		**$12.0**		**$8.0**

ter tax and adjusts them for noncash items and transactions that are not related to the firm's operating activities. Second, the firm's operating activities *include interest expense*, which, in our approach, is part of the firm's financing activities. The indirect method of presenting cash flows has been criticized by many accounting professionals, as Exhibit 4.8 shows.

For OS Distributors in 2010, earnings after tax were $10.2 million (see Exhibit 4.4), and depreciation expense of $8 million is added because this expense is not a cash-related item. The balance of $18.2 million is then adjusted by the $14 million change in the firm's working capital requirement, as shown in Exhibit 4.7. The net cash flow from operating activities is thus $4.2 million ($18.2 million less $14 million). The difference between this amount and the NOCF in Exhibit 4.5 is $7 million ($11.2 million less $4.2 million), which is, not surprisingly, the firm's net interest expense for 2010 (see Exhibit 4.4).

CASH FLOWS FROM INVESTING AND FINANCING ACTIVITIES

The cash flows related to investing and financing activities are reported in the statement of cash flows the same way they are presented in our cash-flow statement,

EXHIBIT 4.8 GO DIRECTLY TO CASH.[1]

Of all the recent financial-reporting reforms, Securities and Exchange Commission chief accountant Donald Nicolaisen thinks the most important has yet to be proposed: requiring companies to use the direct method to report their cash flow.

At a November [2004] conference hosted by Financial Executives International, Nicolaisen said that despite Sarbanes-Oxley and the slew of new rules issued by the Financial Accounting Standards Board, corporate efforts to improve reporting have "fallen short" of his expectations. "The single thing in my view that should go furthest toward improving disclosure" would be to mandate direct-method accounting.

The direct method calculates operating cash flow as a product of actual cash flow in and out—collection from customers, cash payments to suppliers, and so on. The indirect method, by contrast, arrives at that figure by adjusting net income for noncash expenses (such as depreciation and amortization), accruals, deferrals, and changes in working capital accounts. Although both produce the same number, "the indirect method can hide a multitude of sins," says Charles Mulford, an accounting professor at the Georgia Institute of Technology.

Still, the indirect method had always been the method of choice for many companies. Back in 1987, when FASB 95 established the standards for cash-flow reporting, FASB left the indirect method as an alternative, bowing to corporate concerns about the expense of tracking all cash items, recalls Grant Thornton CEO Ed Nusbaum. And since companies using the direct method must provide a reconciliation to net income using the indirect method anyway, says Mulford, it's no surprise that most simply continue to use the latter.

To date, Nicolaisen has never directly suggested that the SEC or FASB change the requirement. At the November conference, however, he did remark that "there's more that we have to do." The question, then, says Nusbaum, who is also a member of FASB's advisory council, is whether analysts and other financial-statement users really want to make the change.

Still, the cash-flow methods may soon find their way to the table. "This is a back-burner item that is slowly moving forward," says Mulford.

[1]"Go Directly to Cash" by Tim Reason. Reprinted with permission from *CFO* online, January 27, 2005. Visit our website at www.cfo.com. © CFO Publishing LLC. All Rights Reserved. Foster Printing Service: 866-879-9144, www.marketingreprints.com.

except that (1) interest payments are not shown as a financing activity and (2) interest and dividends received from financial investments are not recorded as an investing activity. Because these items are already taken into account in the earnings after tax, they are already included in the operating activities section of the statement. The differences between the two variations of the cash-flow statement can be seen by comparing the statements in Exhibits 4.7 and 4.5.

CASH FLOW FROM ASSETS OR FREE CASH FLOW

A popular measure of a firm's cash flow is the cash flow generated by the firm's assets, that is, by both its operating and investing activities. In other words, it is a measure of the total net cash flow generated by the firm *excluding* all financing transactions. As such, it is a measure of the cash flow available to those who *finance* the firm's activities, that is, the firm's lenders and the firm's shareholders (the suppliers of capital to the firm). We show in Chapter 6 and Chapter 12 that **cash flow from assets (CFA)**, also called **free cash flow (FCF)**, is a key input to value investment projects and businesses.

Given that cash flow from assets, or free cash flow, is a measure of the firm's total net cash flow *excluding* all financing transactions, we can write the following:

$$\begin{aligned}\text{Free cash flow} &= \text{Cash flow from operations} + \text{Cash flow from investing activities}\\ &= \text{EBIT} + \text{Depreciation expense} - \text{Tax expense} - \Delta\text{WCR}\\ &\quad - \text{Net capital expenditure}^{6}\end{aligned}$$

Because free cash flow excludes all financial transactions, it can be thought of as the cash flow the firm will generate if it did not borrow. In this case, its taxable profit is EBIT (because there is no interest expense). If T_C is the corporate tax rate, then tax expense is $T_C \times \text{EBIT}$. Factoring EBIT in the above equation gives us the following:

$$\begin{aligned}\textbf{Free cash flow} &= \textbf{EBIT}(\mathbf{1} - \mathbf{T_C}) + \textbf{Depreciation expense} - \mathbf{\Delta WCR}\\ &\quad - \textbf{Net capital expenditure}\end{aligned} \tag{4.5}$$

In this equation, the term $\text{EBIT} \times (1 - T_C)$ is often referred to as **net operating profit after tax (NOPAT)** or **net operating profit less adjusted taxes (NOPLAT)**.

Applied to the case of OS Distributors (whose tax rate is 40 percent), we get this:

$$\begin{aligned}\text{Free cash flow}_{2009} &= \$18.3 \text{ million} \times (1 - .40) + \$5 \text{ million} - \$4 \text{ million} - \$0\\ &= \$12 \text{ million}\end{aligned}$$

$$\begin{aligned}\text{Free cash flow}_{2010} &= \$24 \text{ million} \times (1 - .40) + \$8 \text{ million} - \$14 \text{ million} - \$10 \text{ million}\\ &= -\$1.6 \text{ million}\end{aligned}$$

During 2009, OS Distributors generated from its assets a free cash flow of \$12 million, whereas cash flow from operating activities was \$14 million (see NOCF in Exhibit 4.5). How can we account for the \$2 million difference given that net capital expenditures were zero in 2009? Free cash flow is \$2 million lower because it *excludes* interest expense and the tax reduction that goes with it, called the **interest tax shield.** In 2009, this tax shield is equal to 40 percent of OS Distributors' interest expense of \$5 million, that is, \$2 million (0.40 × \$5 million). We show in Chapters 8 and 12 how to use free cash flow to estimate the market value of a firm's assets.

MANAGERIAL IMPLICATIONS

Let's go back to NOCF, defined in equation 4.1. It is an indicator of a company's ability to generate cash from *operating its business* as opposed to generating cash from *selling assets* (a cash flow from investing activities) or *borrowing* (a cash flow from financing activities). It is a key component of a company's total net cash flow because no firm can survive if its *operating* cash flow keeps shrinking: it

---

[6] "Net capital expenditure" is the same as "cash flow from investing activities." The negative sign indicates that capital expenditure represents a net cash outflow.

EXHIBIT 4.9 MARGIN AND INVESTMENT COMPONENTS FOR OS DISTRIBUTORS' NET OPERATING CASH FLOW.

FIGURES IN MILLIONS

	2009	2010	Percent Change
Sales	$420.0	$480.0	14.3%
less COGS	(353.0)	(400.0)	
less SG&A expenses	(43.7)	(48.0)	
less tax expense	(5.3)	(6.8)	
= margin component	**$18.0**	**$25.2**	40.0%
Working capital requirement at the beginning of the year	$59.0	$63.0	
less working capital requirement at the end of the year	63.0	77.0	
= investment component	**($4.0)**	**($14.0)**	250.0%
NOCF = Margin – Investment	**$14.0**	**$11.2**	–20.0%

may be able to temporarily offset that weakness by raising cash through asset sales or borrowing (assuming lenders are ready to provide cash), but unless operating cash flow is strengthened, the firm will not survive.

We can better understand how management decisions affect operating cash flow by rewriting NOCF, shown in equation 4.1, as the difference between a margin component and an investment component:

Net operating cash flow = Margin component – Investment component (4.6)

The margin component is defined as sales less the sum of COGS, SG&A expenses, and tax expense. The investment component is the change in the firm's working capital requirement.

Exhibit 4.9 shows the two components of OS Distributors' NOCF in 2009 and 2010. Sales grew by 14.3 percent between 2009 and 2010, and the margin component increased by 40 percent. If the performance of OS Distributors' managers is measured only in terms of their contribution to profits, their 2010 performance would be remarkable. However, to generate this higher margin in 2010, managers had to increase investment in the firm's operating cycle (working capital requirement) from $4 million to $14 million, a year-to-year growth of 250 percent. The net result is not flattering for OS Distributors' operating cash flow. Because the investment component of NOCF grew much faster than its margin component, the firm's NOCF actually *declined* by 20 percent. The implication is clear: *if margin decisions are made without considering their effects on the firm's investment in its operating cycle, the result may be disastrous for operating cash flow.*

Equation 4.6 indicates that firms should run and monitor their operating activities on the basis of NOCF rather than margin. Monitoring the performance of operating managers on the basis of their contribution to the growth of NOCF will encourage them to widen the firm's margin without letting investment in operations (working capital requirement) grow too fast and offset the contribution of wider margins to the firm's operating cash flow. The net effect will be a higher operating cash flow for the firm.

SUMMARY

In its most reductionist form, a firm can be viewed as a "cash machine." It has to make strategic investment and funding decisions to generate more cash than it consumes. Strategic investment decisions include the building of plants, the purchase of equipment, and the acquisition of other businesses. Strategic funding decisions include long-term borrowing, dividend payments, and the issuance of shares. The various cash-flow statements presented in this chapter provide useful information about these decisions by showing how much money the firm has spent and how much money it has earned as a consequence of these decisions.

However, even though *strategic* decisions are the keys to the firm's long-term ability to create value, they do not guarantee that the "machine" will permanently produce excess cash. Only good *operating* decisions, that is, efficient day-to-day management of the firm's operating cycle (the machine's "engine") can, over time, help generate more cash than is consumed.

The relevant measure of the cash flow generated by operations is net operating cash flow (NOCF). It is the net cash flow generated by *running* the business, not by selling some of its assets or borrowing from banks.

There are alternative approaches to calculating a firm's NOCF. One approach is given by equation 4.1. In this formula, NOCF equals sales less the following three items: operating expenses (excluding depreciation expense, a noncash item), tax expense, and the change in the firm's working capital requirement. Another approach is given by equation 4.3. In this case, NOCF equals EBIT plus depreciation expense less tax expense and the change in the firm's working capital requirement (WCR). For a firm with a rising (and positive) working capital requirement, the change in WCR represents the cash used to finance the growth in the firm's net investment in its operating cycle (see Chapter 3). The more cash that goes to fund operations (to support additional inventories and receivables, for example), the weaker the firm's NOCF.

NOCF can also be viewed as the difference between a margin component and an investment component. The margin component is the firm's operating margin (its sales less its operating expenses, excluding depreciation expense); the investment component is the change in the firm's working capital requirement.

Firms generally use two types of cash-flow statements interchangeably. One distinguishes between cash flows generated by the firm's operating activities (its NOCF), its investing activities, and its financing activities. The other one is the statement of cash flows recommended by the Financial Accounting Standards Board.

Obtaining the Net Operating Cash Flow from Balance Sheet and Income Statement Accounts

APPENDIX **4.1**

Net operating cash flow (NOCF) is defined as the difference between the cash inflow and the cash outflow from the firm's operating activities. This appendix shows how these cash flows can be estimated from the balance sheets and income statement, using the estimation of OS Distributors' NOCF in 2010 as an illustration.

MEASURING CASH INFLOW FROM OPERATIONS

As shown in the chapter, cash inflow from sales can be measured by tracing what happens to accounts receivable during the estimation period. This cash inflow is equal to sales adjusted by the change in receivables during the period:

$$\textbf{Cash inflow from sales} = \textbf{Sales} - \Delta\textbf{Accounts receivable} \qquad \text{(A4.1.1)}$$

where ΔAccounts receivable is the change in accounts receivable during the period.

Thus, the cash inflow from sales is calculated using information from the period's income statement and from the opening and closing balance sheets that surround the income statement. For example, what is the cash inflow from sales for OS Distributors in 2010? The balance sheets in Exhibit 4.1 show that accounts receivable at the end of 2009 and 2010 are equal to \$48 million and \$56 million, respectively. Therefore,

$$\Delta\text{Accounts receivable 2010} = 56 \text{ million} - 48 \text{ million} = \$8 \text{ million}$$

The 2010 sales are equal to \$480 million, as shown in the 2010 income statement in Exhibit 4.4. From equation A4.1.1:

$$\text{Cash inflow from sales}_{2010} = \$480 \text{ million} - \$8 \text{ million} = \$472 \text{ million}$$

which is the amount reported in Exhibit 4.2.

MEASURING CASH OUTFLOW FROM OPERATIONS

Cash outflow from operations includes payments to suppliers for purchased goods; cash expenses related to selling, general, and administrative (SG&A) expenses, *excluding* depreciation, which is not a cash item; and tax payments. We can write the following:

$$\text{Cash outflow from operations} = \text{Cash outflow from purchases} + \text{Cash outflow from SG\&A and taxes}$$

CASH OUTFLOW FROM PURCHASES

To determine cash payments to suppliers, we use the same approach as the one used to calculate cash receipts from customers. Instead of tracing what happens to receivables during the estimation period, we trace what happens to payables. Each time the firm receives an invoice from one of its suppliers, accounts payable increase by the amount of the invoice, and each time the firm pays an invoice, accounts payable decrease by the amount paid. Thus, we can write the following:

$$\text{Accounts payable}_{\text{end}} = \text{Accounts payable}_{\text{beginning}} + \text{Purchases} - \text{Cash outflow from purchases}$$

Rearranging the terms of the equation, we get the following:

$$\text{Cash outflow from purchases} = \text{Purchases} - [\text{Accounts payable}_{\text{end}} - \text{Accounts payable}_{\text{beginning}}]$$

This equation can be written as

$$\textbf{Cash outflow from purchases = Purchases} - \boldsymbol{\Delta}\textbf{Accounts payable} \qquad \text{(A4.1.2)}$$

where ΔAccounts payable is the change in payables during the estimation period.

However, unlike sales, purchases are not shown in the income statement. They must be calculated indirectly from the data provided by the income statement and the balance sheets. For a distributor, inventories at the beginning of the period increase by the cost of purchases made during the period. When the firm sells the goods, these costs are released to the cost of goods sold (COGS) account. Thus, we can write the following:

$$\text{Inventories}_{\text{beginning}} + \text{Purchases} - \text{COGS} = \text{Inventories}_{\text{end}}$$

Rearranging the terms of the equation, we get the following:

$$\textbf{Purchases = COGS +} \boldsymbol{\Delta}\textbf{Inventories} \qquad \text{(A4.1.3)}$$

where ΔInventories is the change in inventories during the period.

Equation A4.1.3 could have been obtained directly because, for a distributor, if the amount of goods purchased during the accounting period exceeds the amount of goods sold during that period, the inventories account will increase by the difference. If a distributor sells more goods than it buys during the accounting period, the inventories account will decrease by the difference.

Substituting the value of purchases given by equation A4.1.3 into equation A4.1.2 yields the following value for the firm's cash outflows from purchases:

$$\textbf{Cash outflow from purchases = COGS + Inventories} - \boldsymbol{\Delta}\,\textbf{Accounts payable} \qquad \text{(A4.1.4)}$$

Using the data in OS Distributors' 2010 income statement and in the balance sheets at the end of 2009 and 2010, the cash outflow from the firm's operations in 2010 is as follows:

$$\begin{aligned}\text{Cash outflow from purchases in 2010} &= \$400 \text{ million} + [\$72 \text{ million} - \$57 \text{ million}] \\ &\quad - [\$48 \text{ million} - \$40 \text{ million}] \\ &= \$407 \text{ million}\end{aligned}$$

The first term on the right side of the equation is the COGS in 2010. The second term is the change in the inventories account in 2010. This is the difference between the inventories at year-end 2010 ($72 million) and year-end 2009 ($57 million). The third term is the change in accounts payable between year-end 2010 ($48 million) and year-end 2009 ($40 million).

CASH OUTFLOW FROM SG&A AND TAX EXPENSES

To determine the amount of cash paid for SG&A expenses and tax expenses during the estimation period, we must adjust them for any change in prepaid expenses and accrued expenses. This approach is similar to adjusting purchases for changes in accounts payable to determine the cash payments to suppliers. For example, when OS Distributors' prepaid expenses decreased by $1 million in 2010 (see Exhibit 4.1), cash paid for operating expenses (in this case, rent payments as indicated in Note 2 to the balance sheet) was $1 million less than the expense reported in the income statement for 2010. To convert operating expenses into cash payments, the decrease of $1 million must be deducted from the expenses. If the prepaid expenses had increased, the increase would have been added to the expenses. In 2009, OS Distributors' accrued expenses increased by $2 million. This means that cash paid for operating expenses (in this case, payments for wages and tax, as indicated in Note 4 to the balance sheet) was $2 million lower than the expenses recorded in the 2009 income statement. As a result, the $2 million must be subtracted from operating expenses to arrive at the cash payment. If the accrued expenses had decreased, the decrease would have been added to the operating expenses. Therefore, if ΔAccrued expenses and ΔPrepaid expenses represent the change in the accrued and prepaid expenses accounts, respectively, we can write the following:

$$\textbf{Cash outflow from SG\&A and tax expenses} \\ = \textbf{SG\&A expenses} + \textbf{Tax expenses} + \Delta\textbf{Prepaid expenses} - \Delta\textbf{Accrued expenses} \tag{A4.1.5}$$

Applying equation A4.1.5 to OS Distributors in 2010, we get this:

$$\text{Cash outflow from SG\&A and tax expenses}_{2010} \\ = [\$48\text{ million} + \$6.8\text{ million}] + [\$1\text{ million} - \$2\text{ million}] - [\$4\text{ million} - \$4\text{ million}] \\ = \$53.8\text{ million}$$

The terms in the first set of brackets are the SG&A expenses and tax expenses from the 2010 income statement in Exhibit 4.4. The terms in the second and third sets of brackets are the changes in prepaid expenses and accrued expenses taken from the balance sheets at year-end 2009 and 2010 in Exhibit 4.1.

NET OPERATING CASH FLOW

We can now derive a general formula for a firm's NOCF. Adding the cash outflow from purchases in equation A4.1.4 to the cash outflow from SG&A expenses and tax expenses in equation A4.1.5, we get the total cash outflow from operations:

$$\text{Cash outflow from operations} = \text{COGS} + \Delta\text{Inventories} - \Delta\text{Accounts payable} \\ + \text{SG\&A and tax expenses} + \Delta\text{Prepaid expenses} \\ - \Delta\text{Accrued expenses}$$

Rearranging the terms of the equation, we get the following:

$$\textbf{Cash outflow from operations} = \textbf{COGS} + \textbf{SG\&A expenses} + \textbf{Tax expenses} + \Delta\textbf{Inventories} + \Delta\textbf{Prepaid expenses} - \Delta\textbf{Accounts payable} - \Delta\textbf{Accrued expenses} \quad (A4.1.6)$$

For OS Distributors, using data from the income statements and balance sheets in Exhibits 4.1 and 4.4, we have the following:

$$\begin{aligned}\text{Cash outflow from operations}_{2010} &= [\$400 \text{ million} + \$48 \text{ million} + \$6.8 \text{ million}] \\ &\quad + [\$72 \text{ million} - \$57 \text{ million}] \\ &\quad + [\$1 \text{ million} - \$2 \text{ million}] \\ &\quad - [\$48 \text{ million} - \$40 \text{ million}] \\ &\quad - [\$4 \text{ million} - \$4 \text{ million}] \\ &= \$460.8 \text{ million}\end{aligned}$$

which is the amount shown in Exhibit 4.2.

We can now estimate NOCF by finding the difference between cash inflow from operations, equation A4.1.1, and cash outflow from operations, equation A4.1.6:

$$\begin{aligned}\text{NOCF} = {} & [\text{Sales} - \Delta\text{Accounts receivable}] - [\text{COGS} + \text{SG\&A expenses} \\ & + \text{Tax expenses} + \Delta\text{Inventories} + \Delta\text{Prepaid expenses} \\ & - \Delta\text{Accounts payable} - \Delta\text{Accrued expenses}]\end{aligned}$$

The terms in this equation can be rearranged to yield:

$$\begin{aligned}\text{NOCF} = {} & [\text{Sales} - \text{COGS} - \text{SG\&A expenses} - \text{Tax expenses}] \\ & - [\Delta\text{Accounts receivable} + \Delta\text{Inventories} + \Delta\text{Prepaid expenses} \\ & - \Delta\text{Accounts payable} - \Delta\text{Accrued expenses}]\end{aligned}$$

The first three items in the second set of brackets measure the *changes* in the firm's operating assets, and the last two terms measure the *changes* in its operating liabilities. Recall that the difference between the firm's operating assets and its operating liabilities represents the accounting estimate of the firm's net investment in its operating cycle and is called working capital requirement (WCR). Therefore, the expression in the second set of brackets represents the *change* in the firm's working capital requirement, or ΔWCR. Thus, we get this:

$$\text{NOCF} = \text{Sales} - \text{COGS} - \text{SG\&A expenses} - \text{Tax expenses} - \Delta\text{WCR}$$

which is equation 4.1.

THE HOME DEPOT'S CASH FLOWS

APPENDIX 4.2

The Home Depot's cash-flow statements for 2007 and 2008,[7] taken from the firm's annual reports, are shown on Exhibit A4.2.1. The analysis of these statements shows how the company's three main activities—its operating, investing, and financing activities—have contributed to the changes in its cash position over the two-year period.

RESTRUCTURING THE HOME DEPOT'S CASH-FLOW STATEMENTS

The cash-flow statements in Exhibit A4.2.1 were prepared according to *Standard No. 95* of the Financial Accounting Standards Board (FASB 95). Remember that in this version of the cash-flow statement, the net cash flow provided by the operations includes interest expense, even though this account belongs to the firm's financing activities, not its operating activities. Furthermore, because the FASB does not require firms to provide detailed information on the adjustments needed to reconcile the individual accounts in the three statements (the cash-flow statement, the income statement, and the balance sheets), it is not easy to construct a cash-flow statement from the income statement and the opening and closing balance sheets without the additional information provided in the company's annual reports.

Using the information in The Home Depot's annual reports, the income statements in Exhibit A4.2.2, and the managerial balance sheets in Exhibit A4.2.3, we show how to reconstruct The Home Depot's cash-flow statements into the format shown in Exhibit A4.2.4. We then analyze and interpret these reconstructed statements.

From The Home Depot's income statements in Exhibit A4.2.2, we get net interest expenses of $622 million in 2007 and $606 million in 2008. Adding these amounts to the net cash provided by operating activities eliminates their impact on operating cash flows. Furthermore, note that the cash-flow statement in Exhibit A4.2.1 shows the change in the company's cash and cash equivalents over each of the two fiscal years, excluding the changes in the firm's short-term investments and receivables that are part of the definition of cash in the company's managerial

[7]Years 2007 and 2008 refer to fiscal years ending February 3, 2008, and February 1, 2009, respectively.

EXHIBIT A4.2.1 THE HOME DEPOT, INC.'S CASH-FLOW STATEMENTS.

FROM THE COMPANY ANNUAL REPORTS FOR FISCAL YEARS 2007 AND 2008. FIGURES IN MILLIONS

	2007	2008
Cash flows from operating activities:		
Net earnings	$ 4,395	$ 2,260
Reconciliation of net earnings to net cash provided by operating activities	1,332	3,268
Net cash provided by operating activities	5,727	5,528
Cash flows from investing activities:		
Capital expenditures, net	(3,558)	(1,847)
Proceeds from sale of business, net	8,337	–
Payments for business acquired, net	(13)	–
Proceeds from sales of property and equipment	318	147
Purchases of investments	(11,225)	(168)
Proceeds from sales and maturities of investments	10,899	139
Net cash provided by (used in) investing activities	4,758	(1,729)
Cash flows from financing activities:		
(Repayment of) proceeds from short-term borrowings, net	1,734	(1,732)
Repayments of long-term debt	(20)	(313)
Repurchases of common stock	(10,815)	(70)
Proceeds from sale of common stock	276	84
Cash dividends paid to stockholders	(1,709)	(1,521)
Other financing activities	(105)	(128)
Net cash provided by (used in) financing activities	(10,639)	(3,680)
Increase (decrease) in cash and cash equivalents	(154)	119
Effect of exchange rate changes on cash and cash equivalents	(1)	(45)
Cash and cash equivalents at beginning of the year	600	445
Cash and cash equivalents at end of the year	$ 445	$ 519

balance sheet.[8] In the cash-flow statement, these changes are deducted from net earnings in the reconciliation of net earnings to net cash provided by operating activities; therefore, they also have to be added to the net cash provided by operating activities to get The Home Depot's net operating cash flow (NOCF). The

[8]Short-term investments are investments with maturities of less than a year and readily available for sale. Receivables are credit card payments made by customers in the process of being cleared by the financial institutions. For all practical purposes, both short-term investments and receivables are cash equivalents and must be included in the cash account in the managerial balance sheet.

EXHIBIT A4.2.2 THE HOME DEPOT INC.'S CONSOLIDATED STATEMENTS OF INCOME.

FROM EXHIBIT A2.1.2, APPENDIX 2.1, CHAPTER 2. FIGURES IN MILLIONS

	2006	2007	2008
Net sales	**$79,022**	**$77,349**	**$71,288**
Cost of goods sold	52,476	51,352	47,298
Gross profit	**26,546**	**25,997**	**23,990**
Selling, general, and administrative expenses	16,106	17,053	17,846
Depreciation expense	1,574	1,702	1,785
Operating profit	**8,866**	**7,242**	**4,359**
Special items[1]	495	185	(215)
Earnings before interest and tax (EBIT)	**9,361**	**7,427**	**4,144**
Net interest expense	364	622	606
Earnings before tax (EBT)	**8,997**	**6,805**	**3,538**
Income tax expense	3,236	2,410	1,278
Earnings after tax (EAT)	**$ 5,761**	**$ 4,395**	**$ 2,260**

[1]The special items account includes investment write-downs and profit (loss) from discontinued operations reported in The Home Depot's income statements.

company's balance sheets in Exhibit A2.1.1 (See Chapter 2, Appendix 2.1) provide the data needed to calculate the changes in these two accounts. The change in short-term investments in 2007 is *minus* $2 million ($12 million less $14 million)

EXHIBIT A4.2.3 THE HOME DEPOT'S MANAGERIAL BALANCE SHEETS.

FROM EXHIBIT A3.2.3, APPENDIX 3.2, CHAPTER 3. FIGURES IN MILLIONS

	Jan. 28, 2007		Feb. 3, 2008		Feb. 1, 2009	
Invested capital						
• Cash		$ 3,837		$ 1,716		$ 1,497
• Working capital requirement		1,250		2,299		2,479
• Net fixed assets		34,263		29,650		27,802
Total invested capital		**$39,350**		**$33,665**		**$31,778**
Capital employed						
• Short-term debt		$ 18		$ 2,047		$ 1,767
• Long-term financing		39,332		31,618		30,011
Long-term debt	$11,643		$11,383		$ 9,667	
Other long-term liabilities	2,659		2,521		2,567	
Owners' equity	25,030		17,714		17,777	
Total capital employed		**$39,350**		**$33,665**		**$31,778**

EXHIBIT A4.2.4 THE HOME DEPOT'S RESTRUCTURED CASH-FLOW STATEMENTS.

FIGURES IN MILLIONS

	2007		2008	
• Cash flows from operating activities				
Margin component	$5,432		$6,021	
Investment component:				
(increase) decrease in working capital requirement	1,049		180	
A. Net operating cash flow (NOCF)		**$4,383**		**$5,841**
• Cash flows from investing activities				
Capital expenditures, net of property and equipment sales	(3,240)		(1,700)	
Proceeds from sale of business, net of disposals	8,324		–	
Others	(326)		(29)	
B. Net cash flow from investing activities		**4,758**		**(1,729)**
• Cash flows from financing activities				
Payment of dividends	(1,709)		(1,521)	
Repurchases of common stock	(10,815)		(70)	
Changes in short-term borrowings, net	1,734		(1,732)	
Repayments of long-term debt	(20)		(313)	
Interest payments, net	(622)		(606)	
Others	170		(89)	
C. Net cash flow from financing activities		**(11,262)**		**(4,331)**
D. Total net cash flow (A + B + C)		**($2,121)**		**($219)**
E. Opening cash		**$3,837**		**$1,716**
F. Closing cash (E + D)		**$1,716**		**$1,497**

and *minus* $6 million in 2008 ($6 million less $12 million). The change in receivables is *minus* $1,964 million in 2007 ($1,259 million less $3,223 million) and *minus* $287 million in 2008 ($972 million less $1,259 million). *Adding* $622 million of interest expense and *deducting* $2 million of change in short-term investments and $1,964 million in receivables to the $5,727 million of net cash provided by operating activities in 2007 gives an NOCF of $4,383 million ($5,727 million plus $622 million less $2 million less $1,964 million). The same adjustments for 2008 result in an NOCF of $5,841 million that year.

Data from The Home Depot's managerial balance sheets in Exhibit A4.2.3 show that the company's working capital requirement (WCR) increased by $1,049 million in 2007 ($2,299 million less $1,250 million) and by $180 million in 2008 ($2,479 million less $2,299 million).

The Home Depot's NOCF for 2007 and 2008 can now be reconstructed, showing its margin and investment components, as reported in Exhibit A4.2.4.

The investment component is the change in WCR: $1,049 million in 2007 and $180 million in 2008. The margin component is the NOCF plus the investment component: $5,432 million in 2007 ($4,383 million plus $1,049 million) and $6,021 million in 2008 ($5,841 million plus $180 million).[9]

Exhibit A4.2.4 shows The Home Depot's cash-flow statements after adjusting for the above changes in the firm's operating cash flows. In the following sections, we analyze this statement, showing the contribution of the firm's operating, investing, and financing activities to the company's cash position.

THE HOME DEPOT'S CASH FLOWS FROM OPERATING ACTIVITIES

The Home Depot's NOCF increased by a third in 2008, rising from $4,383 million in 2007 to $5,841 million in 2008. This increase of $1,458 million comes from both an improvement in the margin component, which was $589 million higher in 2008 than in 2007 ($6,021 million less $5,432 million) and a reduction of $869 million in the investment component ($1,049 million less $180 million), despite worsening product market conditions.

Although the margin component increased in 2008, operating profit decreased significantly (see Exhibit A4.2.2). At first glance, this may seem contradictory but it is not. The explanation is that the margin component in the NOCF is based on *real cash* movements, whereas operating profit also includes *noncash* expenses such as depreciation, write-offs, and impairment of assets. In its 2008 annual report, The Home Depot mentions substantial amounts of noncash expenses.

The investment component, which absorbed an extra $1,049 million of cash in the company's operating cycle during 2007, consumed only $180 million during 2008.[10] How do we explain this reduction in the investment component? Exhibit A3.2.4 in Chapter 3, Appendix 3.2 shows that the ratio of WCR to sales increased from 3.0 percent at year-end 2007 to 3.5 percent at year-end 2008, which would imply an increase in the amount of cash absorbed in the operating cycle. However, the company's revenues decreased from $77,349 million in 2007 to $71,288 million in 2008 (see Exhibit A4.2.2). The reduction in revenues more than compensated for the increase in the ratio of WCR to sales, leaving a net increase in the investment component of the NOCF of only $180 million in 2008.

THE HOME DEPOT'S CASH FLOWS FROM INVESTING ACTIVITIES

The Home Depot generated $4,758 million of cash from its investing activities during 2007 while spending a net amount of $1,729 million on the same activities in 2008.

During 2007, the company sold its HD Supply business for $8,324 million. This was much more than the amount spent in the same year on capital expenditures ($3,240 million) and on other investments ($326 million), leaving a cash surplus of $4,758 million.

---

[9]The margin component cannot be calculated directly from the income statements in Exhibit A4.2.2 because operating profit includes a number of noncash expenses that we do not know.

[10]Appendix 3.2 in Chapter 3 provides a detailed analysis of the changes in the company's WCR.

In 2008, responding to worsening market conditions, the company cut its capital expenditures drastically from $3,240 million in 2007 to $1,700 million. Other investment activities marginally increased the cash spent on investments bringing net cash flow from investing activities to negative $1,729 million in 2008.

THE HOME DEPOT'S CASH FLOWS FROM FINANCING ACTIVITIES

After accounting for the net cash flow from operating and investing activities, The Home Depot generated a cash surplus of $9,141 million in 2007 (NOCF of $4,383 million plus $4,758 million of net cash inflow from investing activities). And in 2008, it generated another surplus of $4,112 million ($5,841 million less $1,729 million).

The analysis of The Home Depot's cash flows from financing activities during 2007 shows that the company spent $10,815 million to repurchase some of its common stock in addition to paying $1,709 million of dividends. It also shows that the company's short-term borrowings increased by $1,734 million.

In contrast, during 2008, the company spent only $70 million on shares repurchase. This decision was directly related to the dismal economic environment and market conditions prevailing in 2008. During that same year, the company reduced its short-term debt by $1,732 million (in other words, it repaid its debt by that amount), which was nearly the same amount it had borrowed short term in 2007 ($1,734 million). It also marginally reduced its dividend payment from $1,709 million in 2007 to $1,521 million in 2008.

To summarize, The Home Depot's cash position deteriorated significantly in 2007, decreasing by $2,121 million (from $3,837 million at the beginning of the year to $1,716 million at the end of the year) as shown in lines D to F in Exhibit A4.2.4. In 2007, the company repurchased $10,815 million of its shares and spent $3,240 million on capital expenditures, $1,709 million on dividends, and $622 million on interest payment for a total amount of $16,386 million. To finance these large cash outlays, the company essentially used four sources of cash: (1) the cash surplus generated by its operating activities ($4,383 million); (2) the net proceeds from the sale of its HD Supply business ($8,324 million); (3) an increase in short-term borrowing ($1,734 million); and, finally, (4) cash from its cash account, which decreased by $2,121 million ($3,837 million less $1,716 million). The sum of these four items is $16,562 million.[11]

During 2008, the company's cash position decreased further but much less than the previous year. The major discretionary expenses that took place during that year include a drastically reduced amount of capital expenditures to $1,700 million, the reimbursement of $1,732 million of short-term borrowings, and a slightly reduced dividend payout of $1,521 million for a total of nearly $5,000 million. Most of these cash outflows, plus other less significant ones, were financed with the cash flow generated by the company's operating activities ($5,841 million) and $219 million of cash from its cash account (which decreased from $1,716 million to $1,497 million).

[11]The net cash outflow of $16,386 million and the net cash inflow of $16,562 million do not balance out exactly because we ignored some smaller accounts shown in Exhibit A4.2.4.

FURTHER READING

1. Kieso, Donald, Jerry Weygandt, and Terry Warfield. *Intermediate Accounting*, 13th ed. John Wiley & Sons, 2010. See Chapters 4 and 5.
2. Stickney, Clyde, Roman Weil, Katherine Schipper, and Jennifer Francis. *Financial Accounting*, 13th ed. South-Western, 2010. See Chapter 5.

SELF-TEST PROBLEMS

4.1 CONSTRUCTING AND INTERPRETING CASH-FLOW STATEMENTS.

The financial statements of Allied & Consolidated Clothier (ACC), a manufacturer of coats and other garments, are shown below. ACC's operational efficiency and liquidity position are analyzed in Chapter 3. The income statements span a calendar year, and balance sheets are dated December 31. All figures are in millions of dollars.

a. Prepare a standard cash-flow statement for Year 2 and Year 3. Interpret your results.
b. Calculate net operating cash flow (NOCF) in Year 2 and Year 3, using earnings before interest and tax (EBIT). What is the difference between this approach and the one in the cash-flow statement in the previous question?
c. Calculate net operating cash flow in Year 2 and Year 3, using earnings before interest, tax, depreciation, and amortization (EBITDA). What is the difference between this approach and the ones in the previous two questions?
d. Calculate NOCF as the difference between cash inflows from operations and cash outflows from operations (refer to Appendix 4.1 to measure the latter).
e. What are cash flows from assets in Year 2 and Year 3? What do they measure?
f. Separate the margin component from the investment component in the NOCF in Year 2 and Year 3. What can you conclude?
g. Prepare a statement of cash flows (*Standard No. 95* of the Financial Accounting Standards Board) for Year 2 and Year 3. What is the difference between this type of statement and the one prepared in question (a)?

Balance Sheets (in millions, year-end data)

	Year 1	Year 2	Year 3		Year 1	Year 2	Year 3
Cash	$100	$ 90	$ 50	Short-term debt	$ 80	$ 90	$ 135
Trade receivables	200	230	290	Trade payables	170	180	220
Inventories	160	170	300	Accrued expenses	40	45	50
Prepaid expenses	30	30	35	Long-term debt	140	120	100
Net fixed assets	390	390	365	Owners' equity	450	475	535
Total assets	$880	$910	$1,040	**Total liabilities and owners' equity**	$880	$910	$1,040

Income Statements (in millions)	Year 1	Year 2	Year 3
Net sales	**$1,200**	**$1,350**	**$1,600**
Cost of goods sold	860	970	1,160
Selling, general, and administrative expenses	150	165	200
Depreciation expense	40	50	55
Earnings before interest and tax (EBIT)	**150**	**165**	**185**
Net interest expense	20	20	25
Earnings before tax (EBT)	**130**	**145**	**160**
Income tax expense	40	45	50
Earnings after tax (EAT)	$ 90	$ 100	$ 110
Dividends	$ 75	$ 75	$ 50

4.2 EXAMINING THE OPERATING CASH FLOW OF A RETAILER.

Return to the 2007 and 2008 financial statements for Carrefour, the French retailer whose operational efficiency and liquidity positions are examined in Self-Test Problem 3.2 of Chapter 3.

a. What is the cash flow that Carrefour has generated from its operating activities in 2008?
b. Separate the margin component from the investment component in the net operating cash flow in 2008. What can you conclude about Carrefour's growth strategy?

REVIEW PROBLEMS

1. **Transactions.**
Indicate the effect of the following transactions on working capital requirement (**WCR**), net operating cash flow (**CF_{OPE}**), cash flow from investing activities (**CF_{INV}**), cash flow from financing activities (**CF_{FIN}**), and owners' equity. Use + to indicate an increase, – to indicate a decrease, and 0 to indicate no effect.

		WCR	CF_{OPE}	CF_{INV}	CF_{FIN}	Owners' Equity
1.	Shares are issued for cash					
2.	Goods from inventory are sold for cash					
3.	A fixed asset is sold for cash at a loss					
4.	Corporate income tax is paid					
5.	Cash is obtained through a bank loan					
6.	A cash dividend is paid					
7.	Accounts receivable are collected					
8.	Minority interest in a firm acquired for cash					

		WCR	CF_{OPE}	CF_{INV}	CF_{FIN}	Owners' Equity
9.	A fixed asset is depreciated					
10.	Obsolete inventory is written off					
11.	Insurance premium is paid					
12.	Merchandise is purchased on account					
13.	Interest on debt is paid					
14.	Dividends from a subsidiary are received					

2. **Profits, losses, and cash flows.**
   a. How would you explain that a firm can generate a profit, when at the same time its cash flow from operations is negative?
   b. How would you explain that a firm showing a net loss can have a positive cash flow from operations?

3. **Depreciation and cash flows.**
   Do you agree with the statement that depreciation expenses are one of the firm's most important sources of cash?

4. **Building a cash-flow statement.**
   Based on the following financial statements and information given below, compute the following for the year 2010:
   a. The cash inflow from operations
   b. The cash outflow from operations
   c. The net operating cash flow (NOCF)
   d. The net cash flow from investing activities
   e. The net cash flow from financing activities
   f. The total net cash flow

Income Statement (in thousands)		
		2010
Net sales		**$320,000**
Cost of goods sold		(260,000)
Material cost	$224,000	
Labor expense	36,000	
Selling, general, and administrative expenses		(18,000)
Depreciation expense		(9,000)
Earnings before interest and tax		**$33,000**
Net interest expense		(3,000)
Earnings before tax		**$30,000**
Income tax expense		(10,800)
Earnings after tax		**$19,200**
Dividends		$9,200

Balance Sheets (in thousands)	December 31, 2009	December 31, 2010
Cash	$ 7,500	$ 11,400
Accounts receivable	32,000	38,400
Inventories	28,000	32,000
Prepaid expenses	1,500	2,200
Net fixed assets	76,000	81,000
Total assets	$145,000	$165,000
Short-term debt	$ 7,000	$ 9,000
Accounts payable	30,000	38,000
Accrued expenses	4,000	2,000
Long-term debt	23,000	25,000
Owners' equity	81,000	91,000
Total liabilities and owners' equity	$145,000	$165,000

The firm is a distributor of video games for which you have the following information:

1. Prepaid expenses are prepaid rent and insurance premium
2. The company owes its employees (direct labor force) $4 million at the end of 2009 and $2 million at the end of 2010
3. The company paid in advance $10,800,000 of taxes on December 15, 2010
4. The company did not sell any fixed assets in 2010
5. The company did not issue or repurchase any new shares in 2010
6. The balance of long-term debt was $27 million at the end of 2009, of which $4 million was paid in 2010
7. The company borrowed $6 million long term in 2010
8. The company owed $3 million in short-term debt to its bank at the end of 2009. A year later, it owed $5 million
9. The company paid $9,200,000 of dividends in 2010

5. **Two cash-flow statements.**
Following are the income statement for 2010 and the balance sheets at year-ends 2009 and 2010 for Allied Enterprises Inc.

   a. Prepare the managerial balance sheets for Allied Enterprises at year-ends 2009 and 2010
   b. Prepare the company's cash-flow statement for 2010 according to the direct method, and the indirect method to computing the net operating cash flow per *Standards No. 95* of the Financial Accounting Standards Board

Income Statement (in thousands)	2010
Net sales	**$34,760**
Cost of goods sold	27,610
Selling, general, and administrative expenses	5,500
Depreciation expense	165
Earnings before interest and tax	**1,485**
Net interest expense	286
Earnings before tax	**1,199**
Income tax expense	473
Earnings after tax	$ 726
Dividends	$ 220

Balance Sheet (in thousands)	December 31, 2009	December 31, 2010
Cash	$ 385	$ 330
Accounts receivable	3,410	4,620
Inventories	3,520	4,730
Prepaid expenses	0	0
Net fixed assets[1]	1,430	1,595
Total assets	$8,745	$11,275
Short-term debt	$ 570	$ 2,100
Accounts payable	1,760	2,255
Accrued expenses	286	385
Long-term debt	1,300	1,200
Owners' equity	4,829	5,335
Total liabilities and owners' equity	$8,745	$11,275

[1]The company did not sell any fixed assets in year 2010.

6. **From the statement of cash flows (*Standards No. 95* of the Financial Accounting Standards Board) to the cash-flow statement (direct method).**
From the following Lowe's cash-flow statement, build the firm's cash-flow statement according to the direct method. The interest payments in 2008 were equal to $280 million.

(in millions)	2008
Cash flows from operating activities	
Net earnings	$2,195
Adjustments to reconcile net income to net cash provided by operating activities	1,927
Net cash provided by operating activities	**4,122**
Cash flows from investing activities	
Proceeds from sale of short-term investments, net of sales	221
Purchase of long-term investments, net of sale	(154)
Increase in other long-term assets	(56)
Property acquired, net of disposals	(3,237)
Net cash used in investing activities	**(3,226)**
Cash flows from financing activities	
Net (decrease) increase in short-term borrowing	(57)
Repayment of long-term debt, net	(558)
Proceeds from issuance of common stock	174
Cash dividend payments	(491)
Repurchase of common stock	(8)
Excess cash benefits of share-based payments	1
Net cash used in financing activities	**(939)**
Effect of exchange rate changes on cash	7
Net (decrease) increase in cash and cash equivalents	(36)
Cash and cash equivalents, beginning of year	281
Cash and cash equivalents, end of year	$ 245

7. **Direct versus indirect method to cash-flow estimation.**
   What are the major differences between the cash-flow statement (direct method) and the statement of cash flows (indirect method according to *Standards No. 95* of the Financial Accounting Standards Board)? Which is the most relevant to financial analysis?

8. **Another version of the cash-flow statement.**
   Build a cash-flow statement for Allied Enterprises Inc. (see Review Problem 5) that measures the firm's cash flow from its operating activities in 2010 based on the cash flows the firm was legally obliged to meet that year (its **nondiscretionary cash flows**), and the cash flows that were at the discretion of the management (its **discretionary cash flows**). What would make this version of the cash-flow statement relevant?

9. **The effect of the management of the operating cycle on the firm's cash flows.**
   Following are financial statements for Sentec Inc., a distributor of electrical fixtures, for 2008, 2009, and 2010.

Income Statements (in thousands)	2008	2009	2010
Net sales	**$22,100**	**$24,300**	**$31,600**
Cost of goods sold	17,600	19,300	25,100
Selling, general, and administrative expenses	3,750	4,000	5,000
Depreciation expense	100	100	150
Earnings before interest and tax	**650**	**900**	**1,350**
Net interest expense	110	130	260
Earnings before tax	**540**	**770**	**1,090**
Income tax expense	220	310	430
Earnings after tax	**$ 320**	**$ 460**	**$ 660**
Dividends	$ 180	$ 200	$ 200

Balance Sheets (in thousands)	December 31, 2008	December 31, 2009	December 31, 2010
Cash	$ 600	$ 350	$ 300
Accounts receivable	2,730	3,100	4,200
Inventories	2,800	3,200	4,300
Prepaid expenses	0	0	0
Net fixed assets[1]	1,200	1,300	1,450
Total assets	**$7,330**	**$7,950**	**$10,250**
Short-term debt	$ 300	$ 500	$ 1,900
Accounts payable	1,400	1,600	2,050
Accrued expenses	200	260	350
Long-term debt	1,300	1,200	1,100
Owners' equity	4,130	4,390	4,850
Total liabilities and owners' equity	**$7,330**	**$7,950**	**$10,250**

[1]The company did not sell any fixed assets in years 2009 and 2010.

a. Prepare Sentec Inc.'s managerial balance sheets on December 31, 2008, 2009, and 2010.
b. Prepare Sentec's cash-flow statements for 2009 and 2010 according to the direct method.
c. What accounts for the change in the firm's net operating cash flow over the two-year period?
d. In 2010, firms in the same business sector as Sentec Inc. had an average collection period of thirty days, an average payment period of thirty-three days, and an inventory turnover of eight days. Suppose that Sentec Inc. had managed its operating

cycle like the average firm in the sector. On December 31, 2010, what would its working capital requirement have been? Its net operating cash flow in year 2010?

10. **Seasonal business.**
Mars Electronics is a distributor for the Global Electric Company (GEC), a large manufacturer of electrical and electronics products for consumer and institutional markets. Below are the semiannual financial statements of the company for the last year and a half.

Income Statements (in thousands)

	Six Months to June 30, 2009	Six Months to December 31, 2009	Six Months to June 30, 2010
Net sales	**$10,655**	**$13,851**	**$11,720**
Cost of goods sold	8,940	11,671	9,834
Selling, general, and administrative expenses	1,554	1,925	1,677
Depreciation expense	44	55	76
Interest expense	62	90	70
Income tax expense	23	44	26
Earnings after tax	$ 32	$ 66	$ 37
Dividends	$ 5	$ 44	$ 1

Balance Sheets (in thousands)

	June 30, 2009	December 31, 2009	June 30, 2010
Cash	$ 160	$ 60	$ 70
Accounts receivable	1,953	2,616	2,100
Inventories	1,986	2,694	2,085
Prepaid expenses	80	42	25
Net fixed assets[1]	733	818	830
Total assets	**$4,912**	**$6,230**	**$5,110**
Short-term debt	$ 50	$ 880	$ 50
Accounts payable	1,450	1,950	1,650
Accrued expenses	98	114	138
Long-term debt	800	750	700
Owners' equity	2,514	2,536	2,572
Total liabilities and owners' equity	**$4,912**	**$6,230**	**$5,110**

[1]The firm did not sell any fixed assets over the three-year period.

a. Prepare Mars Electronics' cash-flow statements according to the direct method for the six months ending June 30, 2009, December 31, 2009, and June 30, 2010.
b. What accounts for the changes in the firm's cash flows over the three periods?

Diagnosing Profitability, Risk, and Growth

CHAPTER 5

What effect do managerial decisions have on the firm's profitability? At first glance, this may seem to be an easy question. To find the answer, all you need to do is compare this year's net profit to last year's figure. If you see an increase, you can conclude that managers improved profitability. If you see a decrease, you can assume that managers did not run the firm profitably. Unfortunately, this straightforward comparison may not tell the whole story.

Suppose, for example, that higher profits came from an increase in sales that was achieved by giving customers significantly more time than usual to pay their bills and by simultaneously letting the firm's inventories rise to unusual levels to meet every customer's request promptly. In this case, looking just at profits in the firm's income statement does not provide the full picture. The rises in sales and profits have been achieved by increasing the size of the firm's balance sheet through higher accounts receivable and inventories. And, a larger balance sheet means that more capital is used to finance the firm's activities. Because capital is costly, a larger balance sheet may be detrimental to the firm. You need to know, instead, whether *profits per dollar of capital employed* have increased.

Alternatively, suppose a drop in profits came from a rise in interest expenses because of additional borrowing. This does not mean that financial managers made borrowing decisions that impaired profitability. Borrowing can be advantageous under certain conditions. If this were not the case, then firms wishing to achieve higher levels of profitability would never borrow. Our point is that an increase or a decrease in profits, in and of itself, is not a good indicator of a firm's financial performance.

The integrated approach to profitability analysis presented in this chapter considers the effects of managerial decisions not only on the firm's income statement but also on its balance sheet. For example, the approach is able to differentiate between an increase in profits that is accompanied by a rise in accounts receivable (a balance sheet item) from one that is accompanied by no change in receivables. We also show that an increase in borrowing does not necessarily reduce the firm's profitability. Alternative measures of profitability are discussed, and we explain how they are related to one another. We also show how financial leverage, a measure of the impact of borrowing on a firm's profitability, affects the firm's riskiness. Finally, we review the concept of self-sustainable growth and its application to the management of the firm's growth strategy. As in previous chapters, the financial statements of Office Supplies (OS) Distributors are used to illustrate our analysis. After reading this chapter, you should understand the following:

- How to measure a firm's profitability
- The key drivers of profitability
- How to analyze the structure of a firm's overall profitability
- How business risk and the use of debt financing affect profitability
- How to assess a firm's capacity to finance its expected growth in sales

MEASURES OF PROFITABILITY

Every manager has a favorite measure of profitability. It is usually a ratio calculated by dividing the firm's earnings after tax (EAT) or net profit by (1) sales to get **return on sales (ROS)**, or (2) total assets to get **return on assets (ROA)**[1], or (3) owners' equity to get **return on equity (ROE)**. ROS measures the profit generated by one dollar of sales. It is traditionally used to measure the ability of managers to generate profits from the firm's sales. ROA measures the profit generated by one dollar of assets. It is used to assess the ability of managers to generate profits from the firm's assets. Finally, ROE measures the profit generated by one dollar of equity. It is the standard measure of the profitability to shareholders of the equity capital they invested in the firm.

The measure of profitability that is adopted depends on the manager's area of responsibility. A sales manager would look at ROS; the manager of an operating unit, with responsibility for that unit's assets, would choose ROA. The chief executive, concerned with the firm's profitability to shareholders, would pay attention to ROE.

The three measures of profitability raise a number of questions. How are they related to one another? Which one is the most *comprehensive* indicator of profitability? How does risk affect profitability? What can managers do to raise the profitability of their firm? These questions are answered in this chapter.

RETURN ON EQUITY

ROE is the most comprehensive indicator of profitability because it is the final outcome of *all* the firm's activities and decisions made during the year. It considers the operating and investing decisions as well as the financing and tax-related decisions that the firm's managers have made. The following sections show how to calculate ROE and then explain in detail why it is the most comprehensive measure of profitability.

---

[1]A variation of ROA is **return on investment (ROI)**, where the term *investment* refers to either the firm's total assets or a subset of its assets.

MEASURING RETURN ON EQUITY

ROE measures the firm's profitability from the perspective of the owners, those who invested equity capital in the firm. Their reward is the firm's net profit. The return on their investment is the ratio of EAT to owners' equity:

$$\textbf{Return on equity (ROE)} = \frac{\textbf{Earnings after tax (EAT)}}{\textbf{Owners' equity}} \tag{5.1}$$

The amount of investment in the denominator of a profitability ratio—owners' equity in this case—can be measured at the beginning or the end of the period during which EAT was generated. In general, taking the average of the beginning and ending figures is usually the best alternative. The examples in this chapter use the *year-end* figures in all the profitability ratios because we compare the *three* years of data reported in OS Distributors' financial statements.

Based on the earnings and equity figures in Exhibits 5.1 and 5.2, OS Distributors' ROE rose from 10.9 percent in 2008 (EAT of \$7 million divided by \$64 million of equity) to 13.2 percent in 2010 (EAT of \$10.2 million divided by \$77 million of equity). What are the firm's activities and decisions that produced this rise in ROE? To answer this question, we must first find out how the firm's operating and financing activities affect its ROE.

THE EFFECT OF OPERATING DECISIONS ON RETURN ON EQUITY

Operating decisions, broadly defined, involve the acquisition and disposal of fixed assets and the management of the firm's operating assets (such as inventories and trade receivables) and operating liabilities (mostly trade payables). ROS (net profit per dollar of sales) and ROA (net profit per dollar of total assets) are not appropriate measures of the profitability generated by the firm's operating activities because they are calculated with *net* profit (earnings after tax). Net profit is obtained after deducting *interest expenses*—the outcome of a *financing* decision—from the firm's pre-tax operating profit. ROS and ROA are thus affected by financing decisions and do not reflect *only* operating decisions. The following sections present three ratios that are commonly used as substitutes for ROS and ROA when evaluating the specific contribution of operating decisions to the firm's overall profitability.

RETURN ON INVESTED CAPITAL BEFORE TAX ($ROIC_{BT}$)[2]

A relevant measure of **operating profitability** should have in its numerator the firm's pre-tax *operating* profit, or earnings before interest and tax (EBIT), and should have in its denominator the investments that were made to generate EBIT. EBIT is shown in the firm's income statement (see Exhibit 5.2), and the appropriate investments are shown in its restructured or managerial balance sheet, which was

---

[2]We use the following convention to distinguish *after-tax* returns from *pre-tax* returns: when returns are measured *after tax*, we do not put any subscript; when they are measured *before tax*, we indicate this with the subscript BT ($_{BT}$).

EXHIBIT 5.1 OS DISTRIBUTORS' BALANCE SHEETS.

FIGURES IN MILLIONS

	December 31, 2008		December 31, 2009		December 31, 2010	
Assets						
• **Current assets**						
Cash[1]		$ 6.0		$ 12.0		$ 8.0
Accounts receivable		44.0		48.0		56.0
Inventories		52.0		57.0		72.0
Prepaid expenses[2]		2.0		2.0		1.0
Total current assets		**104.0**		**119.0**		**137.0**
• **Noncurrent assets**						
Financial assets and intangibles		0.0		0.0		0.0
Property, plant, and equipment						
Gross value[3]	$90.0		$90.0		$93.0	
less accumulated depreciation	(34.0)	56.0	(39.0)	51.0	(40.0)	53.0
Total noncurrent assets		56.0		51.0		53.0
Total assets		**$160.0**		**$170.0**		**$190.0**
Liabilities and owners' equity						
• **Current liabilities**						
Short-term debt		$ 15.0		$ 22.0		$ 23.0
Owed to banks	$ 7.0		$14.0		$15.0	
Current portion of long-term debt	8.0		8.0		8.0	
Accounts payable		37.0		40.0		48.0
Accrued expenses[4]		2.0		4.0		4.0
Total current liabilities		**54.0**		**66.0**		**75.0**
• **Noncurrent liabilities**						
Long-term debt[5]		42.0		34.0		38.0
Total noncurrent liabilities		**42.0**		**34.0**		**38.0**
• **Owners' equity**[6]		**64.0**		**70.0**		**77.0**
Total liabilities and owners' equity		**$160.0**		**$170.0**		**$190.0**

[1]Consists of cash in hand and checking accounts held to facilitate operating activities on which the firm earns no interest.
[2]Prepaid expenses is rent paid in advance (when recognized in the income statement, rent is included in selling, general, and administrative expenses).
[3]In 2009, there was no disposal of existing fixed assets or acquisition of new fixed assets. However, during 2010, a warehouse was enlarged at a cost of $12 million and existing fixed assets, bought for $9 million in the past, were sold at their net book value of $2 million.
[4]Accrued expenses consist of wages and taxes payable.
[5]Long-term debt is repaid at the rate of $8 million per year. No new long-term debt was incurred during 2009, but during 2010, a mortgage loan was obtained from the bank to finance the extension of a warehouse (see Note 3).
[6]During the three years, no new shares were issued and none were repurchased.

EXHIBIT 5.2 OS DISTRIBUTORS' INCOME STATEMENTS.

FIGURES IN MILLIONS

	2008	2009	2010
• **Net sales**	**$390.0**	**$420.0**	**$480.0**
Cost of goods sold	328.0	353.0	400.0
• **Gross profit**	**62.0**	**67.0**	**80.0**
Selling, general, and administrative expenses	39.8	43.7	48.0
Depreciation expense	5.0	5.0	8.0
• **Operating profit**	**17.2**	**18.3**	**24.0**
Special items	0.0	0.0	0.0
• **Earnings before interest and tax (EBIT)**	**17.2**	**18.3**	**24.0**
Net interest expense[1]	5.5	5.0	7.0
• **Earnings before tax (EBT)**	**11.7**	**13.3**	**17.0**
Income tax expense	4.7	5.3	6.8
• **Earnings after tax (EAT)**	**$ 7.0**	**$ 8.0**	**$ 10.2**
Dividends	$ 2.0	$ 2.0	$ 3.2
Addition to retained earnings	$ 5.0	$ 6.0	$ 7.0

[1]There is no interest income, so net interest expense is equal to interest expense.

introduced in Chapter 3 (see Exhibit 5.3). The investments are listed on the upper section of the managerial balance sheet and are referred to as **invested capital**. We have the following:

Invested capital = Cash + Working capital requirement + Net fixed assets (5.2)

Cash and net fixed assets are the same as those shown in the standard balance sheets in Exhibit 5.1. Working capital requirement (WCR), a measure of the firm's *net* investment in its operating cycle, is the difference between operating assets (receivables, inventories, and prepaid expenses) and operating liabilities (payables and accrued expenses).

Thus, a firm's operating profitability can be measured by the ratio of its EBIT to its invested capital. This ratio is known as the firm's **return on invested capital before tax** or **$ROIC_{BT}$**:

$$\textbf{Return on invested capital before tax } (ROIC_{BT}) = \frac{\textbf{Earnings before interest and tax (EBIT)}}{\textbf{Invested capital}} \quad (5.3)$$

We can make several noteworthy observations about this definition of operating profitability. First, **ROIC** can be measured before tax, as shown above, or after tax. To get the after-tax ROIC, EBIT in equation 5.3 must be reduced by the amount of tax it generates, which is EBIT × Tax rate, so that the numerator of equation 5.3 becomes EBIT × (1 – Tax rate). We show in Chapter 15 that ROIC

EXHIBIT 5.3 OS DISTRIBUTORS' MANAGERIAL BALANCE SHEETS.

ALL DATA FROM THE BALANCE SHEETS IN EXHIBIT 5.1. FIGURES IN MILLIONS

		December 31, 2008		December 31, 2009		December 31, 2010
Invested capital						
• Cash		$ 6.0		$ 12.0		$ 8.0
• Working capital requirement (WCR)[1]		59.0		63.0		77.0
• Net fixed assets		56.0		51.0		53.0
Total invested capital		**$121.0**		**$126.0**		**$138.0**
Capital employed						
• Short-term debt		$ 15.0		$ 22.0		$ 23.0
• Long-term financing						
Long-term debt	$42.0		$34.0		$38.0	
Owners' equity	64.0	106.0	70.0	104.0	77.0	115.0
Total capital employed		**$121.0**		**$126.0**		**$138.0**

[1]WCR = (Accounts receivable + Inventories + Prepaid expenses) – (Accounts payable + Accrued expenses).

is an important measure of performance when estimating the value created by a business.

Second, the ratio in equation 5.3 can also be interpreted as operating profitability per dollar of **capital employed** because, according to the managerial balance sheet (see Exhibit 5.3), invested capital is equal to capital employed, the sum of all the sources of funds (both debt and equity capital) used to finance the firm's investments. Thus, $ROIC_{BT}$ is the same as **return on capital employed before tax** or **$ROCE_{BT}$**.

Third, because cash is included in the definition of invested capital (see Exhibit 5.3), any interest *income* earned on cash balances should be *included* in EBIT.

Fourth, to evaluate the performance of a business unit that has no control over its cash, a variation of $ROIC_{BT}$ can be constructed. This ratio would *exclude* cash from invested capital and *exclude* interest income from EBIT. This measure of operating profitability can be called pre-tax **return on business assets** or **ROBA** where **business assets** are defined as the sum of WCR and net fixed assets.

Another measure of operating profitability is **return on total assets,** or **ROTA**, the ratio of EBIT to the firm's *total* assets as reported in its standard balance sheet. Note the distinction we make between ROTA and ROA (return on assets). The former is the ratio of EBIT to total assets, whereas the latter is the ratio of EAT to total assets.

In this and the remaining chapters, we measure operating profitability with ROIC. But keep in mind that $ROIC_{BT}$ is the same as $ROCE_{BT}$. Finally, note that $ROIC_{BT}$ can be replaced by either $ROBA_{BT}$ or $ROTA_{BT}$ in the following analysis without any loss of generality.

EXHIBIT 5.4 THE STRUCTURE OF OS DISTRIBUTORS' PRE-TAX RETURN ON INVESTED CAPITAL.

ALL DATA FROM THE INCOME STATEMENTS IN EXHIBIT 5.2 AND THE BALANCE SHEETS IN EXHIBIT 5.3. FIGURES IN MILLIONS

Year	Operating Profit Margin		Capital Turnover		Return on Invested Capital Before Tax
	$\frac{\text{EBIT}}{\text{Sales}}$	×	$\frac{\text{Sales}}{\text{Invested capital}^{1}}$	=	$\frac{\text{EBIT}}{\text{Invested capital}}$
	$\frac{\$17.2}{\$390}$	×	$\frac{\$390}{\$121}$	=	$\frac{\$17.2}{\$121}$
2008	4.4%	×	3.2	=	14.2%
	$\frac{\$18.3}{\$420}$	×	$\frac{\$420}{\$126}$	=	$\frac{\$18.3}{\$126}$
2009	4.4%	×	3.3	=	14.5%
	$\frac{\$24}{\$480}$	×	$\frac{\$480}{\$138}$	=	$\frac{\$24}{\$138}$
2010	5.0%	×	3.5	=	17.4%

[1]Invested capital = Cash + Working capital requirement + Net fixed assets.

OS Distributors' $ROIC_{BT}$ is given in the last column of Exhibit 5.4. It rose from 14.2 percent in 2008 to 17.4 percent in 2010. To understand why this improvement occurred, we need to know what drives operating profitability.

THE DRIVERS OF OPERATING PROFITABILITY

$ROIC_{BT}$ is the ratio of pre-tax operating profit (EBIT) to invested capital, so any improvement in $ROIC_{BT}$ must be the outcome of (1) an increase in EBIT for the *same* level of invested capital or (2) a reduction of invested capital for the *same* level of EBIT.

To find out how these two components of operating profitability affect $ROIC_{BT}$, we write equation 5.3 as follows:

$$ROIC_{BT} = \frac{\textbf{EBIT}}{\textbf{Invested capital}} = \frac{\textbf{EBIT}}{\textbf{Sales}} \times \frac{\textbf{Sales}}{\textbf{Invested capital}} \qquad (5.4)$$

The first ratio on the right side of equation 5.4 (EBIT/Sales) is called the firm's **operating profit margin**, and the second (Sales/Invested capital) is called its **capital turnover**. Thus, a firm's $ROIC_{BT}$ is simply the product of its operating profit margin and its capital turnover:

Return on invested capital before tax = Operating profit margin × Capital turnover

For example, Exhibit 5.4 shows that OS Distributors had an operating profit margin of 4.4 percent in 2008, meaning that it generated that year, on average, $4.40 of pre-tax operating profit (EBIT) per $100 of sales. Its capital turnover was 3.2, indicating that the company needed, on average, $100 of invested capital to generate $320 of sales.

Obviously, the higher a firm's operating profit margin and capital turnover, the higher its operating profitability. A higher operating profit margin is obtained by increasing operating profit (EBIT) more than sales. This can be achieved, for example, by reducing operating expenses without losing sales or by raising sales without increasing operating expenses. A higher capital turnover is obtained through a more efficient use of the assets required to support the firm's sales activities. This can be achieved, for example, through a faster inventory turnover, a shorter collection period for receivables, or fewer fixed assets per dollar of sales.

As shown in Exhibit 5.4, OS Distributors' operating profitability rose slightly from 14.2 percent in 2008 to 14.5 percent in 2009 because of a small rise in capital turnover from 3.2 to 3.3. In 2010, operating profitability increased to 17.4 percent as a result of a rise in operating profit margin from 4.4 percent to 5.0 percent accompanied by an increase in capital turnover from 3.3 to 3.5.

If the key to higher operating profitability is a combination of higher operating profit margin and faster capital turnover, what are the underlying factors that would allow a firm to achieve this outcome? The relative importance of the factors that affect $ROIC_{BT}$ can be determined empirically only by examining the historical relationships between these factors and the pre-tax operating profitability of a large sample of firms. A study of this type was conducted on a sample that included more than 3,000 business divisions that were drawn from some 500 corporations (mostly North American and European) from a wide range of industries.[3]

Three factors emerge from the study as major determinants of operating profitability: (1) the firm's competitive position as measured by its *market share* relative to that of its competitors; (2) the relative *quality of its products and services* as perceived by its customers; and (3) the firm's *cost and assets structures*, namely, the composition and concentration of its assets, the structure of its costs, and its degrees of vertical integration and capacity utilization. The evidence indicates that *high market share* and *superior product quality*, on average, *boost* operating profitability, while *high investments* and *high fixed costs,* on average, *depress* it. In the sample, those businesses with the highest market shares and superior products and services had an average pre-tax operating profitability of 39 percent, while those with the lowest market share and inferior products or services had an average pre-tax operating profitability of only 9 percent. Businesses with low capital turnover—those with relatively higher fixed assets and fixed costs per dollar of sales—were, on average, unable to offset their lower capital turnover with higher operating profit margin and hence, in general, had lower pre-tax operating profitability than businesses with high capital turnover. Businesses with a capital turnover below 1.5 had an average pre-tax operating profitability of 8 percent, whereas those with a capital turnover above 3.3 had an average pre-tax operating profitability of 38 percent.

Why are businesses with low capital turnover usually unable to generate higher profit margins? One explanation is that investment-intensive businesses with low

---

[3]The unit of analysis was not an entire company but a business division within a corporation selling a distinct product or service to an identifiable group of customers. The data were collected by the Profit Impact of Market Strategy (PIMS) Program. For further information, refer to the article by Jagiello and Mandry (2004).

capital turnover usually have relatively high fixed costs and are prone to price and marketing wars that weaken their margin. When economic conditions become unfavorable, these businesses tend to cut prices to maintain high rates of capacity utilization. Furthermore, because these businesses have relatively high amounts of capital tied up in their operations, they cannot easily exit the business (they have high **exit barriers**). They usually try to ride the unfavorable market conditions in the hope of better future days. This behavior is typical in such sectors as airlines, refining, commodity pulp and paper, shipbuilding, and base chemicals.

THE LINK BETWEEN RETURN ON EQUITY AND OPERATING PROFITABILITY

To understand the link between ROE and operating profitability (ROIC), consider the case of a firm that has not borrowed a single dollar; its investments are entirely financed with equity capital. What is the relationship between this firm's ROE and its ROIC? Because the firm has not borrowed a single dollar, it has no interest expense and thus its pre-tax profit, or earnings before tax (EBT), must be equal to its EBIT. And because the firm's investments are entirely financed with equity (recall that the firm does not borrow), its invested capital must be equal to its owners' equity. In other words, *if a firm does not borrow, its ROIC is the same as its ROE.*

THE EFFECT OF FINANCING DECISIONS ON RETURN ON EQUITY

If ROIC and ROE are the same when a firm does not borrow, then any difference between them must be caused by the use of debt to finance the firm's investments. What are the effects of the firm's financing decisions on its ROE?

Let's consider what happens when a firm replaces some of its equity capital with an equal amount of debt. The higher proportion of debt financing resulting from this **recapitalization**[4] increases the firm's **financial leverage** (also called **gearing**). A firm without borrowed funds is said to be **unlevered.** A firm with borrowed funds is said to be levered. And the higher the amount of debt relative to equity, the higher the firm's financial leverage. A higher leverage affects the firm's ROE in two ways. First, the firm's interest expenses increase and its EAT decreases. This will reduce ROE because EAT is the numerator of ROE. Second, owners' equity decreases because debt has replaced equity. This will increase ROE because owners' equity is the denominator of ROE. Conclusion: You cannot predict how financial leverage affects the firm's ROE. There is a **financial cost effect** that *reduces* ROE (EAT goes down because of higher interest expenses) and a simultaneous **financial structure effect** that *increases* ROE (because of lower equity capital). The net effect depends on the strength of the former relative to the latter. If the financial cost effect is weaker than the financial structure effect, higher financial leverage will *increase* the firm's ROE. If it is stronger, higher financial leverage will *decrease* the firm's ROE. The ratios that measure these two effects are discussed in the following sections.

---

[4]Recapitalization referred to the substitution of debt for equity, leaving the firm's assets unchanged. It can be carried out by using the proceeds from borrowing to buy back common stock from shareholders.

THE FINANCIAL COST RATIO

The financial cost effect is captured in the firm's *income statement*. It is measured with the **financial cost ratio**, which is defined as the firm's EBT divided by its EBIT:

$$\text{Financial cost ratio} = \frac{\text{Earnings before tax (EBT)}}{\text{Earnings before interest and tax (EBIT)}} \quad (5.5)$$

As the amount of debt financing *increases*, (1) EBT relative to EBIT *decreases*, (2) the financial cost ratio *decreases*, and (3) the firm's ROE *decreases*, all else the same. If the firm is entirely equity financed, then the ratio is equal to one because EBT and EBIT are equal in this case. This is the *maximum* value of the ratio. If the firm borrows, its financial cost ratio will be smaller than one.

OS Distributors' financial cost ratios are given in the fourth column of Exhibit 5.5. The ratio was 0.68 in 2008, 0.73 in 2009, and 0.71 in 2010. The ratios indicate that OS Distributors had interest expenses during the three years (the three ratios are smaller than one), and that interest expenses relative to pre-tax operating profit (EBIT) were highest in 2008 (the ratio is lowest that year).

A popular ratio, similar to the financial cost ratio, is the **times-interest-earned ratio** or **interest coverage ratio**. It is defined as EBIT divided by interest expenses:

$$\text{Times-interest-earned ratio} = \frac{\text{Earnings before interest and tax (EBIT)}}{\text{Interest expenses}} \quad (5.6)$$

This ratio indicates how many times the firm's pre-tax operating profit (EBIT) covers its interest expenses. For example, OS Distributors' 2010 income statement in Exhibit 5.2 shows that the firm's EBIT of $24 million covered its $7 million of interest expenses 3.4 times ($24 million divided by $7 million). The higher the ratio, the higher the firm's ability to meet its interest payments.

THE FINANCIAL STRUCTURE RATIO

The financial structure effect is captured in the firm's balance sheet. It is measured with the **financial structure ratio**, also known as the **equity multiplier**. It is the ratio of invested capital to owners' equity:

$$\text{Financial structure ratio} = \frac{\text{Invested capital}}{\text{Owners' equity}} \quad (5.7)$$

For a given amount of invested capital, as the amount of debt financing *increases*, (1) owners' equity *decreases*, (2) the financial structure ratio *increases*, and (3) the firm's ROE *increases*, all else the same. If the firm's invested capital is entirely financed with equity, then invested capital is equal to owners' equity and the financial structure ratio is equal to one, its *minimum* value. It can reach, theoretically, very large values as more debt is used to finance the firm's investments.

OS Distributors' financial structure ratios are given in the fifth column of Exhibit 5.5. The ratio went from 1.89 in 2008 to 1.79 in 2010, indicating that the *proportion* of OS Distributors' investments that was financed with debt decreased during that period as can be verified in Exhibit 5.3 and discussed below.

EXHIBIT 5.5 THE STRUCTURE OF OS DISTRIBUTORS' RETURN ON EQUITY.

ALL DATA FROM THE INCOME STATEMENTS IN EXHIBIT 5.2 AND THE BALANCE SHEETS IN EXHIBIT 5.3. FIGURES IN MILLIONS

Year	Return on Equity	=	Operating Profitability			×	Financial Leverage Multiplier			×	Tax Effect
	ROE	=	[Operating profit margin]	×	Capital turnover	×	Financial cost ratio	×	Financial structure ratio	×	Tax effect ratio
	$\frac{\text{EAT}}{\text{Owners' equity}}$	=	$\frac{\text{EBIT}}{\text{Sales}}$	×	$\frac{\text{Sales}}{\text{Invested capital}}$	×	$\frac{\text{EBT}}{\text{EBIT}}$	×	$\frac{\text{Invested capital}}{\text{Owners' equity}}$	×	$\frac{\text{EAT}}{\text{EBT}}$
			Pre-tax return on invested capital ($ROIC_{BT}$)				**Financial leverage multiplier**				
	$\frac{\$7}{\$64}$	=	$\frac{\$17.2}{\$390}$	×	$\frac{\$390}{\$121}$	×	$\frac{\$11.7}{\$17.2}$	×	$\frac{\$121}{\$64}$	×	$\frac{\$7}{\$11.7}$
2008	10.9%	=	4.4%	×	3.2	×	0.68	×	1.89	×	0.60
			14.2%				1.29				
	$\frac{\$8}{\$70}$	=	$\frac{\$18.3}{\$420}$	×	$\frac{\$420}{\$126}$	×	$\frac{\$13.3}{\$18.3}$	×	$\frac{\$126}{\$70}$	×	$\frac{\$8}{\$13.3}$
2009	11.4%	=	4.4%	×	3.3	×	0.73	×	1.80	×	0.60
			14.5%				1.31				
	$\frac{\$10.2}{\$77}$	=	$\frac{\$24}{\$480}$	×	$\frac{\$480}{\$138}$	×	$\frac{\$17}{\$24}$	×	$\frac{\$138}{\$77}$	×	$\frac{\$10.2}{\$17}$
2010	13.2%	=	5.0%	×	3.5	×	0.71	×	1.79	×	0.60
			17.4%				1.27				

OTHER MEASURES OF FINANCIAL LEVERAGE

The financial structure ratio is one of several debt ratios used to measure the firm's borrowing relative to its equity financing. Other popular ratios include the **debt-to-equity ratio** (debt divided by owners' equity) and the **debt-to-invested capital ratio** (debt divided by invested capital).

Using the data in Exhibit 5.3, we can get the **debt ratios** of OS Distributors in 2010. Its debt-to-equity ratio was 79.2 percent ($61 million of total debt divided by $77 million of equity) and its debt-to-invested capital ratio was 44.2 percent ($61 million of total debt divided by $138 million of invested capital). We examine in Chapter 11 the factors that determine a firm's debt ratio.

THE INCIDENCE OF TAXATION ON RETURN ON EQUITY

The third determinant of a firm's ROE is the incidence of corporate taxation. The higher the tax rate applied to a firm's EBT, the lower its ROE. The incidence of tax is measured by the **tax-effect ratio**—that is, the ratio of EAT to EBT:

$$\textbf{Tax effect ratio} = \frac{\textbf{EAT}}{\textbf{EBT}} = \frac{\textbf{EBT (1 – Effective tax rate)}}{\textbf{EBT}}$$
$$= \textbf{1 – Effective tax rate} \qquad (5.8)$$

Note that because EAT is equal to EBT (1 – Effective tax rate), the tax-effect ratio is equal to one minus the effective corporate tax rate.

As the effective corporate tax rate increases, the tax-effect ratio decreases and the firm keeps a smaller percentage of its pre-tax earnings. Other things being equal, the firm's ROE decreases. Consider OS Distributors. Its pre-tax earnings (EBT) are taxed at the rate of 40 percent; hence, its tax-effect ratio is 60 percent, as shown in the last column of Exhibit 5.5.

The relevant corporate tax rate is the **effective tax rate** the firm pays, not the **statutory tax rate.**[5] The effective tax rate can be significantly lower than the maximum statutory tax rate imposed by the tax authority if some of the firm's earnings are taxed at different rates. For example, the statutory corporate tax rate in the United States was equal to 35 percent in 2008. But data on two firms in the same sector, Hewlett-Packard (HP) and Sun Microsystems, reveal a significant difference between their effective tax rates. As shown in Exhibit 5.6, HP's effective tax rate of 20.5 percent in 2008 was significantly lower than that of Sun Microsystems (33.9 percent). What is the effect on the two firms' ROE? Before tax, HP's ROE was two and a half times higher than Sun's ROE, but after tax it was three times higher. In other words, by having a lower effective tax rate, HP was able to *widen* its ROE gap relative to Sun Microsystems.

HP's lower effective tax rate was caused by lower rates charged in non-U.S. jurisdictions where the firm operates. The implication is that a firm should plan to *minimize* its tax liabilities as early as possible. For example, when evaluating an investment

[5]For information on the latest corporate tax rates prevailing in member countries of the Organisation for Economic Co-operation and Development go to http://www.oecd.org and see Table II.1: *Taxation of Corporate and Capital Income*.

EXHIBIT 5.6 COMPARISON OF EFFECTIVE TAX RATES IN 2008.

FIGURES IN THOUSANDS

Firm	EBT	EAT	Equity	Pre-Tax ROE	After-Tax ROE	Effective Tax Rate
Hewlett-Packard	$10,473	$8,329	$38,942	26.9%	21.4%	20.5%
Sun Microsystems	$610	$403	$5,588	10.9%	7.2%	33.9%

Source: Companies' annual reports.

proposal, it should consider locating in countries or regions that offer significant tax breaks. Achieving higher ROE through a planned reduction in the firm's effective tax rate may be one of the easiest ways to boost the firm's ROE.

PUTTING IT ALL TOGETHER: THE STRUCTURE OF A FIRM'S PROFITABILITY

The previous sections identify five ratios that affect a firm's ROE: (1) its operating profit margin (EBIT/Sales); (2) its capital turnover (Sales/Invested capital); (3) its financial cost ratio (EBT/EBIT); (4) its financial structure ratio (Invested capital/Equity); and (5) its tax-effect ratio (EAT/EBT). The relationship that ties these ratios to the firm's return on equity is straightforward: *ROE is simply equal to the product of these five ratios*:

$$\text{ROE} = \frac{\text{EAT}}{\text{Owners' equity}}$$
$$= \frac{\text{EBIT}}{\text{Sales}} \times \frac{\text{Sales}}{\text{Invested capital}} \times \frac{\text{EBT}}{\text{EBIT}} \times \frac{\text{Invested capital}}{\text{Owners' equity}} \times \frac{\text{EAT}}{\text{EBT}} \qquad (5.9)$$

The product of the five ratios on the right side of equation 5.9 is equal to EAT divided by owners' equity. You can check this by simply canceling EBIT, Sales, Invested capital, and EBT because they appear in both a numerator and a denominator. The only items left are EAT in the numerator and owners' equity in the denominator.

The first two ratios capture the effect of the firm's investing and operating decisions on its overall profitability. Their product is equal to the firm's operating profitability measured by the ROIC_{BT} (see equation 5.4). The third and fourth ratios capture the effect of the firm's financial policy on its overall profitability. We call their product the firm's **financial leverage multiplier**:

$$\textbf{Financial leverage multiplier} = \textbf{Financial cost ratio} \times \textbf{Financial structure ratio} \qquad (5.10)$$

The last ratio captures the effect of corporate taxation on return on equity and, as shown in equation 5.8, is equal to (1 – Effective tax rate). Thus, equation 5.9 can be written as the following:

$$\textbf{ROE} = \textbf{ROIC}_{BT} \times \textbf{Financial leverage multiplier} \times \textbf{(1 – Effective tax rate)} \qquad (5.11)$$

EXHIBIT 5.7 THE DRIVERS OF RETURN ON EQUITY.

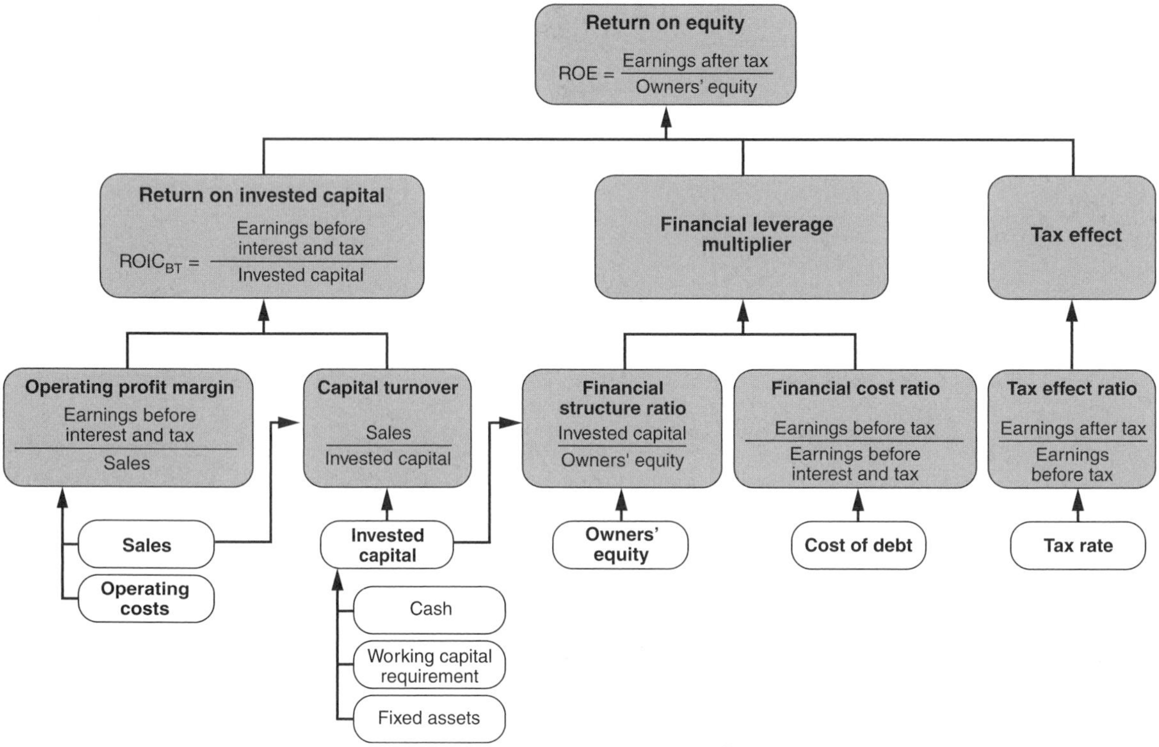

Exhibit 5.7 provides a pictorial representation of the five ratios behind ROE and the way they are related.

If we ignore the incidence of taxes on profitability and focus on ROE before tax (ROE_{BT}), equation 5.11 can be written as follows:

$$ROE_{BT} = ROIC_{BT} \times \text{Financial leverage multiplier}$$

Obviously, if the financial leverage multiplier is greater than one, ROE_{BT} exceeds $ROIC_{BT}$. If it is less than one, ROE_{BT} is lower than $ROIC_{BT}$.

We can now examine the structure of OS Distributors' profitability, shown in Exhibit 5.5. Compare ROE in 2008 with ROE in 2010: it increased from 10.9 percent in 2008 to 13.2 percent in 2010. Is this overall performance improvement the outcome of improved operating management, a higher financial leverage multiplier, or a reduction in OS Distributors' effective tax rate? The exhibit indicates that the improvement in ROE is caused by a better operating profit margin coupled with a higher capital turnover.[6] These two effects pushed operating profitability from 14.2 percent

[6]A firm's capital turnover can increase as a result of the depreciation of fixed assets, which reduces net fixed assets. When this is the case, the improvement in turnover cannot be attributed to better management of the firm's invested capital.

to 17.4 percent. The financial leverage multiplier declined slightly, from 1.29 to 1.27, and the tax effect was unchanged.

THE STRUCTURE OF RETURN ON EQUITY ACROSS INDUSTRIES

The structure of a firm's return on equity depends to a large extent on the nature of the industry in which it operates and the competitive advantages it has been able to achieve over time.

To illustrate this phenomenon, refer to Exhibit 5.8, which reports the ROE structure of five firms in 2008. The companies include a U.S. pharmaceutical company, a U.S. soft-drink company, a European manufacturer of mobile devices, a U.S. chain of retail stores, and a U.S. software company. All are leading firms in their respective sectors. Given the reported ROE structures, try to determine which company belongs to which sector before reading the next paragraphs.

Firm 1 is Microsoft, the software company. It is the most profitable firm with an ROE of 45.3 percent. This is due to the fact that it has the highest operating profit margin in the group (its software has a very high market share and is relatively inexpensive to produce) combined with the third-highest capital turnover of 2.04 (software production is not a capital-intensive activity).

Firm 2 is Coca-Cola Co., the beverage company. It has the second-highest ROE (33.0 percent) driven by the second-highest operating profit margin (its strong brand name gives it pricing power and high market share) and a reduced effective tax rate (its effective tax rate, at 19.5 percent, is the lowest in the group because of its large portion of profits earned outside the United States).

EXHIBIT 5.8 THE STRUCTURE OF RETURN ON EQUITY FOR FIVE FIRMS IN DIFFERENT SECTORS (2008).[1]

Firm[2]	Operating Profit Margin[3] (1)	Capital Turnover[4] (2)	Return on Invested Capital[5] (3) = (1) × (2)	Financial Leverage Multiplier[6] (4)	Pre-Tax Return on Equity[7] (5) = (3) × (4)	Tax Effect[8] (6)	Return on Equity[9] (7) = (5) × (6)
1	37.2%	2.04	75.9%	0.82	62.3%	72.7%	45.3%
2	27.5%	0.95	26.1%	1.57	41.0%	80.5%	33.0%
3	20.8%	0.91	18.9%	1.72	32.5%	66.7%	21.7%
4	9.8%	2.86	28.0%	1.20	33.6%	77.4%	26.0%
5	5.6%	3.51	19.7%	1.60	31.5%	65.3%	20.6%

[1]Compiled by the authors with accounting data from the firms' annual reports.
[2]See text for names of companies.
[3]Operating profit margin = Earnings before interest and tax/Sales.
[4]Capital turnover = Sales/Invested capital, where invested capital = Cash + Working capital requirement + Net fixed assets.
[5]Return on invested capital before tax = Earnings before interest and tax/Invested capital.
[6]Financial leverage multiplier = Pre-tax return on equity/Pre-tax return on invested capital.
[7]Pre-tax return on equity = Earnings before tax/Owners' equity.
[8]Tax effect = Earnings after tax/Earnings before tax = (1 − Effective tax rate).
[9]Return on equity = Earnings after tax/Owners' equity.

Firm 3 is Bristol-Myers Squibb Co, the pharmaceutical company. Although its capital turnover and financial leverage multiplier are not very different from those of Coca-Cola, its ROE is lower because of its lower operating profit margin and higher effective tax rate (33.3 percent).

Firm 4 is Nokia, the European manufacturer of mobile devices. Its operating profit margin is the second lowest in the group at 9.8 percent. Despite a leadership position in its industry, intense global competition in the market for mobile phones keeps the operating margin relatively low. This low margin is somewhat compensated by a high capital turnover, which eventually produces the third-highest after-tax ROE.

Firm 5 is Walmart Stores, the U.S. retail chain. Because it competes on prices, it has the lowest operating profit margin (5.6 percent), which is compensated by the highest capital turnover (3.51) in the group. Half of its assets are inventories of goods that turn over quickly. The resulting 19.7 percent operating profitability, the second lowest in the group, is magnified to a pre-tax ROE of 31.5 percent by a financial leverage multiplier of 1.60. But its high effective tax rate of 34.7 percent (most likely due to relatively fewer non-U.S. activities) puts this firm's ROE at the bottom of the list.

OTHER MEASURES OF PROFITABILITY

The measures of profitability discussed so far are based on the accounting data shown on a firm's income statement and balance sheet. A number of other popular profitability-related ratios combine financial *accounting* data with financial *market* data. These ratios include the firm's **earnings per share**, its **price-to-earnings ratio**, and its **market-to-book ratio**.

EARNINGS PER SHARE (EPS)

Earnings per share, or EPS, is simply the firm's earnings after tax divided by its total number of shares outstanding:

$$\textbf{Earnings per share (EPS)} = \frac{\textbf{Earnings after tax}}{\textbf{Number of shares outstanding}}$$

EPS, a favorite of financial analysts, is essentially a "normalized" measure of the firm's earnings after tax. OS Distributors has 10 million shares outstanding (see Exhibit 2.5 in Chapter 2) and has generated earnings after tax of $10.2 million in 2010. Thus, its EPS in 2010 is equal to $1.02 ($10.2 million divided by 10 million shares).

THE PRICE-TO-EARNINGS RATIO (P/E)

The price-to-earnings ratio (P/E or PER), also known as the firm's **earnings multiple**, is another favorite of financial analysts. It is defined thus:

$$\textbf{Price-to-earnings ratio (P/E)} = \frac{\textbf{Share price}}{\textbf{Earnings per share}}$$

Suppose OS Distributors had shares listed on a stock market. If the quoted price per share was \$14, OS Distributors' P/E would be 13.7 (\$14 divided by \$1.02). In other words, OS Distributors would be trading at 13.7 times its current earnings. (This is why a firm's P/E is also known as its earnings multiple.) Higher P/Es mean that investors in the market are assigning higher values to each dollar of current earnings per share generated by the firm. Chapter 12 examines the determinants of firms' P/E and explains why these ratios vary across firms.

THE MARKET-TO-BOOK RATIO

The third ratio, the market-to-book ratio, is defined as follows:

$$\textbf{Market-to-book ratio} = \frac{\textbf{Share price}}{\textbf{Book value per share}}$$

where book value per share is equal to the firm's owners' equity, as recorded in its balance sheet, divided by the number of shares outstanding.

For OS Distributors, book value per share is \$7.7 at the end of 2010 (\$77 million book value of equity divided by 10 million shares). Given a share price of \$14, the market-to-book ratio is 1.8 (a share price of \$14 divided by a book value per share of \$7.70). In other words, OS Distributors' shares are traded in the market at a premium over book value, that is, 1.8 times their book value. The fact that OS Distributors' shares trade at a premium means the firm is creating value for its shareholders. This is explained in detail in Chapter 15.

FINANCIAL LEVERAGE AND RISK

A firm's financial structure affects its ROE through the financial leverage multiplier. How exactly does financial leverage work? Consider two firms with identical assets that are funded with \$100 million of capital. The only difference between the two firms is their financing strategy. One firm finances its assets *exclusively* with equity (the unlevered firm); the other firm finances half of its assets with \$50 million of equity and the balance with \$50 million of borrowed funds at a cost of debt of 10 percent (the levered firm). For the sake of simplicity, assume that the firms pay no corporate taxes (this assumption does not affect the conclusion).

Let's now introduce risk into the analysis. At the beginning of the year, when the two firms established their **capital structure**, they did not know what their year-end pre-tax operating profit (EBIT) would be. Thus, suppose they forecasted three equally likely levels of EBIT, each based on different expectations about the economic environment during the coming year. If the economic environment was favorable, EBIT would be \$14 million. If the environment was average, EBIT would be \$10 million. And if it was unfavorable, EBIT would be only \$8 million. Which of these three possible levels of EBIT the firm achieved would not be known until the end of the year? This situation is what we call **business risk**. *A firm faces business risk because of its inability to know for certain the outcome of its current investing and operating decisions.* The best a firm can do is to determine alternative outcomes for EBIT and their likelihood of occurrence.

The two firms have invested the same amount of capital and face the same probability distribution of EBIT, so they have the same business risk. How will the

EXHIBIT 5.9 EFFECT OF FINANCING ON PROFITABILITY FOR DIFFERENT LEVELS OF EBIT.

Alternative Levels of Pre-Tax Operating Profit	Profitability of the Firm with 100% Equity Financing		Profitability of the Firm with 50% Equity Financing	
EBIT	$ROIC_{BT}$	ROE_{BT}	$ROIC_{BT}$	ROE_{BT}
$14 million	14%	14%	14%	18%
$10 million	10%	10%	10%	10%
$8 million	8%	8%	8%	6%

difference in their financing strategies affect their profitability? Exhibit 5.9 shows each firm's profitability ratios—return on invested capital ($ROIC_{BT}$) and return on equity (ROE_{BT})—for each of the three possible levels of EBIT. Consider first the case of the unlevered firm. The firm's operating profitability ($ROIC_{BT}$) varies from a high of 14 percent (EBIT of $14 million divided by $100 million of invested capital) to a low of 8 percent. Its ROE_{BT} is equal to its $ROIC_{BT}$ because it has no debt and pays no taxes. (Both its financial leverage multiplier and its tax-effect ratio are equal to one.)

What is the profitability of the levered firm? Its $ROIC_{BT}$ is the same as that of the unlevered firm because both firms have identical assets and operating profit. The firm pays no taxes, its interest expense is $5 million (10 percent of $50 million of debt), and it has $50 million of equity capital. Its ROE_{BT} is thus:

$$ROE_{BT} = \frac{\text{EBIT} - \text{Interest expense}}{\text{Owners' equity}} = \frac{\text{EBIT} - \$5\text{ million}}{\$50\text{ million}}$$

When EBIT is $14 million, ROE_{BT} is 18 percent ($14 million minus $5 million divided by $50 million). In this case, the levered firm's ROE_{BT} is *higher* than that of the unlevered firm (18 percent versus 14 percent). Although the $5 million of interest expenses for the levered firm reduced owners' profit to $9 million ($14 million of EBIT less the $5 million of interest expenses), *profit per dollar of invested equity* (ROE_{BT}) rose to 18 percent because the equity base is smaller for the levered firm than it is for the unlevered firm ($50 million instead of $100 million). In this case, financial leverage is *favorable* to the owners of the levered firm because a positive financial structure effect has more than offset a negative financial cost effect.

When EBIT is equal to $10 million, the levered firm's ROE_{BT} is 10 percent. In this case, financial leverage is neutral because the levered firm's ROE_{BT} is equal to that of the unlevered firm. Finally, when EBIT is equal to $8 million, the levered firm's ROE_{BT} is 6 percent. In this case, financial leverage is *unfavorable* to the firm's owners because the levered firm's ROE_{BT} is lower than that of the unlevered firm (6 percent versus 8 percent). Notice how financial leverage (borrowing at a fixed rate of interest) affects ROE. The unlevered firm's ROE_{BT} varies from a high of 14 percent to a low of 8 percent in response to changes in EBIT, whereas the levered firm's ROE_{BT} varies from a high of 18 percent to a low of 6 percent in response to the same changes in EBIT. The two firms face the same business risk because the changes in EBIT are the same for both. However, the levered firm's ROE_{BT} varies more widely than the ROE_{BT} of the unlevered firm. In other words, *financial leverage (borrowing) magnifies a firm's business risk*. Borrowing at a fixed interest rate adds **financial risk** to the firm's existing business risk. The owners of the levered firm face *both* business risk and financial risk, whereas the owners of the unlevered firm face only business risk. The levered firm is riskier than the unlevered one, and its risk increases with rising levels of borrowing.

HOW DOES FINANCIAL LEVERAGE WORK?

Why is financial leverage favorable to the firm's owners when EBIT is \$14 million (they get a *higher* ROE_{BT} than the firm that has not borrowed), neutral when EBIT is \$10 million (they get the *same* ROE_{BT} as the firm that has not borrowed), and unfavorable when EBIT is \$8 million (they get a *lower* ROE_{BT} than the firm that has not borrowed)? The answer is straightforward. In the first case, the firm's owners borrow at 10 percent to finance assets that generate a pre-tax return of 14 percent ($ROIC_{BT}$ is equal to 14 percent in the first case). You do not have to be a financial wizard to realize that borrowing at 10 percent to achieve a return on investment of 14 percent is a profitable proposition. Financial leverage enhances the firm's overall profitability (its ROE_{BT}). In the second case, the firm borrows at 10 percent to achieve an $ROIC_{BT}$ of 10 percent. Financial leverage is neutral, and ROE_{BT} is the same as if the firm did not borrow. In the third case, the firm borrows at 10 percent to achieve an $ROIC_{BT}$ of only 8 percent. This is clearly a losing proposition. Borrowing, in this case, turns out to be a poor decision.

The relationship that links a firm's after-tax ROE to its pre-tax $ROIC_{BT}$ *for a given cost of debt, tax rate,* and a *debt-to-equity ratio* can be written as follows:

$$ROE = ROIC_{BT}(1 - T_C) + [ROIC_{BT} - \text{Cost of debt}](1 - T_C) \times \frac{\text{Debt}}{\text{Owners' equity}}$$

where T_C is the effective corporate tax rate. For any given debt-to-equity ratio, ROE will be higher than $ROIC_{BT}$ if $ROIC_{BT}$ is higher than the cost of debt. When $ROIC_{BT}$ is equal to the cost of debt, ROE is equal to $ROIC_{BT}$. And when $ROIC_{BT}$ is smaller than the cost of debt, ROE is smaller than $ROIC_{BT}$.

To illustrate this relationship, we return to our earlier example. The 50 percent equity-financed firm has a debt-to-equity ratio of one (\$50 million of debt divided by \$50 million of equity). The cost of debt is 10 percent, and the firm does not pay any tax ($T_C = 0$). Here are the three cases:

1. When $ROIC_{BT}$ = **14%**, ROE = 14% + [14% – 10%] × 1 = 14% + 4% = **18%**
2. When $ROIC_{BT}$ = **10%**, ROE = 10% + [10% – 10%] × 1 = 10% + 0% = **10%**
3. When $ROIC_{BT}$ = **8%**, ROE = 8% + [8% – 10%] × 1 = 8% – 2% = **6%**

Although we can compute a firm's ROE for any combination of $ROIC_{BT}$ and debt-to-equity ratio, the formula will *never* provide the *optimal* or best level of debt for the firm. We return to this issue in Chapter 11 when we examine how a firm should determine its capital structure.

TWO RELATED CAVEATS: RISK AND THE ABILITY TO CREATE VALUE

One obvious conclusion from the previous discussion is that a firm seeking to enhance its ROE should borrow as long as its $ROIC_{BT}$ exceeds its cost of debt, and refrain from borrowing whenever its $ROIC_{BT}$ is lower than its cost of debt. There are, however, two important and related caveats to this conclusion.

The first is that managers do not know their firm's *future* $ROIC_{BT}$ at the time they borrow to fund the firm's assets. Hence, they can only compare the cost of debt with an *expected* (risky) $ROIC_{BT}$ that may or may not be the one the firm will eventually achieve. Risk cannot be ignored when applying the ROE formula. Higher levels of *expected* $ROIC_{BT}$ will produce higher levels of *expected* ROE. However, the *expectation* of achieving a higher ROE must be weighed against the risk of not achieving it. (You hope to achieve 18 percent but you may well end up with only 6 percent; you just don't know!)

The second caveat, which is related to the first, is that a high *expected* ROE does not necessarily mean that the firm is creating value for its owners. Consider again the firm with a debt-to-equity ratio of one that can borrow at 10 percent. Suppose the firm can acquire assets that are expected to generate an $ROIC_{BT}$ of 14 percent. As shown above, financial leverage will have a positive effect on the firm's ROE, which will reach 18 percent. But this does not mean that the firm should acquire the assets. What if the firm's owners expect a return of, say, 25 percent to compensate them for the business and financial risks attached to the equity they have invested in the firm? If this is the case, then the acquisition's expected ROE of 18 percent is not sufficient to remunerate the firm's owners. The acquisition should not be undertaken, because it is not a value-creating proposition. More on this point in Chapter 15.

SELF-SUSTAINABLE GROWTH

Without a sustainable level of profit, a firm will be constrained in its ability to finance its future growth. Consider OS Distributors. Sales in 2010 grew by 14.3 percent, from \$420 million to \$480 million. Suppose OS Distributors expects sales to grow by, say, 15 percent next year. As sales increase, more receivables will be generated, more inventories will be needed, and eventually more fixed assets will be required to support the higher levels of sales. This growth in assets will have to be financed with debt, equity, or a combination of these two sources of funds. How can OS Distributors' management anticipate the financing implications of the expected growth in sales?

Firms can finance their anticipated growth in two ways: (1) internally, through the retention of profits (additions to retained earnings) or (2) externally, through the issuance of shares and through borrowing. Because *external* equity financing is more costly than *internal* equity financing,[7] firms often try to finance their expected growth with internally generated equity (retained earnings). For this reason, managers need to have an indicator of the *maximum* growth their firm can achieve

[7]Raising equity through the issuance of shares involves transaction costs that can add several percentage points to the cost of equity. More on this point in Chapter 11.

without raising external equity. The firm's **self-sustainable growth rate (SGR)** is this indicator. It is *the maximum rate of growth in sales a firm can achieve without issuing new shares or changing either its operating policy (its operating profit margin and capital turnover remain the same) or its financing policy (its debt-to-equity ratio and* **dividend payout ratio** *remain the same)*.

How is the self-sustainable growth rate determined? Let's begin by estimating the rate for OS Distributors at the end of 2010. From the firm's financial data in Exhibits 5.2 and 5.3, we know that the firm's \$70 million of equity at the beginning of 2010 (the same as end of 2009) generated \$10.2 million in earnings after tax. The firm retained \$7 million and distributed the balance of \$3.2 million to owners in the form of dividends. As a result, owners' equity increased by 10 percent, from \$70 million to \$77 million. If the firm expects its equity to increase by the same percentage next year and if it wants to maintain its current debt-to-equity ratio, then its debt must also increase by 10 percent. If both owners' equity and debt increase by 10 percent, their sum, which is equal to the firm's invested capital, will also increase by 10 percent. Furthermore, if the firm's capital turnover (sales divided by invested capital) does not change, sales will also increase by 10 percent. This 10 percent growth in sales is OS Distributors' self-sustainable growth rate. It is equal to the 10 percent growth in the firm's equity and is *the fastest growth rate in sales the firm can achieve without changing its capital structure and operating policy and without raising new equity through a share issue*.

From this example, we can now derive a general formula to compute the self-sustainable growth rate of any firm. We define a firm's **profit retention rate** as the ratio of its addition to retained earnings to its earnings after tax:

$$\text{Profit retention rate} = \frac{\text{Addition to retained earnings}}{\text{Earnings after tax}}$$

Then, the self-sustainable growth rate, which is equal to the rate of increase in owners' equity, can be written as follows:

$$\text{Self-sustainable growth rate} = \frac{\text{Retained earnings}}{\text{Owners' equity}}$$

$$= \frac{\text{Retention rate} \times \text{EAT}}{\text{Owners' equity}}$$

$$\textbf{Self-sustainable growth rate = Retention rate} \times \textbf{Return on equity} \quad (5.12)$$

where ROE is calculated by dividing the year's net profit or EAT by the book value of the firm's equity at the *beginning* of the year.

We know that ROE can be written as the product of operating profit margin, capital turnover, financial leverage multiplier, and the tax-effect ratio (see equations 5.9 and 5.10). Thus, the firm's self-sustainable growth rate can be written as follows:

$$\begin{aligned}\text{Self-sustainable growth rate} = {} & \text{Retention rate} \times \text{Operating margin} \\ & \times \text{Capital turnover} \\ & \times \text{Financial leverage multiplier} \\ & \times (1 - \text{Effective tax rate})\end{aligned}$$

This equation clearly identifies the five factors that determine the firm's capacity to grow *without* raising new equity. The second and third factors reflect the

EXHIBIT 5.10 OS DISTRIBUTORS' SELF-SUSTAINABLE GROWTH RATE COMPARED WITH GROWTH IN SALES.

Year	Retention Rate	Return on Equity	Self-Sustainable Growth Rate	Growth in Sales
2010	$\frac{7.0}{10.2} = 0.69$	$\frac{10.2}{70.0} = 14.6\%$	$0.69 \times 14.6\% =$ **10%**	**14.3%**
2009	$\frac{6.0}{8.0} = 0.75$	$\frac{8.0}{64.0} = 12.5\%$	$0.75 \times 12.5\% =$ **9.4%**	7.7%

firm's operating policy (its operating profit margin and capital turnover), the first and fourth reflect its financing policy (its profit retention rate and financial leverage multiplier), and the fifth reflects the effective rate at which its pre-tax profit is taxed. The point to remember is this: *if these five factors stay fixed, a firm cannot grow its sales faster than its self-sustainable growth rate unless it issues new shares.*

Let's return to OS Distributors. Exhibit 5.10 shows the firm's self-sustainable growth rate in 2009 and 2010, computed according to equation 5.12, and the growth in sales the firm experienced during these two years. OS Distributors' self-sustainable growth rate was 10 percent in 2010, slightly higher than its value of 9.4 percent a year earlier. Its sales, however, grew by 14.3 percent during 2010, a rate almost twice that achieved the previous year (7.7 percent). How did OS Distributors grow its sales by 14.3 percent in 2010 with roughly the same self-sustainable growth rate as in 2009 without issuing new shares? In other words, where did the firm get the additional capital required to grow sales beyond the self-sustainable growth rate of 10 percent? The answer is found in OS Distributors' managerial balance sheet (see Exhibit 5.3). Cash decreased from $12 million at the beginning of 2010 to $8 million at the end of that year, a one-year drop of 33 percent. Thus, OS Distributors used its cash holdings to finance the gap between its self-sustainable growth rate and its growth in sales.

This example illustrates an important point: *firms with sales growing faster than their self-sustainable growth rate will eventually experience a cash deficit; firms with sales growing slower than their self-sustainable growth rate will eventually generate a cash surplus*. This phenomenon is illustrated in Exhibit 5.11. Firms positioned on the line that bisects the plane are in **financial balance**. Their self-sustainable growth rate is equal to their growth in sales. Firms with sales growth exceeding their self-sustainable growth rate are above the line, and firms with sales growth slower than their self-sustainable growth rate are below the line. Cash deficit firms face a *funding problem*; firms with a cash surplus have an *investment problem*—they generate more cash than they can invest.

How can management respond to unsustainable levels of growth in sales, that is, to growth rates that exceed the firm's self-sustainable growth rate? For example, suppose OS Distributors expects its sales to grow by 15 percent next year. This growth rate is clearly unsustainable if OS Distributors maintains its self-sustainable growth rate at its current level of 10 percent (see the initial position of OS Distributors at point A in Exhibit 5.11). If raising new equity is not an option, then OS Distributors' management will have to make operating or financing decisions that will raise the firm's self-sustainable growth rate to 15 percent (see the desired final

EXHIBIT 5.11 SALES GROWTH AND CASH CONDITION.

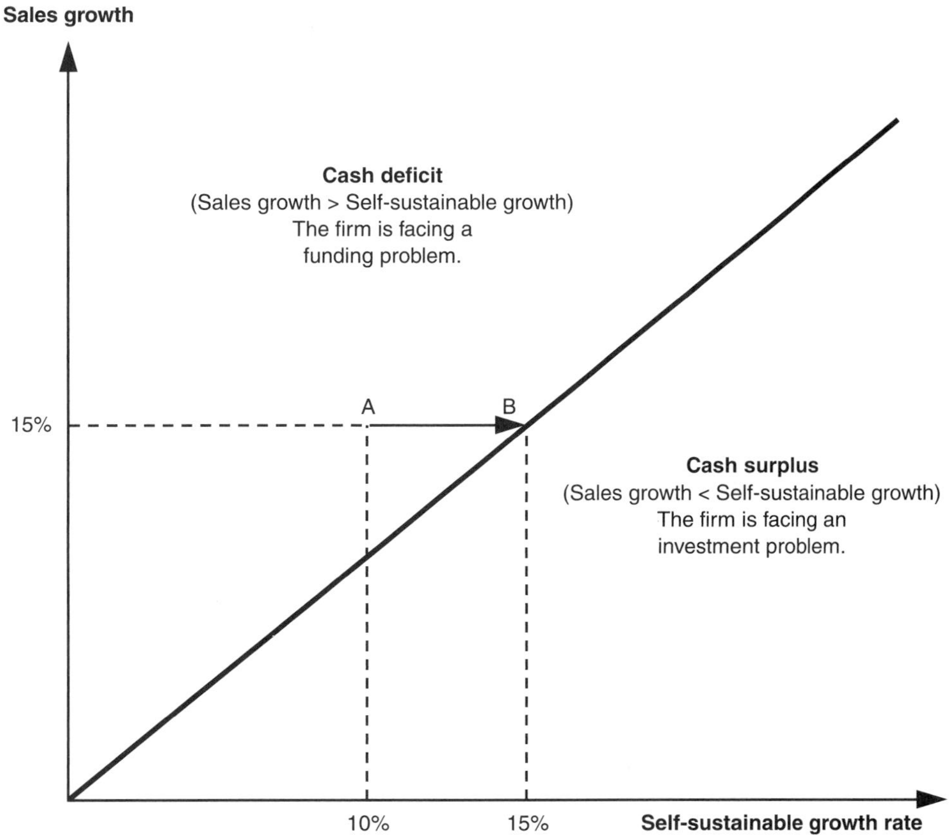

position of OS Distributors at point B in Exhibit 5.11). Otherwise, OS Distributors will experience a continued loss of cash next year that may eventually initiate a funding and liquidity crisis.

Let's examine some of the options available to OS Distributors. If we assume that next year's ROE will be the same as this year's (14.6 percent), then one possible option is to retain 100 percent of the firm's profit. With a retention rate of one, the firm's self-sustainable growth rate will be equal to its ROE. Thus, this option, which implies an elimination of dividend payments, would raise the firm's self-sustainable growth rate to 14.6 percent, a figure close to the firm's 15 percent expected growth in sales. But it is unlikely that the firm's owners will find this option acceptable. They will probably impose some financial constraints on the firm's management. Let's assume (1) they are unwilling to cut dividends below 20 percent of profits and (2) their desired debt-to-equity ratio is one. *After management has met these financial constraints, the firm's self-sustainable growth rate can be increased only through an improvement in the firm's operating profitability.*

How much does OS Distributors' operating profitability, measured by its $ROIC_{BT}$, need to increase to bring its self-sustainable growth rate up to its target rate of 15 percent? To answer this question, we first look at ROE. A firm's self-sustainable growth rate is equal to its retention rate multiplied by its ROE. To achieve a self-sustainable growth rate of 15 percent with a retention rate of 0.80 (which corresponds to a dividend payout ratio of 20 percent), the firm's ROE must be equal to the following (see equation 5.12):

$$\text{ROE} = \frac{\text{Self-sustainable growth rate}}{\text{Retention rate}} = \frac{15\%}{0.80} = 18.7\%$$

To achieve a target self-sustainable growth rate of 15 percent with a retention rate of 80 percent, OS Distributors' ROE must rise to 18.7 percent. What combination of financial leverage and ROIC_{BT} will provide an ROE of 18.7 percent? Rearranging the terms in equation 5.11, we have the following:

$$\text{ROIC}_{\text{BT}} = \frac{\text{ROE}}{\text{Financial leverage multiplier} \times (1 - \text{Effective tax rate})}$$

Recall that the financial leverage multiplier is the product of the financial *structure* (Invested capital/Equity) ratio and the financial *cost* ratio. Given a target debt-to-equity ratio of one, the financial *structure* ratio (Invested capital/Equity) is two. If we assume the financial *cost* ratio will remain at 0.71 as in 2010, then the financial leverage multiplier will be equal to two multiplied by 0.71. With desired ROE of 18.7 percent and a tax rate of 40 percent, the implied return on invested capital (ROIC_{BT}) is as follows:

$$\text{ROIC}_{\text{BT}} = \frac{18.7\%}{2.0 \times 0.71 \times 0.60} = \frac{18.7\%}{0.85} = 22\%$$

Thus, OS Distributors' operating profitability must increase to 22 percent to bring its self-sustainable growth rate up to 15 percent. So, how can the firm's operations achieve an ROIC_{BT} of 22 percent next year? ROIC_{BT} can rise only through a combination of higher operating profit margin and faster capital turnover. Suppose in a previous meeting of OS Distributors' managers, the marketing manager said that operating profit margin is expected to rise to 5.5 percent next year. How high must capital turnover rise to achieve an ROIC_{BT} of 22 percent given that operating profit margin is expected to be 5.5 percent? ROIC_{BT} is the product of capital turnover and operating profit margin, so we can write the following:

$$\text{Capital turnover} = \frac{\text{Pre-tax return on invested capital}}{\text{Operating profit margin}} = \frac{22\%}{5.5\%} = 4.0$$

We now know that OS Distributors must raise its capital turnover to 4.0 next year to raise its self-sustainable growth rate to 15 percent. How can this objective be achieved? The operations manager will have to focus first on the firm's WCR; receivables will have to be collected faster and inventories will have to turn over as quickly as possible. Being in the distribution business, however, OS Distributors uses a relatively small amount of fixed assets, and thus has a lower opportunity to rapidly improve its ***fixed* asset turnover ratio** (sales divided by *fixed* assets). This challenge may have to be addressed eventually if OS Distributors is to raise its self-sustainable growth rate to 15 percent without raising new equity.

The conclusion is inescapable: given OS Distributors' financial constraints, if the firm's management cannot achieve the targeted improvements in the firm's operations, the firm's owners will have to inject new equity into the business, issue new shares, or accept lower-than-expected sales.

SUMMARY

A firm's profitability, risk, and growth are related to one another and must be managed in a way that allows the firm to grow smoothly without impairing its ability to create wealth for its owners. A firm's return on equity (ROE) measures the firm's overall profitability and is affected by the firm's operating, investing, and financing activities as well as its effective tax rate.

The effect of operating and investing activities on ROE is captured by return on invested capital before tax ($ROIC_{BT}$), which is obtained by dividing the firm's earnings before interest and tax (EBIT) by its invested capital (the sum of cash, working capital requirement, and net fixed assets). $ROIC_{BT}$ is equal to the firm's operating profit margin (EBIT/Sales) multiplied by its capital turnover (Sales/Invested capital). Empirical evidence indicates that a firm's $ROIC_{BT}$ is essentially driven by its competitive position (the size of its market share), the relative quality of its products and services, and the structure of its costs and assets.

A firm's financing strategy also has an effect on ROE. A firm's pre-tax ROE is equal to its operating profitability multiplied by the financial leverage multiplier, a measure of the effect of borrowing on the firm's profitability. When operating profitability *exceeds* the cost of debt, the financial leverage multiplier is *higher* than one and financial leverage is *favorable* to the firm's owners. When operating profitability is *lower* than the cost of debt, the firm's financial leverage multiplier is *lower* than one and financial leverage is *unfavorable* to the firm's owners. However, a firm cannot easily take advantage of favorable financial leverage because of business risk (the unpredictable fluctuations in the firm's EBIT and operating profitability). In other words, the firm will generally be unable to predict its operating profitability at the time it borrows to finance its investments. Financial leverage adds another layer of risk to the firm's business risk, and this additional risk, called financial risk, affects the firm's performance.

Finally, taxation affects ROE. Firms should try to minimize the negative effect of corporate taxes on their profitability by taking advantage, whenever possible, of tax breaks and tax subsidies that are offered, for example, by countries or regions that want to attract investments.

Other measures of profitability, besides ROE, include the firm's earnings per share (earnings after tax divided by the number of shares outstanding), its price-to-earnings ratio (share price divided by earnings per share), and its market-to-book ratio (share price divided by book value per share).

The ability of a firm to finance its growth is determined by its self-sustainable growth rate. This rate is equal to the fraction of profits retained by the firm (its retention rate) multiplied by its ROE. A firm's self-sustainable growth rate indicates whether the firm can finance its anticipated growth in sales without raising new equity or changing either its operating policy (its operating profit margin and capital turnover remain the same) or its financing policy (its debt-to-equity and dividend-payout ratios remain the same). A firm that grows its sales faster than its self-sustainable growth rate will eventually experience a cash deficit. If it is unable to raise its self-sustainable growth rate through a higher profit retention rate or a higher ROE, then its only option for eliminating its cash deficit is to issue new equity. A firm that is unable to grow its sales as fast as its self-sustainable growth rate will eventually experience a cash surplus. A firm facing this situation must then decide how to spend its cash surplus to create value for its owners. If it is unable to find value-creating investment opportunities, it should simply return the excess cash to its shareholders through a dividend payment or a share repurchase program.

The Home Depot's Profitability

APPENDIX **5.1**

In this appendix, we analyze The Home Depot's profitability over the three years 2006, 2007, and 2008.[8] Using the return-on-equity (ROE) formula in equation 5.9, we show how the company's operating activity, financial policy, and taxation have contributed to its profitability, and provide some comparison with Lowe's Companies, Inc., The Home Depot's well-known competitor in the home improvement retail industry.

THE HOME DEPOT'S PROFITABILITY STRUCTURE

We apply equation 5.9 to The Home Depot's data taken from its income statements in Exhibit A5.1.1 and managerial balance sheets in Exhibit A5.1.2.[9] The result is presented in Exhibit A5.1.3, which shows the effect of operations, financial policy, and taxation on The Home Depot's ROE in 2006, 2007, and 2008. For comparison purposes, we also show, in the same exhibit, the profitability structure of Lowes' during the same periods.[10]

The Home Depot's ROE increased from 23 percent in 2006 to 24.8 percent in 2007 and then dropped sharply to 12.7 percent in 2008. During the same period, Lowe's ROE increased from 14 percent in 2006 to 17.4 percent in 2007 and then decreased slightly to 17.2 percent in 2008. What accounts for these variations and differences between the two companies? This question is addressed in the next five sections in which we analyze the ROE structure of the two companies based on the data in Exhibit A5.1.3.

The Effect of The Home Depot's Operating Profitability on Its Return on Equity

The Home Depot's return on invested capital before tax ($ROIC_{BT}$) decreased over the three-year period from 23.8 percent in 2006 to 22.1 percent in year 2007 and

[8]Years 2006, 2007, and 2008 refer to fiscal years ending January 28, 2007, February 3, 2008, and February 1, 2009, respectively.

[9]The Home Depot's income statements were presented in Chapter 2, Appendix 2.1, and its managerial balance sheets were presented in Chapter 3, Appendix 3.2.

[10]Lowe's fiscal year 2006 ends on February 2, 2007, fiscal year 2007 ends on February 1, 2008, and fiscal year 2008 ends on January 30, 2009.

EXHIBIT A5.1.1 THE HOME DEPOT'S CONSOLIDATED STATEMENTS OF INCOME.

FROM EXHIBIT A2.1.2, APPENDIX 2.1, CHAPTER 2. FIGURES IN MILLIONS[1]

Fiscal year ended	Jan. 28, 2007	Feb. 3, 2008	Feb. 1, 2009
Net sales	**$79,022**	**$77,349**	**$71,288**
Cost of goods sold	52,476	51,352	47,298
Gross profit	**26,546**	**25,997**	**23,990**
Selling, general, and administrative expenses	16,106	17,053	17,846
Depreciation expense	1,574	1,702	1,785
Operating profit	**8,866**	**7,242**	**4,359**
Extraordinary items[2]	495	185	(215)
Earnings before interest and tax (EBIT)	**9,361**	**7,427**	**4,144**
Net interest expense	364	622	606
Earnings before tax (EBT)	**8,997**	**6,805**	**3,538**
Income tax expense	3,236	2,410	1,278
Earnings after tax (EAT)	**$ 5,761**	**$ 4,395**	**$ 2,260**

[1]Fiscal years ended February 1, 2009 and January 28, 2007 include 52 weeks. Fiscal year ended February 3, 2008 includes 53 weeks.
[2]The extraordinary items account includes investment write-downs and profit (loss) from discontinued operations reported in The Home Depot's income statements (Exhibit A2.1.2, Chapter 2).

EXHIBIT A5.1.2 THE HOME DEPOT'S MANAGERIAL BALANCE SHEETS.

FROM EXHIBIT A3.2.3, APPENDIX 3.2, CHAPTER 3. FIGURES IN MILLIONS

		Jan. 28, 2007		Feb. 3, 2008		Feb. 1, 2009
Invested capital						
• Cash		$ 3,837		$ 1,716		$ 1,497
• Working capital requirement		1,250		2,299		2,479
• Net fixed assets		34,263		29,650		27,802
Total invested capital		**$39,350**		**$33,665**		**$31,778**
Capital employed						
• Short-term debt		$ 18		$ 2,047		$ 1,767
• Long-term financing		39,332		31,618		30,011
Long-term debt	$11,643		$11,383		$ 9,667	
Other long-term liabilities	2,659		2,521		2,567	
Owners' equity	25,030		17,714		17,777	
Total capital employed		**$39,350**		**$33,665**		**$31,778**

EXHIBIT A5.1.3 THE STRUCTURE OF THE HOME DEPOT AND LOWE'S RETURN ON EQUITY.

ALL DATA FROM THE FIRMS' INCOME STATEMENTS AND MANAGERIAL BALANCE SHEETS

Return on Equity = Operating Profitability × Financial Leverage Multiplier = Return on Equity Before Tax × Tax Effect

$$\frac{\text{EAT}}{\text{Owners' equity}} = \frac{\text{EBIT}}{\text{Net sales}} \times \frac{\text{Net sales}}{\text{Invested capital}} \times \frac{\text{EBT}}{\text{EBIT}} \times \frac{\text{Invested capital}}{\text{Owners' equity}} = \frac{\text{EBT}}{\text{Owners' equity}} \times \frac{\text{EAT}}{\text{EBT}}$$

	Return on Equity: EAT / Owners' equity	EBIT / Net sales	Net sales / Invested capital	Return on invested capital before tax ($ROIC_{BT}$)	EBT / EBIT	Invested capital / Owners' equity	Financial leverage multiplier	Return on Equity Before Tax: EBT / Owners' equity	Tax Effect: EAT / EBT
The Home Depot Fiscal Year Ended:									
January 28, 2007	23.0%	11.8%	2.01	23.8%	0.96	1.57	1.51	35.9%	0.64[2]
February 3, 2008	24.8%	9.6%	2.30	22.1%	0.92	1.90	1.74	38.4%	0.65[2]
February 1, 2009	12.7%	5.8%	2.24	13.0%	0.85	1.79	1.53	19.9%	0.64[2]
Lowe's[1] Fiscal Year Ended:									
February 2, 2007	14.0%	7.8%	2.26	17.7%	0.93	1.36	1.26	22.3%	0.63[2]
February 1, 2008	17.4%	9.7%	1.99	19.4%	0.96	1.50	1.44	28.0%	0.62[2]
January 30, 2009	17.2%	11.0%	1.83	20.1%	0.97	1.42	1.38	27.7%	0.62[2]

[1]Note that the date of the end of the reporting period for Lowe's is not exactly the same as that of The Home Depot.

[2]The product of the return on equity before tax and the tax effect, using figures from this exhibit, might not be exactly equal to the return on equity because these figures are limited to one or two decimals.

to 13 percent in 2008. Like the company's ROE, it dropped sharply in 2008. Remember that $ROIC_{BT}$ is driven by operating margin and invested capital turnover. With this in mind, let's see how these two drivers of operating profitability evolved over the period 2006–2008.

THE EFFECT OF OPERATING MARGIN ON THE HOME DEPOT'S OPERATING PROFITABILITY

Note the steady decline in The Home Depot's operating margin over the three-year period—11.8 percent in 2006, 9.6 percent in 2007, and 5.8 percent in 2008. As Exhibit A5.1.4 shows, this decline cannot be attributed to lower gross margins—which were remarkably stable at around 33.6 percent—but rather to the company's selling, general, and administrative (SG&A) expenses, which increased from 20.4 percent of net sales in 2006 to 25 percent in 2008.

A flat gross margin should be expected from most retailers, such as The Home Depot, because most of the costs that make up a retailer's cost of sales are variable, provided that sale prices are not aggressively discounted to limit sales erosion during a recession period like in 2008.

A look at Exhibit A5.1.1 shows that The Home Depot's net sales decreased from $79,022 million in 2006 to $71,288 million in 2008, a 9.8 percent decline over the two-year period. Turning to Exhibit A5.1.4, we see that SG&A expenses as a percentage of sales have risen from 20.4 percent in 2006 to 25 percent in 2008. This increase is due to the fact that SG&A expenses are mostly fixed in the short run and, thus, the higher the proportion of fixed costs in SG&A expenses, the lower the operating margin. This phenomenon was at work at The Home Depot from 2006 to 2008.

During the same three-year period, Lowe's operating margin, which was significantly lower than The Home Depot's operating margin in 2006 (7.8 percent versus 11.8 percent), increased to 11 percent in 2008, almost double that of The Home Depot's (11 percent versus 5.8 percent). Lowe's gross margin, which was slightly higher than that of The Home Depot's, was stable over the period. However, Lowe's sales *increased* by 2.7 percent from $46,927 million 2006 to $48,230 million in 2008 (sales data are from the company's annual reports not shown here). However, as Exhibit A5.1.4 shows, Lowe's SG&A expenses as a percentage of sales increased from 21.1 percent in 2006 to 23.2 percent in 2008. In its annual

EXHIBIT A5.1.4 THE HOME DEPOT AND LOWE'S GROSS MARGIN AND SG&A EXPENSES AS PERCENTAGE OF NET SALES.

FROM THE FIRMS' INCOME STATEMENTS

	The Home Depot			Lowe's		
Fiscal Year End	**Jan. 28, 2007**	**Feb. 3, 2008**	**Feb. 1, 2009**	**Feb. 2, 2007**	**Feb. 1, 2008**	**Jan. 30, 2009**
Gross Margin	33.6%	33.6%	33.7%	34.5%	34.6%	34.2%
Selling, general, and administrative expenses as percentage of net sales	20.4%	22.0%	25.0%	21.1%	22.1%	23.2%

EXHIBIT A5.1.5 THE HOME DEPOT AND LOWE'S NET SALES-TO-FIXED ASSETS RATIO.

FROM THE FIRMS' INCOME STATEMENTS AND BALANCE SHEETS

	The Home Depot			Lowe's		
Fiscal Year End	Jan. 28, 2007	Feb. 3, 2008	Feb. 1, 2009	Feb. 2, 2007	Feb. 1, 2008	Jan. 30, 2009
Net sales-to-fixed assets ratio	2.31	2.61	2.56	2.41	2.18	2.06

reports, Lowe's indicates that the increase in the ratio is related to added administrative costs, such as expenses associated with its employee retirement plans and impairment charges.

THE EFFECT OF INVESTED CAPITAL TURNOVER ON THE HOME DEPOT'S OPERATING PROFITABILITY

The Home Depot generated $2.01 of sales per dollar of invested capital in 2006, $2.30 in 2007, and $2.24 in 2008. A look at Exhibit A5.1.2 indicates that net fixed assets is the largest component of the company's invested capital, representing approximately 87 percent of total invested capital. Turning to Exhibit A5.1.5, we see that The Home Depot's ratio of sales to fixed assets increased from 2.31 in 2006 to 2.56 in 2008, whereas Lowe's ratio decreased from 2.41 to 2.06 during the same period. It would be tempting to conclude that The Home Depot used its fixed assets more efficiently in 2008 than in 2006, and also more efficiently than Lowe's. Unfortunately, reasons other than efficiency can explain the rise in the ratio. The most important one is the impact of a reduction in the book value of fixed assets (also called asset write-down or fixed asset impairment), which lowers the amount of net fixed assets in a discretionary way, thus increasing the ratio of sales to fixed assets. Because The Home Depot's annual reports for 2007 and 2008 indicate significant asset write-downs, the improvement in the ratio of sales to fixed assets and its higher magnitude compared with that of Lowe's, cannot be fully attributed to a better use of its fixed assets to generate sales.

THE EFFECT OF THE HOME DEPOT'S FINANCIAL POLICY ON ITS RETURN ON EQUITY

The Home Depot's financial multiplier in 2006 was 1.51 (see Exhibit A5.1.3). It increased to 1.74 in 2007 and then decreased to 1.53 in 2008, practically to the same level as in 2006. During the same period, Lowe's multiplier was always lower than that of The Home Depot, although it increased from 1.26 to 1.38.

The increase in The Home Depot's financial multiplier in 2007 is directly related to the company's decision to repurchase a substantial amount of its shares. Exhibit A5.1.2 shows that owners' equity decreased from $25,030 million at year-end 2006 to $17,714 million at year-end 2007. This explains the increase in the financial structure ratio from 1.57 to 1.90. The financial structure ratio is directly related to the debt-to-invested capital ratio. Exhibit A5.1.6 shows this ratio for The Home Depot and Lowe's from 2006 to 2008.

EXHIBIT A5.1.6 DEBT RATIOS FOR THE HOME DEPOT AND LOWE'S.

ALL DATA FROM THE FIRMS' MANAGERIAL BALANCE SHEETS

	The Home Depot			Lowe's		
Fiscal Year End	Jan. 28, 2007	Feb. 3, 2008	Feb. 1, 2009	Feb. 2, 2007	Feb. 1, 2008	Jan. 30, 2009
$\frac{\text{Total debt}}{\text{Invested capital}}$	29.6%	39.9%	36.0%	20.8%	19.8%	23.6%

The Home Depot's debt ratio was 29.6 percent at year-end 2006, then, after the shares repurchase, went up to 39.9 percent at year-end 2007 and decreased to 36 percent at year-end 2008. The jump in the debt ratio from 29.6 percent to 39.9 percent triggered a downgrading of the company's senior debt by rating agencies. Standard & Poors revised its rating from AA to BBB+ and has not changed it in 2008 (see Chapter 9 for a discussion on debt ratings). Lowe's debt ratio did not change much during the three-year period, from a low of 19.8 percent at year-end 2007 to a high of 23.6 percent at year-end 2008. This low debt ratio compared with that of The Home Depot implies that Lowe's senior debt is less risky. This is reflected in its debt rating, which was given an A+ by Standard & Poor's in 2008. However, because the two ratings (A+ and BBB+) mean that both companies have an adequate capacity to pay interest and capital, they were not in danger of sudden and unexpected financial trouble at year-end 2008.

THE EFFECT OF TAXATION ON THE HOME DEPOT'S RETURN ON EQUITY

The Home Depot's pre-tax ROE, which was relatively stable at 35.9 percent to 38.4 percent in 2006 and 2007, respectively, dropped to 19.9 percent in 2008. This significant decrease can be traced to the effect, mentioned previously, of a drop in operating margin from 9.6 percent in 2007 to 5.8 percent in 2008. The Home Depot's pre-tax profitability was much higher than that of Lowe's over the first two years of the three-year period. Most of the difference can be attributed to a higher operating margin as well as a higher invested capital turnover. During 2008, however, Lowe's operating margin went up to nearly twice that of The Home Depot (11 percent versus 5.8 percent). As a result, and despite a lower invested capital turnover, Lowe's profitability, measured by its pre-tax ROE, was higher than that of its competitor (27.7 percent versus 19.9 percent). This difference was not significantly affected by taxation, which was practically the same for both companies over the three-year period, ranging from 62 percent to 65 percent, and implying an effective tax rate in the range of 38 percent to 35 percent.

FURTHER READING

1. Jagiello, Kevin, and Gordon Mandry. "Structural Determinants of Performance: Insight from the PIMS Data Base." *The Handbook of Management*. Edited by D. F. Channon. Blackwell, 2004.
2. Rappaport, Alfred. *Creating Shareholder Value*. The Free Press, 2000. See Chapter 2.

SELF-TEST PROBLEMS

5.1 PROFITABILITY ANALYSIS.

The financial statements of Allied & Consolidated Clothier (ACC), a manufacturer of coats and other garments, are shown below. ACC's operational efficiency, liquidity position, and cash-flow statements are analyzed in Chapters 3 and 4. The income statements span a calendar year, and balance sheets are dated December 31. All figures are in millions of dollars.

Balance Sheets (in millions)

Year End	2008	2009	2010		2008	2009	2010
Cash	$100	$ 90	$ 50	Short-term debt	$ 80	$ 90	$ 135
Trade receivables	200	230	290	Trade payables	170	180	220
Inventories	160	170	300	Accrued expenses	40	45	50
Prepaid expenses	30	30	35	Long-term debt	140	120	100
Net fixed assets	390	390	365	Owners' equity	450	475	535
Total assets	$880	$910	$1,040	**Total liabilities & owners' equity**	$880	$910	$1,040

Income Statements (in millions)

	2008	2009	2010
Net sales	**$1,200**	**$1,350**	**$1,600**
Cost of goods sold	860	970	1,160
Selling, general, and administrative expenses	150	165	200
Depreciation expense	40	50	55
Earnings before interest and tax (EBIT)	**150**	**165**	**185**
Net interest expense	20	20	25
Earnings before tax (EBT)	**130**	**145**	**160**
Income tax expense	40	45	50
Earnings after tax (EAT)	**$ 90**	**$ 100**	**$ 110**
Dividends	$ 75	$ 75	$ 50

a. Restructure ACC's balance sheets in their managerial form.
b. Calculate ACC's return on equity (ROE) in 2008, 2009, and 2010 both before and after tax (use year-end owners' equity).
c. Calculate ACC's pre-tax operating profitability in 2008, 2009, and 2010, using year-end data and the three measures of operating profitability presented in the chapter: return on invested capital before tax ($ROIC_{BT}$), return on total assets (ROTA), and return on business assets (ROBA). Explain how these measures are different. Why do these measures of profitability differ from return on assets (ROA), which we defined as net profits over total assets?
d. What is return on capital employed before tax ($ROCE_{BT}$)?
e. What are the drivers of pre-tax ROIC? Provide a measure of these drivers in 2008, 2009, and 2010. What can you conclude when you compare ACC's operating profitability in 2010 with its 2008 performance?
f. Why is pre-tax ROE (see question b) higher than pre-tax ROIC (see question c)?
g. Given your answer to the previous question, is it correct to claim that as long as ACC borrows to finance its investments, its shareholders are better off because they will have a higher ROE?
h. Provide measures of the extent of ACC's borrowing in 2008, 2009, and 2010, using the ratios that follow. Briefly compare the information provided by these financial ratios:

   1. Financial cost ratio
   2. Times interest earned
   3. Financial structure ratio
   4. Debt-to-equity ratio
   5. Debt-to-invested-capital ratio

i. Break down ROE into its five fundamental components in 2008, 2009, and 2010. What can you conclude about the structure of ACC's profitability?
j. Given that ACC has 50 million shares outstanding that were worth $20 at the end of 2008, $24 at the end of 2009, and $30 at the end of 2010, what were ACC's earnings per share, price-to-earnings ratio, and market-to-book ratio on those dates? What information do these measures of profitability provide?

5.2 ROE STRUCTURE ACROSS INDUSTRIES.

Balance sheet and profitability structures for three companies are shown on the following page. The information was drawn from their 2007 annual reports. The companies are Microsoft, the software developer; Boeing, the aircraft manufacturer; and Cathay Pacific, the Asian airline company. Identify each company and explain your choice.

Balance Sheet Structure (in percentage)	Company A	Company B	Company C
Cash and cash equivalent	15%	18%	37%
Accounts receivable	10%	4%	18%
Inventories	16%	1%	2%
Other current assets	5%	5%	7%
Fixed assets	54%	72%	36%
Total assets	100.0%	100.0%	100.0%
Short-term debt	1%	1%	0%
Accounts payable	10%	5%	5%
Accruals and others	42%[1]	17%	33%
Long-term debt	13%	13%	0%
Other long-term liabilities	19%	21%	13%
Owners' equity	15%	43%	49%
Total liabilities and owners' equity	100.0%	100.0%	100.0%

[1]A third represents advance payments made by clients.

Profitability Structure	Company A	Company B	Company C
Return on total assets (ROTA) = Earning before interest and tax (EBIT)/Total assets	10%	7%	32%
Margin = EBIT/Sales	9%	10%	39%
Total asset turnover = Sales/Total assets	1.13	0.64	0.81
Leverage effect = Pre-tax ROE/ROTA	6.87	2.08	2.03
Pre-tax ROE = Earnings before tax (EBT)/Owners' equity	68%	14%	65%
Tax effect = Earnings after tax (EAT)/EBT = (1 − tax rate)	0.66	0.89	0.70
After-tax ROE = EAT/Owners' equity	45%	12%	45%

5.3 SUSTAINABLE GROWTH ANALYSIS.

Return to Allied & Consolidated Clothier (ACC), whose financial statements are reported in problem 5.1.

a. Compare the company's growth rate in sales in 2010 with its sustainable growth rate that same year. What can you conclude?
b. Suppose that ACC expects its sales to grow by 25 percent in 2011.
   1. How much equity capital will it need to finance that growth if it does not modify its financing policy and operational efficiency? How will ACC get this equity capital?

2. What will be the consequence of the 25 percent growth in sales on the firm's debt-to-equity ratio if ACC does not issue new equity, modify its dividend policy, or change its operational efficiency?
3. What will be the consequence of the 25 percent growth in sales on the firm's retention policy if ACC does not issue new equity, modify its debt-to-equity ratio, or change its operational efficiency?
4. How should ACC modify its operational efficiency if it wishes to grow its sales by 25 percent without issuing new equity or modifying its financing policy?

c. Suppose that ACC expects its sales to grow by 10 percent in 2011.

1. What will be the consequence of the 10 percent growth in sales on the firm's cash position if ACC does not modify its financing policy or change its operational efficiency?
2. What can ACC do with the extra cash? What should it do?

REVIEW PROBLEMS

1. **Transactions.**
Indicate the effects of the following transactions on *operating margin, invested capital turnover*, and *debt ratio*. Use + to indicate an increase, – to indicate a decrease, and 0 to indicate no effect.

	Operating margin	Invested capital turnover	Debt ratio
1. Shares are issued for cash			
2. Goods from inventory are sold for cash at a profit			
3. A fixed asset is sold for cash at its book value			
4. A fixed asset is sold for more than its book value			
5. A dividend is declared and paid			
6. Cash is obtained through a bank loan			
7. Accounts receivable are collected			
8. Minority interest in a firm is acquired for cash			
9. A fixed asset is depreciated			
10. Obsolete inventory is written off			
11. Merchandise is purchased on account			
12. Shares are repurchased			

2. **$ROIC_{BT}$, $ROCE_{BT}$, ROBA, and ROTA.**
From the balance sheets and income statements of OS Distributors in Exhibits 5.1, 5.2, and 5.3, compute the firm's return on invested capital before tax ($ROIC_{BT}$), return on capital employed before tax ($ROCE_{BT}$), return on business assets (ROBA), and return on total assets (ROTA) for the year 2010. What are the differences between these different measures of return?

3. **Book versus market return on equity.**
Return on equity (ROE) can be estimated using financial statements (book value) or financial market data (market value). The book value of ROE over an accounting period is earnings after tax divided by owners' equity. The market value of ROE is the return that an investor would have experienced during the same period. It is the difference in share price plus dividend paid during the period divided by the share price at the beginning of the period. Why are the two ratios different? If the market ROE is more relevant to any investor, what is the use of the book ROE?

4. **The structure of a firm's profitability.**
   a. If a firm has a return on equity (ROE) of 15 percent, a financial multiplier of 2, and does not pay any tax, what is its return on invested capital before tax?
   b. If a firm has an ROE of 15 percent, a financial cost effect of 0.9, and an pre-tax ROIC of 10 percent, what is its debt-to-equity ratio (total debt divided by owners' equity)? Assume that the firm does not pay any tax.
   c. Under what condition(s) can a firm have, at the same time, a negative pre-tax ROIC and a positive ROE?

5. **Misuse of the structure of return on equity.**
Cite two cases in which a bad decision (i.e., a decision that negatively affects the market value of a firm) would increase its return on equity.

6. **Financial leverage.**
Under what intuitive condition will increase in debt (either short term or long term) relative to equity always increase a firm's return on equity? Can the structure of return on equity (ROE) relationship be used to determine a firm's optimal debt-to-equity ratio?

7. **Industry effect on the structure of the return on equity.**
Below are summarized balance sheets and income statements of three U.S. companies:

Income Statements (in millions)			
	Firm 1	Firm 2	Firm 3
Revenues	$166,809	$7,132	$22,956
Earnings before interest and tax	10,105	1,419	10,937
Earnings before tax	9,083	1,114	14,275
Earnings after tax	$ 5,745	$ 714	$ 9,421

Balance Sheets (in millions)			
	Firm 1	Firm 2	Firm 3
Cash	$ 1,856	$ 485	$23,798
Accounts receivable	1,341	770	3,250
Inventories	19,793	223	0
Prepaid expenses	1,366	237	3,260
Net fixed assets	45,993	13,816	21,842
Total assets	$70,349	$15,531	$52,150
Short-term debt	$ 5,408	$ 890	$ 0
Accounts payable	13,105	616	1,083
Accrued expenses	7,290	158	8,672[1]
Long-term liabilities	18,712	8,205	1,027
Owners' equity	25,834	5,662	41,368
Total liabilities and owners' equity	$70,349	$15,531	$52,150

[1]Mostly unearned revenues.

a. Compute the working capital requirement of the three firms and prepare their managerial balance sheets.
b. Compute the three firms' operating margin, invested capital turnover, return on capital employed, financial multiplier, and the tax effect. What is the relationship between these ratios and the firms' return on equity?
c. One firm is in the retail (nongrocery) industry, another is a utility firm, and the last one is in the computer (software) industry. Which of the companies corresponds to Firm 1, Firm 2, and Firm 3?

8. **The effect of the management of the operating cycle on the firm's profitability.** Below are the last three years' financial statements of Sentec Inc., a distributor of electrical fixtures.

Income Statements (in thousands)			
	Year 1	Year 2	Year 3
Net sales	$22,100	$24,300	$31,600
Cost of goods sold	17,600	19,300	25,100
Selling, general, and administrative expenses	3,750	4,000	5,000
Depreciation expense	100	100	150
Earnings before interest and tax	650	900	1,350
Net interest expense	110	130	260
Earnings before tax	540	770	1,090
Income tax expense	220	310	430
Earnings after tax	$ 320	$ 460	$ 660
Dividends	$ 180	$ 200	$ 200

Balance Sheets (in thousands)			
	Year 1 December 31	Year 2 December 31	Year 3 December 31
Cash	$ 600	$ 350	$ 300
Accounts receivable	2,730	3,100	4,200
Inventories	2,800	3,200	4,300
Prepaid expenses	0	0	0
Net fixed assets[1]	1,200	1,300	1,450
Total assets	**$7,330**	**$7,950**	**$10,250**
Short-term debt	$ 300	$ 500	$ 1,900
Accounts payable	1,400	1,600	2,050
Accrued expenses	200	260	350
Long-term debt	1,300	1,200	1,100
Owners' equity	4,130	4,390	4,850
Total liabilities and owners' equity	**$7,330**	**$7,950**	**$10,250**

[1]The company did not sell any fixed assets in Years 2 and 3.

a. Compute Sentec Inc.'s working capital requirement (WCR) and prepare its managerial balance sheets at Year-end 1, Year-end 2, and Year-end 3.
b. Compute Sentec's operating margin, invested capital turnover, return on capital employed, financial cost ratio, financial structure ratio, and the tax effect in Year 1, Year 2, and Year 3. What is the relationship between these ratios and Sentec's return on equity (ROE) over the three-year period?
c. What accounts for the change in the firm's ROE over the three-year period?
d. In Year 3, firms in the same business sector as Sentec Inc. had an average collection period of thirty days, an average payment period of thirty-three days, and an inventory turnover of eight days. Suppose Sentec Inc. had managed its operating cycle like the average firm in the sector. What would its WCR, managerial balance sheet, operating margin, invested capital turnover, return on capital employed, financial cost ratio, financial structure ratio, and the tax effect have been in Year 3? Its ROE? *Assume a ratio of interest expense to earnings before interest and tax of 4 percent, and an effective tax rate of 40 percent.*

9. **Seasonal business.**
Mars Electronics is distributor for the Global Electric Company (GEC), a large manufacturer of electrical and electronics products for consumer and institutional markets. On the next page are the semiannual financial statements of the company for the last year and a half.

a. Prepare Mars Electronics' managerial balance sheet on June 30, 2009, December 31, 2009, and June 30, 2010.
b. What was the structure of the return on equity (ROE) of Mars Electronics for the six months ending June 30, 2009, December 31, 2009, and June 30, 2010?
c. What accounts for the changes in the firm's ROE?

Income Statements (in thousands)			
	Six Months to June 30, 2009	Six Months to December 31, 2009	Six Months to June 30, 2010
Net sales	$10,655	$13,851	$11,720
Cost of goods sold	8,940	11,671	9,834
Selling, general, and administrative expenses	1,554	1,925	1,677
Depreciation expense	44	55	76
Interest expense	62	90	70
Tax expense	23	44	26
Earnings after tax	$ 32	$ 66	$ 37
Dividends	$ 5	$ 44	$ 1

Balance Sheets (in thousands)			
	June 30, 2009	December 31, 2009	June 30, 2010
Cash	$ 160	$ 60	$ 70
Accounts receivable	1,953	2,616	2,100
Inventories	1,986	2,694	2,085
Prepaid expenses	80	42	25
Net fixed assets[1]	733	818	830
Total assets	$4,912	$6,230	$5,110
Short-term debt	$ 50	$ 880	$ 50
Accounts payable	1,450	1,950	1,650
Accrued expenses	98	114	138
Long-term debt	800	750	700
Owners' equity	2,514	2,536	2,572
Total liabilities and owners' equity	$4,912	$6,230	$5,110

[1]The firm did not sell any fixed assets over the three-year period.

10. **Self-sustainable growth rate.**
Ambersome Inc. has decided against borrowing and to have all its assets financed by equity. Furthermore, it intends to keep its payout ratio at 40 percent. Its assets turnover ratio is 0.9, its profit margin (defined as earnings before interest and tax divided by sales) is 8 percent, and profits are taxed at 40 percent. The firm's target growth rate in sales is 5 percent.

    a. Is the target growth rate consistent with the firm's financing policy?
    b. If not, how much does it need to increase the assets turnover ratio or profit margin to meet the target growth rate?
    c. Suppose the firm can borrow at 10 percent. Would borrowing help it meet the target growth rate?

CHAPTER 6
USING THE NET PRESENT VALUE RULE TO MAKE VALUE-CREATING INVESTMENT DECISIONS

One of the most important decisions a manager can make is the capital investment decision. This key decision requires spending cash now to acquire long-lived assets that will be a source of cash flows in the future. A successful capital investment program will contribute positively to the firm's financial performance for many years. The firm's managers will be commended for their skills in identifying potentially successful projects and carrying them to fruition (we use the terms *project, investment*, and *proposal* interchangeably). If the capital investment program fails, the firm's performance may be affected negatively for years. Moreover, the firm's suppliers of funds—the shareholders and creditors—could lose confidence in the ability of the firm's managers to make good investment decisions and may become reluctant to provide additional funds in the future.

What is a good investment decision? From a financial management perspective, *a good investment decision is a decision that raises the current market value of the firm's equity, thereby creating value for the firm's owners*. An investment decision can have other objectives, but managers who ignore the value-creation objective may jeopardize both the future of their firms and their employment prospects. The value-creating investment decision must raise *market* value, not *book* value or accounting profit. Shareholders cash in on their investment by selling their shares for cash, not for accounting profits.

Capital budgeting involves comparing the amount of cash spent today on an investment with the cash inflows expected from it in the future. Because future cash flows are spread over time, they cannot be compared directly with cash spent today. Recall that a dollar received later is worth less than a dollar received earlier. One reason for this is that the firm can earn interest on earlier cash inflows. This preference for "early cash" is called the *time value of money*.

Discounting is the mechanism used to convert *future* cash flows into their equivalent value today. In other words, discounting adjusts future cash flows for the time value of money. For example, a riskless cash inflow of $1,100 available one year from now is worth $1,000 today, if the firm can earn 10 percent on cash deposited now in a risk-free savings account. (If a firm deposits $1,000 today in a bank that offers 10 percent, it will have $1,100 in one year.) The $1,000 is the *present value*, or *discounted value*, of the $1,100 of future cash inflow at a discount rate of 10 percent. This chapter shows how to calculate the discounted value of a cash flow occurring at any date in the future.

Apart from the timing issue, the risk associated with future cash flows is also an issue. Future cash flows are risky because of the probability that the cash flows realized in the future may not be the expected ones.

Decision models that consider both the time value of money and the risk of an investment's cash flows are called *discounted cash flow (DCF) models*. This chapter presents the net present value (NPV) model and briefly examines a useful variation, the profitability index (PI). Chapter 7 presents and compares other DCF and non-DCF models and concludes that the NPV approach to investment appraisal is superior to alternative methods.

There are two critical elements in a DCF valuation. One is the identification and measurement of the project's expected cash flows, and the other is the estimation of the appropriate discount rate required to calculate the project's present value. Chapter 8 is devoted entirely to the first issue, and Chapter 10 deals with the second. In this chapter, we assume that both the investment's expected cash-flow stream and its appropriate discount rate are known and show how to calculate the investment's NPV. We also explain what NPV measures and how it should be interpreted.

The valuation of a project is a critical element in the capital investment process, but it is not the only one. Thus, we review the major steps involved in a capital investment decision before we explain how to perform an NPV analysis. After reading this chapter, you should understand the following:

- The major steps involved in a capital budgeting decision
- How to calculate the present value of a stream of future cash flows
- The NPV rule and how to apply it to investment decisions
- Why a project's NPV is a measure of the value it creates
- How to use the NPV rule to choose among projects of different sizes or different useful lives
- How the flexibility of a project can be described with the help of managerial options

THE CAPITAL INVESTMENT PROCESS

The **capital investment decision**, also called the **capital budgeting decision** or **capital expenditure decision**, involves several steps that are summarized in Exhibit 6.1. The process is initiated when the firm *identifies* business opportunities that can be translated into potentially valuable investment proposals. This is arguably the most important step in the process. Management must foster a climate within the firm that is conducive to the generation of ideas and the uncovering of opportunities that could lead to successful long-term investments.

Identified investment proposals must then be *evaluated* financially. The inputs required for the financial evaluation of a project include (1) the estimation of its useful life; (2) the estimation of the cash flows the project is expected to generate

EXHIBIT 6.1 THE CAPITAL INVESTMENT PROCESS.

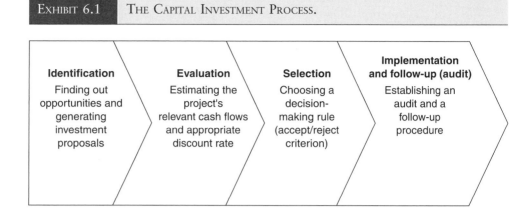

Identification	**Evaluation**	**Selection**	**Implementation and follow-up (audit)**
Finding out opportunities and generating investment proposals	Estimating the project's relevant cash flows and appropriate discount rate	Choosing a decision-making rule (accept/reject criterion)	Establishing an audit and a follow-up procedure
Type of investment	**Input**	**Decision rule**	**Performance evaluation**
• Required investment • Replacement investment • Expansion investment • Diversification investment	• Expected cash-flow stream • Discount rate	• Net present value • Profitability index • Internal rate of return • Payback period	• Monitor the magnitude and timing of cash flows • Check if the project still meets the selection criterion • Decide on continuation or abandonment • Review previous steps if failure rate is high

over that **useful life**; and (3) the appropriate **discount rate** required to calculate the present value of the project's expected cash-flow stream. Estimating the parameters required for the financial analysis of a proposed investment is not an easy task; these estimation procedures are explained in detail in Chapter 8 (cash flows) and Chapter 10 (appropriate discount rate).

Proposals are usually classified by how difficult it is to estimate the key parameters needed for financial evaluation. **Required investments** are those the firm must make to comply with safety, health, and environmental regulations. In this case, managers want to know whether the present value of the cash expenses needed to comply with the regulations is greater than the cost of closing down. If it is, the project should be abandoned. Estimating such expenses should not be too complicated because, in most cases, they are already specified by the regulatory authorities. **Replacement investments** are essentially cost-saving projects that do not generate extra cash inflows. Their future cash benefits (basically cash savings) consist of reductions in anticipated costs that managers can identify with relative ease. Financial evaluation for **expansion investments** is more challenging because these projects require the firm to estimate the additional sales revenues, margins, and working capital that the expansion is expected to generate. Finally, financial evaluation for **diversification investments** is usually the most difficult. The cash flows these proposals are expected to generate are probably the hardest to forecast because the firm will enter an industry it does not know as well as its own.

After the proposal's financial parameters have been estimated, an investment criterion should be applied to *decide* whether the proposal will be accepted or rejected. This chapter examines the **net present value (NPV) rule** in detail and the profitability index briefly. Chapter 7 looks at other popular selection criteria, such as the internal rate of return and the payback period, and discusses the profitability index in more detail.

Finally, accepted proposals must be *implemented*. But the capital investment process does not end at this point. Projects should be *audited* regularly throughout their lives. As projects are being carried out, the magnitude and the timing of their cash flows must be monitored to ascertain that they are in line with budgeted figures. If future cash flows fall short of expectation, the projects will obviously not be as profitable as anticipated. If the audit indicates that the expected remaining benefits of an existing investment are lower than the costs of terminating the investment, the firm should abandon it. The firm's owners will be better off without it than with it. Furthermore, managers should learn from the mistakes uncovered by the regular audits. This information can improve the firm's capital budgeting process by preventing it from repeating the same mistakes on future projects.

We now analyze a simple investment decision to illustrate how an investment's NPV is calculated and how it is used to decide whether to accept or reject an investment proposal.

WOULD YOU BUY THIS PARCEL OF LAND?

Suppose a parcel of land near where you live is on sale for $10,000. If the parcel is not sold today, it will be taken off the market. The parcel is an ideal location for a residential home. Unfortunately, the local authorities have so far refused to allow any construction on it. But you have just learned that they will reverse their decision in the coming year. If you purchase the parcel of land now, you expect to be able to sell it for $10,500 next year when a building permit will be available. The sequence of the two cash flows is shown in Exhibit 6.2, where the cash *outflow* is represented by a descending arrow and the cash *inflow* by an ascending arrow. Given the pattern of cash flows in Exhibit 6.2, you can easily calculate your expected return on investment. It is 5 percent, an expected gain of $500 on an investment of $10,000.

Suppose today is your lucky day and you have just received notification that you have inherited exactly $10,000, available immediately. Should you purchase the parcel of land? Before you can answer this question, you need additional information. One valuable piece of information is the highest return you can earn on a *comparable* investment. Clearly, if you can earn *more* than 5 percent on a truly comparable or **alternative investment**, you should not buy the land.

THE ALTERNATIVE INVESTMENT

The alternative investment and the one under consideration must be compared to see whether they share the same attributes. The most important attribute is **risk**. The parcel of land is a risky investment because you do not know for certain that it will sell for $10,500 next year. Some probability exists that it will sell for more or less than its expected future price. The higher the probability that actual cash

EXHIBIT 6.2 TIME LINE FOR THE PARCEL OF LAND.

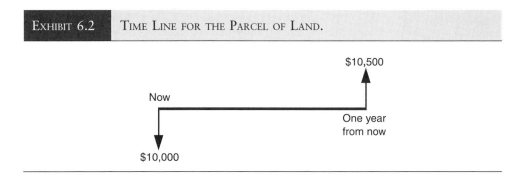

flows will deviate from their expected values, the higher the risk of the expected cash-flow stream. The alternative investment must have the same risk characteristics as the parcel of land. In financial terminology, they should both belong to the same **risk class**.

Another relevant investment characteristic is the *tax treatment* of the investment's expected gains. It must be the same for the two investments because investors are interested only in their *after-tax* return on investment. For the time being and for the sake of simplicity, we assume that you live in a country that does not tax investment income. Thus, the alternative investment has the same tax treatment as the land.

The *liquidity* of the investment, that is, the ability to sell it rapidly at its current market price, is still another investment attribute that might be considered when identifying investments that are similar to the parcel of land. Risk and taxes, however, are the most important characteristics the two investments must share.

THE OPPORTUNITY COST OF CAPITAL

To estimate the rate of return on an alternative investment in the same risk class as the parcel of land, we should look at the return on comparable parcels of land in the market. To simplify the analysis at this stage, we assume that the proposed investment is *riskless* to you. If you sell the land next year for less than $10,500, we will pay you the difference; if you sell it for more than $10,500, you will give us the difference. This deal assures you that you will get $10,500 regardless of the market price of the parcel of land next year. Because the project is now riskless, the alternative investment is the deposit of the inherited $10,000 in a savings account that is government-insured, which is currently offering a 3 percent return. This is the expected return from any project that is riskless. This is also the return that you will give up if you buy the land, so it is called the **project's opportunity cost of capital**, or simply, the **project's cost of capital**. You can think of a project's cost of capital as the interest rate you would pay if you borrowed the $10,000 to buy the land. The project being riskless, you should be able to borrow the $10,000 at 3 percent. In other words, *the project's discount rate is the cost of financing the project.*

Now, should you purchase the parcel of land? The answer is yes because the 5 percent you will earn on the land exceeds the 3 percent you will earn on the savings account. Put differently, you should buy the land because the 5 percent you will earn on that investment exceeds the 3 percent cost of financing it (the opportunity cost of capital).

Comparing a project's return with the return offered by an alternative investment is a simple and straightforward approach to investment analysis. Although this approach works well for one-period projects (such as the parcel of land), we show in Chapter 7 that it may sometimes fail when the project has cash flows spread over several periods. There is, however, another approach to evaluating projects that can deal with any pattern of cash flows: it is the NPV rule explained below.

THE NET PRESENT VALUE RULE

The approach to investment analysis in the previous section compares the rates of return for two investments—the parcel of land and the savings account. An alternative approach is to compare the $10,000 payable *now* to acquire the land with the dollar amount that would have to be invested *now* in the savings account to have $10,500 one year from now. This comparison is the foundation of the NPV rule. It is explained first for a one-period investment.[1]

A ONE-PERIOD INVESTMENT

How much should you invest now in a savings account with a 3 percent interest rate if you want to receive $10,500 in one year? The answer is $10,194. If you invest $10,194 now at 3 percent, in one year you will have $10,500, the sum of your initial deposit ($10,194) and the interest earned on it in one year ($306):

$$\$10{,}194 + [\$10{,}194 \times 3\%] = \$10{,}194 + \$306 = \$10{,}500$$

The left side of the above equation can be rewritten as follows:

$$\$10{,}194 + [\$10{,}194 \times 3\%] = \$10{,}194 \times [1 + 0.03] = \$10{,}500$$

The $10,500 you will receive in one year is called the **future value**, or **compounded value**, of $10,194 at 3 percent for one year. The term (1 + 0.03) is called the one-year **compound factor** at 3 percent. It is equal to 1.03 (1 plus the 3 percent interest rate).

How did we find the $10,194 in the first place? We simply divided the future cash flow of $10,500 by (1 + 0.03), the one-year compound factor:

$$\frac{\$10{,}500}{(1 + 0.03)} = \$10{,}194$$

The left side of the above equation can be rewritten as follows:

$$\$10{,}500 \times \frac{1}{(1 + 0.03)} = \$10{,}500 \times 0.9709 = \$10{,}194$$

The $10,194 you should invest now in the savings account is called the **discounted value**, or **present value (PV)**, of $10,500 at 3 percent for one year. The term $\frac{1}{(1 + 0.03)}$ is called the one-year **discount factor (DF)** at 3 percent. It is equal to 0.9709, the present value, at a 3 percent discount rate, of $1 to be received in one year. In other words,

[1] The period could be of any duration. In this instance, we assume a period of one year.

\$1 in one year is worth approximately \$0.97 today, if the discount rate is 3 percent. **Discounting** has "shrunk" the dollar by roughly 3 percent.

As you may have already noticed, the discount factor is the *inverse* of the compound factor, and discounting is the *reverse* of **compounding**. Compounding provides the future cash flow (\$10,500) if you know the present one (\$10,194) and discounting provides the present cash flow (\$10,194) if you know the future one (\$10,500). In other words, at 3 percent you should be *indifferent* whether you receive \$10,194 now or \$10,500 in one year. *At that rate, the two cash flows are equivalent.*

Let's return to the comparison between the parcel of land and the savings account. The parcel of land costs \$10,000 and generates \$10,500 in one year. The savings account requires a deposit of \$10,194 to generate \$10,500 in one year. Which one do you prefer? Obviously, you would prefer the parcel of land because both investments generate the same cash inflows in one year, but the parcel of land requires a smaller initial investment.

The difference between \$10,194 (the present value at 3 percent of the \$10,500 future cash flow the land will generate in one year) and the initial cash outlay of \$10,000 (the cost of the land) is called the net present value (NPV) of the parcel of land. It is usually presented as follows:

NPV(Land) = –[Initial cash outlay] + [Present value of the future cash flows at the cost of capital]

NPV(Land at 3%) = –[\$10,000] + [\$10,194] = \$194

The NPV is positive, so you should purchase the parcel of land. The present *value* of its future cash inflow is higher than its present *cost*. If the NPV had been negative, you would have invested in the savings account. In general, *an investment should be accepted if its NPV is positive and should be rejected if its NPV is negative.* This is the net present value rule. If the NPV had been zero, you would be indifferent between buying the parcel of land and depositing your money in the savings account.

In Exhibit 6.3, CF_0 designates the initial cash outlay (the cash flow at time zero) and CF_1 designates the cash flow at the end of a one-period project (the cash flow at time one). If k is the opportunity cost of capital, then the NPV of a one-period investment can be written as follows:

$$\text{NPV(Investment)} = -CF_0 + \left[CF_1 \times \frac{1}{(1+k)^1}\right] = -CF_0 + [CF_1 \times DF_1]$$

where $DF_1 = \frac{1}{(1+k)^1}$ is the one-year discount factor at cost of capital k. For the land project, we have

$$\begin{aligned}\text{NPV(Land at 3\%)} &= -\$10{,}000 + [\$10{,}500 \times DF_1] \\ &= -\$10{,}000 + \left[\$10{,}500 \times \frac{1}{(1+0.03)^1}\right] \\ &= -\$10{,}000 + [\$10{,}500 \times 0.9709] \\ &= -\$10{,}000 + \$10{,}194 = \$194\end{aligned}$$

EXHIBIT 6.3 TIME LINE FOR A ONE-PERIOD INVESTMENT.

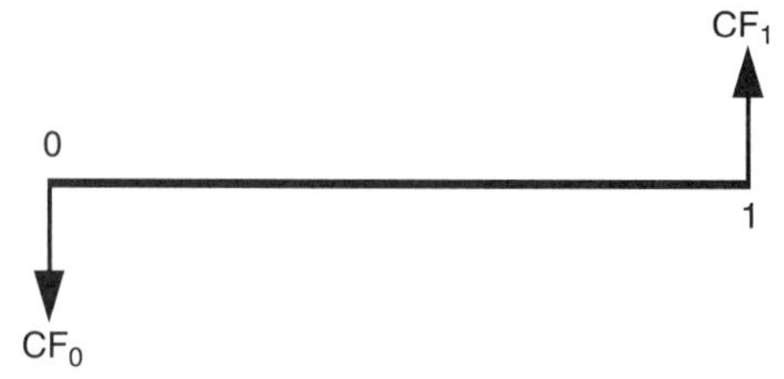

A TWO-PERIOD INVESTMENT WITHOUT AN INTERMEDIATE CASH FLOW

Suppose you will receive the future cash flow of $10,500 for the parcel of land not in one year but in two years, all else unchanged. The sequence of cash flows now looks like the one in Exhibit 6.4. Should you still buy the parcel of land? Before you decide, you need to consider the **time value of money**: $10,500 in two years is not as valuable as $10,500 in one year. How much would you have to invest now in the 3 percent savings account to receive $10,500 two years from now? In other words, what is the present value of a parcel of land that will yield $10,500 in two years if your opportunity cost of capital is 3 percent? It is $9,897 because $9,897 invested at 3 percent per year will produce $10,500 in two years. In one year, the $9,897 will grow to $9,897 × (1 + 0.03). This amount will in turn grow by (1 + 0.03) during the second year. We can write the following equation:

$$[\$9{,}897 \times (1 + 0.03)] \times (1 + 0.03) = \$9{,}897 \times (1 + 0.03)^2$$
$$= \$9{,}897 \times 1.0609 = \$10{,}500$$

where $(1 + 0.03)^2$, which is equal to 1.0609, is the two-year compound factor at 3 percent. The $9,897 present value is found by simply discounting the future value of $10,500 twice at 3 percent, that is:

$$\text{PV}(\$10{,}500 \text{ at } 3\%) = \$10{,}500 \times \frac{1}{(1 + 0.03)(1 + 0.03)}$$
$$= \$10{,}500 \times \frac{1}{(1 + 0.03)^2}$$
$$= \$10{,}500 \times 0.9426 = \$9{,}897$$

where 0.9426 is the two-year discount factor at 3 percent, that is:

$$\text{DF}_2 = \frac{1}{(1 + 0.03)^2} = 0.9426$$

You have to invest only $9,897 in the savings account now to receive $10,500 in two years, whereas you have to invest $10,000 in the parcel of land to receive the same amount at the same date. The savings account is clearly the better investment because it requires a smaller initial cash outlay to generate the same payoff in two years.

EXHIBIT 6.4 TIME LINE FOR THE TWO-PERIOD INVESTMENT, NO INTERMEDIATE CASH FLOW.

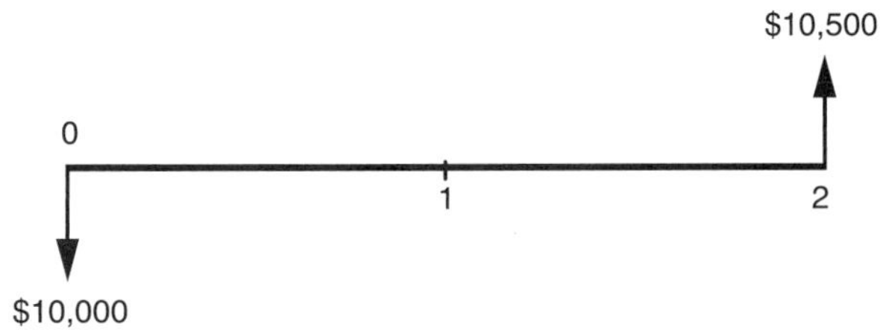

Now, consider the NPV of the land for this case. We have the following:

$$\begin{aligned} \text{NPV(Land at 3\%)} &= -\text{Initial cash outlay} + \text{Present value of \$10,500 at 3\%} \\ &= -\$10{,}000 + \$9{,}897 = -\$103 \end{aligned}$$

The NPV is negative, so the previous NPV rule is still valid: accept a project if its NPV is positive, and reject it if its NPV is negative.

A TWO-PERIOD INVESTMENT WITH AN INTERMEDIATE CASH FLOW

Given the two-year land investment in the previous section, suppose you could rent out the parcel of land during the two years. The land is fertile and you should be able to rent it to a vegetable gardener or farmer for, say, $1,000 per year, payable at the end of each year. The cash-flow profile of the investment in the parcel of land now looks like the one in Exhibit 6.5. The investment requires an initial cash outlay (CF_0) of $10,000, yields a first-year cash flow (CF_1) of $1,000, and a terminal cash flow (CF_2) of $11,500, the sum of the second-year $1,000 rent and the $10,500 resale value of the land. Should you purchase the parcel of land in this case? The present value (PV) of the land's future cash-flow stream ($CF_1 = \$1{,}000$ and $CF_2 = \$11{,}500$) at a cost of capital of 3 percent is as follows:

$$\begin{aligned} PV(CF_1, CF_2 \text{ at } 3\%) &= [CF_1 \times DF_1] + [CF_2 \times DF_2] \\ &= [\$1{,}000 \times 0.9709] + [\$11{,}500 \times 0.9426] \\ &= \$971 + \$10{,}840 = \$11{,}811 \end{aligned}$$

where $DF_1 = 0.9709$ is the one-year discount factor at 3 percent and $DF_2 = 0.9426$ is the two-year discount factor at 3 percent. The present value of the land's future cash-flow stream ($11,811) is greater than its cost ($10,000), so you should purchase the land. The NPV of the parcel of land is the difference between $11,811 and $10,000:

$$\text{NPV(Land)} = -\$10{,}000 + \$11{,}811 = \$1{,}811$$

The NPV is positive, indicating that the investment should be accepted. The NPV rule continues to hold: accept a project when its NPV is positive, and reject it when its NPV is negative.

EXHIBIT 6.5 TIME LINE FOR THE TWO-PERIOD INVESTMENT WITH AN INTERMEDIATE CASH FLOW.

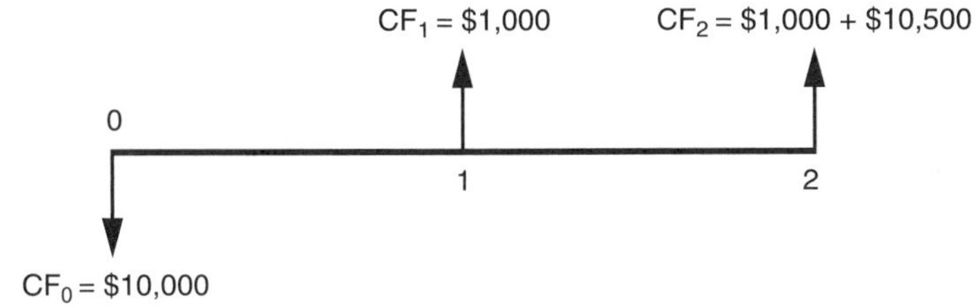

MULTIPLE-PERIOD INVESTMENTS

The analysis of the two-period investment case can be extended easily to a multiple-period investment with any number of intermediate cash flows. The longer the duration of the expected cash-flow stream, the longer the calculation, but the NPV approach still works. A business investment project can always be reduced to a stream of expected periodic cash flows, so the NPV rule can be applied directly to the analysis of any capital expenditure.

Let's call CF_t the expected cash flow at the end of year t from an investment project that requires an initial cash outlay CF_0. Assume that the investment will generate a stream of cash flows for a duration of N years. The cash-flow profile of the investment would now look like the one in Exhibit 6.6. As before, the NPV of the investment is the difference between the present value of its expected cash-flow stream and the investment's initial cash outlay. The present value, $PV(CF_t)$, of a cash flow occurring at time t, at cost of capital k, is as follows:

$$PV(CF_t) = CF_t \times \frac{1}{(1+k)^t} = CF_t \times DF_t$$

where $DF_t = \frac{1}{(1+k)^t}$ is the t-period discount factor at cost of capital k. DF_t is the present value at cost of capital k of *one* dollar of cash flow occurring at time t. It follows that the present value of CF_t dollars of cash flow must be equal to CF_t multiplied by DF_t.

We can express the NPV of an investment with a cash-flow stream lasting for N years and a cost of capital k as follows:

$$\begin{aligned} NPV(k, N) &= -CF_0 + [CF_1 \times DF_1] + [CF_2 \times DF_2] + \cdots \\ &\quad + [CF_t \times DF_t] + \cdots + [CF_N \times DF_N] \end{aligned}$$

The previous decision rule still holds: *an investment should be undertaken if its NPV is positive and should be rejected if its NPV is negative.* If the NPV is zero, you should be indifferent about accepting or rejecting the investment,

EXHIBIT 6.6 TIME LINE FOR A MULTIPLE-PERIOD INVESTMENT.

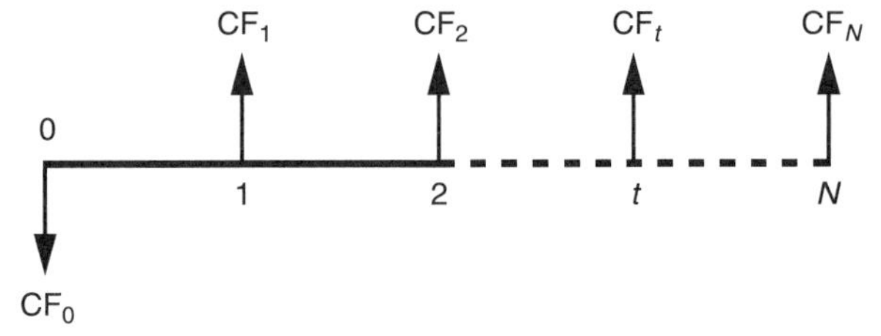

Replacing DF_1 with $\frac{1}{(1+k)^1}$, DF_2 with $\frac{1}{(1+k)^2}$, DF_t with $\frac{1}{(1+k)^t}$, and DF_N with $\frac{1}{(1+k)^N}$ in the above equation, we have another familiar expression for net present value:

$$NPV(k, N) = -CF_0 + \frac{CF_1}{(1+k)^1} + \frac{CF_2}{(1+k)^2} + \cdots + \frac{CF_t}{(1+k)^t} + \cdots + \frac{CF_N}{(1+k)^N}$$

This equation can be written as follows:

$$NPV(k, N) = -CF_0 + \sum_{t=1}^{N} \frac{CF_t}{(1+k)^t}$$

where $\sum_{t=1}^{N} \frac{CF_t}{(1+k)^t}$ means "take the sum of the terms $\frac{CF_t}{(1+k)^t}$ from t equals 1 to t equals N."

APPLYING THE NET PRESENT VALUE RULE TO A CAPITAL INVESTMENT DECISION

Applying the NPV rule to a capital expenditure decision is a straightforward exercise *assuming that all the relevant inputs have been estimated.* These inputs are the stream of cash flows that the project is expected to generate over its anticipated useful life and the cost of capital applicable to the investment under consideration. After these inputs are estimated, the present value of the project's stream of expected cash flows is calculated by discounting the cash flows at the project's cost of capital. Then, the project's initial cash outlay is subtracted from this present value to find the project's NPV. If the NPV is positive, the project is accepted; if the NPV is negative, the project is rejected. We use an example to explain the procedure.

Sunlight Manufacturing Company (SMC) has been successfully producing and selling various types of electrical equipment for the last twenty years and is considering adding a new product, a designer desk lamp, to its existing product line. The firm would have to spend $2,360,000 now to launch the new product, which is expected to be obsolete after five years. The investment is expected to generate an annual net cash flow of \$832,000 at the end of its first year, \$822,000 at the end of its second year, \$692,000 at the end of its third year, \$554,000 at the end of its fourth year, and a terminal net cash flow of \$466,000 at the end of its fifth year. The terminal cash flow includes the estimated resale value of any equipment used to manufacture the product, net of any liquidation cost. The project's estimated cost of capital is 7.6 percent. Should SMC launch the new product? To answer this question, we need to find the project's NPV.

First, the present value of each expected cash flow is calculated by multiplying it by its corresponding discount factor at the cost of capital of 7.6 percent (see Exhibit 6.7, Part I). Then, the initial cash outlay of \$2,360,000 is subtracted from the total present value of the project's expected cash-flow stream to obtain the project's NPV:

$$\text{NPV(New product at 7.6\%)} = -\$2{,}360{,}000 + \$2{,}775{,}083 = \$415{,}083$$

The project's NPV is positive, so SMC should launch the designer desk lamp.

As you may have already noticed, the computation of NPVs for multiple-period projects can be tedious. Fortunately, computer-based spreadsheets can make the task of computing NPVs quite easy. We show in Part II of Exhibit 6.7 how Microsoft Excel™ can be used to compute the NPV of the designer desk-lamp project. Commands are similar for other types of spreadsheet programs. Note also that most electronic financial calculators have several financial functions, including an NPV function. To use this function, simply enter the cash-flow values starting with the initial cash outlay and ending with last period cash flow. Then, enter the investment's cost of capital and press the NPV key. The calculator will compute the present value of the expected cash-flow stream and provide the project's NPV. You can also calculate NPV using the present value table that is inside the front cover of the book. This table shows the present value of \$1 paid or received at the end of any period up to twenty periods and at discount rates ranging from 1 to 20 percent. A far more complex and challenging task is the estimation of the inputs required to perform this calculation, namely, the project's expected cash-flow stream and its corresponding cost of capital. These issues are addressed in Chapters 8 and 10, respectively.

WHY THE NPV RULE IS A GOOD INVESTMENT RULE

The NPV rule is a desirable investment decision rule because, as discussed in this section, it has the following properties:

1. It is a measure of value creation: when the project's NPV is positive, the project creates value, and when it is negative, the project destroys value
2. It adjusts for the timing of the project's expected cash flows
3. It adjusts for the risk of the project's expected cash flows
4. It is additive

The first three properties are essential for any selection criterion used to decide whether to accept or reject a capital investment. In Chapter 7, the comparisons of the NPV rule to alternative selection criteria are based on these important properties.

EXHIBIT 6.7 CALCULATION OF PRESENT VALUES FOR THE SMC DESIGNER DESK-LAMP PROJECT.

Part I Using a calculator

Present value of CF_1	=	$\$832,000 \times \frac{1}{(1+0.076)^1}$	=	$832,000 × 0.92937	=	$773,234
Present value of CF_2	=	$822,000 \times \frac{1}{(1+0.076)^2}$	=	822,000 × 0.86372	=	709,978
Present value of CF_3	=	$692,000 \times \frac{1}{(1+0.076)^3}$	=	692,000 × 0.80272	=	555,483
Present value of CF_4	=	$554,000 \times \frac{1}{(1+0.076)^4}$	=	554,000 × 0.74602	=	413,296
Present value of CF_5	=	$466,000 \times \frac{1}{(1+0.076)^5}$	=	466,000 × 0.69333	=	323,092
Total present values at 7.6%						**$2,775,083**
Initial cash outlay						–$2,360,000
Net present value					=	**$415,083**

Part II Using a spreadsheet

	A	B	C	D	E	F	G
1	Time line	Now	End-of-year 1	End-of-year 2	End-of-year 3	End-of-year 4	End-of-year 5
2	Cash flows	–$2,360,000	$832,000	$822,000	$692,000	$554,000	$466,000
3							
4	Cost of capital	7.60%					
5							
6	Present value of cash inflows	$2,775,083					
7							
8	**Net present value**	**$415,083**					
9							
10	*The formula in cell B6 is =NPV(B4,C2:G2).*						
11	*Note that the formula in cell B6 is identified as NPV even though the formula provides the present value of the future cash-flow stream and not its NPV.*						
12	*The formula in cell B8 is =B2+B6.*						
13	*The cost of capital can be shown in absolute value or in percentage value.*						
14							

The additive property of the NPV rule simply means that if one project has an NPV of $100,000 and another an NPV of $50,000, then the two projects, taken together, have a combined NPV of $150,000, assuming that the two projects are independent. This property has several useful implications.

NPV Is a Measure of Value Creation

At the beginning of this chapter, we define a good investment decision as one that increases the market value of the firm's equity. Would a positive NPV project be one?

Consider again the one-period real estate investment example. Recall that the initial cash outlay is $10,000 and that the present value of its expected cash inflow of $10,500 is $10,194 at 3 percent. Suppose you make the investment and, as soon as you have done so, an interested investor wants to purchase the parcel of land from you.

What *minimum* price should you quote? You should not accept any price less than $10,194. If you sell it for less, say $10,100, the best alternative investment available is to put the $10,100 in a savings account. After a year, you will have $10,403 ($10,100 plus 3 percent of $10,100 or $303). This is less than the $10,500 you will receive in a year from your parcel of land. Clearly, you would not want to sell the land for less than $10,194.

What is the *maximum* price the interested investor would be willing to pay for the parcel of land? The maximum price for the investor is also $10,194. This is the amount the investor would have to spend now on the alternative investment (the savings account) to have an amount in a year equal to the return on the land. At a higher purchase price, the investor will be "poorer" than if the money was put in the alternative investment.

If there is a price that both you and the interested investor can agree on, it is indeed $10,194. This would also be the price at which your new property would be sold to any other buyer in an active real estate market. Thus, $10,194 is the *market value* of the parcel of land. In other words, its present value is also its market value. By extension, this is also true for any capital investment. In fact, *the present value of a project's expected cash-flow stream at its cost of capital is an estimate of how much the project would sell for if a market existed for it.* In other words, the market value of any investment is determined by the present value of the cash flows that it is expected to generate in the future.

The parcel of land you bought for only $10,000 has a market value of $10,194. Thus, your wealth has increased by $194 ($10,194 less $10,000). This is exactly the same as the NPV of the investment. By extension, the *NPV of an investment project represents the immediate change in the wealth of the firm's owners if the project is accepted.* If positive, the project creates value for the firm's owners; if negative, it destroys value. From the perspective of owners, a decision to invest in a positive NPV project is clearly a good investment decision. It increases the owner's current wealth.

Although a project with a positive NPV is expected to create value, NPV does not provide any indication about the source of value creation. Firms can generate positive NPV projects and create value for the firm's owners for many reasons. The firm may have creative managers supported by a superior workforce. It may hold a strong position in a product or service market that makes it difficult for new entrants to compete on an equal footing. More important, some projects cannot be easily replicated by competitors, either because they require expertise that is specific to the firm or because they are protected by patents. For these reasons, a firm may be able to generate cash flows from some of its investments that have present values higher than the cost of investing in these projects.

NPV ADJUSTS FOR THE TIMING OF THE PROJECT'S CASH FLOWS

A good investment decision must take into consideration the timing of the investment's expected cash flows. Does the NPV rule do this? A project's NPV is the difference between the present value of its expected cash flows and its current cost. The present values of these cash flows are obtained by discounting each of them at the project's opportunity cost of capital. The more distant the cash flows, the lower their contribution to the investment's present value because the discount factor, $\frac{1}{(1+k)^t}$, by which the cash flows are multiplied in the net present value formula, becomes smaller as t increases. Thus, the NPV rule adjusts for the timing of a project's expected cash flows through the discount factors.

To illustrate, consider two five-year investments, A and B. Both require an initial cash outlay of $1 million and have a cost of capital of 10 percent. The cash flows expected from the two investments are shown in Exhibit 6.8.

Assume that the investments are **mutually exclusive**, meaning that if one is chosen, the other must be turned down. (An example is the choice between building either a bridge or a tunnel to allow traffic to cross a river.) A firm confronted with this choice should prefer to invest in project A because it would receive cash faster than if it invested in project B. Does the NPV rule lead to the same selection? To find out, compute the present values of the two investments' expected cash flows, as shown in Exhibit 6.9A. The initial cash outflow is $1 million in both cases. Thus, the NPV of the two projects are:

$$\text{NPV(A at 10\%)} = -\$1{,}000{,}000 + \$1{,}722{,}361 = \$722{,}361$$

$$\text{NPV(B at 10\%)} = -\$1{,}000{,}000 + \$1{,}463{,}269 = \$463{,}269$$

Both investments are worth undertaking because both have a positive NPV. However, the NPV of investment A is larger than the NPV of investment B. In other words, the NPV rule favors the investment with the faster cash return.

Exhibit 6.9B shows the calculations using a spreadsheet.

EXHIBIT 6.8 CASH FLOWS FOR TWO INVESTMENTS WITH CF_0 = $1 MILLION AND K = 10%.

End-of-Year	Investment A	Investment B
1	CF_1 = $800,000	CF_1 = $100,000
2	CF_2 = 600,000	CF_2 = 200,000
3	CF_3 = 400,000	CF_3 = 400,000
4	CF_4 = 200,000	CF_4 = 600,000
5	CF_5 = 100,000	CF_5 = 800,000
Total cash flows	**$2,100,000**	**$2,100,000**

EXHIBIT 6.9A PRESENT VALUE OF CASH FLOWS FOR TWO INVESTMENTS USING A CALCULATOR.

FIGURES FROM EXHIBIT 6.8

End-of-Year			Investment A Opportunity Cost of Capital = 10%		
1	PV($800,000)	=	$800,000 × 0.9091	=	$727,273
2	PV($600,000)	=	600,000 × 0.8264	=	495,868
3	PV($400,000)	=	400,000 × 0.7513	=	300,526
4	PV($200,000)	=	200,000 × 0.6830	=	136,602
5	PV($100,000)	=	100,000 × 0.6209	=	62,092
Total present values					**$1,722,361**[1]
Initial cash outlay					–$1,000,000
Net present value					**$722,361**

End-of-Year			Investment B Opportunity Cost of Capital = 10%		
1	PV($100,000)	=	$100,000 × 0.9091	=	$90,909
2	PV($200,000)	=	200,000 × 0.8264	=	165,289
3	PV($400,000)	=	400,000 × 0.7513	=	300,526
4	PV($600,000)	=	600,000 × 0.6830	=	409,808
5	PV($800,000)	=	800,000 × 0.6209	=	496,737
Total present values					**$1,463,269**
Initial cash outlay					–$1,000,000
Net present value					**$463,269**

[1]The present values do not add up exactly to the amount shown because of rounding errors in the discount factors.

NPV ADJUSTS FOR THE RISK OF THE PROJECT'S CASH FLOWS

Does the NPV rule consider the risk of a project? It certainly does. *The risk adjustment is made through the project's discount rate.* As the risk of the stream of future cash flows expected from the investment increases, the discount rate (the opportunity cost of capital) used to calculate the present value of the expected cash-flow stream should also increase. The reason is that investors are **risk averse**. They buy shares of firms with riskier projects only if they expect to earn a higher return to compensate them for the higher risk they have to bear.[2] By

[2]The relationship between the returns investors will require and the risk they are willing to bear is discussed in Chapter 10.

EXHIBIT 6.9B PRESENT VALUE OF CASH FLOWS FOR TWO INVESTMENTS USING A SPREADSHEET.

FIGURES FROM EXHIBIT 6.8

Investment A
Opportunity Cost of Capital = 10%

	A	B	C	D	E	F	G
1		Now	End-of-year 1	End-of-year 2	End-of-year 3	End-of-year 4	End-of-year 5
2	Cash flows	–$1,000,000	$800,000	$600,000	$400,000	$200,000	$100,000
3							
4	Cost of capital	10.00%					
5							
6	**Net present value**	**$722,361**					
7							
8	*The formula in cell B6 is =B2+NPV(B4,C2:G2).*						
9							

Investment B
Opportunity Cost of Capital = 10%

	A	B	C	D	E	F	G
1		Now	End-of-year 1	End-of-year 2	End-of-year 3	End-of-year 4	End-of-year 5
2	Cash flows	–$1,000,000	$100,000	$200,000	$400,000	$600,000	$800,000
3							
4	Cost of capital	10.00%					
5							
6	**Net present value**	**$463,269**					
7							
8	*The formula in cell B6 is =B2+NPV(B4,C2:G2).*						
9							

discounting the future stream of expected cash flows at a rate that increases with risk, the NPV rule adjusts not only for the time value of money but also for the project's risk—that is, the riskier the project, the higher the discount rate and the lower the NPV. In other words, the riskier the project the less valuable it is.

EXHIBIT 6.10 CASH FLOWS FOR TWO INVESTMENTS WITH CF_0 = \$1 MILLION; $K = 8\%$ FOR INVESTMENT C AND $K = 12\%$ FOR INVESTMENT D.

End-of-Year	Investment C	Investment D
1	CF_1 = \$300,000	CF_1 = \$300,000
2	CF_2 = 300,000	CF_2 = 300,000
3	CF_3 = 300,000	CF_3 = 300,000
4	CF_4 = 300,000	CF_4 = 300,000
5	CF_5 = 300,000	CF_5 = 300,000
Total cash flows	**\$1,500,000**	**\$1,500,000**

To illustrate, consider two five-year investments, C and D, both requiring the same initial cash outlay of \$1 million. Investment D is riskier than investment C. As a result, it has an opportunity cost of capital of 12 percent, whereas C has an opportunity cost of capital of only 8 percent. The two investments have the identical expected cash-flow streams shown in Exhibit 6.10.

Assume again that the investments are mutually exclusive; the firm can choose only one of the two. A manager making investment decisions on behalf of risk-averse investors should prefer investment C. Its expected cash flows are identical to those of investment D, but they are *less risky*. Does the NPV rule favor the same investment? To find out, compute the present values of the investments' expected cash flows, as shown in Exhibit 6.11, in Part I using a calculator and in Part II using a spreadsheet.

The initial cash outflow is \$1 million in both cases. Thus, the NPV of the two projects are:

$$\text{NPV(C at 8\%)} = -\$1{,}000{,}000 + \$1{,}197{,}813 = \$197{,}813$$

$$\text{NPV(D at 12\%)} = -\$1{,}000{,}000 + \$1{,}081{,}433 = \$81{,}433$$

The investment with the lower risk (investment C) has the larger NPV. In other words, the NPV rule favors the same investment as the one the firm would select. *The higher the risk attached to a project's stream of expected cash flows, the higher the opportunity cost of capital required to discount those cash flows, and the lower the project's NPV.* In other words, the NPV method adjusts for the risk of a project by raising the project's cost of capital to reflect the higher risk of the project's expected cash flows. The effect of this adjustment is to reduce the project's NPV, thus making it less attractive to the firm.

NPV IS ADDITIVE

The additive property of the NPV rule has practical implications for the capital expenditure decision. Consider again investments A and B presented earlier and assume now that they are no longer mutually exclusive; the firm can choose to

EXHIBIT 6.11 PRESENT VALUE OF CASH FLOWS FOR TWO INVESTMENTS.

FIGURES FROM EXHIBIT 6.10

Part I Using a calculator

End-of-Year			Investment C Opportunity Cost of Capital = 8%		
1	PV($300,000)	=	$300,000 × 0.92593	=	$277,779
2	PV($300,000)	=	300,000 × 0.85734	=	257,202
3	PV($300,000)	=	300,000 × 0.79383	=	238,149
4	PV($300,000)	=	300,000 × 0.73503	=	220,509
5	PV($300,000)	=	300,000 × 0.68058	=	204,174
Total present values					**$1,197,813**
Initial cash outlay					–$1,000,000
Net present value					**$197,813**

Part II Using a spreadsheet

	A	B	C	D	E	F	G
1		Now	End-of-year 1	End-of-year 2	End-of-year 3	End-of-year 4	End-of-year 5
2	Cash flows	–$1,000,000	$300,000	$300,000	$300,000	$300,000	$300,000
3							
4	Cost of capital	8.00%					
5							
6	**Net present value**	**$197,813**					
7							
8	*The formula in cell B6 is =B2+NPV(B4,C2:G2).*						
9							

invest in both projects. Because the NPV rule is additive, the value created by the two investments taken together is equal to the sum of their NPVs:[3]

$$\text{NPV}(A + B) = \text{NPV}(A) + \text{NPV}(B)$$

$$\text{NPV}(A + B) = \$722{,}361 + \$463{,}269 = \$1{,}185{,}630$$

[3]The implicit assumption is that the projects' expected cash-flow streams are independent of each other. Investing in one project will have no effect on the cash-flow stream of the other.

EXHIBIT 6.11 PRESENT VALUE OF CASH FLOWS FOR TWO INVESTMENTS. (*Continued*)

FIGURES FROM EXHIBIT 6.10

Part I Using a calculator

End-of-Year			**Investment D Opportunity Cost of Capital = 12%**		
1	PV($300,000)	=	$300,000 × 0.89286	=	$267,858
2	PV($300,000)	=	300,000 × 0.79719	=	239,157
3	PV($300,000)	=	300,000 × 0.71178	=	213,534
4	PV($300,000)	=	300,000 × 0.63552	=	190,655
5	PV($300,000)	=	300,000 × 0.56743	=	170,229
Total present values					**$1,081,433**
Initial cash outlay					–$1,000,000
Net present value					**$81,433**

Part II Using a spreadsheet

	A	B	C	D	E	F	G
1		Now	End-of-year 1	End-of-year 2	End-of-year 3	End-of-year 4	End-of-year 5
2	Cash flows	–$1,000,000	$300,000	$300,000	$300,000	$300,000	$300,000
3							
4	Cost of capital	12.00%					
5							
6	**Net present value**	**$81,433**					
7							
8	*The formula in cell B6 is =B2+NPV(B4,C2:G2).*						
9							

Thus, to find the NPV of investing in both projects, you do not need to calculate the sum of their combined cash flows, discount them at their cost of capital of 10 percent, and deduct the $2 million initial cash outlay required to launch the two projects. Adding their NPVs produces the same result. Together, the two projects should raise the market value of the firm's equity by an estimated $1,185,630.

The additive property has other useful implications. Suppose that the analysis of investment B overlooked a relevant and recurrent cost that would have reduced each annual cash flow by an estimated $50,000. To determine the investment's NPV with the corrected cash flows, simply calculate the present value of the future stream of "overlooked" cash outflows ($50,000 per year) and add it to the NPV of the original investment. Our calculator indicates the following:

$$\text{NPV}(-\$50{,}000 \text{ for 5 years at } 10\%) = -\$189{,}539$$

The corrected NPV is thus as follows:

$$\begin{aligned}\text{NPV(Corrected)} &= \text{NPV(Original)} + \text{NPV}(-\$50{,}000 \text{ sequence}) \\ &= \$463{,}269 - \$189{,}539 = \$273{,}730\end{aligned}$$

The NPV is still positive. The project remains attractive, but the magnitude of its NPV has been reduced by almost 41 percent to reflect the overlooked costs.

The additive property can also help the firm's managers determine the *change* in the value created by an investment if the risk of its expected cash-flow stream is suddenly revised upward or if the magnitude of its expected cash flows is revised downward. Suppose the risk of investment C, discussed earlier, is revised upward. The appropriate discount rate, which reflects the investment's higher risk, is no longer 8 percent but, say, 12 percent. The firm should expect the upward revision of the risk of investment C to reduce the market value of the firm's equity by $116,380, an amount equal to the NPV of the additional risk:

$$\begin{aligned}\text{NPV(Additional risk)} &= \text{NPV(C at } 12\%) - \text{NPV(C at } 8\%) \\ &= \$81{,}433 - \$197{,}813 = -\$116{,}380\end{aligned}$$

How much can the value of investment C be reduced because of overlooked future costs, initial cost overruns, or higher-than-expected levels of risk and *still earn its cost of capital*? For investment C to still earn its 8 percent cost of capital, its value can be reduced no more than $197,813, the NPV of the original investment. The upward revision of the project's risk (which resulted in an increase in the cost of capital to 12 percent) has already reduced the project's initial NPV by $116,380. If the present value of, say, additional overlooked costs exceeds $81,433 ($197,813 less $116,380), the project's NPV will become negative and will no longer earn its *new* opportunity cost of capital of 12 percent. In other words, an investment's positive NPV is a measure of value creation to the firm's owners *only if the project proceeds according to the budgeted figures*. From the firm's managers' perspective, a project's positive NPV is the maximum present value that they can afford to "lose" on the project (because of downward revision of the project's cash flows or upward revision of the project's risk) and still earn the project's cost of capital. Further "losses" will change the project's NPV to a negative value, and the investment will become a value-destroying proposition.

SPECIAL CASES OF CAPITAL BUDGETING

We have examined how the timing and the risk of expected cash flows affect the NPVs of investments with equal sizes and equal lives. However, projects usually have different sizes or different life spans. Further, a firm's investment budget may not be large enough to allow the firm to fund all its investment proposals that have a positive NPV. When these proposals vary greatly in size (measured by their initial cash outlay), managers have to decide which positive NPV project to accept and which to reject, a process called budgeting under **capital rationing**. Managers may

EXHIBIT 6.12 CASH FLOWS, PRESENT VALUES, AND NET PRESENT VALUES FOR THREE INVESTMENTS OF UNEQUAL SIZE WITH $K = 10\%$.

	Investment E	Investment F	Investment G
(1) Initial cash outlay (CF_0)	$1,000,000	$500,000	$500,000
Year-one cash flow (CF_1)	800,000	200,000	100,000
Year-two cash flow (CF_2)	500,000	510,000	700,000
(2) Present value of CF_1 and CF_2 at 10%	$1,140,496	$603,306	$669,421
Net present value = (2) minus (1)	**$140,496**	**$103,306**	**$169,421**

also have several choices for replacing an aging machine, with each possibility having a different expected useful life. The following sections show how to use the NPV method to select investments with different sizes or different life spans.

COMPARING PROJECTS OF UNEQUAL SIZE

Suppose a firm is considering the three investments described in Exhibit 6.12. According to the NPV rule, all three investments should be undertaken because they all have a positive NPV. This decision assumes that the three projects are not mutually exclusive and that the firm can raise the $2 million it needs to launch the three projects (the sum of their initial cash outlays).

What if the firm can raise only $1 million? In this case, the choice narrows down to either investing only in E or investing in both F and G. Investments F and G are clearly the superior choice because they have a value-creating potential of $272,727 (the sum of their NPVs) compared with only $140,496 for investment E. Thus, *if the total capital available for investment is limited, the firm cannot simply select the project with the highest NPV.*[4] It must first determine the combination of investments with the highest present value of future cash flows *per dollar of initial cash outlay*. This can be done by using the project's **profitability index**. An investment's profitability index is defined as the ratio of the present value of the investment's expected cash-flow stream to the investment's initial cash outlay. The profitability indexes of investments E, F, and G are shown in Exhibit 6.13.

An investment's profitability index is equivalent to a benefit-to-cost ratio. If the investment has a positive NPV, then its benefit (line 2 of Exhibit 6.13) must exceed its cost (line 1 of Exhibit 6.13), and its profitability index is greater than one. If it has a negative NPV, then its cost must exceed its benefit, and its profitability index is less than one. Investments E, F, and G all have a positive NPV, so their profitability indexes are all greater than one. Project E yields $0.14 of *net* present value per $1 of initial investment, project F yields $0.21, and project G yields $0.34.

[4]This problem arises only because the three projects do not have the same initial size. If they did, then the projects should be ranked by decreasing order of their NPV, and the projects with the largest NPV should be selected.

EXHIBIT 6.13 PROFITABILITY INDEXES FOR THREE INVESTMENTS OF UNEQUAL SIZE.

FIGURES FROM EXHIBIT 6.12

	Investment E	Investment F	Investment G
(1) Initial cash outlay	\$1,000,000	\$500,000	\$500,000
(2) Present value of future cash flows	\$1,140,496	\$603,306	\$669,421
(3) Profitability index = $\frac{(2)}{(1)}$	$\frac{\$1,140,496}{\$1,000,000} = 1.14$	$\frac{\$603,306}{\$500,000} = 1.21$	$\frac{\$669,421}{\$500,000} = 1.34$

If the firm has limited funds available for investment, it should first rank the three projects in decreasing order of their profitability indexes (first G, then F, and finally E). Then, *it should select projects with the highest profitability indexes until it has allocated the total amount of funds at its disposal.* In our case, this allocation rule will select project G and then project F for a total investment of \$1 million.

Allocating limited capital to a set of projects on the basis of their profitability indexes does not, unfortunately, resolve the size problem entirely because this method deals with a situation in which the limit on capital expenditures is imposed during the year the projects are under review. In our case, the \$1 million limit applies to the initial year. What will happen next year?

Suppose that the \$1 million limit on capital applies again the following year and that project H, costing \$1.8 million and having an NPV of \$400,000, becomes available. Will the firm be able to finance project H? The firm will have a *maximum* of \$1.3 million of funds to invest: the \$1 million capital budget plus the \$300,000 of cash flow generated by projects F and G at the end of year one. (Recall that the firm selected projects F and G last year and that their combined first-year cash flows are equal to \$300,000, as indicated in Exhibit 6.12.) Project H costs \$1.8 million, so \$1.3 million is not enough to fund it. It will have to be turned down. Conclusion: Because the firm invested in projects F and G last year, it must now turn down a project with a \$400,000 NPV.

If the firm had selected investment E last year, it would be able to fund investment H. Investment E would have generated \$800,000 at the end of year one, which, added to the \$1 million capital budget, would provide the funds required to invest in H. Investments E and H have a combined NPV of \$540,496 (\$140,496 plus \$400,000), a higher value than the combination of F and G (\$103,306 plus \$169,421), even after adjusting the NPV of project H to account for the fact that it occurs a year later.[5]

Thus, *a firm operating under capital constraints should not make today's investment decisions without considering investments that may be available*

[5]The \$400,000 NPV of project H is worth only \$363,636 a year earlier if discounted at the firm's cost of capital of 10 percent.

tomorrow. However, this may be difficult in practice because information about tomorrow's investments may not be readily available today. If the firm does not have enough information on future potential projects, then using the profitability index to make optimal decisions on the basis of currently available information may be the *second-best* solution. The next chapter discusses the profitability index in more detail and reexamines its reliability as a rule to select alternative investments.

Comparing Projects with Unequal Life Spans

We now consider a firm that must make a choice between two investments with unequal life spans. Suppose a firm must decide whether to purchase machine A or machine B. Machine A costs $80,000, has a useful life of two years, and has annual maintenance costs of $4,000. It is assumed to be worthless after two years of operation. Machine B costs $120,000, has a useful life of four years, and has annual maintenance costs of $3,000. It will be worthless in four years. Machine B is 50 percent more expensive than machine A, but its useful life is twice as long and its annual maintenance costs are lower. The two machines are expected to generate the same annual cash flows. The firm's managers want to find out which machine the firm should buy.

If the two machines generate identical future annual cash inflows, the one with the lower present value of overall costs should be preferred because its NPV would be higher. The problem is that the two machines have unequal life spans; machine A will last two years and machine B will last four years. We cannot make a meaningful comparison unless both machines operate over the same period of time. Thus, we assume that at the end of the second year the firm will purchase a new machine A that will last two years. With this approach, we can compare a sequence of *two* machines A lasting four years to *one* machine B, also lasting four years.

Let's assume that the appropriate cost of capital applicable to this type of cost analysis is 10 percent. The relevant streams of cash outflows for two machines A and one machine B and their present values at 10 percent are shown in Exhibit 6.14 (Part I using a calculator to compute the NPV, and Part II using a spreadsheet). The present value of the total cost of a sequence of two machines A ($158,795) is higher than the present value of the total cost of a single machine B ($129,510) over the same span of useful life. The firm should buy machine B even though it is more expensive. The present value of the total cost of a *single* machine A bought today is equal only to $86,924 (not shown in the exhibit). If the firm compares that cost with the cost of machine B ($129,510), it will find machine A cheaper and will incorrectly purchase it.

In the case we have just examined, a sequence of two machines A is equivalent to one machine B. If, for example, machine B had a five-year useful life and machine A had only a three-year life, we would have compared a sequence of *five* machines A against a sequence of *three* machines B to have two sequences with *equal lives* of fifteen years. Fortunately, a shortcut exists that avoids these tedious calculations. We convert each machine's total stream of cash outflows into an equivalent stream of *equal* annual cash flows with the same present value as the total cash-outflow stream (called the **constant annual-equivalent cash flow** or annuity-equivalent cash flow).

EXHIBIT 6.14 CASH OUTFLOWS AND PRESENT VALUES OF COST FOR TWO INVESTMENTS WITH UNEQUAL LIFE SPANS.

Part I Using a calculator

Sequence of Two Machines A					One Machine B	
End-of-Year	Cash Flows Machine 1	Cash Flows Machine 2	Total	Present Value at 10%	Cash Flows	Present Value at 10%
Now	–$80,000		–$80,000	–$80,000	–$120,000	–$120,000
1	–4,000		–4,000	–3,636	–3,000	–2,727
2	–4,000	–$80,000	–84,000	–69,422	–3,000	–2,479
3		–4,000	–4,000	–3,005	–3,000	–2,255
4		–4,000	–4,000	–2,732	–3,000	–2,049
			Present value of costs	**–$158,795**	**Present value of costs**	**–$129,510**

Part II Using a spreadsheet

	A	B	C	D	E	F
1			Sequence of Two Machines A			
2		Now	End-of-year 1	End-of-year 2	End-of-year 3	End-of-year 4
3	Machine 1	–$80,000	–$4,000	–$ 4,000		
4	Machine 2			–$80,000	–$4,000	–$4,000
5	Cash flows	–$80,000	–$4,000	–$84,000	–$4,000	–$4,000
6						
7	Cost of capital	10.00%				
8						
9	**Present value of costs**	**–$158,795**				
10						
11	*The formula in cell B9 is =B5+NPV(B7,C5:F5).*					
12						
13			One Machine B			
14		Now	End-of-year 1	End-of-year 2	End-of-year 3	End-of-year 4
15	Cash flows	–$120,000	–$3,000	–$3,000	–$3,000	–$3,000
16						
17	**Present value of costs**	**–$129,510**				
18						
19	*The formula in cell B17 is =B15+NPV(B7,C15:F15).*					
20						

EXHIBIT 6.15 ORIGINAL AND ANNUITY-EQUIVALENT CASH FLOWS FOR TWO INVESTMENTS WITH UNEQUAL LIFE SPANS.

FIGURES FROM EXHIBIT 6.14 AND APPENDIX 6.1

	Machine A		Machine B	
End of Year	**Original Cash Flows**	**Annuity-Equivalent Cash Flows**	**Original Cash Flows**	**Annuity-Equivalent Cash Flows**
Now	–$80,000		–$120,000	
1	–4,000	–$50,096	–3,000	–$40,855
2	–4,000	–50,096	–3,000	–40,855
3			–3,000	–40,855
4			–3,000	–40,855
Present value at 10%	**–$86,942**	**–$86,942**	**–$129,509**	**–$129,509**

Then, we simply compare the size of the annuities. A firm should select the machine with the lowest annuity-equivalent cash flow. Appendix 6.1 shows how to calculate these constant annual-equivalent cash flows. These cash flows for the original case are shown in Exhibit 6.15.

The total stream of cash outflows generated by machine A has a two-year annuity-equivalent cash outflow of $50,096, and the total stream of cash outflows generated by machine B has a four-year annuity-equivalent cash outflow of $40,855. Because $40,855 is less than $50,096, machine B should be selected. It can be replaced by an *infinite* sequence of machines B with an annual cost of $40,855, whereas machine A is replaceable by an *infinite* sequence of machines A with an annual cost of $50,096.

LIMITATIONS OF THE NET PRESENT VALUE CRITERION

Although the NPV criterion can be adjusted to deal with particular cases, such as the comparison of two projects of unequal size or unequal life spans, in other cases, the required adjustments to the NPV criterion are far too complex to be easily implemented. In most cases, these situations arise because the NPV criterion is a take-it-or-leave-it rule that is based only on the information available at the time the NPV is estimated. Hence, *the NPV criterion ignores the opportunities to make changes to the project as time passes and more information becomes available.*

NPV is estimated from the stream of *expected* cash flows generated by the proposal and discounted at the project's cost of capital, which depends on the project's risk. The estimation of both the cash flows and their corresponding cost of capital depends on information available at the time NPV is calculated. This information involves factors such as the marketability of the product, its selling price, the risk of obsolescence, the technology used in manufacturing the product, and the economic, regulatory, and tax environments.

A project that can be adjusted easily and inexpensively to significant changes in these factors will contribute more to the value of the firm than indicated by its NPV. It will also be more valuable than an alternative proposal with the same NPV that cannot be altered as easily and as cheaply. A project's flexibility, that is, the ability of a project to adjust to changing circumstances, is usually described by **managerial options**, which can be exercised to alter a project during its useful life.

Managerial or Real Options Embedded in Investment Projects

The following sections discuss two important managerial options—the option to switch technologies and the option to abandon a project. We use the designer desk-lamp project of SMC to illustrate the concepts.

The Option to Switch Technologies

Suppose SMC can use two different types of machines to manufacture the designer desk lamp during the five years the project is expected to last. One is a multipurpose standard machine and the other is a single-purpose, untested digitally driven apparatus, which was developed by SMC's research department specifically for the project. Assume that the machine used does not significantly affect the project's NPV. Although engineers at SMC are confident the newer machine will prove to be reliable, the project's manager believes it is possible that the newer machine will not be able to meet the stringent volume and quality requirements of mass production and may have to be scrapped and replaced with the standard machine. If the standard machine is selected, it can easily be replaced with the newer one, after the new machine has successfully passed extra reliability tests, with minimal disruption and adjustment to the manufacturing process. However, the reverse is not true, because replacing the new machine with the standard one would require a complete revamping of the production line. In other words, although management will have the *option to switch* machines while the project is running, this option has more value if the standard machine is chosen.

The importance and the value of the option to switch not only technologies but also production facilities have long been recognized by firms in some industries. For example, some Japanese auto manufacturers have established manufacturing operations in the United States and Europe so that they can switch production from one continent to the other when changes occur in the relative costs of producing a car. If the yen appreciates against the U.S. dollar or against European currencies, cars manufactured in the United States or in Europe can be exported to Japan, where they can be sold at a higher margin than locally made cars.

The Option to Abandon a Project

Suppose SMC's designer desk lamp is a flop and does not sell. Although the decision to go ahead with the project implicitly assumed that it will last five years, SMC's management will always have the *option to abandon* the project at an earlier date. Does this option add value to the project's NPV of $415,083 (see Exhibit 6.7)?

EXHIBIT 6.16 EXPECTED CASH FLOWS, YEARS 2 THROUGH 5, AND THEIR PRESENT VALUES FOR SUCCESS AND FAILURE OF THE SMC DESIGNER DESK-LAMP PROJECT.

	Year 2	Year 3	Year 4	Year 5	Present Value at 7.6%
Expected cash flows according to the initial estimation	$822,000	$692,000	$554,000	$466,000	—
Expected cash flows if the project is successful	$890,000	$783,000	$612,000	$520,000	$2,382,629
Expected cash flows if the project is a failure	$662,000	$480,000	$420,000	$340,000	$1,620,618

To answer this question, we assume that within one year after the project's launch, SMC knows more about the fate of the designer desk lamps. Depending on whether the lamp is a success or a failure, the expected cash flows for the remaining years (from the second to the fifth year) will change as shown in Exhibit 6.16. If the designer desk-lamp project is a success, the present value of the remaining cash flows at the project's cost of capital of 7.6 percent is $2,382,629. If the project turns out to be a failure, the present value is $1,620,618. Assuming that the project can be abandoned at the end of the first year and that the net proceeds from its liquidation will be $1,650,000, what should SMC do one year after it launches the project?

If the designer desk lamps are a success, SMC should continue with the project because the present value of the remaining cash flows ($2,382,629) exceeds the net proceeds from liquidating the project ($1,650,000). But if the lamp is a failure, the present value of the remaining cash flows ($1,620,618) is less than the net proceeds from liquidation, and SMC should abandon the project. Thus, in one year, the investment will be worth either $2,382,629 (with the success scenario) or $1,650,000 (with the failure scenario). If there is a 30 percent chance that the project will fail and a 70 percent chance that it will succeed, the expected value of the project in one year's time will be $2,162,840 (30 percent of $1,650,000 plus 70 percent of $2,382,629).

We can now recalculate the project's NPV taking into account the possibility that it could be abandoned after one year. The initial cash outlay ($2,360,000) and the first year's expected cash flow ($832,000) have not changed, but the cash flows from the second to the fifth years are now replaced by the project's worth at the end of the first year, that is, $2,162,840.[6] Both the first year's cash

[6]The expected cash flows in the original estimation of the project NPV are the same as the average of the expected cash flows under the success and the failure scenarios, weighted by the chances of success (70 percent) and failure (30 percent). For example, the original cash flow in year 3 ($692,000) is equal to 70 percent of $783,000 (cash flow if the lamp is a hit) plus 30 percent of $480,000 (cash flow if the lamp is a flop).

flow and the project's worth at the end of that year need to be discounted at the project's cost of capital of 7.6 percent to obtain the NPV with the abandonment option:

$$NPV_{\text{with abandonment option}} = -\$2,360,000 + \frac{\$832,000 + \$2,162,840}{1 + 0.076} = \$423,309$$

The project's NPV without accounting for the abandonment option was \$415,083. Thus, the option to abandon the project after one year adds \$8,226 of value (\$423,309 less \$415,083). Although \$8,226 represents only 2 percent of the original NPV of the designer desk-lamp project and does not affect the investment decision, this may not always be the case. For example, a proposal that is rejected because its NPV is negative can be turned into a positive NPV project, and consequently accepted, when the abandonment option is considered.

Dealing with Managerial Options

The option to switch technologies and the option to abandon a project are embedded in most investment projects. However, these are not the only managerial options. Managers have many opportunities to enhance the value of an investment during its lifetime as circumstances change. A counterpoint to the option to abandon a project is the *option to expand* the project. For example, suppose the designer desk lamp is a big winner and the project needs to be expanded to meet increased demand. Regardless of the machine used to manufacture the lamps, SMC's management will have the option to expand the production line. But, contrary to the previous cases, it is not clear that the value of this option will be different for different machines because there is no reason to believe that it will be easier to increase the production of lamps with one machine rather than with the other one. However, this is not always the case, and a project that can be expanded is worth more than a project that cannot.

An investment can usually be postponed, so another important managerial option is the *option to defer* an investment. This kind of option is particularly valuable in the mining and oil extraction industries where the output (mineral or oil) prices are particularly volatile. For example, the NPV of an oil reserve may be negative, given the current market expectations about the future price of oil. However, because the development of the reserve can be postponed, sometimes for many years, the capital expenditures needed to start the extraction of oil can be deferred until the market prices rise. And the more volatile the oil prices, the higher the chance that the NPV of the reserve will become positive, and the higher the value of the option to defer the development of the reserve.

The designer desk-lamp example explains how an option to abandon can be estimated. However, our result depended to a large extent on (1) the probability that the project will be either a failure or a success and (2) the date at which this failure or success will be recognized. Unfortunately, it is difficult to make reliable estimates on these uncertain outcomes. An alternative approach is to use the option valuation models that were initially developed to value options on financial securities. But these models require data that are usually difficult to obtain and often unreliable. Furthermore, as mentioned previously, investment projects have a large number of embedded options, and it would be almost impossible to identify and evaluate them all.

In the absence of practical and simple ways to value these options, our advice is to remember that an investment decision should not be based on a single number—that is, its NPV. Before arriving at a decision, managers should conduct a sensitivity analysis to identify the most salient options embedded in the project, attempt to value them as we did for the abandonment option, and exercise sound judgment. Options embedded in a project are either worthless or have a positive value. Thus, the NPV of a project will always *underestimate* the value of an investment project. The larger the number of options embedded in the project and the higher the probability that the value of the project is sensitive to changing circumstances, the greater the value of these options and the higher the value of the investment project.

SUMMARY

An investment proposal can be evaluated by estimating its net present value (NPV). According to the NPV rule, if the investment has a positive (negative) NPV it creates (destroys) value and should be undertaken (rejected). The NPV rule is a good investment decision rule because it adjusts the investment's expected cash flows for both their timing and risk and has the convenient property of being additive. Most important is the capacity of the NPV method to evaluate the value-creating potential of an investment proposal. In addition, the NPV of an investment proposal is an estimate of the current value the proposal will create or destroy if undertaken.

The steps involved in applying the NPV rule to evaluate an investment proposal are summarized in Exhibit 6.17. Two inputs are required to calculate a project's NPV: (1) the expected cash-flow stream that the project will generate over its useful life and (2) the appropriate cost of capital that reflects the risk of the expected cash flows. The cost of capital is the rate at which the project's future cash flows need to be discounted to compare their present value with the investment cost. Chapter 8 shows how to estimate a project's expected cash-flow stream, and Chapter 10 shows how to estimate its appropriate risk-adjusted cost of capital.

After these inputs have been estimated, a financial calculator or any computer equipped with a spreadsheet application can compute the project's NPV. If the NPV is positive, the project creates value and should be undertaken. The present value of its future cash-flow stream is expected to more than compensate for the investment cost. If the project's NPV is negative, the project destroys value and should be rejected. In this case, the present value of its future cash-flow stream is not expected to cover the investment cost.

The NPV rule can be used to choose among projects with different initial sizes or different life spans. If a firm has a limit on the amount of funds it can invest in new projects, it may not be able to undertake all available positive NPV projects. If the alternative projects have different initial cash outlays (different sizes), then the project's profitability index can be used to select the combination of projects that would create the most value. However, if the constraint on the availability of funds is imposed every year, rather than just during the initial year, the profitability index may lead to suboptimal investment decisions. If projects have unequal life spans, the comparison should be made between sequences of projects of the same duration. The calculations for this

EXHIBIT 6.17 STEPS INVOLVED IN APPLYING THE NET PRESENT VALUE RULE.

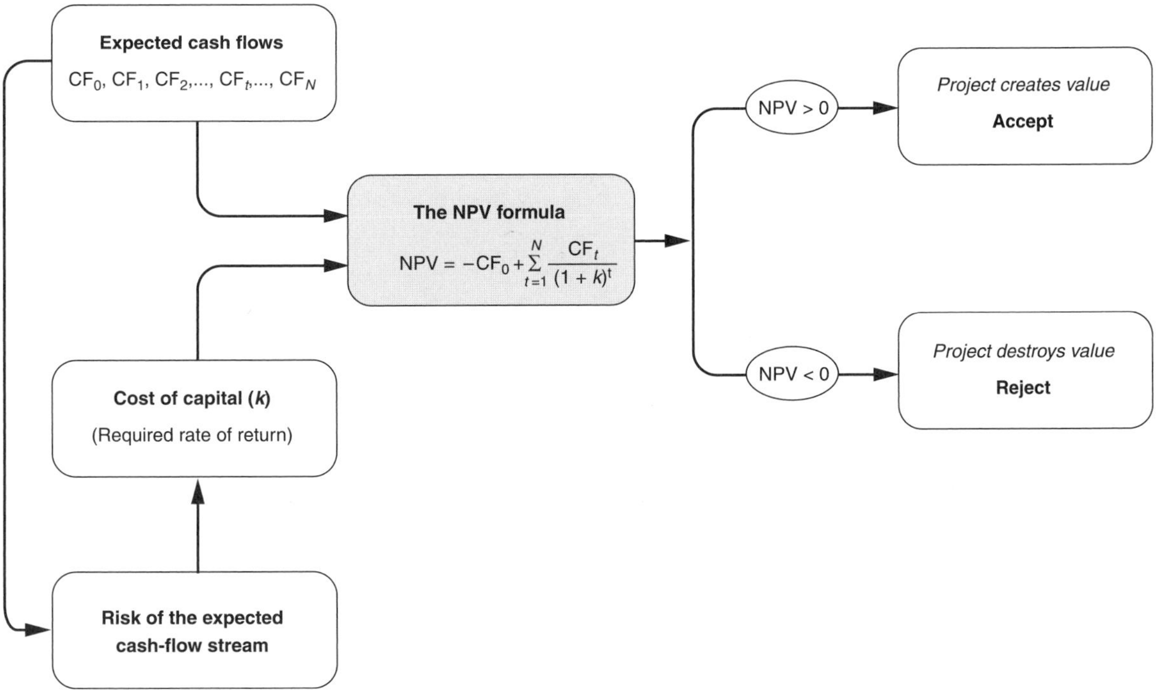

comparison are easier if the projects' annuity-equivalent cash flows are compared. The project with the lowest annuity-equivalent cost or the highest annuity-equivalent benefit should be selected.

Most projects have managerial options, options to change course after the project is launched, which are ignored in standard NPV analysis. The added value provided by these options is difficult to estimate. Although sensitivity analysis is not a perfect substitute, it can identify the most critical options embedded in a project, thus providing valuable information for the final decision to accept or reject.

Calculation of the Present Value of an Annuity and the Constant Annual-Equivalent Cash Flow of a Project's Cash-Flow Stream

APPENDIX 6.

PRESENT VALUE OF AN *N*-PERIOD ANNUITY

If a cash-flow stream is composed of *equal* and *uninterrupted* periodic cash flows lasting for N periods, then the cash-flow stream is called an N-period **annuity**. Consider a project that is expected to generate the same annual cash flow of \$20,000 at the end of each year for the next five years. Its expected cash-flow stream is composed of equal and uninterrupted periodic cash flows, and it is, thus, an annuity. What is the present value of that annuity ($PV_{annuity}$) if the project's cost of capital is 12 percent? It is the sum of the present values of the five \$20,000 annual cash flows:

$$PV_{annuity} = \frac{\$20{,}000}{1+0.12} + \frac{\$20{,}000}{(1+0.12)^2} + \frac{\$20{,}000}{(1+0.12)^3} + \frac{\$20{,}000}{(1+0.12)^4} + \frac{\$20{,}000}{(1+0.12)^5} \quad \text{(A6.1.1)}$$

Performing the calculations on a financial calculator gives $PV_{annuity}$ = \$72,096. Thus, a project that generates \$20,000 at the end of every year for the next five years is today worth \$72,096 at a cost of capital of 12 percent. If the project's initial cash outlay is less than \$72,096, the project should be undertaken.

It is not necessary to calculate the present value of each cash flow and add them to determine their present value. A simple formula provides the present value of an annuity. We begin by multiplying both sides of equation A6.1.1 by (1 + 0.12):

$$(1+0.12) \times PV_{annuity} = \$20{,}000 + \frac{\$20{,}000}{1+0.12} + \frac{\$20{,}000}{(1+0.12)^2} + \frac{\$20{,}000}{(1+0.12)^3} + \frac{\$20{,}000}{(1+0.12)^4}$$

Subtracting equation A6.1.1 from this equation gives the following:

$$(1 \times 0.12) \times PV_{annuity} - PV_{annuity} = \$20{,}000 - \frac{\$20{,}000}{(1+0.12)^5}$$

which can be rewritten as follows:

$$0.12 \times PV_{annuity} = \$20{,}000 - \frac{\$20{,}000}{(1+0.12)^5}$$

Dividing both sides by 0.12 and factoring out the \$20,000 gives the following:

$$PV_{annuity} = \$20{,}000 \times \frac{1 - \dfrac{1}{(1 + 0.12)^5}}{0.12} = \$20{,}000 \times 3.6048 = \$72{,}096$$

Generalizing, the present value of any N-period annuity can be computed using the following formula:

$$\mathbf{PV_{annuity} = Annuity\ cash\ flow \times \frac{1 - \dfrac{1}{(1 + \mathit{k})^{\mathit{N}}}}{\mathit{k}}} \qquad \text{(A6.1.2)}$$

where k is the discount rate.

The term $\dfrac{1 - \dfrac{1}{(1 + k)^N}}{k}$ is referred to as the **annuity discount factor (ADF)**. If DF designates the discount factor of the *Nth* annuity cash flow, we have the following:

$$\mathbf{ADF = \frac{1{-}DF}{\mathit{k}}}$$

In our example,

$$DF = \frac{1}{(1 + 0.12)^5} = 0.5674$$

and

$$ADF = \frac{1 - 0.5674}{0.12} = \frac{0.4326}{0.12} = 3.6048$$

If you know the value of the DF, you can easily calculate the corresponding value of the ADF.

As you can guess, a spreadsheet will instantly give you the value of an entire annuity directly if you provide the inputs. In Microsoft Excel, the formula is *PV (cost of capital, number of periods N, annuity value)*, or *PV (k, N, annuity)*. You can also use a financial calculator or use the *annuity present value* table on the inside covers at the back of the book, which gives the present value of a \$1 annuity paid or received at the end of any period up to twenty periods and for discount rates ranging from 1 to 20 percent.

PRESENT VALUE OF AN INFINITE ANNUITY OR PERPETUITY

As a special application of equation A6.1.2, let's determine the present value of a **perpetuity**, that is, an annuity for which N is an infinite number. If N is infinitely large, the term $\dfrac{1}{(1 + k)^N}$ can be considered as equal to zero and equation A6.1.2 reduces to the annuity cash flow divided by the discount rate:

$$\mathbf{PV_{perpetuity} = \frac{Annuity\ cash\ flow}{Discount\ rate}} \qquad \text{(A6.1.3)}$$

For example, if the \$20,000 annuity was a perpetuity and the discount rate was 12 percent, its present value would be \$166,667, that is, \$20,000 divided by 0.12.

EXHIBIT A6.1.1 ORIGINAL AND ANNUITY-EQUIVALENT CASH FLOWS FOR MACHINE B.

FIGURES FROM EXHIBIT 6.15

End of Year	Original Cash Flows	Annuity-Equivalent Flows
Now	$120,000	
1	3,000	$ 40,855
2	3,000	40,855
3	3,000	40,855
4	3,000	40,855
Present value at 10%	**$129,509**	**$129,509**

CONSTANT ANNUAL-EQUIVALENT CASH FLOW

The cash-flow stream of machine B and its constant annual-equivalent cash flow are shown as part of Exhibit 6.15 and repeated in Exhibit A6.1.1. How did we find the $40,855 constant annual-equivalent cash flow? The constant annual-equivalent cash-flow stream must have the same present value as the original cash-flow stream, and the four-year ADF at a cost of capital of 10 percent is equal to 3.1699. We can now write the following:

$$\$129{,}509 = (\text{Constant annual-equivalent cash flow}) \times (3.1699)$$

and thus

$$\text{Constant annual-equivalent cash flow} = \frac{\$129{,}509}{3.1699} = \$40{,}855$$

More generally, we have the following:

$$\textbf{Constant annual-equivalent cash flow} = \frac{\textbf{Present value of original cash flow}}{\textbf{Annuity discount factor}} \qquad \text{(A6.1.4)}$$

FURTHER READING

1. Amran, Martha, and Navil Kulatikala. *Real Options: Managing Strategic Investments in an Uncertain World*. Harvard Business School Press, 1999.
2. Brealey, Richard, Stewart Myers, and Franklin Allen. *Principles of Corporate Finance*, 9th ed. McGraw-Hill, 2008. See Chapters 2, 3, 6, 10, 11, and 23.
3. Copeland, Tom, and Peter Tufano. "A Real-World Way to Manage Real Options." Harvard Business School Publishing Corporation, March 2004.
4. Damodaran, Aswath. *Corporate Finance: Theory and Practice*, 2nd ed. John Wiley & Sons, 2001. See Chapters 3 and 10.
5. Luehrman, Timothy. "Investment Opportunities as Real Options: Getting Started on the Numbers." *Harvard Business Review*, July-August 1998.
6. Ross, Stephen, Randolph Westerfield, and Jeffrey Jaffe. *Corporate Finance*, 8th ed. McGraw-Hill Irwin, 2008. See Chapters 4 and 8.

SELF-TEST PROBLEMS

6.1 PRESENT VALUES AND THE COST OF CAPITAL.

What is meant by each of the following statements?

a. "The present value of the future cash flows expected from an investment project is $20,000,000."
b. "The net present value (NPV) of an investment project is $10,000,000."
c. "A project's cost of capital is 10 percent."

6.2 MANAGERIAL OPTIONS.

What are managerial options embedded in an investment project? Give some examples.

6.3 NET PRESENT VALUE.

The Blaker Company is considering undertaking a project that is expected to generate the following cash-flow stream:

	Expected Cash Flow
Now	–$100,000
End-of-Year 1	50,000
End-of-Year 2	50,000
End-of-Year 3	50,000

a. If the project's cost of capital is 12 percent, what is the present value of the project's expected cash-flow stream?
b. What is the net present value of the project?
c. What is the profitability index of the project?
d. Should the project be undertaken? Explain.

6.4 CHOOSING BETWEEN TWO INVESTMENTS WITH UNEQUAL COSTS AND LIFE SPANS.

Perfect Color Company (PCC) is in the business of dyeing material. Business is booming, and PCC is considering buying a new color printer. Two printers are available on the market: printer X costs $50,000, requires $5,000 per year to operate, and has a useful life of two years; printer Y costs $60,000, requires $7,000 per year to operate, and will need to be replaced every three years. PCC's cost of capital is 10 percent.

a. What are the present values of the total costs of the two printers over their useful life?
b. Why are the two present values not comparable?
c. What is the annual-equivalent cost for each of the printers?
d. Which printer should PCC purchase?

6.5 REPLACING AN EXISTING MACHINE WITH A NEW ONE.

Pasta Uno is operating an old pasta-making machine that is not expected to last more than two years. During that time, the machine is expected to generate a cash inflow of $20,000 per year. It could be replaced by a new machine at a cost of $150,000. The new machine is more efficient than the current one and, as a result, is expected to generate a net cash flow of $75,000 per year for three years. The management of Pasta Uno is wondering whether to replace the old machine now or wait another year. Pasta Uno's cost of capital is 10 percent.

a. Assume that the current resale value of the old machine is zero and that the new machine will also have a zero resale value in the future. What is the annual-equivalent cash flow of using the new machine?
b. What should the management of Pasta Uno do? Explain.

REVIEW PROBLEMS

1. **Future values.**
Suppose you deposit $1,000 in one year, $2,000 in two years, and $4,000 in three years. Assume a 4 percent interest rate throughout.

   a. How much will you have in five years?
   b. Suppose you plan to withdraw $1,500 in four years and there is no penalty for early withdrawal. How much will you have in five years?

2. **Present values.**
A basketball player has just signed a $30 million contract to play for three years. She will receive $5 million as an immediate cash bonus, $5 million at the end of the first year, $8 million at the end of the second year, and the remaining $12 million at the end of the contract. Assuming a discount rate of 10 percent, what is the value of the package?

3. **Present values.**
You can invest in a machine that costs $500,000. You can expect revenues net of any expense, except maintenance costs, of $150,000 at the end of each year for five years. You will subcontract the maintenance costs at a rate of $20,000 a year, to be paid at the beginning of each year. You expect to get $100,000 from selling the machine at the end of the fifth year. All these revenues and costs are after tax, as is the 10 percent cost of capital. Should you buy the machine?

4. **Buying a car.**
You are buying a car. No Better Deals will give you $500 off the list price on a $10,000 car.

   a. You can get the same car from Best Deals if you pay $4,000 down and the rest at the end of two years. If the interest rate were 12 percent, where would you buy the car?

b. Best Deals has revised its offer. You now pay $2,000 down, $3,000 at the end of the first year, and $5,000 at the end of the second year. If the interest rate were still 12 percent, where would you buy the car?

c. No Better Deals, in turn, makes a new offer. You pay $10,000, but you can borrow the sum from the dealer at 0.5 percent per month for thirty-six months even though the going market rate is 1 percent per month, with the first payment made when the car is delivered. If you accept the offer, (1) What would your monthly payments be? (2) What would the cost of the car to you be?

Note: *The objective of this exercise* ***is not*** *to learn how to use present value tables or the present value macro of a spreadsheet, but rather to explicitly identify the financial decisions underlying the different alternatives.*

5. **Saving for college.**

You expect that your daughter will go to college ten years from now. Taking account of inflation, you estimate that you will need $160,000 to support her during her years in college. Assume an interest rate of 4 percent on your saving accounts. How much will you have to pay into those accounts in the next ten years to get $160,000 by then?

6. **Saving for retirement.**

Suppose you have decided to set up a personal pension fund for your retirement. You just turned twenty-five. You expect to retire at age sixty-five and believe it is reasonable to count on living at least twenty years after retirement. Furthermore, you wish to have an annual income of $100,000 during your retirement starting when you turn sixty-five, and that upon receipt of the twentieth payment, the entire capital sum would have been distributed. You have been offered two investment plans by your financial adviser: (1) an "aggressive" portfolio of well-diversified equities that promise to yield on average a 12 percent rate and (2) a "conservative" portfolio of government bonds that promise to yield on average a 6 percent rate.

a. How much must you invest in each of the two savings schemes each year, starting now until you retire, to ensure that you receive the $100,000 per year retirement income?

b. What investment strategy would you recommend?

7. **Financial deals.**

Five years ago, your favorite aunt won a $1,000,000 lottery. The prize money is paid out $50,000 per year for twenty years. Unfortunately, your aunt needs as much as $250,000 cash now to pay for medical bills that she and your uncle incurred as a result of an accident. A local finance company has proposed to provide her with the $250,000 cash in return for the $50,000 annual payments over the next nine years.

a. What is the interest rate implicit in the local finance company proposal?

b. What advice would you give to your aunt?

8. **Value of a firm.**
   Hellenic Vultures is expected to generate $100,000 of net cash flows next year, $120,000 the year after, and $150,000 for the following three years. It is expected that the firm could be sold for $500,000 at the end of the fifth year. The owners of Hellenic Vultures, who would like to sell their firm, strongly believe that their investment in the firm should generate a 10 percent return. What is the minimum price at which they should sell the firm?

9. **Competing investment projects.**
   Lolastar Co. is evaluating two competing investment projects. They both require an investment of $25 million. The company cost of capital is 10 percent for projects of this type. The expected cash flows are as follows:

	Project I (millions)	Project II (millions)
End-of-Year 1	$ 3	$12
End-of-Year 2	5	9
End-of-Year 3	8	7
End-of-Year 4	10	4
End-of-Year 5	13	3
Total cash flows	$39	$35

   a. Which of the two projects would you recommend? Why?
   b. Will your choice be the same whatever the cost of capital?

10. **Comparing projects with unequal economic life.**
    Rollon Inc. is comparing the operating costs of two types of equipment. The standard model costs $50,000 and will have a useful life of four years. Operating costs are expected to be $4,000 per year. The superior model costs $90,000 and will have a useful life of six years. Its operating costs are expected to be $2,500 per year. Both models will be able to operate at the same level of output and quality and generate the same cash earnings. Rollon's cost of capital is 8 percent.

    a. Compute the present values of the cash costs over the useful life of each model.
    b. Can the two present values be compared? If not, why not?
    c. What is the *annuity-equivalent cost* of each model?
    d. Which model should the company purchase? Explain.

ALTERNATIVES TO THE NET PRESENT VALUE RULE

CHAPTER 7

The net present value (NPV) rule is not the only criterion available to evaluate a capital investment proposal. You may be familiar with the payback period, the internal rate of return, or another criterion. This chapter examines and explains how to apply five alternatives to the NPV rule: the ordinary payback period rule, the discounted payback period rule, the internal-rate-of-return (IRR) rule, the profitability index (PI) rule, and the average accounting return rule. Exhibit 7.1 shows the criteria used by a large sample of companies when making capital budgeting decisions, with the NPV and IRR rules being the most popular and the average accounting return and PI rules being the least popular. We analyze whether these five alternatives to the NPV rule satisfy the conditions of a good investment decision rule.

Recall that a good investment decision rule must take into account the timing of a project's expected cash flows and the project's risk. In addition, it should select projects that increase the market value of the firm's equity.

In our analysis of the alternative rules, we identify a number of cases in which these methods lead to a decision that contradicts the NPV rule. We explain why these conflicts occur and why some firms still use some of these techniques to screen investment proposals. We use six projects to illustrate how the five alternatives to the NPV rule are usually applied in making investment decisions and compare their performance with that of the NPV rule. After reading this chapter, you should understand the following:

- A project's ordinary payback period, discounted payback period, internal rate of return, profitability index, and average accounting return, and how to calculate these measures
- How to apply the alternative rules to screen investment proposals
- The major shortcomings of the alternative rules
- Why these rules are still used even though they are not as reliable as the NPV rule

EXHIBIT 7.1 POPULARITY OF DIFFERENT CAPITAL BUDGETING TECHNIQUES: PERCENTAGE USED BY COMPANIES.

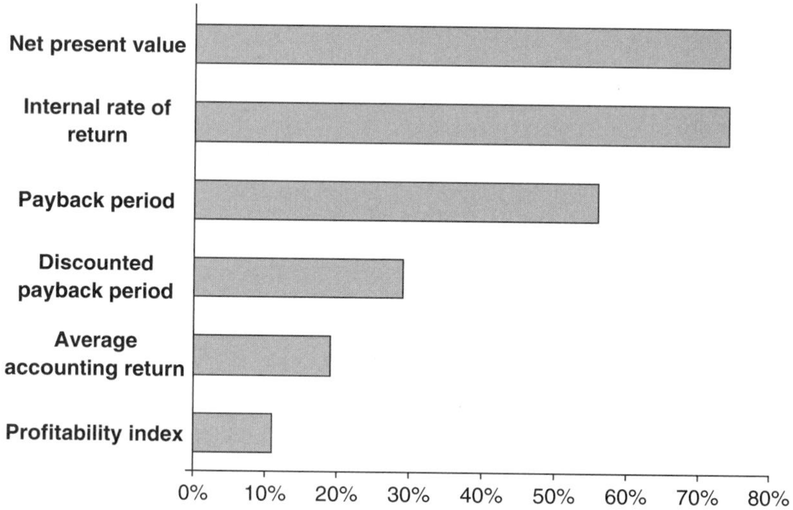

John R. Graham, Campbell R. Harvey. *The Journal of Applied Corporate Finance*, Vol. 14, No. 4, 2002.

THE PAYBACK PERIOD

A project's **payback period** is the number of periods (usually measured in years) required for the sum of the project's expected cash flows to equal its initial cash outlay. In other words, the payback period is the time it takes for a firm to recover its initial investment. Consider investment A, whose characteristics are reported in Exhibit 7.2 and whose expected and cumulative cash flows are shown in Exhibit 7.3. The investment's payback period is the length of time it takes for the firm to get back its initial cash outlay of $1 million.

As indicated in Exhibit 7.3, we assume that the cash flows occur at the end of each year. Project A has a payback period of three years because it takes exactly three years for the project's *cumulative* cash flows to reach a value equal to the initial cash flow of $1 million.

Sometimes, a project's payback period includes a fraction of a year. For example, investment E requires an initial cash outlay of $1 million and generates a cumulative cash flow of $975,000 after three years and $1,300,000 after four years (see Exhibit 7.4). The project's payback period is between three and four years. It is equal to three years plus the *fraction* of the Year 4 cash flow ($325,000) required to recover the initial investment:

$$\text{Payback period(E)} = 3 + \frac{\text{Initial cash flow} - \text{Cumulative cash flow to year 3}}{\text{Year 4 cash flow}}$$

$$= 3 + \frac{\$1{,}000{,}000 - \$975{,}000}{\$325{,}000}$$

$$= 3 \text{ years} + 0.08 \text{ year} = 3.08 \text{ years}$$

EXHIBIT 7.2 EXPECTED CASH-FLOW STREAMS, COST OF CAPITAL, AND NET PRESENT VALUES OF ALTERNATIVE INVESTMENT PROPOSALS.

ALL INVESTMENTS ARE FIVE YEARS LONG AND REQUIRE AN INITIAL CASH OUTLAY OF $1 MILLION

Investments A and B		
End-of-Year	Investment A	Investment B
1	$ 600,000	$ 100,000
2	300,000	300,000
3	100,000	600,000
4	200,000	200,000
5	300,000	300,000
Total cash flows	$1,500,000	$1,500,000
Cost of capital	10%	10%
NPV	$ 191,399	$ 112,511

Investments C and D		
End-of-Year	Investment C	Investment D
1	$ 250,000	$ 250,000
2	250,000	250,000
3	250,000	250,000
4	250,000	250,000
5	250,000	250,000
Total cash flows	$1,250,000	$1,250,000
Cost of capital	5%	10%
NPV	$ 82,369	$ –52,303

Investments E and F		
End-of-Year	Investment E	Investment F
1	$ 325,000	$ 325,000
2	325,000	325,000
3	325,000	325,000
4	325,000	325,000
5	325,000	975,000
Total cash flows	$1,625,000	$2,275,000
Cost of capital	10%	10%
NPV	$ 232,006	$ 635,605

EXHIBIT 7.3 EXPECTED AND CUMULATIVE CASH FLOWS FOR INVESTMENT A.

EXPECTED CASH FLOWS FROM EXHIBIT 7.2

End-of-Year	Expected Cash Flows	Cumulative Cash Flows
1	$600,000	$ 600,000
2	300,000	900,000
3	100,000	1,000,000
4	200,000	1,200,000
5	300,000	1,500,000

Exhibit 7.4 shows how to use a spreadsheet to compute payback periods, taking investment E as an example. The payback periods for the investment proposals defined in Exhibit 7.2 are shown in Exhibit 7.5.

THE PAYBACK PERIOD RULE

According to the **payback period rule**, *a project is acceptable if its payback period is shorter than or equal to a specified number of periods called the* **cutoff period.** If the choice is between several mutually exclusive projects with payback periods shorter than the cutoff period, the one with the shortest payback period should be selected.

If the firm reviewing projects A–F adopts a cutoff period of four years, then all six projects are acceptable. None of their payback periods exceeds the firm's four-year cutoff period (see Exhibit 7.5). If the choice is between projects A and B, or C and

EXHIBIT 7.4 COMPUTING THE PAYBACK PERIOD FOR INVESTMENT E USING A SPREADSHEET.

EXPECTED CASH FLOWS FROM EXHIBIT 7.2

	A	B	C	D	E	F	G
1		0	1	2	3	4	5
2	Cash flows	–$1,000,000	$325,000	$325,000	$325,000	$ 325,000	$ 325,000
3	Cumulative cash inflows		$325,000	$650,000	$975,000	$1,300,000	$1,625,000
4							
5	**Payback period**		–	–	–	3.08	–
6							
7	*0 is now; 1, 2, 3,... is end of year.*						
8	*The formula in cell C3 is =C2. The formula in cell D3 is =C3+D2. Then copy formula in cell D3 to next cells in row 3.*						
9	*The formula in C5 is =IF(OR(C3<=–$B$2,B3>–$B$2),"–",B1+(–$B$2–B3)/C2). Then copy formula in cell C5 to next cells in row 5.*						
10							

EXHIBIT 7.5 PAYBACK PERIODS FOR THE SIX INVESTMENTS IN EXHIBIT 7.2.

Investment	A	B	C	D	E	F
Payback period (in years)	3.00	3.00	4.00	4.00	3.08	3.08

D, or E and F, then each project within a pair is as good as the other because they have the same payback period. If the choice is between projects A, C, and E, then A should be selected because it has the shortest payback period.

DOES THE PAYBACK RULE ADJUST FOR THE TIMING OF CASH FLOWS?

Consider investments A and B. They require the same initial cash outlay, have the same useful life, and carry the same risk (they have the same cost of capital). Their payback periods are also the same, but the timing of their cash flows differs. The largest cash inflow ($600,000) occurs at the end of the *first* year for investment A; it occurs at the end of the *third* year for investment B. Thus, the payback period rule does *not* take into consideration the timing of the cash flows. It simply adds them and ignores the time value of money.

DOES THE PAYBACK RULE ADJUST FOR RISK?

Now, consider investments C and D. They are both five-year projects and have the same initial cash outlay and expected annual cash flows of $250,000. Even though the expected cash-flow stream of investment D is riskier than that of investment C (the cost of capital for D is higher than the cost of capital for C), their payback periods are identical (four years). Thus, the payback period rule ignores risk.

DOES THE PAYBACK RULE MAXIMIZE THE FIRM'S EQUITY VALUE?

It is unlikely that an investment decision rule that ignores the timing and the risk of a project's expected cash flows would systematically select projects that maximize the market value of the firm's equity. Furthermore, when managers apply the payback period rule, they must have the "right" cutoff period. Unfortunately, there is no objective reason to believe that a particular cutoff period exists that is consistent with the maximization of the market value of the firm's equity. The choice of a cutoff period is always *arbitrary*.

One consequence of this shortcoming is illustrated by comparing investments E and F. The payback period rule does not discriminate between the two projects because they both have the same payback period of 3.08 years. But the firm's managers would certainly prefer to invest in F because, all else being equal, at the end of Year 5 that project is expected to generate a cash inflow that is three times larger than the one generated by project E. Clearly, the payback period rule ignores expected cash flows after the cutoff period. As far as the firm is concerned, these cash flows are simply irrelevant. In other words, this decision rule is biased against long-term investments.

Why Do Managers Use the Payback Period Rule?

Despite its well-known shortcomings, many managers still use the payback period rule. All the studies that survey the techniques that managers use to make investment decisions reveal a large proportion of payback period users.[1] Which redeeming qualities does the payback period rule offer that can explain its popularity among managers?

The payback period's strongest appeal is its simplicity and ease of application. Managers in large companies make many accept/reject decisions on small and repetitive investments with typical cash-flow patterns. Over time, these managers may develop good intuition regarding the appropriate cutoff periods for which these investments have a positive NPV. Under these circumstances, it is possible that the "cost" of occasionally making wrong decisions with the payback period rule is lower than the "cost" of using more elaborate and time-consuming decision rules.

Another reason why managers use the payback period rule is that it favors projects that "pay back quickly" and, thus, contribute to the firm's overall cash availability. This could be an important consideration for small firms that rely primarily on internally generated funds to finance their activities because they do not have easy access to long-term funding through their banks or the financial markets.

Sometimes, two projects have the *same* NPV but have *different* payback periods. In this case, selecting the project with the shortest payback makes sense. To illustrate, we compare investment A in Exhibit 7.2 with investment G; the latter requires the same initial cash outlay as A ($1 million), has the same cost of capital (10 percent), and generates the expected cash flows shown in Exhibit 7.6. At a cost of capital of 10 percent, the two investments have the same NPV of $191,399. However, the payback period of investment A is three years, whereas that of G is one year longer. According to the NPV rule, a firm should be indifferent in its choice

Exhibit 7.6 Comparison of Two Investments with the Same NPV and Different Payback Periods.

End-of-Year	Investment A	Investment G
Now	–$1,000,000	–$1,000,000
1	600,000	200,000
2	300,000	200,000
3	100,000	300,000
4	200,000	300,000
5	300,000	666,740
NPV at 10%	$ 191,399	$ 191,399
Payback period	3 years	4 years

[1]However, most payback period users usually use this method in addition to other approaches (such as NPV or IRR). The payback period method is rarely used alone to evaluate large projects.

between the two investments, but the payback period rule clearly favors investment A because of its shorter payback period (essentially because of its first-year cash inflow of $600,000).

Finally, because the payback period rule tends to favor short-term projects over long-term ones, it is often used when future events are difficult to quantify, such as for projects subject to political risk. Suppose a firm has a choice between two investments in a foreign country, one with a three-year payback period and one with a ten-year payback period. An election *may* take place in the foreign country in four years, and there is *some* chance that a new government *may* harden its policy towards foreign investments. It is very difficult (1) to estimate the probability of the occurrence of this type of event and (2) to quantify its implications on the magnitude of the project's expected cash flows and cost of capital. Even if the longer project has a higher positive NPV than the shorter investment, the firm's managers may opt for the project with the three-year payback period. Many risk-averse managers believe that this type of trade-off is relevant.

THE DISCOUNTED PAYBACK PERIOD

A project's **discounted payback period**, also known as the **economic payback period**, is the number of periods—usually measured in years—required for the sum of the *present values* of the project's expected cash flows to equal its initial cash outlay. To illustrate, we calculate the discounted payback period of investment A. The cumulative sums of the present values of its expected cash flows, at a cost of capital of 10 percent, are shown in the last column of Exhibit 7.7, indicating a discounted payback period slightly less than four years (recall that investment A requires an initial cash outlay of $1 million). The discounted payback periods of the investment proposals presented in Exhibit 7.2 are shown in Exhibit 7.8, where we find that project A's discounted payback period is 3.96 years. Exhibit 7.9 shows how to calculate discounted payback periods using a spreadsheet, taking project E as an example.

The discounted payback periods are *longer* than the ordinary payback periods calculated earlier (compare the data in Exhibit 7.8 with the data in Exhibit 7.5).

EXHIBIT 7.7 DISCOUNTED PAYBACK PERIOD CALCULATIONS FOR INVESTMENT A.

EXPECTED CASH FLOWS FROM EXHIBIT 7.2

End-of-Year	Expected Cash Flows	Discount Factor at 10%[1]	Present Value	Cumulative Present Value of Cash Flows
1	$600,000	0.9091	$545,455	$ 545,455
2	300,000	0.8264	247,934	793,389
3	100,000	0.7513	75,131	868,520
4	200,000	0.6830	136,603	1,005,123
5	300,000	0.6209	186,276	1,191,399

[1]The discount factors are four-digit approximations, but the present values are calculated on the basis of more exact approximations.

EXHIBIT 7.8 DISCOUNTED PAYBACK PERIODS FOR THE SIX INVESTMENTS IN EXHIBIT 7.2.

Investment	A	B	C	D	E	F
Discounted payback period (in years)	3.96	4.40	4.58	More than 5	3.86	3.86

This is not surprising because the discounted payback periods are measured with discounted cash flows that are smaller than the undiscounted cash flows used to calculate the ordinary payback periods. Notice also that the *ranking* of the investments according to their discounted payback periods is different from the ranking according to their ordinary payback periods. Furthermore, note that investments A and B as well as C and D no longer have the same payback periods.

THE DISCOUNTED PAYBACK PERIOD RULE

As for the ordinary payback period rule, the **discounted payback period rule** says that *a project is acceptable if its discounted payback period is shorter than or equal*

EXHIBIT 7.9 COMPUTING THE DISCOUNTED PAYBACK PERIOD FOR INVESTMENT E USING A SPREADSHEET.

EXPECTED CASH FLOWS FROM EXHIBIT 7.2

	A	B	C	D	E	F	G
1		0	1	2	3	4	5
2	Cash flows	–$1,000,000	$325,000	$325,000	$325,000	$ 325,000	$ 325,000
3							
4	Cost of capital	10.00%					
5							
6	Discounted cash flows		$295,455	$268,595	$244,177	$ 221,979	$ 201,799
7	Cumulative discounted cash flows		$295,455	$564,050	$808,227	$1,030,206	$1,232,005
8							
9	**Discounted payback period**		–	–	–	3.86	–
10							
11	*0 is now; 1, 2, 3,... is end of year.*						
12	*The formula in cell C6 is =C2/(1+$B$4)^C1. Then copy formula in cell C6 to next cells in row 6.*						
13	*The formula in cell C7 is =C6. The formula in cell D7 is =C7+D6. Then copy formula in cell D7 to next cells in row 7.*						
14	*The formula in cell C9 is =IF(OR(C7<=–$B$2,B7>–$B$2),"–",B1+(–$B$2–B7)/C6). Then copy formula in cell C9 to next cells in row 9.*						
15							

to a specified number of periods called the cutoff period. If the choice is among several projects, the one with the shortest discounted payback period should be selected.

If the cutoff period is maintained at four years, only investments A, E, and F are acceptable. In the case of the ordinary payback period rule, all six investments could be undertaken.

DOES THE DISCOUNTED PAYBACK RULE ADJUST FOR THE TIMING OF CASH FLOWS?

Consider investments A and B in Exhibit 7.2. They are identical except that the first-year and third-year cash flows have been interchanged. The largest cash flow of $600,000 occurs at the end of the first year for investment A; it occurs at the end of the third year for investment B. The discounted payback period takes this difference into account because the discounted payback period of A (3.96 years) is shorter than that of B (4.40 years). Thus, the discounted payback period rule takes the time value of money into account but *only* for the cash flows occurring up to the discounted payback period. Those following the payback period are still ignored.

DOES THE DISCOUNTED PAYBACK RULE ADJUST FOR RISK?

Consider investments C and D. They have an identical cash-flow stream, but investment C is less risky than D. The discounted payback period of C (4.58 years) is shorter than that of D (more than 5 years). Thus, the discounted payback period rule takes the risk of a project's expected cash flows into consideration but, as in the previous case, *only* for those cash flows occurring up to the discounted payback period. The cash flows after the discounted payback period, as well as their risk, are ignored.

DOES THE DISCOUNTED PAYBACK RULE MAXIMIZE THE FIRM'S EQUITY VALUE?

According to the discounted payback period rule, the present value of a project's expected cash flows up to their discounted payback period is equal to the project's initial cash outlay. In other words, if we calculate the project's NPV for the cash flows that occur up to the project's discounted payback period, we will find that it is equal to zero. *This means that a project's discounted payback period is equal to its "break-even" period.* For example, investment A, which has a discounted payback period of 3.96 years, creates value only if it lasts *more* than 3.96 years. If we then include cash inflows expected to occur *after* the discounted payback period, the project's NPV will be positive. Thus, if a project's cutoff period is *longer* than its discounted payback period, the project's NPV, estimated with cash flows up to the cutoff period, is always positive.

We cannot, however, conclude that the discounted payback period will systematically select those projects that contribute the most to the wealth of the firm's owners. A "right" cutoff period must be determined, and this is an arbitrary decision. Consider investments E and F. Their discounted payback period is the same and equal to 3.86 years. Like the ordinary payback period rule, the discounted payback period rule cannot discriminate between the two investments because it ignores the fifth year's cash flow, which is three times larger for F than it is for E.

Thus, the discounted payback period rule ignores cash flows beyond the cutoff period and is biased against long-term investments.

THE DISCOUNTED PAYBACK PERIOD RULE VERSUS THE ORDINARY PAYBACK PERIOD RULE

The discounted payback period rule has two major advantages over the ordinary payback period rule: it considers the time value of money, and it considers the risk of the investment's expected cash flows. However, it considers these conditions of a good investment rule only for cash flows expected to occur up to the discounted payback period. The discounted payback period is certainly superior to the ordinary payback period as an indicator of the time necessary to recover the project's initial cash outlay because it takes into consideration the opportunity cost of capital. But it is more complicated to estimate than the ordinary payback period. Indeed, it requires the same inputs as the NPV rule, that is, the project's useful life, its expected cash-flow stream, and its cost of capital. This may explain why the discounted payback period rule is less frequently used than the ordinary payback period rule, particularly for managers making frequent accept/reject decisions.

THE INTERNAL RATE OF RETURN

A project's **internal rate of return (IRR)** is the discount rate that makes the NPV of the project equal to zero. For example, to compute the IRR of investment A, we set NPV(A) equal to zero and find the discount rate that satisfies this condition. That rate is the investment's IRR:

$$\text{NPV(A)} = 0 = -\$1{,}000{,}000 + \frac{\$600{,}000}{(1 + \text{IRR})^1} + \frac{\$300{,}000}{(1 + \text{IRR})^2} + \frac{\$100{,}000}{(1 + \text{IRR})^3} + \frac{\$200{,}000}{(1 + \text{IRR})^4} + \frac{\$300{,}000}{(1 + \text{IRR})^5}$$

Unfortunately, there is no simple way to compute the IRR of a cash-flow stream except for the trivial case in which the project is a one-period investment or an annuity.[2] For example, if a project requires an initial investment of \$10,000 and will generate an expected cash flow of \$12,000 in one year, then its IRR is simply equal to 20 percent. For investments with longer lives, we can try to find the IRR by trial and error: we first guess a rate, use it to calculate the project's NPV, and then adjust the rate until we find the one that makes the NPV equal to zero. As you can imagine, this is a tedious and time-consuming exercise, especially if we want a precise number. Fortunately, any financial calculator or computer spreadsheet application will have an IRR function. Both search for the IRR by the trial-and-error method but do so quickly and accurately. Exhibit 7.10 shows how to compute investment E's IRR using a spreadsheet, and Exhibit 7.11 presents the IRR for the investment proposals defined in Exhibit 7.2.

---

[2] An annuity is a cash-flow stream with equal annual cash flows. The calculation of the present value of an annuity is presented in Appendix 6.1.

EXHIBIT 7.10 COMPUTING THE INTERNAL RATE OF RETURN OF INVESTMENT E USING A SPREADSHEET.

EXPECTED CASH FLOWS FROM EXHIBIT 7.2

	A	B	C	D	E	F	G
1		0	1	2	3	4	5
2	Cash flows	–$1,000,000	$325,000	$325,000	$325,000	$325,000	$325,000
3							
4	**Internal Rate of Return**	18.72%					
5							
6	*0 is now; 1, 2, 3,... is end of year.*						
7	*The formula in cell B4 is =IRR(B2:G2,.1) where .1 or 10 percent is a guess value for the IRR.*						

In general, if $CF_1, CF_2, \ldots, CF_t, \ldots, CF_N$ is the sequence of expected cash flows from an investment of N periods with an initial cash outlay of CF_0, then the investment's IRR is the solution to the following equation:

$$0 = CF_0 + \frac{CF_1}{(1 + IRR)^1} + \frac{CF_2}{(1 + IRR)^2} + \ldots + \frac{CF_t}{(1 + IRR)^t} + \ldots + \frac{CF_N}{(1 + IRR)^N}$$

All that is needed to calculate the IRR of an investment is the sequence of cash flows the investment is expected to generate. In effect, an investment's IRR summarizes its expected cash-flow stream with a single rate of return. The rate is called *internal* because it considers only the expected cash flows related to the investment and does not depend on rates that can be earned on alternative investments.

THE IRR RULE

Consider investment A. Its IRR is 19.05 percent, and its opportunity cost of capital is 10 percent. Recall that investment A's opportunity cost of capital is the highest return a firm can get on an alternative investment with the same risk as A.[3] Should the firm accept investment A? Yes, because the project's IRR (19.05 percent) is greater than the highest return the firm can get on another investment with the same risk (the 10 percent opportunity cost of capital).

EXHIBIT 7.11 IRR FOR THE SIX INVESTMENTS IN EXHIBIT 7.2.

Investment	A	B	C	D	E	F
Internal rate of return	19.05%	13.92%	7.93%	7.93%	18.72%	28.52%

[3]See Chapter 6 for a definition of an investment's opportunity cost of capital.

According to the **internal rate of return rule**, *an investment should be accepted if its IRR is higher than its cost of capital and should be rejected if its IRR is lower.* If the investment's IRR is equal to the cost of capital, the firm should be indifferent about accepting or rejecting the project.

A project's IRR can be interpreted as a measure of the profitability of its expected cash flow *before* considering the project's cost of capital. Thus, if a project's IRR is *lower* than its cost of capital, the project does not earn its cost of capital and should be rejected. If it is *higher*, the project earns more than its cost of capital and should be accepted.[4]

When used in comparison with the IRR, the investment's opportunity cost of capital is usually referred to as the **hurdle rate**, the **minimum required rate of return**, or, simply, the investment's *required return*. In other words, if a project's IRR is lower than its required return, it should be rejected; if it is higher, it should be accepted.

DOES THE IRR RULE ADJUST FOR THE TIMING OF CASH FLOWS?

Consider investments A and B in Exhibit 7.2. As pointed out earlier, investment A is preferable to investment B because its largest cash flow ($600,000) occurs earlier. The IRR rule indicates the same preference because the IRR of investment A (19.05 percent) is higher than the IRR of investment B (13.92 percent). Thus, the IRR rule takes into account the time value of money.

DOES THE IRR RULE ADJUST FOR RISK?

Compare investments C and D shown in Exhibit 7.2. They have the same expected cash-flow stream, but investment D, with a cost of capital of 10 percent, is riskier than investment C, whose cost of capital is only 5 percent. The two investments have the same IRR of 7.93 percent. Does the IRR rule take the risk of the two investments into consideration? Yes, it does, indirectly, through the comparison of the investment's IRR with its cost of capital. The IRR of investment C (7.93 percent) is greater than the minimum required return of 5 percent for this type of investment, so it should be accepted. Investment D should be rejected because its IRR of 7.93 percent is lower than the hurdle rate of 10 percent that the firm wants to earn on riskier investments similar to investment D.

The risk of an investment does not enter into the *computation* of its IRR, but the IRR *rule* does consider the risk of the investment because it compares the project's IRR with the minimum required rate of return, which is a measure of the risk of the investment.

DOES THE IRR RULE MAXIMIZE THE FIRM'S EQUITY VALUE?

A project's IRR is determined by setting its NPV equal to zero, so we would expect a project's NPV to be related to its IRR. To illustrate, we compute the NPV of investment E for various discount rates, as shown in Exhibit 7.12.

---

[4]The IRR should not be confused with the average accounting rate of return sometimes used to evaluate investment proposals. The latter is discussed in the last section of this chapter.

Exhibit 7.12 Net Present Value of Investment E for Various Discount Rates.

Discount Rate	0%	5%	10%	15%	20%	25%	30%
NPV(E)	$625,000	$407,080	$232,006	$89,450	–$28,050	–$125,984	–$208,440

From the figures in Exhibit 7.12, we can draw a graph that shows the changes in NPV(E) as the discount rate varies. The graph, known as the project's **NPV profile**, is shown in Exhibit 7.13. NPV(E) is on the vertical axis and the discount rate is on the horizontal axis.

The graph shows an *inverse* relationship between NPV(E) and the discount rate. As the discount rate increases, NPV(E) decreases because its expected cash flows are discounted at increasingly higher rates. The NPV curve intersects the horizontal axis at the point at which NPV(E) is equal to zero. At this point, the discount rate used to calculate the NPV of investment E must be equal to the IRR of investment E because the IRR is the discount rate at which the NPV is equal to zero. This discount rate is 18.72 percent (see Exhibit 7.13).

According to the IRR rule, investment E should be accepted if its cost of capital is lower than its IRR of 18.72 percent and should be rejected if its cost of capital is higher. The graph indicates that for discount rates (or costs of capital) lower

Exhibit 7.13 The NPV Profile of Investment E.

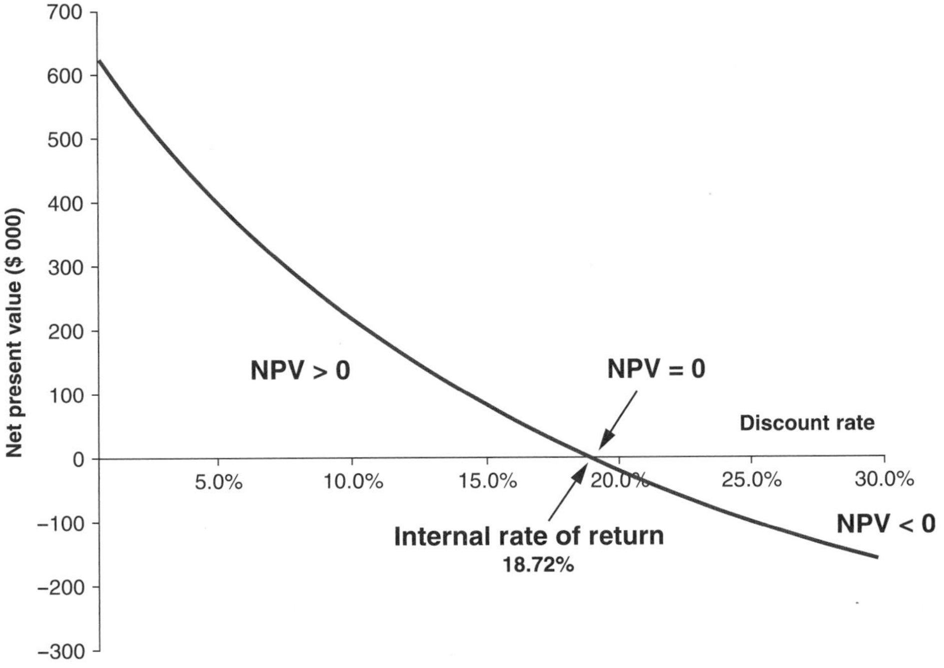

than 18.72 percent, the project's NPV is positive, and for discount rates higher than 18.72 percent, the project's NPV is negative. In other words, the graph indicates that when the NPV is positive, the IRR is higher than the cost of capital, and when it is negative, the IRR is lower than the cost of capital. The two rules are thus equivalent. And because the NPV rule is consistent with the maximization of the firm's equity value, so is the IRR rule.

THE IRR RULE MAY BE UNRELIABLE

The IRR rule may sometimes provide the *incorrect* investment decision when (1) the firm is reviewing two mutually exclusive investments (the firm cannot invest in both; if it accepts one, it must reject the other), and (2) the project's cash-flow stream changes signs more than once (the sequence of *future* cash flows contains at least one negative cash flow after a positive one).

THE CASE OF MUTUALLY EXCLUSIVE INVESTMENTS

When two projects are **mutually exclusive**, the IRR rule and the NPV rule may, under certain circumstances, select different investment proposals. Suppose we compare investment E in Exhibit 7.2 with investment H in Exhibit 7.14. They have the same useful life (five years), the same initial cash outlay ($1 million), and the same cost of capital (10 percent). Investment E has an IRR of 18.72 percent, and investment H has an IRR of 16.59 percent.

Both investments have an IRR that exceeds the cost of capital of 10 percent, so they should both be accepted according to the IRR rule. However, the investments are mutually exclusive, so the firm can accept only one. Which should it select? Intuition suggests the selection of investment E because it has a higher IRR than investment H. Unfortunately, intuition does not always lead to the correct decision. According to the NPV rule, investment H is preferable to investment E: at a cost of capital of 10 percent, the NPV of investment H is $282,519, whereas that of investment E is only $232,006 (see Exhibit 7.2).

The NPV profiles of investments E and H in Exhibit 7.15 show why the IRR and NPV rules disagree. The graph indicates that both the NPV and IRR rules

EXHIBIT 7.14 COMPARISON OF TWO MUTUALLY EXCLUSIVE INVESTMENTS WITH DIFFERENT CASH FLOWS AND IRR.

USEFUL LIFE = 5 YEARS; INITIAL CASH OUTLAY = $1 MILLION; COST OF CAPITAL = 10%

End-of-Year	Investment E	Investment H
1	$325,000	$ 100,000
2	325,000	100,000
3	325,000	100,000
4	325,000	150,000
5	325,000	1,500,000
IRR	**18.72%**	**16.59%**

favor investment E when the discount rate is higher than 12.94 percent (the rate at which the two NPV curves intersect)[5] and lower than 18.72 percent. For rates above 18.72 percent, the two projects should be rejected; both have a negative NPV and a discount rate higher than the IRR. For rates lower than 12.94 percent, the NPV rule favors investment H, but the IRR rule still favors investment E (it has a higher IRR than H).

This situation usually arises when the cash-flow patterns of two mutually exclusive investments differ widely, as in the case of investments E and H. Investment E's cash flows are evenly distributed during the project's life, whereas those of H are concentrated in the last year of the project's life. At high discount rates, the discounting effect (the "shrinking" of cash flows resulting from discounting) on distant cash flows is more pronounced than when the rate is low. As a consequence, when the discount rate increases, the NPV of the investment with cash flows concentrated at the end of the project's life (such as investment H) decreases more rapidly than the NPV of the investment whose cash flows arise earlier (such as investment E). The two projects have the same NPV at the point at which their NPV curves intersect. After that point, the NPV ranking of the two projects changes.

With a cost of capital of 10 percent, project H is the better investment because its NPV is larger than that of project E, thus creating more value to the firm's owners. Because the IRR approach would lead to the opposite choice, it would also have the opposite effect. In general, when a firm wants to rank projects according

EXHIBIT 7.15 THE NPV PROFILES OF INVESTMENTS E AND H.

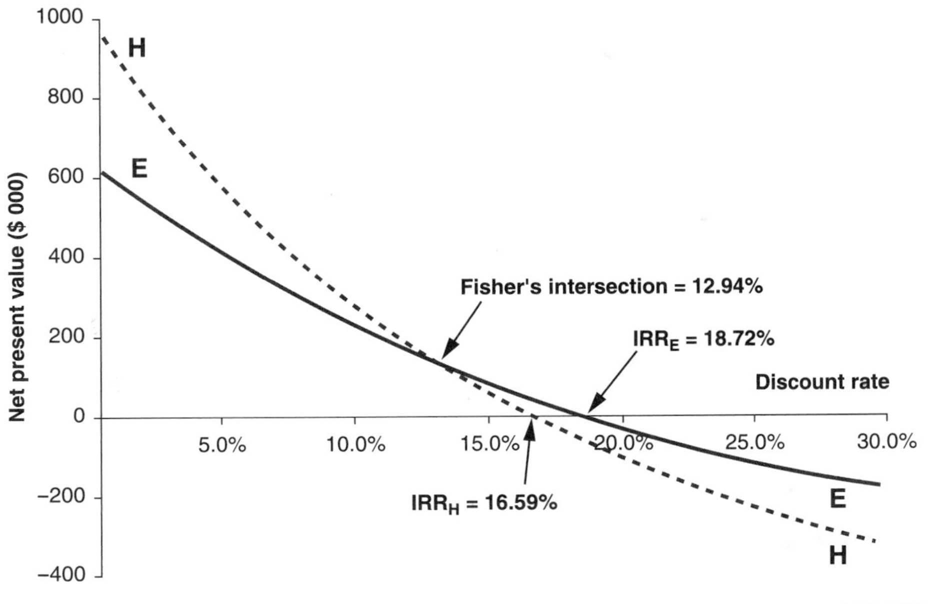

[5]The intersection rate is often referred to as **Fisher's intersection**, named after the economist Irving Fisher, who was among the first to study this phenomenon.

to their contribution to the value of the firm's equity, it should use the NPV rule rather than the IRR rule.

THE CASE OF INVESTMENTS WITH SOME NEGATIVE FUTURE CASH FLOWS

The IRR rule may be unreliable when a project's stream of expected cash flows includes negative cash flows. Negative cash flows can occur when an investment requires the construction of several facilities that are built at different times in the future. During the year when a new unit is built, the cash flow generated by the previously installed unit might not be large enough to cover the cost of the new one. The result is that the project's total cash flow for that year becomes negative. A project can also have a negative future cash flow if the project's termination requires a major capital expenditure, such as for a strip-mining project. Closing the mine and restoring the area's landscape at the end of the project's useful life may make the project's terminal cash flow negative.

When negative cash flows occur, a project may have more than one IRR or none at all. We illustrate this phenomenon with a two-year project that has a cost of capital of 20 percent and the pattern of expected cash flows shown in Exhibit 7.16.

The project has an IRR of 5 percent and an IRR of 40 percent. (If you check this, you will find that the project's NPV is zero at both 5 percent and 40 percent.) If the project has a cost of capital of 20 percent, it should be rejected if its IRR is 5 percent and accepted if its IRR is 40 percent. The choice is not obvious. What should the firm's managers do in this case? They should ignore the IRR rule and use the NPV rule instead. At a cost of capital of 20 percent, the project has a positive NPV of $20,833 and should be undertaken.

WHY DO MANAGERS USUALLY PREFER THE IRR RULE TO THE NPV RULE?

Despite its shortcomings, the IRR rule is popular among managers. One reason may be that the calculation of a project's IRR requires a single input, the cash-flow stream that the project is expected to generate. An estimate of the project's cost of capital is not necessary, whereas the calculation of a project's NPV requires estimates of both the expected cash-flow stream and the cost of capital. However, the application of the IRR *rule* requires both inputs. To decide whether to invest, managers

EXHIBIT 7.16 EXPECTED CASH FLOWS, IRR, AND NPV OF A PROJECT WITH NEGATIVE CASH FLOWS AND COST OF CAPITAL = 20%.

End-of-Year	Cash Flow
Now	–$1,000,000
1	+2,450,000
2	–1,470,000
IRR	**5% and 40%**
NPV at 20%	$20,833

must compare the project's IRR to its cost of capital. Thus, even though the IRR can be computed without knowing the project's cost of capital, the cost of capital is still needed to decide whether to undertake the project. If both methods require the same inputs to select projects, what is the advantage of using the IRR rule?

The advantage may be that it is easier to estimate a project's IRR than its NPV when the project's cost of capital is uncertain (the *computation* of the IRR does not require knowing the cost of capital). Then, the decision whether to accept or reject the project is made after an appropriate required return is determined.[6] Our suspicion is that managers favor the IRR rule for a simpler reason: it is easier for them to communicate a project's potential profitability using its IRR than its NPV. When "selling" an investment proposal, you will certainly be more convincing if you indicate that the proposal has a potential return of 35 percent than if you say it has an NPV of $4,531,284. Managers usually have a good understanding of what an investment should "return" (partly because they are accustomed to measuring business performance with indicators such as return on sales and return on assets). A comparison of that implicit "return" with the project's IRR is straightforward. A comparison with the project's NPV is not so obvious.

Our advice: a project's NPV can be estimated with the same information required to apply the IRR rule, so you should compute both. When both rules lead to the same recommendation, mention the project's IRR instead of its NPV. When the outcome of your analysis indicates a conflict between the two methods, you should trust the NPV rule.

THE PROFITABILITY INDEX

A project's **profitability index (PI)** is equal to the ratio of the present value of its expected cash-flow stream to its initial cash outlay (CF_0):

$$\textbf{PI(project)} = \frac{(CF_1 \times DF_1) + \ldots + (CF_t \times DF_t) + \ldots + (CF_N \times DF_N)}{CF_0}$$

where DF_t is the discount factor calculated with the project's cost of capital k. The PI is a benefit-to-cost ratio because it is the ratio of the benefit derived from the investment (the present value of its expected cash flows at the cost of capital) to its cost (the initial cash outlay).

Applying the definition to investment A in Exhibit 7.2 (all financial figures in thousands of dollars), we get the following:

$$\text{PI(A)} = \frac{(\$600 \times 0.9091) + (\$300 \times 0.8264) + (\$100 \times 0.7513) + (\$200 \times 0.6830) + (\$300 \times 0.6209)}{\$1{,}000}$$

$$\text{PI(A)} = \frac{\$1{,}191}{\$1{,}000} = 1.19$$

[6] This would usually happen if the firm adopted a "bottom-up" approach to capital budgeting for some of its difficult-to-assess projects. In this approach, divisions submit projects with their IRR to a committee. The decision to invest is made after collecting all submitted projects and comparing their IRR with risk-adjusted required returns established by the investment committee.

EXHIBIT 7.17 COMPUTING THE PROFITABILITY INDEX OF INVESTMENT E USING A SPREADSHEET.

EXPECTED CASH FLOWS FROM EXHIBIT 7.2

	A	B	C	D	E	F	G
1		0	1	2	3	4	5
2	Cash flows	–$1,000,000	$325,000	$325,000	$325,000	$325,000	$325,000
3							
4	Cost of capital	10.00%					
5							
6	**Profitability index**	**1.23**					
7	*0 is now; 1, 2, 3,... is end of year.*						
8	*The formula in cell B6 is =NPV(B4,C2:G2)/–B2.*						
9							

Exhibit 7.17 shows how to compute PIs using a spreadsheet, taking investment E as an example. Exhibit 7.18 presents the PIs of the investment proposals in Exhibit 7.2.

THE PROFITABILITY INDEX RULE

According to the **profitability index rule**, *a project should be accepted if its PI is greater than one and rejected if it is less than one.* If the investment's PI is equal to one, the firm should be indifferent about whether to accept or reject the project. According to this rule, all projects except project D should be accepted (see Exhibit 7.18).

DOES THE PROFITABILITY INDEX RULE ADJUST FOR THE TIMING OF CASH FLOWS?

The PI rule takes into account the time value of money because the projects' expected cash flows are discounted at their cost of capital. Like the NPV and IRR rules, the PI rule favors project A over project B (see Exhibit 7.18), and the only difference between these two projects is the timing of their respective expected cash flows.

DOES THE PROFITABILITY INDEX RULE ADJUST FOR RISK?

The PI rule considers the risk of an investment because it uses the cost of capital (which reflects the risk of the expected cash-flow stream) as the discount rate. Again, like the NPV and IRR rules, the PI rule chooses investment C over riskier investment D, even though the two investments have the same expected cash-flow stream.

EXHIBIT 7.18 PROFITABILITY INDEXES FOR THE SIX INVESTMENTS IN EXHIBIT 7.2.

Investment	A	B	C	D	E	F
Profitability index	1.19	1.11	1.08	0.95	1.23	1.64

EXHIBIT 7.19 COMPARISON OF TWO MUTUALLY EXCLUSIVE INVESTMENTS WITH DIFFERENT INITIAL CASH OUTLAYS AND EXPECTED CASH FLOWS.

End-of-Year	Investment A	Investment K
Now	–$1,000,000	–$2,000,000
1	600,000	100,000
2	300,000	300,000
3	100,000	600,000
4	200,000	200,000
5	300,000	2,100,000
NPV at 10%	$ 191,399	$ 230,169
Profitability index	1.19	1.12

DOES THE PROFITABILITY INDEX RULE MAXIMIZE THE FIRM'S EQUITY VALUE?

When a project has a PI greater than one, the present value of its expected cash flows is greater than the initial cash outlay, and the project's NPV is positive. Conversely, if the PI is less than one, the project's NPV is negative. It may seem to follow that the PI rule is a substitute for the NPV rule and will select projects that contribute the most to enhancing the firm's market value.

Unfortunately, the PI rule may lead to an incorrect decision when it is applied to two mutually exclusive investments with *different* initial cash outlays. To illustrate, we compare investment A in Exhibit 7.2 with investment K, which has the same useful life (five years) and the same cost of capital (10 percent), but investment K requires an initial cash outlay twice as large as that of investment A and has a different cash-flow stream. The cash-flow streams, the NPVs, and the PIs for the two investments are shown in Exhibit 7.19.

Investment A's PI (1.19) is higher than that of investment K (1.12). Before concluding that investment A is superior to K, we should first compare the NPV of the investments. Investment A has a lower NPV than investment K, so the PI has chosen the investment that creates the *least* value to the firm's owners. Conclusion: The PI rule is not consistent with the maximization of the firm's market value when used to make a choice between mutually exclusive projects with different initial cash outlays.

USE OF THE PROFITABILITY INDEX RULE

Despite the problem that occurs when the choice is between mutually exclusive projects of unequal sizes, the PI is a useful substitute for the NPV rule. Like the IRR, it is easier to communicate the potential profitability of an investment proposal with the PI than with the NPV. The reason is that both the PI and the IRR are *relative* measures of an investment's value, whereas the NPV is an *absolute* measure. The index tells how much present benefit a project is expected to generate *per dollar* of investment, whereas the NPV provides the present value of the benefits net of the project's initial cost.[7]

THE AVERAGE ACCOUNTING RETURN

Although many measures of **average accounting returns (AAR)** are applied to investment proposals, they are always defined as the ratio of some measure of average accounting profit expected from the proposal to some average amount of assets that the investment is expected to use over its useful life. The most general measure of average accounting return is defined as follows:

$$\text{AAR} = \frac{\textbf{Average earnings after tax expected from the project}}{\textbf{Average book value of the project}}$$

As an example, let's assume that project P requires an initial cash outlay of $1 million for the purchase of a piece of equipment that it is expected to last five years. The investment will be depreciated at a rate of $200,000 a year over its useful life. The project is expected to generate annual earnings after tax of $100,000, $80,000, $60,000, $40,000, and $20,000 in Years 1, 2, ..., 5, respectively. Thus the average expected earnings after tax is as follows:

$$\frac{\$100{,}000 + \$80{,}000 + \$60{,}000 + \$40{,}000 + \$20{,}000}{5} = \$60{,}000$$

The initial book value of the investment is $1,000,000 and is zero at the end of its useful life. Thus the average book value of the investment is $500,000 and the average accounting return of the project is as follows:

$$\text{AAR} = \frac{\$60{,}000}{\$500{,}000} = 12 \text{ percent}$$

THE AVERAGE ACCOUNTING RETURN RULE

According to the average accounting return rule, *a project is acceptable if its average accounting return is higher than a target average return.*

DOES THE AAR RULE ADJUST FOR THE TIMING OF CASH FLOWS?

The rule relies on accounting numbers such as earnings after tax and book value of investments, which are not cash flows. Like the payback period rule, it does not account for the time value of money. But, unlike the payback period, which can be improved to account for the timing of cash flows by discounting them at the cost of capital, the average accounting return rule does not adjust for the timing of earnings.

DOES THE AAR RULE ADJUST FOR RISK?

In the discounted cash-flow rules, such as the NPV or IRR rules, the risk of the project is accounted for in the cost of capital. By extension, we would expect that

[7]Chapter 6 shows how the PI rule can be used to compare investments of unequal sizes (investments with different cash outlays).

risk in the average accounting return rule is taken care of in the target return. This may be the case, but there is no objective way to adjust the target return to the project's risk.

Does the AAR Rule Maximize the Firm's Equity Value?

It is unlikely that the average accounting return rule would always select investment proposals that maximize shareholder value because it is based on accounting data (as opposed to cash flows), ignores the time value of money, and treats risk on an *ad hoc* basis.

Given the rather serious shortcomings of the average accounting return, why do 20 percent of the chief financial officers in the survey presented in Exhibit 7.1 use this rule? We suggest two reasons. First, the rule is easy to apply because it uses accounting numbers that are usually readily available. Second, because most measures of performance used in compensation and reward systems are still based on accounting figures, it makes sense that managers may want to check the accounting return of their investment proposals.

SUMMARY

Our analysis of the alternatives to the net present value (NPV) rule has shown that the NPV rule is the best criterion for selecting desirable investment proposals (projects that are expected to raise the market value of a firm's equity and, thereby, increase the wealth of the firm's owners). This conclusion does not imply that the alternative capital budgeting techniques presented in this chapter should be discarded. A project's profitability index, internal rate of return, payback period, and average accounting return may provide useful information to managers and are often easier to interpret and communicate than the NPV.

As Exhibit 7.1 shows, companies rarely rely on a single method to screen investment proposals. Most firms using the NPV rule also use alternative decision criteria. But this observation should not distract from the facts that *all* the alternatives to the NPV method have some shortcomings and that some have serious weaknesses in assessing the value-creating capacity of a project.

Exhibit 7.20 summarizes the properties of the five alternative investment evaluation methods. Our final recommendation: when alternative methods provide conflicting signals, the value-creating manager should trust the NPV approach.

EXHIBIT 7.20 PROPERTIES OF ALTERNATIVE CAPITAL BUDGETING RULES.

Evaluation method	Inputs required		Decision rule		Does the rule adjust cash flows for		Is the rule consistent with the maximization of the firm's equity value?
	for calculation	for decision	Accept	Reject	Time?	Risk?	
Net present value (NPV)	• Cash flows • Cost of capital (k)	• NPV	NPV > 0	NPV < 0	Yes	Yes	Yes, a project's NPV is a measure of the value the project creates or destroys.
Profitability index (PI)	• Cash flows • Cost of capital (k)	• PI	PI > 1	PI < 1	Yes	Yes	Yes, but *may* fail to select the project with the highest NPV when projects are mutually exclusive.
Internal rate of return (IRR)	• Cash flows	• IRR • Cost of capital (k)	IRR > k	IRR < k	Yes	Yes	Yes, but *may* fail when: • projects are mutually exclusive • cash flows change signs more than once
Discounted payback period (DPP)	• Cash flows • Cost of capital (k)	• DPP • Cutoff period	DPP < Cutoff period	DPP > Cutoff period	Only within DPP	Only within DPP	Only when the project's discounted payback period is *shorter* than its cutoff period.
Payback period (PP)	• Cash flows	• PP • Cutoff period	PP < Cutoff period	PP > Cutoff period	No	No	No

FURTHER READING

1. Damodaran, Aswath. *Corporate Finance: Theory and Practice*, 2nd ed. John Wiley & Sons, 2001. See Chapter 10.
2. Ross, Stephen, Randolph Westerfield, and Jeffrey Jaffe. *Corporate Finance*, 8th ed. McGraw-Hill Irwin, 2008. See Chapter 6.

SELF-TEST PROBLEMS

7.1 SHORTCOMINGS OF THE PAYBACK PERIOD.

What are the shortcomings of the payback period rule, and why, despite these shortcomings, do many firms still use the payback period as an important input in the investment decision?

7.2 INTERNAL RATE OF RETURN VERSUS COST OF CAPITAL.

What is the difference between a project's cost of capital and its internal rate of return?

7.3 INTERNAL RATE OF RETURN VERSUS RETURN ON INVESTED CAPITAL.

What is the difference between the internal rate of return and the return on invested capital?

7.4 SHORTCOMINGS OF THE INTERNAL RATE OF RETURN AND THE PROFITABILITY INDEX RULES.

Under which circumstances may the internal rate of return rule and the profitability index rule lead to the wrong investment decision?

7.5 EVALUATING TWO PROJECTS USING ALTERNATIVE DECISION RULES.

Two projects have the expected cash flows shown below. The projects have similar risk characteristics, and their cost of capital is 10 percent.

	Project A	Project B
Now	–$2,000,000	–$2,000,000
End-of-Year 1	200,000	1,400,000
End-of-Year 2	1,200,000	1,000,000
End-of-Year 3	1,700,000	400,000

a. Calculate the net present value (NPV) of each project. According to the NPV rule, which project should be accepted if they are independent? If they are mutually exclusive?
b. Calculate the payback period and the discounted payback period of each project. If the two projects are mutually exclusive, which project should be accepted?

c. Calculate the internal rate of return of each project. Which project should be accepted if they are independent? If they are mutually exclusive?
d. Calculate the profitability index of each project. Which project should be accepted if they are independent? If they are mutually exclusive?
e. Based on your answers to questions a–d, which criterion leads to the best investment decision if the projects are independent? If they are mutually exclusive?

REVIEW PROBLEMS

1. **Investment criteria.**
The Global Chemical Company (GCC) uses the following criteria to make capital investment decisions:

1. Effect on earnings per share *(must be positive)*
2. Payback period *(must be less than six years)*
3. Internal rate of return *(must be at least 12 percent)*
4. Net present value *(must be positive at a 12 percent discount rate)*

a. What are the advantages and disadvantages of each of these measures?
b. Why do you think GCC uses all of these measures rather than just one of them?

2. **Relationship between investment criteria.**
A project with a cash outlay now is followed by positive expected cash flows in the future and a positive net present value. What does this information tell you about the project's discounted payback period, internal rate of return, profitability index, and average accounting return?

3. **Net present value and payback period.**
A project with a cash outlay now is followed by positive expected cash flows in the future and a payback period less than its economic life. Is its net present value positive or negative? Explain.
Now suppose that the discounted payback period is less than the useful life of the project. Is its net present value positive or negative? Explain.

4. **The internal rate of return of mutually exclusive projects.**
The following chart plots the net present value (NPV) of projects A and B at different discount rates. The projects have similar risk and are mutually exclusive.

a. What is the significance of the point on the graph where the two lines intersect?
b. What is the significance of the points on the graph where the two lines cross the zero NPV axis?
c. What is the likely explanation for the differences in net present value at the various discount rates?
d. Which project would you recommend? Why?

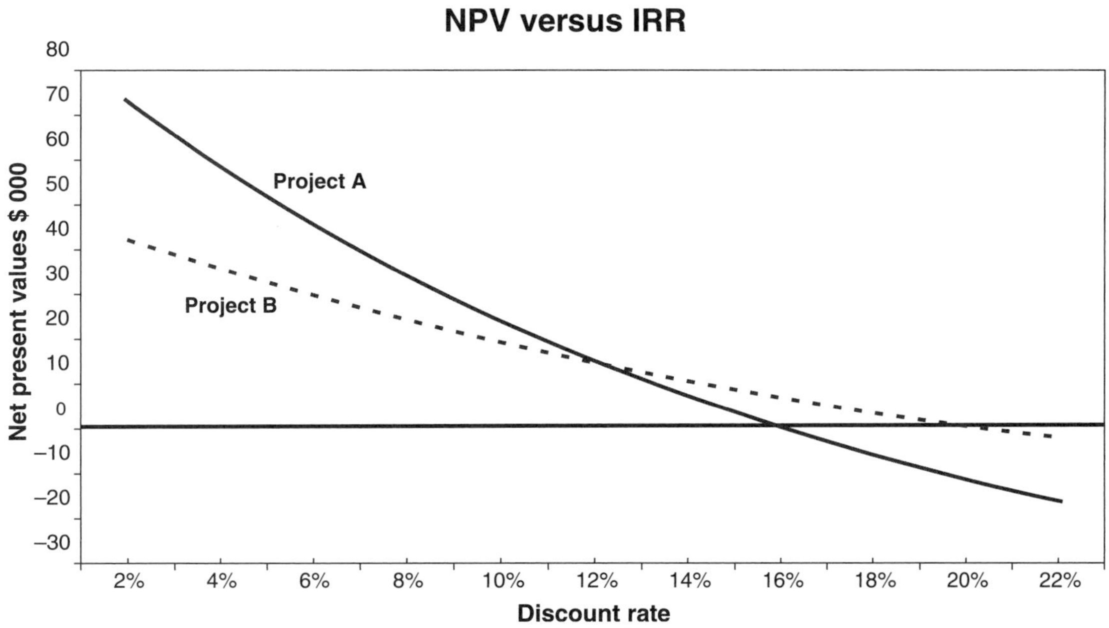

5. **The case of multiple internal rates of return.**
The International Industrial Company has an investment project with the following cash flows:

	Cash Flow	Type of Cash Flow
Now	–$200	Purchase of equipment
End-of-Year 1	600	Cash earnings from project
End-of-Year 2	–400	Cash earnings from project less cleanup costs

a. What is the net present value of these cash flows at 0, 25, 50, and 100 percent discount rates?
b. What is the internal rate of return of this project?
c. Under what conditions should the project be accepted?

6. **The net present value rule versus the internal rate of return.**
You must choose *between* the two projects whose cash flows are shown below. The projects have the same risk.

	Project A	Project B
Now	–$12,000	–$2,400
End-of-Year 1	7,900	2,500
End-of-Year 2	6,850	950

a. Compute the internal rate of return and the net present value for the two projects. Assume a 10 percent discount rate.
b. Which of the projects is better according to each of the two methods?
c. What is the explanation for the differences in rankings between the net present value and the internal rate of return?
d. Which method is correct? Why?
e. Compute the internal rate of return for the incremental cash flows (project A minus project B). For discount rates below this internal rate of return, which project is best? For discount rates above this IRR, which project is best? Is this consistent with your answer to question d?

7. **The internal rate of return rule and the net present value rule.**
Consider the three projects A, B, and C. The cost of capital is 12 percent, and the projects have the following expected cash flows:

	Project A	Project B	Project C
Now	–$150,000	–$300,000	–$150,000
End-of-Year 1	120,000	200,000	110,000
End-of-Year 2	80,000	180,000	90,000

a. What is the internal rate of return of the three projects?
b. What is the net present value of the three projects?
c. If the three projects are independent, which projects should be accepted?
d. If the three projects are mutually exclusive, which project should be selected?
e. If the total budget for the three projects is limited to $450,000, which projects should be selected?

8. **The net present value rule versus the profitability index rule.**
You must choose *between* the two projects whose cash flows are shown below. The projects have the same risk.

	Project A	Project B
Now	–$16,000	–$3,200
End-of-Year 1	10,500	3,300
End-of-Year 2	9,100	1,260
End-of-Year 3	3,000	600

a. Compute the net present value (NPV) and the profitability index (PI) for the two projects. Assume a 10 percent discount rate.
b. Which of the projects is better according to each of the two methods?
c. What is the explanation for the differences in rankings between the NPV and PI methods of analysis?
d. Which method is correct? Why?

9. **The average accounting return.**
The Alpha Printer Company is considering the purchase of a $2 million printing machine. Its economic life is estimated at five years, and it will have no resale value after that time. The machine would generate an additional $200,000 of earnings after tax for the company during the first year of operation that will grow at a rate of 10 percent per year afterward. The company applies straight-line depreciation to its property, plant, and equipment assets. What is the average accounting return of the investment? Should the machine be bought if the firm's target average accounting return on its investment is 20 percent? Would you feel comfortable with your decision based on this approach to capital budgeting? Why or why not?

10. **Investment criteria.**
The Great Eastern Toys Company is evaluating a new product. The cash flows that are expected from this product over its five years' expected life are shown below. Note that the final year's cash flow includes $2,000 of working capital to be recovered at the end of the project.

	Cash Flow
Now	–$18,000
End-of-Year 1 to 4	5,200
End-of-Year 5	7,200

a. Compute the following measures:
   1. Payback period
   2. Discounted payback period at a 10 percent discount rate
   3. Net present value at a 10 percent discount rate
   4. Internal rate of return
   5. Profitability index

b. Should the project be undertaken?

IDENTIFYING AND ESTIMATING A PROJECT'S CASH FLOWS

CHAPTER 8

Chapters 6 and 7 explain rules that help managers make capital expenditure decisions. All these rules require the estimation of the cash-flow stream the investment is expected to generate in the future. This chapter shows how to identify and estimate the cash flows that are relevant to an investment decision.

Two fundamental principles provide some guidance in the determination of a project's cash flows: the *actual cash-flow principle* and the *with/without principle.* According to the first, cash flows must be measured *at the time they actually occur,* that is, during the period cash is actually received or paid out. According to the second, the cash flows relevant to an investment decision are only those that change the firm's *overall* cash position if the investment is undertaken.

First, we present and explain these principles, and then we show how to apply them. Sunlight Manufacturing Company's designer desk-lamp project, whose net present value (NPV) was first computed in Chapter 6, is used to illustrate our approach. After reading this chapter, you should understand the following:

- The actual cash-flow principle and the with/without principle, and how to apply them to make capital expenditure decisions
- How to identify a project's relevant cash flows
- Sunk costs and opportunity costs
- How to estimate a project's relevant cash flows

THE ACTUAL CASH-FLOW PRINCIPLE

According to the **actual cash-flow principle**, an investment's cash flows must be measured at the time they actually occur. For example, suppose a proposal is expected to generate a tax expense next year that will be paid the following year. The cash outflow must be taken into account the year the tax is paid, not the year the tax expense is recorded in the firm's income statement.

Investment proposals are often supported with data obtained from projected income statements that show the expected effect of the project on the firm's accounting earnings. But like tax expense, revenues and expenses reported in the income statement are generally not cash-flow figures. Thus, it is incorrect to use the investment's contribution to the firm's accounting earnings as a proxy for cash flows. This chapter shows how to convert accounting flows into cash flows for the purpose of making investment decisions.

Another implication of the actual cash-flow principle is that the dollar value of a project's future cash flows must be calculated with the prices and costs that are expected to prevail in the future, not with today's prices and costs. In other words, if the prices and costs associated with a project are expected to rise because of inflation, **nominal cash flows**, the cash flows that incorporate anticipated inflation, should be estimated. Furthermore, if the decision to invest is made on the basis of the project's NPV or its internal rate of return (IRR), then the cost of capital used to calculate the project's NPV or to compare with the project's IRR must also incorporate the anticipated rate of inflation.

If the effect of future inflation rates on the project's cash flows is too difficult to estimate, such as in countries subject to hyperinflation or a volatile inflation rate, a project's expected **real cash flows** can be estimated instead of its expected nominal cash flows. Real cash flows are the values of cash flows calculated with the assumption that prices and costs will not be affected by anticipated inflation. In this case, however, the project's cost of capital also must be estimated without the effect of anticipated inflation. Inflation must be treated consistently. If it is excluded from the cash flows, it also must be excluded from the cost of capital. If it is taken into account, it should be incorporated in both the project's expected cash flows and its cost of capital.

Finally, a project's expected cash flows must be measured in the same currency. When an investment decision involves prices or costs that are denominated in a foreign currency, these variables must be converted to their equivalent domestic values at the exchange rates that are expected to prevail in the future. This requirement necessitates forecasting future exchange rates, an issue we address in Chapter 14.

THE WITH/WITHOUT PRINCIPLE

The second guiding principle in estimating an investment's cash flows is the **with/without principle**. According to this principle, the **relevant cash flows** associated with an investment decision are only those cash flows that will *change* the firm's overall future cash position as a result of the decision to invest. In other words, relevant cash flows are **incremental**, or **differential**, **cash flows**.[1] They are equal to the difference between the firm's expected cash flows if the investment is made (the firm "with" the project) and its expected cash flows if the investment is rejected (the firm "without" the project). If CF_t denotes the cash flows occurring during period t,

$$\begin{aligned}\textbf{Project's } \mathbf{CF}_t &= \textbf{Firm's incremental } \mathbf{CF}_t \\ &= \textbf{Firm's } \mathbf{CF}_t\textbf{(with the project)} - \textbf{Firm's } \mathbf{CF}_t\textbf{(without the project)}\end{aligned}$$

---

[1]A similar notion, used in economic analysis, is the concept of marginal cost. The difference between a marginal cost and an incremental cost is that the former usually refers to the additional cost of, say, producing *one* more unit of a product, whereas the latter refers to the *total* extra cost resulting from the acceptance of a project.

To illustrate, consider trying to decide whether to drive to work or take public transportation. Suppose you are currently driving to work (this is your situation *without* the project). Last month, you took the train and found it less tiring than driving. The monthly train tickets cost $140. You want to know whether commuting by train on a regular basis (your situation *with* the project) is cheaper than driving. These are the monthly cash expenses related to your car:

1.	Insurance	$120
2.	Rent on the garage near your apartment	$150
3.	Parking fees near your office	$ 90
4.	Gas and car service related to commuting	$110

If you take the train, your *total* monthly cash expenses will include the cost of the train tickets, and the insurance and garage rental costs, which you will still have to pay (we assume you will not sell your car):

$$\begin{aligned}\text{CF(with the project)} = \text{CF(train)} &= -\text{ Insurance cost} - \text{Garage rental cost} \\ &\quad - \text{Train tickets cost} \\ &= -\$120 - \$150 - \$140 = -\$410\end{aligned}$$

If you drive your car, your *total* monthly cash expenses will include the office parking fees, gas and car service costs, and insurance and garage rental costs. Therefore,

$$\begin{aligned}\text{CF(without the project)} = \text{CF(car)} &= -\text{ Insurance cost} - \text{Garage rental cost} \\ &\quad - \text{Office parking fees} - \text{Gas and service cost} \\ &= -\$120 - \$150 - \$90 - \$110 = -\$470\end{aligned}$$

If you take the train, your total monthly cash outflow is $410. If you take the car, it is $470. The project's incremental monthly cash flow is thus $60:

$$\begin{aligned}\text{Project's CF} = \text{Incremental CF} &= \text{CF(train)} - \text{CF(car)} \\ &= [-\$410] - [-\$470] = \$60\end{aligned}$$

The $60 incremental cash flow can be determined directly if you identify which of the four expenses are relevant to commuting by train and which are irrelevant. The **relevant costs** are those cash expenses that will increase your monthly *total* or *overall* expenses; the **irrelevant costs** are those cash expenses that will not affect them. The first two costs (insurance and garage rental) are irrelevant to your decision because they will be incurred regardless of whether or not you take the train. In other words, they are **unavoidable costs**. The third and fourth costs (office parking fees and gas and car service) are relevant costs because they can be saved if you decide to take the train. They are **avoidable costs**. They amount to $200 per month ($90 plus $110). Because the monthly train ticket costs $140, the train is the cheaper commuting alternative. Every month, you would save $60, the difference between $200 and $140, which is exactly the project's monthly incremental cash flow that we found previously. The difference from the previous approach is that we ignored the common expenses of insurance ($120) and garage rental ($150) because they are irrelevant to the decision.

The $140 you paid *last month* to take the train on a trial basis is irrelevant to your decision. That money has already been spent and will not be recovered whether or not you decide to go to work by car or by train in the future. These types of costs are called **sunk costs.**

Now, let's add a small complication to the choice between the car and the train. Suppose you drive a colleague to work twice a week with the understanding that he will fill your gas tank once a month at a cost of $35. Is this a relevant cost to your commuting decision? Yes, it is, because if you take the train, you will no longer receive the $35. In this situation, the advantage of taking the train instead of the car will drop to $25 a month ($60 less $35). The cost we have just described is called an **opportunity cost.** It is relevant because it represents a loss of income if the train alternative is adopted. Sunk costs and opportunity costs are discussed in more detail later in the chapter in the context of Sunlight Manufacturing Company's designer desk-lamp project.

The assumption so far is that your car will stay in the garage. But what if your daughter decides to drive to college twice a week now that the car is available? If the monthly cost of these trips (gas and parking) exceeds $25, then commuting to work by train will be more expensive than driving your car. This example illustrates an important point. When estimating a project's incremental cash flows, *all* the side effects must be identified. This can be a challenging task for many investments. But you cannot estimate a project's expected cash flows properly if you have not considered *all* the relevant costs and benefits.

A final comment: the relevant benefits and costs associated with a project cannot all be quantified easily. For example, our analysis indicates that commuting by car is more expensive than taking the train. But you may find that driving is more convenient and less time-consuming. Although putting a dollar value on these benefits may not be simple, you must do so because they may justify taking the car.

We now turn to the analysis of a complex case—the designer desk-lamp project whose NPV is computed in Chapter 6.

THE DESIGNER DESK-LAMP PROJECT

Recall that Sunlight Manufacturing Company (SMC) has been successfully producing and selling electrical appliances for the past twenty years and is considering a possible extension of its existing product line. The company's general manager has recently proposed that SMC enter the relatively high-margin, high-quality designer desk-lamp market. This section describes the project's characteristics, which are summarized in Exhibit 8.1.

A consulting company was hired to do a preliminary study of the potential market for this type of product. Its report indicates that SMC can sell as many as 45,000 lamps the first year of the project, 40,000 the second year, 30,000 the third year, 20,000 the fourth year, and 10,000 the fifth year, after which the project will be terminated. The lamps can be sold for $40 each the first year, and that price can be raised annually by no more than 3 percent, a rate of increase equal to the rate of inflation expected to prevail during the project's five-year life. The consulting company billed SMC $30,000 for the study and was paid a month later.

SMC's sales manager is concerned that the new product will reduce the sales of SMC's standard desk lamps. She fears that potential customers will switch from buying standard desk lamps to buying the new designer desk lamps and estimates that SMC's potential losses could reduce the firm's after-tax operating *cash flows* by as much as $110,000 per year.

EXHIBIT 8.1 DATA SUMMARY OF THE DESIGNER DESK-LAMP PROJECT.

Item	Corresponding Units or Value	Type	Timing
1. Expected annual unit sales	45,000; 40,000; 30,000; 20,000; 10,000	Revenue	End-of-Year 1 to 5
2. Price per unit	$40 the first year, then rising annually at 3%	Revenue	End-of-Year 1 to 5
3. Consulting company's fee	$30,000	Expense	Already incurred
4. Losses on standard lamps	$110,000	Net cash loss	End-of-Year 1 to 5
5. Rental of building to outsiders	$10,000	Revenue	End-of-Year 1 to 5
6. Cost of the equipment	$2,000,000	Asset	Now
7. Straight-line depreciation expense	$400,000 ($2,000,000 divided by 5 years)	Expense	End-of-Year 1 to 5
8. Resale value of equipment	$100,000	Revenue	End-of-Year 5
9. Raw material cost per unit	$10 the first year, then rising annually at 3%	Expense	End-of-Year 1 to 5
10. Raw material inventory	7 days of sales	Asset	Now
11. Accounts payable	4 weeks (or 28 days) of purchases	Liability	Now
12. Accounts receivable	8 weeks (or 56 days) of sales	Asset	Now
13. In-process and finished goods inventories	16 days of sales	Asset	Now
14. Direct labor cost per unit	$5 the first year, then rising annually at 3%	Expense	End-of-Year 1 to 5
15. Energy cost per unit	$1 the first year, then rising annually at 3%	Expense	End-of-Year 1 to 5
16. Overhead charge	1% of sales	Expense	End-of-Year 1 to 5
17. Financing charge	12% of the net book value of assets	Expense	End-of-Year 1 to 5
18. Tax expense on income	40% of pre-tax profits	Expense	End-of-Year 1 to 5
19. Tax expense on capital gains	40% of pre-tax capital gains	Expense	End-of-Year 5
20. After-tax cost of capital	7.6% (see Chapter 10)	Not a cash flow	

If SMC decides to produce the designer desk lamp, it will use a building it already owns that is unoccupied. Recently, SMC received a letter from the vice president of a nearby department store who wanted to know whether SMC would be willing to rent the building as a storage area. SMC's accounting department indicates that, given current market rates, the building can be rented for $10,000 a year for five years.

The engineering department has determined that the equipment needed to produce the lamps will cost $2 million, shipped and installed. For tax purposes, the equipment can be depreciated using the straight-line method over the next five years, that is, at a rate of $400,000 per year ($2 million divided by five). The resale value of the equipment is estimated at $100,000 if it is sold at the end of the project's fifth year.

After consulting a few suppliers, the purchasing department says that the raw materials required to produce the designer desk lamp will cost $10 per lamp the first year of the project and will most likely rise at the annual expected rate of inflation of 3 percent. To avoid disruption in supply, SMC will need seven days of raw material inventory. The firm pays its suppliers, on average, four weeks (twenty-eight days) after the raw materials are delivered, and receives payment from its customers, on average, eight weeks (fifty-six days) after the products are shipped.

The production department has estimated that the project's necessary amount of work in process and finished goods inventories will be worth sixteen days of sales. Furthermore, SMC's direct labor costs will rise by $5 per lamp and its energy costs will rise by $1 per lamp the first year of the project. These costs will rise at the expected annual rate of inflation of 3 percent during the project's life. Because the company's existing personnel and organizational structure are expected to be able to support the sale of the new product, the firm will not have additional selling, general, and administrative expenses.

To cover SMC's overhead costs (corporate fixed costs), the accounting department charges new projects a standard fee equal to 1 percent of the projects' sales revenues. New projects are also charged an additional fee to cover the cost of financing the assets used to support the projects. This financing charge is equal to 12 percent of the book (accounting) value of the assets employed.

Tax laws allow the $2 million worth of equipment to be fully depreciated on a straight-line basis over a five-year period if the equipment has a terminal book value of zero. A terminal or residual book value greater than zero is considered a capital gain. SMC is subject to a 40 percent tax on both earnings and capital gains.

The firm's financial manager must now estimate the project's expected cash flows and find out whether the investment is a value-creating proposal. We show later that the after-tax cost of capital that SMC uses for projects similar to the designer desk-lamp project is 7.6 percent.

IDENTIFYING A PROJECT'S RELEVANT CASH FLOWS

In the commuting example earlier in the chapter, the project's relevant cash flows were reasonably easy to determine because the alternative situation was clearly defined: it was to continue driving to work. But for many investments, the alternative scenario (the firm's *future* situation if the project is *not* undertaken) is not clearly defined. This complicates the identification of the project's relevant cash flows, as illustrated below for the designer desk-lamp project.

SUNK COSTS

A sunk cost is a cost that has already been paid and that has no alternative use at the time when the decision to accept or reject the project is being made. The with/without principle *excludes* sunk costs from the analysis of an investment because they are irrelevant to the decision to invest. The firm has already paid them. For the designer desk-lamp project, the $30,000 fee paid to the consulting company (item 3 in Exhibit 8.1) is a sunk cost. It should not affect the decision to produce and launch the new lamp. Most sunk costs are costs related to research and development and to market tests performed *before* the investment decision is made.

To further clarify the point, assume for a moment that the designer desk-lamp project has an NPV of \$10,000, *excluding* the *after-tax* consulting fee of \$18,000 (\$30,000 × (1 – 40%)). What should SMC's managers do in this case? Should they reject the project because its NPV does not cover the after-tax consulting fee (NPV *with* the fee is a *negative* \$8,000) or go ahead with the project? The correct decision is to go ahead with the project because the consulting fee cannot be recovered if the project is *not* undertaken. Taking it into account means that it is counted twice: once when it was paid and again against the project's future cash flows. Accepting the project does not destroy \$8,000 of value; it creates \$10,000 of value.

Opportunity Costs

Based on the discussion about sunk costs, it may seem logical to ignore any costs related to the use of the unoccupied building in which the equipment will be installed because SMC has already paid for the building. However, the building can be rented for \$10,000 a year if it is not used for manufacturing the new product (item 5 in Exhibit 8.1). In other words, the decision to undertake the designer desk-lamp project means that SMC must forfeit \$10,000 annual rental income for the next five years. This "loss" of potential cash is the direct consequence of undertaking the project. According to the with/without principle, it represents a \$10,000 annual reduction in cash flow.

Costs associated with resources that the firm could use to generate cash if it does not undertake a project are called opportunity costs. These costs do not involve any movement of cash in or out of the firm. But the fact that they are not recorded as a transaction in the firm's books does not mean they should be ignored. The cash revenues a firm can earn if it does *not* undertake a project are equivalent to a loss of cash if the project is undertaken.

Opportunity costs are not always easy to identify and quantify. In the case of the unused building, SMC has an offer to rent the building and a market price can be established for the rent. But what if the building cannot be rented because there is no practical way to allow outsiders access to the building without disturbing SMC's normal operations? In this case, an opportunity cost still exists. If the designer desk-lamp project occupies the building, then other projects that arise in the future will not be able to use it and new facilities will have to be built. Estimating the dollar value of that potential displacement is not easy but should nevertheless be done. Assigning the empty building free of charge to the designer desk-lamp project *understates* the real cost of the project.

Costs Implied by Potential Sales Erosion

Recall that SMC's sales manager is concerned about the potential loss of sales for standard desk lamps if the designer desk-lamp project is launched (item 4 in Exhibit 8.1). In this case, the cash flows that the new lamps are expected to generate must be reduced by the estimated loss of cash flows caused by the sales erosion of standard desk lamps. This appears to be another example of an opportunity cost, similar to the potential loss of rental income if the project is launched.

Sales erosion, however, is more complicated than loss of rental income because sales erosion can be caused by SMC or by a competing firm. Lost sales should be counted as relevant costs *only* if they are directly related to SMC's decision to produce the new lamps. What if SMC will lose sales on its existing standard lamps even if it does *not* launch the new lamps? How could this be possible? This situation can occur if *competitors* decide to launch newly designed desk lamps that compete directly with SMC's standard desk lamps. In this case, the loss of sales will occur *anyway* and the erosion should *not* be counted as a relevant cost in the decision to launch the new product. It is an irrelevant cost because it is a part of the "SMC-without-the-project" scenario. If this occurs, sales erosion is no longer similar to an opportunity cost but, rather, is comparable to a sunk cost.

The question that SMC's managers must answer is this: what will happen to the firm's future cash flows if it does *not* launch the designer desk lamp? In other words, what is the scenario if SMC does *not* undertake the project (the "without" situation)? If SMC's managers believe that some sales erosion will take place, then the corresponding loss of cash flows should be ignored; in this case, they are similar to a sunk cost. Our point is that a firm cannot evaluate an investment properly if it does not know what will happen *if it does not invest.* We return to the issue of sales erosion when we estimate the NPV of the designer desk-lamp project.

ALLOCATED COSTS

Like many firms, SMC spreads its overhead costs over a number of projects using standard allocation rules. But according to the with/without principle, these allocated costs are irrelevant because the firm will have to pay them even if the project is not undertaken. *Only increases in overhead cash expenses resulting from the project should be taken into account.* The project should not have to pay a share of the existing overhead expenses. Because no increases in overhead expenses are expected to occur for the designer desk lamp, it would be incorrect to charge this project a fee of 1 percent of sales as required by the accounting department (item 16 in Exhibit 8.1).

DEPRECIATION EXPENSE

If SMC decides to buy the \$2 million piece of equipment, it will incur an initial cash outflow of \$2 million. The equipment will be listed as a fixed asset on SMC's balance sheet and depreciated at a rate of \$400,000 per year (item 7 in Exhibit 8.1). Recall that depreciation expense does not involve any cash outflows; it is not paid to anyone and is thus irrelevant to the investment decision.

However, firms must pay taxes. Even though depreciation does not affect *pre-tax* cash flows, it has an effect on *after-tax* cash flows. When the firm pays taxes, depreciation becomes relevant because it reduces the firm's taxable profit. With a lower taxable income, the firm pays less in taxes and saves an equivalent amount of cash. With a corporate tax rate of 40 percent (item 18 in Exhibit 8.1), SMC saves \$0.40 of taxes for every \$1 of depreciation expense.[2]

---

[2]The tax savings from depreciation expenses must be computed from the amount of depreciation expenses allowed by the tax authorities. This is not necessarily the same amount the firm reports in its income statement (see Chapter 2).

TAX EXPENSE

If an investment is profitable, the firm will have to pay more taxes. According to the with/without principle, the *additional* tax the firm must pay as a result of the project's acceptance is a relevant cash outflow. To compute this additional tax payment, we must first estimate the incremental earnings before interest and tax (EBIT) that the project is expected to generate if adopted. The contribution of the project to the firm's total tax bill is then found by multiplying the incremental EBIT by the corporate tax rate applicable to the extra amount of pre-tax profit. This rate is known as the marginal corporate tax rate. We have

$$\text{Project tax} = \text{Project EBIT} \times \text{Marginal corporate tax rate}$$

where

$$\text{Project EBIT} = \text{Project revenues} - \text{Project operating expenses} - \text{Project depreciation}$$

We use the project's EBIT to calculate the project tax so we can account for the tax savings that result from the depreciation of the project's assets. However, the project's EBIT is the incremental profit *before* the deduction of interest expense. Thus, we seem to have ignored the corporate tax reduction that results from the deduction of interest expenses on the funds borrowed to finance the project. This is not the case. We ignore it in the cash flows, but, as shown below, we account for it in the cost of capital, which is measured on an *after-tax* basis. In other words, *the tax savings from the deductibility of interest expense are not taken into account in the project's cash flows but in the project's estimated after-tax cost of capital.*

What would happen if SMC has a loss next year and thus has no taxes to pay? Obviously, in this case, the tax savings from the deduction of depreciation and interest expenses will not be available. To get the tax savings, SMC must pay some taxes in the first place. If no taxes are paid, then none can be saved. Fortunately, the tax authorities in most countries allow companies to carry forward or carry back their tax savings. This means that companies that cannot take advantage of the tax savings during the current tax year (because they made no profit) can do so against profits generated during the previous three to five years (the **carry-back** method) or during the forthcoming three to five years (the **carry-forward** method).

FINANCING COSTS

The cost of financing an investment is certainly a relevant cost when deciding whether to invest. But financing costs are cash flows *to* the investors who fund the project, not cash flows *from* the project. If a project is analyzed using the NPV rule, the project's expected cash-flow stream is discounted at the project's cost of capital. And the project's cost of capital is the return required by the investors who will finance the project. Thus, *the cost of capital is the cost of financing the project.* If financing costs are deducted from the project's expected cash-flow stream, the present value calculations will count them twice—once in the expected cash flows and a second time when the cash flows are discounted. Hence, *financing costs should be ignored when estimating a project's relevant cash flows.* They will be captured in the project's cost of capital.

To illustrate the distinction that must be made between cash flows *from* the project (investment-related cash flows) and cash flows *to* the suppliers of capital (financing-related cash flows), consider the case of a one-year investment that requires an initial cash outlay of $1,000 and will generate a future cash inflow of $1,200. Suppose that the investment is financed with a $1,000 loan at 10 percent. The firm borrows $1,000 from a bank (an initial cash inflow) to finance the project and repays $1,100 at the end of the year (a year-end cash outflow). The cash-flow streams related to the investment and financing decisions, the total cash flows, and the NPVs are shown in Exhibit 8.2.

The cash flows related to the financing decision have an NPV of zero. Hence, the project's NPV is the same as the total NPV, which takes into account the cash flows from both the investment decision and the financing decision. Deducting the $100 of financing expense (10 percent of $1,000) from the project's $1,200 future cash flow, and then discounting the difference at the cost of capital of 10 percent, will introduce the double counting mentioned earlier.

How can we estimate the appropriate cost of capital for the designer desk-lamp project? In the previous example, the investment was financed entirely with debt, so the cost of debt is the cost of capital. Chapter 10 shows that 30 percent of the designer desk-lamp project will be financed with debt borrowed at 6.8 percent and the remaining 70 percent will be financed with equity capital provided by SMC's shareholders, who expect to earn a 9.1 percent return on their equity investment. The 9.1 percent return expected by SMC's shareholders is SMC's cost of equity.

Given the financing structure and costs, what is the designer desk-lamp project's overall cost of capital? It is the weighted average of the project's *after-tax* cost of debt (because interest expenses are tax deductible) and the project's cost of equity. Shareholders receive dividend payments that are *not* tax deductible at the corporate level, so the cost of equity is not measured on an after-tax basis. The weights used in the calculation are the proportions of debt and equity financing. With a pre-tax cost of debt of 6.8 percent, a tax rate of 40 percent, a proportion of debt financing of 30 percent, a cost of equity of 9.1 percent, and a proportion of equity financing of 70 percent, the project's weighted average cost of capital, k, writes as follows:

$$\begin{aligned}\text{Project's cost of capital } (k) &= [6.8\% \times (1 - 0.40) \times 30\%] + [9.1\% \times 70\%] \\ &= 7.6\%\end{aligned}$$

The project's appropriate cost of capital is 7.6 percent. It is not the 12 percent rate that SMC's accounting department applies to the book value of the project's assets (item 17 in Exhibit 8.1). The reason is twofold. First, a financing cost should

EXHIBIT 8.2 INVESTMENT- AND FINANCING-RELATED CASH-FLOW STREAMS.

Type of Cash-Flow Stream	Initial Cash Flow	Terminal Cash Flow	NPV at 10%
Investment-related cash flows	–$1,000	+$1,200	+$91
Financing-related cash flows	+$1,000	–$1,100	Zero
Total cash flows	**Zero**	**+$100**	**+$91**

not affect the project's expected cash flows; it affects the project's discount rate or cost of capital. But more to the point, the 12 percent charge is an inappropriate estimate of the project's cost of capital because it is an allocated financial expense that does not reflect the actual opportunity cost of the funds required to finance the project.

INFLATION

The 3 percent annual rate of inflation expected to prevail during the life of the project will affect several of the project's variables. The lamp's price (item 2 in Exhibit 8.1), the cost of raw material (item 9), and the labor and energy costs (items 14 and 15) are all expected to increase at the 3 percent anticipated rate of inflation. SMC's management has little or no control over the expected rise in the costs of raw material, energy, and labor unless SMC can exert pressure on its suppliers and prevent wages from rising, an unlikely outcome given competitive market forces. But management *can* decide not to raise the price of SMC's lamps by the 3 percent annual inflation rate if, for example, competitors keep the price of their products constant.

Inflation is also involved in another cost over which management has no influence. The firm's 7.6 percent cost of capital, which is entirely determined by the financial markets, is assumed to incorporate the market's 3 percent expected rate of inflation. The suppliers of capital will obviously require compensation to cover the potential erosion of their purchasing power caused by price inflation.

How will the 3 percent expected inflation rate affect the project's evaluation? If the cost of capital already incorporates the market's anticipated rate of inflation, then consistency requires that the inflation rate also be incorporated in the cash-flow stream that the project is expected to generate. In other words, the project's cash flows should be measured in nominal terms, inflation included. The only component of cash flows that does not need to incorporate the 3 percent anticipated inflation rate is the lamp's selling price.[3] For competitive reasons, management can decide to keep that price at a constant $40. In the following analysis of the designer desk-lamp project, we first assume that the price of the lamp will rise by the 3 percent expected inflation rate and later examine what would happen to the project's profitability if the price remains constant at $40.

ESTIMATING A PROJECT'S RELEVANT CASH FLOWS

We let CF_t designate the project's relevant cash flow at the *end* of year *t*.[4] Then, CF_0 denotes the project's initial cash outflow, CF_1 to CF_{N-1} denote the project's intermediate cash flows from year 1 to year N–1, and CF_N denotes the **terminal cash**

[3]One other component of a project's cash flows that may not be affected by inflation is the tax savings from depreciation expense. In most countries, accounting conventions do not allow firms to change their depreciation expense to compensate for the effect of inflation on the value of assets.

[4]This assumption is made for computational convenience because discounting requires that the cash flow occur at a specific point. If this assumption is not realistic for the project being analyzed, the length of the cash-flow period should be shortened to six months or less.

flow, which is the cash flow at the end of year N, the last year of the project. As shown in Chapter 6, the project's NPV can be expressed as follows:

$$\text{NPV(project)} = \text{CF}_0 + \frac{\text{CF}_1}{(1+k)^1} + \frac{\text{CF}_2}{(1+k)^2} + \ldots + \frac{\text{CF}_t}{(1+k)^t} + \ldots + \frac{\text{CF}_N}{(1+k)^N} \quad (8.1)$$

where k = the project's cost of capital;

$\frac{\text{CF}_t}{(1+k)^t}$ = the present value of CF_t at the project's cost of capital k; and

N = the project's **economic** or **useful life**, that is, the number of years over which the project is expected to provide benefits to the firm's owners.

Recall that if a project has a positive NPV, it is a value-creating proposition and should be undertaken. If it has a negative NPV, it should be rejected. As an illustration, we will estimate the NPV of the designer desk-lamp project using an economic life equal to five years ($N = 5$), the same as its **accounting life** or number of years over which the project's fixed assets are depreciated (item 7 in Exhibit 8.1). However, the project may have an economic or useful life that is longer than five years, meaning that the project may still generate *positive* net cash flows beyond the fifth year. If this occurs, the project will be continued if its NPV at the end of Year 5 is higher than the net cash flow resulting from the project's termination at that time.

MEASURING THE CASH FLOWS GENERATED BY A PROJECT

According to the with/without principle, CF_t, the cash flow generated by a project in year t is equal to the *change* in the firm's *overall* cash flow in year t if the project is undertaken. It is given by the following general expression (see Chapter 4 for details):

$$\textbf{CF}_t = \textbf{EBIT}_t(1 - \textbf{Tax}_t) + \textbf{Dep}_t - \Delta\textbf{WCR}_t - \textbf{Capex}_t \quad (8.2)$$

where CF_t = the incremental cash flow generated by the project in year t, which is assumed to occur at the end of the year.

EBIT_t = the incremental earnings before interest and tax, or pre-tax operating profit, generated by the project in year t; it is equal to sales_t *less* $\text{operating expenses}_t$ *less* $\text{depreciation expense}_t$.

Tax_t = the marginal corporate tax rate applicable to the incremental EBIT_t.

Dep_t = the depreciation expense in year t that is related to the fixed assets used to support the project.

ΔWCR_t = the incremental working capital required in year t to support the sales that the project is expected to generate *the following* year;[5] WCR_t is equal to the project's operating assets (mostly accounts receivable and inventories) *less* its operating liabilities (mostly accounts payable).

Capex_t = capital expenditures or incremental investment in fixed assets in year t.

---

[5]WCR builds up throughout the year. Recognizing the change in WCR at the beginning rather than the end of the year will *reduce* the project's NPV, because the change in WCR reduces cash flows. This is preferable to recognizing the investment later and *overstating* the project's NPV.

CF_t, the cash flow *from* the project, excludes all cash movements related to the financing of the project, such as the cash inflows from borrowing or the cash outflows associated with interest and dividend payments made to lenders and shareholders. As discussed earlier, these financing costs are captured by the project's weighted average cost of capital.

Because we want to exclude financing costs from the project's cash flows, the first term in equation 8.2 is the after-tax profit generated from the project's *operations.* It is the earnings before interest and taxes (EBIT) adjusted by the corporate tax rate: $EBIT_t(1 - Tax_t)$.[6] This after-tax operating profit is then converted into an after-tax cash flow by making three adjustments (see Self-Test Problem 8.2):

1. Depreciation expense (Dep_t) is added because it is not a cash expense[7]
2. Any cash used to finance the growth of the working capital required to support the sales generated by the project (ΔWCR_t) is subtracted
3. The cash used to acquire the fixed assets needed to launch the project and keep it going over its useful life ($Capex_t$) is subtracted

The following sections examine the estimation of a project's initial, intermediate, and terminal cash flows using the designer desk-lamp project as an illustration. A summary of the estimation procedure is presented in Exhibit 8.3.

ESTIMATING THE PROJECT'S INITIAL CASH OUTFLOW

The project's initial cash outflow, CF_0, includes the following items:

1. The cost of the assets acquired to launch the project
2. Any setup costs, including shipping and installation costs
3. Any additional working capital required to support the sales that the project is expected to generate the first year
4. Any tax credits provided by the government to induce firms to invest
5. Any cash inflows resulting from the sale of existing assets when the project involves a decision to replace assets, including any taxes related to that sale

All these costs must be *cash* costs and should not include any sunk costs, such as those related to research and development or market research, if these expenses occurred before the decision to accept or reject the project.

For the designer desk-lamp project, the initial cash outflow is equal to the sum of the following:

1. The $2 million cost of acquiring and installing the equipment in the existing building (item 6 in Exhibit 8.1)
2. The initial working capital required to support the first year of sales the project is expected to generate

---

[6]The actual tax payment the firm must make is obtained by applying the corporate tax rate to profits *after deducting interest expenses.* However, as discussed earlier, applying the tax rate to EBIT does not ignore interest expenses and the corresponding reduction in taxes they provide; both are accounted for in the project's cost of capital.

[7]Depreciation expense is included in EBIT. After we have calculated the tax expense by applying the tax rate to EBIT, we must add depreciation expense to remove its effect on cash flow. We need depreciation expense in the first place only to calculate the tax liability triggered by the project.

We can estimate the project's working capital requirement (WCR) from the information reported in Exhibit 8.1. WCR is usually expressed as a percentage of sales. In other words, if we know the expected sales in year *t,* we can estimate the amount of working capital that is required at the beginning of the year to support these sales. For the designer desk-lamp project,

$$\text{Working capital requirement} = \text{Receivables} + \text{Inventories} - \text{Payables}$$

Receivables are equal to fifty-six days of sales (item 12 in Exhibit 8.1), and inventories are equal to twenty-three days of sales (items 10 and 13). Payables are equal to four weeks of purchases (item 11), which is equivalent to one week (seven days) of sales because the $10 cost for raw material is one-fourth of the $40 lamp price, and one-fourth of four weeks is one week. It follows that the project's WCR is equal to seventy-two days of sales (fifty-six days of receivables plus twenty-three days of inventories less seven days of payables). This is equivalent to 20 percent of annual sales (seventy-two days of sales divided by 360 days of annual sales).

The next step is to estimate sales revenues at the end of the first year. From items 1 and 2 in Exhibit 8.1:

$$\text{Sales revenues at the end of Year 1} = 45{,}000 \text{ units} \times \$40 = \$1{,}800{,}000$$

This figure is reported in Exhibit 8.3A in line 3 of the column labeled "End-of-Year 1." WCR is equal to 20 percent of sales:

$$\text{Initial WCR} = 20\% \times \$1{,}800{,}000 = \$360{,}000$$

Thus, the total initial cash outlay required to launch the project is as follows:

$$CF_0 = \$2{,}000{,}000 + \$360{,}000 = \$2{,}360{,}000$$

The $360,000 initial WCR and the total initial cash flow of $2,360,000 are reported in the "Now" column of Exhibit 8.3A, lines 19 and 22, respectively. Note that CF_0 can be obtained as a special case of equation 8.2, the general cash-flow equation. In the case of CF_0, EBIT and depreciation expense are zero (there are no initial profit and no depreciation expense), the change in WCR is $360,000 (more precisely, it is $360,000 minus zero because $360,000 is the initial investment in working capital), and capital expenditures are $2 million.

ESTIMATING THE PROJECT'S INTERMEDIATE CASH FLOWS

The estimates of the desk-lamp project's intermediate cash flows (CF_1 to CF_4) are based on the information in Exhibit 8.1 and are calculated using the project's cash-flow formula given in equation 8.2. Exhibit 8.3A shows the inputs and summarizes the cash-flow estimates.

We illustrate the procedure for CF_1, the cash flow that the project is expected to generate the first year. Sales revenues, as computed earlier, are $1,800,000 (line 3 in Exhibit 8.3A).

Total operating expenses are $1,130,000 (line 12). They include the total material expense (line 5), total direct labor expense (line 7), total energy expense (line 9), loss of rental income (line 10), and depreciation expense (line 11). They exclude the $30,000 fee paid to the consulting company (a sunk cost), the overhead charge of 1 percent of sales (SMC's overhead expenses are not expected to rise if

EXHIBIT 8.3A ESTIMATION OF THE CASH FLOWS GENERATED BY THE DESIGNER DESK-LAMP PROJECT USING A CALCULATOR.

FIGURES IN THOUSANDS. DATA FROM EXHIBIT 8.1

	Now	End-of-Year 1	End-of-Year 2	End-of-Year 3	End-of-Year 4	End-of-Year 5
I. Revenues						
1. Expected unit sales in thousands		45	40	30	20	10
2. Price per unit, rising at 3% per year		*$40.00*	*$41.20*	*$42.44*	*$43.71*	*$45.02*
3. Total sales revenues (line 1 × line 2)		**$1,800**	**$1,648**	**$1,273**	**$874**	**$450**
II. Operating expenses						
4. Material cost per unit, rising at 3% per year		*$10.00*	*$10.30*	*$10.61*	*$10.93*	*$11.26*
5. Total material cost (line 1 × line 4)		450	412	318	219	113
6. Labor cost per unit, rising at 3% per year		*5.00*	*5.15*	*5.30*	*5.46*	*5.63*
7. Total labor cost (line 1 × line 6)		225	206	159	109	56
8. Energy cost per unit, rising at 3% per year		*1.00*	*1.03*	*1.06*	*1.09*	*1.13*
9. Total energy cost (line 1 × line 8)		45	41	32	22	11
10. Loss of rental income (opportunity cost)		10	10	10	10	10
11. Depreciation expense ($2,000/5)		400	400	400	400	400
12. Total operating expenses (lines 5+7+9+10+11)		**$1,130**	**$1,069**	**$919**	**$760**	**$590**
III. Operating profit						
13. Pre-tax operating profit (EBIT) (line 3 – line 12)		$670	$579	$354	$115	($140)
14. Less tax at 40% (when positive, it is a tax credit)		(268)	(232)	(142)	(46)	56
15. After-tax operating profit (line 13 + line 14)		**$402**	**$347**	**$212**	**$69**	**($84)**
IV. Cash flow generated by the project						
16. After-tax operating profit (line 15)		$402	$347	$212	$69	($84)
17. Depreciation expense (line 11)		400	400	400	400	400
18. Working capital requirement at 20% of next year's sales	*360*	*330*	*255*	*175*	*90*	*0*
19. Change in working capital requirement from previous year	360	(30)	(75)	(80)	(85)	(90)
20. Capital expenditure	2,000	0	0	0	0	0
21. Recovery of the after-tax resale value of equipment						60
22. Cash flow from the project (lines 16+17–19–20+21)	**($2,360)**	**$832**	**$822**	**$692**	**$554**	**$466**

EXHIBIT 8.3B ESTIMATION OF THE CASH FLOWS GENERATED BY THE DESIGNER DESK-LAMP PROJECT USING A SPREADSHEET.

FIGURES IN THOUSANDS. DATA FROM EXHIBIT 8.1

	A	B	C	D	E	F	G
1		Now	End-of-Year 1	End-of-Year 2	End-of-Year 3	End-of-Year 4	End-of-Year 5
2							
3	*I. Revenues*						
4	Expected unit sales in thousands		45	40	30	20	10
5	Price increase			3.0%	3.0%	3.0%	3.0%
6	Price per unit		$40.00	$41.20	$42.44	$43.71	$45.02
7	**Total sales revenues**		**$1,800**	**$1,648**	**$1,273**	**$874**	**$450**
8							
9	*Values in rows 4 and 5 are data.*						
10	*Value in cell C6 is data. Formula in cell D6 is =C6*(1+D5). Then copy formula in cell D6 to next cells in row 6.*						
11	*The formula in cell C7 is =C4*C6. Then copy formula in cell C7 to next cells in row 7.*						
12							
13	*II. Operating expenses*						
14	Increase in unit of material cost			3.0%	3.0%	3.0%	3.0%
15	Per unit material cost		$10.00	$10.30	$10.61	$10.93	$11.26
16	Total material cost		$450	$412	$318	$219	$113
17	Increase in unit of labor cost			3.0%	3.0%	3.0%	3.0%
18	Per unit labor cost		$5.00	$5.15	$5.30	$5.46	$5.63
19	Total labor cost		$225	$206	$159	$109	$56
20	Increase in unit of energy cost			3.0%	3.0%	3.0%	3.0%
21	Per unit energy cost		$1.00	$1.03	$1.06	$1.09	$1.13
22	Total energy cost		$45	$41	$32	$22	$11
23	Loss of rental income		$10	$10	$10	$10	$10
24	Depreciation expense		$400	$400	$400	$400	$400
25	**Total operating expenses**		**$1,130**	**$1,069**	**$919**	**$760**	**$590**
26							
27	*Values in rows 14, 17, 20, and 23 are data.*						
28	*Values in cells C15, C18, and C21 are data.*						
29	*Formula in cell C24 is =SLN(2000,0,5) where 2000 is the equipment cost. Then copy formula in cell C24 to next cells in row 24.*						
30	*Formulas in cells D15, D18, and D21 are =C15*(1+D14), =C18*(1+D17), and =C21*(1+D20), respectively. Then copy formulas in cells D15, D18, and D21 to next cells in rows 15, 18, and 21, respectively.*						
31							
32							

EXHIBIT 8.3B ESTIMATION OF THE CASH FLOWS GENERATED BY THE DESIGNER DESK-LAMP PROJECT USING A SPREADSHEET. (*CONTINUED*)

	A	B	C	D	E	F	G
33	*III. Operating profit*						
34	Pre-tax operating profit (EBIT)		$670	$579	$354	$115	($140)
35	Income tax rate		40.0%	40.0%	40.0%	40.0%	40.0%
36	Income tax effect		($268)	($232)	($142)	($46)	$56
37	**After-tax operating profit**		**$402**	**$347**	**$212**	**$69**	**($84)**
38							
39	*Formula in cell C34 is =C7–C25. Then copy formula in cell C34 to next cells in row 34.*						
40	*Values in row 35 are data.*						
41	*Formula in cell C36 is =C34*C35. Then copy formula in cell C36 to next cells in row 36.*						
42	*Formula in cell C37 is =C34–C36. Then copy formula in cell C37 to next cells in row 37.*						
43							
44	*IV. Cash flow generated by the project*						
45	Working capital requirement/Sales$_{t+1}$		20.0%	20.0%	20.0%	20.0%	
46	Working capital requirement	$360	$330	$255	$175	$90	$0
47	Change in working capital requirement	$360	($30)	($75)	($80)	($85)	($90)
48	Capital expenditure	$2,000	$0	$0	$0	$0	$0
49	After-tax resale of equipment						$60
50	**Cash flow from the project**	**($2,360)**	**$832**	**$822**	**$692**	**$554**	**$466**
51							
52	*Values in rows 45 and 48 are data.*						
53	*Working capital requirement in B46 is from text. Formula in cell C46 is =C45*C7. Then copy formula in cell C46 to next cells in row 46.*						
54	*Formula in cell G49 is =100*(1–G35), where 100 is the dollar resale value of the equipment.*						
55	*Formula in cell C50 is =C37+C24–C47–C48+C49. Then copy formula in cell C50 to next cells in row 50.*						

the project is adopted), and the 12 percent financing charge required by the accounting department (financing costs are captured by the project's 7.6 percent weighted average cost of capital). They also exclude the effect of sales erosion. This item will be examined later.

With $1,800,000 of sales revenues and $1,130,000 of total operating expenses, the project's pre-tax operating profit (EBIT) is $670,000 (line 13). Deducting 40 percent of tax expense (line 14), we get an after-tax operating profit of $402,000 (line 15). In section IV of Exhibit 8.3A, this figure is converted into a cash flow by adding back $400,000 of depreciation expense (line 17) and deducting $30,000 (line 19), the *change* in WCR. (Line 18 shows that WCR *decreased* from $360,000 to $330,000.) Thus, the project's cash flow is $832,000 at the end of the first year (line 22) because there is no additional capital expenditure in Year 1 ($Capex_1 = 0$). Using equation 8.2:

$$CF_1 = (\$1{,}800{,}000 - \$1{,}130{,}000) \times (1 - 40\%) + \$400{,}000 - (-\$30{,}000) - \$0$$

$$CF_1 = \$402{,}000 + \$400{,}000 + \$30{,}000 = \$832{,}000$$

WCR declines after the first year because sales decline after the first year and working capital requirement is based on next year's sales. Thus, SMC needs to invest a decreasing amount of cash in its operating cycle to support the project's sales. As a consequence, the changes in WCR from Year 1 to Year 5 are negative. Note that the sum of all the changes in WCR over a project's life must equal zero because the firm recovers its initial investment in WCR during the project's duration. For the designer desk-lamp project, we have the following:

Sum of the *changes* in WCR =

$$\$360{,}000 - \$30{,}000 - \$75{,}000 - \$80{,}000 - \$85{,}000 - \$90{,}000 = 0$$

ESTIMATING THE PROJECT'S TERMINAL CASH FLOW

The incremental cash flow for the last year of any project, its terminal cash flow, should include the following items:

1. The last incremental net cash flow the project is expected to generate
2. The recovery of the project's incremental working capital requirement, if any
3. The after-tax resale value of any physical assets acquired earlier in relation to the project
4. Any capital expenditure and other costs associated with the termination of the project

At the end of a project, inventories associated with the project are sold, accounts receivable are collected, and accounts payable are paid. In other words, the cash value of the project's contribution to the firm's WCR is recovered. For the designer desk-lamp project, the WCR that will be recovered at the end of the fifth year is worth $90,000.

Some of a project's fixed assets may have a resale value when the project is terminated. The sale of these assets will generate a cash inflow that must be counted in the project's terminal cash flow after adjustments for the incidence of any taxes associated with the sale. The resale value of the assets, also known as their **residual value** or **salvage value**, affects the firm's overall tax bill *only if it is different from the assets' book value.* If the resale value is higher than the book value, the project's termination will generate a taxable capital gain (equal to the difference between the resale value and the book value) that will increase the firm's overall tax bill. If they are equal, there are no tax implications. And if the resale value is lower than the book value, then the project's termination will generate a capital loss that will reduce the firm's overall tax bill.

For the designer desk-lamp project, the initial equipment has an expected residual value of $100,000 (see item 8 in Exhibit 8.1) and a book value of zero at the end of Year 5 (see item 7 in Exhibit 8.1). The sale of that asset is thus expected to generate a capital gain of $100,000 that will be taxed at 40 percent (see item 19 in Exhibit 8.1). As a result, the project's terminal cash flow, CF_5, should increase by

\$60,000 (\$100,000 less 40 percent of \$100,000), an amount equal to the expected *after-tax* resale value of the equipment.

Combining the various items that contribute to the project's terminal cash flow, we have the following:

$$CF_N = EBIT_N(1 - Tax_N) + Dep_N - \Delta WCR_N + \text{After-tax residual value}_N$$

Applying this formula to the designer desk-lamp project, as shown in the last column of Exhibit 8.3A, provides a total terminal cash flow, CF_5, of \$466,000:

$$CF_5 = -\$84,000 + \$400,000 - (-\$90,000) + \$60,000 = \$466,000$$

The last operating "profit" for the project (line 13 in Exhibit 8.3A) is in fact a loss of \$140,000. SMC's overall taxable income will be reduced by that amount, providing a tax saving of \$56,000 (40 percent of \$140,000) and yielding an *after-tax* operating loss of \$84,000 for the project. Although the after-tax net income is negative, the net cash flow from the project is positive, and the decision to invest should be based on cash flows, not profits.

The same analysis we performed with a calculator in Exhibit 8.3A is reproduced in Exhibit 8.3B using a spreadsheet.

SHOULD SMC LAUNCH THE NEW PRODUCT?

We have now identified and estimated the entire cash-flow stream the designer desk-lamp project is expected to generate during the next five years. It is shown in the last row of Exhibit 8.3A. The project's cost of capital is 7.6 percent (item 20 in Exhibit 8.1). The calculations for the project's NPV according to equation 8.1 are shown in Exhibit 8.4. Part I shows the calculations using a calculator, and Part II shows the calculations using a spreadsheet.

The designer desk-lamp project has a positive NPV of \$415,083, so SMC should launch the new product.[8] Before concluding, however, we should perform a sensitivity analysis on the project's NPV because the \$415,083 ignores two important elements: (1) SMC may not be able to raise the price of its new lamps above \$40 and (2) SMC may incur net cash losses of as much as \$110,000 per year (item 4 in Exhibit 8.1) as a result of a potential reduction in the sales of SMC's standard desk lamps due to sales erosion. We did not consider the potential sales erosion in our earlier analysis because we assumed it would occur whether or not SMC launched the new lamps. However, if the sales erosion will occur *only as a result of the launch of the new lamps,* then it must be considered in the calculation of the project's NPV.

SENSITIVITY OF THE PROJECT'S NPV TO CHANGES IN THE LAMP PRICE

What will happen to the project's net present value if SMC is unable to raise the price of lamps by the 3 percent expected increase in the annual rate of inflation? If SMC keeps the price constant at \$40 while costs are rising by 3 percent, the

[8]Alternatively, the project's internal rate of return (IRR) is equal to 14.8 percent. Because the project's IRR exceeds the 7.6 percent cost of capital, the project is a value-creating proposal.

EXHIBIT 8.4 CALCULATION OF NET PRESENT VALUE FOR SMC'S DESIGNER DESK-LAMP PROJECT.

FIGURES FROM EXHIBIT 8.3

Part I Using a calculator

Initial cash outlay CF_0	=				−$2,360,000
Present value of CF_1	=	$\$832{,}000 \times \dfrac{1}{(1+0.076)^1}$	= $832,000 × 0.92937	=	$773,234
Present value of CF_2	=	$822{,}000 \times \dfrac{1}{(1+0.076)^2}$	= 822,000 × 0.86372	=	709,978
Present value of CF_3	=	$692{,}000 \times \dfrac{1}{(1+0.076)^3}$	= 692,000 × 0.80272	=	555,483
Present value of CF_4	=	$554{,}000 \times \dfrac{1}{(1+0.076)^4}$	= 554,000 × 0.74602	=	413,296
Present value of CF_5	=	$466{,}000 \times \dfrac{1}{(1+0.076)^5}$	= 466,000 × 0.69333	=	323,092
Net present value at 7.6%					**$415,083**

Part II Using a spreadsheet

	A	B	C	D	E	F	G
1		Now	End-of-Year 1	End-of-Year 2	End-of-Year 3	End-of-Year 4	End-of-Year 5
2							
3	Cash flows	−$2,360,000	$832,000	$822,000	$692,000	$554,000	$466,000
4							
5	Cost of capital	7.6%					
6							
7	**Net present value**	**$415,083**					
8							
9	*The formula in cell B7 is =B3+NPV(B5,C3:G3).*						
10							

project's NPV drops from $415,083 to $304,190, a 27 percent reduction.[9] But the project is still worth undertaking because its NPV remains positive.

By using a spreadsheet like the one presented in Exhibit 8.3B you can perform sensitivity analysis rapidly and efficiently. Just change the values of the variables that are expected to deviate significantly from their expected value. The spreadsheet will automatically be updated and show the NPV under each scenario.

[9]The estimation procedure is the same as the one shown in Exhibit 8.3A except that the price of a lamp remains at $40. Note, however, that in this case WCR will be *less* than 20 percent of sales. Accounts payable are going to be *higher* than one week of sales, because the cost of raw material is rising by 3 percent while the price of a lamp remains constant. We kept WCR at 20 percent of sales in our calculation. A lower ratio would have produced larger cash flows and a higher NPV.

SENSITIVITY OF NPV TO SALES EROSION

The present value at 7.6 percent of the loss of annual net cash flows of $110,000 for five years is equal to $443,872.[10] If we deduct this amount from the project's NPV of $415,083, we have the following:

NPV(project with erosion) = NPV(project without erosion) – NPV(erosion)
= $415,083 – $443,872 = –$28,789

Thus, with $110,000 yearly sales erosion, the designer desk-lamp project is no longer a value-creating proposal. However, the project can withstand some sales erosion and still have a positive NPV. The project will break even if the annual reduction in net cash flow is $102,866.[11] In other words, if sales erosion is expected to reduce SMC's net cash flows by more than $102,866 per year for the next five years, then the project will no longer be acceptable. If annual sales erosion is less than $102,866, the project has a positive NPV and may still be acceptable.

The preceding analysis clearly indicates that the magnitude of the potential annual reduction in sales and net cash flows due to sales erosion must be determined by SMC's managers before they decide whether to launch the designer desk-lamp project. In other words, SMC's managers must have a clear understanding of their firm's competitive position in the standard desk-lamp market before they evaluate the value-creating potential of the new product.

Will competitors enter the standard desk-lamp market with a competing product that will erode SMC's position in that market? If the answer is yes, then the effect of erosion on the project's cash flows can be ignored. The sales erosion will happen anyway and thus is irrelevant to the decision to produce the designer desk lamps. In this case, the project's NPV is positive, and SMC should launch the new product. If the answer is that erosion will take place *only* if SMC launches the new lamp, then the effect of erosion on the firm's net cash flows should be carefully estimated and taken into account. If erosion is expected to reduce the firm's annual net cash flows by less than $102,866, the project is still worth undertaking because its NPV is still positive. If management believes that erosion will reduce cash flows by more than $102,866 a year, the project should be rejected.

Sensitivity analysis is a useful tool when dealing with project uncertainty. By showing how sensitive NPV is to changes in underlying assumptions, it identifies those variables that have the greatest effect on the value of the proposal and indicates where more information is needed before a decision can be made.

---

[10]This cash-flow stream is an annuity. Appendix 6.1 shows that the present value of an annuity is equal to the constant cash flow multiplied by the annuity discount factor (ADF), where ADF is equal to (1 – Discount factor) divided by k. With $k = 7.6\%$ and $N = 5$, ADF = (1 – 0.6933)/0.076 = 4.0352 and the present value of the $110,000 annuity is $110,000 × 4.0352 = $443,872.

[11]The break-even point is obtained when the project's NPV is equal to the present value of the annuity. We have $415,083 = Annuity × ADF. With ADF equal to 4.0352, the annuity is equal to $415,083 divided by 4.0352, that is, $102,866.

SUMMARY

Managers can use a number of principles and rules to identify and estimate the cash flows that are relevant to an investment decision. Relevant cash flows are the ones that should be discounted at the project's estimated cost of capital to obtain the project's net present value (NPV) or used to calculate the project's internal rate of return (IRR). The decision of whether to invest should be made using only relevant cash flows.

Remember the two fundamental principles when estimating a project's cash flows. The first is the *actual cash-flow principle*, according to which a project's relevant cash flows must be measured at the time they occur. Relevant cash flows *exclude* any financing costs associated with the project because these costs are already taken into account in estimating the project's weighted average cost of capital. The weighted average cost of capital is the discount rate that must be used to convert a project's expected future cash-flow stream into its present-value equivalent. Deducting the project's initial investment from this present value provides an estimate of the project's NPV. If it is positive, the project is a value-creating proposition and should be undertaken.

The second principle is the *with/without principle*, according to which a project's relevant cash flows are those that are expected to either increase or decrease the firm's *overall* cash position if the project is adopted. Examples of cash outflows that should be ignored are those related to *sunk costs*. These are costs that are incurred *before* the project's net present value is estimated. These costs cannot be recovered, so they should be ignored. Asking the project to cover them means that the firm pays twice for these costs.

Examples of cash flows indirectly related to a project that should nevertheless be taken into account are those related to *opportunity costs*. These are usually cash inflows the firm will have to give up if it undertakes the project. Contrary to sunk costs that are relatively easy to determine because they have already been paid, opportunity costs are usually difficult to identify because they involve *potential future* cash flows rather than *actual past* cash flows.

One of the most difficult types of costs to identify is the effect that competitors may have on a firm's existing and potential products or services. For example, a firm's managers considering the launch of a new product must find out whether the new product will erode the sales of the firm's existing products. To make the proper decision to invest or not, managers must first forecast the firm's future development if the firm does *not* go ahead with the project (the firm without the project). Then, they must compare the firm's future prospect *with* the project against its future outlook *without* the project. If sales erosion is expected to occur even if the firm does not launch the new product, then the sales erosion of existing products is irrelevant to the decision of whether to launch the new product.

FURTHER READING

1. Damodaran, Aswath. *Corporate Finance: Theory and Practice*, 2nd ed. John Wiley & Sons, 2001. See Chapter 9.
2. Ross, Stephen, Randolph Westerfield, and Jeffrey Jaffe. *Corporate Finance*, 8th ed. McGraw-Hill Irwin, 2008. See Chapter 7.

SELF-TEST PROBLEMS

8.1 INTEREST PAYMENTS AND PROJECT'S CASH FLOW.

Why is interest paid on the debt raised to finance an investment project not included in the estimation of the cash flows that are relevant to the evaluation of the project?

8.2 UNDERSTANDING THE STRUCTURE OF THE CASH-FLOW FORMULA.

The estimation of a project's cash flows is usually based on the formula Cash flow = EBIT(1 − Tax) + Depreciation − ΔWCR − Capex, where EBIT = Earnings before interest and tax, Tax = Marginal tax rate, ΔWCR = Change in working capital requirement, and Capex = Capital expenditures required to support the project. Neither EBIT nor depreciation expense is a cash-flow item. Why do they appear in the cash-flow formula?

8.3 ALTERNATIVE FORMULA TO ESTIMATE A PROJECT'S CASH FLOW.

The cash-flow formula Cash flow = EBIT(1 − Tax) + Depreciation − ΔWCR − Capex is sometimes replaced by the following formula: Cash flow = EBITDA(1 − Tax) + (Tax × Depreciation) − ΔWCR − Capex, where EBIT, Tax, ΔWCR, and Capex are defined as in Self-Test Problem 8.2, and EBITDA is earnings before interest and tax, depreciation, and amortization. Show that the two formulas are equivalent.

8.4 IDENTIFYING A PROJECT'S RELEVANT CASH FLOWS.

Your company, Printers Inc., is considering investing in a new plant to manufacture a new generation of printers developed by the firm's research and development (R&D) department. Comment on the analysis of the proposal that is summarized below.

1. *Project's useful life:* The company expects the plant to operate for five years
2. *Capital expenditures:* $6 million, which includes the construction costs and the costs of machinery and installation. The plant will be built on a parking lot owned by the company.
3. *Depreciation:* For tax purposes, the building and equipment will be depreciated over ten years using the straight-line method
4. *Revenue:* The company expects to sell 5,000 printers in Year 1, 10,000 in Year 2, and 20,000 thereafter. The printers will be sold at $800 each
5. *R&D costs:* $1 million spent a year ago and this year
6. *Overhead costs:* 3.75 percent of the project revenues, as stipulated by the corporate manual
7. *Operating costs:* Direct and indirect costs are expected to be $500 per unit produced
8. *Inventories:* The initial investment in raw material, work in process, and finished goods inventories is estimated at $1,500,000

9. *Financing cost:* 10 percent of capital expenditures per year, as stipulated by the corporate manual
10. *Tax rate:* 40 percent (includes federal and state taxes)
11. *Discount rate:* 8 percent. This is Printers Inc.'s current borrowing rate.
12. *Cash-flow stream and net present value (figures are in thousands of dollars; figures from Year 1 to Year 5 are at the year end):*

	Now	Year 1	Year 2	Year 3	Year 4	Year 5
1. Capital expenditures	–$6,000					
2. Inventories	–1,500					
3. R&D expenses	–1,000					
4. Revenue		$4,000	$8,000	$16,000	$16,000	$16,000
5. Overhead costs		–150	–300	–600	–600	–600
6. Operating costs		–2,500	–5,000	–10,000	–10,000	–10,000
7. Depreciation		–600	–600	–600	–600	–600
8. EBIT		750	2,100	4,800	4,800	4,800
9. EBIT(1 – Tax rate)		450	1,260	2,880	2,880	2,880
10. Add depreciation		1,050	1,860	3,480	3,480	3,480
11. Net cash flow	–$8,500	$1,050	$1,860	$3,480	$3,480	$3,480
12. Discount rate	8%					
13. **Net present value**	$1,755					

8.5 ESTIMATING A PROJECT'S RELEVANT CASH FLOWS AND NET PRESENT VALUE.

Suppose you are given the following additional information on the investment proposal described in Self-Test Problem 8.4. What is the net present value of the project? Should it be accepted?

1. Salvage value at the end of Year 5 is $3 million
2. Tax rate on capital gains is 20 percent
3. Ratio of working capital requirement to sales is 30 percent
4. Because of competitive pressure, the printer's sale price is expected to decrease at the following rate: $800 in Year 1, $700 in Year 2, and $600 thereafter
5. Fixed operating costs are $800,000 per year
6. Variable operating costs are $400 per unit produced
7. Overhead costs will not be significantly affected by the project
8. Printers Inc. will have to rent parking spaces for its employees at an estimated cost of $50,000 per year
9. Expected inflation rate is 3 percent. Inflation is expected to affect only the operating costs that can be assumed to grow at the inflation rate.
10. Cost of capital is 12 percent

REVIEW PROBLEMS

1. **Pondering an investment offer.**
Your brother-in-law offers you the opportunity to invest $15,000 in a project that he promises will return $17,000 at the end of the year. Because you have only $3,000 in cash, you will have to borrow $12,000 from your bank. The bank charges interest at 12 percent. After reflection, you decide not to accept the offer because you figure the net return would be only $15,560 ($17,000 less $1,440 of interest paid to the bank). When your brother-in-law asks why, you tell him that because the bank charges you 12 percent, it is ridiculous for him to expect you to invest in a risky project that returns less than 4 percent. Please comment. Is the offer that "ridiculous"?

2. **The effect of inflation on the investment decision.**
The company's financial manager and accountant were arguing over how to properly take account of inflation when analyzing capital investment projects. The accountant typically included estimates of price-level changes when estimating and projecting future cash flows. For this, he took the government's gross domestic product (GDP) price deflator as the best estimate for the future inflation rate. This was 5 percent per year. He therefore believed that the company's discount rate should take into account inflation and that the standard 12 percent they used should be increased by 5 percent to avoid biasing the analysis and overestimating the net present value of the project. The financial manager disagreed, arguing that what the accountant was proposing would really underestimate the net present value. The 12 percent discount rate had been computed by taking the firm's 10 percent expected borrowing rate from its bank, its estimated cost of equity of 15 percent, and a 25 percent corporate tax rate. Who is correct in this argument? Please elaborate.

3. **Changing machines in a world without taxes.**
The Clampton Company is considering the purchase of a new machine to perform operations currently being performed on different, less efficient equipment. The purchase price is $110,000, delivered and installed. A Clampton production engineer estimates that the new equipment will produce savings of $30,000 in labor and other direct costs annually, compared with the present equipment. He estimated the proposed equipment's economic life at five years, with zero salvage value. The present equipment is in good working order and will last, physically, for at least ten more years. The company requires a return of at least 10 percent before taxes on an investment of this type. Taxes are to be disregarded.

   a. Assuming the present equipment has zero book value and zero resale value, should the company buy the proposed piece of equipment?
   b. Assuming the present equipment is being depreciated at a straight-line rate of 10 percent, that is, it has a book value of $40,000 (cost, $80,000; accumulated depreciation, $40,000) and has zero net resale value today, should the company buy the proposed equipment?

   The Clampton Company decides to purchase the equipment, hereafter called Model A. Two years later, even better equipment (called Model B) is available on the market and makes the other equipment completely obsolete, with no resale value. The Model B equipment costs \$150,000 delivered and installed, but it is expected to result in annual savings of \$40,000 over the cost of operating the Model A equipment. The economic life of Model B is estimated to be five years. It will be depreciated at a straight-line rate of 20 percent.

c. What action should the company take?
d. The company decides to purchase the Model B equipment, but a mistake has been made somewhere, because good equipment, bought only two years previously, is being scrapped. How did this mistake come about?

4. **Changing machines in a world with taxes.**
Assume that the Clampton Company in the previous problem expects to pay income taxes of 40 percent and that a loss on the sale or disposal of equipment is treated as an ordinary deduction, resulting in a tax savings of 40 percent. The Clampton Company wants to earn 8 percent on its investment after taxes. Depreciation for tax purposes is computed on the straight-line method.

a. Should the company buy the equipment if the facts are otherwise as described in the first scenario from the previous problem?
b. Should the company buy the equipment if the facts are otherwise as described in the second scenario from the previous problem?

5. **Investing in the production of toys.**
The Great Eastern Toy Company management is considering an investment in a new product. It would require the acquisition of a piece of equipment for \$16 million with a ten-year operational life, providing regular maintenance is carried out. Salvage value of the equipment is estimated at \$800,000. The product's economic life is expected to be five years, with annual revenues estimated at \$10.8 million during this period. Raw material for the new product is estimated at \$95 per unit produced, and an inventory equivalent to one month's production, or 3,000 units, would be needed. Direct costs of manufacture are expected to be \$130,000 per month. Work-in-progress and finished goods inventories would rise by \$150,000. For tax purpose, fixed assets must be depreciated according to the straight-line method. The corporate income tax rate is 40 percent and so is the capital-gain tax rate. The company's cost of capital is 12 percent.

a. Based on the above data, set out the cash flows expected from the project.
b. What is the net present value of the project?

6. **The effect of accounts receivable, accounts payable, overhead, and financial costs on the investment decision.**
Reviewing the cash-flow forecasts of a new investment project that appear in the following table, the Avon company's finance manager noted that there was no mention of any effect of the investment on the firm's accounts receivable and payable. The average collection period on the new product was expected to be fifty days, and new raw material purchases were expected to be settled in thirty-six days on average. Also, he noted that the standard charges of 1 percent of sales

revenues from new projects had not been made, nor the annual financing charge of 10 percent levied against the book value of the assets used by the project. How would the project's profitability be affected by including its effect on Avon's:

a. accounts receivable and accounts payable;
b. overhead costs; and
c. financial charges?

(in thousands)	Now	Years 1 to 4	Year 5
1. Revenues		$12,000	$12,000
2. Raw materials cost		4,000	4,000
3. Direct costs		1,000	1,000
4. Depreciation expense		4,000	4,000
5. Pre-tax operating profit		3,000	3,000
6. Tax rate		40%	40%
7. After-tax operating profit		1,800	1,800
8. Increase in inventories	$ 400	0	-400
9. Capital expenditures	20,000	0	0
10. After-tax resale value of equipment			0
11. Cash flow from the project	-20,400	5,800	6,200
12. Project net present value at 11% cost of capital	**$ 1,274**		

7. **The effect of depreciation for tax purposes.**
According to the Modified Accelerated Cost Recovery System (MACRS) of depreciation imposed by U.S. tax law, autos and computers must be depreciated the following way for tax purposes:

Year 1	Year 2	Year 3	Year 4	Year 5	Year 6
20.00%	32.00%	19.20%	11.52%	11.52%	5.76%

a. What is the present value of the interest tax shield from the purchase of an automobile for $50,000, with a cost of capital of 10 percent and a tax rate of 34 percent?
b. What would be the effect of a change in the tax law from MACRS to straight-line depreciation?

8. **The effect of cannibalization.**
Although he was initially satisfied by the apparent profitability of the new project, the Avon company's chief executive officer (CEO) was troubled by some other aspects of the project that he thought the finance manager had left out of the analysis. First, he was concerned about whether the new project could possibly cannibalize sales of the firm's existing products. In a worst-case scenario, he believed that a negative effect on after-tax cash flows by as much as $650,000 per

year was possible. Second, a building owned by the company, but unoccupied, would be used to produce the new product. They had recently received an offer from an adjacent business to rent this property for $100,000 per year. Finally, the firm had commissioned and already paid to a consultant $500,000 for a market study of the new product. How would the project's profitability be affected by including these items in the cash-flow estimates that are shown on the table in Review Problem 6?

9. **Break-even analysis.**
   Suppose Snowmobile Inc. is considering whether or not to launch a new snowmobile. It expects to sell the vehicle for $10,000 over five years at a rate of 100 per year. The variable costs of making one unit are $5,000, and the fixed costs are expected to be $125,000 per year. The investment would be $1 million and would be depreciated according to the straight-line method over five years with zero salvage value. Snowmobile Inc.'s cost of capital is 10 percent. The corporate tax rate is 40 percent. The investment would not require any significant addition to the firm's working capital requirement.

   a. What is the net present value of the investment?
   b. How many snowmobiles would the company need to sell to break even (i.e., for the project to have a zero net present value)?
   c. At the break-even level, what would be the project's discounted payback period and internal rate of return?

10. **Bid price.**
    Maintainit Inc. is asked to submit a bid for watering and spraying trees in a housing development for the next five years. To provide this service, Maintainit would have to buy new equipment for $100,000 and invest $30,000 in working capital requirement. The equipment would be depreciated straight-line to zero salvage value over the five-year period. Total labor and other costs would be $80,000 a year. The tax rate is 40 percent and Maintainit's cost of capital is 10 percent. What would Maintainit's minimum bid price need to be?

Raising Capital and Valuing Securities

CHAPTER 9

Firms need cash to finance new investments in fixed assets and working capital. For most firms, the major source of funds is the cash they generate from their operations, net of the cash used to service existing debt (pay interest expenses and repay loans), settle taxes, and pay dividends to shareholders. When internally generated cash is not sufficient to maintain existing assets and finance all its new, value-creating investment opportunities, the firm has to raise additional funds from external sources in the form of debt or equity capital. Sources of borrowed funds include *bank loans, leases,* and the sale of debt securities to investors; external sources of equity include the sale of *preferred* and *common stocks* to existing and new shareholders. These various sources of capital are surveyed in this chapter. As in previous chapters, the words *funds, financing,* and *capital* are used interchangeably.

Although new funds are usually used to finance asset growth, a firm may borrow to restructure its capital, that is, to repay part of its existing debt or to buy back some of its outstanding shares. Chapter 11 explains why a firm might want to modify its capital structure. The focus here is on the description of the various forms of debt and equity capital available to firms, the methods used to raise these funds, and the valuation of the most common types of securities a firm can issue. After reading this chapter, you should understand the following:

- How to estimate the amount of external funds a firm needs to finance its growth
- How the financial system works and what functions it performs
- The differences between the various sources of debt and equity capital
- How firms raise capital in the financial markets
- How to value the securities issued by firms

ESTIMATING THE AMOUNT OF REQUIRED EXTERNAL FUNDS

To determine the amount of external funds it will need, say, next year, a firm must estimate (1) the amount by which its investments are expected to grow during the coming year and (2) the amount of *internal* funds the firm expects to generate next year. If **internally generated funds** are less than the amount by which the firm's assets are expected to grow, the difference is the amount of external funds the firm will need to raise.

Recall from Chapter 3 that a firm's investments include cash and cash-equivalent assets (such as marketable securities), working capital requirement (WCR, a measure of the firm's net investment in its operating cycle), and fixed assets. The firm will need to finance any expected growth in these investments. Of course, any reduction in growth would be a source of funds. More precisely, we have the following:

$$\text{Funding needs} = \Delta\text{Cash} + \Delta\text{WCR} + \Delta\text{Fixed assets}$$

where we define ΔCash as the change in the firm's cash and cash-equivalent holdings; ΔWCR as the change in working capital requirement (any change in inventories, accounts receivable, and prepaid expenses less any change in accounts payable and accrued expenses); and ΔFixed assets as *new* capital expenditures and acquisitions less cash raised from the sale of existing fixed assets (disposals and divestitures).

The source of internally generated funds is the firm's retained earnings, that is, the portion of its net profit that is not distributed as dividends. However, depreciation expenses are charged against the firm's net profit but are not cash expenses, so they must be added to retained earnings to obtain the firm's internally generated funds.[1] In general, we have the following:

$$\text{Internally generated funds} = \text{Retained earnings} + \text{Depreciation expense}$$

We can now write:

$$\text{External funds need} = [\text{Funding needs}] - [\text{Internally generated funds}]$$

which can be expressed as follows:

$$\begin{aligned}\textbf{External funds need} = {} & [\boldsymbol{\Delta}\textbf{Cash} + \boldsymbol{\Delta}\textbf{WCR} + \boldsymbol{\Delta}\textbf{ Fixed assets}] \\ & - [\textbf{Retained earnings} + \textbf{Depreciation expense}]\end{aligned} \qquad (9.1)$$

Any funds needed to pay interest on existing debt and dividends to shareholders are already accounted for in equation 9.1 because retained earnings are calculated after deducting both interest expenses and dividend payments from operating profit.

To illustrate equation 9.1, we revisit Office Supplies (OS) Distributors, the firm we analyzed in Chapters 2 through 5. We assume it is the end of 2009, and we want to estimate the amount of funds OS Distributors will need to raise externally in 2010. Exhibit 9.1 shows the firm's balance sheet at year-end 2009 in managerial

---

[1] If other noncash expenses are charged to the firm's net profit, such as provisions against bad debt, they should be added back to retained earnings.

form (see Chapter 3). Exhibit 9.2 shows the asset side of the firm's pro forma (projected) balance sheet at year-end 2010 and its 2010 pro forma income statement. From the pro forma income statement, we see that OS Distributors expects to generate $7 million of retained earnings in 2010. Adding the $8 million of depreciation expense reported in the income statement, we conclude that OS Distributors expects to generate internally $15 million in 2010.

What are OS Distributors' **funding needs** for 2010? A comparison of the balance sheets at the end of 2010 and 2009 (see Exhibits 9.1 and 9.2) indicates that OS Distributors' invested capital should grow from $126 million to $138 million: cash holdings should decrease by $4 million (from $12 million to $8 million), working capital requirement should increase by $14 million (from $63 million to $77 million), and net fixed assets should rise by $2 million (from $51 million to $53 million). However, the net fixed assets reported in the balance sheets are *net* of depreciation expense, so the $2 million increase in *net* fixed assets is not the expected increase in fixed assets. The latter figure is $10 million: $12 million for the enlargement of the warehouse less $2 million expected from the sale of existing assets. (See Note 1 at the bottom of the balance sheet in Exhibit 9.2.) In total, OS Distributors' funding needs for 2010 can be estimated at $20 million: $14 million to finance the rise in working capital requirement plus $10 million to finance the increase in fixed assets less $4 million of cash reduction.

To summarize, OS Distributors expects to generate internally $15 million in 2010, and its funding needs are expected to amount to $20 million during that period. To bridge the gap, OS Distributors will have to raise $5 million.

EXHIBIT 9.1 OS DISTRIBUTORS' BALANCE SHEET ON DECEMBER 31, 2009.

FIGURES IN MILLIONS

Invested Capital		
• Cash		$ 12.0
• Working capital requirement[1]		63.0
• Net fixed assets		51.0
Gross value	$90.0	
Accumulated depreciation	(39.0)	
Total invested capital		$126.0
Capital Employed		
• Short-term debt		$ 22.0
• Long-term debt[2]		34.0
• Owners' equity		70.0
Total capital employed		$126.0

[1]WCR = (Accounts receivable + Inventories + Prepaid expenses) – (Accounts payable + Accrued expenses).
[2]Long-term debt is repaid at a rate of $8 million per year.

EXHIBIT 9.2 OS DISTRIBUTORS' 2010 PRO FORMA FINANCIAL STATEMENTS.

FIGURES IN MILLIONS

Pro Forma (Projected) Balance Sheet
Invested Capital Side

		December 31, 2010
Invested Capital		
• Cash		$ 8.0
• Working capital requirement		77.0
• Net fixed assets		53.0
Gross value[1]	$ 93.0	
Accumulated depreciation	(40.0)	
Total invested capital		$138.0

Pro Forma (Projected) Income Statement

		Year 2010
• **Net sales**		$480.0
Cost of goods sold	(400.0)	
• **Gross profit**		80.0
Selling, general, and administrative expenses	(48.0)	
Depreciation expense	(8.0)	
• **Operating profit**		24.0
Special items	0	
• **Earnings before interest and tax (EBIT)**		24.0
Net interest expense[2]	(7.0)	
• **Earnings before tax (EBT)**		17.0
Income tax expense	(6.8)	
• **Earnings after tax (EAT)**		$ 10.2
Dividends		$ 3.2
• Addition to retained earnings		$ 7.0

[1]In 2010, a warehouse will be enlarged at a cost of $12 million, and existing assets, bought for $9 million in the past, are expected to be sold at their book value of $2 million.
[2]There is no interest income, so net interest expense is equal to interest expense.

If OS Distributors is like most firms, it will raise the $5 million it needs through borrowing.[2] Aggregate figures on the funding structures of nonfinancial

[2]You can check that this is indeed the case by examining OS Distributors' balance sheet in 2010 in Exhibit 2.1 in Chapter 2. You will see that the firm increased its short-term borrowing by $1 million and its long-term borrowing by $4 million.

EXHIBIT 9.3 SOURCES OF FUNDING FOR NONFARM, NONFINANCIAL U.S. FIRMS, 1965–2008.

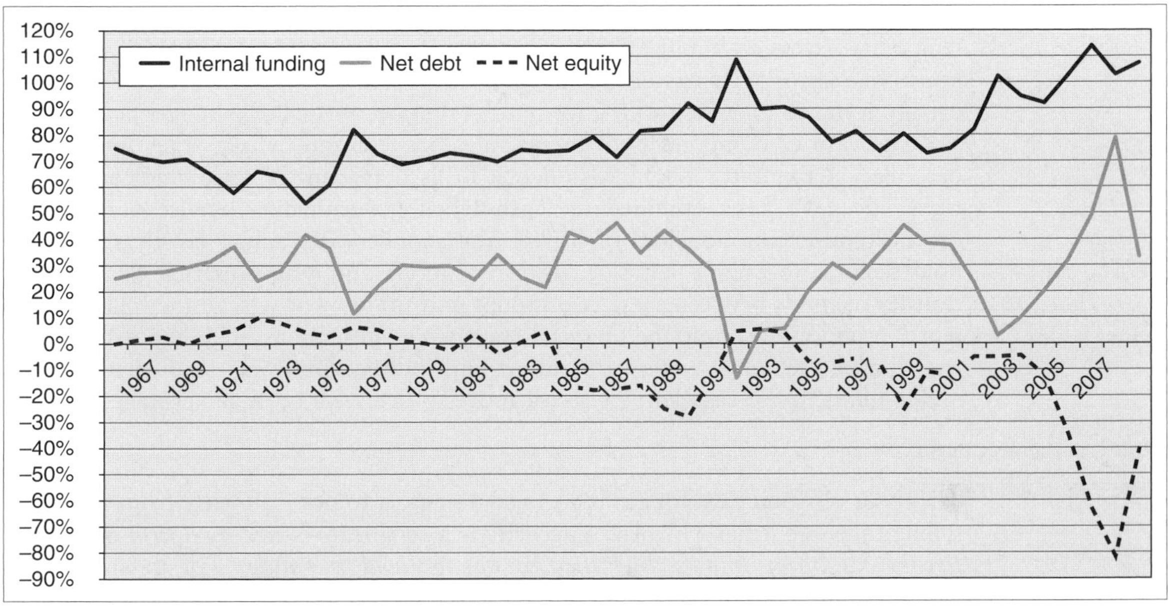

Source: Board of Governors of the Federal Reserve System, *Flow of Funds Accounts* (www.federalreserve.gov/releases/Z1). Net debt is the amount of long-term and short-term debt issued less debt repayments. Net equity is the amount of equity issued less the amount of equity repurchased. Negative net equity indicates that more equity was repurchased than issued during that year.

firms in the world's largest economies show that more than half of the funds needed to finance new investments are generated by the firm's own activities, with the balance mostly raised through borrowing. As an illustration, we show in Exhibit 9.3 the relative weight of the sources of financing for a very large sample of nonfinancial U.S. corporations from 1965 to 2008 (negative *net* equity means more equity was repurchased than issued). Over this period of time, *most of the firms outside the financial sector have relied primarily on borrowed funds to cover their cash deficits*. Possible reasons for this behavior are examined in Chapter 11. Other statistics indicate that 60 to 80 percent of total funds available are used to finance capital expenditures, with the balance going to finance investment in working capital requirement and cash holdings.

The rest of this chapter explains how firms raise external funds through the **financial system**, so we begin with a description of the structure of that system and the functions it performs.

THE FINANCIAL SYSTEM: ITS STRUCTURE AND FUNCTIONS

The fundamental role of a financial system is to act as a conduit through which the cash surplus of "savers" is channeled to firms that need cash. A financial system that performs this cash-transfer role efficiently—that is, cheaply, rapidly, and safely—is a major driver of sustained corporate growth. Without a financial system, entrepreneurs would have to finance their activities exclusively with their own savings and their firm's internally generated funds. The financial system provides another option by allowing firms with a cash shortage to tap the cash surplus sectors of the economy. Most of that surplus is supplied by the **household sector**, individuals who, on aggregate, save more than they consume. In addition, firms with temporary excess cash may lend it to cash-deficit firms for *short* periods of time. The household sector's savings do not all go to cash-starved firms, however. Companies usually compete for funds with governments that need to finance budget deficits.

The various components of the financial system and the way they interact are described in Exhibit 9.4. The cash-deficit firms that want to raise funds are on the right side. (We have excluded the cash-deficit governments because our focus is on the fund-raising activities of firms.) The suppliers of capital, mostly the household sector, are on the left side. The institutions and processes that facilitate the transfer of funds between these two groups constitute what we call the financial system. To understand how the financial system operates, we examine the two alternative financing channels, known as **direct** and **indirect financing**, through which the excess funds of the cash surplus sector move to firms with a cash shortage.

DIRECT FINANCING

The most obvious way for firms to raise money is to get it *directly* from savers by selling them securities for cash. A **security** *is a certificate issued by a firm that specifies the conditions under which the firm has received the money*. For an equity security, called a share of **stock**, the certificate recognizes an *ownership* position in the firm. It provides the holder with a *residual* claim (after all contractual claims have been settled) to the firm's earnings and assets and entitles the holder to vote on matters brought up at shareholder meetings, such as the selection of the firm's board of directors. For a debt security, called a **bond**, the certificate acknowledges a *creditor* relationship with the firm. It provides the holder with a *priority* claim (before shareholders) to the firm's earnings and assets. A bond certificate stipulates the conditions and terms under which the money was borrowed, including the amount borrowed, the duration of the loan, the interest rate the firm must pay, any restrictions on the use of the money, and the rights of the lender if the firm defaults on its obligation. When a security is **negotiable**, it can be traded in the **securities markets**, shown at the center of Exhibit 9.4 and described in the following section. The methods used by firms to sell securities to potential buyers are examined in a later section.

INDIRECT OR INTERMEDIATED FINANCING

Although direct financing may make a lot of sense, many firms are not able to access the financial markets to sell their securities directly to investors. This is the case for many newly established firms and for firms that are too small to issue a sufficiently large amount of securities to appeal to investors. Investors are generally reluctant to buy the securities of little-known firms or firms with relatively small amounts of shares, either because it is difficult to assess the risk of the issuer or because the securities do not have much **liquidity**, meaning that they cannot be sold rapidly at a price that is close to their perceived fair value. These firms must rely on *indirect* or *intermediated* financing to raise equity and debt capital. Sometimes, large, well-established firms also rely on indirect financing, particularly to raise short-term funds.

EXHIBIT 9.4 THE FINANCIAL SYSTEM.

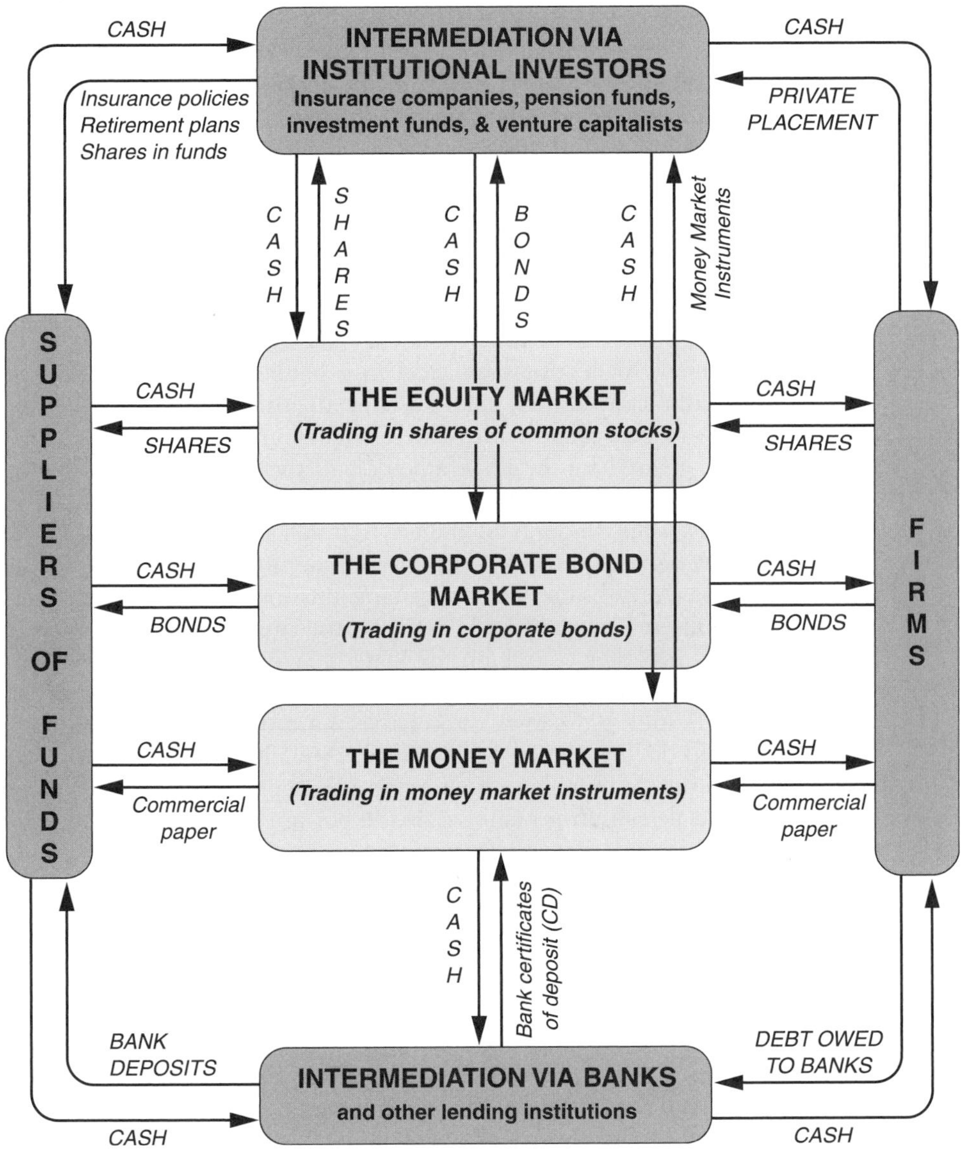

Indirect financing refers to raising capital through **financial intermediaries**, institutions such as **commercial banks**, insurance companies, pension funds, and venture capital firms that act as agents between the ultimate recipients of capital (the firms with a cash shortage) and the ultimate providers of capital (the cash surplus households). Commercial banks typically offer short- to medium-term loans with terms of one day to ten years. Longer-term debt and equity capital can be obtained through **private placement** of securities, usually with insurance companies, pension funds, or **venture capital firms**, the latter specializing in supplying equity to recently established firms with limited track records.

To see how financial intermediation works, consider a commercial bank. As shown on the bottom of Exhibit 9.4, a bank gets cash from depositors in the form of checking and savings accounts and from investors to whom it sells short-term securities, also called **negotiable certificates of deposit** or **CDs**. The bank then lends these funds to firms by extending short- to medium-term loans.

Note the fundamental difference between direct and indirect financing. In the case of direct financing, ultimate savers hold securities (bonds and stocks) issued by *firms*. In the case of indirect financing, ultimate savers hold securities issued by *banks*, such as checking and savings accounts and CDs. Bank-intermediated financing is important because it *facilitates* and *increases* the flow of funds between ultimate savers and cash-deficient firms. Individual savers may be reluctant to lend their excess cash directly to firms (will they get their money back?), but they may find it convenient to deposit their cash in a bank that can then lend it to firms. Banks offer **indirect securities**, such as bank deposits, that are attractive to savers because they can be opened with relatively small amounts of money, they are safe and generally insured by the government, and they can usually be withdrawn on demand. Banks extend loans that are convenient to firms because these loans involve relatively large amounts of money that can be borrowed rapidly for several years and can be renegotiated if the firm encounters some difficulties. Of course, banks must be compensated for performing this intermediation function. Their reward is the difference, or spread, between the interest rate they offer depositors and the higher rate they charge on the loans they extend to firms.

Financing via intermediaries is the dominant channel through which companies raise money. Exhibit 9.5 shows the relative share of assets held by different financial institutions in the United States since 1860. Note the following two trends: (1) the rise in the dollar value, though not adjusted for inflation, of financial assets held by financial institutions (shown at the bottom of the Exhibit 9.5); and (2) the decline in the share of financial assets held by banks and the corresponding rise in the share held by pension funds and investment funds. Since the early 1990s, nonbanking institutions have held more than two-thirds of the securities issued by firms. They purchase them directly from firms or buy them in the securities markets with the cash they receive from ultimate savers.[3] As shown in the upper part of Exhibit 9.4, these savers receive insurance policies, retirement plans, and shares in investment funds in exchange. Nonbanking intermediaries offer insurance and pension products to savers and, in the case of investment funds, convenient and cheap access to the securities markets, risk diversification, and investment management.

Why would a firm borrow from a bank if it can sell debt securities to nonbanking institutions or individual investors? This question brings up a subtle function performed by banks, called *monitoring*. To understand what this function achieves, think of the problem investors face when they consider buying bonds. They wonder whether the issuing firm has told them everything about its ability to

[3]With the exception of the United Kingdom, the predominance of banks among financial institutions is generally more pronounced in other countries than in the United States. However, the trends observed in the United States are also at work in other industrial countries around the world.

EXHIBIT 9.5 RELATIVE SHARE OF ASSETS HELD BY FINANCIAL INSTITUTIONS IN THE UNITED STATES FROM 1860 TO 2008.[1]

Types of Financial Intermediary	1860	1900	1939	1970	1980	1990	2000	2008
Banks[2]	89%	81%	65%	58%	56%	43%	29%	37%
Insurance companies[3]	11	14	27	19	16	16	14	13
Pension funds	0	0	2	13	17	23	26	19
Investment funds	0	0	2	4	4	10	22	21
Other	0	5	4	6	7	8	9	10
	100%	100%	100%	100%	100%	100%	100%	100%
Total (in billions)	**$1**	**$16**	**$129**	**$1,328**	**$4,025**	**$11,503**	**$28,570**	**$43,226**

[1]From 1860 to 1980, adapted from Kaufman and Mote, *Economic Perspectives* (pp. 2–21, May/June 1994), Federal Reserve Bank of Chicago. From 1990 to 2008, from the Board of Governors of the Federal Reserve System, *Flow of Funds Account.*
[2]Includes commercial and savings banks.
[3]Includes life and property and casualty insurances companies.

service its debt. What if the firm has withheld information that would indicate some potential difficulties in repaying the borrowed funds? Investors try to protect themselves by imposing protective **covenants** in the written contract between the bond issuer and the lenders, known as **indenture**. These covenants would, for example, require the firm to maintain a minimum amount of working capital and restrict its ability to sell assets, pay dividends, or issue new debt. But covenants are not as good as an insider watching over managers' shoulders and preventing them from taking actions that are detrimental to the **debt holders**. A bank is expected to be this insider. In performing this task, the bank is playing a monitoring role that provides bond buyers with additional protection. In other words, although large firms can sell debt securities directly to investors, they are willing to borrow from banks and pay higher rates to reassure the potential buyers of their bonds. In this case, the firm's choice is not between borrowing from a bank or issuing debt securities: some bank borrowing may be needed to facilitate the firm's access to the debt market.

SECURITIES MARKETS

We now turn to the description of the markets in which **listed securities**, such as debt and equity securities, are issued and then traded among investors. Securities markets, shown at the center of Exhibit 9.4, can be classified along several dimensions: whether they are primary or secondary markets, whether they trade equity securities or debt securities, and whether they are domestic (within one country) or international (outside the reach of domestic regulators).

PRIMARY VERSUS SECONDARY MARKETS

Primary markets are the markets in which *newly* issued securities are sold to investors for the first time. When a firm sells equity securities to the general public for the first time, the issue is called an **initial public offering (IPO)**.[4] When the firm returns to the market for another public issue of equity, usually a few years later, the process is referred to as a **seasoned issue**. A seasoned issue should not be confused with a **secondary public offering**, or a **secondary distribution**, which is the sale to the public of a relatively large block of equity held by an investor who acquired it earlier directly from the firm. An example of a secondary public offering would be the public sale by the Ford Foundation of a block of shares it received initially from the Ford Motor Company.

After they are issued, securities are traded in the **secondary market**, where they are bought and sold by investors. These transactions no longer provide cash to the issuing firm. The securities are exchanged among investors at a price established by the interaction of demand and supply. In the process, the market performs two important functions: it enables the quoted prices to reflect all publicly available information, and it provides the **liquidity** required to facilitate transactions. These functions are performed through the continuous trading of securities among investors on the basis of **fair prices**, prices that can be observed during the time the markets are open and that allow potential buyers and sellers to quickly trade securities and settle their transactions at a relatively low cost.

What exactly are fair prices? The answer to this question can easily fill an entire chapter. Suffice it to say that an extensive body of accumulated empirical evidence indicates that well-developed market economies have reasonably **efficient securities markets**, meaning that security prices in these markets reflect all available *public* information regarding the firm that has issued the securities. In other words, they are fair prices in the sense that they provide the best *estimate* of the true, but *unobservable,* value of a firm's securities. The existence of a secondary market is critical for the trading of the securities issued by corporations because investors are more inclined to purchase securities in the primary market when they know they can sell them later in an active and efficient secondary market.

EQUITY VERSUS DEBT MARKETS

Equity securities, or shares in firms' stock, are traded in the equity, or **stock markets**. These markets, shown in the center of Exhibit 9.4, can be either **organized stock exchanges** or **over-the-counter (OTC) markets**. The former are regulated markets and allow firms to list their securities only if the firms meet a number of stringent conditions.[5] In an organized stock exchange, shares are traded by **members of the exchange**, who may act as **dealers** or as **brokers**. Dealers trade shares that they own; brokers trade on behalf of a third party and do not own the traded

---

[4]Launching an IPO is a costly and complex process. Beyond the difficulties of going to the stock market and complying with all the IPO's rules and regulations, there is the issue of pricing. Setting the correct offering price in an IPO is not an easy task. If it is set too high, investors might be reluctant to buy the issue, which may lead to its withdrawal. If it is set too low, the company's existing shareholders would give away the difference between the true value of their shares and the offering price. Empirical studies show that IPOs are often significantly underpriced. We show in Chapter 12 different approaches to value a firm's equity.

[5]They must have a minimum acceptable number of publicly held shares, a minimum asset size, and a history of dividend payments, and they must publish financial reports that provide relevant and timely information.

shares. **Unlisted securities**, usually shares of small companies, trade in OTC markets. These markets do not require companies to meet the listing requirements of organized exchanges. In OTC markets, shares are traded through dealers connected by a telephone and computer network rather than on the floor of an organized exchange.

In most industrial countries, the bulk of the trading in the stock markets is done by **institutional investors**. The activities of institutional investors provide an example of another type of financial intermediation, illustrated at the top of Exhibit 9.4: an insurance company or a pension fund issues indirect securities to ultimate savers in the form of insurance policies in the former case and pension contracts in the latter. The funds collected are then invested in securities issued by cash-deficit firms. These securities can be purchased either in the financial markets or directly from the issuing firm. The latter channel, called private placement, shown on the upper-right side of Exhibit 9.4, is discussed in the next section.

Debt securities trade in the debt or **credit markets**. Credit markets are usually identified by the **maturity** of the debt securities that are traded in them. Debt securities with an **original maturity** not exceeding one year, known as **money market instruments**, are issued and traded in the **money market**. **Corporate notes** have maturities ranging from one to five years, and **corporate bonds** have maturities exceeding five years. These securities trade in the **bond market**.[6] Two money market instruments are shown in Exhibit 9.4: (1) certificates of deposit issued by banks, which we mentioned earlier in the discussion of financial intermediation; and (2) **commercial paper (CP)**, which is issued by firms with high credit standing to raise short-term debt from the market as an alternative to borrowing short term from banks. The volume of securities issued in the U.S. financial markets in 1970, 1980, 1990, 2000, and 2008 is reported in Exhibit 9.6. Note the growth in the volume of securities issued after 1990 and the dominance of debt instruments over common stocks, preferred stocks, and convertible securities.[7]

DOMESTIC VERSUS INTERNATIONAL MARKETS

Large and well-established firms can raise funds outside their domestic financial markets by selling their securities in the domestic markets of another country. These **foreign securities** can be denominated in the currency of the foreign country or in the currency of the issuer's country. For example, a U.S. company can sell **foreign bonds** in the Japanese corporate bond market denominated either in Japanese yen or in U.S. dollars.[8]

---

[6]The term *financial markets* usually refers to all security markets, whereas the term *capital market* usually refers to the market for long-term securities only, that is, equity and debt securities with a maturity exceeding one year. Thus, financial markets can be divided into capital and money markets, and capital markets can be divided into equity and bond markets.

[7]These securities are examined later in the chapter.

[8]If the bonds are denominated in yen, they are called **Samurai bonds**. They are called **Shogun bonds** if they are denominated in U.S. dollars. Bonds issued by foreign firms in the United States (denominated in U.S. dollars or other currencies) are called **Yankee bonds**.

EXHIBIT 9.6 SECURITIES ISSUED PUBLICLY IN THE UNITED STATES.

FIGURES IN BILLIONS

Types of Security	1970	1980	1990	2000	2008
Debt instruments	$23	$37	$108	$1,243	$1,548
Common stocks	4	13	20	169	166
Preferred stocks	0	2	4	12	51
Convertible debt	3	4	5	16	21
Total	**$30**	**$56**	**$137**	**$1,440**	**$1,786**

Source: *Securities Data Corporation Platinum.*

Alternatively, a firm can sell bonds in the **Euromarket**,[9] a market that is outside the direct control and jurisdiction of the issuer's country of origin. For example, a U.S. company can simultaneously sell **Eurobonds** denominated in either U.S. dollars (**Eurodollar bonds**) or Japanese yen (**Euroyen bonds**) to German, French, and Japanese investors. In this situation, a group of international banks acts as selling agents through, for example, British investment accounts. Eurobonds, which are sold outside the holder's country of residence, are **bearer bonds** and are not subject to the laws, taxes, and regulations that affect domestic issues.[10] As a result, firms can issue Eurobonds at a lower rate than that on an equivalent taxable bond sold in their domestic market or in the domestic market of another country.

If a company issues bonds in a foreign-denominated currency, it is exposed to the risk of unexpected movements in the value of the foreign currency, a risk known as **currency** or **foreign exchange risk**. This risk is examined in detail in Chapter 14.

In addition to foreign bonds and Eurobonds, other securities in international markets include foreign equity (stocks sold in a foreign country), **Euroequity** (stocks sold in the Euromarkets), and **Eurocommercial paper (EuroCP)**. The first two are the equity equivalent of foreign and Eurobonds, and the third is the Euromarket variation of domestic CP.

HOW FIRMS ISSUE SECURITIES

Firms can sell their debt and equity securities to the public at large through a **public offering**, or they can sell them to **qualified investors** (individuals and financial institutions that meet some minimum standards set by regulatory authorities) through a private placement. Both distribution channels are usually regulated. In the United States, the regulatory agency is the **Securities and Exchange Commission**

[9]The prefix "Euro" in "Euromarkets" and "Eurosecurities" means "external to a domestic market." It does not refer to the "euro," the currency of some European countries.

[10]The holder's name does not appear on a bearer bond. Domestic bonds are usually **registered bonds** and identify the holder's name.

(SEC). Most countries with developed securities markets have institutions that perform similar functions. The reasons why some firms choose private placement and the mechanisms through which securities are distributed in a public issue are discussed in this section.

PRIVATE PLACEMENT

A firm that chooses to sell securities privately can have the issue tailored to meet specific needs, such as the option to renegotiate the issue in response to unexpected events. Furthermore, unlike a public issue, a private placement does not have to be registered with a government agency, which is a costly process. Clearly, private placement provides a firm with a flexible, discreet, and speedy method of raising funds. The drawback is that the absence of organized trading in privately placed securities makes it difficult for the investors who subscribed to the issue to easily resell the securities. As a result, it is generally more expensive for a firm to place its securities privately than it is to issue them to the public at large. Even so, this may be the only way little-known companies can raise cash.

PUBLIC OFFERINGS

Relatively large firms can offer their securities to the public after they have registered them with a government agency that approves the issuance and distribution of securities and regulates their subsequent trading on public markets. To help with the public offering process, firms use the services of an **investment bank.**[11] At the earliest stage, the bank advises the firm about the type and amount of securities it should be issuing. Then, the investment bank seeks the approval of all the supervising government agencies, determines an appropriate selling price for the securities (a price that is both acceptable to the firm and attractive to buyers), and determines the best period of time for the offering. Finally, the investment bank ensures that the securities are purchased by investors by stimulating widespread interest in the offering. The last step, which involves the marketing and distribution of the securities to the public, is the most important function the investment bank plays in a public offering.

We illustrate this process using a new equity issue, as shown in Exhibit 9.7. Aside from a private placement, a firm can offer its shares to any interested buyer through a **general cash offering** or can offer its shares exclusively to its *existing* stockholders through a **rights offering**.

GENERAL CASH OFFERINGS

In a general cash offering, the investment bank can either do its best to sell the securities on behalf of the firm or buy the securities and then resell them to the public *at its own risk*. In the first case, the investment bank acts as an agent for the firm, distributing securities on a **best efforts basis**. In a best efforts deal, if the investment bank fails to distribute a predetermined minimum number of shares during a specified period of time, the offering is canceled.

---

[11]Firms may also use the services of investment banks to help them place their securities privately.

EXHIBIT 9.7 ALTERNATIVE METHODS USED BY FIRMS AND THEIR INVESTMENT BANKS TO DISTRIBUTE EQUITY SECURITIES.

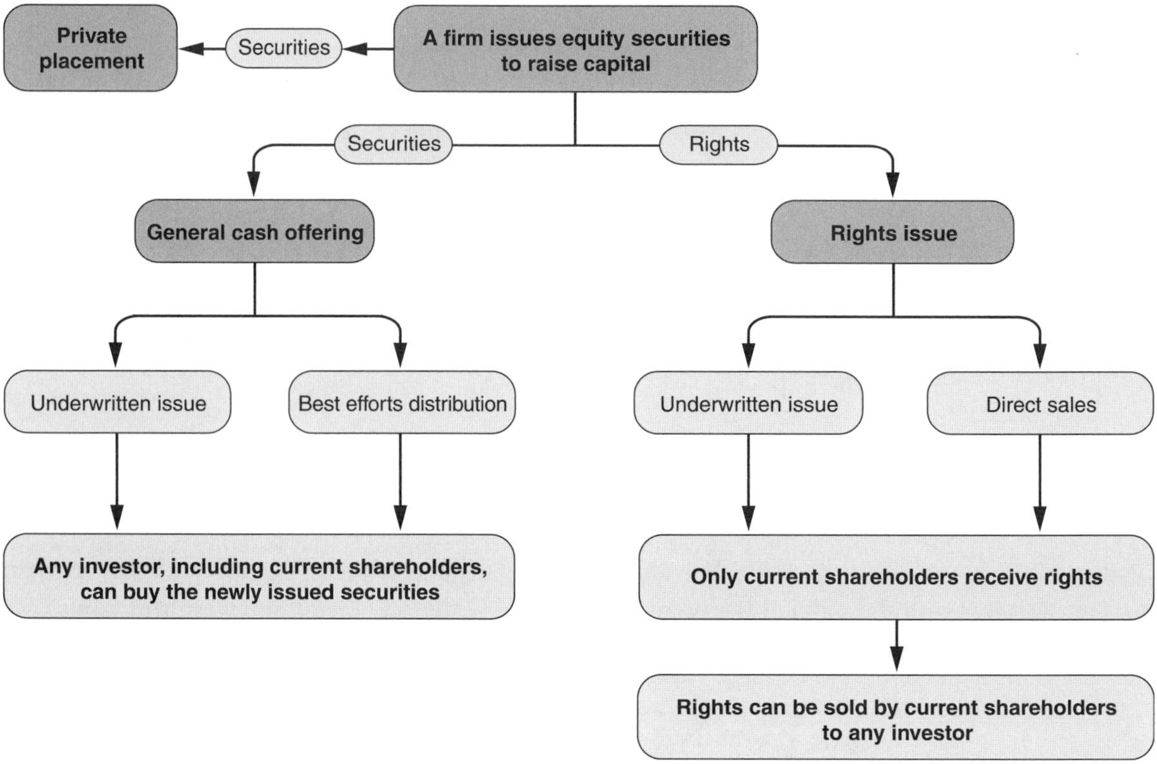

In the second case, the investment bank is said to act as an **underwriter**. When an issue is underwritten, the bank *buys* the securities from the firm in order to resell them to the public at a higher price. The **spread** between the price at which the issue is sold to the public and the price paid to the issuing firm is the investment bank's compensation. Studies of underwritten equity issues in the United States indicate that the spread is between 2 and 8 percent of the value of the issue, depending on its size and quality, and the market conditions. To reduce the risk of being unable to sell the securities at a profit and to reach as many potential buyers as possible, the investment bank that has initiated the deal, called the **originating house**, **lead manager**, or **book runner**, forms an **underwriting syndicate** with other investment banks.[12] The originating house then sells some of the securities to the members of the syndicate, which they, in turn, sell to the public. To further

[12] It is worth pointing out that the underwriting risk in the United States is not very high because the price of the issue is usually set the day before the offering is made. Any price risk before that day is actually borne by the issuer, not the investment bank. In the United Kingdom, however, the underwriting risk is higher because the price is announced a few weeks before the issue is available for trading.

broaden and speed distribution, a **selling group** is formed to bring in additional investment banks that agree to sell the securities allocated to them for a fee. (Members of the selling group do not act as underwriters.) If needed, during the distribution period, the members of the underwriting group may buy the security in the open market to support its price and ensure the success of the offering. How is the spread shared among the various intermediaries? In a typical transaction, the originating house receives 15 to 20 percent of the spread, 20 to 30 percent goes to the members of the underwriting syndicate, and the balance is paid to members of the selling group as a **selling concession**.

Although new issues of equity and debt are generally underwritten, in many cases, securities are distributed on a best efforts basis. Issues sold this way usually fall into two extreme categories. One category includes small and risky firms that are involved in IPOs for which investment banks are reluctant to bear the underwriting risk; the other category includes large and well-established companies whose strength and reputation allow them to issue securities that are not underwritten, thus saving the underwriting commission and related expenses.

An investment bank that underwrites a securities issue is providing more than a mechanism to sell securities. The bank is also telling the market that it believes that the securities are of sufficient quality; otherwise, it would not have underwritten them. In other words, the bank is playing a **certification role**. Clearly, top-quality firms may not need this seal of approval. Also, banks may be reluctant to "certify" the securities of risky firms, fearing that if the issue turns out to be a failure, their reputations may be damaged.

RIGHTS ISSUES

When a firm sells common stocks exclusively to *new* investors, it obviously reduces the fraction of the firm's equity held by its *existing* shareholders. One way to prevent this **dilution** of property rights is to give existing shareholders the right to buy the portion of a new stock issue that will preserve their fractional ownership. The charters of most European companies require them to raise equity capital through rights issues only. This is not the case in the United States, where firms usually issue shares through general cash offers.

We illustrate the mechanics of a rights offering using an example that ignores **issuance costs** for the sake of simplicity. Suppose European Engines Corporation (EEC) has just announced that it will issue 1 million new shares of common stock through a rights issue at the **subscription price** of \$80. (The subscription price is the selling price of the new shares.) Before the announcement, EEC shares were trading at \$100 and there were 4 million shares outstanding. Next, EEC will notify its shareholders that they are granted one **right** for every share they hold and that the rights will expire at a specific future date (usually a few weeks after the offer date). Before that date, the shares are usually referred to as **rights-on shares**; afterward, they are called **ex-rights shares**. Shareholders have three possibilities: (1) they can exercise their rights and subscribe to the issue; (2) they can sell their rights to interested investors if they do not want to buy new shares; or (3) they can do nothing and let the rights expire.

There are several questions to answer at this point: (1) Why is the subscription price (\$80) set below the market price prevailing immediately before the announcement of the rights issue ($100)? (2) How many rights are needed to buy one new share? (3) What will happen to the share price when the shares become ex-rights shares, and what is the value of one right? (4) What effect does the issue have on the wealth of existing shareholders? (5) What is the role played by investment banks in a rights offer?

Setting an Appropriate Subscription Price The subscription price ($80) is set below the market price ($100) because the rights offer is good for a few weeks. If the market price falls below the subscription price by the time the offer expires, no rational shareholder will exercise the right to buy a share for more than its prevailing market price. Thus, to ensure the success of the issue, the firm must set the subscription price at a sufficiently large discount to reduce the risk that the market price may drop *below* the subscription price during the period the offer is outstanding.

Number of Rights Required to Buy One New Share There were 4 million shares outstanding before the issue was announced, so there will be 4 million rights granted by EEC. This represents four rights per new share issued (4 million "old" shares divided by 1 million new shares). In other words, any investor, including the current shareholders, will need to own four rights to be able to buy one new share. Generalizing, if N_0 is the number of "old" shares and N_n is the number of new shares, the number of rights required to acquire one new share is $N = N_0/N_n$.

The Ex-Rights Price of a Share and the Value of a Right Before the offer was announced, a shareholder who owned four shares had a holding worth $400 (four times $100). Because she holds four rights, she now has the opportunity to get a fifth share for $80. If she purchases the share, she will have five EEC shares worth $480 ($400 + $80). It follows that the price of a share after the offer will no longer be $100 but $96 ($480 divided by five). The only difference between the $100 shares and the $96 shares is that the former are rights-on shares (they have a right attached to them) and the latter are ex-rights shares (they no longer carry rights). Consequently, the $4 difference between the two prices represents the price of a right.

To generalize the results, if N is the number of rights required to buy one new share, the ex-rights price is given by the following formula:

$$\textbf{Ex-rights price} = \frac{N \times \textbf{Rights-on price} + \textbf{Subscription price}}{N + 1} \qquad (9.2)$$

and the value of a right is the difference between the rights-on price and the ex-rights price:[13]

$$\textbf{Value of one right} = \textbf{Rights-on price} - \textbf{Ex-rights price} \qquad (9.3)$$

---

[13]Using the ex-rights price given by equation 9.2, the value of one right is the following:

$$\text{Value of one right} = \frac{\text{Rights-on price} - \text{Subscription price}}{N + 1} = \frac{\$100 - \$80}{4 + 1} = \frac{\$20}{5} = \$4$$

EXHIBIT 9.8 EFFECT OF RIGHTS ISSUE ON THE WEALTH OF EXISTING SHAREHOLDER.

Initial Wealth	Decision	Ending Wealth
4 shares at $100 = $400 Cash = 80 Total = $480	*Case 1:* Tender 4 rights and buy 1 new share at $80	5 shares at $96 = $480 Cash = 0 Total = $480
	Case 2: Sell 4 rights at $4 for $16	4 shares at $96 = $384 Cash ($80 + $16) = 96 Total = $480

Effect of the Rights Issue on the Wealth of Existing Shareholders A right is an option issued by the firm to its existing shareholders, giving them the privilege, but *not* the obligation, to buy shares of the firm at a fixed price (the subscription price) over a fixed period of time (the life of the right). This is known as a **call option**. As mentioned, a shareholder who has received rights can exercise them and buy new shares at the subscription price, can sell them to other investors, or can let the rights "die."

Whether the shareholder exercises his option by tendering his rights to buy new shares or sells his option, his initial wealth will not change, as shown in Exhibit 9.8. Starting with an initial holding of $480 that consists of four EEC shares and $80 in cash, an investor will end up with the same amount of wealth. Only when the shareholder lets his rights expire (usually by ignorance or because the expiration date has passed before he could exercise or sell them) will his wealth be affected by the issue because the rights are then worthless.

The Role of Investment Banks in Rights Offerings In a rights offering, a firm can sell shares directly to its shareholders (and some firms do), but the possibility always exists that the market price will fall below the subscription price or that some investors may not exercise their rights to buy the new shares. To avoid this situation, the firm can arrange a **standby agreement** with an underwriting syndicate of investment banks. The syndicate agrees to buy any shares that have not been sold during the period the rights offering is outstanding at the subscription price less a **take-up fee**. In this case, investment banks underwrite only the unsold portion of the rights offering for a **standby fee**.

ISSUANCE COSTS OF PUBLIC OFFERINGS

Data indicate that issuance costs of public offerings, measured as a percentage of the gross amount raised, are higher for small issues than for large ones. Furthermore, rights offerings are less expensive than underwritten issues, and a rights offering without a standby agreement is the least expensive method for firms to raise new equity capital.

DEBT CAPITAL: CHARACTERISTICS AND VALUATION

We now examine the alternative sources of debt financing available to firms and show how to value the debt securities issued by companies. For most firms, the primary source of borrowed funds is bank loans. These loans can be supplemented by leasing contracts and, for relatively large firms with high credit standing, by the issue of commercial paper and corporate bonds.

BORROWING THROUGH BANK LOANS

Bank loans, particularly short-term loans, are the dominant source of debt. If a firm cannot access the corporate debt markets, then bank loans (short term, medium term, and long term) are the only source of borrowed funds.

SHORT-TERM BANK LOANS

Firms that need to finance the seasonal buildup in their working capital requirement usually resort to short-term bank loans. These loans are described as **self-liquidating** loans because banks expect firms to repay the loans with the cash that will be released by the subsequent reduction in working capital requirement. For example, a company selling toys will need to borrow to finance the buildup of its inventory before the holiday season. After the goods are sold, some of the collected cash will be used to repay the bank loan. These loans can be extended for several months, after which they must be repaid or renewed for another period. How do banks ensure that firms that have borrowed short term do not use the loan to finance long-term investments? To protect themselves, banks usually impose a **cleanup clause** that requires the firm to be completely out of debt to the bank for at least one month during the year.

Short-term bank loans are often **unsecured loans**, meaning that the firm does not have to provide any assets as **collateral**, or guarantee, in case of default. When a short-term loan is a secured loan, assets such as accounts receivable and inventories are pledged as collateral. Three forms of unsecured loans are commonly used: (1) a **transaction loan**, which is a one-time loan used to finance a specific, nonrecurrent need; (2) a **line of credit**, which is a nonbinding arrangement in which the bank lends the firm a stated amount of money over a fixed, but renewable, period of time, usually a year; and (3) a **revolving credit agreement**, which is the same as a line of credit except that the bank is *legally committed* to lend the money, a guarantee for which the bank charges a commitment fee on the unused portion of the credit line.

These loans are extended at the **bank prime rate** (the reference rate for the pricing of loans to domestic borrowers) plus a spread over prime to reflect the specific risk of the borrowing firm. For example, if the prime rate is 5 percent, a firm that is charged a 3 percent spread over prime will borrow at 8 percent.

Medium- and Long-Term Loans

Medium- and long-term loans are extended by banks and insurance companies and are known as **term loans**. Their duration is between one and ten years, and they are usually repaid in equal periodic installments that include the loan reimbursement as well as interest on the loan. This repayment schedule is known as an **annuity**. Contrary to most short-term loans, term loans are backed by collateral, meaning that the firm must provide the lender with assets to secure the loan. For example, a **mortgage loan** is backed by real estate and an **equipment financing loan** (which is often extended by the **captive finance subsidiary** of the equipment manufacturer) is backed by the piece of machinery. These types of loans are also known as **asset-based borrowing**. A popular alternative to term loans is **lease financing**.

Borrowing through Lease Agreements

Leasing is an alternative source of debt capital that allows firms to finance the *use* of assets—such as computers, copiers, trucks, utility vehicles, and aircraft—without actually owning them. It is estimated that as much equipment is financed with leasing as through any other source of capital.

A lease is a contractual agreement between the owner of the asset, known as the **lessor**, and the user of the asset, known as the **lessee**. The agreement says the lessee has the right to use the asset in exchange for periodic payments to the lessor. The lessor can be a manufacturer, a financial institution, or an independent leasing company. When the lessor is not the manufacturer, the asset is sold by the manufacturer to the lessor, who, in turn, leases it to the lessee. When the contract expires, the asset is returned to the lessor, or, if the contract gives the lessee the option of purchasing the asset, the lessee may decide to buy it.

This section describes two of the most common types of leases: **operating leases** and **financial leases**.[14] Then, after showing that a long-term lease is just another way of borrowing and using the proceeds to purchase the leased asset, we present a procedure for analyzing a leasing-versus-borrowing decision, using a long-term equipment lease as an illustration.

Operating Leases

An operating lease is a short-term lease that usually, but not always, has the following characteristics. First, the length of the contract is shorter than the useful life of the asset, which means that the lessor must re-lease the asset or sell it at the expiration of the contract to recover its full cost. Second, the lessor is responsible for the maintenance and insurance costs while the asset is leased. Third, the lessee has the right to cancel the lease contract before it expires. This option is particularly valuable to the lessee when the asset leased is a piece of equipment that can quickly become obsolete because of rapid technological advances. However, to cancel the contract, the lessee may have to pay a cancellation fee.

[14]Accountants classify leases as capital leases or operating leases. A capital lease is recorded both in the assets and liabilities sides of the balance sheet with the same amount, which is equal to the present value of the future lease payments. Operating leases do not appear in the balance sheet. However, information on these leases must be disclosed elsewhere in the firm's annual report.

FINANCIAL LEASES

A financial lease is a long-term lease that differs significantly from an operating lease. Contrary to an operating lease, it usually extends over most of the useful life of the asset; it is the lessee, not the lessor, that pays the maintenance and the insurance costs; and, generally, it cannot be canceled.

Most financial leases are one of the following: **direct lease**, **sale and leaseback**, or **leveraged lease**. A direct lease is a contract between the lessee and the owner of the asset. The owner can be the manufacturer of the asset or a leasing company that bought the asset from the manufacturer for the purpose of leasing it. Under a sale and leaseback lease, the firm owning the asset sells it to the leasing company, which immediately leases it back to the firm. Finally, in a leveraged lease, the leasing company finances the purchase of the asset with a substantial level of debt, using as collateral the lease contract and the **salvage value** of the asset—its value at the end of the lease contract.

LEASING AS AN ALTERNATIVE TO BORROWING

Suppose a firm has decided to change ten forklifts used in its plants and is considering leasing the new ones instead of purchasing them. Because the plants will be in operation for many more years, the lease must be a long-term, or financial, lease. The decision to lease or buy will not affect the way the vehicles are used, their useful life, or the cost of insuring and maintaining them. Thus, the difference between leasing and purchasing is only financial. If the firm decides to lease, it will not incur any initial large cash outlay to buy the equipment. Instead, it will have to make annual payments to the leasing company. If the firm decides to purchase the forklifts, it will incur a large initial cash outlay equal to the purchase price of the new forklifts. In this case, if the investment is financed with equity, the firm will also have to pay dividends to its shareholders, or, if it is financed by debt, make interest payments to its banks and bondholders.

Lease payments, like interest payments, are *fixed* obligations. Thus, the *relevant comparison is between lease financing and debt financing*, not equity financing. In other words, a financial lease is just an alternative to borrowing and using the proceeds of the loan to purchase the (leased) assets. This is why financial analysts count financial leases as debt in calculating a firm's debt ratios.

DECIDING WHETHER TO LEASE OR BORROW

Chapter 6 explains that the best management decisions are those with the highest net present value (NPV) because these decisions will maximize the firm's equity value. One way to apply the NPV rule to the decision of whether to lease or to borrow and buy is to compute the NPV of the *difference* in cash flows between leasing and buying. This NPV is known as the **net advantage to leasing** or **NAL**. If NAL is positive, the asset should be leased; if it is negative, it should be bought.

To illustrate, we return to the firm that needs to replace ten forklifts. The replacement decision has a positive NPV. The question is whether the firm should lease the equipment or borrow money and buy it. If purchased, the cost is \$10,000 per vehicle, for a total of \$100,000. This expenditure will be financed

EXHIBIT 9.9 SUMMARY OF DIFFERENCE IN CASH FLOWS WHEN FORKLIFTS ARE LEASED RATHER THAN PURCHASED.

Lease versus Buy	Now	Year 1	Year 2	Year 3	Year 4	Year 5
After-tax lease payments	–$9,000	–$9,000	–$9,000	–$9,000	–$9,000	
Loss of tax savings on depreciation		–8,000	–8,000	–8,000	–8,000	–8,000
Loss of the after-tax scrap value						–10,000
Cash saved because the forklifts are not bought	+100,000					
Total differential cash flows	**$91,000**	**–$17,000**	**–$17,000**	**–$17,000**	**–$17,000**	**–$18,000**

over the equipment's useful life of five years with a $100,000 loan of the same maturity. The interest rate on the loan is 5 percent. The vehicles will be depreciated for fiscal purposes over five years, according to the straight-line method. In other words, the annual depreciation expense will be $2,000 per vehicle ($10,000 divided by five) or $20,000 for the whole fleet (ten times $2,000). The *after-tax* scrap or salvage value of each vehicle is estimated at $1,000, meaning that in five years' time the firm should get $10,000 (ten times $1,000) from the sale of the forklifts. The corporate tax rate is 40 percent.

If the firm leases the forklifts, the terms of the lease call for annual payments of $1,500 per vehicle or $15,000 for all of them. The lease payments are payable at the *beginning* of the year. The firm is responsible for the maintenance and insurance on the vehicles, regardless of whether it leases or buys.

Exhibit 9.9 summarizes the *difference* between the cash flows from leasing the forklifts and the cash flows from buying them. There are four differences in these cash flows. First, we have the *after-tax* annual lease payments, the first one due *immediately* (the "Now" column in the exhibit). The tax rate is 40 percent, so these annual payments, net of tax savings, will amount to $9,000 (60 percent of $15,000). Second, because the vehicles will be leased, the firm cannot depreciate them for tax purposes. It will therefore *lose* the tax savings from depreciation it would have had if it had owned the equipment. The annual tax *saving* resulting from the deductibility of annual depreciation expense amounts to $8,000 ($20,000 multiplied by a tax rate of 40 percent; it is the amount of tax the firm would have saved if it had been able to depreciate the assets). Third, the firm will not get the $10,000 after-tax scrap value of the vehicles at the end of the fifth year because it will not own the forklifts. Fourth, if the vehicles are leased, the firm will not have to spend $100,000 to buy them.

The initial differential cash flow is positive, whereas those from Year 1 to Year 5 are negative. This reflects the fact that leasing the forklifts allows the firm to exchange the purchase price of $100,000 for cash outflows in the following five years. Because leasing is comparable to borrowing, the relevant discount rate is simply the after-tax cost of debt, that is, 3 percent [5% × (1 – 0.40)]. Discounting the total differential cash flows at 3 percent,[15] we found a positive NPV, or net advantage of leasing, of $12,282. Conclusion: Leasing is "cheaper" than borrowing. The firm should lease the forklifts instead of borrowing to buy them.

BORROWING BY ISSUING SHORT-TERM SECURITIES

As mentioned earlier, large firms with high-credit standings can raise short-term funds by issuing commercial paper (CP) in their domestic money markets and EuroCP in the Euromarkets. Commercial paper is usually unsecured; that is, the holder has no claim on the firm's income or assets if the issuing firm defaults. However, a CP issue is almost always backed by bank lines of credit, meaning that the bank agrees to lend money to the firm to repay the CP when it is due if, at the CP's maturity date, the firm is unable to issue new securities on preferential terms to repay the maturing paper.

Commercial paper is usually sold in large denominations ($5 million and higher), at a **discount from face value**, and with a maturity of 2 to 270 days in the U.S. market and up to 360 days in the Euromarkets.[16] The paper can be issued either directly to investors or through brokers specializing in the distribution of commercial paper. In general, firms that are able to access the CP market find this debt instrument slightly cheaper and more flexible than a short-term bank loan.

BORROWING BY ISSUING CORPORATE BONDS

The alternative to borrowing medium- and long-term funds through bank loans and lease agreements is to borrow by issuing corporate bonds that can be either sold to the public at large or placed privately. Corporate bonds are long-term securities issued by firms to raise debt capital over periods ranging from five years to as many as 100 years, although most corporate bonds are issued with a maturity ranging between five and thirty years. As pointed out earlier, issues with a maturity longer than one year but shorter than five years are usually called corporate notes. For the sake of simplicity in the following discussion, we will not make any distinction between bonds and notes, calling any corporate debt security with a maturity longer than a year a bond.

The issuing firm has a contractual obligation to pay bondholders a fixed annual **coupon payment** over the bond's life and to repay the borrowed funds on the day the bonds have reached their **maturity date**. (Coupons are sometimes paid semiannually.) Corporate bonds denominated in U.S. dollars are usually issued at a **par value** or **face value** of $1,000, which is the amount of money that the firm must repay at maturity. (A bond's par value is also called its **nominal value, redemption value**, or **principal**.)

---

[15]If the salvage value is uncertain, it should be discounted at a higher rate to adjust for the additional risk.

[16]The terms *price discount, face value,* and *maturity* are explained in the following section on corporate bonds.

Suppose that Allied Equipment Corporation (AEC) issues 50,000 bonds with a par value of $1,000, a maturity date of five years, and a **coupon rate** of 5 percent. The buyer of one bond will receive a coupon payment of $50 each year (5 percent of $1,000) and will receive $1,000 at the end of the fifth year. If the bond is held to maturity, the holder earns an annual rate of return equal to the 5 percent coupon rate, because buying the bond is equivalent to depositing $1,000 in a bank account, receiving an annual interest rate of 5 percent for five years, and withdrawing the $1,000 at the end of the fifth year. If the bonds are priced at par value, AEC will receive $50 million ($1,000 multiplied by 50,000 bonds) less the cost of issuing the bonds, called **flotation costs**. If the bonds are offered at a discount, AEC will receive less than $50 million. For example, if the **original price discount** is 2 percent, the bonds will sell at $980 apiece (2 percent less than the par value) and AEC will receive $49 million less the cost of issuing the bonds. Note that bond prices are usually quoted as a percentage of par value. AEC's bond price will thus be quoted at 98 percent, which is equivalent to $980 per $1,000 of face value. We explain later why AEC would issue its bonds at a discount.

SECURITY, SENIORITY, SINKING FUNDS, AND CALL PROVISIONS

Corporate bonds are usually issued with a number of provisions attached to them that provide specific rights to either the bond buyer or the issuing firm. The buyer is protected by the bond's security, seniority, and sinking funds provisions. The issuing firm is protected against a possible drop in interest rates by a **call provision.**

Security The issuer of a **secured bond** has provided collateral to the lender. For example, a firm issuing a **mortgage bond** offers as collateral the property it buys with the cash raised from the sale of the bond. If the firm fails to service the bond, the lenders, acting through their **trustee**, can seize and resell the property. **Unsecured bonds**, sometimes called **debentures**, are supported only by the general credit standing of the issuing firm.[17]

Seniority A **senior bond** has a claim on the firm's assets (in the event of liquidation) that precedes the claim of **junior** or **subordinated debt**, which, in turn, takes precedence over the claims of the firm's stockholders.

Sinking Fund Provision A **sinking fund provision** requires the bond issuer to set aside cash in a special **trust** account according to a regular schedule. This cash accumulates during the bond's life to allow the firm to either **redeem the bonds** at maturity or redeem parts of the outstanding bonds before they reach their maturity date. Because the trust is legally separated from the issuer's assets, a sinking fund provision reduces the risk that the issuer will be unable to redeem the bonds at maturity.

Call Provision The issuer of a **callable bond** has the option of **redeeming the bond** before it reaches its maturity date. For example, suppose AEC issues a

---

[17]This is the terminology used in the United States. In the United Kingdom, debentures refer to secured bonds.

five-year, 5.25 percent coupon bond at par ($1,000) that is callable at 2 percent over par ($1,020) any time *after* two years. (In this case, the bond has a **deferred call provision.**) The call option gives AEC the right to buy the bond from its holder at a **call value** that is 2 percent higher than its par value.

A callable bond is clearly less valuable to its *holder* than an identical bond that is not callable. The issuer will most likely call the bond when it can issue new ones at a lower coupon rate, thus forcing the holder to replace the original bond with a lower coupon one. This is why the issuer must compensate the holder with a redemption value that exceeds par value and with a higher coupon rate. (AEC's callable bond has a coupon rate of 5.25 percent, whereas the identical noncallable bond has a 5 percent coupon rate.) From the issuer's point of view, the call provision is valuable because it gives the option to retire the bond and refinance at a lower rate if market rates fall. But this option is costly to the issuer because a callable bond's coupon rate exceeds the rate of an identical, noncallable bond.

FINDING THE YIELD OF A BOND WHEN ITS PRICE IS KNOWN

We return to AEC's noncallable bond issue and assume the bonds are sold at $980, below their par value of $1,000. Although the bonds are issued at a **discount** from their par value, they still provide the *buyer* with the same cash-flow stream as if they were issued at par. The holder of one bond is expected to receive $50 each year for the following *four* years and $1,050 the *fifth* year if the bond is held until maturity (the fifth payment includes the last $50 coupon and the $1,000 face value). Thus, the bond's expected return is higher than the 5 percent coupon rate because when the bond is redeemed in five years, the holder will realize a capital gain of $20 ($1,000 less $980). What is the bondholder's expected return? It is the rate that makes the bond price equal to the *present value* of the bond's future cash-flow stream. This rate is called the bond **market yield, yield to maturity,** or **redemption yield.**[18]

The cash-flow stream expected from the AEC bond is $50 a year for five years plus a principal repayment of $1,000 the fifth year. If y denotes the bond's yield to maturity, the present value of the cash-flow stream is the following:

$$\text{Present value of the cash flows expected from the bond} =$$
$$\frac{\$50}{(1+y)^1}+\frac{\$50}{(1+y)^2}+\frac{\$50}{(1+y)^3}+\frac{\$50}{(1+y)^4}+\frac{\$1,050}{(1+y)^5}$$

Setting the present value of the expected cash flows equal to the bond price of $980, we have the following:

$$\$980=\frac{\$50}{(1+y)^1}+\frac{\$50}{(1+y)^2}+\frac{\$50}{(1+y)^3}+\frac{\$50}{(1+y)^4}+\frac{\$1,050}{(1+y)^5}$$

[18]The bond's yield to maturity is the internal rate of return (IRR), as defined in Chapter 7, of the investment in the bond. Thus, a bond's net present value (NPV) calculated at its market yield must be zero because the IRR is the rate that makes the NPV zero. Buying a bond at its market price is thus a zero NPV investment.

This equation can be solved using a financial calculator or a spreadsheet as follows:

	A	B	C	D	E	F	G
1	Number of periods	5					
2							
3	Coupon payment	\$50					
4							
5	Market price	\$980					
6							
7	Principal repayment	\$1,000					
8							
9	**Yield to maturity**	5.47%					
10							
11	*Formula in cell B9 is =RATE(B1,B3,–B5,B7)*						
12							

Our spreadsheet indicates that the yield to maturity is 5.47 percent. This means that investors who buy the bonds at \$980 a piece and hold them to maturity can expect to earn a return of 5.47 percent. It also means that AEC is actually borrowing at a cost of 5.47 percent and not at the 5 percent coupon rate or at the bond's **current yield** of 5.1 percent (the \$50 coupon payment of the bond divided by its \$980 price). The bond market yield (5.47 percent) is higher than its coupon rate (5 percent) because the bond is issued at a price (\$980) that is lower than the bond face value (\$1,000). The \$20 of capital gains at maturity is the reason why the yield exceeds the coupon rate.

Why would AEC issue its bonds at a discount? Why not issue them at par and thus borrow at the 5 percent coupon rate instead of the higher 5.47 percent market yield? AEC cannot issue its bonds at par because firms do not set the yield on their bonds—the market does. The yield of 5.47 percent is the return required by investors to compensate them for the risk of holding a five-year, 5 percent coupon bond issued by AEC. Had AEC set the coupon rate at 5.47 percent, it would have issued its bonds at par.

THE YIELD OF A BOND IS DETERMINED BY ITS RISK

A bondholder faces two major sources of risk, and the higher these risks, the higher the yield at which the issuing firm will have to sell its bonds. **Market risk** (also called **price risk** or **interest rate risk**) occurs because the price of bonds fluctuates unpredictably in response to unexpected changes in the level of interest rates. This risk is discussed in a later section. **Credit risk** (also called **default risk**) occurs because the issuing firm may not be able to service its bonds (it may not be able to pay the promised coupons on their scheduled dates and repay the principal on the bond maturity date).

Firms that want to sell their bonds to the public are usually required to first obtain a **credit rating** from a bond rating agency, such as Moody's or Standard & Poor's. That rating provides an overall assessment of the bond's credit risk. At

EXHIBIT 9.10 BOND RATINGS AND MARKET YIELDS ON JANUARY 13, 2010.

TWENTY-YEAR U.S. GOVERNMENT AND INDUSTRIAL BONDS[1]

Bond Rating	Market Yield	Spread over Government Bond
Government	4.23%	–
AAA	5.17%	0.94% (94 basis points)
AA	5.51%	1.28% (128 basis points)
A	6.11%	1.88% (188 basis points)
BBB	6.69%	2.46% (246 basis points)

[1]Yield on 20-year government bonds is taken from the yield curve.

Source: www.bondsonline.com.

Standard & Poor's, issues with the highest financial strength are assigned a AAA rating, followed by AA, A, and BBB ratings. Bonds that have been assigned one of these four top ratings are known as **investment-grade bonds**. Bonds with lower ratings (BB, B, and CCC) are known as **speculative-grade bonds** or **junk bonds**.[19] Their prices are more sensitive to unexpected changes in the firm's financial condition. Thus, they are more risky and investors require higher yields to hold them.

The yield investors require depends on the bond's rating and the rate at which the government is borrowing for the same maturity. The rate for government borrowing is usually the minimum rate for the given maturity because the government cannot *technically* default on debt denominated in its own, domestic currency. (It can always print money to repay investors.)

An example of the credit-risk structure of bonds with a twenty-year maturity is shown in Exhibit 9.10. The higher the credit risk, the lower the **bond rating** and the higher the bond's market yield. Note that the lower the bond rating, the wider its **yield spread** or **credit spread** over the government bond with the same maturity. (One **basis point** is equal to one-hundredth of 1 percent.) The size of the spread is obviously not fixed; it varies over time with changes in market conditions and outlook.

FINDING THE PRICE OF A BOND WHEN ITS YIELD IS KNOWN

Suppose that a year has passed since AEC issued its five-year, 5 percent coupon bonds. The **current maturity** of the bonds is thus four years. Suppose further that you bought a bond for $980 a year ago and that you wish to sell it today. You cannot sell it back to the issuer. You will have to sell it to another investor through a bond dealer. Ignoring **transaction costs**, what price can you expect to receive for your bond? The answer depends on the yield at which *new* corporate bonds, *similar* to yours, are currently being issued. Similar bonds are those with a four-year maturity and with the same risk as the bonds issued by AEC. Let's assume that

[19]Institutional investors such as pension funds and insurance companies are usually restricted by regulation to only buy investment-grade bonds.

newly issued four-year corporate bonds with the same credit risk as AEC's bonds are being sold at par ($1,000) with a 4.5 percent coupon rate. Thus, investors can earn a 4.5 percent yield on newly issued, four-year corporate bonds similar to AEC's bonds. But your bond offers a higher coupon rate of 5 percent and is, thus, *more valuable* than the newly issued 4.5 percent bonds. You should be able to sell it for more than $1,000. The price should be the one at which a buyer will earn a yield of 4.5 percent on a 5 percent coupon bond. Indeed, by paying *more* than $1,000 for the bond, the buyer will incur a capital *loss* at maturity that will reduce the bond yield to 4.5 percent.

Earlier, we knew the bond price ($980) and we wanted to find its yield (which we found to be 5.47 percent). Now, we know the bond's yield (4.5 percent) and we want to find its price. The bond price must be the present value at 4.5 percent of the remaining four $50 coupons and the $1,000 principal repayment at the end of the fourth year:

$$\text{Bond price} = \frac{\$50}{(1+0.045)^1} + \frac{\$50}{(1+0.045)^2} + \frac{\$50}{(1+0.045)^3} + \frac{\$1,050}{(1+0.045)^4} = \$1,017.94$$

The bond price of $1,017.94 can be found using the spreadsheet function *PV* as follows:

	A	B	C	D	E	F	G
1	Number of periods	4					
2							
3	Coupon payment	$50					
4							
5	Market rate	4.50%					
6							
7	Principal repayment	$1,000					
8							
9	**Bond price**	**$1,017.94**					
10							
11	*Formula in cell B9 is =PV(B5,B1,B3,B7)*						
12							

Because the bond yield is now *lower* than its coupon rate, the bond price is at a $17.94 **premium** over its $1,000 face value. Recall that when the bond price was at a $20 **discount** from its face value, its 5.47 percent yield was *above* its 5 percent coupon rate. In general, when the yield is *below* the coupon rate, the bond price is at a *premium* over face value; when the yield is *above* the coupon rate, the price is at a *discount* from face value.

ZERO-COUPON BONDS

As their name indicates, **zero-coupon bonds** do not pay any coupon. Bondholders earn their return on investment entirely through capital gains (the difference between the price at which the bond is issued and its face value). To show how this type of bonds is priced, consider a firm that wishes to issue a ten-year zero-coupon bond.[20] If investors require a 5 percent yield to hold this type of bond, at what price should the bonds be issued if their face value is $1,000? The price must be equal to the present value of $1,000 in ten years at a discount rate of 5 percent:

$$\text{Zero-coupon bond price} = \frac{\$1,000}{(1+0.05)^{10}} = \$613.91$$

The bond price of $613.91 can be found using again the *PV* function of a spreadsheet:

	A	B	C	D	E	F	G
1	Number of periods	10					
2							
3	Coupon payment	$0					
4							
5	Market rate	5%					
6							
7	Principal repayment	$1,000					
8							
9	**Bond price**	**$613.91**					
10							
11	*Formula in cell B9 is =PV(B5,B1,B3,B7)*						
12							

Alternatively, we could have used the present value table inside the front cover of the book to find that the present value of $1 in ten years at 5 percent is 0.61391, which is the discount factor at 5 percent for ten years. The price of the bond is thus $613.91 ($1,000 multiplied by 0.61391). The firm must issue the bonds at an original discount of 38.61 percent of face value ($1,000 less $613.91, divided by $1,000). If the firm wishes to raise $100 million (before flotation costs), it will have to sell 162,890 bonds ($100 million divided by $613.91).

In general, the price of a zero-coupon bond can be written as follows:

$$\textbf{Zero-coupon bond price} = \frac{\textbf{Face value}}{(\mathbf{1+y})^{N}} = \textbf{Face value} \times \textbf{DF}(\mathbf{y}, N) \qquad (9.4)$$

where DF(y, *N*) is the discount factor at the market yield y for *N* years.

PERPETUAL BONDS

Perpetual bonds are bonds that never mature; the issuer continues to pay the coupon forever. This raises the immediate question of whether the issuing entity will be around forever. Because of this uncertainty, *noncallable* perpetual bonds have usually been

[20]The first public issue of a zero-coupon bond in the U.S. market was made in April 1981 by JC Penney (a department store). In June of the same year, Pepsico Overseas issued a three-year zero-coupon Eurobond at 67.25 percent of face value to yield 14.14 percent.

issued only by governments, such as the British and Canadian governments, although some nongovernment entities, such as banks, have also issued such bonds in the past.

Suppose a firm wishes to raise funds through an issue of perpetual bonds with a 5 percent coupon rate and a $1,000 face value. If investors require a yield of 6 percent on this type of bond, what should the issue price be? It must be the present value of an infinite **annuity** or **perpetuity**. In Appendix 6.1 of Chapter 6, we show that it is equal to the perpetual annual cash flow (here the annual coupon payment of $50 (5 percent of $1,000)) divided by the market rate (here the market yield of 6 percent). Therefore, the price of the perpetual bond is as follows:

$$\text{Perpetual bond price} = \frac{5\% \times \$1{,}000}{6\%} = \frac{\$50}{0.06} = \$833.33$$

In general, we can write,

$$\textbf{Perpetual bond price} = \frac{\textbf{Coupon rate} \times \textbf{Face value}}{\textbf{Market yield}} \tag{9.5}$$

Although perpetual bonds are rarely issued, a number of firms have issued bonds with a 100-year maturity.[21]

HOW CHANGES IN MARKET YIELD AFFECT BOND PRICES

By calculating the price of a bond as a function of its term to maturity, coupon rate, and market yield, we can show how a change in the market yield affects the price of a bond. To illustrate, we examine the price behavior of the three bonds shown in Exhibit 9.11, where the bond prices were calculated using a spreadsheet as shown in the previous sections. The first bond is a ten-year, 10 percent coupon bond; the second is a ten-year, zero-coupon bond; and the third is a 10 percent perpetual bond. All have a $1,000 face value. We can draw several general conclusions from the graphs in Exhibit 9.11:

1. The price of bonds is *inversely* related to the market yield, as shown in the first graph: when the yield increases, the price of *all* bonds fall; when the yield decreases, the price of *all* bonds rise
2. The *longer* a bond's term to maturity (all else the same), the *higher* the price sensitivity of the bond to a change in market yield. To see this, compare the ten-year, 10 percent coupon bond with the 10 percent perpetual bond in the second graph: they have the same coupon rate (10 percent), but the perpetual bond has a longer maturity and its price is much more sensitive to changes in market yield
3. The *lower* a bond coupon rate (all else the same), the *higher* the price sensitivity of the bond to a change in market yield. To see this, compare the ten-year, 10 percent coupon bond with the ten-year, zero-coupon bond in the second graph: they have the same maturity (ten years), but the zero-coupon bond has a lower coupon rate and its price is much more sensitive to changes in market yield

Thus, a bond's market risk, which reflects the sensitivity of its price to a change in the market yield, *increases* when the bond's term to maturity *increases*

[21]During the 1990s, more than forty U.S. companies issued so-called **century bonds**, including IBM.

EXHIBIT 9.11 THE RELATION BETWEEN MARKET YIELDS AND BOND PRICES FOR DIFFERENT TYPES OF BONDS.

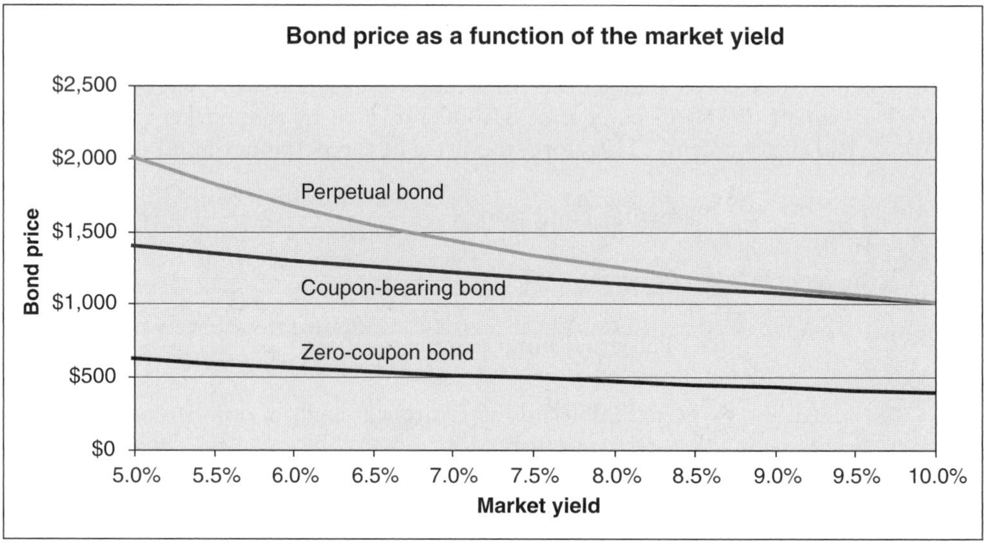

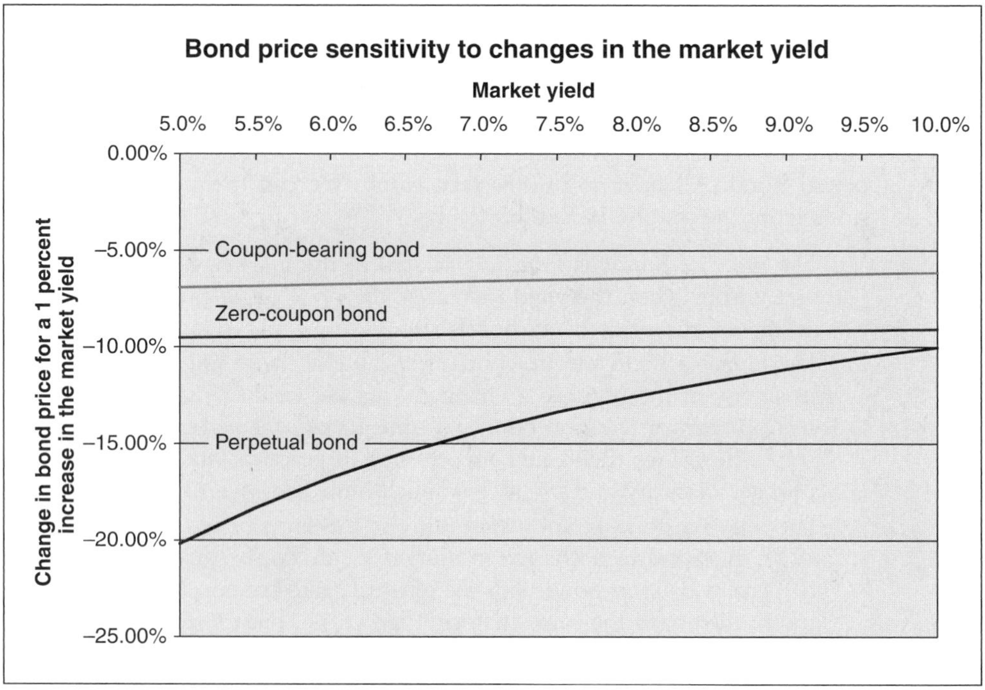

and the bond's coupon rate *decreases*. If the three bonds shown in Exhibit 9.11 have the same credit risk (assume they are issued by the same firm), then the perpetual bond has more market risk than the zero-coupon bond, which has more market risk than the 10 percent coupon bond.

Floating Rate and Variable Rate Bonds

Some corporate bonds are called **floating rate bonds** because they have floating coupon rates; their coupon rates are related to another rate, called the **reference** or **benchmark rate**, which usually changes every six months. The reference rate is often the interest rate at which *international* banks lend U.S. dollars to one another, known as the **London Interbank Offering Rate (LIBOR)**. To illustrate, suppose AEC wants to issue five-year bonds but does not wish to pay a fixed coupon rate for the next five years because it expects rates to drop in the future. A **floater** may be the answer. The coupon rate that AEC will pay during the ten consecutive six-month periods over the next five years is the six-month LIBOR prevailing at the beginning of each period, plus a *fixed* **spread** of, say, eighty-five basis points (0.85 percent above LIBOR). The five-year floater allows AEC to eliminate its **refinancing risk** (the risk of not being able to renew the loan during the five-year period) while still bearing the risk of changing interest rates.

A floating rate bond should not be confused with a **variable rate bond**. The latter is a bond that has a coupon rate set at more than one level; for example, a fifteen-year bond may have a zero-coupon rate during its first five years and a 10 percent coupon rate during its remaining ten-year life. This pattern of coupon payments is attractive to a firm planning to invest the funds in a long-term project that is not expected to generate positive cash flows before its fifth year.

Convertible Bonds

As its name indicates, a **convertible bond** can be converted into the firm's common stock at the option of the bondholder. This conversion option, called a **sweetener** or an **equity kicker**, makes these bonds more attractive to investors. At the same time, firms can issue them at a lower rate than bonds without a conversion option. To illustrate, suppose General Beverage Company (GBC) issues ten-year, 5 percent bonds at $1,000 par value that are convertible into ten shares of GBC (this is the bond's **conversion ratio**) at a price of $100 per share (this is the **conversion price**). Shares of GBC are currently trading at $80, so the **conversion premium** is 25 percent ($100 less $80, divided by $80) and the bond's **conversion value** is $800 (ten times $80). If GBC issued ten-year *straight* bonds, it would have to pay a coupon rate of 6 percent. Thus, GBC has reduced its cost of debt by a full percentage point by giving investors the option to convert their bonds into equity.

The value of the conversion option is equal to the difference between the value of the convertible bond and the value of the bond if it were not convertible (which is called the **bond value of the convertible bond**). We know that GBC issued the convertible bond at $1,000, so this is its value. What is the bond value of the convertible bond, that is, its value if it were not convertible? It is the value of a bond with a face value of $1,000, a coupon rate of 5 percent, a term to maturity of ten years, and a yield of 6 percent (the rate it would have if it were not convertible). Entering these figures in the bond-price spreadsheet presented earlier gives a value of $926.40. Thus, the value of the conversion option is as follows:

$$\begin{aligned}\text{Option value} &= \text{Value of convertible} - \text{Bond value}\\ &= \$1{,}000 - \$926.40 = \$73.60\end{aligned}$$

The convertible bond that GBC has sold to investors is equivalent to a package containing a ten-year, 5 percent *straight* bond worth $926.40 plus an *option* to buy ten shares of GBC at $100 per share (the option to buy equity) worth $73.60.

Note that the option allows investors to buy shares, currently worth $80, for $100. The option is valuable because there is a chance that GBC's share price will rise above $100 during the next ten years. If it does, and if it exceeds the convertible bond value, investors will exercise their right to convert, and GBC will have to issue equity at $100 in exchange for the bonds. Does the deal make sense for GBC?

If the convertible bond is properly priced, then its option value ($73.60) is the appropriate "payment" that the firm must make to lower its cost of debt financing (from 6 percent to 5 percent). The convertible bond is, in this case, a fair deal that should neither reduce nor enhance the firm's value. Firms do not issue convertible bonds because the interest cost of a convertible bond is lower than the interest cost of a straight bond. The embedded option gives bondholders the right to convert the bond into the firm's common stock, and we have just shown that this option is valuable to bondholders. As a consequence, they are willing to accept a lower rate of return on the bond portion of the issue. In equilibrium, there should be a perfect trade-off, which explains why the value of the firm should not be affected by a convertible issue.

Firms may decide to issue convertible bonds for two main reasons. First, the lower coupon rate of a convertible, compared with that of a straight bond issue, can be attractive to high-growth, high-risk, cash-starved firms. For these firms, the cash flows from operations may not be high enough to fund their large capital expenditures programs. Furthermore, their level of risk may command high interest rates. By issuing convertibles that have lower coupon rates than straight bonds, the pressure on the firm's cash flows can be somewhat relieved and, to some extent, transformed instead into a pressure to generate capital gains for investors.

Second, convertible bonds may be attractive to bondholders who find it difficult to assess the risk of the firm issuing the securities or who fear that the firm's management may not act in their best interests. The straight-bond portion of the convertible package, which obliges the firm to make coupon payments and repay the principal, provides bondholders with some protection if the firm does not do well, and the option to convert the bonds into the firm's stock allows them to share in the increase in the firm's value if the firm does well.

EQUITY CAPITAL: CHARACTERISTICS AND VALUATION

External equity capital comes from two sources: **common stock** and **preferred stock**. Their comparative characteristics are summarized in Exhibit 9.12. Preferred stockholders have priority over common stockholders in the payment of dividends and have a prior claim on the firm's assets in the event of liquidation (if there is anything left after debt holders and creditors have been paid). Preferred stockholders usually have no voting rights, but they may have **contingent voting rights**, such as the right to elect members to the board of directors *if* the company has skipped dividend payments for a specified number of quarters. Preferred shares, like bonds, may have sinking funds, can be callable, and can be converted into common equity.

EXHIBIT 9.12 COMPARATIVE CHARACTERISTICS OF COMMON AND PREFERRED STOCKS.

Characteristic	Common Stocks	Preferred Stocks
Control and voting rights		
	Common stockholders have full control and voting rights	Preferred stockholders have no control but some voting rights only if the firm skips dividend payments for a specified number of periods
Dividend payments		
Seniority	Can be paid only after payment to preferred stockholders	Paid before payment to common stockholders but after interest payments to debt holders
Are they cumulative?[1]	No	Most preferred are cumulative
Can they vary?	Yes, according to the firm's dividend payment policy	Yes, with payments often linked to money market rates
Is there a maximum payment?	No	There is usually an upper limit
Are they tax deductible for the issuing corporation?	No	No
Provisions		
Any sinking fund provision?	No	Some preferred have sinking funds
Is it callable by the firm?	Cannot be called	Some preferred are callable
Is it convertible into another type of security?	Cannot be converted	Some preferred are convertible into common stocks
Why and when are they usually issued?		
	To raise permanent equity capital to fund the firm's growth	To allow owners to raise quasi-equity without losing control. Often used as payment when buying another company
Pricing		
	See common stock valuation in Appendix 9.1	A straight preferred is priced like a perpetual bond (fixed dividend divided by market yield). See equation 9.6
Flexibility to issuing firm		
	The most flexible type of security a firm can issue	More flexible than bonds but less flexible than common stocks
Risk		
	Higher than preferred stocks and bonds	Higher than bonds but lower than common stocks

[1]Cumulative dividends means that if the firm skips the payment of dividends for a period of time, it will have to pay the missed dividends (called **arrearage**) when it resumes paying dividends.

THE VALUATION OF PREFERRED STOCKS

Because straight preferred stocks pay a constant perpetual dividend, they are priced like perpetual bonds. To illustrate, suppose two years ago Consolidated Motor Company (CMC) issued straight preferred stocks that pay a constant dividend of \$6. A company in the same sector and with the same risk profile as CMC has just issued straight preferred stocks at \$50 that promise to pay a constant dividend of \$4. What is the current price of one share of CMC preferred stocks given that both CMC and the similar company quote their dividend payment on the basis of a face value of \$100? The market yield of the similar preferred stock is 8 percent (\$4 divided by \$50). This is the yield that investors will require to hold CMC's preferred stocks. Again, recognizing that the value of a preferred stock—as the value of a perpetual bond—is the present value of an infinite annuity (in our case, an annual dividend payment of \$6), CMC's preferred stock price, according to equation 9.5, is the following:

$$\text{Preferred stock price} = \frac{\text{Annual dividend payment}}{\text{Market yield}} = \frac{\$6}{0.08} = \$75 \qquad (9.6)$$

If the preferred stocks are both callable and convertible into common stock, the \$75 price will have to be *reduced* by the estimated value of the call option (which the holder has in effect *sold* to CMC) and *increased* by the estimated value of the option to convert into common stock (which the holder has in effect *purchased* from CMC).

THE VALUATION OF COMMON STOCKS

Suppose the International Manufacturing Company (IMC) is expected to pay its common stockholders a \$2 cash dividend at the end of the year (DIV_1 = \$2) and that one share of IMC will be worth \$30 at the same date (P_1 = \$30). What is the estimated value that one share should have today (P_0) if investors require a return of 12 percent to hold IMC's common stock ($k_E = 0.12$, E for equity)? As in the case of a bond, it is the present value of the cash flow expected from holding the security and selling it in one year. At the end of the year, a holder of one share of IMC's common stock is expected to receive DIV_1 plus P_1. At a discount rate of k_E, the present value of this year-end cash flow is the following:

$$P_0 = \frac{DIV_1 + P_1}{1 + k_E} = \frac{\$2 + \$30}{1.12} = \frac{\$32}{1.12} = \$28.57$$

We can extend this formula to the next period, with a second-year expected cash dividend of DIV_2 and a share valued at P_2 at the end of Year 2. We have the following:

$$P_0 = \frac{DIV_1}{1 + k_E} + \frac{DIV_2 + P_2}{(1 + k_E)^2}$$

If we carry this logic to an infinitely large number of periods, we get the following:

$$P_0 = \frac{DIV_1}{1 + k_E} + \frac{DIV_2}{(1 + k_E)^2} + \ldots + \frac{DIV_N}{(1 + k_E)^N} + \ldots = \sum_{t=1}^{\text{infinity}} \frac{DIV_t}{(1 + k_E)^t}$$

where $\sum_{t=1}^{\text{infinity}}$ means "take the sum of the present values of the cash dividends from year one (t = 1) to infinity." This equity valuation formula is known as the **dividend discount model (DDM)**.

THE CONSTANT GROWTH DIVIDEND DISCOUNT MODEL

To find the value of equity using the dividend discount model, we need to know the stream of cash dividends the firm is expected to pay in the future. As you can imagine, a firm's future dividend stream is not easy to predict, making the dividend discount model difficult to apply. As a convenient shortcut, we can assume that cash dividends are expected to grow at a *constant* annual rate g forever. In this case, the dividend discount model reduces to the ratio of next year's dividend to the difference between the required return k_E and the constant annual growth rate g (see Appendix 9.1):

$$P_0 = \frac{DIV_1}{k_E - g} \tag{9.7}$$

Equation 9.7 is known as the **constant growth dividend discount model**. Although it is an extreme simplification of reality, it is a convenient formula that we use in Chapters 10 and 12.

To illustrate, suppose that Consolidated Utilities is expected to pay a \$2.60 cash dividend per share next year that is anticipated to grow at a constant annual rate of 3 percent forever. If investors require a return of 10 percent to hold common stocks of Consolidated Utilities (k_E = 0.10), the present value of one share of Consolidated Utilities' common stock is as follows:

$$P_0 = \frac{\$2.6}{0.10 - 0.03} = \frac{\$2.6}{0.07} = \$37.14$$

There are two points to note about the growth rate used in this valuation formula. The first point is related to the theoretical validity of the formula: the growth rate must be lower than the required rate of return by shareholders; otherwise, the formula becomes meaningless. (The growth rate can be negative, however, if dividends are *declining* at a constant rate.) The second point is related to the practical application of the formula: the growth rate should not exceed the average expected rate of growth of the economy in which the firm operates; otherwise, the firm would one day be as large as the economy. We return to these issues in Chapter 12.

MARKET EFFICIENCY AND EQUITY PRICING

If investors, on average, have the same required rate of return and make the same forecast of a firm's expected stream of dividend payments, then the observed market price of one share should be the same as the share value inferred from our valuation formula. In this case, the market is efficient in the sense that the price at which shares trade in the market reflects investors' consensus forecast about the future cash flows they expect to receive from their investment. Thus, in an **efficient market**, the observed share price is the best estimate of the value of a share. What you pay is, on average, what the share is worth.

TRACKING STOCK

A **tracking stock** is a special class of common stock carrying claims on the cash flows of a particular segment of a company, such as a subsidiary, division, or business unit.[22] Holders of tracking stocks receive dividends linked to the performance of the segment, but they neither legally own the assets of the segment nor have full voting rights. Diversified companies use these stocks to unlock the value of a specific activity for the benefit of investors who prefer having a direct equity claim on that activity instead of sharing it with claims on the company's other businesses.

EQUITY WARRANTS

Warrants are options sold by firms that give the holder the right to buy a specific number of shares of common stock at a fixed price (the **exercise price**) during the life of the warrant. In other words, these instruments are **call options** (an option to buy). Warrants are usually issued by firms as a sweetener attached to bonds or preferred shares, although firms have issued "plain" warrants that are not attached to any securities.

An issue of straight bonds sold with warrants is similar to a convertible bond issue. Both combine the features of a straight bond and an option on the firm's common stock and are appropriate financing instruments for high-growth, high-risk, cash-hungry companies. However, there are some differences. A convertible bond does not permit the holder to separate the bond from the option to convert, whereas warrants can be detached and sold separately from the bond. Also, when investors exchange their convertibles into equity, the firm's total capital does not change because the firm issues equity to replace debt. But when investors exercise their warrants, equity is issued (in return for cash), whereas debt is not automatically retired.

CONTINGENT VALUE RIGHTS

Contingent value rights (CVR) are options sold by companies that give the holder the right to *sell* a fixed number of shares to the issuing company at a fixed price during the life of the CVR. These option-type instruments are called **put options.** They are valuable to investors who believe the share price of the issuing firm is currently *overvalued* and who expect the share price to fall *below* the exercise price of the CVR before their expiration date.

---

[22]The first notable issue of tracking stock took place in 1984 when General Motors (GM) acquired Electronic Data Systems. To finance the deal, GM issued stock that would track the performance of the new acquisition, rather than that of all GM's subsidiaries and business units. The phenomenon amplified in the late 1990s and early 2000s. For example, in 2000, AT&T Corp. issued $10.6 billion of tracking stock for its Wireless Group, one of the largest public offerings in U.S. history.

Why would a firm want to issue this type of financial instrument? One reason is to raise funds; another is to signal to the market that the firm believes that its stock price is *not* overvalued. (If the firm thought its shares were overvalued, it would not issue the CVR.) A third reason is that when the CVR are sold in conjunction with a stock issue, they are an insurance given to the subscribers. The value of the shares they bought cannot be lower than the exercise price of the CVR because they can sell the shares back to the issuing firm at that price (at least until the CVR expire).

SUMMARY

Most of the funds needed to finance a firm's growth are generated by its internal activities. When firms experience a cash deficit, they must raise external funds. External funds are usually borrowed via bank loans and the issuance of debt securities; however, at times, they are supplemented with new issues of equity.

The source of internally generated funds is retained earnings, adjusted for noncash expenses such as depreciation. The amount of external financing the firm needs is the difference between these internally generated funds and the expected growth in the firm's investment in working capital requirement and fixed assets.

External funds are raised through the financial system, which acts as a conduit for savers' excess cash to be channeled to the firms that need it. Funds can be transferred directly from savers to firms or can be transferred indirectly via financial intermediaries. In the first case, the firms sell securities to savers in the form of shares or bonds. In the second case, an intermediary, such as a bank, receives funds from savers, typically in the form of deposits, and lends these funds to firms in the form of loans. Firms can place their debt and equity securities privately with financial institutions, such as insurance companies and pension funds. Alternatively, they can sell them in the securities markets, where they can then be traded among investors.

The function of primary markets is to ensure the success of new issues; the function of secondary markets is to ensure that investors can buy and sell existing securities at a fair price, a price that reflects all available public information. In addition to the distinction between primary and secondary markets, securities markets can be classified according to whether they are organized exchanges or over-the-counter markets, equity or debt markets, and domestic or international markets.

Firms issue shares and bonds either through private placement or through public offerings. For an equity issue, firms can raise capital through a general cash offering or via a rights issue. In a rights issue, current shareholders are given subscription rights that allow them to purchase new shares; in a general cash offering, shares are offered to the public at large and no distinction is made between current shareholders and other investors. The various sources of debt financing available to firms include bank loans, lease agreements, and bond issues.

A firm can issue a wide range of securities in addition to common stocks and straight bonds. These include convertibles, perpetual bonds, preferred shares, warrants, and contingent value rights. We explained why these securities are issued by firms and why they appeal to investors. Finally, we discussed various valuation formulas that can be used to price a security traded in an efficient market.

The Valuation Formula for the Constant Growth Dividend Model

APPENDIX 9.1

According to the constant growth dividend model, the current stock price (P_0) is equal to the discounted value, at the return required by stockholders (k_E), of the expected stream of dividend payments (DIV_t) that are anticipated to grow at a constant rate (g) forever. We can write the following:

$$P_0 = \frac{DIV_1}{1 + k_E} + \frac{DIV_2}{(1 + k_E)^2} + \frac{DIV_3}{(1 + k_E)^3} + \ldots$$

Because annual dividend payments are expected to grow at the constant rate g, we have the following:

$$DIV_2 = DIV_1(1 + g)$$

$$DIV_3 = DIV_2(1 + g) = DIV_1(1 + g)(1 + g) = DIV_1(1 + g)^2$$

and thus we have the following:

$$P_0 = \frac{DIV_1}{1 + k_E} + \frac{DIV_1(1 + g)}{(1 + k_E)^2} + \frac{DIV_1(1 + g)^2}{(1 + k_E)^3} + \ldots$$

Multiplying the above equation by $(1 + k_E)$ and dividing it by $(1 + g)$, we obtain

$$\frac{(1 + k_E)}{(1 + g)} \times P_0 = \frac{DIV_1}{(1 + g)} + \frac{DIV_1}{(1 + k_E)} + \frac{DIV_1(1 + g)}{(1 + k_E)^2} + \ldots$$

Subtracting the first equation from the second, we get the following:

$$\frac{(1 + k_E)}{(1 + g)} \times P_0 - P_0 = \frac{DIV_1}{(1 + g)}$$

Then, multiplying by $(1 + g)$, we get the following:

$$(1 + k_E)P_0 - (1 + g)P_0 = DIV_1$$

Rearranging the terms yields equation 9.7, the constant growth dividend valuation model shown in the chapter:

$$P_0 = \frac{DIV_1}{k_E - g}$$

FURTHER READING

1. Brealey, Richard, Stewart Myers, and Franklin Allen. *Principles of Corporate Finance*, 9th ed. McGraw-Hill, 2008. See Chapters 14, 15, and 16.
2. Damodaran, Aswath. *Corporate Finance: Theory and Practice*, 2nd ed. John Wiley & Sons, 2001. See Chapters 15 and 16.
3. Ross, Stephen, Randolph Westerfield, and Jeffrey Jaffe. *Corporate Finance*, 8th ed. McGraw-Hill Irwin, 2008. See Chapters 5, 14, 19, 20, and 21.
4. Smith, Roy, and Ingo Walter. *Global Banking*. Oxford University Press, 2003. See Chapters 1, 8, 9, 10, and 11.

SELF-TEST PROBLEMS

9.1 STRUCTURE AND CHARACTERISTICS OF FINANCIAL MARKETS.

Briefly explain the distinction between the two items that make up each of the following pairs:

a. Direct financing versus indirect financing
b. Primary markets versus secondary markets
c. Organized exchanges versus over-the-counter markets
d. Domestic securities versus international securities
e. Domestic securities versus foreign securities
f. Private placement versus public offering

9.2 ESTIMATING EXTERNAL FUNDING NEEDS.

Office Supplies (OS) Distributors wants to estimate the external funds it will need in 2011 based on the data available in Exhibit 9.2 and the following information and assumptions for 2011:

- Cash need: same as in 2010
- Working capital requirement: up 10 percent
- Capital expenditure: $10 million with $1 million annual depreciation
- Depreciation on existing assets: same as in 2010
- Net profit: up 10 percent
- Retention rate: same as in 2010

a. What are OS Distributors' expected total funding needs for 2011?
b. What are OS Distributors' expected internally generated funds in 2011?
c. What are expected external funding needs for 2011?
d. What should OS Distributors do to cover its external funding needs?

9.3 LEASING.

Do you agree with these statements?

a. Different tax rates between lessees and lessors may affect the magnitude of lease payments

b. A lease reduces uncertainty
c. An operating lease will reduce the liabilities of the firm as opposed to a purchase financed by debt

9.4 SEMIANNUAL COUPON BONDS.

Bonds issued in the United States often pay coupons twice a year. For example, if an ordinary ten-year, $1,000 semiannual coupon bond has a coupon rate of 8 percent, the bondholder will receive $40 every six months for a total of $80 (8 percent of $1,000) per year during ten years. Answer the following questions with the assumption that the current market rate for such a bond is 9 percent, that is, 4.5 percent every six months.

a. What is the bond price?
b. What is the bond effective yield to maturity, given that the owner will receive half of the annual coupons six months in advance?

9.5 VALUATION OF COMMON STOCKS.

National Equipment Company (NEC) has common stocks outstanding. NEC has just paid a $2 dividend per share of common stock.

a. Assume NEC's dividend per common share is expected to increase by 8 percent per year during the next three years and then rise at a constant rate of 4 percent forever. What is the estimated value of NEC's common stock if the required rate of return for this type of investment is 12 percent?
b. Suppose NEC's common stocks are currently trading at $29.12. How can you interpret the difference between the estimated value and the observed market price?

REVIEW PROBLEMS

1. **Structure and characteristics of financial markets.**
Briefly explain the distinction between the two items that make up each of the following pairs:

a. Rights issue versus general cash offering
b. Underwritten issue versus best efforts distribution
c. Originating house versus selling group
d. Seasoned issue versus secondary distribution
e. Credit risk versus market risk
f. Investment-grade bonds versus speculative-grade bonds

2. **Rights issue.**
Micro-Electronics Corporation (MEC) has just announced that it will issue 10 million shares of common stock through a rights issue at a subscription price of $20. Before the announcement, MEC shares were trading at $26, and there were 50 million shares outstanding.

- How many rights will MEC grant to its existing shareholders?
- How many rights will an investor need to buy one new share?

- What will happen to MEC's share price when the rights issue is announced?
- What should be the value of one right?

3. **Leasing versus borrowing.**
Office Supplies (OS) Distributors needs a new truck. It can buy it for $24,000, depreciate it over four years at an annual rate of $6,000, and finance the purchase with a four-year loan at 10 percent. The truck could be sold for $5,000 in four years. Alternatively, it can lease the truck and make four annual lease payments of $6,500 (payments are made at the *beginning* of the year). OS Distributors is subject to a 40 percent corporate tax rate and is responsible for the maintenance and insurance of the truck, regardless of whether it leases or buys.

   a. Should OS Distributors lease or buy the truck?
   b. What resale value of the truck in four years will make OS Distributors indifferent about buying versus leasing?

4. **Leasing.**
Thorenberg Inc. is considering the purchase of a machine from Hydraulic Engineering Company (HECO) to make hard pressed-metal sheets. The machine will cost $100,000 and would replace the currently used one. Savings are expected to be $60,000 per year, and the new machine is expected to last five years with proper maintenance. For tax purposes, the machine would be depreciated according to the straight-line method, and the tax rate is 36 percent. As an alternative to buying the machine, Thorenberg could lease it from Foster Leasing Corporation at a rate of $25,000 a year for five years, with payments made at the beginning of the year. All insurance, maintenance, and the cost of operating the machine would be the responsibility of Thorenberg. The interest rate at which Thorenberg can borrow on a medium- or long-term basis is 8 percent.

   a. What are the cash flows from leasing relative to buying for Thorenberg Inc.? Should Thorenberg Inc. lease or buy the new machine?
   b. What are the after-tax cash flows to Foster Leasing Corporation from buying and then leasing the machine to Thorenberg? Why are they the exact opposite of the cash flows to Thorenberg? (Assume that the two companies have the same effective corporate tax rate.)
   c. If the cash flows to the lessee (Thorenberg) and the cash flows to the lessor (Foster) are exactly the opposite, why would the leasing nevertheless take place?

5. **Bond valuation.**
Consider the following three bonds with $1,000 face value:

   Bond A: 10-year, 10 percent coupon bond
   Bond B: 10-year, zero-coupon bond
   Bond C: 20-year, 10 percent coupon bond

Compute the market values of each of the three bonds when the market interest rate varies from 0 to 14 percent. What is your interpretation of the decreasing relationship between bond market prices and interest rates?

6. **Bond valuation.**
Thalin Inc. has decided to extend its current product line. To finance the project, the firm is considering issuing a ten-year, $1,000 face value, 10 percent coupon bond. The firm has made public that its target debt-to-equity ratio of 30 percent is not going to change in the foreseeable future. Two years ago the firm issued a twelve-year, $1,000 face value, 10 percent coupon bond to finance a similar project. The current market price of the bond is $1,065. At what rate should the firm issue the new bond?

7. **Bond valuation.**
Consider the following four bonds:

	Coupon Issue	Zero Coupon	Perpetual	Convertible
Maturity	5 years	5 years	Infinity	5 years
Coupon rate	6 percent	Zero	6 percent	5 percent

a. If the market yield is 7 percent, what are the values of the three first bonds (assume a face value of $1,000)?
b. Why are the values of the bonds lower than their face values?
c. Why is the coupon rate for the convertible bond lower than that for the non-convertible, coupon issue?
d. Given that the convertible bond is trading at $1,040, what is the value of the option to convert?
e. Suppose that the market yield rises to 7.5 percent. What are the bond values at that yield? Explain why the change in the value of the bonds is different.

8. **Common stock valuation.**
Financial analysts expect Theron Co.'s earnings and dividends to grow at a rate of 16 percent during the next three years, 12 percent in the fourth and fifth years, and at a constant rate of 6 percent thereafter. Theron's dividend, which has just been paid, was $1.20. If the expected rate of return on the stock is 12 percent, what is the price of the stock today?

9. **Growth stocks versus income stocks.**
Therol Inc. has no debt. Its invested capital generates $5 of earnings per share, and all these earnings are paid out as dividends.

a. Suppose that Therol's shareholders require a return of 10 percent on their investment in the firm. What is Therol's stock price if the firm's earnings per share stays at $5 and if its dividend policy does not change over the foreseeable future?
b. Suppose that Therol pays out 60 percent of its earnings from existing invested capital and reinvests the remaining 40 percent in new plant and equipment,

from which it expects a return of 10 percent. What would be the effect on Therol's stock price? Compare it with the stock price found in question (a) and explain.

c. What if the return on new plant and equipment is 15 percent instead of 10 percent? What is your interpretation of the difference in the stock price?

10. **Valuation of preferred shares and common stocks.**
East Harbor Company (EHC) has both preferred and common stocks outstanding. EHC has just paid a $4 dividend per share of preferred stock and a $3.50 dividend per share of common stock.

a. Assume the dividend on the preferred is constant and that preferred stocks with similar risk to that of EHC are yielding 8.6 percent. What is its estimated value of EHC's preferred stock?
b. Suppose EHC's preferred stocks are currently trading at $48.68. How can you interpret the difference between the estimated value and the observed market price?
c. Assume EHC's dividend per common share is expected to increase by 8 percent per year during the next three years and then rise at a constant rate of 4 percent forever. What is the estimated value of EHC's common stock if the required rate of return for this type of investment is 12 percent?
d. Suppose EHC's common stocks are currently trading at $53.24. How can you interpret the difference between the estimated value and the observed market price?

ESTIMATING THE COST OF CAPITAL

CHAPTER 10

Firms need cash to finance their investment projects. Usually, this cash is generated internally from the firm's operations. If there is a shortage of internally generated funds, firms will ask investors (lenders and shareholders) to supply them with additional cash. Chapter 9 shows how firms can raise cash from external sources. Whatever its origin, cash is not free; it comes at a price. The price is the cost to the firm of using investors' money. When this cost is expressed as the return expected by investors for the capital they supply, it is called the *cost of capital.* Chapter 6 shows that the cost of capital is the rate at which a project's stream of future cash flows must be discounted to estimate its net present value (NPV) and to decide whether the project is worth undertaking, that is, whether it has the potential to create value. Chapter 7 shows that it is also the rate against which the project's internal rate of return (IRR) must be compared for the same purpose of deciding whether to accept or reject the project.

This chapter shows how to estimate the cost of capital to be used in the NPV, the IRR, or any other discounted cash-flow method applied to the analysis of an investment project. This cost of capital is called the *project's* cost of capital, not to be confused with the *firm's* cost of capital. The latter is the return expected by investors from *all* the assets acquired and managed by the firm.

As mentioned in Chapter 6, the rate investors require from their investment in a project is the return they expect to receive from investing their cash in alternative investments that have the same risk profile as the risk profile of the project. Thus, to estimate the cost of capital for a particular project, we first need to identify similar projects available to investors. The problem is that investors usually do not invest directly in projects; they invest in the firms that undertake projects. The challenge, then, is to identify firms that exhibit the same risk characteristics as the project under consideration. These comparable firms are called *proxies* or *pure-plays.*

After a proxy company has been identified, we must estimate the returns expected by the investors who hold the securities (bonds and shares) the proxy firm has issued. These investors have claims on the cash flows generated by the proxy's assets, which differ depending on the *type* of security held. Debt holders and shareholders of the same company have claims on the same cash flows generated by the firm's assets, but debt holders have a prior and fixed claim on these cash flows and thus bear *less* risk than shareholders. Consequently, the return expected from holding debt is *lower* than the return expected from holding shares of the same company. This chapter shows how to estimate the expected returns from the two most common financial instruments, straight bonds and common stocks, using financial market data.

The return expected from the assets acquired and managed by a firm belongs to the investors who financed these assets and to no one else. Thus, this return must be the total of the returns expected by debt holders and shareholders, weighted by their respective contribution to the funding of these assets. In other words, a firm's cost of capital must be equal to the weighted average of the costs of each of its financing sources. This cost of capital, which is first mentioned in Chapter 1, is known as the firm's weighted average cost of capital (WACC). Although we cannot directly measure the return investors expect from the assets managed by firms, we can use the firm's WACC as a surrogate. We show how to estimate a firm's WACC and how to find a project's cost of capital based on the WACC of proxy firms.

As an illustration, we estimate the cost of capital of Sunlight Manufacturing Company's (SMC) desk-lamp project that is introduced in Chapter 6 and analyzed in detail in Chapter 8. Because this project has the *same* risk profile as SMC's overall risk, the project's cost of capital is, in this case, the same as the firm's cost of capital. We also discuss another example that illustrates how to estimate the project's cost of capital when the project has a risk that *differs* from the risk of the firm that would undertake it.

Remember that the terms *cost of capital, investors' required return,* and *investors' expected return* mean the same thing and can thus be used interchangeably. A firm's cost of equity capital is the return expected by investors who hold stock in the firm; a firm's cost of debt capital is the return expected by investors who hold the loans and bonds the firm has issued. After reading this chapter, you should understand the following:

- How to estimate the cost of debt capital
- How to estimate the cost of equity capital
- How to combine the cost of different sources of financing to obtain a project's weighted average cost of capital (WACC)
- The difference between the cost of capital for a firm and the cost of capital for a project

IDENTIFYING PROXY OR PURE-PLAY FIRMS

Identifying the alternative investments that have risks similar to those of the project is the first and most crucial step in the estimation of a **project's cost of capital**. Data from these investments are the inputs for the models that are used to estimate the project's cost of capital. Regardless of the degree of sophistication of the models, the reliability of the estimated cost of capital always depends on the quality of the inputs chosen to perform the estimation. (Remember GIGO: garbage in, garbage out.)

When a project is in the same line of business as the firm that would undertake it—in other words, when the project's risk profile is *similar* to the firm's risk profile—the proxy is the firm itself. This is the case for the designer desk-lamp project from Chapter 8, because the firm that wanted to launch the project, Sunlight Manufacturing Company, specializes in the production of small light fixtures.

When the risk of the project is *different* from the risk of the firm that would undertake it, we need to identify **proxy** or **pure-play firms**. These are firms that have a single line of business, are in the same industry as the project, and compete in the same input and output markets. Pure-plays are usually selected using industry classification codes that identify firms according to their type of business. Unfortunately, these classification systems are far from perfect. The sample of firms must be examined critically, and only those firms that replicate as closely as possible the business of the investment project should be selected. Exact duplication is unlikely, and often a choice must be made between a small sample of closely comparable companies and a larger sample of firms that are loosely comparable to the project.

In a small sample, the proxies will be more representative of the business to which the project belongs. But if some of the proxies' data have large measurement errors, the sample may be too small for these errors to wash out when the data are averaged across the proxies. In a larger sample, the proxies will be less comparable to the project, but the effect of large measurement errors may be greatly reduced in the averaging process.

Having indicated how to identify pure-plays, we show in the next sections how to estimate the return investors expect from holding debt securities (bonds) and common stocks (shares) issued by firms. These returns are, respectively, estimates of the **cost of debt** and the **cost of equity**.

ESTIMATING THE COST OF DEBT

A firm can borrow from a bank by taking out a loan. In this case, the firm's cost of debt is simply the interest rate the bank charges the firm. Alternatively, if the firm is large enough, it can borrow directly from investors by selling them bonds. (Bonds are debt securities described in Chapter 9.) This section shows how to use the market price of a firm's bonds to estimate the firm's cost of debt. We use SMC (the company that is considering the investment in the designer desk-lamp project) as an illustration.

Assume that *five* years ago SMC publicly issued 100,000 bonds with an *original* maturity of *ten* years. This means the bonds will be repaid *five* years from now. (Their *current*, or remaining, maturity is five years.) Each bond has a par value of \$1,000 and an annual coupon payment of \$80. The bonds' coupon rate is thus 8 percent (\$80 divided by \$1,000). The current market price of the bonds is \$1,050. The bond's expected rate of return, also known as its **market yield to maturity**, is an estimate of SMC's cost of debt. How can we calculate that rate?

An investor buying an SMC bond now and planning to keep it until maturity can expect to receive from SMC \$80 every year for the next five years plus \$1,000 at the end of the fifth year. As shown in Chapter 9, in a well-functioning bond market, the \$1,050 bond price must be equal to the present (or discounted) value of the future stream of cash payments the bondholder is expected to receive during the next five years. We can write the following:

$$\$1{,}050 = \frac{\$80}{1 + k_D} + \frac{\$80}{(1 + k_D)^2} + \frac{\$80}{(1 + k_D)^3} + \frac{\$80}{(1 + k_D)^4} + \frac{\$1{,}080}{(1 + k_D)^5} \qquad (10.1)$$

where k_D, the bondholders' expected return, is the firm's estimated cost of debt. To solve this valuation formula for k_D, we used a spreadsheet as follows:

	A	B	C	D	E	F	G
1	Number of years	5					
2							
3	Coupon payment	$80					
4							
5	Market price	$1,050					
6							
7	Principal repayment	$1,000					
8							
9	**Yield to maturity**	6.79%					
10							
11	*Formula in cell B9 is =RATE(B1,B3,–B5,B7)*						
12							

Our calculation indicates that k_D is 6.8 percent (rounded up from 6.79 percent).

To summarize, if we know the price of the bond, its coupon payments, and its par value, the valuation formula can be solved for the rate of return investors require to hold the security. *This rate is an estimate of the cost of debt for the issuer.* Why is the bond's 6.8 percent *market yield* (its expected return) the relevant cost of debt instead of the bond's 8 percent *coupon rate*, or the bond's *current yield* of 7.6 percent (a bond's current yield is found by dividing its coupon payment [$80] by its price [$1,050])? The reason is simple: SMC's cost of debt is the interest rate it will have to pay if it decided *today* to issue *new* bonds to investors. This rate is the market yield of 6.8 percent. Both the coupon rate and the current yield are based on an interest rate that was set five years ago when the bond was originally issued. If SMC issues new bonds today that have a five-year maturity, it will have to offer investors a yield of 6.8 percent, not 8 percent (the coupon rate on the previously issued bond) or 7.6 percent (the current yield of the previously issued bond).

If the firm has no bonds outstanding, its cost of debt for a given maturity can be estimated by adding to the prevailing market yield on *government* bonds with the *same* maturity, an estimate of the firm's credit-risk spread (see Chapter 9 for a discussion on how to estimate a firm's credit-risk spread):

$$\textbf{Cost of debt} = \textbf{Market yield on government bonds} + \textbf{Estimated credit-risk spread} \qquad (10.2)$$

To illustrate, suppose you want to estimate the ten-year cost of debt of Allied Distribution Stores (ADS). If the market yield on ten-year government bonds at the time of the analysis is 4.2 percent and firms with a credit risk similar to ADS can borrow, on average, at 3 percent above the yield on government bonds, then ADS's estimated cost of debt is 7.2 percent (4.2 percent plus 3 percent).

Regardless of the method used to estimate the firm's cost of debt, the cost needs to be adjusted for corporate taxes. Because interest expenses are tax deductible, the **after-tax cost of debt** to the firm is less than its *pre-tax* cost. For example, if SMC has a marginal tax rate of 40 percent, then every dollar of interest expense reduces the firm's tax bill by \$0.40 and the after-tax interest expense is only \$0.60 cents per \$1 of interest expense (\$1 less \$0.40 of tax saved). Given SMC's pre-tax cost of debt (k_D) of 6.8 percent and a marginal corporate tax rate (T_C) of 40 percent, the after-tax cost of debt is 4.1 percent:

$$\begin{aligned}\textbf{After-tax cost of debt} &= k_D \times (1 - T_C) \\ &= 6.8\% \times (1 - 40\%) = 4.1\%\end{aligned} \qquad (10.3)$$

Remember that the above relationship is valid only if (1) the firm is profitable enough to take full advantage of the tax deductibility of interest expenses; or (2) the firm is not profitable enough during the current period, but the tax authority allows it to deduct current interest expenses from past or future profits, a rule known as the **carry-back** or **carry-forward** method. (See Chapter 8.)

ESTIMATING THE COST OF EQUITY USING THE DIVIDEND DISCOUNT MODEL

Equity securities are financial instruments that give their holders a proportional right to ownership of the firm's assets. The standard type of equity security is common stock (described in Chapter 9). Owners of common stock have a *residual* claim on any cash left after the firm has paid all its obligations, including interest and principal on debt. **Cash dividends** are paid by the firm to its shareholders as a return on their investment.

We use $DIV_1, DIV_2, DIV_3, \ldots, DIV_t, \ldots$ to represent the stream of future annual cash dividends expected from an investment in one share of a company and k_E to represent the expected return from that share. We know that the expected return k_E is the cost of equity for the firm that issued the share. According to the **dividend discount model** (DDM, see Chapter 9), the price of a share should be equal to the present (or discounted) value of the stream of cash dividends shareholders are expected to receive:

$$P_0 = \frac{DIV_1}{1 + k_E} + \frac{DIV_2}{(1 + k_E)^2} + \ldots + \frac{DIV_t}{(1 + k_E)^t} + \ldots \qquad (10.4)$$

This formula does not explicitly take into account the future prices of the share. As explained in Chapter 9, this does not mean that future share prices are ignored. They are implicitly taken into account by the valuation formula because, for example, the share price in two years can be expressed as a function of the expected cash dividends that will be received after the second year.

We can use equation 10.4 to estimate the firm's cost of equity if we know the firm's share price and the dividends it is expected to pay. The procedure is similar to the one used to estimate the cost of debt. Unfortunately, although we know the expected coupon payments for bonds (because they are contractual), we do not know the expected dividend payments for shares. We can circumvent this difficulty if we make some simplifying assumptions about the growth of future dividends. The next section examines the particular case in which dividends are expected to grow forever at a constant rate.

ESTIMATING THE COST OF EQUITY WHEN DIVIDENDS GROW AT A CONSTANT RATE

Suppose we assume the dividend DIV_1 that a firm is expected to pay next year will grow at a constant rate g forever. Then, the DDM reduces to the following:

$$P_0 = \frac{DIV_1}{k_E - g}$$

This valuation formula, first presented in Chapter 9, is known as the constant growth DDM. The terms of the formula can be rearranged to express the expected cost of equity k_E as a function of next year's dividend, the current share price, and the expected constant growth rate:[1]

$$k_E = \frac{DIV_1}{P_0} + g \tag{10.5}$$

Equation 10.5 indicates that the firm's estimated cost of equity is the sum of two components. The first is the firm's expected **dividend yield**, that is, the firm's expected dividend payment per share divided by its current share price. The second is the expected growth rate in future dividends.

To illustrate, we consider the case of All Bearing Company (ABC). The company's stock is selling at \$50, the company is expected to pay a dividend per share of \$3 next year, and the dividend per share is anticipated to grow at 3 percent a year forever. According to equation 10.5, ABC and *all firms that have the same risk profile as that of ABC* have the following estimated cost of equity:

$$k_E = \frac{\$3}{\$50} + 3\% = 9\%$$

ESTIMATING THE COST OF EQUITY: HOW RELIABLE IS THE DIVIDEND DISCOUNT MODEL?

In its general form, the DDM shown in equation 10.4 is not very useful because it requires forecasting an infinite number of dividends. The model can be reduced to a more manageable form under some simplifying assumptions about the future growth of the firm's dividends. Unfortunately, these assumptions are unrealistic.[2]

---

[1]Multiply both sides of the price formula by $(k_E - g)$, divide both sides by P_0, and move g from the left to the right side of the equation.

[2]The exception is the dividend from *preferred* stock, which is fixed and does not have a maturity date. In this case, we can apply equation 10.5 with a growth rate equal to zero. For example, if a share of preferred stock sells for \$10 and pays a dividend of \$1 per share, the expected return from the stock is 10 percent (\$1 divided by \$10).

Casual observation of series of dividends paid on common stocks shows that dividends neither stay constant forever nor grow at a constant rate for very long. Furthermore, a number of firms pay no dividends at all, at least for a certain period of time. For these firms, we would have to estimate the date at which the payment of dividends will resume in addition to estimating the dividend's magnitude and its future rate of growth—quite a challenging task.

The simplified version of the DDM (equation 10.5) can be reliably applied only to the small subset of firms that pay regular dividends with a fairly stable pattern of growth, such as utility companies. For the vast majority of companies, the simplistic and unrealistic assumptions underlying the reduced version of the DDM are not acceptable.

The following section presents an alternative valuation model that directly relates the expected return on any security to its risk. When this model, called the **capital asset pricing model,** or **CAPM,** is applied to common stocks, it provides a better estimate of a firm's cost of equity capital because it does not rely on forecasting future patterns of dividend payments.

ESTIMATING THE COST OF EQUITY USING THE CAPITAL ASSET PRICING MODEL

We know that the return required by investors on an investment depends on that investment's risk: *the greater the risk, the higher the expected return.* But what is the nature of risk, and how is it measured? These topics are considered in this section, along with an examination of the relationship between expected return and risk. This relationship, known as the capital asset pricing model, is used to estimate the cost of equity capital.

DIVERSIFICATION REDUCES RISK

Suppose there is an island in the Caribbean where the sun shines half the time and it rains the other half. There are two companies on the island: one company, Sun Cream Inc., sells suntan lotion; the other, Umbrella & Co., sells umbrellas. The shares of the two firms trade on the local stock exchange. An analysis of their historical monthly returns reveals that they have identical *average* returns of 15 percent. As illustrated in Exhibit 10.1, the actual monthly returns for both stocks vary over time, meaning that investing in either stock is risky. Note that the amplitude and frequency of the returns on both stocks are the same. In other words, their **volatility**, and thus their risk, is identical.

Suppose you have $1,000 to invest in the two companies' stocks. What investment strategy should you use? Should you invest in only one of the two stocks because they both have the same average return and risk? If you do so, you will become a victim of "weather risk." If you buy shares of Sun Cream Inc., your investment will perform well when the sun shines but not when it rains. If you buy shares of Umbrella & Co., the opposite will occur: your investment will do well when it rains but not when the sun shines. A smarter strategy, based on the principle of "not putting all your eggs in one basket," would be to buy $500 worth of shares in each of the two firms. Any loss on one share would be offset by a gain on the other, whatever the weather turns out to be. In other words, as shown at the bottom of Exhibit 10.1, regardless of the weather conditions, the strategy locks

EXHIBIT 10.1 RISK AND RETURN FOR THE SUN CREAM AND UMBRELLA INVESTMENTS.

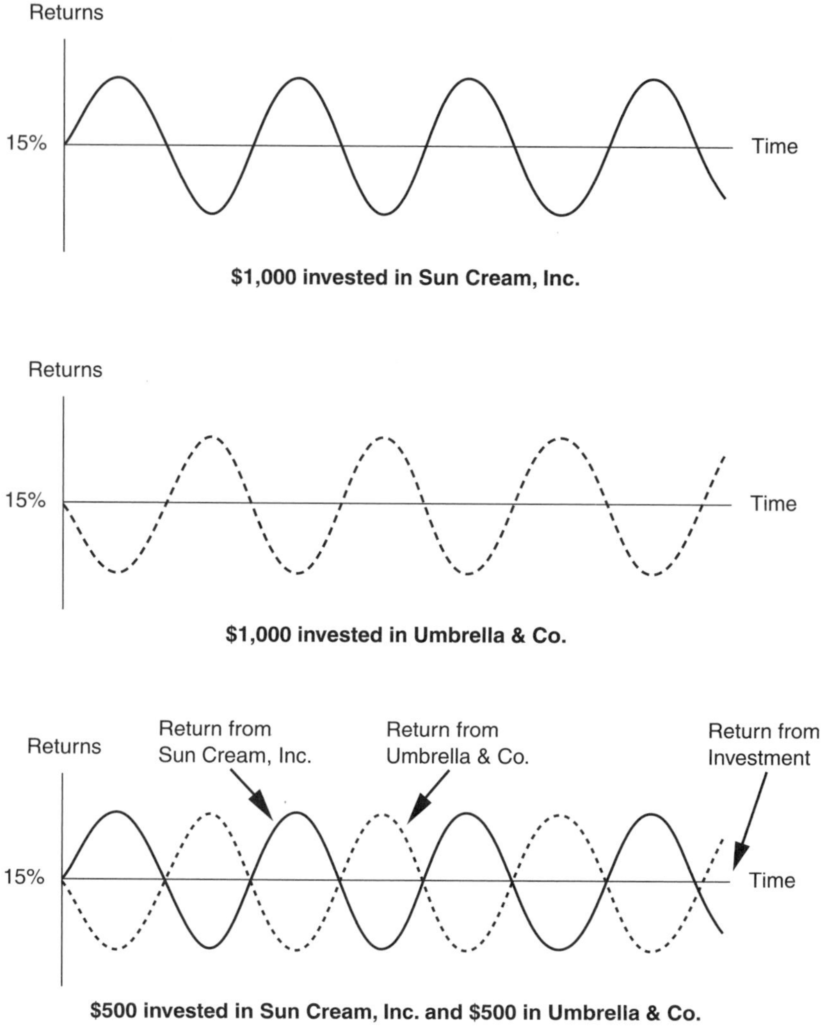

in a *riskless* return of 15 percent, which is the expected return on an investment in either one of the two stocks.

This example is obviously unrealistic because it is impossible to find two investments whose returns move in exactly opposite directions and in the same proportions. Nevertheless, it does illustrate an important phenomenon: *diversification helps reduce risk*. When the shares of different firms are held together in a diversified portfolio, variations in their returns tend to average out and the risk of the portfolio goes down rapidly. Studies that have analyzed the effect of diversification on portfolio risk show that portfolios made up of about twenty randomly chosen stocks have a risk that can be as low as 20 percent of the average risk of their component securities. Moreover, investing in twenty stocks is not significantly more costly than investing the same amount of money in a single stock, so portfolio diversification costs almost nothing. As a result, any rational investor who dislikes risk will choose to hold a diversified portfolio of stocks rather than invest his entire wealth in a single asset.

A major implication of the above analysis is that the risk of holding a single stock can be divided into two types of risks. One risk can be eliminated through portfolio diversification; the other risk remains despite the risk reduction property of diversification. The first is called **diversifiable,** or **unsystematic, risk.** The second is called **undiversifiable,** or **systematic, risk.** We can now express the total risk of a stock as follows:

Total risk = Systematic risk + Unsystematic risk

The source of unsystematic risk is firm-specific events that may have either a positive or a negative effect on share prices. Examples of positive, or favorable, events are the unanticipated win of a liability lawsuit, the discovery of a new product, or the announcement of higher-than-expected earnings. Examples of negative, or unfavorable, events include a labor strike, an accident that temporarily shuts down major production facilities, or an unanticipated liability lawsuit. Those events, taken together, are unlikely to have a significant effect on the returns of a *well-diversified* portfolio, because the positive effect of favorable events for some stocks will *cancel out* the negative effect of the unfavorable ones for the other stocks. The portfolio's unsystematic risk will approach zero.

The source of systematic (or undiversifiable) risk is events that affect the entire economy instead of only a single stock. These include changes in the economy's growth rate, inflation rate, and interest rates as well as changes in the political and social environments. These market-wide events tend to affect all share prices in the *same* fashion. For example, if the market expects the central bank to raise interest rates, an event that is usually interpreted as unfavorable to the stock market, the price of most shares should go down. Because this type of risk affects most shares in a similar fashion, it is called *systematic* risk. And because it cannot be eliminated or reduced through diversified portfolio holdings, it is also called *undiversifiable* risk. Note, however, that some stocks will exhibit more (or less) systematic risk than others because they are more (or less) sensitive to market-wide events.

To summarize, a stock's total risk has two components. One, called *unsystematic risk*, can be eliminated or reduced at very low cost through diversification. The other, called *systematic risk*, cannot be eliminated or reduced through diversified portfolio holdings. This separation of risk between a systematic component and an unsystematic component has an important implication for the determination of the return required by shareholders.

Because unsystematic risk can be eliminated through diversification at practically no significant cost, the financial market will not reward it. Put another way, the financial market will reward only the risk that investors cannot avoid, that is, systematic or undiversifiable risk. We have said many times that the return required from a financial asset depends on the risk of that asset. We can now say: *the only risk that matters in determining the required return on a financial asset is the asset's systematic risk*. The implication is so important that it is worth repeating: *the required rate of return on a financial asset depends only on the asset's systematic risk*. Which leads to the next question: how is systematic risk measured?

MEASURING SYSTEMATIC RISK WITH THE BETA COEFFICIENT

The systematic risk of an individual stock is usually measured *relative* to a benchmark portfolio called the **market portfolio**. Theoretically, the market portfolio contains all the assets in the world—not just stocks but also bonds, domestic and foreign assets, currencies, and even real estate. It is the portfolio that ensures maximum diversification and, thus, provides maximum risk reduction. The variations in the returns of this portfolio reflect only the effect of market-wide events, which are the source of systematic risk. In practice, building such a portfolio is a formidable, if not impossible, task. Instead, when estimating an individual stock's systematic risk, analysts use a domestic stock market index that is sufficiently broad, such as the Standard & Poor's Composite Index (S&P 500) in the United States and the Financial Times All Share Index (FT-A) in the United Kingdom.

Measuring the systematic risk of an individual stock relative to the market portfolio boils down to measuring the sensitivity of the stock's returns to changes in the returns of a broad stock market index. This measure of sensitivity is called the stock's **beta coefficient** or simply its **beta**. We show how to estimate a stock's beta using Sunlight Manufacturing Company (SMC) as an illustration.

The graph in Exhibit 10.2 shows the monthly returns of SMC's stocks plotted against the monthly returns of the S&P 500 during the five-year period from January 2004 to December 2008. The sixty monthly returns to SMC stockholders, r_{SMC}, were computed as follows:

$$r_{SMC} = \frac{\text{End of month stock price} + \text{Dividend (if any)} - \text{Beginning of month stock price}}{\text{Beginning of month price}}$$

The corresponding monthly returns for the stock market index were computed the same way. Each point on the graph represents a pair of monthly returns (one for SMC's stock and the other for the S&P 500). For example, as shown in Exhibit 10.2, during August 2006, the price of SMC's shares increased by 3.6 percent while the S&P 500 rose by 2.4 percent.

On the graph in Exhibit 10.2, we have drawn the line that is closest to *all* the points. This line is called the security's **characteristic line.**[3] Its slope is 1.09, indicating that for each increase (or decrease) of 1 percent in the S&P 500, SMC's stock return increases (or decreases) by 1.09 percent, *on average*. In other words, *the slope of the characteristic line measures the sensitivity of SMC's stock returns to changes in the returns of the market index*. Therefore, it is an estimate of the beta coefficient of SMC's stock.

The return on the market index measures the reaction of the stock market to economy-wide events. For example, in August 2006, these events had a positive

[3]In statistics, the characteristic line would be called a *regression line*. Most spreadsheets contain an application usually called *regression analysis,* which can be used to draw the characteristic line.

EXHIBIT 10.2 SMC MONTHLY RETURNS VERSUS THE S&P 500 MONTHLY RETURNS.

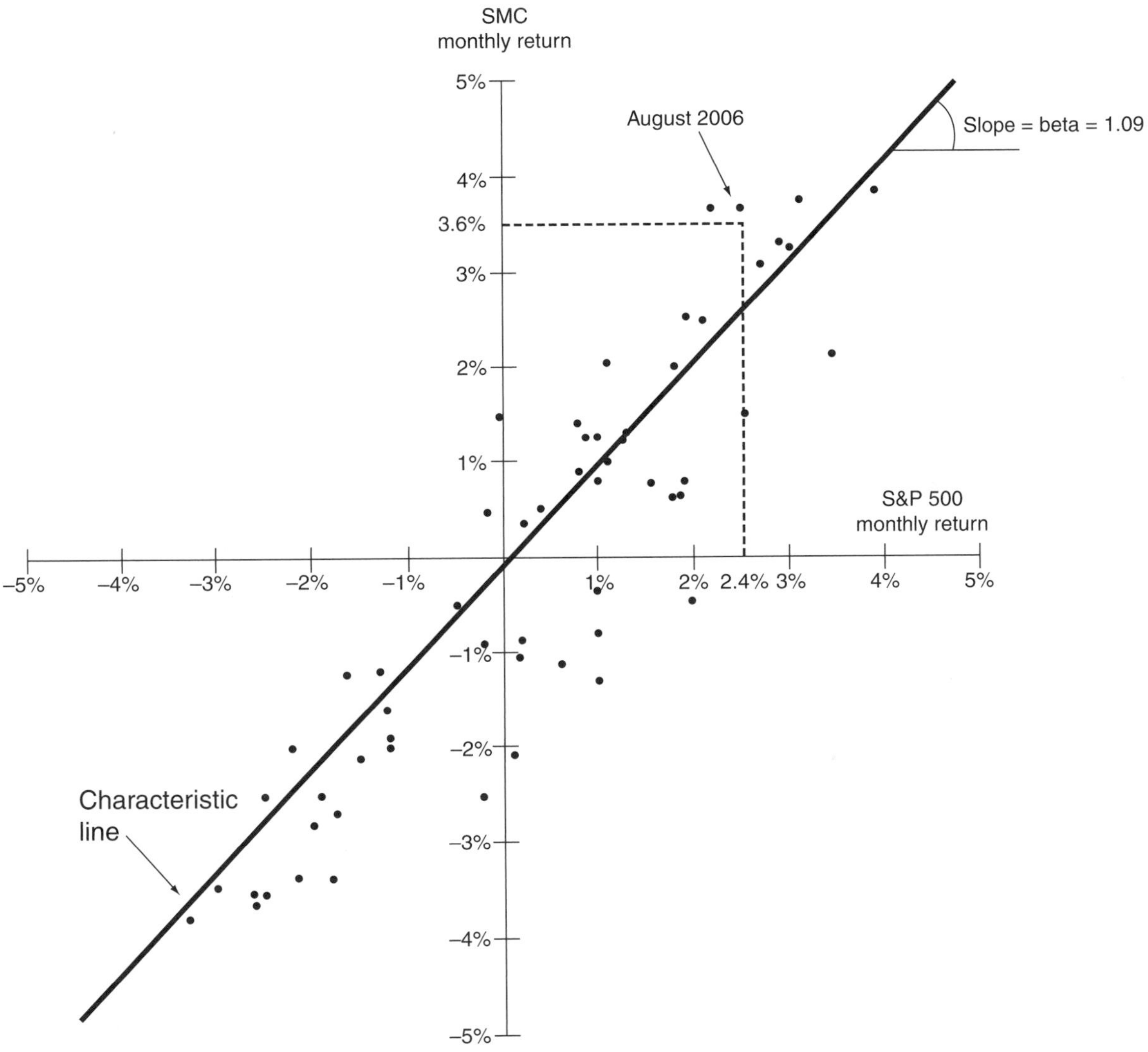

effect on the market because the index rose by 2.4 percent. During the same month, SMC's stock increased by 3.6 percent. The return on SMC's stock can be divided into two parts. One part reflects the impact of the economy-wide events on SMC's stock, and the other part reflects the effect of events that are specific to SMC, such as the success of a marketing campaign or the successful launch of a new product. What is the contribution of each type of event to the 3.6 percent return achieved in August 2006? The positive economy-wide events contributed 2.6 percent (a market return of 2.4 percent multiplied by a beta of 1.09) and favorable SMC-specific events contributed the remaining 1 percent (the 3.6 percent total return less the 2.6 percent contributed by the economy-wide events). The fluctuation

EXHIBIT 10.3 BETA COEFFICIENTS OF A SAMPLE OF INTERNATIONAL STOCKS AND THE STOCK EXCHANGE IN WHICH THEY ARE LISTED.

	Beta	Exchange		Beta	Exchange
Whirlpool Corporation	1.77	NYSE	Hewlett-Packard	0.94	NYSE
General Electric	1.51	NYSE	Toyota Motors	0.88	Tokyo
Goldman Sachs Group	1.47	NYSE	Singapore Airlines	0.80	Singapore
Citigroup	1.43	NYSE	Vodafone Group	0.78	London
Air France–KLM	1.32	Paris	Walgreen	0.75	NYSE
Black & Decker	1.31	NYSE	Carrefour	0.70	Paris
Boeing	1.25	NYSE	Charoen Pokphand Foods	0.68	Bangkok
Nokia	1.22	Helsinki	Total	0.66	Paris
Texas Instruments	1.21	NYSE	Nestlé	0.62	Zurich
Intel	1.20	Nasdaq	Dow Chemicals	0.58	Brussels
BASF	1.19	Frankfurt	Verizon Communications	0.58	NYSE
Bank of China	1.17	Hong Kong	Coca-Cola	0.55	NYSE
Anheuser-Busch	1.06	Brussels	American Electric Power	0.55	NYSE
Southwest Airlines	1.06	NYSE	Exxon Mobil	0.54	NYSE
Cisco Systems	1.04	Nasdaq	Unilever	0.47	Amsterdam

Source: Computed by the authors, using a spreadsheet regression application and monthly stock price data over five years (Mid 2004–Mid 2009) from *Datastream*. Beta are estimated with a maximum of 5 years' worth of monthly returns prior to the publication date using an index of the market in which the stock is listed and adjusted for exceptional price movements. NYSE is the New York Stock Exchange, and Nasdaq (the National Association of Securities Dealers Automated Quotations) is another U.S.-based stock exchange.

of the first part is the systematic risk of SMC's stock, whereas the fluctuation of the second part is its unsystematic risk, which can be eliminated through diversification.

Each stock has its own beta. Think of it as an identification number that measures the stock's systematic risk exposure to economy-wide events. A stock with a beta of one fluctuates, *on average,* the same as the market index against which its movement is measured because, by definition, the beta of the market index is one. Stocks with a beta higher than one are more sensitive to economy-wide events than the market index is. And stocks with a beta lower than one are less sensitive to economy-wide events than the market index. Exhibit 10.3 shows the beta coefficients of the stocks of a number of firms listed on the stock exchange of various countries. Note that companies with relatively low business risk, such as utilities (American Electric Power) and consumer goods companies (Coca-Cola and Unilever), have significantly lower betas than companies with higher business risk, such as financial institutions (Goldman Sachs Group and Citigroup).

Managers do not have to estimate betas. The betas of most listed companies around the world are available from a number of information services firms. These firms estimate betas from market data, updating them regularly and often making them available online through a subscription service.

THE EFFECT OF BORROWING ON A COMPANY'S STOCK BETA

Most firms finance their activities with both debt and equity capital. Both debt holders and shareholders have claims on the cash flows generated by the firm's assets and both are affected by the volatility, or risk, of these cash flows. This risk, which originates from the firm's assets, is called **business risk**. Debt holders, however, have a priority claim over shareholders on the firm's cash flows (they receive interest payments *before* shareholders receive dividends). As a consequence, shareholders bear *more* risk than debt holders. This additional risk, which results from the decision to borrow, is called **financial risk**. (See Chapters 1 and 5 for details.) As the firm increases its debt relative to its equity capital, financial risk will rise. Conclusion: A firm's beta coefficient will be affected by both business risk and financial risk, and the higher these risks, the higher the firm's beta. How can we measure the respective effect of business risk and financial risk on beta?

We use the words **asset beta** or **unlevered beta** (designated by β_{asset}) to refer to the beta of a stock *when the firm is all-equity financed*. In this case, the firm's owners face only business risk. There is no financial risk because there is no debt. Hence, the firm's asset or unlevered beta captures the firm's business risk. We use the words **equity beta, levered beta,** or **market beta** (designated by β_{equity}) to refer to the beta of a stock when the firm has borrowed. In this case, the firm's owners face both business risk and financial risk and the firm's equity, or levered, beta captures both sources of risk. The relationship between a company's unlevered, or asset, beta and its levered, or equity, beta, can be expressed as follows:

$$\beta_{equity} = \beta_{asset}\left[1 + (1 - \text{Tax rate})\frac{\text{Debt}}{\text{Equity}}\right] \tag{10.6}$$

where debt and equity are measured at their *market* value and not at their book, or accounting, value. As the amount of borrowing increases relative to equity financing, the firm's debt-to-equity ratio increases, the firm's financial risk increases, and the firm's equity, or levered, beta increases.

The terms of equation 10.6 can be rearranged to express asset beta as a function of equity beta. We get the following:

$$\beta_{asset} = \frac{\beta_{equity}}{\left[1 + (1 - \text{Tax rate})\frac{\text{Debt}}{\text{Equity}}\right]} \tag{10.7}$$

Consider SMC. We will show that the firm currently has a debt-to-equity ratio of three to seven. It is taxed at the marginal rate of 40 percent. Its levered, or equity, beta was estimated earlier at 1.09. Its unlevered, or asset, beta is thus:

$$\beta_{asset,SMC} = \frac{1.09}{\left[1 + (1 - 0.40)\frac{3}{7}\right]} = 0.87$$

Note that slightly less than 80 percent of SMC's beta (0.87 divided by 1.09) originates from business risk, and the remaining 20 percent comes from financial risk.

THE CAPITAL ASSET PRICING MODEL

Exhibit 10.4 shows the average annual returns for three types of securities—common stocks, long-term government bonds, and short-term government bills—in the United States, the United Kingdom, and the rest of the world over the period from 1900 to 2008.

Not surprisingly, common stocks offered the highest returns, followed by long-term government bonds and short-term government bills. These three categories of assets have different returns because they have different risks, and, as expected, the higher the risk of a type of security, the higher its return.

Common stocks generate the highest average returns because they are the riskiest type of security: they do not promise fixed payments and shareholders receive whatever is left after all debt holders are paid. Government bonds are much less risky because they promise bondholders regular, government-guaranteed coupon payments and the repayment of the amount borrowed when the bonds mature. Finally, government bills offer, on average, a lower return than government bonds because bills, which are very short-term securities, are much less sensitive to changes in the rate of inflation than long-term bonds. All factors considered, bills are the safest investment available. This is why their rate of return is usually taken as a surrogate for the riskless rate, or **risk-free rate**.

Referring to the U.S. data in Exhibit 10.4, the difference of 5.2 percent between the average return on common stocks (9.2 percent) and the average return on Treasury bills (4 percent) represents the average *historical* compensation received by investors who have chosen to invest in the riskiest class of assets (common stocks) rather than in the safest one (government bills). In other words, the average U.S. historical stock **market risk premium** over government bills is 5.2 percent. The same phenomenon occurred in the United Kingdom and the rest of the world. In the United Kingdom, the average historical stock market risk premium

EXHIBIT 10.4 AVERAGE ANNUAL RATE OF RETURN ON COMMON STOCKS, GOVERNMENT BONDS, AND BILLS IN THE UNITED STATES, THE UNITED KINGDOM, AND THE REST OF THE WORLD (IN U.S. DOLLARS).[1]

	United States 1900 to 2008	United Kingdom 1900 to 2008	Rest of the World[2] 1900 to 2008
Average Annual Rate of Return			
Common stocks	9.2%	9.2%	7.9%
Government bonds	5.2%	5.4%	4.2%
Government bills	4.0%	5.0%	4.0%
Average Market Risk Premium: Return on Stocks *minus* Return on Government Securities			
Stocks *minus* bills	5.2%	4.2%	3.9%
Stocks *minus* bonds	4.0%	3.8%	3.7%

[1]Source: Elroy Dimson, Paul Marsh, and Mike Staunton, *Credit Suisse Global Investment Returns Sourcebook* 2009.

[2]The "Rest of the World" includes 16 countries (12 European plus Australia, Japan, South Africa, and Canada) with returns converted into U.S. dollars. Risk premia outside the United States vary from a low of 2.1% in Spain to a high of 5.9% in Australia.

over government bills is 4.2 percent. In the rest of the world it is lower, at 3.9 percent.

In general, the difference between the *expected* return on any security, such as bonds or stock, and the risk-free rate is the risk premium of that security:

Security's risk premium = Security's expected return − Risk-free rate

Rearranging the terms of the above equation, we have the following:

Security's expected return = Risk-free rate + Security's risk premium (10.8)

When the risk premium is computed for the portfolio of *all* existing common stocks, it is called the stock market risk premium, or simply the market risk premium:

Market risk premium = Market portfolio expected return − Risk-free rate (10.9)

The historical market risk premia reported in Exhibit 10.4 have been measured over a sufficiently long period of time (108 years) to allow us to use them with confidence as forecasts of expected market risk premia. Thus, we can assume that 5.2 percent is a good estimate of the expected, or *future,* market risk premium (over government bills) in the United States. For other countries, we can take the average figure of 4 percent (3.9 percent rounded up to 4 percent; see Exhibit 10.4) unless we have actual data from that country (for actual data for sixteen countries, see the reference at the bottom of Exhibit 10.4).[4]

We know that the beta of a security measures its risk relative to the market portfolio. Thus, the risk premium of a *security* must be equal to the market risk premium multiplied by the security's beta coefficient:

Security's risk premium = Market risk premium × Security's beta

We can now write equation 10.8 as follows:

Security's expected return = Risk-free rate + Market risk premium × Security's beta

With symbols, we have the following:

$$\boldsymbol{R_i = R_F + (R_M - R_F) \times \beta_i} \qquad (10.10)$$

where R_i is the expected return on security i, R_F is the risk-free rate, β_i is the security's beta, and R_M less R_F is the market risk premium as expressed in equation 10.9. This formula, which relates a security's expected return to its systematic risk or beta, is the capital asset pricing model (CAPM). Its interpretation is quite straightforward. It says that the expected return on any security is the sum of two factors: (1) the risk-free rate, which measures the compensation for investing money without taking any risk and (2) the expected reward for bearing systematic risk, which is equal to the market risk premium multiplied by the security's beta coefficient.

The CAPM is a linear relationship between expected return and risk. This relationship is shown in the graph drawn in Exhibit 10.5. Expected returns are plotted against betas according to the CAPM, where the risk-free rate is set equal to a

[4]Risk premia differ across countries because market conditions, attitudes toward risk, and the structure and organization of financial markets are not the same in all countries.

EXHIBIT 10.5 THE CAPITAL ASSET PRICING MODEL.

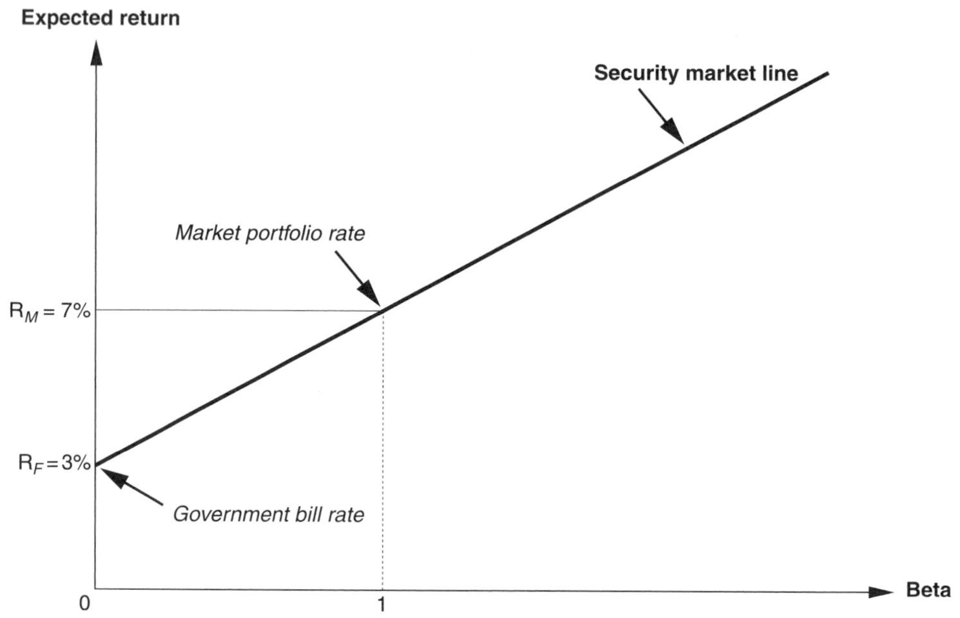

government bill rate assumed to be 3 percent at the time the graph was drawn. The line starts at the point that represents the investment in government bills. That investment bears no risk, so its beta is equal to zero. The line then passes through the point that identifies the market portfolio. By definition, this portfolio has a beta of one. Its expected return is 7 percent, the sum of a risk-free rate of 3 percent and a market risk premium of 4 percent. The line, called the **security market line (SML)**, has a positive slope. This is not surprising, because the higher the beta, the higher the systematic risk and the higher the expected return.

USING THE CAPM TO ESTIMATE SMC'S COST OF EQUITY

We have identified the relevant risk of a stock, we know how to measure this risk, and we know how to relate the risk to the stock's required return. We are now in a position to estimate the cost of equity for any firm. If $k_{E,i}$ denotes the cost of equity of firm i and $\beta_{equity,i}$ denotes the firm's equity beta, then according to the CAPM, we can write the following:

$$k_{E,i} = R_F + (R_M - R_F) \times \beta_{equity,i} \tag{10.11}$$

However, the CAPM expressed in equation 10.10 applies to short periods of time, because the risk-free rate is measured by the return on government bills, which mature in less than one year. Consequently, a firm's cost of equity derived from equation 10.10 is relevant only for a short period of time, say one year. Because firms' activities continue over many years, we would need, theoretically, to estimate a cost of equity for each coming year, depending on the government bill rate that is expected to prevail that year. In practice, given the difficulties of estimating future bill rates, only one cost of equity is estimated. This cost of equity, which is an estimate of the average of its expected future values, is obtained from a version of the CAPM in which the government bill rate is replaced by the rate on government bonds. Thus, the relevant market risk premium in equation 10.11 $(R_M - R_F)$ is equal to the difference between the return on the market portfolio and the return on government *bonds*. For U.S. stocks, this average premium, reported in Exhibit 10.4, is equal to 4 percent, the difference between the 9.2 percent stock market return and the 5.2 percent average return on government bonds. For non-U.S. stocks, we could also use 4 percent by rounding up the figures shown in Exhibit 10.4 (for actual data for sixteen countries, see the reference at the bottom of Exhibit 10.4).

To illustrate, we compute SMC's cost of equity $k_{E,SMC}$. We know that SMC's equity beta is 1.09 and that the market risk premium over the government bond rate is 4 percent. If we assume that the yield on long-term government bonds is 4.7 percent at the time of the analysis, then SMC's estimated cost of equity is as follows:

$$k_{E,SMC} = 4.7\% + (4\% \times 1.09) = 4.7\% + 4.4\% = 9.1\%$$

ESTIMATING THE COST OF CAPITAL OF A FIRM

We have defined a project's cost of capital as the return that investors can get from similar investments with the same risk profile. Unfortunately, the proxy firms that have undertaken similar investments do not publish their returns. We are therefore left with the task of estimating the proxy's cost of capital using only information that is publicly available. In this section, we estimate the cost of capital of a *firm,* leaving the estimation of a *project's* cost of capital to the following section.

WHAT IS THE FIRM'S COST OF CAPITAL?

Suppose that a firm is considering a one-year project that requires an initial investment of $30 million to be financed two-thirds with equity ($20 million) and one-third with debt ($10 million). If the project and the firm have the same risk profiles, the firm's debt holders will require a return on the debt portion of the investment that is equal to the firm's cost of debt. And shareholders will expect a return on the equity portion of the investment that is equal to the firm's cost of equity. If the firm's cost of debt is 6 percent and its cost of equity is 12 percent, the firm is expected, next year, to pay its debt holders $10,600,000 (the initial $10 million plus 6 percent of $10 million) and give its shareholders $22,400,000 (the initial $20 million plus 12 percent of $20 million).

The project will meet debt holders' and shareholders' expectations only if its return on the initial $30 million investment generates a net cash flow of at least $33 million ($10,600,000 plus $22,400,000). This is equivalent to a 10 percent rate of return ($30 million plus 10 percent of $30 million). This rate is the project's cost of capital or the project's **weighted average cost of capital (WACC)**. It is the *minimum* rate of return the project must generate to meet the return expectations of its suppliers of capital. And, because we assumed that the project has the *same* *risk* as the firm, this rate is also the **firm's cost of capital** (or its WACC). Generalizing from our example, if a firm finances its activities with E dollars of equity and D dollars of debt, the project's WACC must be as follows:

$$(E + D) \times (1 + \text{WACC}) = D \times (1 + \text{Cost of debt}) + E \times (1 + \text{Cost of equity})$$

which can be written as follows:

$$\text{WACC} = \text{Cost of debt} \times \frac{D}{E + D} + \text{Cost of equity} \times \frac{E}{E + D}$$

To account for the tax deductibility of interest expenses, the cost of debt must be calculated on an after-tax basis. According to equation 10.3, the after-tax cost of debt is $k_D\ (1 - T_C)$ where k_D is the pre-tax cost of debt and T_C is the marginal corporate tax rate. If, as before, k_E denotes the firm's cost of equity, then the WACC of any firm that finances its investment projects with debt and equity is as follows:

$$\textbf{WACC} = k_D(1 - T_C)\frac{D}{E + D} + k_E\frac{E}{E + D} \qquad (10.12)$$

Equation 10.12, which considers a firm financed with only debt and equity, can be easily extended to a firm that also uses other sources of funds such as, for example, PR dollars of preferred stocks with a cost equal to k_{PR}. In this case, we can write the following:

$$WACC = k_D(1 - T_C)\frac{D}{E + D + PR} + k_E\frac{E}{E + D + PR} + k_{PR}\frac{PR}{E + D + PR} \qquad (10.13)$$

In the following sections, we consider only firms that are financed with a mix of debt and equity. Thus, to estimate a firm's WACC according to equation 10.12, we need four inputs:

1. The debt and equity ratios, $\frac{D}{E + D}$ and $\frac{E}{E + D}$
2. The cost of debt, k_D
3. The marginal corporate tax rate, T_C
4. The cost of equity, k_E

THE FIRM'S TARGET CAPITAL STRUCTURE

The debt-equity mix to use in the estimation of a firm's WACC must reflect the relative proportions of debt and equity that the firm intends to use in financing its investment projects. We call this mix the firm's **target capital structure.** In this chapter, these proportions are given; Chapter 11 discusses how a firm determines its target capital structure. However, there are two caveats when estimating the relevant proportions of debt and equity in the WACC formula (equation 10.12).

First, the firm's current capital structure may *not* be its target capital structure. Issuing securities is costly, so firms typically do not issue debt and equity simultaneously when they raise capital. A firm may, for example, issue debt today, which will move the firm away from its target capital structure. To restore capital structure to its target values, the firm will have to issue equity at a later date. Because of this process, the firm's capital structure changes over time and the structure we observe at one particular point in time may not be the firm's target capital structure. In computing the WACC, the long-run target capital structure must be used.

EXHIBIT 10.6 SMC'S MANAGERIAL BALANCE SHEET.

Invested Capital		
• Cash		$ 5,000,000
• Working capital requirement[1]		75,000,000
• Net fixed assets		170,000,000
Total invested capital		**$250,000,000**
Capital Employed		
• Long-term debt[2]		$100,000,000
100,000 bonds at par value $1,000		
• Owners' equity		$150,000,000
25,000,000 shares at par value[3] $2	50,000,000	
Retained earnings	100,000,000	
Total capital employed		**$250,000,000**

[1]WCR = [Accounts receivable + Inventories + Prepaid expenses] – [Accounts payable + Accrued expenses].
[2]SMC has no short-term debt.
[3]The par value of common stocks is an arbitrary fixed value assigned to shares when they are initially issued.

Second, the proportions of debt and equity financing in the WACC should be estimated with the *market values* of debt and equity, not with their *accounting* or *book values*. Firms issue stocks and bonds at their market values, not at their book values. Thus, the firm's current book values of debt and equity are irrelevant. To illustrate this point, consider again the case of SMC. The firm's managerial balance sheet,[5] shown in Exhibit 10.6, indicates that the firm's book value of debt is $100 million and book value of equity is $150 million. Hence, the *book* values of the financing proportions in equation 10.12 are 40 percent debt ($100 million divided by $250 million, the sum of debt and equity) and 60 percent equity.

To estimate the *market values* of the debt and equity ratios, we need the market values of the firm's debt and equity. SMC's only debt consists of 100,000 bonds (see Exhibit 10.6). Recall that the market value of one bond is $1,050, so the market value of SMC's debt is $105 million ($1,050 times 100,000). SMC's share price is currently $9.80 (given). With 25 million shares outstanding (see Exhibit 10.6), the market value of SMC's equity is thus $245 million ($9.80 times 25 million). Based on these market values, the debt ratio is as follows:

$$\text{Debt ratio at market value} = \frac{\$105{,}000{,}000}{\$105{,}000{,}000 + \$245{,}000{,}000} = 30\%$$

Thus, the equity ratio is 70 percent. The debt ratio is 40 percent when measured at *book* value and 30 percent when measured at *market* value. Likewise, the equity

[5]The managerial balance sheet is a modified version of the standard balance sheet introduced in Chapter 3. On the upper part of the balance sheet, it reports the firm's investment in cash, operations (working capital requirement), and fixed assets. On the lower part, it shows the amount of capital (borrowed funds and owners' equity) employed to finance these investments.

ratio is 60 percent at book value and 70 percent at market value. In practice, such large differences are not uncommon.

Clearly, estimating the debt and equity ratios at market value requires knowing the market values of the firm's debt and equity. When the firm's shares are publicly traded, as in the case above, the market value of equity is simply the share price multiplied by the number of shares outstanding. The estimation of the market value of debt is more complicated because the debt securities of most firms are not publicly traded. One way to circumvent this difficulty is to apply the bond valuation formula (see equation 10.1) to each of the firm's debt issues and then add these values to obtain the total market value of the firm's debt.

In practice, many analysts would simply use the book value of debt as a surrogate for its unavailable market value. When the firm's shares are not publicly traded, the book value of equity is used as a substitute for its market value. These approximations are less than satisfactory because ratios based on market values can be quite different from their book value equivalents. As an alternative, we suggest using the market value ratios of proxy firms that have publicly traded bonds and stocks.

THE FIRM'S COSTS OF DEBT AND EQUITY

The previous sections present a number of models that can be used to estimate a firm's costs of debt and equity. Let's briefly recapitulate.

1. The cost of debt k_D can be estimated using the bond valuation formula (equation 10.1) or the credit-risk spread equation (equation 10.2). Recall that if we know the bond price, its promised coupon payments, and its face value, the valuation formula (equation 10.1) can be solved for k_D. When we applied this technique to SMC, we found k_D equal to 6.8 percent.

   In practice, firms do not have to perform these calculations. They either use the credit-risk spread approximation (equation 10.2) or simply call their bank. Indeed, banks and other financial institutions constantly follow changes in bond prices and market interest rates. Thus, a less time-consuming way to estimate k_D is to ask your banker, who will quote you a rate when needed. This alternative is particularly useful for firms that do not have publicly traded bonds from which they can estimate their most recent cost of debt.
2. The cost of equity k_E can be estimated with the help of the CAPM using equation 10.11. To estimate k_E, we need the prevailing market yield on government bonds, the market risk premium, and the firm's equity beta. The market yield on government bonds is regularly published in the business pages of major daily newspapers. The historical market risk premium over government bonds is 4 percent in the United States (see Exhibit 10.4). Most industrial countries with an active equity market have a historical market risk premium in the range of 3 percent to 6 percent. The betas of publicly traded stocks can easily be obtained from information services firms.

   Using a government bond yield of 4.7 percent and an equity beta of 1.09, we found that SMC has an estimated cost of equity of 9.1 percent. Recall that we need share prices to estimate betas. However, even when there are no available share prices, which is the case of firms whose shares are not publicly traded, the CAPM can still be applied. In this case, the betas of proxy (similar) firms are used. This approach is described later in the chapter.

SUMMARY OF THE FIRM'S WACC CALCULATIONS

Exhibit 10.7 summarizes the four steps required to estimate a firm's WACC. Each of the first three steps corresponds to a particular component of the WACC. For each, the exhibit indicates how to estimate its value and shows the results of the estimation for SMC. The last step is simply the computation of the WACC using equation 10.12. SMC's financing ratios at market value are 30 percent debt and 70 percent equity. Its pre-tax cost of debt is 6.8 percent, its cost of equity is 9.1 percent, and the tax rate is 40 percent. Applying equation 10.12, we find the following:

$$WACC_{SMC} = [6.8\% \times (1 - 0.40) \times 30\%] + [9.1\% \times 70\%] = 7.6\%$$

This is the discount rate that SMC should use when making investment decisions involving projects that have the same risk profile as that of the firm. Any proposal that has a risk profile similar to that of SMC but does not expect to generate a return in excess of 7.6 percent should be rejected. This is the discount rate we used in Chapter 8 to evaluate SMC's investment in the designer desk-lamp project, a project with the same risk profile as SMC.

ESTIMATING THE COST OF CAPITAL OF A PROJECT

A project's cost of capital is primarily determined by the project's *risk*, which can be classified into one of two categories. The first category includes projects that have risk characteristics *similar* to those of the firm that would undertake them. SMC's designer desk-lamp project belongs to this category.

The second category includes projects that have a risk profile *different* from the risk profile of the firm that would undertake them. As an illustration of this type of project, we use a fictitious food-processing company called Fine Foods. Managers at Fine Foods, convinced that their company will benefit from vertical integration into fast-food restaurants, are considering opening a chain of restaurants similar to McDonald's under the name Buddy's. The Buddy's restaurants project belongs to the second category because the firm that would undertake the project, Fine Foods, is in the food-processing business, not the fast-food restaurant business.

The following sections show how to estimate the cost of capital for these two types of projects.

THE PROJECT'S RISK IS SIMILAR TO THE RISK OF THE FIRM

If the project's risk is the same as the risk of the firm, then the firm is the appropriate proxy for the project, and the project's WACC is simply the firm's WACC. The estimation procedure for the firm's WACC is described in the previous section and summarized in Exhibit 10.7. The designer desk-lamp project has the same risk as SMC's risk, so the 7.6 percent WACC of SMC is the appropriate cost of capital for that project. This is the discount rate we used in Chapter 6 to estimate the net present value of the project.

EXHIBIT 10.7 THE ESTIMATION OF A FIRM'S WEIGHTED AVERAGE COST OF CAPITAL (WACC), INCLUDING AN APPLICATION TO SUNLIGHT MANUFACTURING COMPANY (SMC).

Steps to Follow	How To	SMC
Step 1: Estimate the firm's relative proportions of debt (D) and equity (E) financing: $\frac{D}{E+D}$ and $\frac{E}{E+D}$	• Use the firm's market values of debt and equity • The market value of debt is computed from data on outstanding bonds using the bond valuation formula (equation 10.1) • The market value of equity is the share price multiplied by the number of shares outstanding • If the firm's securities are not publicly traded, use the market value ratios of proxy firms	\$105,000,000 \$245,000,000 $\frac{D}{E+D} = 0.3$ $\frac{E}{E+D} = 0.7$
Step 2: Estimate the firm's after-tax cost of debt: $k_D(1 - T_C)$	• If the firm has outstanding bonds that are publicly traded, use equation 10.1 to estimate k_D • Otherwise, use the credit-spread equation 10.2 or ask the bank • Use the marginal corporate tax rate for T_C	$k_D = 6.8\%$ $T_C = 40\%$ $k_D(1 - T_C) = 6.8\% \times (1 - 0.40) = 4.1\%$
Step 3: Estimate the firm's cost of equity: k_E	• Use the capital asset pricing model (equation 10.11) • The risk-free rate is the prevailing rate on government bonds • The market risk premium is 4% (historical average) • Use the beta of the firm's stock. If the firm's shares are not publicly traded, estimate beta from proxies	4.7% 4% 1.09 $k_E = 4.7\% + (4\% \times 1.09) = 9.1\%$
Step 4: Calculate the firm's weighted average cost of capital (WACC)	• WACC = $k_D(1 - T_C)\frac{D}{E+D} + k_E\frac{E}{E+D}$	WACC = (4.1% × 0.30) + (9.1% × 0.70) = 7.6%

THE PROJECT'S RISK IS DIFFERENT FROM THE RISK OF THE FIRM

When a project has a different risk profile from the risk profile of the firm that would undertake it, such as in the case of the Buddy's restaurants project, the firm is no longer the right proxy for the project because investors require the project's cost of capital to reflect the risk of the *project*, not the risk of the *firm*. As indicated at the beginning of the chapter, investors expect a return from the project that is at least equal to the return they would get from the proxy firms.

How should the project's cost of capital be estimated in this case? Should it be set equal to the average value of the proxies' WACC, where the WACC of each proxy is estimated as in the previous section? One potential problem with this approach is that the project may have different target debt and equity ratios than those of the proxy firms. Another problem is that the marginal corporate tax rate of the firm that would undertake the project may differ from the average tax rate of the proxy firms. A solution to these problems is to estimate the cost of capital of the proxy firms *assuming that they have no debt financing*. Then, these estimates are adjusted to reflect the project's target capital structure and specific tax rate. This procedure is illustrated using the Buddy's restaurants project.

THE PROJECT'S TARGET CAPITAL STRUCTURE

Chapter 11 explains that many factors affect a firm's capital structure, among them the type of assets owned by the firm. Because proxy firms operate in the same line of business as the project and are expected to own assets that are similar to those of the project, it is generally assumed that their capital structure is a good approximation of the degree of financial leverage that investors would require for the project. In other words, the project's financing ratios can be set equal to the *average* of the proxies' financing ratios.

To estimate the proxies' financing ratios, the same approach is used as in the case where the firm itself (SMC) is the proxy. The two caveats mentioned earlier are still valid. First, market values should be used instead of book values. Second, the *observed* capital structure of a particular proxy firm may not be that firm's target structure. However, taking the mean of the proxies' financing ratios should reduce the effect of most measurement errors.

Exhibit 10.8 reports the financing ratios for the Buddy's restaurants proxy firms. The three proxies selected from the U.S. restaurant industry are McDonald's Corp. and CKE Restaurants, Inc., both listed on the New York Stock Exchange, and Jack in the Box, Inc., listed on the Nasdaq.

THE PROJECT'S COSTS OF DEBT AND EQUITY

As mentioned earlier, both the cost of debt and cost of equity depend on the firm's debt ratio. The higher the debt ratio, the higher the financial risk and the greater the returns required by shareholders and debt holders. Therefore, if we want to use the proxies' costs of debt and equity to estimate the project's cost of capital, we must first adjust these costs to account for the differences in debt ratios between the proxies and the project. In practice, however, it is assumed that the cost of debt is less sensitive to changes in financial leverage than the cost of equity,[6] so only the latter is adjusted for differences in capital structure.

---

[6]At least for firms that do not exhibit an extreme degree of financial leverage.

EXHIBIT 10.8 PROXIES FOR THE BUDDY'S RESTAURANTS PROJECT.

FISCAL YEAR ENDING 2008[1]

	Equity Beta	Debt / Equity	Tax Rate	Asset Beta[2]
McDonald's Corp.	0.67	0.22	30%	0.58
Jack in the Box, Inc.	0.91	0.82	36%	0.60
CKE Restaurants, Inc.	1.19	1.30	41%	0.65
Average betas of proxies	**0.92**			**0.61**

[1]Source: Data for equity betas, debt ratios, and tax rates are from *Yahoo! Finance*. Debt is measured at book value, and equity at market value.

[2]Asset betas are calculated according to equation 10.7 using the data in the exhibit.

ESTIMATING THE COST OF DEBT FOR THE BUDDY'S RESTAURANTS PROJECT

To estimate the rate of interest at which the three proxy firms could borrow, we need their credit ratings and the corresponding rates.[7] In early 2009, McDonald's Corp. was rated A, and the other two companies were rated BB at Standard & Poor's. At that time, A-rated firms could borrow long term at 6.6 percent. BB-rated firms, however, had difficulty accessing the bond market in early 2009.[8] Because Fine Foods has a credit rating closer to that of McDonald's than the other two companies, we take 6.6 percent as our estimate of the rate of interest Fine Foods would be charged to finance its project. Given that Fine Foods has a marginal tax rate of 35 percent, the project's after-tax cost of debt is:

$$k_D(1 - T_C) = 6.6\% \times (1 - 0.35) = 4.3\%$$

In practice, firms do not need to compute the required rates of interest because these rates are readily available from banks and other financial institutions. However, banks will often quote a rate for a company as a whole, not for a specific project. We can use this rate as long as the project's risk is not very different from the risk of the company. But if this is not the case, the bank should quote the rates for proxy firms, not the rate for the company.

ESTIMATING THE COST OF EQUITY FOR THE BUDDY'S RESTAURANTS PROJECT

Recall that a firm's beta coefficient increases with financial leverage. Thus, if we employ the CAPM to estimate a project's cost of equity, we want to ensure that the beta coefficient we use reflects the effect of the project's target capital structure.

[7]Credit ratings and their providers, the rating agencies, are discussed in Chapter 9.

[8]Information on the three companies, their ratings, and the corresponding rates are publicly available. They are updated daily on the Web sites of the main rating agencies such as Moody's and Standard & Poor's.

If proxies have different capital structures than the project's target capital structure, their betas need to be adjusted to account for the difference. The adjustment is done in two steps. First, each of the proxies' equity beta is "unlevered," meaning that its corresponding unlevered or asset beta is calculated using equation 10.7. Second, the *mean* of the "unlevered" betas is "relevered" at the *project's* target capital structure using equation 10.6 to obtain the *project's* equity beta. This is the beta coefficient that should be used to estimate the project's cost of equity according to the CAPM.

We illustrate this procedure using the Buddy's restaurants project. The unlevered, or asset, betas of the proxies are shown in Exhibit 10.8. They are calculated using equation 10.7 and the information on each proxy firm is reported in Exhibit 10.8. The betas have a mean value of 0.61. Note that the estimates of asset betas are much closer to one another than the estimates of equity betas because the three proxies have similar assets but different debt ratios and tax rates. This is why we want to remove the effects of borrowing and taxation from the proxy equity betas, and relever the average asset beta of 0.61 at the debt-to-equity ratio and tax rate of the Buddy's restaurants project.

What should Fine Foods take as a target debt-to-equity ratio for its Buddy's restaurants project? The debt-to-equity ratios of the proxy companies range from a low of 0.22 (McDonald's) to a high of 1.30 (CKE Restaurants). Because CKE Restaurants is highly leveraged, its debt-to-equity ratio is not a good proxy for the financial risk of fast-food restaurants. We should thus drop CKE Restaurants and take the average debt-to-equity ratio of the other two proxy companies as Fine Foods target debt-to-equity ratio, which is equal to 0.52 (0.22 plus 0.82 divided by 2). This is equivalent to 34 percent debt-to-total financing and 66 percent equity-to-total financing.[9]

We now need to relever the average asset beta of 0.61 to the target debt-to-equity ratio of 0.52. Applying equation 10.6 with a corporate tax rate of 35 percent for Fine Foods, we get the following:

$$\beta_{\text{equity,Buddy's}} = 0.61 \times [1 + (1 - 0.35) \times 0.52] = 0.82$$

The estimated equity beta of 0.82 for the project is significantly different from the average equity beta of 0.92 shown in Exhibit 10.8. This explains why it is important to go through all the steps required to get a proper estimate of the project's equity beta. Just taking the average equity beta of the proxy companies would not produce a good estimate when the debt ratios and tax rates of the proxy firms are far apart.

Applying the CAPM expressed in equation 10.11 with an equity beta of 0.82, a risk-free rate of 4.7 percent (this was the yield on long-term government bonds at the time of the analysis), and a market risk premium of 4 percent, we get the following estimate of the cost of equity for the Buddy's restaurants project:

$$k_{E,\text{Buddy's}} = 4.7\% + (4\% \times 0.82) = 8\%$$

[9] Note that $\dfrac{D}{E+D} = \dfrac{D/E}{1+(D/E)} = \dfrac{0.52}{1+0.52} = 34\%$.

ESTIMATING THE WACC FOR THE BUDDY'S RESTAURANTS PROJECT

Exhibit 10.9 summarizes the steps required to estimate the cost of capital when the project's risk is different from the firm's risk. Each step shows the application to the Buddy's restaurants project. Recall that Buddy's target debt-to-equity ratio is 52 percent, which means that its target financing ratios are 34 percent debt and 66 percent equity. Its pre-tax cost of debt is 6.6 percent, its cost of equity is 8 percent, and the tax rate is 35 percent. Applying the WACC formula in equation 10.12, we get the following:

$$WACC_{Buddy's} = [6.6\% \times (1 - 0.35) \times 0.34] + [8\% \times 0.66] = 6.74\%$$

This is the appropriate rate that managers of Fine Foods should use to decide whether to open a chain of Buddy's fast-food restaurants.

THREE MISTAKES TO AVOID WHEN ESTIMATING A PROJECT'S COST OF CAPITAL

We close this section by discussing three mistakes that are commonly made when estimating a project's cost of capital. These mistakes reveal some dangerous misconceptions about the precise meaning and the correct estimation of a project's cost of capital.

MISTAKE NUMBER 1

The project is going to be financed entirely with debt, so its relevant cost of capital is the interest rate on the debt.

Or:

The project is going to be financed entirely with equity, so its relevant cost of capital is the cost of equity.

Suppose that SMC, being short of funds, decided to borrow $2 million to finance the entire cost of its designer desk-lamp project at an interest rate of 6.8 percent (the same rate as the one used earlier) or 4.08 percent after tax [6.8% × (1 – 0.40)]. If we mechanically apply the WACC formula (equation 10.12), the project's cost of capital would be 4.08 percent because there is no equity financing in this case. If you think something is wrong with this, you are right. Let's see why.

First, the firm could borrow $2 million at 6.8 percent, not on the merit of the project but because it has enough equity and other valuable assets that serve as guarantees for the lender. Although SMC as a whole can borrow $2 million, no bank or any other potential lender would be willing to lend the full cost of the designer desk-lamp project with the project's assets as sole guarantee. Second, and more fundamentally, the WACC formula was incorrectly used. Remember that the cost of capital of the desk-lamp project is the rate of return that the project needs to generate to meet investors' return expectations. Because the project has the same risk as SMC's risk, the relevant cost of capital for the project must be the same as SMC's cost of capital. The latter can be estimated using the WACC formula *applied to SMC*, which, we know, is *not* 100 percent financed by debt.

EXHIBIT 10.9 THE ESTIMATION OF A PROJECT'S WEIGHTED AVERAGE COST OF CAPITAL (WACC), WHEN RISK IS DIFFERENT FROM THE RISK OF THE FIRM, INCLUDING AN APPLICATION TO THE BUDDY'S RESTAURANTS PROJECT.

Steps to Follow	How To	Buddy's Restaurant
Step 1: Estimate the project's relative proportions of debt (D) and equity (E) financing: $\frac{D}{E+D}$ and $\frac{E}{E+D}$	• Use the proxies' market values of debt and equity • The market value of debt is calculated from data on outstanding debt using the bond valuation formula (equation 10.1) • The market value of equity is the share price times the number of shares outstanding • Take the mean of the proxies' ratios	$\frac{D}{E+D} = 0.34$ $\frac{E}{E+D} = 0.66$
Step 2: Estimate the project's after-tax cost of debt: $k_D(1 - T_C)$	• Use the proxies' credit ratings and the corresponding borrowing rates • Take the mean of the proxies' borrowing rates • Use the marginal corporate tax rate for T_C	$k_D = 6.6\%$ $T_C = 35\%$ $k_D(1 - T_C) = 6.6\% \times (1 - 0.35) = 4.3\%$
Step 3: Estimate the project's cost of equity: k_E	• Use the capital asset pricing model (equation 10.11) • The risk-free rate is the prevailing rate on government bonds • The market risk premium is 4% (historical average) • Unlever the proxies' equity beta using equation 10.7 to get their unlevered asset betas • Relever the mean of the proxies' asset betas at the project's target debt-to-equity ratio using equation 10.6 to get the project's equity beta • Apply the CAPM to the project's equity beta to get the project's cost of equity k_E	4.7% 4% 0.61 0.82 $k_E = 4.7\% + (4\% \times 0.82) = 8.0\%$.
Step 4: Calculate the project's weighted average cost of capital (WACC)	• WACC = $k_D(1 - T_C)\frac{D}{E+D} + k_E\frac{E}{E+D}$	WACC = $(4.3\% \times 0.34) + (8.0\% \times 0.66)$ = **6.74%**

MISTAKE NUMBER 2

> *Although the project does not have the same risk as the firm, its relevant cost of capital should be equal to the firm's WACC because the firm's shareholders and debt holders are paid with cash from the firm's cash flows, not from the project's cash flows.*

It is true that dividends and interest expenses are paid out of the firm's cash flows. However, this does not imply that the cost of capital of any project undertaken by the firm must be the same as the firm's cost of capital. The return that investors want to earn on a project is the same as the one they would get from an alternative investment with the same risk characteristics, irrespective of the return they are currently getting from the firm. For example, should the cost of capital of the investments to be made by Buddy's (a chain of fast-food restaurants) be the same as the cost of capital of Fine Foods (a food-processing company)? The answer is no, because investors will certainly not view investments made in the fast-food restaurant sector in the same way they view investments in the food-processing industry. They would rather compare them to investments made by firms that invest exclusively in fast-food restaurants. Remember: it is not the *firm's* cost of capital that determines a *project's* cost of capital; it is the *other way around.* Each project has its own cost of capital, and the firm's cost of capital is simply the weighted average of the capital costs of the various projects that the firm has undertaken.

Unfortunately, many firms still use a company-wide cost of capital, often called the **hurdle rate**, which they apply indiscriminately to all projects. Unless all these projects have the same risk, this procedure is incorrect.

To illustrate this point, we consider MultiTek, a firm that is using the company's WACC to evaluate all its projects. To simplify, suppose that MultiTek has no debt and that its beta is equal to one. Suppose further that the rate on government bonds is 5 percent and that the market risk premium is 4 percent. According to the CAPM, expressed in equation 10.11, MultiTek's cost of equity, which is also its WACC because the firm has no debt, is equal to the following:

$$k_{E,\text{MultiTek}} = \text{WACC}_{\text{MultiTek}} = 5\% + (4\% \times 1) = 9\%$$

Note that 9 percent is also the expected return on the market portfolio because MultiTek has a beta coefficient equal to one. Because MultiTek uses its WACC to evaluate its investment proposals, it will accept any project that has a return higher than 9 percent and reject any project that has a return lower than 9 percent. This decision rule is illustrated in Exhibit 10.10, where the 9 percent line separates the point at which projects are accepted from the point at which they are rejected.

We have also drawn the security market line (SML), which provides a project's expected return given that project's beta coefficient. It starts at 5 percent, the prevailing risk-free rate at that time, and passes through point M, the market expected return of 9 percent. If MultiTek used the projects' betas instead of the firm's beta to evaluate its investment projects, it would reject any project *below* the SML and accept any project *above* the SML because the SML represents the relationship between any investment's expected returns and its corresponding beta coefficient. Exhibit 10.10 shows that using a single rate for all types of projects may lead

MultiTek to incorrectly accept some high-risk projects and incorrectly reject some low-risk projects.

To see why this would happen, suppose MultiTek has two divisions: a low-risk one in the education sector and a high-risk one in the software-publishing sector. Let's assume that proxy firms for the former have an average asset beta of 0.50, while the proxies for the latter have an average asset beta of 1.50. Because MultiTek does not carry any debt, the cost of capital for each of the divisions is its cost of equity. Using the CAPM to estimate each division's cost of capital, we find the following:

$$k_{E,\text{Education}} = 5\% + (4\% \times 0.50) = 7\%$$
$$k_{E,\text{Software}} = 5\% + (4\% \times 1.50) = 11\%$$

If the education division is considering an investment with an IRR of 8 percent (see Exhibit 10.10), the project should be accepted because it would provide MultiTek's shareholders with a return that is higher than the required 7 percent return. If the software-publishing division has a project with an IRR of 10 percent (see Exhibit 10.10), it should be rejected because its IRR is lower than the 11 percent return required by MultiTek's shareholders. However, under the decision rule applied by MultiTek, the first project is rejected because its expected return is less than the company-wide WACC of 9 percent and the second is accepted because its expected return is higher than the WACC. If MultiTek continues to use its WACC of 9 percent as a cutoff rate for all types of investment, it will, at times, accept unprofitable risky investments and reject profitable and less risky ones. As a result,

EXHIBIT 10.10 COMPANY-WIDE COST OF CAPITAL AND PROJECTS' EXPECTED RATES OF RETURN

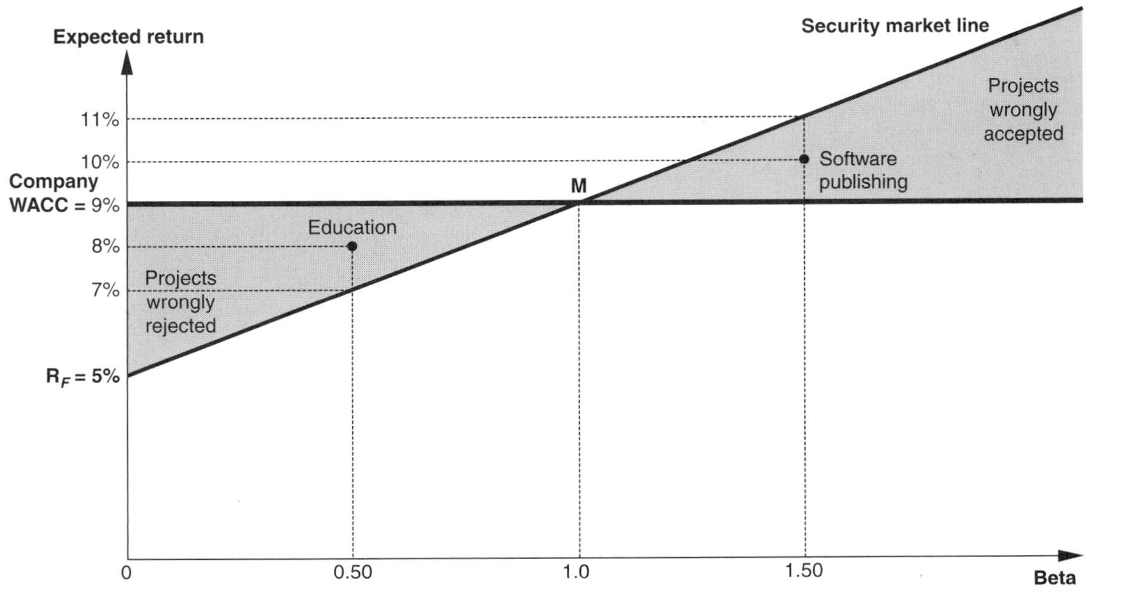

the risk of the firm will rise over time, its risk-adjusted profitability will decline, and its value will go down.

MISTAKE NUMBER 3

> *When a project's risk is different from the risk of the firm, the project's cost of capital should be lowered to account for the risk reduction that diversification brings to the firm.*

It is true that a project whose returns do not vary like those of the firm's existing investments will reduce the firm's overall risk through diversification. For example, you may argue that by diversifying into fast-food restaurants, Fine Foods' total risk will be reduced because earnings in both industries do not move in steps. When the earnings from the food-processing industry go up (or down), earnings from the fast-food industry may also go up (or down), but not necessarily in the same proportions. As a result, the volatility of Fine Foods' earnings will be smoother if it decides to invest in fast-food restaurants. You may, therefore, conclude that using fast-food restaurant chains as proxies for Buddy's without accounting for this risk reduction effect is incorrect.

Although it is true that the total risk of the firm will be reduced if it invests in fast-food restaurants, the effect is irrelevant to its shareholders because they can benefit directly from the same risk reduction by buying shares in McDonald's, Jack in the Box, or CKE Restaurants. Consequently, they would certainly not accept that the return they require from the project be reduced because of the risk diversification that they can achieve in their personal portfolio without the help of Fine Foods' managers.

AVOIDING MISTAKES

Mistakes made when estimating a project's cost of capital can lead to a distorted allocation of capital among projects and eventually to value destruction, as in the case of a firm using a company-wide cost of capital irrespective of the systematic risk (beta) of the project it evaluates. When in doubt, always remember that *a project's cost of capital is determined by financial markets, not by managers.* What you can do, and must do, is use market data, such as market interest rates, betas, and the capital structure of proxies, to determine the return that the market is expecting from the project being evaluated. What you should *not* do is set values for the WACC that are based on internally generated data, such as accounting data. Doing so could incorrectly influence the outcome of your evaluation.

SUMMARY

The *firm's* cost of capital is simply the return that investors expect to earn on the firm's invested capital. When a project has the *same* risk profile as that of the firm that would undertake it, the *project's* cost of capital is the same as the firm's cost of capital. But when a project's risk is different from the firm's risk, the firm's cost of capital is no longer the appropriate cost of capital for the project.

In this case, proxies, or pure-plays, that have the *same* risk as the project's risk must be identified, and the proxies' cost of capital must be used to evaluate the project.

Unfortunately, a firm's cost of capital is not directly observable. It must be inferred from the return investors expect to earn on the capital they invest in the firm. This expected return can be estimated using data on the securities the firm has issued. We showed how to calculate the cost of debt using bond prices and how to estimate the cost of equity using either the dividend discount model (DDM) or the capital asset pricing model (CAPM). The DDM can be applied only to companies that pay regular and stable dividends. The CAPM is more general and is the standard model used to estimate the cost of equity.

To determine the overall cost of capital, we simply find the weighted average of the cost of debt and the cost of equity, where the weights are the proportions of debt and equity the firm has raised to finance its investments. This overall cost of capital is called the weighted average cost of capital (WACC).

The firm's WACC is also the project's cost of capital when the project risk is similar to the risk of the firm. When the project's risk differs from that of the firm, the firm's WACC no longer represents the return that investors require from the project. We showed how to estimate the project's WACC in this case using the cost of equity and the cost of debt of proxy firms that have the same risk as that of the project.

Finally, the chapter discusses three mistakes that are often made when estimating a project's cost of capital. These mistakes can be traced to some misconceptions about a project's cost of capital, and they can be easily avoided by remembering that a project's cost of capital is determined by financial markets, not by managers.

FURTHER READING

1. Brealey, Richard, Stewart Myers, and Franklin Allen. *Principles of Corporate Finance*, 9th ed. McGraw-Hill, 2008. See Chapters 8 to 10.
2. *Yearbook, 2009*. Credit Suisse Global Investment Returns, 2009.
3. Damodaran, Aswath. *Corporate Finance: Theory and Practice*, 2nd ed. John Wiley & Sons, 2001. See Chapter 6.
4. Koller, Tim, Marc Goedhart, and David Wessels. *Valuation: Measuring and Managing the Value of Companies*, 4th ed. John Wiley & Sons, 2005. See Chapter 10.
5. Ross, Stephen, Randolph Westerfield, and Jeffrey Jaffe. *Corporate Finance*, 8th ed. McGraw-Hill Irwin, 2008. See Chapters 9, 10, and 12.

SELF-TEST PROBLEMS

10.1 COST OF DEBT VERSUS COST OF EQUITY.

When we say that a firm, a division, or a project has a cost of equity capital of 10 percent and a cost of debt of 8 percent, what do we mean? Why is the cost of debt lower than the cost of equity?

10.2 CASH FLOWS FROM BONDS AND STOCKS.

What are the cash flows associated with a bond? With a share of common stock? How are these cash flows related to the market value of the bond? The market value of the share of common stock?

10.3 THE CAPITAL ASSET PRICING MODEL.

What does the capital asset pricing model (CAPM) claim?

10.4 THE COST OF CAPITAL OF A FIRM.

Vanhoff Line Corp. has an equity beta of 1.16 and a debt-to-equity ratio of 1. The expected market portfolio return is 10 percent. The interest rate on government bonds is 5 percent. Vanhoff Line can borrow long term at a rate of 6 percent. The corporate tax rate is 40 percent.

a. What is Vanhoff's cost of equity?
b. What is Vanhoff's cost of capital?

10.5 AN ESTIMATE OF THE COST OF CAPITAL.

Your company, PacificCom, manufactures telecommunication equipment and communication software. You have just received a copy of a consultant's report that strongly recommends that investment proposals be accepted only if their internal rate of return is higher than 8 percent. The rate of 8 percent is presented as the weighted average cost of capital (WACC) of PacificCom and was computed as follows:

$$\text{WACC} = [5.78\% \ (1 - 40\%) \times 40\%] + [11\% \times 60\%] = 7.99\% \text{ rounded to } 8\%$$

where k_D = 5.78 percent is the rate at which PacificCom can borrow from its banks; T_C = 40 percent is the firm's marginal corporate tax rate; $[D/(E + D)]$ = 40 percent and $[E/(E + D)]$ = 60 percent are PacificCom financing ratios, and D and E are the amounts of debt and equity taken from the firm's most recent balance sheet; and k_E = 11 percent is PacificCom's cost of equity. The rate was calculated using the capital asset pricing model, with a risk-free rate equal to the government bond rate of 5 percent, a market risk premium of 5 percent, and a firm's beta coefficient of 1.2 $[k_E = 5\% + (1.2 \times 5\%)]$ = 11 percent.

Do you agree with the consultant's estimate of PacificCom's cost of capital?

REVIEW PROBLEMS

1. **Historical returns.**

The following table shows the annual realized returns on the following U.S. securities from 1994 to 2007: the stock market (S&P 500), corporate bonds, government bonds, and Treasury bills. The annual inflation rate for each period is shown in the last column.

Time Period	S&P 500	Corporate Bonds Rate	Government Bonds Rate	Treasury Bills Rate	Inflation Rate
1994	1.31%	-5.76%	-7.77%	3.90%	2.67%
1995	37.43	27.20	31.67	5.60	2.54
1996	23.07	1.40	-0.93	5.21	3.32
1997	33.36	12.95	15.85	5.26	1.70
1998	28.58	10.76	13.06	4.86	1.61
1999	21.04	-7.45	-8.96	4.68	2.68
2000	-9.11	12.87	21.48	5.89	3.39
2001	-11.88	10.65	3.70	3.83	1.55
2002	-22.10	16.33	17.84	1.65	2.38
2003	28.70	5.27	1.45	1.02	1.88
2004	10.87	8.72	8.51	1.20	3.26
2005	4.91	5.87	7.81	2.98	3.42
2006	15.80	3.24	1.19	4.80	2.54
2007	5.49	2.60	9.88	4.66	4.08
Annual arithmetic averages:					
1994–2007	11.96	7.48	8.20	3.97	2.64
1926–2007	12.30	6.20	5.80	3.80	3.10

Source: Ibbotson Associates, *2008 Yearbook*

a. Theory suggests that the riskier the investment, the higher the expected return. To what extent is that illustrated by the data in the table?

b. How do you explain the relatively high volatility in the annual returns on both corporate and government long-term bonds?

c. What was the market risk premium of the S&P 500 for each of the years from 1994 to 2007? What was it over the two periods 1994–2007 and 1926–2007? What conclusions can you draw from your observations?

2. **Risk and return.**
Do you agree or disagree with the following statements? Explain.

a. "The best forecast of future returns on the stock market is the average over the past ten years of historical returns."

b. "Because stocks offer a higher return over the long term than bonds, all rational investors should prefer stocks."

c. "Because a government bond is considered risk-free, that means an investor would never suffer a loss."

3. **The cost of equity and the cost of debt.**
Your chief operating officer argues the following:

a. "Our stock price is currently \$60, and our dividend per share is \$6. It means that it costs us 10 percent to use shareholders' cash (\$6 divided by \$60)."

b. "From our balance sheet our liabilities are $80 million. From our income statement our interest expenses are $5 million. Thus our cost of debt is 6.25 percent ($5 million divided by $80 million)."
Which statement is true or false?

4. **The cost of debt.**
Cordona Corp. has bonds outstanding that will mature twelve years from now. These bonds are currently quoted at 110 percent above par value. The issue makes annual payments of $80 on $1,000 bond face value. What is Cordona's cost of debt?

5. **The cost of equity.**
The dividend of Onogo Inc. is currently $2 per share and is supposed to grow at 5 percent a year forever. Its share price is $50. Its beta is 1.08. The market risk premium is 5 percent and the risk-free rate is 4 percent. What is your best estimate of Onogo's cost of equity?

6. **Practical application of the capital asset pricing model.**
According to the capital asset pricing model:

$$R_i = R_F + (R_M - R_F) \times \beta_i$$

where R_i, the expected return on security i, is the sum of R_F, the return on a risk-free investment, and $(R_M - R_F) \times \beta_i$ is the expected extra return over the risk-free rate for taking on the risk of holding the security. β_i measures the relative sensitivity of the security's returns to changes in the return of a market index. R_M is the expected return on a market index, and $(R_M - R_F)$ is the difference between the expected market return and the risk-free rate, otherwise known as the market risk premium.

In recent years, there has been considerable debate about the size of the market risk premium. Most textbooks, including this one, give a range between 4 percent and 6 percent. However, some of the major investments banks are using market risk premium as low as 3 percent when they are computing the cost of capital for valuing a company in mergers or other transactions.

How could rates as low as 3 percent be justified? What are the possible arguments used by the banks? If you were buying another company, would you agree to such a low rate? What if you were the selling firm?

7. **Calculating the weighted average cost of capital.**
Suppose that Tale Inc. has the following target capital structure: 50 percent stock, 40 percent debt, and 10 percent preferred stock. Its cost of equity is estimated at 10 percent, that of debt 6 percent, and that of preferred stock 4.5 percent. The tax rate is 35 percent.

a. What is Tale's cost of capital?
b. Should Tale use more preferred stock financing than debt financing since it is cheaper?

8. **Estimating the cost of capital of a firm.**
You have been asked to estimate the cost of capital for the CAT corporation. The company has 4 million shares and 125,000 bonds of par value $1,000

outstanding. In addition, it has $20 million in short-term debt from its bank. The target capital structure ratio is 55 percent equity, 40 percent long-term debt, and 5 percent short-term debt. The current capital structure has temporarily moved slightly away from the target ratio.

The company's shares currently trade at $50 with a beta of 1.03. The book value of the shares is $16. The annual coupon rate of the bonds is 9 percent, they trade at 108 percent of par, and they will mature in ten years. Interest on the short-term debt is 3.5 percent. The current yield on ten-year government bonds is 5.2 percent. The market risk premium is 5 percent. The corporate tax rate applicable is expected to be 35 percent.

Based on these data, calculate the cost of capital for the CAT corporation.

9. **Estimation of the cost of capital of a division.**
FarWest Inc. manufactures telecommunication equipment and communication software. The equipment division is asking the finance department of FarWest for an estimate of its cost of capital. FarWest can borrow long term at 7 percent; its corporate tax rate is 40 percent. Its target debt ratio is 30 percent (debt to total financing ratio). Its beta coefficient is 1.05. The rate of interest on government bonds is currently 5.2 percent, and the market risk premium is 5 percent.

The finance department has identified three single business companies with activities that are similar to those of the equipment division of FarWest Inc. Their beta coefficient and debt-to-equity ratios are as follows:

	Proxy A	Proxy B	Proxy C
Equity beta	0.70	1.00	1.02
Debt-to-equity ratio at market value	1.00	0.80	0.70

How would you estimate the equipment division's weighted average cost of capital (WACC) if that division's target debt-to-equity ratio is 1.20?

10. **Estimation of cost of capital for a spinoff.**
A diversified company plans to sell a division as part of a restructuring program. The division to be sold is a regional airline that was acquired by a previous management. The finance department has been asked by the chief executive officer (CEO) to estimate what they consider an acceptable price before entering into discussion with their investment bankers. The chief financial officer (CFO) intends to value the division on the basis of the present value of its future cash flows. He agrees with the CEO on the major assumptions that will affect the cash flows. But they disagree on the appropriate discount rate. The CEO believes that they should use the company's weighted average cost of capital (WACC), which at present is 6.4 percent and calculated as follows:

- Debt-to-equity ratio (D/E) = 0.5; cost of debt (k_D) = 6 percent; risk-free rate (R_F) = 5 percent; corporate tax rate = 30 percent; market risk premium = 5 percent; company beta = 0.5

- Cost of equity k_E:

$$k_E = R_F + (R_M - R_F) \times \beta$$

where R_F = 5 percent is the risk-free rate, $(R_M - R_F)$ = 5 percent is the market risk premium, and β = 0.5 is the company's beta coefficient. Thus,

$$k_E = 5\% + 5\% \times 0.50 = 7.50\%$$

- $$WACC = k_D(1 - T_C)\frac{D}{E + D} + k_E\frac{E}{E + D}$$
$$= 6\% \times (1 - 0.3) \times \frac{1}{3} + 7.50\% \times \frac{2}{3}$$
$$= 6.4\%$$

The CFO disagrees, arguing that the airline is a completely different type of business and that it carries much more debt than the other divisions because of very large equipment purchases. Therefore, the corporate WACC is completely inappropriate for valuing the cash flows of the airline division. They should base the valuation on a cost of capital typical for the airline industry. To do this, the CFO obtains the following data for a sample of pure-play airline companies.

	Airline A	Airline B	Airline C	Airline D	Airline E
Equity beta	1.20	0.95	1.35	1.45	1.55
Debt-to-equity ratio at market value	1.25	1.85	1.35	1.70	3.40
Average cost of debt	6%	7%	7.50%	7.25%	8.50%

a. The cost of borrowing and the debt-to-equity ratio for the division were to be set at the average for the group of airlines shown in the table. Based on the comparative data shown in the table, a risk-free rate of 5 percent, a market risk premium of 5 percent, and a tax rate of 30 percent, estimate the division's WACC.

b. If the company's WACC had been used instead of the divisional WACC you have just computed, what effect would that have on the valuation?

Designing a Capital Structure

CHAPTER 11

Broadly speaking, managers need to make two major decisions. They need to decide which investment projects create the most value, and they need to decide which mix of sources of capital is best for financing the firm's investments. Previous chapters show how managers should select value-creating projects. This chapter shows how they should design a value-creating capital structure, keeping in mind that the opportunities to create value through a change in the mix of debt and equity capital are more limited than those available through the selection of superior investment projects.

The decision to finance part of the firm's assets with borrowed funds has important managerial implications. If the firm finds it increasingly difficult to service its debt (paying interest and repaying the borrowed funds) because of excessive borrowing, its management will be under pressure to make decisions that may not be in the best interest of shareholders. For example, management may have to quickly sell *value-creating* assets, for less than they are worth to the firm, to raise the cash needed to make the payments required to service the firm's debt. Conversely, a firm with too little debt may pass up the opportunity to reduce its tax payments and increase its value through tax savings (the more interest the firm pays, the less taxes it owes because interest payments reduce taxable income). By replacing equity with debt, the firm can deduct more interest expenses from its taxable income and save an equivalent amount of cash that would have been used to pay taxes. If too much debt is damaging and too little debt is fiscally inefficient, what, then, is the right amount of debt? This is the question we answer in this chapter.

Managers can choose from a variety of sources of funds to finance their businesses. Most of these are hybrids of two basic types of capital: debt, such as bank loans and bonds; and equity, which includes retained earnings and common stocks. This chapter examines how managers should combine debt and equity financing to establish a capital structure that *maximizes the value of the firm's assets and equity*. A firm's capital structure is usually identified by its *debt ratios*, either its debt-to-equity ratio (the amount of borrowing divided by the amount of equity) or its debt-to-assets ratio (the portion of the firm's assets financed with borrowed funds). These two debt ratios are often used interchangeably.

The firm's *optimal capital structure* is the debt ratio that maximizes the market value of the firm's assets. We show that this is generally the same as maximizing the market value of the firm's *equity* and *minimizing* its cost of capital. The optimal debt ratio depends on several factors; some are easily identifiable and measurable, others are not. To find out what these factors are and how they affect the firm's profitability and value, we analyze how a change in the firm's debt ratio affects (1) its profitability, measured with earnings per share (EPS), that is, earnings after tax divided by the number of shares outstanding; (2) the market value of its assets; (3) its share price; and (4) its cost of capital.

After reading this chapter, you should understand the following:

- How changes in capital structure affect the firm's EPS, asset value, equity value, share price, and cost of capital
- The trade-offs that are implied in the capital structure decision
- How corporate taxes and the *costs of financial distress* affect the capital structure decision
- Why firms in different industries and countries can have different capital structures
- The factors, in addition to taxes and the costs of financial distress, which must be taken into account when establishing an optimal capital structure, including agency *costs* and the presence of *information asymmetry* between managers and outside investors

THE CAPITAL STRUCTURE DECISION IN A WORLD WITHOUT TAXES AND FINANCIAL DISTRESS COSTS

This section examines how changes in capital structure affect the firm's profitability, the market value of its assets and equity, its share price, and its cost of capital in a world in which firms do *not* pay corporate income taxes and do *not* face **financial distress costs**—that is, costs that result from excessive borrowing that affect the firm's ability to perform efficiently and reduce its value. These two restrictions are lifted in the following sections. Beginning our analysis without the complications of taxes and financial distress costs will make it easier to understand the more general model presented later.

EFFECTS OF BORROWING ON THE FIRM'S PROFITABILITY (NO TAXES AND NO FINANCIAL DISTRESS COSTS)

In physics, leverage refers to the increase in power that comes from using a lever. In finance, **leverage**, or **gearing**, refers to the increase in profitability, usually measured with EPS, that can come from using debt financing.[1] To see why and how

[1]The effect of borrowing on another measure of profitability, the firm's return on equity, is examined in detail in Chapter 5.

borrowing affects EPS, we examine the Jolly Bear Company (JBC). JBC is currently *all-equity* financed with 2 million shares outstanding worth $100 each. The firm's equity value is thus $200 million ($100 times 2 million shares). Because the firm has no debt, the value of its assets is the same as the value of its equity ($200 million). JBC's chief financial officer, Ms. Johnson, is considering borrowing $100 million at 10 percent and using the cash to repurchase one-half of the firm's shares at $100 per share (we explain later why the share price is not affected by the repurchase). She wants to know how this change in JBC's capital structure might affect the firm's EPS.

Exhibit 11.1 illustrates the effect of this **recapitalization** decision on EPS for three possible scenarios for the future performance of the economy—recession, expected performance, and expansion. The firm's profit from operations, that is, its earnings before interest and tax (EBIT), is not affected by the decision to borrow. Operating profit is $10 million under the recession scenario, $30 million under the expected performance scenario, and $40 million under the expansion scenario, irrespective of the amount of debt Ms. Johnson decides to issue.

Consider first the case of the expected scenario. With no debt (upper part of Exhibit 11.1), net earnings are $30 million, the same as EBIT, because there are no interest or tax payments. With 2 million shares outstanding, EPS is equal to $15 ($30 million divided by 2 million shares). With $100 million of debt at an

EXHIBIT 11.1 JBC'S EARNINGS PER SHARE UNDER THE CURRENT AND PROPOSED CAPITAL STRUCTURES AND IN THE ABSENCE OF TAXES.

Current capital structure: no debt and 2 million shares at $100 per share

	Recession	Expected	Expansion
Earnings before interest and tax (EBIT)	$10,000,000	$30,000,000	$40,000,000
Less interest expenses	0	0	0
Less tax	0	0	0
Equals net earnings	$10,000,000	$30,000,000	$40,000,000
Divided by the number of shares	2,000,000	2,000,000	2,000,000
Equals earnings per share (EPS)	$ 5	$ 15	$ 20

Proposed capital structure: borrow $100 million at 10 percent and use the cash to repurchase 1 million shares at $100 per share

	Recession	Expected	Expansion
Earnings before interest and tax (EBIT)	$10,000,000	$30,000,000	$40,000,000
Less interest expenses	(10,000,000)	(10,000,000)	(10,000,000)
Less tax	0	0	0
Equals net earnings	$ 0	$20,000,000	$30,000,000
Divided by the number of shares	1,000,000	1,000,000	1,000,000
Equals earnings per share (EPS)	$ 0	$ 20	$ 30

interest rate of 10 percent (lower part of Exhibit 11.1), the interest payment is $10 million and net earnings drop to $20 million. Before concluding that borrowing has a negative effect, we should examine its impact on EPS. Because there are only 1 million shares after the share repurchase, EPS is now $20 ($20 million divided by 1 million shares). Thus, debt financing boosts expected EPS from $15 to $20. **Financial leverage** seems to have the same effect as leverage has in the world of physics.

Leverage also works to the advantage of shareholders in the expansion scenario, with EPS rising by 50 percent, from $20 to $30 (see Exhibit 11.1). Under the recession scenario, however, EPS, which is positive in the no-debt case, is zero in the borrowing case.

We can see this phenomenon graphically by plotting EPS against EBIT for the current and proposed capital structure, as shown in Exhibit 11.2. The no-debt line starts at the origin because EPS is zero when EBIT is zero. As EBIT increases, EPS increases $0.50 for each $1 million rise in EBIT. With $100 million of debt, the line starts with a negative $10 EPS; at this point, EBIT is zero, but JBC still has to pay $10 million of interest expenses. The result is a loss of $10 million. Divided by 1 million shares, this loss produces a $10 loss per share. When EBIT rises, EPS increases twice as fast as when there is no debt, that is, EPS increases $1 for each $1 million rise in EBIT. The reason should be clear: the number of shares outstanding is reduced by half when the firm borrows $100 million to repurchase equity.

Now, consider the point at which the two lines intersect. For values of EBIT less than its value at the intersection point, EPS is higher if JBC selects an all-equity capital structure. At the point at which the lines intersect, EPS is the same for both

EXHIBIT 11.2 JBC'S EARNINGS PER SHARE UNDER DIFFERENT CAPITAL STRUCTURES.

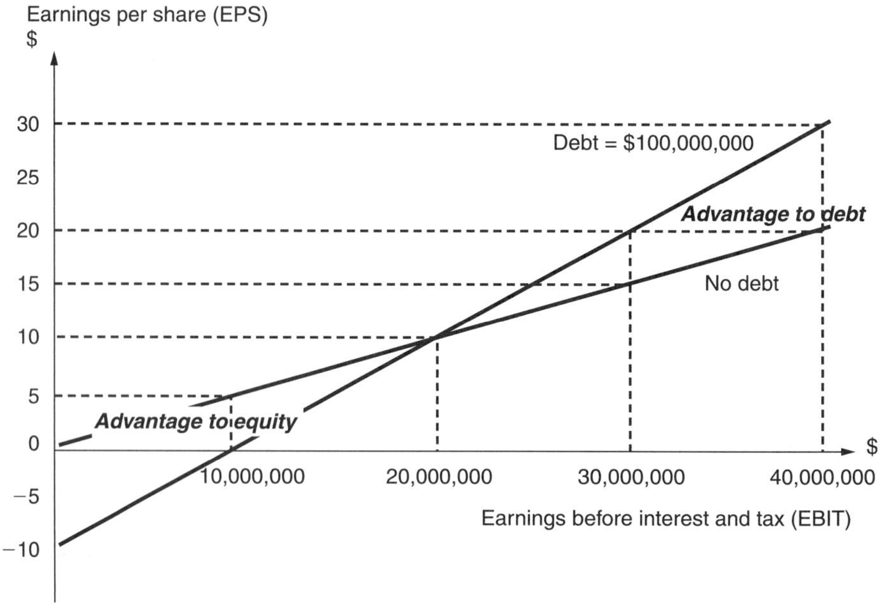

financing alternatives. For values of EBIT greater than its value at the intersection point, EPS is higher with debt financing. We determine the values of EBIT and EPS at the intersection point by using the fact that, at this point, EPS with no debt is equal to EPS with $100 million of debt. For the no-debt line, EPS equals EBIT divided by 2 million shares outstanding, as shown on the left side of the equation below. With $100 million of debt financing, EPS equals EBIT less $10 million of interest expenses divided by 1 million shares, as shown on the right side of the equation. At the intersection point, the two are the same:

$$\text{EPS} = \frac{\text{EBIT}}{2{,}000{,}000} = \frac{\text{EBIT} - \$10{,}000{,}000}{1{,}000{,}000}$$

from which we get

$$\text{EBIT} = \$20{,}000{,}000$$

and

$$\text{EPS} = \frac{\$20{,}000{,}000}{2{,}000{,}000} = \$10$$

Thus, when EBIT equals $20 million, EPS is $10 for both capital structures. Note that when EBIT is $20 million, JBC's return on assets is 10 percent ($20 million of EBIT divided by $200 million of assets), which is the same as the rate of interest on the debt. As long as JBC earns a return on its assets that is higher than its cost of debt, its shareholders are better off with debt financing.[2] From this analysis, Ms. Johnson can draw the following tentative conclusions:

1. The capital structure decision affects the firm's profitability measured by EPS
2. Financial leverage increases EPS as long as EBIT is higher than $20 million, which is the same as saying that return on assets exceeds the 10 percent cost of debt
3. At the $30 million expected level of EBIT, EPS are $15 with no debt financing and $20 with $100 million of debt financing

Clearly, under the *expected* scenario, borrowing would benefit JBC's shareholders. However, Ms. Johnson knows that she cannot make a decision on the basis of a single scenario. There is some probability that the economy will fall into a recession, in which case borrowing will hurt rather than benefit shareholders. Before Ms. Johnson makes her decision, she must consider the *risk* that EBIT and return on assets are lower than their threshold values of $20 million and 10 percent, respectively.

THE TRADE-OFF BETWEEN PROFITABILITY AND RISK

The relationship between borrowing and risk is illustrated in the graph shown in Exhibit 11.3. The lines represent the changes in JBC's EPS as a function of time

[2] The same result was obtained in Chapter 5. Remember, however, the two limitations we mention in that chapter. The discussion ignores risk and does not examine whether the higher leverage is accompanied by an increase in the value of the firm. These issues are discussed later in this chapter.

EXHIBIT 11.3 BORROWING AND RISK.

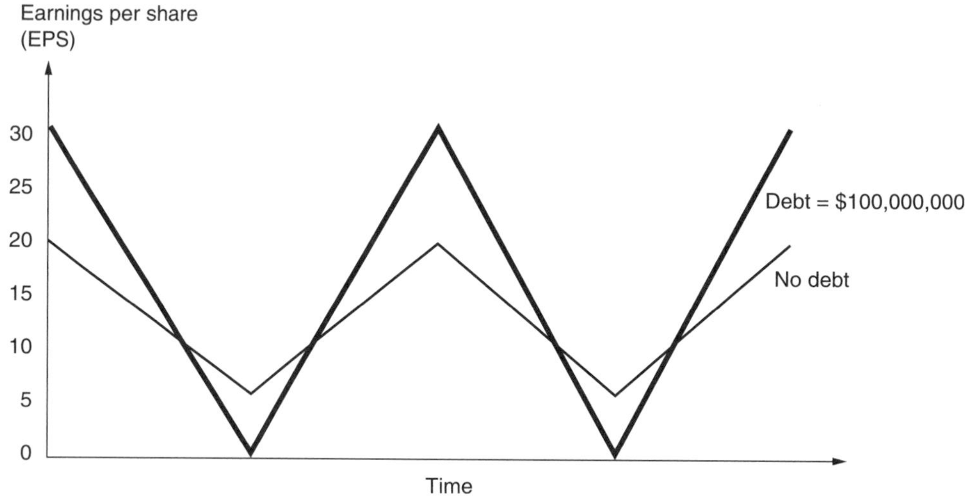

for the two capital structures of the last section: no debt financing and $100 million of debt financing. EPS is calculated for values of EBIT that vary over time between the recession and the expansion scenarios, that is, between $10 million and $40 million. In the absence of debt, EPS varies between $5 and $20, as shown in Exhibit 11.1. The variations in EPS result from changes in general economic conditions and from factors affecting the industry to which JBC belongs. (Examples of such factors include changes in input and output prices, technology, and competition.) The risk generated by these changes, which originates from the business environment in which the firm operates, is rightly called **business risk**. This type of risk is independent of JBC's capital structure. In other words, business risk is the same for any amount of funds that Ms. Johnson decides to borrow.

In the presence of debt, EPS varies between $0 and $30. The graph in Exhibit 11.3 clearly shows that debt financing *amplifies* the variability of EPS. The extra risk related to this magnifying effect is called **financial risk**. If Ms. Johnson decides to finance a portion of JBC's assets with debt, the risk borne by JBC's shareholders will rise. Ms. Johnson is thus faced with a trade-off between the following:

1. She can issue debt to increase JBC's *expected* EPS, but the firm's shareholders will have to take on more risk
2. She can maintain all-equity financing to reduce risk, but JBC's shareholders will end up with lower *expected* EPS

Unfortunately, the analysis performed so far does not tell us what to do. To find out, we must determine how debt financing affects the firm's *value*, not just EPS. The alternative that produces the highest value for the firm would be preferred. How, then, does debt financing affect the firm's value in the absence of taxes and financial distress costs? The so-called pizza theory of capital structure provides the answer.

Effect of Borrowing on the Value of the Firm's Assets and Its Share Price (No Taxes and No Financial Distress Costs)

In its culinary version, the so-called pizza theory says that no one can increase the size of a pizza by slicing it. In its corporate finance version, we could think of the market value of the firm's assets as a gigantic pizza and the firm's shareholders and debt holders as the claimants to the slices, where the slices represent the cash flows generated by the assets. The pizza theory says that the market value of the firm's assets (the pizza) cannot be increased by changing the proportions of the cash flows (the slices) going to the firm's shareholders and debt holders, *provided these cash flows are not taxed.* In other words, the market value of the firm's assets is determined only by the cash flows the assets generate and is not affected by the relative proportions of debt and equity capital used to finance the assets.

To illustrate this phenomenon, suppose that Ms. Johnson decides to borrow the $100 million and buy back half of the firm's 2 million shares. Consider the implications of this recapitalization on the wealth of JBC's shareholders. Before the change in capital structure, their claim against JBC's assets amounted to the market value of the entire firm ($200 million) because the firm had no debt. After JBC is levered up, shareholders' claims against the $200 million of assets are reduced by $100 million, which represents the value of the debt now owed by JBC. But this reduction in value is exactly offset by the $100 million shareholders received from the 1 million shares they sold back to the firm. Shareholders will be as well off after the change in capital structure as they were before. (Their collective and aggregate wealth remains at $200 million.) Thus, the change should not have any effect on JBC's share price.

The formal proof of the theory that changes in the firm's capital structure do not affect its total market value or share price was provided by Nobel Prize laureates Franco Modigliani and Merton Miller (MM) in two seminal papers published in 1958 and 1961. The intuition behind the theory is straightforward: the value of a firm's assets is determined only by the ability of its managers to generate as much cash flow as possible from these assets. Simply reshuffling paper claims on these cash flows does not add value to or subtract value from the firm's assets. Furthermore, it does not affect the firm's share price. In other words, the price of a pizza is independent of the way you slice it.

Let's follow MM's reasoning as it applies to JBC's capital structure. If JBC borrows $100 million, EPS are $0 under the recession scenario, $20 under the expected scenario, and $30 under the expansion scenario. The computations are reproduced on the upper part of Exhibit 11.4, which also shows the corresponding returns on shareholders' equity investment obtained by dividing the EPS by $100, the price of one share. The return is 0 percent under the recession scenario, 20 percent under the expected scenario, and 30 percent under the expansion scenario.

Suppose now that Ms. Johnson decides *not* to change JBC's capital structure. (She does not borrow the $100 million and JBC remains with its initial debt-free capital structure.) You, a shareholder with one share, would have preferred that the firm borrows the $100 million because you like the higher EPS that would result if the economy expands. What can you do? You can try to persuade Ms. Johnson to change her mind, but you would probably be wasting your time unless you own a substantial number of shares. Well, you do not need to bother Ms. Johnson. *You can get the capital structure you want even if JBC remains debt-free.* How is

EXHIBIT 11.4 CORPORATE LEVERAGE VERSUS HOMEMADE LEVERAGE.

Shareholder's return on a $100 investment when JBC borrows $100 million.

	Recession	Expected	Expansion
JBC's net earnings with debt (from Exhibit 11.1)	$ 0	$20,000,000	$30,000,000
Divided by the number of shares	1,000,000	1,000,000	1,000,000
Equals earnings per share (EPS)	$ 0	$ 20	$ 30
Return on investment (EPS divided by $100)	0%	20%	30%

Shareholder's return on a $100 net investment when JBC maintains the all-equity capital structure. The investor buys two shares of JBC, one with his own money and the other with borrowed money.

	Recession	Expected	Expansion
JBC's net earnings with no debt (from Exhibit 11.1)	$10,000,000	$30,000,000	$40,000,000
Divided by the number of shares	2,000,000	2,000,000	2,000,000
Equals earnings per share (EPS)	$ 5	$ 15	$ 20
Earnings on two shares	10	30	40
Less interest payment of 10% on $100	(10)	(10)	(10)
Equals net earnings	$ 0	$ 20	$ 30
Return on investment (net earnings divided by $100)	0%	20%	30%

this possible? The trick is to manufacture your own *personal* leverage that will replicate the returns JBC would have delivered if Ms. Johnson had decided to borrow the $100 million.

All you have to do is borrow $100 *at 10 percent* and use the cash to buy another share of JBC. You now own two shares, the one you already had plus the one you just bought. These transactions have created a **homemade leverage**, that is, a personal financial leverage as opposed to a corporate financial leverage. The lower part of Exhibit 11.4 shows how to calculate the returns on your investment under the three scenarios using JBC's EPS with all-equity financing (see Exhibit 11.1). Because you own two shares of JBC, you get twice the EPS in each of the three scenarios. However, your earnings are reduced in each scenario by the $10 interest payment you have to make on the $100 you borrowed (10 percent of $100). The last row of Exhibit 11.4 shows the net returns on your $100 investment. (Although you *own* two shares, your *personal* investment, net of borrowing, is only $100.) *These returns are exactly the same as those you would have achieved if the firm had decided to recapitalize.* In other words, it does not matter whether the firm borrows to leverage its assets or whether investors borrow to leverage their own share holdings. What firms can do to their capital structures, investors can replicate on their own. Therefore, investors would neither reward nor penalize the firm if it changes its capital structure. Under those conditions, the firm's share price must remain the same.

You may have noticed the two critical assumptions required to reach this conclusion. The first assumption is that the changes in capital structure must occur in a world without taxes. The second assumption is that investors can borrow at the same rate as the firm (10 percent in the JBC example). Later in this chapter, we examine what happens without the first assumption, that is, when the changes in capital structure occur in a world *with* taxes. You may think the second assumption is unrealistic because interest rates on personal borrowing are usually higher than the rates at which firms borrow. But investors do not have to borrow directly to build up their homemade leverage. To understand why, recall that investors diversify their investments. They do not buy only the shares of a single firm; they buy shares of other firms as well (see Chapter 10). Consequently, it is the financial leverage of all the firms in the investor's portfolio that is relevant, not just that of a particular firm in the portfolio. Given the large number of publicly traded companies offering a wide range of debt ratios, investors can easily reach any degree of financial leverage *in their portfolios* by constructing them in such a way that its average debt ratio is the one they want. And they do not need to borrow to achieve this; the firms in their portfolios have already done the borrowing.

The **MM theory of capital structure** does not mention risk. But, in the previous section, we show that any increase in the firm's debt ratio increases the risk borne by its shareholders. How can JBC's share price *not* go down as a result of the increase in risk generated by the firm's decision to borrow $100 million? The answer is straightforward: the increase in risk is exactly offset by the rise in the EPS the shareholders can expect from higher financial leverage. In a world without taxes, the trade-off between risk and higher expected EPS that confronts Ms. Johnson does not actually exist. Whichever debt ratio she chooses, JBC's share price will not change because shareholders are exactly compensated for the higher risk with higher expected EPS. However, the *return* expected by shareholders from their equity investment in JBC—which is JBC's cost of equity—will rise to reflect the higher risk. We show this in the next section.

EFFECT OF BORROWING ON THE FIRM'S COST OF CAPITAL (NO TAXES AND NO FINANCIAL DISTRESS COSTS)

If JBC's capital structure remains debt-free, the return expected by its shareholders from their investment in the firm (which is the firm's cost of equity capital) is equal to the return expected from its assets, because in this case shareholders are the only claimants to the cash flows generated by the firm's assets. If r_A denotes the expected return from the firm's assets and k_E^U denotes the firm's cost of equity when the firm does not borrow (called the unlevered cost of equity), then, in the absence of debt and taxes, the two rates are the same ($r_A = k_E^U$).

If the firm decides to replace some equity with debt, the debt holders will also have claims on the firm's cash flows. In other words, r_A will be split into the return expected by shareholders when the firm borrows (called the levered cost of equity, k_E^L) and the rate required by its debt holders (denoted by k_D). Their claims on the firm's return on assets will be proportional to their respective contributions to the funding of the firm's assets. If E is the amount of equity funding and D the amount of debt funding, then their relative contributions to the total funding of JBC's assets are $\frac{E}{E+D}$ and $\frac{D}{E+D}$, respectively. We can write the following:

$$r_A = k_E^L \frac{E}{E+D} + k_D \frac{D}{E+D} \tag{11.1}$$

The right side of the relationship is the firm's weighted average cost of capital (the WACC), which was discussed in Chapter 10. Assuming a fixed interest rate (k_D) on the firm's debt, equation 11.1 indicates that any change in the proportions of equity and debt financing must be compensated for by a change in the cost of equity (k_E^L) because the return on assets (r_A) is not affected by the way returns are split between shareholders and debt holders. To show how the cost of equity varies when the **debt-to-equity ratio** increases, we can rearrange the terms of equation 11.1 to express k_E^L as a function of r_A, k_D, and the debt ratio. We get the following:

$$k_E^L = r_A + (r_A - k_D)\frac{D}{E} \equiv k_E^U + (k_E^U - k_D)\frac{D}{E} \tag{11.2}$$

Note the two *identical* versions of the levered cost of equity in equation 11.2: in the version on the right, we have simply replaced r_A by k_E^U because they are the same. To illustrate, we consider JBC under the expected scenario. JBC's expected return on assets, r_A, is 15 percent (EBIT of \$30 million divided by \$200 million of assets) and its cost of debt, k_D, is 10 percent. Exhibit 11.5 shows JBC's cost of equity and WACC for two alternative debt-to-equity ratios, 0.25 (20 percent debt and 80 percent equity) and 1.00 (50 percent debt and 50 percent equity, the capital structure Ms. Johnson has proposed). With a debt-to-equity ratio of 0.25, JBC's shareholders require a return of 16.25 percent, which is JBC's cost of equity. With a debt-to-equity ratio of 1.00, they require 20 percent to compensate them for the additional financial risk generated by the increase in leverage. Note, however, that the firm's WACC, which is the expected return on assets, is a constant 15 percent irrespective of the debt-to-equity ratio.

Exhibit 11.6 shows how the return on assets (r_A), the WACC, the cost of equity (k_E^L), and the cost of debt (k_D) vary when the debt-to-equity ratio increases. When the firm carries no debt, its cost of equity and WACC are 15 percent, the

EXHIBIT 11.5 JBC'S COST OF EQUITY AND WACC FOR TWO DEBT-TO-EQUITY RATIOS, $r_A = 15\%$ AND $k_D = 10\%$.

Debt-to-Equity Ratio	$\frac{\text{Debt}}{\text{Equity}} = \frac{0.20}{0.80} = 0.25$	$\frac{\text{Debt}}{\text{Equity}} = \frac{0.50}{0.50} = 1.00$
Cost of equity from equation 11.2	15% + [(15% − 10%) × 0.25] = **16.25%**	15% + [(15% − 10%) × 1.00] = **20%**
Weighted average cost of capital from the right side of equation 11.1	(16.25% × 0.80) + (10% × 0.20) = **15%**	(20% × 0.50) + (10% × 0.50) = **15%**

EXHIBIT 11.6 THE COST OF CAPITAL AS A FUNCTION OF THE DEBT-TO-EQUITY RATIO ACCORDING TO THE MM THEORY IN THE ABSENCE OF TAXES.

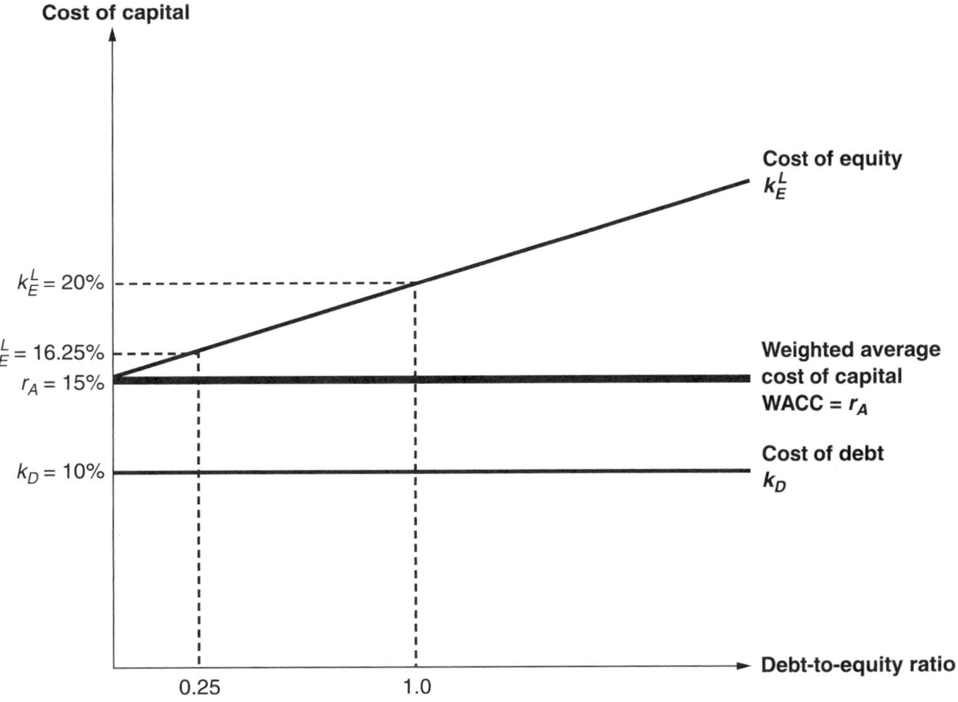

same as the expected return on the firm's assets. As the firm replaces equity with debt, shareholders bear increasing levels of financial risk and, therefore, expect higher returns from their investment; however, the firm's WACC remains equal to 15 percent, the return expected from the firm's assets.

An increasing cost of equity is not in contradiction with a constant share price. Shareholders expect a higher return from higher risk and, as shown earlier, they get it through higher expected EPS. As a result, the firm's share price does not move. It stays at \$100 as shown in Exhibit 11.7. When there is no debt in the capital structure, the firm does not carry any financial risk and the market value of its assets (\$200 million) is also the market value of its equity. With 2 million shares outstanding, the share price is \$100. As the proportion of assets financed by debt rises, financial risk increases. If the firm wants to finance 20 percent of its assets with debt, it must borrow \$40 million (20 percent of \$200 million) and repurchase 400,000 shares at \$100 each. When the recapitalization is over, the firm's equity is \$160 million (\$200 million minus \$40 million worth of repurchased shares) and the number of shares outstanding is 1,600,000 (2 million shares minus 400,000 shares repurchased), yielding a share price of \$100 (\$160 million divided by 1,600,000 shares). Applying the same reasoning to the case in which the firm finances 50 percent of its assets with debt shows that the share price remains at \$100.

EXHIBIT 11.7 JBC'S SHARE PRICE FOR DIFFERENT CAPITAL STRUCTURES.

Capital Structure	Financial Risk	Market Value of Assets (1)	Amount of Debt Financing (2)	Market Value of Equity (1) – (2) = (3)	Number of Shares (4)	Price per Share (3)/(4)
No debt	None	$200 million	None	$200 million	2,000,000	$100
20% debt	Low	$200 million	$ 40 million	$160 million	1,600,000	$100
50% debt	Higher	$200 million	$100 million	$100 million	1,000,000	$100

To summarize, in a world without taxes and financial distress costs, the MM theory of capital structure says that *a firm's* ***financial structure decision*** *does not affect the market value of its assets, its share price, or its weighted average cost of capital.* We show in the next section that this is no longer true when taxes are included in the analysis.

THE CAPITAL STRUCTURE DECISION IN A WORLD WITH CORPORATE INCOME TAXES BUT WITHOUT FINANCIAL DISTRESS COSTS

The analysis so far has ignored corporate income taxes. What would happen to JBC's profits, market value of assets, and share price if a 50 percent tax were imposed on the firm's earnings? To answer this question, we have to refer again to the MM theory of capital structure, but this time in the presence of corporate income taxes. Consider first the case in which JBC is all-equity financed. The EPS reported in the upper part of Exhibit 11.1 will be reduced by 50 percent, from $5 to $2.50 in the recession scenario, from $15 to $7.50 in the expected scenario, and from $20 to $10 in the expansion scenario. With EPS cut in half, JBC's share price and market value will drop by 50 percent as a result of the tax. Share price will go from $100 to $50 and market value from $200 million to $100 million. (The 2 million shares are now worth $50 each.)

Exhibit 11.8 summarizes the consequences of a change in capital structure from a situation of no-debt financing to a situation with 50 percent debt financing under two tax regimes: no corporate income tax and a corporate income tax rate of 50 percent. The exhibit shows how the tax affects the value of the firm's assets and equity, its share price, and its cost of capital when expected EBIT is $30 million (the expected scenario). As mentioned, the change in the capital structure will be carried out by borrowing and using the cash to buy back shares.

The upper part of Exhibit 11.8 reproduces the results of our previous analysis (no taxes). The lower left side shows the consequences of the imposition of the 50 percent corporate tax with no-debt financing, as described above. The cost of equity and the WACC are still 15 percent, as in the no-tax case. This is why JBC's share price and market value lost half their value. The business risk underlying the firm's assets is not affected by the tax rate, so investors still want to earn 15 percent. With profits and EPS at half their original amount, JBC's share price and value must decrease by 50 percent for investors to still earn 15 percent

EXHIBIT 11.8 EFFECTS OF CHANGES IN CAPITAL STRUCTURE ON THE FIRM'S EARNINGS PER SHARE, SHARE PRICE, MARKET VALUE, AND COST OF CAPITAL WITHOUT CORPORATE TAXES AND WITH A 50 PERCENT CORPORATE TAX RATE.

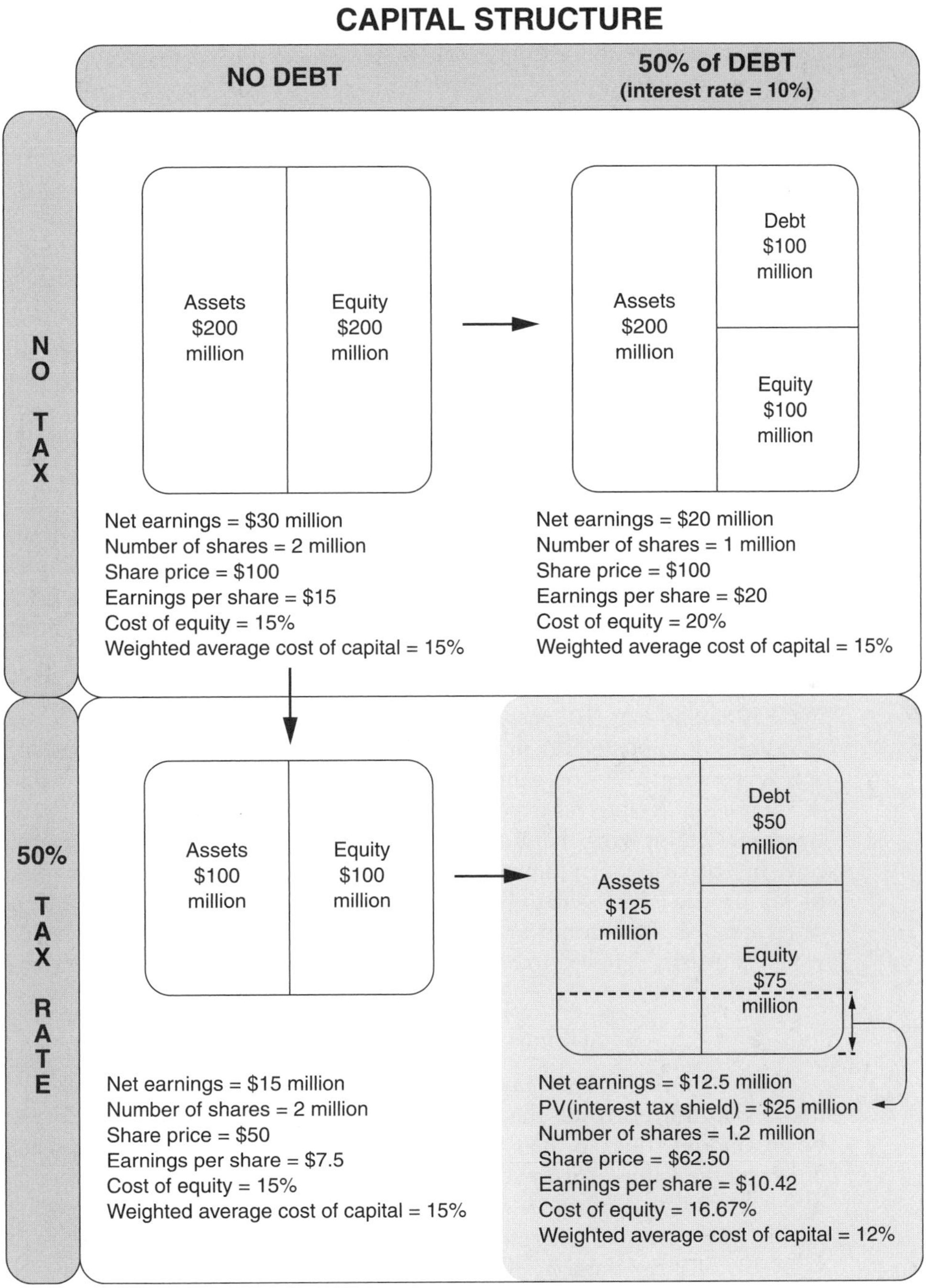

on shares purchased after the tax was imposed. Obviously, investors who held JBC's shares *before* the tax was imposed lost 50 percent of the value of their investment.

We now want to find out what will happen to JBC's asset value, equity value, share price, and cost of capital if Ms. Johnson decides to change JBC's capital structure by borrowing $50 million (half the value of assets) to repurchase an equal amount of equity. Will the value of JBC's assets and its share price remain the same as in the case of no taxes? The answer is no. In the presence of corporate income taxes, both the value of the firm's assets and its share price will *rise* as debt replaces equity in the firm's balance sheet, as shown in the lower-right side of Exhibit 11.8. In the next sections, we explain why this happens.

EFFECT OF BORROWING ON THE VALUE OF A FIRM'S ASSETS (WITH CORPORATE INCOME TAXES AND NO FINANCIAL DISTRESS COSTS)

Corporate tax laws favor debt financing because interest paid by the company to its creditors is a tax-deductible expense, whereas dividends and retained earnings are not. Replacing equity with debt financing reduces the amount of tax JBC must pay and thus increases the *after-tax* cash flow generated by the firm's assets. A higher cash flow from assets raises the market value of assets.

To illustrate the tax effect on asset value, we estimate the amount of taxes JBC will save if Ms. Johnson decides to borrow $50 million at 10 percent and use the cash to repurchase equity. JBC will pay $5 million of interest every year, and its taxable income will drop to $25 million ($30 million of EBIT less $5 million of interest expenses). As a result, it will pay $12.5 million in taxes (50 percent of $25 million). If the firm does not borrow, its expected annual tax payment will be $15 million (50 percent of an expected EBIT of $30 million). Thus, by borrowing $50 million at 10 percent, JBC can save $2.5 million in taxes every year ($15 million minus $12.5 million), and the annual cash flows generated by its assets will increase by the same amount. Because taxable income is reduced by an amount equal to interest expense, this annual tax savings can be calculated directly by simply multiplying the amount of interest expense by the corporate income tax rate. In our case, $5 million multiplied by 50 percent is equal to the $2.5 million of tax saved. More generally, if k_D is the cost of debt, T_C is the corporate tax rate, and D is the amount of debt, then the annual tax saving from debt financing, which is usually referred to as the annual **interest tax shield (ITS)**, can be expressed as follows:

$$\textbf{Annual interest tax shield} = T_C \times k_D \times D \qquad (11.3)$$

How will this interest tax shield affect the value of the firm's assets? We know that if the firm borrows, the cash flows generated by its assets will rise every year by an amount equal to the annual interest tax shield. Consequently, when the firm borrows, the value of its assets today is the sum of two components: (1) the value of its assets *if the firm does not borrow* and (2) the *present value* of the stream of all the *future* annual interest tax shields its debt will create. If V_L is the market value of the firm's assets when debt is used to finance these assets (the value of the levered firm), V_U is their value without debt (the value of the unlevered or all-equity financed firm), and PV_{ITS} is the present value of the stream of future interest tax shields, we have the following:

$$V_L = V_U + PV_{ITS} \tag{11.4}$$

In other words, the value of a firm's assets financed with debt (V_L) is equal to its value if it were financed only with equity (V_U), plus the present value of the interest tax shields that debt financing is expected to generate in the future (PV_{ITS}).[3]

Let's apply this valuation formula to JBC. We know V_U is \$100 million when the corporate income tax rate is 50 percent (see the lower left side of Exhibit 11.8); we want to find V_L if JBC borrows \$50 million and uses the cash to repurchase \$50 million of equity. We know the \$50 million debt will generate a recurrent annual interest tax shield of \$2.5 million. If we assume the interest tax shield has the *same* risk as the debt itself, its present value, PV_{ITS}, is the present value of a perpetual annuity (\$2.5 million every year forever) discounted at the rate of interest on debt.

The present value of a perpetual cash flow is simply the recurrent cash flow divided by the discount rate (see equation A6.1.3 in Appendix 6.1). JBC borrows \$50 million at 10 percent and its annual interest tax shield is \$2.5 million, so the present value of the entire stream of future interest tax shields is the following:

$$PV_{ITS} = \frac{T_C \times k_D \times D}{k_D} = \frac{0.5 \times 0.10 \times \$50{,}000{,}000}{0.10} = \frac{\$2{,}500{,}000}{0.10} = \$25{,}000{,}000$$

Thus, \$2.5 million of interest tax shield every year forever is worth \$25 million today.[4] According to equation 11.4,

$$V_L = \$100 \text{ million} + \$25 \text{ million} = \$125 \text{ million}$$

By replacing \$50 million worth of equity with debt, Ms. Johnson can increase the value of JBC's assets by \$25 million, as shown in the lower-right side of Exhibit 11.8. Note that the more JBC borrows, the larger the present value of the interest tax shield and the higher the value of the firm's assets. This phenomenon is reported in the first four columns in Exhibit 11.9 and is illustrated in the rising graph in Exhibit 11.10. As JBC increases its borrowing, the value of its assets increases. This happens because, as the amount of borrowing increases, the firm's interest tax shield increases and its tax payment decreases. With lower tax payments, the value of the firm's assets goes up.

Consider the result of JBC's proposed recapitalization: by borrowing \$50 million to finance the firm's assets, Ms. Johnson can increase the value of the assets by 25 percent, *even though they are exactly the same assets the firm had before borrowing*. The reason they are more valuable is that the recapitalization reduces the portion of these cash flows paid out as corporate tax. By refinancing JBC's assets with debt, Ms. Johnson can make a value-creating *financing* decision.

There is another way to think about the effect of financial leverage. Suppose another company wants to buy JBC's assets and plans to finance the acquisition

---

[3]Our result ignores the effect of investors' personal taxes, a point we discuss later in this chapter.

[4]When the tax shield is a perpetual annuity, PV_{ITS} is simply equal to T_C multiplied by Debt. In our case, it is 50% × \$50 million = \$25 million.

EXHIBIT 11.9 EFFECT OF BORROWING ON JBC'S ASSET VALUE, EQUITY VALUE, AND SHARE PRICE WITH A 50 PERCENT CORPORATE TAX RATE.

Amount of Borrowing (1)	Present Value of ITS (2) = 50% × (1)	Unlevered Value of Assets (3)	Levered Value of Assets (4) = (2) + (3)	Levered Value of Equity (5) = (4) – (1)	Unlevered Number of Shares (6)
Zero	Zero	$100 million	$100 million	$100 million	2,000,000
$ 20 million	$10 million	$100 million	$110 million	$ 90 million	2,000,000
$ 50 million	$25 million	$100 million	$125 million	$ 75 million	2,000,000
$100 million	$50 million	$100 million	$150 million	$ 50 million	2,000,000

Unlevered Share Price (7) = (3)/(6)	Present Value of ITS per Share (8) = (2)/(6)	Levered Share Price (9) = (7) + (8)	Number of Shares to Buy (10) = (1)/(9)	Number of Shares Left (11) = (6) – (10)	Levered Value of Equity (12) = (9) × (11)
$50.00	Zero	$50.00	Zero	2,000,000	$100 million
$50.00	$ 5.00	$55.00	363,636	1,636,364	$ 90 million
$50.00	$12.50	$62.50	800,000	1,200,000	$ 75 million
$50.00	$25.00	$75.00	1,333,333	666,667	$ 50 million

with $50 million of debt. This company would be ready to pay up to $125 million to acquire JBC's assets: $100 million for the capacity of these assets to generate operating cash flows (V_U in equation 11.4), and an additional $25 million for the present value of the taxes that will be saved through the $50 million debt financing (PV_{ITS} in equation 11.4).

EFFECT OF BORROWING ON THE FIRM'S MARKET VALUE OF EQUITY (WITH CORPORATE INCOME TAXES AND NO FINANCIAL DISTRESS COSTS)

As JBC increases its borrowing and uses the money to repurchase its equity, the firm's equity goes down. If we denote the value of equity (when the firm borrows) by E_L, we can write the following:

$$E_L = V_L - D \tag{11.5}$$

where V_L is still the value of the firm's assets when the firm borrows and D is the amount of borrowing. The declining value of JBC's equity as the firm increases its borrowing is shown in the fifth column of Exhibit 11.9 and illustrated in the descending graph in Exhibit 11.10.

EFFECT OF BORROWING ON THE FIRM'S SHARE PRICE (WITH CORPORATE INCOME TAXES AND NO FINANCIAL DISTRESS COSTS)

You may ask at this point, why should the firm borrow if the result is a reduction in the value of its equity? Is this financing policy advantageous to its shareholders? The answer is yes, because what matters to shareholders is not the total value of equity

EXHIBIT 11.10 THE VALUE OF JBC'S ASSETS AND EQUITY AS A FUNCTION OF ITS BORROWING WITH A 50 PERCENT CORPORATE TAX.

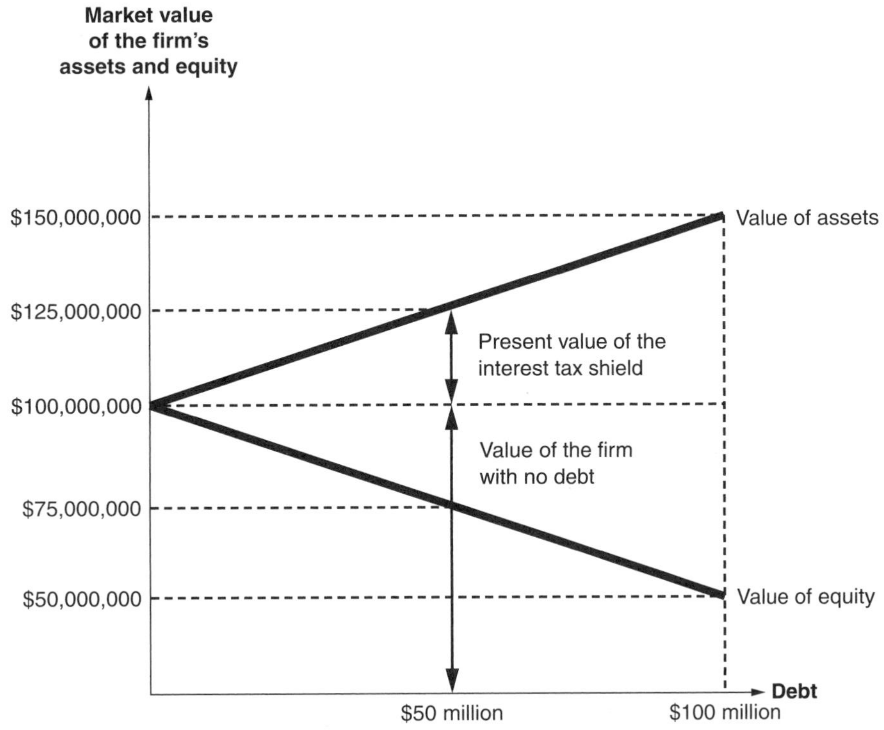

but the price per share. When the firm borrows to buy back its shares, the number of shares obviously goes down, but as we will show, the price per share goes up.

We can illustrate this phenomenon in the case of JBC. When the firm has no debt, its share price is $50 as shown at the bottom left side of Exhibit 11.8 and column 7 in Exhibit 11.9. What will happen to JBC's share price if Ms. Johnson decides to borrow $50 million to repurchase equity? As soon as this recapitalization decision is announced, JBC's share price will rise to reflect the increase in the value of the firm's assets. We know that the value of assets will go up by an amount equal to the present value of the interest tax shield, which is worth $25 million (50 percent of $50 million of borrowing as indicated in column 2 in Exhibit 11.9). Because JBC has 2 million shares, each share will rise by $12.50, which is equal to the present value of the interest tax shield (PV_{ITS}) of $25 million divided by the 2 million shares. If we use P_L to designate the share price with borrowing (the levered share price), P_U, the share price without borrowing (the unlevered share price), and N_U, the number of shares *before* recapitalization, then we can write the following:

$$P_L = P_U + \frac{PV_{ITS}}{N_U} \qquad (11.6)$$

In the case of JBC, we can write the following:

$$P_L = \$50 + \frac{\$25{,}000{,}000}{2{,}000{,}000} = \$50 + \$12.50 = \$62.50$$

as shown at the bottom right side of Exhibit 11.8 and in column 9 of Exhibit 11.9. How many shares can JBC buy with the \$50 million it has borrowed? Given that each share will rise to \$62.50 when *the announcement is made*, this is the price per share JBC will have to pay. The number of shares it can buy is thus equal to \$50 million divided by \$62.50, that is, 800,000 shares, as shown in column 10 in Exhibit 11.9. The number of shares that will remain in the hands of shareholders after the share repurchase is 1,200,000 (2 million less 800,000) as indicated in column 11 in Exhibit 11.9. We know that the total value of equity after the share buy back is \$75 million (see column 5 in Exhibit 11.9). You can now check for consistency: if you multiply the number of shares after the buyback (1,200,000) by their price (\$62.50), you should find \$75 million. This is indeed the case as shown in column 12 in Exhibit 11.9 and on the bottom right side of Exhibit 11.8.

We have shown so far that the levered value of JBC's assets (V_L) and its share price (P_L) keep rising as JBC increases its borrowing. How long can this process go on? When we carry the logic of debt financing to its extreme, a problem occurs because managers who wish to maximize the value of their firm's assets and its share price would be advised to borrow as much as possible. This advice will have to be reexamined because the excessive use of debt generates a number of problems that we have not yet considered. Before we do so, we examine how the cost of capital is affected by corporate income taxes.

EFFECT OF BORROWING ON THE COST OF CAPITAL (WITH CORPORATE INCOME TAXES AND NO FINANCIAL DISTRESS COSTS)

When a firm has no debt and pays income taxes, the return expected by its shareholders from their equity investment—the firm's unlevered cost of equity (k_E^U)—is still equal to the return on the firm's assets (r_A). However, when the firm has debt in its capital structure and pays taxes, we must account for the tax reduction resulting from the deductibility of interest expenses. In this case, equation 11.1, which relates r_A to the levered cost of equity (k_E^L) and the cost of debt (k_D), is no longer valid. It can be shown that it must be replaced with the following to reflect the tax effect:

$$r_A = k_E^L \frac{E}{E + D(1 - T_C)} + k_D(1 - T_C)\frac{D}{E + D(1 - T_C)}$$

where T_C is the corporate income tax rate. Rearranging the terms of the above equation to express the cost of equity (k_E^L) as a function of the other variables, we get the following:

$$k_E^L = r_A + (r_A - k_D)(1 - T_C)\frac{D}{E} \equiv k_E^U + (k_E^U - k_D)(1 - T_C)\frac{D}{E} \quad (11.7)$$

Note the two *identical* versions of the levered cost of equity in equation 11.7: in the version on the right, we have simply replaced r_A by k_E^U because they are the same.

Furthermore, because of the tax deductibility of interest expenses, the relevant cost of debt is now the *after-tax* cost of debt, that is, $k_D(1 - T_C)$, so that the after-tax WACC becomes as follows:

$$\text{WACC} = k_E^L \frac{E}{E + D} + k_D(1 - T_C)\frac{D}{E + D} \tag{11.8}$$

Exhibit 11.11 shows how the cost of equity (k_E^L) in equation 11.7 and the WACC in equation 11.8 vary when the debt-to-equity ratio increases according to the MM theory of capital structure in the presence of corporate income taxes. As in a world without corporate income taxes, the cost of equity (k_E) increases with debt because of the financial risk that comes with debt financing. The WACC decreases when the firm's borrowing rises because the extra return from the interest tax shield and the lower after-tax cost of debt more than offset the higher financial risk generated by higher levels of debt.

To illustrate, we again consider JBC, where the expected return on assets (which is the same as the unlevered cost of equity) is 15 percent, the cost of debt is 10 percent, and the corporate income tax rate is 50 percent. The previous analysis showed that with \$20 million of debt, the market value of JBC's equity is \$90 million; with \$50 million of debt, it is \$75 million. Exhibit 11.12 shows JBC's cost of equity and WACC in this situation. As leverage increases, the cost of equity rises but the WACC declines, as shown in Exhibit 11.11.

EXHIBIT 11.11 THE COST OF CAPITAL AS A FUNCTION OF THE DEBT-TO-EQUITY RATIO ACCORDING TO THE MM THEORY WITH A 50 PERCENT CORPORATE TAX RATE.

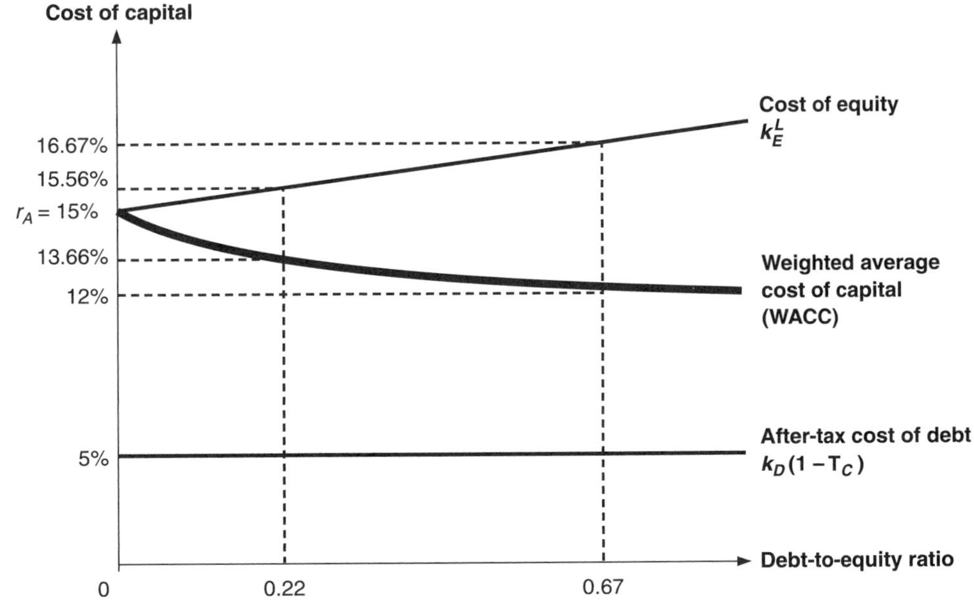

EXHIBIT 11.12 JBC'S COST OF EQUITY AND WACC FOR TWO DEBT-TO-EQUITY RATIOS; $r_A = 15\%$, $k_D = 10\%$, AND $T_C = 50\%$.

VALUE OF EQUITY FROM EXHIBIT 11.9

Amount Borrowed	$20 Million	$50 Million
Value of equity	$90 million	$75 million
Debt-to-equity ratio	$\frac{\$20 \text{ million}}{\$90 \text{ million}} = 0.22$	$\frac{\$50 \text{ million}}{\$75 \text{ million}} = 0.67$
$\frac{D}{D+E}$	$\frac{\$20 \text{ million}}{\$110 \text{ million}} = 0.18$	$\frac{\$50 \text{ million}}{\$125 \text{ million}} = 0.40$
Cost of equity from equation 11.7	15% + [(15% – 10%) × (1 – 50%) × 0.22] **= 15.56%**	15% + [(15% – 10%) × (1 – 50%) × 0.67] **= 16.67%**
Weighted average cost of capital from equation 11.8	(15.56% × 0.82) + (5% × 0.18) **= 13.66%**	(16.67% × 0.60) + (5% × 0.40) **= 12.00%**

Exhibit 11.13 provides a list of valuation formulas (referred to as MM valuation formulas) with and without borrowing in the presence of corporate tax.

According to the MM theory of capital structure *when taxes are taken into account, the firm's financing decision affects the value of its assets, its share price, and its cost of capital. When more and more debt replaces equity in the firm's capital structure, the value of the firm's assets and its share price increase, whereas its WACC decreases.* The implication, we know, is awkward but clear: when corporate taxes are taken into account, the capital structure that maximizes the value of the firm's assets and its share price is close to 100 percent debt financing. This result, however, is inconsistent with what we observe in practice: most companies do not carry very large amounts of debt. The reasons are discussed in the rest of this chapter.

THE CAPITAL STRUCTURE DECISION WHEN FINANCIAL DISTRESS IS COSTLY

Debt puts pressure on firms because interest and principal payments are contractual obligations firms must meet. If a firm finds it increasingly difficult to service its debt, it will face a situation that is referred to as financial distress and may ultimately go bankrupt. Financial distress generates costs, described below, that reduce the cash flows expected from the firm's assets. In the context of the pizza theory of capital structure, we can say that financial distress costs reduce the size of the pizza, leaving less of it for investors (both debt holders and shareholders). And as the pizza shrinks, the firm's value and its share price go down. Shareholders bear most of the financial distress costs because debt holders have a prior and fixed claim on the smaller pizza.

The **direct costs of financial distress** are the actual costs the firm incurs if it becomes legally bankrupt. **Bankruptcy** is a legal procedure through which the ownership

EXHIBIT 11.13 SUMMARY OF MODIGLIANI AND MILLER VALUATION FORMULAS WITHOUT AND WITH BORROWING IN THE PRESENCE OF CORPORATE TAX (T_C).

	No Borrowing[1] *The firm's assets are unlevered (subscript U means unlevered)*	**With Borrowing (D)** *The firm's assets are levered (subscript L means levered)*
Value of assets[2,3] **(V)** *See equation 11.4*	(1) $V_U = P_U \times N_U$ (2) $V_U = \frac{EBIT(1 - T_C)}{K_U}$	$V_L = V_U + PV_{ITS}$ $V_L = V_U + (T_C \times D)$
Value of equity[4] **(E)** *See equation 11.5*	$E_U \equiv V_U$	$E_L = V_L - D$
Share price[5] **(P)** *See equation 11.6*	$P_U = \frac{E_U}{N_U}$	$P_L = P_U + \frac{PV_{ITS}}{N_U}$
Cost of debt[6] **(k_D)** *See equation 10.3*	$k_D^{BT} = 0$	$k_D^{AT} = k_D^{BT}(1 - T_C)$
Cost of equity[7] **(k_E)** *See equation 11.7*	$k_E^U \equiv r_A$	$k_E^L = k_E^U + (k_E^U - k_D^{BT})(1 - T_C)\frac{D}{E_L}$
Weighted average cost of capital[8] **(WACC)** *See equation 11.8*	$WACC_U = k_E^U$	$WACC_L = k_E^L\frac{E}{E + D} + k_D^{BT}(1 - T_C)\frac{D}{E + D}$

[1]"No borrowing" is a special case of "with borrowing"; to get the formulas with "no borrowing," simply set to zero the tax rate (T_C), the amount of borrowing (D), and the cost of debt (k_D) in the "with borrowing" formulas.
[2]V_U is the unlevered value of assets; referring to Exhibit 11.8, we have V_U = \$100 million. We get this value by either multiplying the \$50 share price (P_U) by the 2 million shares (N_U) or, assuming perpetual valuation, by dividing net earnings (EBIT) of \$15 million by the 15% unlevered cost of equity (k_E^U).
[3]PV_{ITS} is the present value of interest tax shield; referring to Exhibit 11.8, we have $PV_{ITS} = T_C \times D$ = \$25 million (50% of \$50 million).
[4]E is the market value of the firm's equity; referring to Exhibit 11.8, we have E_U = \$100 million and E_L = \$75 million (\$125 million less \$50 million).
[5]P is the price per share; referring to Exhibit 11.8, we have P_U = \$50 and P_L = \$62.50 (\$50 plus \$25 million divided by 2 million shares).
[6]k_D^{BT} is the pre-tax cost of debt (10%), and k_D^{AT} is the after-tax cost of debt (5%).
[7]k_E^U is the unlevered cost of equity, r_A the unlevered return on assets, and k_E^L the levered cost of equity; referring to Exhibit 11.8, we have $k_E^U = r_A$ = 15% and k_E^L = 16.67% (see Exhibit 11.12).
[8]$WACC_U$ and $WACC_L$ are, respectively, the unlevered and levered weighted average cost of capital; referring to Exhibit 11.8, we have $WACC_U$ = 15% and $WACC_L$ = 12% (see Exhibit 11.12).

of the firm's assets is transferred to debt holders. Associated with this transfer are legal and administrative costs and lawyers' and consultants' fees.

Before a firm legally declares bankruptcy, it may have already incurred significant **indirect costs of financial distress**. The increasing probability that it will have to declare bankruptcy creates a situation that prevents the firm from operating at maximum efficiency. With too much debt outstanding, the firm may have to pass up valuable investment opportunities, cut research and development activities, or reduce marketing expenses to conserve cash and avoid bankruptcy. Customers may question the firm's long-term ability to deliver reliable goods and services and decide to switch to other companies. Suppliers may be reluctant to provide trade credit. Valuable employees may leave. Conflicts of interest between managers, shareholders, debt holders, and employees may arise, with each group trying to pursue a different strategy of self-preservation. All these indirect costs, which have a negative effect on the firm's value, become increasingly significant as the firm's indebtedness rises.

The previous section shows that when the proportion of debt in the firm's capital structure increases, the firm's value rises because of larger interest tax shields. However, in the presence of costly financial distress, these tax-related gains are eventually offset by the expected costs of financial distress. The relationship between the value of the levered firm (V_L), its unlevered value (V_U), and the present value of the interest tax shield (PV_{ITS}) expressed in equation 11.4 must be modified to account for this offsetting effect. If PV_{CFD} is the present value of the expected costs of financial distress, we can adjust the valuation formula to reflect the reduction in value generated by these costs:

$$V_L = V_U + PV_{ITS} - PV_{CFD} \tag{11.9}$$

How large is the present value of the expected costs of financial distress (PV_{CFD})? The question can be answered only empirically. The evidence indicates that these costs are not insignificant. They can reach 10 to 15 percent of the value of the firm's assets as early as several years before filing for bankruptcy.

Exhibit 11.14 shows the rising value of the firm's assets (the straight line first presented in Exhibit 11.10) from which we deducted the present value of the costs

EXHIBIT 11.14 THE VALUE OF A FIRM IN THE PRESENCE OF CORPORATE TAXES AND FINANCIAL DISTRESS COSTS AS A FUNCTION OF BORROWING.

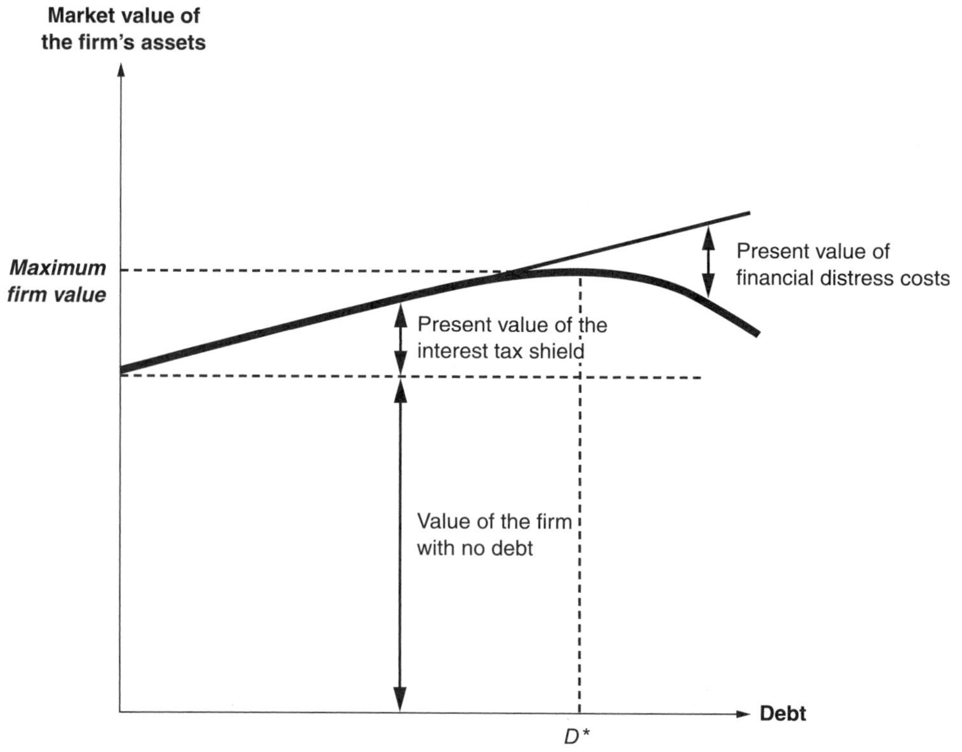

of financial distress. At low to moderate levels of debt, the probability of financial distress is negligible and the firm can capture the entire value of the interest tax shield. As more and more debt replaces equity, the probability of financial distress rises and the present value of the associated costs grows at an increasing rate. At some debt level, denoted D*, the increase in the present value of financial distress costs arising from an extra dollar of borrowing exactly offsets the increase in the present value of the interest tax shield. At that point, the firm has reached its **optimal capital structure**. This is the firm's best capital structure because it is the one that maximizes the value of its assets and share price.

Exhibit 11.15 illustrates the effect of changes in capital structure on the firm's cost of capital in the presence of financial distress costs. As shown earlier in Exhibit 11.11, in which case financial distress costs were nonexistent, the cost of equity first increases proportionally with a rise in the debt-to-equity ratio. When the present value of financial distress costs becomes significant, the cost of equity begins to rise at a faster rate. For the same reason, the cost of debt also begins to rise at some point. The WACC declines until the benefit of the interest tax shield is offset by the negative effect of expected financial distress on the costs of equity and debt. At this point, the firm has reached its optimal capital structure: its WACC is at its minimum, its debt-to-equity ratio is at its optimal value (D/E)*, and the value of the firm's assets and its share price are maximized. This model of debt financing is known as the **trade-off model of capital structure**.

The conclusion is that an optimal capital structure exists, at least conceptually, that is the outcome of a trade-off between the benefit of the interest tax shield and the cost of financial distress arising from an increasing use of debt financing.

EXHIBIT 11.15 THE COST OF CAPITAL AS A FUNCTION OF THE DEBT-TO-EQUITY RATIO IN THE PRESENCE OF CORPORATE TAXES AND FINANCIAL DISTRESS COSTS.

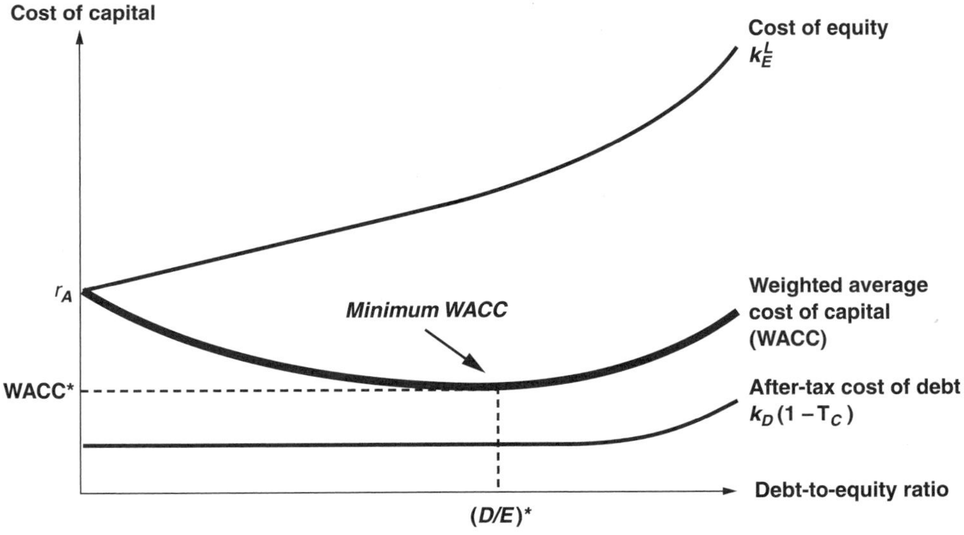

Unfortunately, we cannot tell you how to determine that optimal debt ratio because it is impossible to estimate financial distress costs precisely. However, this does not mean that the information in this chapter is not useful for managers. On the contrary, as shown next, it provides a solid conceptual framework within which the firm's managers can formulate a capital structure policy for their firm.

FORMULATING A CAPITAL STRUCTURE POLICY

The previous analysis of the trade-off model of capital structure looks at the two major determinants of a firm's borrowing decision: the value-creating effect of the tax deductibility of interest expenses and the value-destroying effect of financial distress costs. This section extends the basic trade-off model by examining additional factors that have an effect on the formulation of a capital structure policy. We first examine two questions related to the trade-off model:

1. How do personal taxes, which investors must pay on the income they receive from firms, affect the size of the interest tax shield?
2. Which types of firms are more likely to experience a state of financial distress?

We then look at a number of issues that go beyond the standard trade-off model of capital structure to shed more light on the underlying variables that shape a firm's capital structure:

1. Are there reasons for firms to borrow *even if debt does not provide tax savings*?
2. Are there reasons for firms to abstain from borrowing *even if debt financing generates little or no financial distress costs*?
3. Why do firms prefer to finance their activities with internally generated funds (retained earnings) rather than external funds?

The answers to these questions provide additional insights into the factors that affect a firm's capital structure decision and help both managers and firms' owners establish an appropriate capital structure for their companies.

A CLOSER LOOK AT THE TRADE-OFF MODEL OF CAPITAL STRUCTURE

This section examines two issues that are related to the major determinants of the trade-off model of capital structure. First, we want to determine how personal income taxes influence the value-creating effect of the tax deductibility of corporate interest expenses. Second, we want to find out which types of firms are more likely to be affected by the value-destroying effect of financial distress costs.

THE EFFECT OF PERSONAL TAXES

The interest tax shield given in equation 11.3 ignores the tax that debt holders and shareholders must pay on the income they receive from their investments in the firm. Debt holders receive interest payments. Shareholders receive cash dividends, and they receive capital gains if they sell shares at a price higher than their purchase price. If the personal tax rate on interest income is T_D and the *average* personal tax rate on equity income (dividends and capital gains) is T_E, it can be shown that the interest tax shield is in this case:

$$\textbf{Interest tax shield} = \left[1 - (1 - T_C) \times \frac{(1 - T_E)}{(1 - T_D)}\right] \times k_D \times D \qquad (11.10)$$

When the personal tax rates on debt and equity income are equal ($T_D = T_E$), equation 11.10 reduces to $T_C \times k_D \times D$, which is the annual interest tax shield when personal taxes are ignored (equation 11.3). But the personal tax rate on equity income is generally *lower* than that on interest income because capital gains are usually taxed at a lower rate than interest income. In this case, the annual interest tax shield is lower than in the case in which personal taxes are not considered.

To illustrate, consider a firm with \$50 million of debt, a cost of debt of 10 percent, a corporate tax rate of 50 percent, and personal tax rates of 50 percent on interest income and 25 percent on equity income. The interest tax shield according to equation 11.10 is as follows:

$$\text{Interest tax shield} = \left[1 - (1 - 0.50) \times \frac{(1 - 0.25)}{(1 - 0.50)}\right]$$
$$\times\ 0.10 \times \$50 \text{ million} = \$1.25 \text{ million}$$

This is half the \$2.5 million of interest tax shield when the personal tax rates on debt and equity income are equal ($T_C \times k_D \times D = 50\% \times 10\% \times \$50$ million = \$2.5 million). Hence, ignoring the possibility that the personal tax rate on equity income can be lower than the personal tax rate on income from debt is likely to *overestimate* the true tax benefit of debt financing.

FACTORS AFFECTING THE RISK AND COST OF FINANCIAL DISTRESS

When a firm increases its borrowing, it also increases the probability that it will experience a state of financial distress and incur (financial distress) costs that will reduce its value. But not every firm is exposed to the same **risk of financial distress** or bears the same costs of financial distress. Some may reach a state of financial distress at lower debt ratios than others. In this section, we identify a number of firm-specific factors that are likely to increase the probability that a firm will experience a state of financial distress. We would expect firms with a higher risk of financial distress to have relatively lower debt ratios, which will move their optimal amount of debt financing to the left in Exhibit 11.14.

The Volatility of the Firm's Operating Profits A firm that has highly volatile and cyclical operating cash flows (that is, a firm with high *business* risk) faces a higher probability of experiencing financial distress than a firm that has steady operating cash flows, assuming both firms have the *same* debt ratio. This is why firms with high business risk, such as software publishing companies and semiconductor manufacturers, have lower debt ratios than, say, textile mills and water utilities, as shown in Exhibit 11.16. Utilities are usually able to generate a steadier and more predictable stream of operating profits and cash flows and hence have relatively low business risk. In other words, firms with low business risk can afford higher financial risk (higher debt ratios) than firms with high business risk. A simple way to find out whether a company can take full advantage of the interest tax shield is to draw an after-tax EPS-EBIT graph like the one shown in Exhibit 11.2. Simply check to see whether the probability of falling below the break-even point is negligible.

EXHIBIT 11.16 DEBT RATIOS FOR SELECTED U.S. INDUSTRIES.[1]

Industries with high ratios of debt as a percentage of debt plus equity		Industries with low ratios of debt as a percentage of debt plus equity	
Textile mills	53%	Software publishing	19%
Building construction	50	Semiconductor manufacturing	16
Real estate companies	47	Educational services	15
Paper manufacturing	47	Internet companies[2]	14
Hotels	44	Pharmaceutical preparation manufacturing[3]	14
Maritime transportation	43	Surgical instrument manufacturing	11
Water utilities	43	Gold and silver ore mining	11
Iron and steel mills	40	Lessors of nonfinancial intangible assets[4]	9

[1]Debt ratios are calculated by dividing debt by the sum of debt and equity. Debt is measured at book value, and equity at market value. Industry ratios in the exhibit are the average of the ratios of the individual companies in the industry measured at the end of the fiscal year over the four-year period 2004–2007, computed by the authors using data from *Compustat North America.*

[2]Including Internet publishing and broadcasting as well as web search portals.

[3]This industry comprises establishments primarily engaged in manufacturing in vivo diagnostic substances and pharmaceutical preparations (except biological) intended for internal and external consumption in dose forms, such as ampoules, tablets, capsules, vials, ointments, powders, solutions, and suspensions.

[4]This industry comprises establishments primarily engaged in assigning rights to assets, such as patents, trademarks, brand names, and/or franchise agreements for which a royalty payment or licensing fee is paid to the asset holder.

The Type of Assets the Firm Holds When financial distress occurs, creditors are less likely to extend credit to firms with few tangible assets (such as software companies, education services, and Internet companies) than to firms with assets that can be valuable in case of liquidation (such as real estate and hotel companies). Thus, firms that have relatively large investments in human capital, research, brands, and other intangible assets face higher costs of financial distress than firms that have the *same* debt ratio but that have large investments in land, buildings, and similar tangible assets that can be sold in case of bankruptcy. Firms with relatively large proportions of intangible assets can reduce the probability of financial distress by borrowing less than firms with relatively large proportions of tangible and liquid assets. This may explain why software companies, education services firms, and Internet companies, which have comparatively lower amounts of tangible assets, have lower debt ratios than real estate and hotel companies, which have comparatively higher amounts of tangible assets, as reported in Exhibit 11.16.

The Type of Products or Services the Firm Sells When the firm sells a commodity or when the firm's service can be obtained elsewhere, customers do not usually care whether their supplier goes bankrupt, because another firm will always fill the void. When the product or service is unique, however, customers are concerned about the consequences of their supplier experiencing financial distress. Thus, a commodity supplier faces lower costs of financial distress than a supplier of unique goods or services with the *same* debt ratio. The former can afford relatively large levels of debt without making its customers nervous, but the supplier of a unique product or service would rather rely on relatively less debt to reassure its customers that its future viability will not be jeopardized by an excessive debt burden (again, compare the utility companies with the software publishers shown in Exhibit 11.16).

Even if the product is a commodity, however, customers may be concerned if the product needs future service or repair. For example, if you believe a car manufacturer will go bankrupt, you will probably not buy one of its cars. But if bankruptcy threatens a food company, you may still buy its products, because they do not need to be serviced or repaired.

The Structure of the Country's Financial System The risk of a firm experiencing financial distress is not related just to factors specific to the firm or its industry. It is also affected by the structure of the financial system in which the firm operates. In countries in which some of the banks are owned or controlled by the state or in countries that allow banks to own shares of companies, firms usually have higher debt ratios than in countries in which banks are in the private sector and must restrict their activities only to lending.

When banks are state owned and can be both lenders and shareholders of the same company, they are more likely to help that company avoid bankruptcy, particularly if the company is large. State-owned banks may continue to lend to a company if the state wants to keep the company afloat. Banks that are allowed to own shares in companies may accept converting excessive debt into equity. This may explain why some large companies in countries such as France, Germany, Italy, and Japan usually have higher debt ratios than their counterparts in the United States or the United Kingdom.

FACTORS OTHER THAN TAXES THAT MAY FAVOR BORROWING

The major benefit of debt financing is the tax savings that come from the deductibility of interest expenses. If the tax reductions associated with debt were no longer available (either because the tax authority denies them or because firms cannot take advantage of them), would a firm's owners still have an incentive to borrow? Yes, they would. A firm's owners may want to borrow for several reasons that are not based on the tax advantage of debt financing.

DEBT IS A DEVICE THAT HELPS REDUCE THE AGENCY COSTS ARISING FROM THE SEPARATION OF OWNERSHIP FROM CONTROL

Managers may not always act in the best interest of shareholders. They sometimes make decisions that benefit themselves but that reduce the firm's value. Suppose that a firm has generated a large cash surplus because it had an exceptionally good year. Managers may be tempted to spend this cash unwisely, such as on expensive and often useless perquisites that are not really needed, or on "empire-building" investments that allow the firm to grow in revenues and size but do not create value.

This behavior illustrates what is called an **agency problem**. It arises from the separation of ownership and control. When managers run a firm on behalf of shareholders (they act as the agents of shareholders), they may not always make decisions that benefit shareholders. They may make decisions that increase their own level of comfort and satisfaction but reduce the firm's value. An example is an executive who buys a corporate plane when such an acquisition has no identifiable benefit beyond enhancing the executive's status. This executive reduces the firm's value by an amount equal to the after-tax cost of the plane. This value reduction is referred to as an **agency cost of equity financing**.

Consider another example, directly related to the capital structure decision. The income and wealth of managers are generally not as well diversified as those of shareholders. Managers' income, their job tenure, and most of their wealth depend on the firm that employs them, whereas most shareholders invest only a small fraction of their total wealth in a single firm. Because they are poorly diversified, managers are more exposed to risk than their well-diversified shareholders. Consequently, they may adopt a more conservative debt policy than the one that maximizes the firm's value. The difference between the firm's value under the conservative debt policy and its potential maximum value with more debt financing is another example of an agency cost of equity financing.

One way to reduce agency costs is to turn managers into partial owners by giving them either shares in the firm or options to buy shares at a predetermined fixed price. However, the number of shares or options owned by the managers needs to be substantial to induce them to make the maximization-of-shareholder-value their overriding concern. What if shareholders are reluctant to distribute large amounts of shares or options to managers?

Debt financing can be another solution to the agency problem. Issuing debt and using the cash to buy back shares reduces the agency costs of equity in two ways. First, the portion of the firm's cash flow that goes to shareholders falls because there are fewer shares. The portion that goes to debt holders rises because managers must now allocate a larger part of the firm's cash flows to service debt. This means that managers have less of that cash flow to squander on things such as airplanes. Second, if managers already have some equity in the firm, their *percentage share* of the firm's ownership rises, because, even though they hold the same amount of equity, they now own a bigger portion of the firm's total equity. Both of these debt effects should motivate managers to act in the interest of shareholders. The first effect acts as the proverbial stick, the second as the carrot. Thus, debt financing becomes a device that helps reduce the agency costs associated with equity financing by aligning managers' interests with those of shareholders.

In this case, borrowing should increase the market value of the firm and its share price through two distinct channels. One is through the tax-induced gains generated by debt financing and the other is through the reduction in the agency costs of equity. The latter results from the increased focus and discipline imposed on managers by higher debt levels and the enhanced motivation provided by a higher fractional ownership of the firm for managers who held shares before the recapitalization.

DEBT IS A DEVICE THAT ALLOWS CURRENT OWNERS TO RETAIN CONTROL

The choice of debt over new equity may be dictated by the desire of current owners to retain **control** of their firm. Fresh equity, supplied by new investors, reduces the percentage of the firm's equity capital controlled by the original owners, but debt financing avoids this **dilution** effect. Thus, if the firm needs outside funding and the current owners wish to retain control, they will prefer that the firm borrow rather than issue new shares, regardless of tax considerations.

If the decision to issue debt rather than equity is motivated by control considerations, we can expect the firm's shares to trade at a discount, because that will greatly diminish the ability of outsiders to take over the company. If the present value of the tax gains generated by the debt issued to retain control is smaller than the market discount caused by a tight control, the net effect is a *lower* equity value. But this does not mean that shareholders are necessarily worse off. Control may generate nonmonetary benefits that are more valuable to them than the loss of market value.

Debt Is a Device that Helps Resolve the Problem of Information Asymmetry between Managers and Outside Investors

Asymmetric information is present when management knows more about the future prospects of their firm than outside investors (shareholders and creditors) know. This occurs when it is expensive for a company to keep outside investors informed about the firm's current condition and future prospects. It can also arise when management does not want future plans to be public knowledge because such information might be valuable to its competitors. Let's see why the presence of asymmetric information can create a managerial preference for debt financing.

Suppose JBC has decided to invest in a new project that will require external financing. Ms. Johnson could either issue shares at the current market price of, say, \$70 or issue bonds. Suppose Ms. Johnson is convinced that the firm's future is more promising than the financial market expects. She believes JBC's equity is *underpriced* and JBC's shares are worth at least \$90. What should she do? If she issues undervalued shares, she penalizes the current shareholders by handing a gift to new shareholders who would pay only \$70 for what she values at \$90. Ms. Johnson, who cares about the firm's existing shareholders, would rather issue bonds. Now consider the opposite case in which Ms. Johnson believes JBC's shares are *overpriced* and a price of \$60 would be more in line with her expectation regarding JBC's future prospects. If she issues bonds, the required interest and principal payments may create an added burden when she should focus her full attention on improving the firm's prospects. She should issue shares. If she could issue shares at a price close to their current price of \$70, she would provide a windfall profit to current shareholders at the expense of new shareholders.

There is another point to consider, however. If investors are aware that firms issue shares only when managers think the firm's equity is overvalued, they will revise their expectations downward when a firm announces its intention to issue shares and bid down its share price. The evidence seems to support this view because the price of existing shares usually goes down on the day firms announce their intention to issue new shares. Managers, who typically do not like to see a drop in their firm's share price, are often reluctant to issue shares, whether or not they find their equity underpriced or overpriced. This may explain why, for most corporations, debt is the favored means of external financing, irrespective of the tax benefit it procures.

FACTORS OTHER THAN FINANCIAL DISTRESS COSTS THAT MAY DISCOURAGE BORROWING

Although debt financing provides valuable tax reductions, increasing borrowing eventually generates financial distress costs that rise with higher debt ratios. The question, then, is whether firms would increase borrowing even if financial distress costs were insignificant. Some firms may deliberately decide to refrain from borrowing even if financial distress costs are moderate or nonexistent because the debt the firm must issue to take advantage of the tax savings may create a number of constraints that owners and managers find too costly. If these expected costs are higher than the potential tax benefits of debt financing, the firm may decide not to issue additional debt.

EXCESSIVE DEBT MAY PREVENT FIRMS FROM TAKING FULL ADVANTAGE OF THE INTEREST TAX SHIELD

To take advantage of the tax savings from interest expenses, a firm needs to generate relatively large operating profits so that it may deduct the full amount of interest expenses. Firms that operate in capital-intensive industries can already reduce their tax liability through accelerated depreciation schedules. Consequently, they may not have sufficient pre-tax operating profits to benefit fully from the additional tax savings offered by the interest expenses generated by high levels of debt.

EXCESSIVE DEBT MAY CREATE COSTLY CONFLICTS OF INTEREST BETWEEN SHAREHOLDERS AND DEBT HOLDERS

Excessive debt may give rise to costly conflicts of interest between shareholders and lenders that can affect the firm's capital structure decision. We use an extreme example to illustrate the point. Suppose that management, acting on the instructions of shareholders, borrows $8 million at 10 percent to invest in a $10 million project that is risky. Furthermore, assume that the lenders do not have all the details about the riskiness of the project. In one year, the project should yield either $30 million or nothing, with an equal probability of occurrence. If the project goes well, the shareholders repay $8.8 million to the lenders (the $8 million loan plus 10 percent interest) and keep the rest ($21.2 million). If the project fails, everyone loses, but the lenders will lose more than the shareholders, because they financed 80 percent of the project. This is rightly described as "gambling away" lenders' money. The lenders, of course, anticipate this type of behavior and try to protect their investment by imposing restrictions on the firm's ability to spend the borrowed funds as it wishes. In other words, the lenders make it more expensive for the shareholders to raise debt capital.

The protection the suppliers of debt demand takes the form of **restrictive covenants** in the formal agreement between the borrowing firm and its lenders. For example, these covenants may impose limits on the amount of dividends the firm is allowed to pay, the amount of additional debt it can borrow, or the type of assets it can acquire or sell. The more debt the firm already has, the more restrictive the protective covenants associated with additional borrowing become. In other words, additional debt becomes increasingly costly, not only in terms of the higher interest payments lenders may demand but also in the loss of managerial flexibility. The costs eventually reach the point at which they offset the benefit of the interest tax shield.

These **bonding** and **monitoring costs** are also referred to as **agency costs of debt financing** because they are the outcome of another type of agency problem. In this case, the shareholders are the agents of the debt holders because they decide how debt holders' funds will be spent. You could argue that agency costs of debt are actually a subset of financial distress costs. Like financial distress costs, they are expected to discourage firms from borrowing too much.

The agency costs of *debt* financing and the agency costs of *equity* financing have *opposite* effects on the firm's value. When a firm increases its borrowing, its agency costs of debt *rise* and the value of the firm's assets and share price *fall* (additional debt gets more costly). Simultaneously, its agency costs of equity *fall* and the value of the firm's assets and share price *rise*. The net effect depends on the relative magnitude of the two types of agency costs.

EXCESSIVE DEBT MAY CONSTRAIN THE FIRM'S ABILITY TO PAY STABLE DIVIDENDS

Managers generally prefer to adopt **stable dividend policies**. They try to distribute dividends regularly and to increase their amount steadily over time to keep pace with the rise in the firm's share price. This maintains a **dividend yield** (dividend per share divided by share price) acceptable to the market. The objective is usually to attain an unbroken record of dividend payments. When a firm faces a temporary liquidity problem, it will try not to cut its dividend. Cutting or skipping a dividend payment may be interpreted by the market as a signal that the firm is facing a fundamental cash-flow problem that will prevent it from paying dividends for the foreseeable future. The market reaction can be a sharp drop in the firm's share price. To avoid these negative **signaling effects**, firms try to pursue stable dividend policies unless they face a severe cash-flow problem and have no choice but to cut dividends.

The implication for the capital structure decision is clear: firms with excessive debt may be unable to maintain a stable dividend policy. Consider JBC's alternative capital structures reported in Exhibit 11.1. Suppose the firm pays a $5 dividend per share. With no debt in its capital structure, JBC will be able to pay its dividend even if the worst-case scenario occurs. If recession hits, EPS will be $5, enough to cover the $5 dividend. But with $100 million of debt, JBC will be unable to pay dividends if recession occurs. No cash may be available after paying the $10 million of interest on the debt.

If a firm adopts a stable dividend policy and if the market prefers stable dividends, the value of the firm should rise. But this potential increase in value will be offset by the loss of the tax benefits of debt *not* issued. The value of the firm's assets and its share price will rise only if the gains derived from a stable dividend policy exceed the foregone tax benefits of debt financing.

EXCESSIVE DEBT MAY REDUCE THE FIRM'S FINANCIAL FLEXIBILITY AND AFFECT ITS CREDIT RATING

Some firms are tempted to build up cash during good times. This cash buildup, often referred to as **financial slack**, may be valuable because it is immediately available if a value-creating investment opportunity is found. In addition, a cash buildup contributes to increasing the firm's **debt capacity**, that is, its ability to quickly raise debt in the future if the need for funds arises unexpectedly. Clearly, a firm with excessive debt will not be able to enjoy this sort of flexibility. **Financial flexibility** may be valuable to managers, but does it create value to shareholders? This is a difficult question to answer. Holding cash and reducing debt should have a negative effect on the firm's value because cash does not earn high returns and debt reduction means that valuable tax savings are lost. The net effect on value will be positive only if the expected gains from acting rapidly to take advantage of investment opportunities exceed these negative effects.

Another illustration of how financial flexibility may lead to a capital structure with less than optimal debt is managers' desire to retain or improve the **credit rating** of their firm's debt. Companies that issue debt securities are required to obtain a rating from a **credit rating agency**. This rating reflects the agency's assessment of the quality of the firm's debt (see Chapter 9 for details). If the agency downgrades the firm's debt, the firm's cost of debt will rise and its ability to raise debt quickly may be impaired, thus reducing the firm's financial flexibility. For this reason, most managers avoid borrowing in excess of the amount that may trigger a credit downgrade, even if more debt makes sense otherwise. Again, the net effect on share price is not obvious.

IS THERE A PREFERENCE FOR RETAINED EARNINGS?

Managers seem to have a marked preference for retained earnings over external financing, whether in the form of debt or new equity. How can we explain this reticence toward external financing, and what are its implications for the capital structure decision?

CONTRARY TO SECURITIES, RETAINED EARNINGS DO NOT HAVE ISSUE COSTS

Contrary to bond and stock issues, retained earnings do not have any **flotation** or **issue costs** and are, thus, less expensive than a stock issue. Flotation costs include administrative costs (such as filing fees, legal fees, and printing fees), taxes, and the costs of using the services of investment banks that sell the firm's securities to the public (see Chapter 9). Most of these costs are fixed, so the total cost of selling bonds and stocks is proportionally lower for large issues than for small ones. This may explain why firms raise large amounts of external funds infrequently rather than small amounts more often. (For issues of the same size, it has been shown that the cost of raising equity is higher than the cost of raising debt.)

DO FIRMS HAVE A PREFERRED ORDER IN THEIR CHOICE OF FINANCING?

Evidence suggests that firms usually raise capital according to a **pecking order**, meaning that they rely first on retained earnings and then, if external financing is needed, issue debt before raising new equity. Some of the reasons why firms issue bonds rather than stocks were reviewed in the previous section. They include the desire of current owners to retain control, the role of debt as a mechanism to reduce the agency costs of equity, and the negative market reaction to the announcement of a new equity issue, a reaction arising from asymmetric information between managers and outside investors. Firms may prefer to issue bonds rather than stocks, but why would they prefer internal financing (retained earnings) to external financing?

One reason is that no issue costs are associated with retained earnings, whereas significant costs are associated with any form of external financing. Another reason is that firms do not have to provide so much information to outsiders to justify a retention of profits as when making a new issue of stocks or bonds. This argument, often defended by the need to prevent competitors from getting valuable information, is generally not well received by shareholders, who interpret it as an excuse for not providing them with valuable information on the use of their funds. This is the dilemma created by shareholders' demand for **transparency**. More transparency should enhance the firm's value, but it could also harm the firm if competitors use the information to their advantage.

One implication of the pecking order hypothesis is that *firms may not have a specific target debt ratio* or, if they have one, they do not aim for it consistently. When they have investment opportunities, they retain earnings to fund them. If an investment requires more funds than available internally, the firm will first issue debt and then raise new equity, thus allowing its capital structure to vary over time in response to investment opportunities.

Putting It All Together

We would have liked to provide a formula that ties together all the factors that influence a firm's capital structure and market value, and that identifies an optimal debt ratio for a firm. Unfortunately, such a formula does not exist. All we have is a basic framework that tells us an optimal capital structure is reached at the point at which the tax benefit of an additional amount of debt is offset by the present value of the expected financial distress costs created by the additional borrowing. From this point, we must make adjustments to reflect the influence of a number of factors that would justify a lower or higher debt-to-equity ratio. These factors are summarized in Exhibit 11.17.

The combined effect of all these factors on the firm's optimal capital structure and market value is practically impossible to estimate with any degree of precision. You will have to exercise a lot of judgment to determine a firm's appropriate capital structure. In making that judgment, the average debt ratio of similar firms in the sector is the best starting point for the analysis. These industry ratios, such as those shown in Exhibit 11.16, must then be adjusted upward or downward to reflect the firm's particular conditions and specific situation with respect to the factors surveyed in this section.

After a firm has established a desirable **target capital structure**, it should make financing decisions that are consistent with that target structure. This does not mean that the firm's actual debt ratio must always be equal to its target value. If a firm needs external funds, it does not necessarily need to issue debt and equity in the same proportion as dictated by the target debt ratio. Furthermore, financial market conditions may, at times, favor one type of financing over the other. This means that *firms may have to deviate temporarily from their target debt ratio*. The objective is to ensure that, *over time,* the firm's average debt ratio is close to its target value. And if the business and financial environments that led to the choice of a

EXHIBIT 11.17 FACTORS AFFECTING THE CAPITAL STRUCTURE DECISION.

Factors That Favor Borrowing	
Primary Factor	
Corporate income tax	Debt is a device that allows firms to reduce their corporate income tax because interest expenses are tax deductible, whereas dividends and retained earnings are not. However, the interest tax shield at the corporate level may be reduced by the impact of personal income taxes.
Important Secondary Factors	
Agency costs of equity	Debt is a device that helps *reduce* the agency costs of equity arising from the tendency of managers to make decisions that are not always in the best interest of shareholders. Debt increases the firm's value because debt servicing imposes focus and discipline on managers, who will then be less likely to "waste" shareholders' funds.
Retention of control	Debt allows current owners to retain control of the firm. This factor, however, may reduce share price because of the inability of outsiders to take over the company when its ownership is not dispersed.
Information asymmetry	Issuing debt instead of equity allows the firm to avoid the drop in share price that usually accompanies a new equity issue. This drop occurs because outside shareholders think that managers issue shares only when they believe the firm's shares are overvalued.

Factors That Discourage (Excessive) Borrowing	
Primary Factor	
Costs of financial distress	Excessive debt increases the probability that the firm will experience financial distress. And the higher the probability of financial distress, the larger the present value of the expected costs associated with financial distress and the lower the value of the firm. Firms that face higher probability of financial distress include companies with pre-tax operating profits that are cyclical and volatile, companies with a relatively large amount of intangible and illiquid assets, and companies with unique products and services or with products that require after-sale service and repair.
Important Secondary Factors	
Agency costs of debt	Additional borrowing comes with strings attached. Lenders impose increasingly constraining and costly protective covenants in new debt contracts to protect themselves against the potential misallocation of borrowed funds by managers acting on behalf of shareholders.
Dividend policy	Excessive debt may constrain the firm's ability to adopt a stable dividend policy.
Financial flexibility	Excessive debt may reduce the firm's financial flexibility, that is, its ability to quickly seize a value-creating investment opportunity.

particular target debt ratio change, the firm should adjust its target capital structure to reflect the new environment.

As a final note, we present two exhibits on the use of debt by U.S. firms. Exhibit 11.18 shows the changes in the debt ratio for a very large sample of nonfinancial corporations from 1945 up to 2007. Notice the steady decline in equity financing from around 75 percent of total financing in the late 1940s to close to 50 percent from the 1990s onward.

The last exhibit, Exhibit 11.19, shows the result of a survey among chief financial officers that indicates the most important factors they refer to when deciding the debt level of their companies: financial flexibility and avoidance of credit ratings downgrades seem to be a higher priority than the tax advantage of interest payment or the costs of financial distress.

SUMMARY

The choice of funds used to finance a firm's investments is important, and certain factors need to be taken into account when designing an optimal capital structure, namely, a capital structure that maximizes the firm's value and share price. Our analysis of the capital structure decision begins with how changes in the firm's debt-to-equity ratio affect the firm's profitability, measured by its earnings per share (EPS). By increasing its financial leverage (higher debt ratios), a firm can increase its *expected* EPS, but it must bear the increasing financial risk (wider swings in EPS) that accompanies higher levels of debt. Unfortunately, the EPS approach to capital structure—although providing useful insights about the capital structure decision—does not identify the ideal trade-off between higher expected EPS and wider fluctuations in EPS. We need to know how debt affects the firm's value.

The MM theory of capital structure provides a starting point for understanding how debt financing affects the firm's value. The theory says that, like a pizza whose size cannot be increased by slicing it, the value of a firm and its share price cannot be increased by changing the proportions of debt and equity in its capital structure, *provided there are no corporate income taxes.* According to this theory, developed by Modigliani and Miller, as the firm increases its financial leverage, the extra benefits accruing to shareholders from higher expected EPS is a compensation for the extra risk brought about by that leverage. Although the cost of equity increases with leverage, the firm's weighted average cost of capital (WACC), and thus the value of the firm's assets, do not change.

When corporate income taxes are considered, debt financing is definitely better than equity financing because the annual interest tax shield resulting from the tax deductibility of interest expenses provides value to shareholders. Similarly, the firm's WACC falls, and the value of the firm rises, as the relative amount of debt financing increases. However, if investors' revenues from equity investment (dividends and capital gains) are taxed at a lower rate than investors' income from holding the firm's debt, then the annual interest tax shield may be lower than predicted. Nevertheless, in a world with corporate income taxes, it appears initially that firms should maximize their value by financing their assets with close to 100 percent debt, which is an awkward policy, never observed in reality.

EXHIBIT 11.18 CAPITAL STRUCTURE OF NONFINANCIAL U.S. FIRMS.

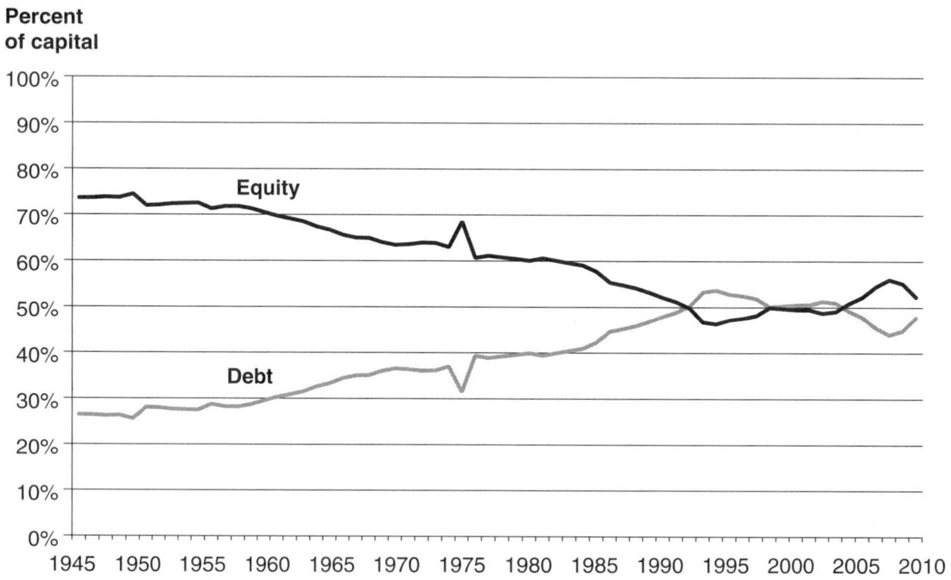

Source: The Board of Governors of the Federal Reserve System, *Flow of Funds Account.*

EXHIBIT 11.19 HOW FIRMS DECIDE ABOUT THEIR DEBT LEVEL.

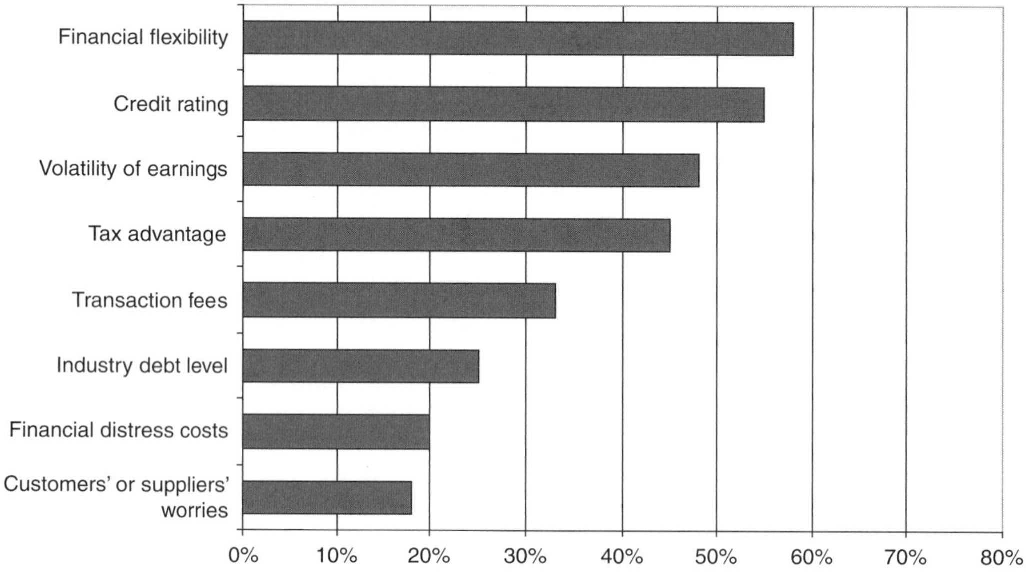

Source: Graham, John R., and Campbell R. Harvey. "How do CFOs make capital budgeting and capital structure decisions?" *The Journal of Applied Corporate Finance* 14, No. 4 (2002).

When financial distress costs are considered, high levels of debt financing become less desirable. Financial distress arises when the firm begins to encounter some difficulties in servicing its debt. When a firm is affected by financial distress, managers' ability to conduct business is impaired; acute conflicts of interest between managers, shareholders, and debt holders emerge; and customers, suppliers, and employees worry about the firm's capacity to meet its contractual obligations. All these factors generate increasing costs that reduce the firm's value as its debt ratio rises.

An optimal level of debt financing is reached when the marginal benefit derived from the interest tax shield is exactly compensated by the additional costs of financial distress. At this level of debt, the firm's WACC is at its lowest and the firm's assets and share price have reached their maximum value. This should be the firm's target debt ratio. This model of optimal financing is called the trade-off model of capital structure.

Finally, a number of additional factors (other than taxes and financial distress costs) need to be examined when formulating a firm's capital structure policy. These factors include the volatility of the firm's operating profits (in other words, its business risk), the type of assets the firm holds, the type of products and services it sells, the presence of agency costs associated with both equity and debt financing, the constraints imposed by dividend policy, the importance of asymmetric information between managers and outside investors, and the existence of a pecking order in the choice of financing sources.

Unfortunately, a formula does not exist that integrates all these factors to provide managers with their firm's optimal debt ratio. Designing the right capital structure involves more than applying formulas. It is the art of combining the conceptual framework provided here with judgment, insight, and timing to establish a viable debt ratio for the firm.

FURTHER READING

1. Brealey, Richard, Stewart Myers, and Franklin Allen. *Principles of Corporate Finance*, 9th ed. McGraw-Hill, 2008. See Chapters 18, 19, and 20.
2. Damodaran, Aswath. *Corporate Finance: Theory and Practice*, 2nd ed. John Wiley & Sons, 2001. See Chapters 17, 18, and 19.
3. Ross, Stephen, Randolph Westerfield, and Jeffrey Jaffe. *Corporate Finance*, 8th ed. McGraw-Hill Irwin, 2008. See Chapters 15, 16, and 30.
4. Shivdasani, Anil, and Mark Zenner. "How to Choose a Capital Structure: Navigating the Debt-Equity Decision." *Journal of Applied Corporate Finance* 17, no. 1 (Winter 2005).

SELF-TEST PROBLEMS

11.1 EFFECT OF BORROWING ON SHARE PRICE.

An increase in debt makes equity riskier because the volatility of the earnings per share increases with debt. Suppose there are no taxes and no financial distress costs. Does that necessarily mean that the share price of a firm must decrease when its indebtedness increases? Answer the same question as if there are taxes and financial distress costs.

11.2 RISK OF DEBT AND EQUITY AND RISK OF THE FIRM.

Increasing debt financing makes the firm's equity riskier. It also makes the firm's debt riskier, because the probability that the firm will default increases with more debt. Because both equity and debt become riskier, the risk of the firm as a whole should increase. True or false?

11.3 FACTORS AFFECTING THE OPTIMAL DEBT-TO-EQUITY RATIO.

Assume that the debt-to-equity ratio of Alternative Solutions Inc. is optimal. Under which of the following circumstances should the ratio be changed to still be optimal?

a. An increase in the corporate tax rate
b. An increase in the personal capital gains tax rate
c. The firm, which specializes in the development of software products, acquires an office building
d. Management believes strongly that their firm's shares are grossly undervalued
e. The firm's working capital requirement (the amount it invests in its operating cycle) keeps on decreasing
f. The firm is taken over by a competitor

11.4 EARNINGS BEFORE INTEREST AND TAX: EARNINGS PER SHARE ANALYSIS.

Albine Inc. has no debt. It has 10,000 shares of equity outstanding with a market price of $100. It is considering two alternative recapitalization plans. The low-debt plan calls for issuing $200,000 of debt, whereas the high-debt plan would imply issuing $400,000 of debt. In both cases, the cost of debt would be 10 percent. The firm does not pay any tax.

a. Earnings before interest and tax (EBIT) are projected to be either $90,000 or $170,000. What would be Albine's earnings per share (EPS) in both scenarios under each of the two refinancing plans? Suppose that both scenarios are equally likely so that the expected EBIT is $130,000. What would the expected EPS be?
b. If EBIT will be equal to $100,000, what would EPS be under each of the two recapitalization plans? Why are they the same?

11.5 THE VALUE OF THE INTEREST TAX SHIELD.

Ilbane Corp. has no debt, and the market value of its equity is $100 million. It can borrow at 5 percent. If the corporate tax rate is 35 percent, what will be the value of Ilbane Corp. if it borrows the following amounts and uses the proceeds to repurchase stock?

a. $20 million
b. $80 million

REVIEW PROBLEMS

1. **Earnings before interest and tax: Earnings per share analysis.**
Chloroline Inc. has 2 million shares outstanding and no debt. Earnings before interest and tax (EBIT) are projected to be $15 million under normal conditions, $5 million for a downturn in the economic environment, and $20 million for an economic expansion. Chloroline considers a debt issue of $50 million with an 8 percent interest rate. The proceeds would be used to buy back 1 million shares at the current market price of $50 a share. The corporate tax rate is 40 percent.
   a. Calculate Chloroline's earnings per share (EPS) and return on investment (EPS divided by share price) under the two scenarios, first before any new debt is issued and then after the recapitalization.
   b. From your answers to part a, would you recommend that Chloroline goes ahead with the recapitalization?

2. **Firm value and capital structure in the absence of tax.**
Assume a zero corporate tax rate. Because both the risk of a firm's equity and debt increase with debt financing, then the value of the firm should decrease when it uses more and more debt. True or false?

3. **Homemade leverage.**
Alberton Inc., an all-equity-financed equipment manufacturer, has announced that it will change its capital structure to one that will have 30 percent of debt, using the proceeds from the debt issue to buy back shares. The firm has 1 million shares outstanding and the share price is $60. Its operating margin, or earnings before interest and tax (EBIT), is expected to stay at its current level of $4 million in the foreseeable future. The interest rate on the debt that will be issued is 10 percent, and the firm does not pay any tax. Furthermore, Alberton has a dividend payout ratio of 100 percent, that is, all its earnings are distributed as dividends.
   a. Mr. Robert owns 140,000 shares of stock. How much Mr. Robert will receive every year from Alberton under the current capital structure?
   b. What will his cash flow be under the new capital structure, assuming that Mr. Robert keeps all of his shares?
   c. Why will the cash flow received by Mr. Robert under the new capital structure be lower than under the current one? What can he do to avoid this cash loss and keep getting the same cash flow from the amount he invested in Alberton?

4. **Cost of debt versus cost of equity.**
Because the cost of debt is lower than the cost of equity, firms must increase their use of debt as much as possible to increase the firm's value. What is your answer to this argument?
From the capital asset pricing model presented in Chapter 10, how can you show that the cost of equity changes with the use of debt?

5. **Changes in capital structure and the cost of capital.**
Starline & Co. has no debt, and its cost of equity is 14 percent. It can borrow at 8 percent. The corporate tax rate is 40 percent.
    a. Calculate the cost of equity and the weighted average cost of capital (WACC) of Starline if it decides to borrow up to the equivalent of 25, 50, 75, or 100 percent of its current equity. The proceeds would be used to buy back shares of the firm.
    b. Draw a graph showing how Starline's cost of equity, cost of debt, and WACC vary with the debt-to-equity ratio.
    c. On the basis of your results, would you recommend that Starline change its capital structure?

6. **The cost of equity, the weighted average cost of capital, and financial leverage.**
Albarval Co. expects its return on assets to be stable at 12 percent, assuming a target capital structure of 80 percent equity and 20 percent debt. Suppose that the firm's borrowing rate is 8 percent, for a wide range of capital structures.
    a. Suppose that Albarval does not pay any tax. What is Albarval's cost of equity? Hint: Refer to equation 11.2. What would Albarval's cost of equity be if the target capital structure is 50 percent equity, 50 percent debt? Show that under both capital structures the firm's weighted average cost of capital (WACC) is the same and that it is equal to 12 percent.
    b. Suppose now that the firm's tax rate is 40 percent. What is the cost of equity and the WACC under the two capital structures? Hint: Refer to equations 11.7 and 11.8. Why are the cost of equity and the WACC different under the two capital structures?

7. **The value of the interest tax shield.**
Lannion Co. is a manufacturing firm with no debt outstanding. It is considering borrowing $25 million at 8 percent and using the proceeds to buy back shares. Its equity market value is $100 million, and its profits are taxed at 35 percent.
    a. What would be the present value of the interest tax shield if the debt is permanent? If it matures in five years?
    b. What would be the present value of the interest tax shield if the interest rate increases to 9 percent immediately after the debt is issued?

8. **Industry influence on the capital structure.**
How would you rank these three firms in decreasing order of expected debt ratios: a biotechnology firm, an auto-parts firm, and an electric utility? Explain.

9. **Board of directors and management.**
Why are companies with a weak board of directors likely to be underlevered (they would use less debt than the optimal amount they could issue)?

10. **Agency costs.**
How can shareholders expropriate wealth from bondholders?

VALUING AND ACQUIRING A BUSINESS

CHAPTER 12

Should you replace an existing piece of equipment with a newer, more efficient one? Build a plant to launch a new product? Acquire a competitor? You should go ahead with these investments only if you are sufficiently confident that undertaking them will raise your firm's market value. This occurs only if the estimated *value* of the assets purchased is higher than the *price* paid to buy them. This chapter shows how to value a business. The business can be either an entire firm or only part of a firm, such as one of its divisions. In the valuation of an entire firm, we must distinguish between the value of the firm's assets and the value of its equity, where the value of equity represents the claims of shareholders on the firm's assets. Obviously, these values are related, because the value of a firm's equity is the difference between the value of its assets and the value of its debts. The value of a division is simply the value of the division's assets.

The most common application of business valuation is the estimation of the price at which the shares of a firm can be acquired. For example, in a takeover, one firm (the bidding company) wants to acquire all or a portion of another firm's shares and needs to determine the price at which the shares of the target firm should be bought. The target firm may be a public firm whose shares are traded and quoted in a stock exchange, or it may be a privately held company with no quoted price. To decide if the acquisition is a value-creating proposal, the bidding firm needs to determine how much the target firm's shares are worth to it (the bidder). If the shares of the target firm are quoted at \$20 a share and the bidder estimates their value at \$30, buying them for *less* than \$30 is a value-creating decision. In this case, the acquisition is a value-creating investment because the shares are worth *more* to the *bidding* firm than the price it has to pay for them. Any acquisition price *above* an average price of \$30 per share is a value-destroying acquisition because the shares are worth *less* to the *bidder* than the price it has to pay for them.

An *initial public offering* (IPO) is another typical situation that requires the valuation of a company's equity. In an IPO, a privately held company is considering issuing shares to the public for the first time. An offer price that will ensure the success of the sale to the public must be estimated. A similar situation occurs when state-owned firms are privatized, that is, sold to the public.

After a brief introduction to the main valuation methods, this chapter focuses on the methods that are most commonly used. First, we present *valuation by comparables,* which values a firm using stock market data on firms similar to the business or the firm we want to value. As an illustration, we apply the method to the valuation of Office Supplies (OS) Distributors, a firm we analyze in Chapters 2–5. Then, we present the *discounted cash-flow* (DCF) approach, which values a firm's assets by discounting the future cash flows expected from these assets. The estimated value of the firm's equity is the difference between the estimated value of its assets and the value of its debts. We show how the method can be implemented by estimating two different values of OS Distributors' equity: (1) its *"stand-alone"* or *"as-is"* value and (2) its value as an acquisition target (its target value). We examine in detail the sources of value creation in an acquisition and show how to estimate them. We also describe why a conglomerate merger, which is the combination of unrelated businesses, is not likely to create value. Finally, we present the *adjusted present value* (APV) method, a variation of the DCF approach. OS Distributors is again used to illustrate this method, this time as a *leveraged buyout* (LBO) target, meaning that the firm's assets will be financed with an unusually high proportion of debt. After reading this chapter, you should understand the following:

- The alternative methods used to value businesses and how to apply them in practice to estimate the value of a company
- Why some companies acquire other firms
- How to value a potential acquisition
- Why a high proportion of acquisitions usually fail to deliver value to the shareholders of the acquiring firm
- Leveraged buyout deals and how they are put together

ALTERNATIVE VALUATION METHODS

Suppose the asking price of a 2,000-square-foot house you wish to buy is $220,000. You want to find out whether $220,000 is a fair price for this piece of property. There are two basic ways to estimate the value of the house. First, you can find the selling price of a *similar* house. A real estate agent tells you that a 1,500-square-foot house on the same street sold for $150,000 last week. What can you conclude? The comparable house was sold for $100 per square foot ($150,000 divided by 1,500 square feet). Applying that rate to the house you want to buy gives a value of $200,000 (2,000 square feet times $100 per square foot), $20,000 less than the asking price of $220,000. You have just estimated the value of the house using a method called **valuation by comparables**. By comparing a company with similar firms in its sector, the same procedure can be used to value that company.

The second approach to estimating the value of the house is to determine its rental value. The real estate agent says that you could expect an annual net rental income of $21,000 for the house. This amount needs to be compared with what you could earn on your savings if you did not buy the house. An investment in long-term, high-grade corporate bonds, which you consider as risky as owning this particular house, is currently offering a 10 percent annual return. How much should you pay for the house to earn the same 10 percent return based on a $21,000 annual rental income? The answer is $210,000 (because an annual rate of 10 percent applied to $210,000 yields an income of $21,000 per year). You have just estimated the value of the house using the **discounted cash-flow (DCF) valuation** method. If rented, the house will generate a constant annual cash flow of $21,000. Discounting this cash-flow stream at a required rate of return of 10 percent provides a DCF value of $210,000. This estimated value is $10,000 less than the asking price of $220,000.

Recall that the **comparables** approach produced an estimated value of $200,000. Different valuation methods usually lead to different estimations, but the differences should not be too large. If different methods produce a wide spread in estimated values (say, more than 20 percent), the validity of the assumptions underlying the alternative methods and the reliability of the data used in the valuation process should be checked. For example, the other house on the street should be as similar as possible to the one you want to buy (ideally, it should be identical), and the 10 percent return on long-term high-grade corporate bonds should be a good substitute for your required return on the rented house (these two investments should have similar risk characteristics). Poorly estimated input data will lead to unreliable estimated values. (Remember GIGO, "garbage in, garbage out.")

To conclude, what should you offer for the house? An offer between $200,000 and $210,000 would be reasonable, based on your estimates. A higher offer would exceed your estimated values and produce an investment with a negative *net present value* (NPV), that is, an investment whose price is higher than its estimated value. Of course, it would be best to buy the house at the lowest possible price. But if the real estate market is reasonably efficient, it has few real bargains to offer.

Although valuation by comparables and DCF valuation are the most common approaches to valuing a business, they are not the only methods. Two other possible estimated values are the **liquidation value** and the **replacement value** of a firm's assets. The liquidation value of a firm's assets is the amount of cash you would receive if you sold separately the various items that make up the firm's assets (its trade receivables, inventories, equipment, land, and buildings). The replacement value of a firm's assets is what it would cost today to replace these assets with similar ones to start a new business with the same earning power as the one you wish to purchase. Clearly, the liquidation value of a business is the *minimum* price you would expect to pay for its assets. If you could buy the assets for less than their liquidation value and resell them immediately at that value, you would earn a sure profit, a situation unlikely to occur in a properly functioning market. Although the replacement value of a *tangible* asset, such as a building, is the *maximum* price you would pay for it—you would not pay more for a building than what it would cost to build a similar one—you may be ready to offer a higher price for a business if it has some *intangible* assets that are valuable to you and that cannot be replaced, such as patents or trademarks.

VALUING A FIRM'S EQUITY USING COMPARABLE FIRMS

OS Distributors is an unlisted, privately owned firm whose financial performance is analyzed in Chapters 2–5. The balance sheets of OS Distributors, a nationwide distributor of office equipment and supplies, are reported in Exhibit 12.1 at the

EXHIBIT 12.1 OS DISTRIBUTORS' BALANCE SHEETS.

FIGURES IN MILLIONS

	December 31, 2008		December 31, 2009		December 31, 2010	
Assets						
• **Current assets**						
Cash[1]		$ 6.0		$ 12.0		$ 8.0
Accounts receivable		44.0		48.0		56.0
Inventories		52.0		57.0		72.0
Prepaid expenses[2]		2.0		2.0		1.0
Total current assets		**104.0**		**119.0**		**137.0**
• **Noncurrent assets**						
Financial assets and intangibles		0.0		0.0		0.0
Property, plant, and equipment						
Gross value[3]	$90.0		$90.0		$93.0	
less accumulated depreciation	(34.0)	56.0	(39.0)	51.0	(40.0)	53.0
Total noncurrent assets		56.0		51.0		53.0
Total assets		**$160.0**		**$170.0**		**$190.0**
Liabilities and owners' equity						
• **Current liabilities**						
Short-term debt		$ 15.0		$ 22.0		$ 23.0
Owed to banks	$ 7.0		$14.0		$15.0	
Current portion of long-term debt	8.0		8.0		8.0	
Accounts payable		37.0		40.0		48.0
Accrued expenses[4]		2.0		4.0		4.0
Total current liabilities		**54.0**		**66.0**		**75.0**
• **Noncurrent liabilities**						
Long-term debt[5]		42.0		34.0		38.0
Total noncurrent liabilities		**42.0**		**34.0**		**38.0**
• **Owners' equity**[6]		64.0		70.0		77.0
Total liabilities and owners' equity		**$160.0**		**$170.0**		**$190.0**

[1]Consists of cash in hand and checking accounts held to facilitate operating activities on which the firm earns no interest.
[2]Prepaid expenses is rent paid in advance (when recognized in the income statement, rent is included in selling, general, and administrative expenses).
[3]In 2009, there was no disposal of existing fixed assets or acquisition of new fixed assets. However, during 2010, a warehouse was enlarged at a cost of $12 million and existing fixed assets, bought for $9 million in the past, were sold at their net book value of $2 million.
[4]Accrued expenses consist of wages and taxes payable.
[5]Long-term debt is repaid at the rate of $8 million per year. No new long-term debt was incurred during 2009, but during 2010, a mortgage loan was obtained from the bank to finance the extension of a warehouse (see Note 3).
[6]During the three years, no new shares were issued and none were repurchased.

EXHIBIT 12.2 OS DISTRIBUTORS' INCOME STATEMENTS.

FIGURES IN MILLIONS

	2008	2009	2010
• **Net sales**	**$390.0**	**$420.0**	**$480.0**
Cost of goods sold	328.0	353.0	400.0
• **Gross profit**	**62.0**	**67.0**	**80.0**
Selling, general, and administrative expenses	39.8	43.7	48.0
Depreciation expense	5.0	5.0	8.0
• **Operating profit**	**17.2**	**18.3**	**24.0**
Special items	0.0	0.0	0.0
• **Earnings before interest and tax (EBIT)**	**17.2**	**18.3**	**24.0**
Net interest expense[1]	5.5	5.0	7.0
• **Earnings before tax (EBT)**	**11.7**	**13.3**	**17.0**
Income tax expense	4.7	5.3	6.8
• **Earnings after tax (EAT)**	**$ 7.0**	**$ 8.0**	**$ 10.2**
Dividends	$ 2.0	$ 2.0	$ 3.2
Addition to retained earnings	$ 5.0	$ 6.0	$ 7.0

[1]There is no interest income, so net interest expense is equal to interest expense.

end of years 2008, 2009, and 2010. Its income statements for the years 2008, 2009, and 2010 are presented in Exhibit 12.2. We want to estimate the equity value of OS Distributors in early January 2011 (which we assume to be the same as the end of December 2010).

The balance sheet at year-end 2010 indicates that the company's accounting, or book, value of equity is $77 million. This value, recorded as "owners' equity" at the bottom of the balance sheet, measures the *net* cumulative amount of equity capital the firm's shareholders have invested in the company since the company was first established. It is a measure of the aggregate amount of net equity capital injected into the firm over time, up to the date of the balance sheet. It is *not* a measure of what shareholders would expect to receive from the sale of their shares. Nor is it a measure of what the firm's equity would be worth if it was listed on a stock market.

The firm has a recent record of steadily increasing profits and dividend payments, and it is likely this trend will continue in the future. Thus, the *market value* of OS Distributors' equity, which is the price it would sell for, should be higher than its book value of $77 million. Because the ownership of a share in a firm's equity entitles the shareholder to receive *future* dividend payments as well as a share of any *future* appreciation in the firm's value, the equity value that matters to investors is the market value, not the book value. The book value of equity, which reflects *past* earnings performance and *past* dividend distributions, is relevant only to the extent that it provides some useful information about the *firm's future* performance.

DIRECT ESTIMATION OF A FIRM'S EQUITY VALUE BASED ON THE EQUITY VALUE OF COMPARABLE FIRMS

What would the value of OS Distributors' equity be if the firm was listed on a stock market? One way to estimate this value is to use data from comparable firms whose shares are listed on a stock exchange. The first step is to identify these companies. One of these companies is General Equipment and Supplies (GES). GES is also a distributor of office equipment and supplies. It is larger than OS Distributors but is similar in asset and cost structures.[1]

Exhibit 12.3 shows comparable accounting and financial market data for the two companies. Items 1 to 8 are from the companies' financial statements. Items 9 and 10 correspond to items 7 and 3 restated on a per share basis. Item 11 is the market price of a share in early January 2011, which is available only for GES.

Using this information, we can calculate the following two ratios for GES (these are items 14 and 15 in Exhibit 12.3):

$$\text{Price-to-earnings ratio} = \frac{\text{Share price}}{\text{Earnings per share}} = \frac{\$20}{\$0.8} = 25$$

$$\text{Price-to-book ratio} = \frac{\text{Share price}}{\text{Book value per share}} = \frac{\$20}{\$6.36} = 3.14$$

These two ratios depend on GES's share price, which is determined by the market. This is why these ratios are also referred to as **market multiples** or **equity multiples**. The **price-to-earnings ratio** (or **P/E ratio**) of twenty-five times is also called GES's **earnings multiple**. It indicates that GES's shares were trading in early January 2011 at a price equal to twenty-five times the firm's most recent **earnings per share (EPS)** (twenty-five times \$0.80 equals \$20). The **price-to-book ratio** (or **P/B ratio**) of 3.14 is also called GES's **book-value multiple**. It indicates that GES's shares were trading in early January 2011 at a price equal to 3.14 times GES's most recent book value per share (3.14 times \$6.36 equals \$20).

Could we construct another multiple by taking, for example, the ratio of share price to earnings before interest and tax (EBIT) per share? Would this make sense? Not really, because this ratio would relate only the firm's operational contribution to its share price (recall that EBIT is a measure of earnings from operations) when we know that share price is also affected by nonoperational decisions, such as financing decisions. Note that the two multiples discussed above are consistent because they are defined as the ratio of share price to an accounting number that incorporates all the firm's decisions that affect its share price, either earnings after tax (EAT) per share (EAT is net profit to equity holders) or book value of equity per share.

These market multiples are called **historical**, or **trailing, multiples**. They are calculated using *past* earnings and book values. If we had a forecast of the earnings or book value for the *next* period, we could have calculated **expected**, or **prospective, multiples.**

We can now estimate the equity value of OS Distributors based on the comparable market multiples of GES. According to this approach, *comparable firms*

---

[1]If we could not find a firm similar enough to OS Distributors, we would have compared OS Distributors with the wholesale merchandise sector.

EXHIBIT 12.3 ACCOUNTING AND MARKET-BASED DATA FOR OS DISTRIBUTORS AND GES, A COMPARABLE FIRM.

	GES	OS Distributors
Accounting data (2010)		
Balance sheet data		
1. Cash	$70 million	$8 million
2. Debt	$430 million	$61 million
3. Book value of equity	$318 million	$77 million
4. Number of shares outstanding	50 million shares	10 million shares
Income statement data		
5. EBIT[1]	$102 million	$24 million
6. Depreciation expense	$33 million	$8 million
7. EAT[2]	$40 million	$10.2 million
8. EBITDA[3] = EBIT + Depreciation expense	$135 million	$32 million
On a per-share basis		
9. Earnings per share (EPS) = [(7)/(4)]	$0.80	$1.02
10. Book value of equity per share = [(3)/(4)]	$6.36	$7.70
Market-based data (January 2011)		
11. Share price	$20	Not available
12. Market capitalization[4] = [(11) × (4)]	$1,000 million	Not available
13. Enterprise value (EV) = [(12) + (2) − (1)]	$1,360 million	Not available
Multiples		
14. Price-to-earnings ratio (P/E) = [(11)/(9)]	25.00	Not available
15. Price-to-book ratio (P/B) = [(11)/(10)]	3.14	Not available
16. EV-to-EBITDA ratio = [(13)/(8)]	10.10	Not available

[1]EBIT = Earnings before interest and tax.
[2]EAT = Earnings after tax (same as net income).
[3]EBITDA is an approximation of the firm's cash flow from assets (see Chapter 4).
[4]Market capitalization is the total market value of a company's equity at a given date; it is equal to its share price on that day multiplied by the total number of shares the company has issued.

should trade at the same market multiples (historical or expected). In other words, if OS Distributors is similar to GES, then GES's market multiples can be used to estimate the value that OS Distributors' equity would have if it were listed on a stock market.[2] This is the same procedure we used to estimate the value of the

[2]No two firms are exactly the same. We know that GES is significantly larger than OS Distributors. Furthermore, GES is a listed company known to the market, whereas OS Distributors is not. This means that OS Distributors' (unobservable) multiples would most likely not be identical to those of GES. Applying GES multiples to OS Distributors' earnings and book value figures provides approximate values.

house in the previous section using the price per square foot of the comparable house. For OS Distributors (OSD), we have the following two estimates of equity value:

$$\begin{aligned}\text{Estimated equity value of OSD} &= [\text{OSD's EAT}] \times [\text{GES's P/E ratio}] \\ &= [\$10.2 \text{ million}] \times [25] \\ &= \$255 \text{ million}\end{aligned}$$

$$\begin{aligned}\text{Estimated equity value of OSD} &= [\text{OSD's Book value}] \times [\text{GES's P/B ratio}] \\ &= [\$77 \text{ million}] \times [3.14] \\ &= \$242 \text{ million}\end{aligned}$$

These two estimates of OS Distributors' equity value are based on GES's historical market multiples. The highest is $255 million and the lowest $242 million. As pointed out earlier, different valuation approaches usually produce different estimated values. Valuation is not a precise exercise, and as long as the spread is within a reasonable range, you should not be concerned. The highest estimated value for OS Distributors ($255 million) is 5.4 percent higher than the lowest estimated value ($242 million), a relatively narrow spread.

Is one multiple more appropriate than the other? Some analysts recommend the use of a particular multiple to value certain types of businesses, suggesting, for example, earnings multiples for industrial companies and book-value multiples for financial services firms, such as banks and insurance companies.

Which one of these two estimated values should we take for OS Distributors' equity? We will answer this question after we estimate the equity value of OS Distributors using two other valuation methods. Before we do this, we first examine the factors that explain the magnitude of earnings multiples. For example, why is the P/E ratio of GES equal to 25 and not a higher or lower number?

FACTORS THAT DETERMINE EARNINGS MULTIPLES

This section reviews the factors that affect the P/E ratio (Chapter 15 looks at the P/B ratio; see Appendix 15.2).

The value of a company is affected by the general market environment, such as the prevailing level of interest rates, and by factors unique to that company, such as its expected growth and the perceived risk of its future earnings. Companies with *higher* expected rates of *growth* in earnings and *lower* perceived *risk* in earnings (earnings that will not deviate much from their expected value) usually have relatively higher values and thus trade at *higher* multiples. The reason is straightforward: because investors prefer higher growth to lower growth and less risk to more risk, high-growth, low-risk companies have higher values than low-growth, high-risk companies. This phenomenon is illustrated later in this chapter. In addition to the growth and risk of earnings, the other factor that affects P/E ratios is the level of interest rates: everything else the same, the *lower* the rate of interest, the *higher* the market multiples because investors can borrow at attractive rates to purchase shares of companies.

Accounting rules and tax regulations also affect multiples. To illustrate the effect on P/E ratios, consider the stock market multiples shown in Exhibit 12.4. These are P/E ratios for an index of firms listed in each of the three countries' stock

Exhibit 12.4 Earnings Multiples in the U.S., U.K., and Japanese Equity Markets on January 21, 2010.[1]

	United States	United Kingdom	Japan
Price-to-earnings ratio[2]	22.2	12.3	35.9

[1]Source: *ThomsonReuters* (reported in the *Financial Times*, January 25, 2010).
[2]Based on a sample of stocks that covers at least 75 percent of each market capitalization. Losses are excluded from the calculations of the price-to-earnings ratios.

exchanges in January 2010. What factors can explain why the Tokyo market has an earnings multiple significantly higher than the one prevailing in New York or London? Relatively small differences between the expected rates of growth in earnings and the level of interest rates in Japan compared with the United States or the United Kingdom cannot explain the wide differences between these countries' market multiples. The other factors at play are accounting conventions and tax regulations.

The magnitude of after-tax profits reported by companies is affected by accounting and tax rules. In some countries, such as Japan, companies are allowed to depreciate their assets rapidly and make generous provisions against potential losses. The result is *lower* after-tax profits and *higher* earnings multiples (recall that an earnings multiple is share price *divided* by net profit per share) than in countries whose tax laws do not provide similar advantages, such as the United States and the United Kingdom. When comparing the value of companies in different countries, analysts usually try to eliminate the distortions created by differences in accounting rules and taxation across countries; otherwise, the comparison would not be meaningful. We present in the next section an alternative valuation ratio that addresses some of these issues.

Indirect Estimation of a Firm's Equity Value Based on the Enterprise Value of Comparable Firms

In the previous section, we presented two *direct* estimates of a firm's equity value based on two different equity multiples of a comparable firm. There is an alternative, *indirect* method to estimate a firm's equity value: we first get an estimate of the value of the firm's *assets* from which we deduct the value of the firm's *debt* to obtain an indirect value of the firm's *equity*. We first illustrate this method using the data from OS Distributors and GES, its comparable firm, in Exhibit 12.3. We then explain the logic of the indirect method and its advantages over the direct approach.

The first step is to estimate the value of the **business assets** of the comparable firm. This is the value of the firm's assets *excluding* cash and other financial assets the firm may hold. It is called the firm's **enterprise value** (EV). Equation 12.1 below and Exhibit 12.5 show how to calculate a firm's enterprise value:

Enterprise value (EV) = Equity value + Debt − Cash and other financial assets (12.1)

EXHIBIT 12.5 GES ENTERPRISE VALUE BASED ON DATA IN EXHIBIT 12.3.

GES MARKET VALUE BALANCE SHEET

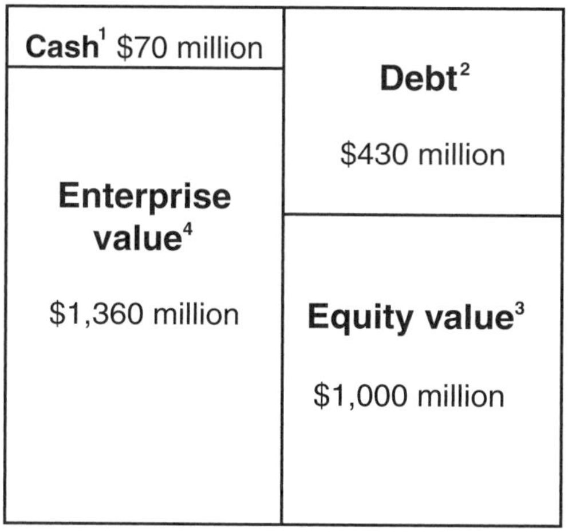

[1]The only financial asset GES has is cash: see item 1 in Exhibit 12.3.
[2]Interest-bearing debt has a market value equal to its book value. See item 2 in Exhibit 12.3 and footnote 11 on page 417.
[3]Equity value is the market capitalization of GES: see item 12 in Exhibit 12.3.
[4]Enterprise value is the value of assets *excluding* cash and other financial assets. We can write:
Enterprise value = Equity value + Debt – Cash = $1,360 million.

In the case of GES, equity value (also called **market capitalization**) is $1,000 million (item 12 in Exhibit 12.3), debt is $430 million (item 2 in Exhibit 12.3), and cash is $70 million (item 1 in Exhibit 12.3). Using equation 12.1, we find an enterprise value of $1,360 million for GES (item 13 in Exhibit 12.3).

The second step is to calculate GES's **earnings before interest, tax, depreciation, and amortization (EBITDA)**. EBITDA is equal to EBIT plus depreciation and amortization (see Chapter 4). In the case of GES, there is no amortization, and its EBITDA of $135 million is equal to EBIT plus depreciation expense (item 8 in Exhibit 12.3).

The third step is to calculate the ratio of GES's enterprise value to EBITDA, also called the **EBITDA multiple:**

$$\text{Enterprise value-to-EBITDA multiple} = \frac{\text{EV}}{\text{EBITDA}} = \frac{\$1{,}360 \text{ million}}{\$135 \text{ million}} = 10.1$$

The fourth step is to apply this **asset multiple** to the EBITDA of OS Distributors ($32 million; item 8 in Exhibit 12.3) to get an estimate of the enterprise value of OS Distributors (OSD):

$$\begin{aligned}\text{Enterprise value of OSD} &= [\text{OSD's EBITDA}] \times [\text{GES's EBITDA multiple}] \\ &= [\$32 \text{ million}] \times [10.1] = \$323 \text{ million}\end{aligned}$$

The final step is to add cash and other financial assets to this enterprise value and deduct debt to obtain an *indirect* estimate of the firm's equity value:

Equity value = Enterprise value + Cash and other financial assets – Debt (12.2)

Applying the above to the case of OS Distributors (OSD), we get the following (the data are from Exhibit 12.3):

Equity value of OSD = \$323 million + \$8 million – \$61 million
= \$270 million

This *indirect* estimate of OS Distributors' equity value is higher than those obtained with the direct method but still within an acceptable range. It is 12 percent higher than the lowest of the two direct equity values we found earlier (\$242 million, based on the book-value multiple of GES).

What are the advantages of using an asset multiple, such as the Enterprise value/EBITDA ratio, over an equity multiple such as the P/E ratio? Suppose you want to compare the values of a number of Telecom companies that have *different* debt ratios and *different* effective tax rates. In this case, the P/E ratio approach may not provide a good estimate of equity value because that ratio assumes that the firms have similar debt ratios and tax rates (recall that earnings in the P/E ratio are measured *after* interest payment and taxes). In this case, however, because the Enterprise value/EBITDA ratio ignores debt and tax rates (EBITDA are measured *before* interest and tax payments), it provides more reliable estimates.

VALUING A FIRM'S BUSINESS ASSETS AND EQUITY USING THE DISCOUNTED CASH-FLOW APPROACH

Before we estimate the value of OS Distributors using the general discounted cash-flow (DCF) approach, we examine a simpler case to explain the logic behind DCF valuation and to identify the data required to obtain the DCF value of a firm's business assets (its enterprise value) and equity.

ESTIMATING THE DCF VALUE OF A FIRM'S BUSINESS ASSETS (ITS ENTERPRISE VALUE)

According to the DCF method, *the value of an asset is determined by the capacity of that asset to generate future cash flows.* When a buyer purchases a company's assets, he acquires the entire stream of cash flows these assets are *expected* to produce in the future. In other words, owning an asset is the same as owning the entire stream of cash flows that asset is expected to generate in the *future.* How are these cash flows estimated and how are they valued?

Consider the case of the National Engineering Company (NEC). Next year, its business assets will generate a cash flow of either \$110 or \$90 with a 50 percent chance that each of the cash flows will occur. The average, or expected, value of that risky cash flow is \$100 (one-half of \$110 plus one-half of \$90). Let's assume that this expected cash flow (CF_1) will then grow forever at a constant annual rate (g) of 4 percent and that NEC's weighted average cost of capital is 8 percent (see Chapter 10). Given these inputs, what should be the value today of NEC's business assets?

We show in Appendix 9.1 in Chapter 9 that the present value (which is the same as the DCF value), at a required rate of return k, of a cash flow CF_1 that grows forever at the rate g is as follows:[3]

$$\textbf{DCF value(constant growth)} = \frac{CF_1}{k - g} \tag{12.3}$$

Note that the expected cash flow (CF_1) on the numerator is the cash flow that is expected to occur at the *end* of the year. Applying this *constant-growth formula* to value NEC's business assets, we get the following:

$$\text{DCF value of NEC's assets(Enterprise Value)} = \frac{CF_1}{k - g} = \frac{\$100}{0.08 - 0.04} = \$2{,}500$$

where the required rate of return (k) is NEC's weighted average cost of capital of 8 percent (we explain this later).

THE EFFECT OF THE GROWTH OF CASH FLOWS ON THEIR DCF VALUE

Assume that the growth rate of NEC's cash flows is now zero instead of 4 percent. What is NEC's enterprise value in this case? With a zero growth rate, the DCF value of NEC's business assets drops from \$2,500 to \$1,250:

$$\text{NEC's enterprise value(zero growth)} = \frac{CF_1}{k} = \frac{\$100}{0.08} = \$1{,}250$$

Thus, reducing the growth rate from 4 percent to zero cuts NEC's enterprise value by 50 percent (from \$2,500 to \$1,250). This shows how sensitive the DCF value of a cash-flow stream is to its assumed future rate of growth. In general, *the faster the growth rate of the cash flows, the higher their DCF value*. We return to this observation when we value OS Distributors later in the chapter.

THE EFFECT OF THE RISK ASSOCIATED WITH CASH FLOWS ON THEIR DCF VALUE

Assume now that NEC's cash flow (CF_1) takes the values of either \$120 or \$80 with a 50 percent chance of occurrence for each (instead of \$110 and \$90). The *expected* value of the cash flow is still \$100 (one-half of \$120 plus one-half of \$80). It is now riskier, however, because its two outcomes are farther away from their average value. In other words, the spread or volatility in the cash flows is wider. Because the cash flow is now riskier, investors (shareholders and debt holders) require a higher rate of return to compensate them for the higher risk. As a consequence, let's assume that the discount rate (k) rises to 9 percent (from 8 percent) to reflect the higher risk. At this rate, the DCF value of NEC's assets is as follows:

$$\text{NEC's enterprise value} = \frac{CF_1}{k - g} = \frac{\$100}{0.09 - 0.04} = \$2{,}000$$

---

[3]The growth rate g must be smaller than k for the formula to hold. If g is higher than k, the cash flows are growing at a faster rate than the rate k at which they are discounted back to the present. In this case, the value of the company becomes infinitely large.

The DCF value of the cash-flow stream is 20 percent lower with the riskier expected cash flow ($2,000 instead of $2,500). In general, the *higher the risk of a cash-flow stream, the lower its DCF value.*

A GENERAL FORMULA TO ESTIMATE A FIRM'S ENTERPRISE VALUE

The cash flows generated by a firm's business assets usually do not grow at a constant rate forever. We need a valuation formula that gives the present value of a stream of future cash flows that is applicable to any growth pattern. This valuation formula, which we use in Chapter 6 to estimate the present value of an investment, is expressed as follows:

$$\text{DCF value} = \frac{CFA_1}{1+k} + \frac{CFA_2}{(1+k)^2} + \ldots + \frac{CFA_t}{(1+k)^t} + \ldots \tag{12.4}$$

where CFA_1, CFA_2, ..., CFA_t, ... are the cash flows that the firm's business assets are expected to generate, and k is the rate of return required to invest in these assets. These cash flows are also called **free cash flows (FCF)**, but because analysts have different definitions of free cash flow, we prefer the more explicit term **cash flow from business assets (CFA)**. *The present value of a firm's expected future CFAs is its enterprise value.* The estimation of these cash flows is presented in Chapter 4, and the estimation of the risk-adjusted discount rate (k) is discussed in Chapter 10. We briefly review these topics in the remainder of this section.

ESTIMATING THE CASH FLOWS GENERATED BY BUSINESS ASSETS

CFA is the cash flow generated by the firm's asset-based activities, namely, from the firm's *operating* and *investing* activities. This cash flow *excludes* any items related to the firm's *financing* activities, such as interest or dividend payments. We show in Chapter 4 (see equation 4.5) that this cash flow is expressed as follows:

$$\begin{aligned}\textbf{CFA} = &\ \textbf{EBIT}(\textbf{1} - \textbf{T}_\textbf{C}) + \textbf{Depreciation expense} \\ &- \boldsymbol{\Delta}\textbf{WCR} - \textbf{Net capital expenditure}\end{aligned} \tag{12.5}$$

where EBIT is earnings before interest and tax, T_C is the corporate income tax rate, and ΔWCR is the *change* in working capital requirement. Recall that WCR is the firm's investment in its operating cycle (see Chapter 3). It is measured by taking the difference between the firm's operating assets (accounts receivable plus inventories plus prepaid expenses related to operations, if any) and the firm's operating liabilities (accounts payable plus accrued expenses related to operations, if any).

We can use equation 12.5 to find the cash flow generated by NEC's business assets. Suppose next year's EBIT is expected to be $180, the tax rate is 40 percent, depreciation expense is $20, the change in WCR is $4, and **net capital expenditure** is $24. In this case, we have the following:

$$CFA = \$180(1 - 40\%) + \$20 - \$4 - \$24 = \$100$$

which is the value we used for CF_1 in equation 12.3.

ESTIMATING THE RATE OF RETURN REQUIRED TO DISCOUNT THE CASH FLOWS

We show in Chapter 10 that the *minimum* rate of return that should be used to discount the cash flows generated by business assets must be equal to the cost of financing these assets. For example, if the cost of financing an asset is 8 percent, then the required return on investment in this asset must be at least 8 percent, otherwise the investment will not cover the cost of financing it. What, then, is the cost of financing an asset? This cost depends on the sources of capital employed (equity capital and borrowed funds) and their respective proportions and costs. It is the **weighted average cost of capital (WACC)**, which is analyzed in detail in Chapter 10. The WACC is defined as follows:

$$\text{WACC} = \left(\frac{\textbf{Equity}}{\textbf{Equity + Debt}} \times k_E\right) + \left(\frac{\textbf{Debt}}{\textbf{Equity + Debt}} \times k_D(\textbf{1 - Tax rate})\right) \quad (12.6)$$

where k_E is the estimated cost of equity, k_D is the estimated pre-tax cost of debt, and the weights are the respective proportions of equity and debt used to finance the asset.

Suppose that 66 percent of NEC's business assets are financed with equity capital at an estimated cost of 10 percent and 34 percent are borrowed at a cost of 7 percent (the interest rate the bank will charge). If the tax rate is 40 percent, NEC's WACC is equal to the following:

$$\text{WACC} = [66\% \times 10\%] + [34\% \times 7\%(1 - 40\%)] = 8\%$$

We estimated NEC's cost of equity capital at 10 percent using the capital asset pricing model (CAPM) discussed in Chapter 10. According to the CAPM, the rate of return required by equity investors (which is the same as the firm's cost of equity) is equal to the rate of return they can get from investing in a *riskless* government bond (R_F) plus a risk premium that will compensate them for the risk of holding the firm's shares. That risk premium is estimated by multiplying the firm's **beta coefficient** (β)[4] by the market risk premium (which is the risk premium of the entire stock market). We can write:

$$\boldsymbol{k_E = R_F + (\textbf{Market risk premium} \times \beta)} \quad (12.7)$$

Suppose that the yield on ten-year government bonds is 4.8 percent and the *historical* market risk premium is 4 percent, meaning that in the past, on average, the market returns exceeded the yield on government bonds by 4 percent. Let's say that NEC's estimated beta is 1.3. Inserting these three figures ($R_F = 4.8\%$, market risk premium = 4%, and $\beta = 1.3$) into the CAPM formula (equation 12.7) provides an estimate of NEC's cost of equity. We have the following:

$$k_E = 4.8\% + (4\% \times 1.3) = 4.8\% + 5.2\% = 10\%$$

which is the cost of equity we used in equation 12.6 to get NEC's WACC of 8 percent.

[4]A company's beta coefficient is a measure of the sensitivity of its stock returns to the overall market movements. By definition, the market has a beta of one. Companies whose stock returns fluctuate *more* than the overall market movements are riskier than the market and have betas higher than one. Those with stock returns that fluctuate *less* than the overall market movements are less risky than the market and have betas that are less than one (see Chapter 10). For example, if a company has a beta of 1.50, it means that, on *average*, when the market rises (drops) by 1 percent, the company's share price increases (decreases) by 1.5 percent.

ESTIMATING THE DCF VALUE OF A FIRM'S EQUITY

The preceding analysis produced an enterprise value of $2,500 for NEC by discounting next year's expected cash flow (CF_1) from business assets of $100 at a WACC of 8 percent, assuming a constant growth rate of 4 percent. However, buying a firm's *assets* is not the same as buying its *equity*. Suppose NEC has $100 of cash and $900 of debt outstanding (debt it has not yet repaid). If a company buys NEC's equity from its existing owners, it will own NEC's assets, *including* its cash holding of $100, and will also assume NEC's existing debt of $900 (meaning that the debt will now be a liability of the company that made the purchase). Because both the firm's cash and debt are now owned by the buyer, the estimated DCF value of the *firm's equity* is only $1,700, the difference between the estimated value of its total assets ($2,500 plus $100 of cash) and the value of its outstanding debt ($900). According to equation 12.2, we can write the following:

$$\begin{aligned}\text{DCF value of NEC's equity} &= \text{Enterprise value} + \text{Cash} - \text{Debt}\\ &= \$2{,}500 + \$100 - \$900 = \$1{,}700\end{aligned}$$

ESTIMATING OS DISTRIBUTORS' ENTERPRISE AND EQUITY VALUES

Now that we have reviewed the various elements required to estimate the DCF value of a firm's business assets and equity, we can turn to the valuation of OS Distributors in early January 2011 (the same as in December 31, 2010). In this section, we assume that OS Distributors stays **as-is**, meaning that its operating efficiency remains the same as in 2010, the most recent year for which data are available. In other words, we estimate the firm's **stand-alone value**. The four steps required to obtain this value are summarized as follows:

Step 1	Estimate the future stream of expected cash flows that the firm's business assets (CFA) will generate using equation 12.5
Step 2	Estimate the rate at which the cash flows from business assets must be discounted to the present. This rate is the WACC, which is estimated using equation 12.6, where the cost of equity is estimated with the capital asset pricing model given in equation 12.7
Step 3	Calculate the DCF value of the firm's business assets (its enterprise value) by discounting the expected cash-flow stream generated by its business assets (CFA) at a discount rate equal to the firm's WACC (see equation 12.4)
Step 4	To get the estimated DCF value of the firm's *equity*, add cash holding and other financial assets to its enterprise value and deduct any debt outstanding, as shown in equation 12.2

As you can imagine, the application of DCF models to the valuation of a firm's business assets, more specifically to the valuation of the stream of cash flows expected from these assets, requires numerous and repetitive computations. Using a spreadsheet to do these computations can save time and, as we will see later in the chapter, can allow for an easy analysis of the sensitivity of the DCF value to changes in the valuation inputs. For these reasons, the exhibits illustrating the valuation examples in the rest of the chapter will be shown as spreadsheets. We present them in a format that can also be used with a financial calculator.

STEP 1: ESTIMATION OF THE CASH FLOW FROM BUSINESS ASSETS

When estimating the DCF value of a firm's business assets, the usual forecasting period is five years. A firm, however, should be valued as a **going concern** (the assumption is that it will operate forever), so we need to account for the cash flows that will occur beyond the fifth year. We do this by estimating the DCF value of the firm's business assets *at the end of the forecasting period.* The estimation of this **terminal value** is based on the cash flows the firm's business assets are expected to generate *beyond the forecasting period.* Applying this approach to the valuation of OS Distributors, we first develop a forecast of that company's cash flows during the *five*-year period from 2011 to 2015. We then added a forecast for 2016 which is needed to estimate the firm's terminal value at the end of 2015.

ESTIMATING THE CASH FLOWS FROM BUSINESS ASSETS UP TO YEAR 2016

Our forecast of the cash flows that OS Distributors' business assets are expected to generate from 2011 to 2016 is shown in Exhibit 12.6. Before we show how to generate these forecasts, we review OS Distributors' *past* performance. The firm's historical efficiency ratios (from 2008 to 2010) are summarized in rows 5 through 8. Sales grew by 7.7 percent during 2009 and by 14.3 percent during 2010. Operating expenses, expressed as a percentage of sales, declined during the period, with the cost of goods sold (COGS) decreasing from 84.1 percent of sales in 2008 to 83.33 percent of sales in 2010. Similarly selling, general, and administrative expenses (SG&A) decreased from 10.21 percent of sales to 10 percent of sales during the period. The efficiency with which the firm managed its operating cycle, measured by the ratio of WCR to sales, however, deteriorated. In 2008, OS Distributors used \$15.13 of working capital to generate \$100 of sales. Two years later, that figure rose to \$16.04.

We now examine the logic behind our forecasting method with particular attention to the first year's forecast (2011). Row 9 gives the annual sales forecast based on the growth rates assumed in row 5. Note that we assume the growth rate will decline steadily, from its peak value of 14.3 percent achieved in 2010 to a terminal rate of 3 percent beyond the fifth year. In other words, *after* year 2015, sales are assumed to grow at a constant rate of 3 percent *forever*. The higher growth rate achieved in 2010 is caused by particular circumstances that are not expected to occur again. These assumptions about the sales growth rate are critical because the rest of the forecast is based on these assumed growth rates. If they are unrealistic, the estimated DCF value will not be realistic. (Remember our earlier observation that DCF values are highly sensitive to the assumed rates at which cash flows grow.)

What is a realistic assumption about growth rates? Unless you have strong evidence and a high level of confidence that the firm's sales will grow at exceptionally high rates for a number of years, you should, without being overly conservative,

EXHIBIT 12.6 DISCOUNTED CASH FLOW (DCF) VALUATION OF OS DISTRIBUTORS' EQUITY AT THE BEGINNING OF JANUARY 2011.

FIGURES IN MILLIONS

	A	B	C	D	E	F	G	H	I	J
1		Historical data			Estimated cash flows to year 2016					
2										
3		2008	2009	2010	2011	2012	2013	2014	2015	2016
4										
5	Sales growth rate		7.70%	14.30%	10.00%	8.00%	7.00%	5.00%	4.00%	3.00%
6	COGS[1] as percent of sales	84.10%	84.05%	83.33%	83.33%	83.33%	83.33%	83.33%	83.33%	83.33%
7	SG&A[1] as percent of sales	10.21%	10.40%	10.00%	10.00%	10.00%	10.00%	10.00%	10.00%	10.00%
8	WCR[1] as percent of sales	15.13%	15.00%	16.04%	16.04%	16.04%	16.04%	16.04%	16.04%	16.04%
9	Sales	$390.0	$420.0	$480.0	$528.0	$570.2	$610.2	$640.7	$666.3	$686.3
10	*less COGS*	*(328.0)*	*(353.0)*	*(400.0)*	*(440.0)*	*(475.2)*	*(508.5)*	*(533.9)*	*(555.2)*	*(571.9)*
11	*less SG&A*	*(39.8)*	*(43.7)*	*(48.0)*	*(52.8)*	*(57.0)*	*(61.0)*	*(64.1)*	*(66.6)*	*(68.6)*
12	*less depreciation expense*	*(5.0)*	*(5.0)*	*(8.0)*	*(8.0)*	*(8.0)*	*(7.0)*	*(6.0)*	*(6.0)*	*(6.0)*
13	equals EBIT[1]	17.2	18.3	24.0	27.2	30.0	33.7	36.7	38.4	39.8
14	**EBIT(1 – Tax rate of 40%)**	10.3	11.0	14.4	16.3	18.0	20.2	22.0	23.1	23.9
15	**plus depreciation expense**	5.0	5.0	8.0	8.0	8.0	7.0	6.0	6.0	6.0
16	*WCR at year-end*	*59.0*	*63.0*	*77.0*	*84.7*	*91.5*	*97.9*	*102.8*	*106.9*	*110.1*
17	**less ΔWCR** [change in (16)]		(4.0)	(14.0)	(7.7)	(6.8)	(6.4)	(4.9)	(4.1)	(3.2)
18	**less net capital expenditure**		$ 0.0	$ (10.0)	$ (8.0)	$ (8.0)	$ (7.0)	$ (6.0)	$ (6.0)	$ (6.0)
19										
20	**equals cash flow from business assets**			$ (1.6)	$ 8.6	$ 11.2	$ 13.8	$ 17.1	$ 19.0	$ 20.6
21										
22	**Terminal value of business assets year-end 2015**								$412.9	

(Continued)

EXHIBIT 12.6 DISCOUNTED CASH FLOW (DCF) VALUATION OF OS DISTRIBUTORS' EQUITY AT THE BEGINNING OF JANUARY 2011. *(CONTINUED)*

	A	B	C	D	E	F	G	H	I	J
23										
24	**Beginning 2011**									
25										
26	WACC[1]	8.00%								
27	**DCF value of business assets at 8%**	$335								
28	*plus cash*	*$ 8*								
29	*less book value of debt*	*$ (61)*								
30	**equals DCF value of equity**	**$282**								
31										
32	*Rows 5 to 8, 12, 15, 18, 26, 28, and 29 plus cell B9 are data.*									
33	*Formula in cell C9 is =B9*(1+C5). Then copy cell C9 to next cells in row 9.*									
34	*Formula in cell B10 is =–B6*B9. Then copy cell B10 to next cells in row 10.*									
35	*Formula in cell B11 is =–B7*B9. Then copy cell B11 to next cells in row 11.*									
36	*Formula in cell B13 is =sum(B9:B12). Then copy cell B13 to next cells in row 13.*									
37	*Formula in cell B14 is =B13*(1–.4). Then copy cell B14 to next cells in row 14.*									
38	*Formula in cell B16 is =B8*B9. Then copy cell B16 to next cells in row 16.*									
39	*Formula in cell C17 is =–(C16–B16). Then copy cell C17 to next cells in row 17.*									
40	*Formula in cell D20 is =D14+D15+D17+D18. Then copy cell D20 to next cells in row 20.*									
41	*Formula in cell I22 is =J20/(B26–J5).*									
42	*Formula in cell B27 is =NPV(B26,E20:I20)+I22/(1+B26)^5.*									
43	*Formula in cell B30 is =B27+B28–B29.*									
44										

[1]COGS = Cost of goods sold; SG&A = Selling, general, and administrative expenses; WCR = Working capital requirement; EBIT = Earnings before interest and tax; WACC = Weighted average cost of capital.

assume that the growth rate will eventually drop to its terminal level of *no more than a few percentage points*. Think of it this way: no company can grow forever at a rate faster than the entire economy. If it did, it would eventually overtake the economy. The *long-term real* growth rate of developed economies is about 2 to 3 percent. Adding a long-term inflation rate of 2 to 3 percent (a reasonable assumption in most well-developed countries)[5] gives a *long-term nominal* growth rate of 4 to 6 percent. *Assuming a figure significantly higher than 4 to 6 percent for the terminal growth of a company would be unrealistic.* Many analysts take the most conservative view and assume a *zero growth rate* beyond the forecasting period. In this case, the cash flows after the forecasting period are assumed to remain the same forever, which, in effect, means that they decline in *real terms* when the expected inflation rate is taken into account. What if you are dealing with the valuation of a company that is expected to sustain an above-average rate of growth beyond five years? In this case, you should extend the forecasting period to, say, eight to ten years, rather than assume a higher terminal growth rate.

After the sales growth rates are estimated, expenses are calculated as a percentage of sales as shown in Exhibit 12.6. These percentages depend on the efficiency with which OS Distributors will manage its operations. Because we are valuing the company "as is," we assume that the operating efficiency ratios are equal to their latest historical values. (Later in this chapter, we revalue OS Distributors under alternative assumptions about its operating efficiency.) Thus, COGS is 83.33 percent of sales, SG&A is 10 percent of sales, and WCR is 16.04 percent of sales from 2011 to 2016.

Based on these assumptions, the expected cash flow from OS Distributors' assets (CFA) in 2011 can be estimated using equation 12.5:

$$\begin{aligned} \text{CFA} = \text{EBIT}(1 - T_C) &+ \text{Depreciation expense} \\ &- \Delta\text{WCR} - \text{Net capital expenditure} \end{aligned}$$

To estimate EBIT in 2011, we start with sales of $528 million (row 9) and deduct the COGS (row 10), the SG&A expenses (row 11), and depreciation expense (row 12, assumed to be $8 million, the same as in 2010). Thus, EBIT is equal to $27.2 million (row 13). EBIT adjusted for taxes is $16.3 million (row 14).[6] We then add back the $8 million of depreciation expense (row 15) and deduct the *change* in WCR (row 17). The $7.7 million growth in WCR in 2011 is the difference between WCR at the end of 2011 and WCR at the end of 2010. The $84.7 million of WCR at the end of 2011 is obtained by multiplying the sales figure in row 9 by the ratio of WCR to sales in row 8; the $77 million of WCR at year-end 2010 is computed directly from the balance sheet in Exhibit 12.1. Finally, we deduct the expected net capital expenditure of $8 million for 2011 (row 18) to get an estimated CFA of $8.6 million in 2011.

---

[5]For example, between 1926 and 2008, the Consumer Price Index in the United States increased at an average annual rate of 3.15 percent.

[6]The corporate tax rate is assumed to be the same as the historical one. Unless you know that the rate is expected to change, taking the historical corporate tax rate is the standard assumption. As pointed out earlier, the tax is calculated on the basis of EBIT because cash flows from business assets ignore interest expenses, which reflect financing activities.

We assume annual net capital expenditure equal to depreciation expense (compare row 18 with row 12) because we are valuing OS Distributors "as is." Thus, we do not expect any major investment beyond the *maintenance of existing assets,* and we assume that maintenance cost will be exactly the same as the annual depreciation expense. Although we assume depreciation expense in 2011 and 2012 is the same as its 2010 historical value of $8 million, we expect depreciation expense to drop to $7 million in 2013 and $6 million in 2014 and remain at that level thereafter. Depreciation expense declines in line with the reduction in sales growth and capital expenditure. It is important to be consistent in our assumptions. If the firm's activities slow down, so will its capital expenditure and depreciation expense.[7] Applying the same approach for the next five years yields the expected cash-flow stream up to year 2016 shown on row 20. We now need to estimate the terminal value of OS Distributors' assets at the end of year 2015 based on the estimated cash flow in 2016.

ESTIMATING THE TERMINAL VALUE OF BUSINESS ASSETS AT THE END OF YEAR 2015

To estimate the terminal value of OS Distributors' business assets at the end of year 2015, we need two pieces of information. First, we need to know the rate at which the cash flows from the firm's assets will grow in perpetuity *after* the year 2016. We argue earlier that we should assume a constant rate of growth that is close to the growth rate of the entire economy. For OS Distributors, we assume a rate of 3 percent, the same as that of sales.[8] We also need an estimate of the firm's WACC, the rate at which the cash flows beyond year 2010 will be discounted to the year 2010. We can then use the constant-growth DCF formula (equation 12.3) to estimate the terminal value of business assets as follows:[9]

$$\text{Terminal value of business assets at the end of year 2015} = \frac{\text{Cash flow in 2016}}{\text{WACC} - \text{Growth rate}}$$

On the basis of a 3 percent growth rate in sales, the expected cash flow in 2016 is $20.645 million (row 20, column J).[10] The next section shows that OS Distributors' estimated WACC is 8 percent. We insert these estimates into the above valuation formula to find the terminal value of business assets at the end of year 2015:

$$\text{Terminal value of assets at the end of year 2015} = \frac{\$20.645 \text{ million}}{0.08 - 0.03} = \$412.9 \text{ million}$$

[7]There are alternative models for estimating future capital expenditure; most of these models relate capital expenditure to sales forecast. A popular one uses historical ratios between annual capital expenditure and previous years' sales and applies the ratio to future annual sales to get the desired estimate.
[8]If the growth rate in sales is constant and capital expenditure is equal to depreciation expense, then the growth of cash flows is close to the growth in sales (even though not identical because of fixed operating costs). We nevertheless assume that, beyond 2016, cash flows grow at the same rate as sales.
[9]Note that we need to estimate the cash-flow stream for 6 years in order to get an estimate of the terminal value because the latter depends on the estimated cash flow in year 6 (2016 in our case) which, in turn, depends on the previous five years' cash flows.
[10]The estimated figures in Exhibit 12.6 have been rounded up or down to the nearest decimal point.

STEP 2: ESTIMATION OF THE WEIGHTED AVERAGE COST OF CAPITAL

The relevant rate at which to discount the cash flows from business assets is the WACC in equation 12.6. The WACC reflects the proportion of debt and equity employed to finance the assets and their respective costs. We first estimate the costs of debt and equity capital and then address the issue of the appropriate proportions of debt and equity we should use to get OS Distributors' WACC.

The cost of debt is the after-tax cost of *new* borrowing (short term and long term). As mentioned earlier, the relevant cost of debt must be calculated after taxes because interest payments are tax-deductible expenses. OS Distributors can borrow at an average cost of 7 percent (see Chapter 10 for details about estimating the cost of debt). Given a tax rate of 40 percent, OS Distributors' after-tax cost of debt is thus 4.2 percent [7 percent × (1 – 40%)].

The cost of equity is the cost of raising *new* equity funds. It can be estimated using the CAPM formula (equation 12.7). We need the following data: (1) the yield on long-term government securities (assumed to be 4.8 percent in January 2011); (2) the market risk premium (we use the historical average of 4 percent); and (3) OS Distributors' estimated beta coefficient.

Because OS Distributors is not a listed company, we do not have a beta coefficient for it. However, GES, the comparable firm we used in the section on valuation by comparables, has an estimated beta coefficient of 1.20. We can use this figure for the unobservable beta coefficient of OS Distributors. Applying the CAPM formula, we can write the following:

$$\text{Cost of equity } (k_E) = 4.8\% + (4\% \times 1.20) = 4.8\% + 4.8\% = 9.6\%$$

The appropriate proportions of equity and debt financing must be based on the *market values* of equity and debt, not their accounting or book values (see Chapter 10). Unfortunately, we cannot observe the market values of OS Distributors' equity and debt because neither the firm's equity nor its debt is traded on a stock exchange. We have no choice but to resort to the procedure of using the data from GES, the comparable firm whose equity is listed on a stock exchange.

The market value of GES's equity in early January 2011 was $1,000 million (GES has 50 million shares with an average price of $20; see Exhibit 12.3). Its balance sheet at the end of December 2010 (not provided here) shows $430 million of total debt.[11] We thus have the following:

$$\textbf{Proportion of equity} = \frac{\textbf{Market value of equity}}{\textbf{Market value of equity + Value of debt}} \tag{12.8}$$

$$= \frac{\$1{,}000 \text{ million}}{\$1{,}000 \text{ million} + \$430 \text{ million}} = \frac{\$1{,}000 \text{ million}}{\$1{,}430 \text{ million}} = 70\%$$

and the proportion of debt is 30 percent.

[11]We should estimate GES's debt at its market rather than book value. However, if we assume that the average rate of interest OS Distributors is paying on the funds it has borrowed in the past is close to the current market rate of interest, market and book values are not significantly different. The relationship between the market value of debt and interest rates is presented in Chapter 9.

We now have all the elements we need to estimate OS Distributors' WACC according to equation 12.6:

$$\text{WACC of OS Distributors} = (70\% \times 9.6\%) + (30\% \times 4.2\%)$$
$$= 7.98\% \text{ rounded up to } 8\%$$

This is the WACC shown in row 26 in Exhibit 12.6. It is an estimate of the required rate of return on the cash flows generated by OS Distributors' business assets.

STEP 3: ESTIMATION OF THE DCF VALUE OF BUSINESS ASSETS

We can now estimate the value of OS Distributors' business assets using the general valuation formula (equation 12.4). The formula gives the present value of a stream of cash flows expected from a firm's business assets. For OS Distributors, the cash flows are our forecasts from 2011 to 2015, including the terminal value of assets at year-end 2015 (shown in rows 20 and 22 in Exhibit 12.6). The appropriate discount rate is OS Distributors' WACC of 8 percent. We have the following (dollar figures in millions):

DCF value of OS Distributors' business assets(its enterprise value)

$$= \frac{\$8.6}{(1+0.08)} + \frac{\$11.2}{(1+0.08)^2} + \frac{\$13.8}{(1+0.08)^3} + \frac{\$17.1}{(1+0.08)^4} + \frac{\$19.0}{(1+0.08)^5} + \frac{\$412.9}{(1+0.08)^5}$$
$$= \$7.96 + \$9.60 + \$10.95 + \$12.57 + \$12.93 + \$281.01 = \$335$$

which is shown in Exhibit 12.6, row 27.

Note the magnitude of the terminal value in comparison with the yearly cash-flow estimates. Its present value at 8 percent is $281 million, which represents 84 percent of the $335 million DCF value of OS Distributors' business assets. This high percentage is not unusual, particularly in cases in which the growth rates during the forecasting period are not exceptionally high and are assumed to decline steadily toward their perpetual level. This is why we insist that great care be given to the estimation of the perpetual growth rate beyond the forecasting period.

STEP 4: ESTIMATION OF THE DCF VALUE OF EQUITY

The estimated value of OS Distributors' *equity* is found using equation 12.2. It is equal to its estimated enterprise value ($335 million) plus its cash holding of $8 million less the $61 million of debt in 2010 (the sum of short-term debt and long-term debt in Exhibit 12.1):

$$\text{DCF value of OS Distributors' equity} = \$335 \text{ million} + \$8 \text{ million} - \$61 \text{ million}$$
$$= \$282 \text{ million}$$

COMPARISON OF DCF VALUATION AND VALUATION BY COMPARABLES

We now have four estimates for the value of OS Distributors' equity. In increasing order, they are as follows: $242 million (based on a book-value multiple of 3.14), $255 million (based on an earnings multiple of 25), $270 million (based on an EBITDA multiple of 10.1), and $282 million (DCF value). The highest estimate ($282 million) is 17 percent higher than the lowest ($242 million), so the estimated values are within an acceptable range.

We can conclude that a figure in the range of \$240 million to \$280 million would be a fair estimate of OS Distributors' equity value if the company were listed and traded on a stock exchange. Given that OS Distributors has 10 million shares outstanding (see Exhibit 12.3), these estimates are equivalent to a share price of \$24 to \$28. If you owned OS Distributors and wanted to sell it, you would ask *at least* \$280 million. If you were the buyer, you would obviously wish to pay *no more* than \$240 million. The price at which a transaction may take place will be the outcome of a negotiation process. That price may or may not be within the estimated price range.

ESTIMATING THE ACQUISITION VALUE OF OS DISTRIBUTORS

The DCF equity value of \$282 million for OS Distributors is an estimated value of the equity of the firm "as is." It does not take into account any potential improvement in the way the firm is managed. If you acquire OS Distributors and enhance its performance, its value to you is obviously more than \$282 million.

Suppose a number of improvements can raise OS Distributors' estimated DCF equity value to \$340 million. This represents a *potential* value creation of \$58 million (\$340 million less \$282 million). Acquiring the company for less than \$340 million is a positive NPV investment, an investment whose price is *lower* than its estimated value. Suppose you end up paying \$300 million to acquire OS Distributors. This represents a **takeover premium** of \$18 million over its stand-alone value of \$282 million (\$300 million less \$282 million). In this case, the acquisition's NPV is the difference between the potential value creation and the takeover premium:

$$\begin{aligned}\text{NPV(Acquisition)} &= \text{Potential value creation} - \text{Takeover premium}\\ &= \$58\text{ million} - \$18\text{ million} = \$40\text{ million}\end{aligned}$$

You must be careful not to give OS Distributors' shareholders most of the future value *you* will create *after* you buy the company (the potential value creation) by paying too high a takeover premium. In general, the higher the potential value creation relative to the takeover premium, the larger the acquisition's NPV.

To estimate the acquisition value of OS Distributors, we must first identify the potential sources of value creation in an acquisition. We then show that when these sources are not present, such as when unrelated businesses are combined in a **conglomerate merger**, an acquisition is not likely to create value. After examining a conglomerate merger, we provide a complete analysis of the estimated acquisition value of OS Distributors.

IDENTIFYING THE POTENTIAL SOURCES OF VALUE CREATION IN AN ACQUISITION

The easiest way to identify potential sources of value creation in an acquisition is to look at how the DCF value is determined. In the simple case of a business expected to generate a **perpetual cash-flow stream** growing at a constant rate, the valuation formula (equation 12.3) shows that the DCF value is equal to next year's CFA divided by the difference between the WACC and the growth rate in the cash flows:

$$\text{DCF value of business assets} = \frac{\text{Next year's CFA}}{\text{WACC} - \text{Growth rate}}$$

where CFA is given by equation 12.5 and WACC is given by equation 12.6. Thus, to create value, that is, to raise the DCF value of the **target firm's** assets, an acquisition must achieve one of three things, all else being the same:[12]

1. Increase the cash flows generated by the target firm's business assets (CFA)
2. Raise the growth rate of the target firm's sales
3. Lower the WACC of the *target* firm

If the acquiring firm is unable to make one or more of the above changes in the target firm, the acquisition should not be carried out. These changes will happen if either or both of the following conditions are met:

1. The target firm is not currently managed at (1) its most efficient level (it has excessive costs and inefficient asset usage), (2) its highest growth rate in sales, or (3) its optimal capital structure (it has too little or too much debt financing), *and* the acquiring firm's managers believe they can do a better job of running the target firm. Those conditions are usually referred to as the **inefficient management** explanation of why acquisitions occur. In this case, an acquisition does not actually have to take place to enhance value. The target's current managers can, in principle, improve their firm's performance if they have the will and the required skills. This is why managers are often advised to run their firm as if it were a potential target
2. Combining the target firm with the acquiring company creates **economies of scale** that lead to cost and market synergies. This is known as the **synergy** explanation of why acquisitions take place. **Cost synergies** can be achieved, for example, in administration, marketing, and distribution if the target firm's costs and investments can be reduced, because these activities can be fully or partly carried out at a *lower* combined cost. Typically, this means eliminating redundancy in management, streamlining management information systems, and reducing sales forces. **Market synergies** can be achieved, for example, by distributing the target firm's products and services through the acquiring company's distribution channels for the purpose of increasing sales

Together, inefficient management and potential synergy provide the most powerful reasons to justify an acquisition. Other, less convincing reasons include the **undervaluation hypothesis**, according to which the acquiring company has superior skills in finding undervalued target firms that can be bought cheaply, and the **market power hypothesis**, which claims that after an acquisition the acquiring firm has a larger market share that may enable it to raise the price of its products or services and thus increase its cash flow and value (assuming, of course, that the government does not block the merger for anticompetitive reasons). Although these are plausible hypotheses as to why some acquisitions take place, indirect empirical evidence (from U.S. and other stock markets around the world) indicates that they are not

[12]Strictly speaking, an acquisition creates value if the value of the merged firms after the acquisition is higher than the *sum* of their respective values before the merger. Here, the focus is exclusively on the potential value creation the acquirer can achieve by improving the performance of the target firm.

the major sources of value creation behind most acquisitions.[13] We now examine the three specific sources of value creation in an acquisition, which were listed earlier.

INCREASING THE CASH FLOWS GENERATED BY THE TARGET FIRM'S ASSETS

A reduction in both the COGS and SG&A expenses will widen the target firm's operating margin and thus increase its operating profits (EBIT). According to equation 12.5, an increase in EBIT will increase a firm's cash flow. A reduction in tax expenses will have the same effect.

Tax expenses merit a special comment. Suppose the acquiring firm has a pre-tax profit of $100 million and the target firm has a pre-tax loss of $40 million. Their combined profits will be $60 million, and the acquirer will pay less tax after the merger than it would have paid on its pre-merger pre-tax profit of $100 million. However, firms seldom buy each other simply to reduce their tax liabilities, because the tax reduction is usually a one-time gain whose magnitude rarely justifies an acquisition. Furthermore, in most countries, the tax authorities do not allow the reduction in tax liability if the *only* purpose of the acquisition is to reduce taxes; a "business reason" has to support the acquisition.

Another way to increase the cash flows generated by the target firm's assets involves using the assets more efficiently. A more efficient use of assets will result in higher sales and higher cash flows per dollar of assets employed. A more efficient use of assets can be achieved in several ways. Any overinvestment, particularly in cash and in WCR, should be rapidly reduced to a level that is justified by the firm's current operations and near-term developments. Any excess cash that cannot be invested in a value-creating project should be returned to shareholders through a **share repurchase program** or a special dividend payment. If the firm holds excessive WCR that is not justified by the firm's current and expected level of operations, it should be reduced to its optimal level via faster collection of receivables and higher inventory turnover (see Chapter 3). The same logic applies to long-term assets if they are currently underutilized and have no identifiable use in the near future to support for the firm's value-creating activities.

RAISING THE SALES GROWTH RATE

Assuming the target firm is already creating value or will create value under the management of the bidding firm, then, all other things being equal, faster growth in sales will create additional value. This can be achieved by increasing the volume of goods and services sold by the target firm or by raising their price (without an

[13]If the undervaluation hypothesis were valid, then target firms whose share price rises on the announcement of an acquisition (because the market becomes aware of their undervaluation) should *maintain their higher value if the acquisition fails to take place.* The empirical evidence indicates that the share prices of unsuccessful target firms usually drop back to their pre-announcement level, a behavior that is inconsistent with the undervaluation hypothesis. If the market power hypothesis were valid, then the share prices of *all firms* in a sector should rise on the announcement day of a specific acquisition, because all firms in the sector should benefit from a potential increase in the price of the product or service, not just the merging firms. The empirical evidence indicates that this is generally not the case.

offsetting reduction in volume) via superior marketing skills and strategies. A more effective advertising campaign, a better mix of products, a wider or different distribution network, a closer relationship with customers, and the development of new markets, both domestically and abroad, are just a few of the possibilities worth exploring to improve the growth prospects of the target firm.

LOWERING THE COST OF CAPITAL

If the target firm's capital structure is not close to its optimal level (too little or too much borrowing compared with the optimal debt ratio), then changing the firm's capital structure should lower its WACC and raise its value. As shown in Chapter 11, the major advantage of debt financing is that it allows a firm to reduce its taxes (because of the deductibility of interest expenses) and thus enhance its after-tax cash flow and value. But the excessive use of debt will expose the firm to financial distress and possibly bankruptcy, which are costly. Hence, the existence of an optimal capital structure at the point at which the marginal tax advantage of debt financing is exactly offset by the marginal costs of financial distress and bankruptcy. It follows that if the target firm has too little or too much debt in its capital structure, a change in the proportion of debt financing relative to equity will lower its WACC and raise its value.

The target firm's WACC, as well as that of the **bidder,** will also decline if, after the merger, their costs of equity and debt are lower than before the merger. A merger is unlikely to lead to a reduction in the cost of equity (see discussion below), but it is often argued that if the merged firms are perceived by their creditors to be less likely to fail as a combination than as separate entities (this is usually referred to as the **coinsurance effect**), then their post-merger cost of debt should, in principle, be lower. However, a lower cost of debt should be accompanied by an increase in the cost of equity. Equity is now riskier because shareholders have, in effect, given debt holders a superior guarantee against failure. This increase in the cost of equity should balance the decrease in the cost of debt, leaving the firm's WACC unchanged.

WHY CONGLOMERATE MERGERS ARE UNLIKELY TO CREATE LASTING VALUE THROUGH ACQUISITIONS

A conglomerate merger is a combination of two or more unrelated (or independent) businesses for which no obvious synergy exists. A firm that grows through conglomerate mergers is unlikely to create lasting value for its shareholders because adding an unrelated business to its existing ones will neither enhance its cash flows by more than the target's cash flows nor reduce its cost of capital. It may, under certain circumstances, increase the conglomerate's earnings per share (EPS), but the growth in EPS is unlikely to be accompanied by a permanent rise in shareholder value.

ACQUIRING UNRELATED BUSINESSES IS UNLIKELY TO CREATE LASTING VALUE

Suppose a personal computer (PC) firm buys a life insurance company because it believes the merger will provide an opportunity to reduce the business risk of the combined firms via the diversification of their activities. The regular and predictable revenues generated by the life insurance business will smooth out the cyclical revenues from the PC business. The resulting reduction in risk should, in principle, reduce the conglomerate's cost of equity and thus raise the market value of its equity beyond the sum of the market values of the two pre-merger firms' equity.

Although this diversification strategy may make sense from the perspective of the PC company's managers, it is unlikely to generate the anticipated increase in market value. The reason is that *investors can achieve the same diversification themselves by combining shares of the PC and the insurance companies in their personal portfolios*. And one could argue that this **homemade diversification** is superior to that of the PC company's diversification strategy because it is cheaper to implement and allows investors to set their own proportions of holdings. Thus, it is doubtful that investors will be willing to pay a higher price for the diversified firm. As a result, it is unlikely that the financial market will value the combination of the two firms for more than the sum of their pre-merger values.

As pointed out earlier, the only types of business combinations that are likely to create lasting value are those that result in managerial improvements or synergistic gains. An example of such a combination is a **horizontal merger** (two firms in the same sector pooling their resources). Even **vertical mergers** (the integration of, say, a car manufacturer with its major supplier or its major distributor) are not likely to achieve lasting value creation; there is no obvious reason why a vertical merger will result in sales growth or cost reductions in a competitive environment. This explains why some of *the most successful value-creating firms focus their efforts on a single activity for which they have developed over time a unique set of skills and competencies that existing and potential competitors cannot easily imitate. It is these "difficult-to-replicate" skills and competencies that are the sources of a sustained increase in their market values.*

RAISING EARNINGS PER SHARE THROUGH CONGLOMERATE MERGERS IS UNLIKELY TO CREATE LASTING VALUE

Some conglomerates grow rapidly by continually buying firms that have a *lower* P/E ratio than the P/E of the conglomerate firm. The premise is that the market will value the combination for more than the sum of the pre-merger firms. Consider the conglomerate merger described in Exhibit 12.7. The most recent figure for the EAT of the acquiring firm is $300 million, whereas that of the target firm is $200 million (line 1). The acquiring firm has 150 million shares outstanding and the target firm has 100 million (line 2), so their EPS are the same and equal to $2 (line 3). The acquirer has a P/E ratio of 20, whereas the target has a P/E ratio of only 10 (line 4), a reflection of the market expectation of a much higher growth rate for the acquirer than for the target. The corresponding share prices and aggregate equity market values are, respectively, $40 and $6 billion for the acquirer and $20 and $2 billion for the target firm (lines 5 and 6).

Suppose the acquirer can buy the target firm at its prevailing market value of $2 billion and pay for the purchase by offering its own shares (worth $40 each) in exchange for those of the target firm (worth $20 each). The acquirer will have to issue 50 million shares ($2 billion divided by $40) to raise $2 billion. When the acquisition is complete, the shares of the target firm will no longer exist and the

EXHIBIT 12.7 DATA FOR A CONGLOMERATE MERGER BASED ON RAISING EPS.

	The Acquiring Firm	The Target Firm
1. Earnings after tax	$300 million	$200 miillion
2. Number of shares	150 million	100 million
3. Earnings per share (EPS) = (1)/(2)	$2.00	$2.00
4. Price-to-earnings (P/E) ratio	20	10
5. Share price = (3) × (4)	$40	$20
6. Total value = (2) × (5)	**$6,000 million**	**$2,000 million**

	Value of the merged firms if the market assigns the combination a P/E that:	
	Is value neutral	**Exceeds value neutrality**
1. Earnings after tax	$500 million	$500 million
2. Number of shares	200 million	200 million
3. Earnings per share (EPS) = (1)/(2)	$2.50	$2.50
4. Price-to-earnings (P/E) ratio	16	18
5. Share price = (3) × (4)	$40	$45
6. Total value = (2) × (5)	**$8,000 million**	**$9,000 million**

acquirer will have 200 million shares, the original 150 million plus the additional 50 million issued to pay for the acquisition.

If the acquisition is a simple combination that does not create any value, that is, if the merger is "value neutral," then the merged firms must have (1) an aggregate market value of $8 billion, the sum of the acquiring and target firms' pre-merger values; (2) a total profit of $500 million, the sum of the acquiring and target firms' pre-merger profits; and (3) a price per share of $40, the same price the acquirer had before the merger.

What is the acquirer's EPS after the acquisition is completed? With 200 million shares and $500 million of total profit, the resulting EPS is $2.50 ($500 million divided by 200 million shares). The acquirer has increased its EPS from a pre-merger value of $2 to a post-merger value of $2.50, a 25 percent rise. Not bad for a value-neutral acquisition, but do not be fooled. This higher EPS does not increase the value of the combined firms to more than $8 billion because the market assigns an earnings multiple (P/E ratio) of 16 that leaves the share price unchanged ($2.50 times 16 equals $40).

What if the market is fooled and assigns an earnings multiple exceeding 16? In this case, the acquirer's share price will rise to more than $40. If, for example, the post-merger market multiple is 18, then the post-merger share price would be $45 ($2.50 multiplied by 18). The acquirer could then use its higher share price to make another acquisition and another and another until the bubble bursts. This phenomenon happened in the U.S. market in the 1960s.

THE ACQUISITION VALUE OF OS DISTRIBUTORS' EQUITY

We now return to DCF valuation. The greatest advantage of this valuation approach over the comparables, or multiples, method is its ability to provide an estimate of the potential value that a particular managerial action can create. The potential value created by increasing OS Distributors' sales, reducing its operating expenses per dollar of sales, managing its WCR tighter, or lowering its average cost of capital, can be determined by modifying the original forecasts in Exhibit 12.6 and recalculating the DCF value of OS Distributors' equity. First, however, it must be determined that OS Distributors' current performance can be improved. If there is indeed room for improvement, a credible **restructuring plan** should be formulated.

In a horizontal merger, the obvious starting point to determine whether the performance of a target company can be improved is to compare it with that of the acquirer. Clearly, if the target underperforms relative to the acquirer, there are ways to get its performance up to the level of the acquiring firm. In addition, the performance of the target can be improved beyond just better management if room exists for synergistic gains after the acquisition is completed.

Let's assume that your company, which is in the same business as OS Distributors, is considering acquiring it. After a careful analysis of OS Distributors' current performance and its comparison with that of your company, you conclude that a combination of better management and the realization of significant economies of scale in marketing, distribution, and administration can produce the following improvements in the future performance of OS Distributors (without producing any significant changes in the performance of your firm):

1. A reduction of its COGS by a full percentage point (from 83.33 percent of sales to 82.33 percent of sales)
2. A reduction of its SG&A expenses, essentially overhead expenses, by half a percentage point (from 10 percent of sales to 9.5 percent of sales)
3. A decrease of its WCR from its current level of 16.04 percent of sales to 13 percent of sales
4. An increase of its sales growth rates from 2011 to 2015 by 2 percentage points above the figures shown in line 5 in Exhibit 12.6 with no increase in the growth rate after 2015

How much are these changes in future performance worth today to your firm? If you can answer this question, you will know how much your company should pay to acquire OS Distributors and still have a positive NPV acquisition. The analysis required to answer this question is shown in Exhibits 12.8 and 12.9. The first exhibit shows the separate effects of a reduction in the COGS, SG&A, and WCR. The second shows the effect of a higher growth rate in sales and the cumulative effect of improved operational efficiency and faster sales growth. The DCF values are all calculated using the same spreadsheet as in Exhibit 12.6 with a WACC of 8 percent, the same as the one used to value OS Distributors' equity "as is."

EXHIBIT 12.8 **EFFECT OF IMPROVED OPERATIONAL EFFICIENCY ON THE ESTIMATED VALUE OF OS DISTRIBUTORS' EQUITY AT THE BEGINNING OF JANUARY 2011.**

FIGURES IN MILLIONS

	Beginning 2011	End 2011	End 2012	End 2013	End 2014	End 2015	2016 and Beyond
Value of OS Distributors' Equity As Is (see Exhibit 12.6)							
Growth in sales		10%	8%	7%	5%	4%	3%
COGS[1] as % of sales		83.33%	83.33%	83.33%	83.33%	83.33%	
SG&A[1] as % of sales		10.00%	10.00%	10.00%	10.00%	10.00%	
WCR[1] as % of sales		16.04%	16.04%	16.04%	16.04%	16.04%	
Cash flow from business assets		**$8.6**	**$11.2**	**$13.8**	**$17.1**	**$ 19.0**	
Terminal value of assets at end-of-year 2015[2]						**$412.9**	
DCF value of business assets at 8%	$335						
plus cash less debt[3]	*$(53)*						
DCF value of equity	**$282**						
Effect of a Reduction in the Cost of Goods Sold							
COGS[1] as % of sales		82.33%	82.33%	82.33%	82.33%	82.33%	
Cash flow from business assets		**$11.8**	**$14.7**	**$17.5**	**$21.0**	**$ 23.0**	
Terminal value of assets at end-of-year 2015[2]						**$495.5**	
DCF value of business assets at 8%	$406						
plus cash less debt[3]	*$(53)*						
DCF value of equity	**$353**						
Potential value creation[4]	**$ 71**						
Effect of a Reduction in Selling, General, and Administrative Expenses							
SG&A[1] as % of sales		9.50%	9.50%	9.50%	9.50%	9.50%	
Cash flow from business assets		**$10.2**	**$13.0**	**$15.7**	**$19.1**	**$ 21.0**	
Terminal value of assets at end-of-year 2015[2]						**$454.4**	
DCF value of business assets at 8%	$370						
plus cash less debt[3]	*$(53)*						
DCF value of equity	**$317**						
Potential value creation[4]	**$ 35**						
Effect of a Decrease in the Ratio Working Capital Requirement to Sales							
WCR[1] as % of sales		13%	13%	13%	13%	13%	
Cash flows from business assets		**$24.7**	**$12.5**	**$15.0**	**$18.1**	**$ 19.7**	
Terminal value of assets at end-of-year 2015[2]						**$425.3**	
DCF value of business assets at 8%	$362						
plus cash less debt[3]	*$(53)*						
DCF value of equity	**$309**						
Potential value creation[4]	**$ 27**						

[1]COGS = Cost of goods sold; SG&A = Selling, general, and administrative expenses; WCR = Working capital requirement.
[2]Terminal value is $CF_{2016}/(8\% - 3\%)$.
[3]Cash of $8 million less book value of debt of $61 million equals $53 million.
[4]Potential value creation = DCF value of equity less $282 million (the value of OS Distributors' equity as is).

EXHIBIT 12.9 EFFECT OF FASTER GROWTH IN SALES AND IMPROVED OPERATIONAL EFFICIENCY ON THE ESTIMATED VALUE OF OS DISTRIBUTORS' EQUITY AT THE BEGINNING OF JANUARY 2011.

FIGURES IN MILLIONS

	Beginning 2011	End 2011	End 2012	End 2013	End 2014	End 2015	2016 and Beyond
Value of OS Distributors' Equity As Is (see Exhibit 12.6)							
Growth in sales		10%	8%	7%	5%	4%	3%
COGS[1] as % of sales		83.33%	83.33%	83.33%	83.33%	83.33%	
SG&A[1] as % of sales		10.00%	10.00%	10.00%	10.00%	10.00%	
WCR[1] as % of sales		16.04%	16.04%	16.04%	16.04%	16.04%	
Cash flow from business assets		**$8.6**	**$11.2**	**$13.8**	**$17.1**	**$ 19.0**	
Terminal value of assets at end-of-year 2015[2]						**$412.9**	
DCF value of business assets at 8%	$335						
plus cash less debt[3]	*$(53)*						
DCF value of equity	**$282**						
Effect of Faster Growth in Sales							
Growth in sales		12%	10%	9%	7%	6%	3%
COGS[1] as % of sales		83.33%	83.33%	83.33%	83.33%	83.33%	
SG&A[1] as % of sales		10.00%	10.00%	10.00%	10.00%	10.00%	
WCR[1] as % of sales		16.04%	16.04%	16.04%	16.04%	16.04%	
Cash flow from business assets		**$7.5**	**$10.2**	**$13.1**	**$16.8**	**$ 19.0**	
Terminal value of assets at end-of-year 2015[2]						**$460.4**	
DCF value of business assets at 8%	$365						
plus cash less debt[3]	*$(53)*						
DCF value of equity	**$312**						
Potential value creation[4]	**$ 30**						
Effect of Faster Growth in Sales and Improved Managerial Efficiency							
Growth in sales		12%	10%	9%	7%	6%	3%
COGS[1] as % of sales		82.33%	82.33%	82.33%	82.33%	82.33%	
SG&A[1] as % of sales		9.50%	9.50%	9.50%	9.50%	9.50%	
WCR[1] as % of sales		13%	13%	13%	13%	13%	
Cash flow from business assets		**$28.7**	**$17.2**	**$20.5**	**$24.3**	**$ 26.9**	
Terminal value of assets at end-of-year 2015[2]						**$609.2**	
DCF value of business assets at 8%	$508						
plus cash less debt[3]	*$(53)*						
DCF value of equity	**$455**						
Potential value creation[4]	**$173**						

[1]COGS = Cost of goods sold; SG&A = Selling, general, and administrative expenses; WCR = Working capital requirement.
[2]Terminal value is $CF_{2016}/(8\% - 3\%)$.
[3]Cash of $8 million less book value of debt of $61 million equals $53 million.
[4]Potential value creation = DCF value of equity less $282 million (the value of OS Distributors' equity as is).

EXHIBIT 12.10 SUMMARY OF DATA IN EXHIBITS 12.8 AND 12.9.

Sources of Value Creation	Potential Value Creation	
1. Reduction in the cost of goods sold to 82.33% of sales	$ 71 million	(41%)
2. Reduction in overheads to 9.50% of sales	$ 35 million	(20%)
3. Reduction of working capital requirement to 13% of sales	$ 27 million	(16%)
4. Faster growth in sales (2 percentage points higher)	$ 30 million	(17%)
5. Interaction of growth and improved operations	$ 10 million	(6%)
Total potential value creation	**$173 million**	(100%)

The effect of the improved performance on value creation is summarized in Exhibit 12.10. The reduction in the COGS and overhead is worth $106 million; the reduction of WCR relative to sales is worth $27 million; and the faster growth in sales is worth $30 million. The four *separate* improvements add to a potential value creation of $163 million. But taken *together*, they produce a potential aggregate value of $173 million (see Exhibit 12.10), which represents an increase of 61 percent over the DCF value of OS Distributors "as is." The extra $10 million (the difference between $173 million and $163 million) is generated by the *interaction* of more efficient operating performance on faster growth.

Depending on your confidence in achieving one or more of the changes described above, the target value of OS Distributors' equity could be as high as $455 million ($282 million "as is" plus $173 million of potential value creation). We did not consider the possibility of a reduction in OS Distributors' cost of capital if it is taken over. If its WACC can be lowered below 8 percent, then all the potential value creations mentioned above will be higher.

An acquiring firm, however, must not become overconfident about its ability to realize (or even exceed) the full potential value of a target. This overconfidence can lead to paying too much for the target. Unfortunately, the evidence indicates that this often occurs, and the result is an acquisition with an NPV close to zero. This means that most, if not all, of the gains from the acquisition end up in the pockets of the target company's shareholders.

ESTIMATING THE LEVERAGED BUYOUT VALUE OF OS DISTRIBUTORS

In a typical **leveraged buyout (LBO)**, a group of **private equity investors** purchases a presumably underperforming firm by raising an unusually large amount of debt relative to equity capital (up to $5 of debt for every dollar of equity). The investors often include the firm's managers in association with private equity investors and possibly a **venture capital firm** (an investment firm specializing in the financing of small and new ventures). The strategy is to restructure the firm, rapidly improve its performance, and increase the cash flows generated by the firm's assets to repay a large part of the initial debt within a reasonable period of time (three to five years). *The new shareholders do not normally receive any cash dividends during* *the restructuring period.* They anticipate cashing in on their investment at the end of that period by selling some (or all) of their shares to the general public. As an alternative to this **exit strategy**, the firm can be sold to another company or to a new group of private investors.

Suppose OS Distributors' owners wish to retire. In January 2011, four of the firm's most senior managers, in association with a private equity firm, agree to buy the firm's assets for $300 million, including the $8 million of cash. They believe that the owners have a conservative management policy and that significant value can be unlocked if the firm is managed more aggressively through a combination of tighter control of expenses, better use of assets, and faster growth in sales. The acquisition will be financed with $220 million of debt and $80 million of equity (the management team will invest $30 million, and the private equity firm another $50 million).

To keep the analysis as simple as possible, we assume the $220 million of debt consists of a single loan at a fixed interest rate of 8 percent. The loan must be repaid at the rate of $20 million per year for the next five years, with the first payment due at the end of 2011. After the fifth year, any repayment on the balance of the loan can be refinanced with new borrowing. The cost of debt is one full percentage point higher than the 7 percent rate on new borrowing that OS Distributors' current owners can obtain. The higher borrowing rate reflects the higher risk borne by the lenders in a leveraged deal such as an LBO.

We can compare the financial structure of OS Distributors before and after the LBO (but before any improvement in the firm's performance) by constructing a reduced form of the balance sheet after the LBO and contrasting it with its actual balance sheet at the end of 2010, as shown in Exhibit 12.11.[14]

EXHIBIT 12.11 COMPARISON OF OS DISTRIBUTORS' BALANCE SHEET BEFORE AND AFTER THE LBO.

BEFORE-LBO FIGURES FROM EXHIBIT 12.1. FIGURES IN MILLIONS

Balance Sheet	Before the LBO		After the LBO	
Cash	$ 8	(6%)	$ 8	(3%)
Working capital requirement	77	(56%)	77	(26%)
Net fixed assets	53	(38%)	215	(71%)
Invested capital	**$138**	**(100%)**	**$300**	**(100%)**
Total debt	$ 61	(44%)	$220	(73%)
Equity	77	(56%)	80	(27%)
Capital employed	**$138**	**(100%)**	**$300**	**(100%)**

[14]The reduced form of the balance sheet is similar to the managerial balance sheet (see Chapter 3). The current liabilities associated with the operating cycle (accounts payable and accrued expenses) are accounted for in the working capital requirement, where they are deducted from the receivables, inventories, and prepaid expenses.

The acquiring team has estimated that OS Distributors' long-term assets are grossly undervalued and believes that they are worth at least $215 million, more than four times the book value of $53 million reported in the firm's balance sheet. Long-term assets are hence recorded in the post-LBO balance sheet at $215 million and will be depreciated on the basis of their higher value. The *additional* yearly depreciation expenses resulting from the revaluation of fixed assets are assumed to equal $20 million for the next ten years and are fully tax deductible.[15] Cash and WCR are reported in the post-LBO balance sheet at their pre-LBO accounting values. Notice the highly leveraged capital structure in the **pro forma** balance sheet (the *expected* balance sheet after the LBO). The $300 million of assets are financed with $220 million of debt and $80 million of equity, giving the post-LBO firm a debt ratio (debt divided by total capital) of 73 percent, which is significantly higher than the pre-LBO debt ratio of 44 percent.

The structure of debt used to finance a typical LBO is far more complex than that of the single loan we assume for OS Distributors. In practice, a package of different types of loans is put together by the private equity firm and its advisors. At the top of the package is the **senior debt** secured by the firm's assets. (A secured loan is one for which the firm has pledged some of its assets—such as property, trade receivables, or inventories—as **collateral**, which the lender can seize and sell if the firm fails to service the loan.) This collateralized debt is also known as **top-floor financing**. It is senior to the **subordinated,** or **junior debt**, which is usually **unsecured** (no collateral is offered) and more expensive. This type of debt is often referred to as **mezzanine financing** because it is positioned between top-floor financing and equity capital, which is known as **ground-floor financing.**

Two key issues should be examined in relation to the LBO of OS Distributors. The first is whether the acquisition of the firm's assets for $300 million is a value-creating investment, that is, an investment with a positive net present value. The second is whether these assets will generate sufficient cash to service the $220 million loan (both interest payments and debt repayment) during the next five years.

ESTIMATING THE LEVERAGED BUYOUT VALUE OF BUSINESS ASSETS

To find out whether the OS Distributors' LBO is a positive NPV acquisition, we must estimate the value of OS Distributors' business assets based on the cash flows they are expected to generate under the new and more efficient management. If this estimated asset value exceeds $300 million (the purchase price), the acquisition is a positive NPV investment. In principle, we can estimate the LBO value of OS Distributors' assets using the DCF approach. However, this approach assumes that the WACC remains constant, an assumption that cannot be maintained in the case of an LBO. Remember that the post-LBO debt ratio is 73 percent (see Exhibit 12.11). The rapid repayment of the loan during the next five years means that the firm's debt ratio will decline during that period. In other words, the firm's WACC will not remain constant during these years. If we want to use the DCF approach to value the LBO, we need to estimate a different WACC for each of the five years, quite a cumbersome task. Fortunately, a variant of the DCF valuation approach, called the **adjusted present value (APV)** method, circumvents this problem.

[15] In some countries, the tax authority may deny the tax reductions resulting from these depreciation expenses.

THE ADJUSTED PRESENT VALUE METHOD

According to the APV method, the valuation of a firm's business assets is carried out in two separate steps. In the first step, the DCF value of the assets is estimated *assuming they are entirely financed with equity*. This all-equity-financed value is called the **unlevered asset value.** If assets are unlevered, then the WACC used in estimating their DCF value must be constant and equal to the cost of equity for an all-equity-financed firm. (This cost is referred to as the **unlevered cost of equity**.) This procedure clearly solves the problem of a WACC changing over time. But ignoring debt means that we fail to take into account the major benefit of debt financing—the reduction in the firm's taxes resulting from the deductibility of the interest expenses related to borrowed funds.[16] The second step in the APV approach corrects for this failure. In this step, the present value of the tax savings the firm will realize in the future if it borrows today to finance its assets is added to the DCF value of the unlevered assets. Thus, according to the APV method, the DCF value of a firm's **levered assets** (the assets financed with debt and equity) can be expressed as follows:

DCF value of *levered* assets =
DCF value of *unlevered* assets + DCF value of future tax savings

The DCF value of unlevered assets is estimated by discounting the cash flows generated by these assets at the unlevered cost of equity. The DCF value of future tax savings from interest expenses is estimated by discounting the future stream of tax savings at the cost of debt.[17]

THE LEVERAGED BUYOUT VALUE OF OS DISTRIBUTORS' BUSINESS ASSETS

We can now apply the APV approach to estimate the LBO value of OS Distributors' business assets. The new management team believes that it can improve operating efficiency by (1) reducing the COGS to 82.33 percent of sales (from the current 83.33 percent level), (2) cutting the SG&A expenses to 9.5 percent of sales (from their current 10 percent level), and (3) lowering the WCR to 13 percent of sales (from the current 16.04 percent level). The team also believes it can add two percentage points to the growth in sales for the next five years. This, as you may have noticed, is the restructuring plan we analyze earlier in the context of a potential merger. However, a major difference exists between a potential merger and an LBO. In a merger, some of the performance improvements are expected to come from synergistic gains resulting from combining the two businesses. In an LBO, there is no merger, and thus, there are no opportunities for synergistic gains. *All the improved performance must come from better management of the firm.*

When OS Distributors is valued as a potential target, the successful implementation of the restructuring plan has a value-creating potential of $173 million (see the

[16]The effect of debt financing on the firm's value is examined in detail in Chapter 11.

[17]Each cash-flow stream should be discounted to the present at a rate that reflects its particular risk. We assume here that the tax savings are less risky than the cash flows from assets and should, therefore, be discounted at a lower rate than the unlevered cost of equity. The standard procedure is to take the cost of debt.

bottom of Exhibit 12.10). Unfortunately, we cannot use this figure as a measure of the potential value the LBO deal can create because, as discussed previously, the WACC will change over time. We now explain how to use the APV approach to estimate the leveraged value of OS Distributors' assets under the LBO financing plan.

OS Distributors' Unlevered Cost of Equity According to the capital asset pricing model (see equation 12.7), a firm's cost of equity is equal to the risk-free rate plus the product of the market risk premium and the firm's beta coefficient. The risk-free rate in early 2011 is assumed to be 4.8 percent, and the market risk premium is the historical rate of 4 percent. We want to estimate the *unlevered* cost of equity, so the beta coefficient must be that of an all-equity financed firm. Chapter 10 shows that this beta, called **asset beta,** can be estimated as follows:

$$\textbf{Asset beta} = \frac{\textbf{Equity beta}}{1 + \left[(1 - \text{Tax rate}) \times \left(\dfrac{\text{Debt}}{\text{Equity}}\right)\right]}$$

The equity, or levered, beta for OS Distributors is 1.20 (estimated earlier from a comparable firm); the tax rate is 40 percent; and the ratio of debt to equity is 30 percent debt to 70 percent equity (see equation 12.8). Thus, we have the following:

$$\text{OS Distributors' asset beta} = \frac{1.20}{1 + \left[(1 - 40\%) \times \left(\dfrac{0.30}{0.70}\right)\right]} = 0.95$$

Applying the capital asset pricing model (equation 12.7) using the asset or **unlevered beta** of OS Distributors provides an estimate of that firm's unlevered cost of equity:

$$\text{OS Distributors' unlevered cost of equity} = 4.8\% + (4\% \times 0.95) = 8.6\%$$

OS Distributors' Estimated Asset Value The APV valuation steps are described in Exhibit 12.12. We start with the cash flows from business assets given at the bottom of Exhibit 12.9. We can use the cash flows that we estimated in the merger valuation approach because the expected improvements in performance are the same as for the merger. (Because the cash flow for the year 2016 is not shown in Exhibit 12.9, we calculated it using the spreadsheet in Exhibit 12.6 assuming the performance expectations of the LBO.) Next, we estimate the assets' terminal value at the end of year 2015 (row 9) the same way we estimated the terminal value for OS Distributors in the previous sections, but this time we use the *unlevered* cost of equity of 8.6 percent instead of a WACC of 8 percent (row 8).[18] Finally, we discount the CFA and the terminal value at the unlevered cost of equity of 8.6 percent (row 10), obtaining a DCF value of $453 million for the unlevered assets of OS Distributors. We then determine the tax savings generated by the additional depreciation

[18]Recall that when the firm is unlevered, it has no debt and its WACC is equal to its unlevered cost of equity.

EXHIBIT 12.12 ESTIMATED VALUE OF OS DISTRIBUTORS' UNLEVERED ASSETS AT THE BEGINNING OF JANUARY 2011.

FIGURES IN MILLIONS

	A	B	C	D	E	F	G	H
1		Beginning 2011	End 2011	End 2012	End 2013	End 2014	End 2015	End 2016
2								
3								
4	**Value of Unlevered Assets**							
5								
6	Cash flows from business assets (see bottom of Exhibit 12.9)		$28.7	$17.2	$20.5	$24.3	$ 26.9	$30.5
7	Growth rate of cash flows after 2015							3.0%
8	Unlevered cost of equity	8.6%						
9	Terminal value of unlevered assets						$544.6	
10	**DCF value of unlevered assets**	$453						
11								
12	Value of Tax Savings on Additional Depreciation Expenses							
13								
14	Additional depreciation expenses for 10 years		$ 20	$ 20	$ 20	$ 20	$20	
15	Tax savings (tax rate = 40%)		8.0	8.0	8.0	8.0	8.0	
16	Discount rate	8.0%						
17	Terminal value of tax savings						$ 31.9	
18	**DCF value of tax savings from depreciation expenses**	$54						
19								
20	**Value of Tax Savings on Interest Expenses**							
21								
22	Debt outstanding at the beginning of the year		$ 220	$ 200	$ 180	$ 160	$ 140	$120
23	Debt repayment		20	20	20	20	20	
24	Debt outstanding at the end of the year		$ 200	$ 180	$ 160	$ 140	$ 120	$124
25	Interest rate	8.0%						
26	Interest expenses		17.6	16.0	14.4	12.8	11.2	9.6
27	Tax savings (tax rate = 40%)		$ 7.0	$ 6.4	$ 5.8	$ 5.1	$ 4.5	$ 3.8
28	Tax savings growth rate after 2015							3.0%
29	Terminal value of tax savings						$ 76.8	
30	**DCF value of tax savings from interest expenses**	$76						
31								
32	**Leveraged Buyout Value**							
33								
34	Unlevered asset value	$453						
35	Overall tax savings value	$130						
36	**Leveraged buyout value**	$583						
37								
38	*Rows 6, 7, 8, 14, 16, 23, 25, and 28 and cell C22 are data.*							
39	*Formula in cell G9 is =H6/(B8–H7).*							
40	*Formula in cell B10 is =NPV(B8,C6:G6)+G9/(1+B8)^5.*							
41	*Formula in cell C15 is =C14*.4. Then copy cell C15 to next cells in row 15.*							
42	*Formula in cell G17 is =–PV(B16,5,G14), where 5 is the number of remaining tax savings periods.*							
43	*Formula in cell B18 is =NPV(B16,C15:G15)+G17/(1+B16)^5.*							
44	*Formula in cell D22 is =C22–C23. Then copy cell D22 to next cells in row 22.*							
45	*Formula in cell C24 is =D22. Then copy cell C24 to cells D24 to G24. Formula in cell H24 is =H22*(1+.03).*							
46	*Formula in cell C26 is =B25*C22. Then copy cell C26 to next cells in row 26.*							
47	*Formula in cell C27 is =C26*.4. Then copy cell C27 to next cells in row 27.*							
48	*Formula in cell G29 is =H27/(B25–H28).*							
49	*Formula in cell B30 is =NPV(B25,C27:G27)+G29/(1+B25)^5.*							
50	*Formula in cell B34 is =B10.*							
51	*Formula in cell B35 is =B18+B30.*							
52	*Formula in cell B36 is =B34+B35.*							
53								

expenses provided by the revaluation of fixed assets and the interest expenses provided by the $220 million loan. The present values of these tax savings are then added to the DCF value of the unlevered assets to obtain the LBO value of OS Distributors' assets. Let's illustrate this procedure with the data in Exhibit 12.12.

With a corporate tax rate of 40 percent, the additional depreciation expenses will generate annual tax savings of $8 million for ten years ($20 million times 40 percent). This is the amount of tax OS Distributors will *not* pay because its pre-tax profit is reduced by the $20 million of annual depreciation. The tax savings from year 2011 to year 2015 are shown in row 15. The terminal value of the additional depreciation expenses at the end of year 2015 (row 17) is $31.9 million. (This is the present value of $8 million every year for the remaining five years of depreciation discounted at the cost of debt of 8 percent.) The total DCF value of the tax savings from depreciation, using a discount rate of 8 percent, is $54 million (row 18).[19]

To estimate the tax savings from interest expenses, we first need to estimate the interest expenses. Row 22 shows the amount of outstanding debt at the *beginning* of each year from 2011 to 2016. Because of high annual debt repayments, OS Distributors' debt is expected to decrease rapidly. Based on the initial borrowing of $220 million and annual repayments of $20 million, the amount of outstanding debt by the end of 2015 will be reduced to $120 million. Assuming that the large debt repayments will stop after 2016, we can expect that debt, interest expenses, and tax savings will then increase at the same rate as the growth in sales, expected to be 3 percent per year. The annual interest expenses in row 26 are obtained by multiplying the amount of debt outstanding at the end of the previous year by the interest rate of 8 percent. Row 27 shows the corresponding tax savings using a tax rate of 40 percent. Row 29 gives the terminal value of the tax savings from the expected annual interest after 2015. It is calculated, once again, with equation 12.3, which gives the present value of a constant growth annuity. In this case, the following year's cash flow is $3.8 million (the tax savings of 2016), the required return is 8 percent (the cost of debt), and the growth rate is 3 percent. Adding the present value of the annual tax savings from 2011 to 2015 to that of the terminal value of the tax savings estimated at $76.8 million in 2015 gives a total tax savings from interest expenses of $76 million (row 30).

Adding the DCF values of the tax savings from depreciation and interest expenses ($130 million in row 35) to the unlevered asset value of $453 million (row 34) yields an estimated DCF value of $583 million for OS Distributors' business assets (row 36), which is the LBO's *enterprise value*.

Note that this value is double the $292 million the LBO team will have to pay for the business assets ($300 million less $8 million of cash). The LBO, if successful, has the potential to create $291 million of value ($583 million less $292 million).[20]

---

[19]The five-year annuity discount factor at 8 percent is 3.9927 (see the table inside the cover pages at the end of book). Multiplying this by $8 million gives $31.9 million.

[20]Note that the LBO's enterprise value ($583 million) is significantly larger than the DCF value of $508 million shown at the bottom of Exhibit 12.9. Because both valuations assume the same improvements in operational efficiency and sales growth, the difference comes from the tax savings provided by the LBO deal.

Will OS Distributors Be Able to Service Its Debt?

We now consider the issue of whether OS Distributors will be able to service its $220 million loan. Although the LBO deal makes sense from a value-creation perspective (its NPV is positive), OS Distributors' management must still meet the challenge of servicing an inordinate amount of debt, particularly the heavy burden of early and rapid principal repayment. *The question is whether the firm's assets under new management will generate enough cash flows to service the firm's debt.* If they do *not*, the financing plan must be revised, that is, borrowing should be reduced and replaced with equity. If additional equity cannot be obtained, the deal may have to be abandoned even though it is a value-creating proposal.

The cash-flow analysis from 2011 to 2016 is summarized in Exhibit 12.13. Part I reports the effect on cash flows of the LBO deal. The total CFAs in row 8 are the cash flows from assets estimated in the merger valuation plus the tax savings from the additional depreciation expenses, both taken from Exhibit 12.12. Are these cash flows high enough to service the $220 million loan?

The amount of cash required to service the loan is shown in row 14 and its calculation in rows 10 to 14. The amount of debt outstanding at the beginning of each year, the annual interest expenses, and the debt repayments are from Exhibit 12.12. Interest expenses are tax deductible, and they have been adjusted using a tax rate of 40 percent. The cash flows to equity holders are given in row 16 with their cumulative values in row 17. The firm has enough cash to pay the debt holders, but the years 2012 and 2013 will be critical. An unexpected decline in the cash flows from business assets, even if relatively small, may cause a serious liquidity problem.

Part II of the exhibit presents the *pro forma* (i.e., future) income statements based on current expectations. The EBIT are computed as in Exhibit 12.6 but with the operational efficiency ratios and the growth rates in sales expected from the LBO restructuring plan. The EAT, obtained after deducting the additional depreciation expenses and the interest expenses from EBIT, show a marginal loss the first year of the LBO followed by a steady increase in profits.

Assuming that the firm will not pay any dividends until after 2016, the firm's equity will increase each year by the amount of earnings after tax. Starting with a book value of equity at $77 million in 2010, we can estimate the book values of equity at the end of each year until 2016. These values are shown in Part III of the exhibit, along with the total capital (equity plus debt outstanding) and the debt ratios (debt-to-total capital) at year-end. The figures show a continuous decrease in the debt ratio. However, it will take more than five years for the firm to return to the pre-LBO ratio of 44 percent and presumably to start paying dividends.

Should the management team go ahead with the deal? Only those directly involved can answer that question. The $300 million price tag is not excessive if the management team is confident that it can rapidly improve the firm's performance according to the restructuring plan. But they will have to keep a close watch on the firm's cash position to avoid any major liquidity problems.

The preceding discussion illustrates an important aspect of an LBO deal: good candidates for an LBO acquisition are generally *underperforming* firms that are expected to generate *stable* and *predictable* cash flows. An LBO involving a firm with

EXHIBIT 12.13 FINANCING OS DISTRIBUTORS' LEVERAGED BUYOUT.

FIGURES IN MILLIONS

	A	B	C	D	E	F	G	H
1		2010	2011	2012	2013	2014	2015	2016
2								
3	**I. Cash Flow Implications**							
4								
5	**Total cash flow from business assets**							
6	Cash flow from business assets		$ 28.7	$ 17.2	$ 20.5	$ 24.3	$ 26.9	$ 30.5
7	Tax savings on additional depreciation expenses		8.0	8.0	8.0	8.0	8.0	0.0
8	**Total cash flow from business assets**		$ 36.7	$ 25.2	$ 28.5	$ 32.3	$ 34.9	$ 30.5
9	**Total cash flow to debt holders**							
10	Debt outstanding at the beginning of the year		$220.0	$200.0	$180.0	$160.0	$140.0	$120.0
11	Interest payment		17.6	16.0	14.4	12.8	11.2	9.6
12	After-tax interest payment (tax rate = 40%)		10.6	9.6	8.6	7.7	6.7	5.8
13	Debt repayment		20.0	20.0	20.0	20.0	20.0	0.0
14	**After-tax cash flow to debt holders**		$ 30.6	$ 29.6	$ 28.6	$ 27.7	$ 26.7	$ 5.8
15								
16	**Cash flow to equity holders**		$ 6.1	$ (4.4)	$ (0.1)	$ 4.6	$ 8.2	$ 24.7
17	**Cumulative cash flow to equity holders**		$ 6.1	$ 1.7	$ 1.6	$ 6.2	$ 14.4	$ 39.1
18								
19	**II. Pro Forma Income Statements**							
20								
21	**Earnings before interest and tax (EBIT)**							
22	*Sales growth rate*		*12.0%*	*10.0%*	*9.0%*	*7.0%*	*6.0%*	*3.0%*
23	*COGS[1] as percent of sales*		*82.33%*	*82.33%*	*82.33%*	*82.33%*	*82.33%*	*82.33%*
24	*SG&A[1] as percent of sales*		*9.5%*	*9.5%*	*9.5%*	*9.5%*	*9.5%*	*9.5%*
25	Sales	$480.0	$537.6	$591.4	$644.6	$689.7	$731.1	$753.0
26	less COGS	(400.00)	(442.61)	(486.87)	(530.68)	(567.83)	(601.90)	(619.96)
27	less SG&A	(48.00)	(51.07)	(56.18)	(61.24)	(65.52)	(69.45)	(71.54)
28	less initial depreciation expenses	(8.00)	(8.00)	(8.00)	(7.00)	(6.00)	(6.00)	(6.00)
29	less additional depreciation expenses		(20.00)	(20.00)	(20.00)	(20.00)	(20.00)	(20.00)
30	equals EBIT	$ 24.0	$ 15.9	$ 20.3	$ 25.7	$ 30.3	$ 33.7	$ 35.5

(Continued)

EXHIBIT 12.13 CONTINUED

	A	B	C	D	E	F	G	H
31	**Earnings before tax**							
32	Interest expenses	$ (7.0)	$(17.6)	$(16.0)	$(14.4)	$(12.8)	$(11.2)	$ (9.6)
33	**Earnings before tax**	**$ 17.0**	**$ (1.7)**	**$ 4.3**	**$ 11.3**	**$ 17.5**	**$ 22.5**	**$ 25.9**
34	**Earnings after tax**							
35	Tax at 40%	(6.8)	0.7	(1.7)	(4.5)	(7.0)	(9.0)	(10.4)
36	**Earnings after tax**	**$ 10.2**	**$ (1.0)**	**$ 2.6**	**$ 6.8**	**$ 10.5**	**$ 13.5**	**$ 15.6**
37								
38	**III. Capital and Debt Ratios**							
39								
40	**Total capital**							
41	Debt outstanding end-of-year	$ 61.0	$200.0	$180.0	$160.0	$140.0	$120.0	$123.6
42	Equity capital	77.0	76.0	78.6	85.4	95.9	109.4	125.0
43	**Total capital**	**$138.0**	**$276.0**	**$258.6**	**$245.4**	**$235.9**	**$229.4**	**$248.6**
44	**Debt ratio**							
45	**Ratio of debt to total capital**	**44%**	**72%**	**69%**	**64%**	**59%**	**52%**	**49%**
46								
47	*Column B, rows 6, 7, 11, 13, 22, 23, 24, 28, 29, 32, and 41, and cell C10 are data.*							
48	*Formula in cell C8 is =C6+C7. Then copy cell C8 to next cells in row 8.*							
49	*Formula in cell D10 is =C10–C13. Then copy cell D10 to next cells in row 10.*							
50	*Formula in cell C12 is =C11*(1–.4). Then copy cell C12 to next cells in row 12.*							
51	*Formula in cell C14 is =C12+C13. Then copy cell C14 to next cells in row 14.*							
52	*Formula in cell C16 is =C8–C14. Then copy cell C16 to next cells in row 16.*							
53	*Formula in cell C17 is =C16. Formula in cell D17 is =C17+D16. Then copy cell D17 to next cells in row 17.*							
54	*Formula in cell C25 is =B25*(1+C22). Then copy cell C25 to next cells in row 25.*							
55	*Formula in cell C26 is =–C23*C25. Then copy cell C26 to next cells in row 26.*							
56	*Formula in cell C27 is =–C24*C25. Then copy cell C27 to next cells in row 27.*							
57	*Formula in cell C30 is =SUM(C25:C29). Then copy cell C30 to next cells in row 30.*							
58	*Formula in cell C33 is =C30–C32. Then copy cell C33 to next cells in row 33.*							
59	*Formula in cell C35 is =.4*C33. Then copy cell C35 to next cells in row 25.*							
60	*Formula in cell C36 is =C33–C35. Then copy cell C36 to next cells in row 36.*							
61	*Formula in cell C42 is =77+C36. Formula in cell D42 is =C42+D36. Then copy cell D42 to next cells in row 42.*							
62	*Formula in cell C43 is =C41+C42. Then copy cell C43 to next cells in row 43.*							
63	*Formula in cell C45 is =C41/C43. Then copy cell C45 to next cells in row 45.*							
64								

[1]COGS = Cost of goods sold; SG&A = Selling, general, and administrative expenses.

volatile and unpredictable cash flows from assets is not recommended because the chances of servicing its debt successfully are lower than in the case of a firm with stable cash flows. Furthermore, because private equity firms are often providers of both equity capital and junior debt financing (which are the riskiest types of financing an LBO), they usually impose a rapid repayment of debt that is easier to achieve with stable and predictable cash flows from assets. Why impose a rapid debt repayment schedule? Because it is the best guarantee for private equity investors that the management team will do its utmost to achieve the *restructuring* plan that will allow investors to get the returns they expect from their contribution to the financing of the LBO. Indeed, a rapid restructuring of the firm's assets is ultimately the key to a successful LBO.

SUMMARY

One approach to the valuation of a firm's equity is based on the market multiples of firms comparable to the one being valued. Although this valuation technique is easy to apply, it does not allow you to test the effect on the firm's value of alternative assumptions about operational efficiency, growth in sales, and different capital structures (this exercise is called sensitivity analysis). Nor can you estimate the potential value that a particular managerial action is expected to create.

The second approach to valuation, the discounted cash-flow (DCF) method, is more complex. First, the future cash-flow stream expected from the firm's business assets must be estimated. Then, these cash flows must be discounted to the present at the firm's weighted average cost of capital (WACC) to obtain the DCF value of the firm's business assets, also called its enterprise value. To get an estimate of the firm's equity value, add cash and deduct current debt from the estimated enterprise value.

The advantage of the DCF approach is that, contrary to the valuation by comparables, it allows managers to do sensitivity analysis to find out how a change in one or more of the valuation parameters under their control will ultimately affect the firm's DCF value. We show that this approach is a valuable tool to assess the potential value creation of an acquisition; it is also a powerful diagnostic technique that can be used to examine whether a change in management strategy and policies could be a source of value creation.

A variation of the DCF approach, the adjusted present value (APV) method, is also explained. The advantage of the APV method is in its ability to value a firm whose capital structure is expected to change over time. Therefore, it is particularly suitable for valuing a leveraged buyout (LBO) deal. We illustrate in the chapter how to implement the alternative DCF valuation methods to the case of OS Distributors for which three different values are estimated: its "as-is" value, its potential acquisition or target value, and its LBO value.

The various valuation methods presented in the chapter are summarized in Exhibit 12.14. On the upper-left side is the equity-multiple approach (or valuation by comparables). On the lower-left side is the DCF approach based on the WACC, and on the lower-right side is the APV approach. At the bottom is the valuation based on earnings before interest, tax, depreciation, and amortization (EBITDA) multiples. For each approach, Exhibit 12.14 shows the steps and the required inputs needed to obtain an estimated value of equity.

EXHIBIT 12.14 ALTERNATIVE EQUITY VALUATION MODELS.[1]

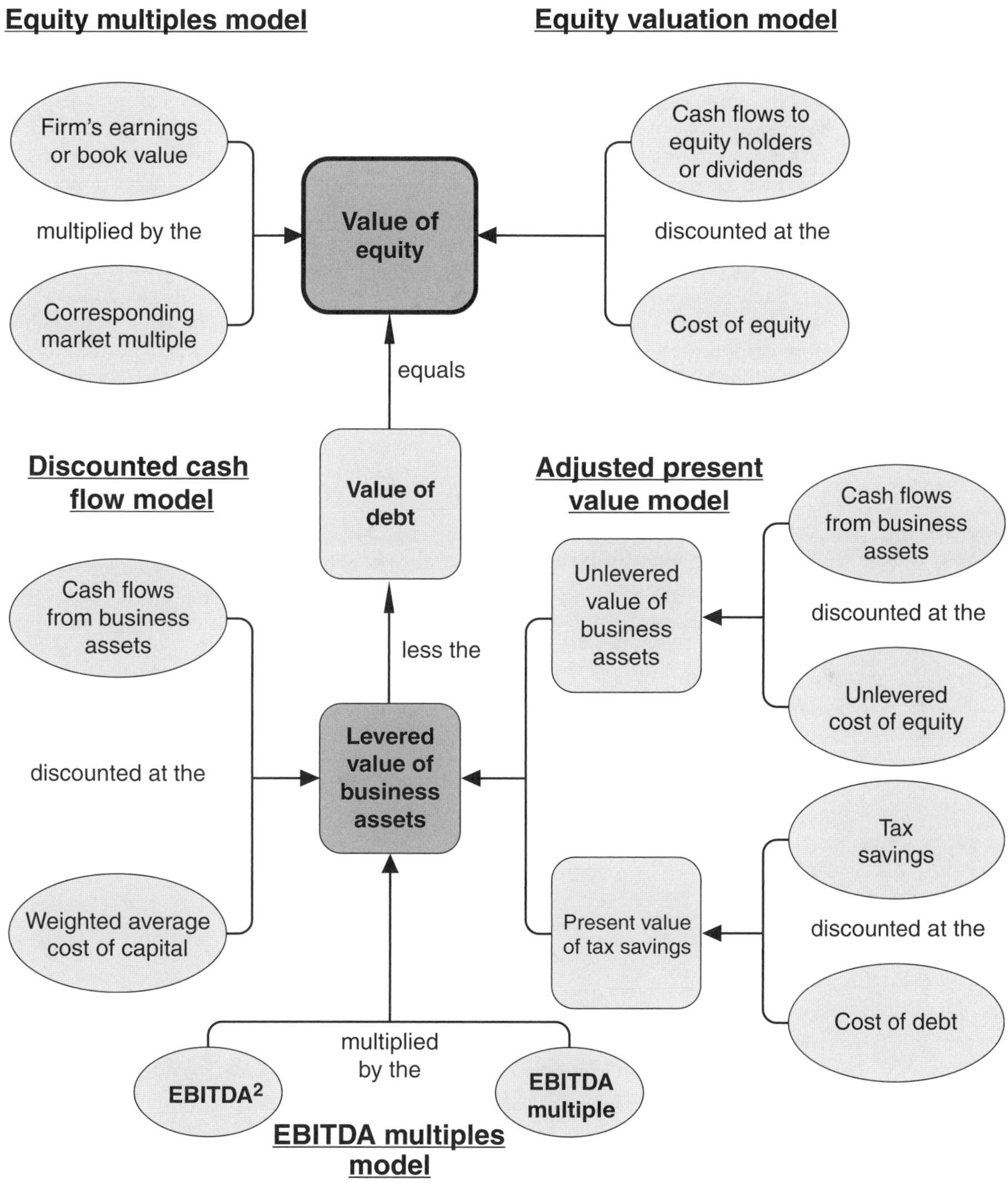

[1]All the valuation models exclude non-operating cash held by the firm.

[2]EBITDA = Earnings before interest, tax, depreciation, and amortization.

The exhibit shows another valuation approach that is not presented in the chapter. It is shown on the upper-right side of the exhibit. The equity valuation model provides a direct estimate of the firm's equity value by discounting at the *cost of equity* the stream of cash flows the firm is expected to distribute to its *shareholders*. This approach is described in Appendix 12.1. Conceptually, the three DCF methods (the WACC, the APV, and the equity valuation model) should provide the same estimate of a firm's equity value. In practice, they will not, because the assumptions made to estimate the cash flows and the discount rates used in the DCF formulas are usually not perfectly consistent across the three methods.

Which of the valuation methods described in this chapter do practitioners use when they value companies? The valuation by multiples is the most commonly employed, with DCF valuation a close second. We recommend the use of both methods. Each has its own merits, and they are not mutually exclusive. The multiple approach is relatively easy to implement and, because it is based on comparables, provides a good approximation of the firm's "as-is" value. The DCF approach is more complicated but is superior when the acquisition of a firm is expected to generate additional value through improved performance or synergistic gains or, in the case of an LBO, through significant tax savings.

The Direct Discounted Cash-Flow Valuation of a Firm's Equity

APPENDIX 12.1

The discounted cash-flow (DCF) model presented in the chapter values a firm's equity in two steps: first, the firm's enterprise value is estimated by discounting the firm's cash flows from business assets (CFA) at the weighted average cost of capital (WACC); cash is then added to enterprise value (EV), and debt (D) is deducted to get the estimated value of the firm's equity (V_E). We show in the chapter that one advantage of that *indirect* equity-valuation approach is that managers can find out how their firm's equity value would change in response to changes in the management of the firm's assets. But we can also use the DCF model to *directly* value the firm's equity in one step.

The direct method is straightforward: in equation 12.4, replace CFA by *cash flow to equity holders* (CFE) and discount them at the estimated cost of equity (k_E) given by equation 12.7.

Notice the difference between the two approaches: the *indirect* approach discounts CFA at the WACC to get enterprise value. Cash is then added to enterprise value and debt deducted to obtain equity value (V_E = EV + Cash − Debt); the *direct* approach discounts CFE at the cost of equity k_E to get V_E directly. How is CFE estimated?

To get the CFE, start with the CFA given in equation 12.5 and deduct the cash flow that goes to debt holders. What is the cash flow that goes to debt holders? It is interest payment on existing debt (taken after tax because the firm saves the tax on interest payments as the result of the tax deductibility of interest payments) and the repayment of debt issued in the past. We can write the following:

$$\textbf{CFE = CFA − Interest payment} \times (1 - T_C) \textbf{ − Debt repayment} \quad \text{(A12.1.1)}$$

We can now illustrate the direct approach with a numerical example and compare it to the indirect approach using the case of a no-growth firm. We know that the value of a no-growth firm is equal to its constant annual cash flow divided by the appropriate discount rate that reflects the risk of the cash flow stream.

Let's assume that the firm's earnings before interest and tax (EBIT) are \$120, its tax rate is 25 percent, its cost of equity is 12 percent, and its cost of debt is 6 percent, and that 40 percent of its assets are financed with debt. The firm does not hold cash, so its total assets are only business assets. Because the firm is not growing, its perpetual CFA is simply its after-tax EBIT (because no-growth means that ΔWCR is zero and depreciation expense equals capital expenditure). Its WACC is given by equation 12.6. We have the following:

$$\text{CFA} = \text{EBIT}(1 - T_C) = \$120(1 - 25\%) = \$90$$

$$\text{WACC} = [60\% \times 12\%] + [40\% \times 6\% \times (1 - 25\%)] = 9\%$$

$$V_A = \frac{\text{CFA}}{\text{WACC}} = \frac{\$90}{0.09} = \$1{,}000$$

The firm's enterprise value is $1,000. It has no cash and $400 of perpetual debt (40 percent of $1,000). Its indirect equity value is thus $600:

$$V_E = \text{EV} + \text{Cash} - \text{Debt} = \$1{,}000 + \$0 - \$400 = \$600$$

Turning now to the direct equity valuation, we first need to estimate the cash flow that goes to equity holders. It is given in equation A12.1.1. Because debt is perpetual, there is no debt repayment, interest payment is $24 (6 percent of $400), and CFE is as follows:

$$\begin{aligned}\text{CFE} &= \text{EBIT}(1 - T_C) - \text{Interest payment} \times (1 - T_C)\\ &= \$90 - \$24 \times (1 - 25\%) = \$90 - \$18 = \$72\end{aligned}$$

Given that the cost of equity is 12 percent, the direct DCF value of the firm's equity is as follows:

$$V_E = \frac{\text{CFE}}{k_E} = \frac{\$72}{0.12} = \$600$$

It is the same as the one found earlier with the indirect DCF method.

Finally, note that the direct DCF approach to equity valuation is similar to the **dividend discount model** we present in Chapter 9. That method calls for discounting the firm's dividend stream at the cost of equity to get a *direct* estimate of the firm's equity value. In our case, because the firm is not growing, it distributes as dividends to shareholders all its equity cash flow (CFE). In this case, replace CFE by dividend payments to get the firm's equity value according to the dividend discount model.

FURTHER READING

1. Damodaran, Aswath. *Damodaran on Valuation*, 2nd ed. John Wiley & Sons, 2006.
2. Damodaran, Aswath. *Corporate Finance: Theory and Practice*, 2nd ed. John Wiley & Sons, 2001. See Chapters 23 through 25.
3. Koller, Tim, Marc Goedhart, and David Wessels. *Valuation: Measuring and Managing the Value of Companies*, 4th ed. John Wiley & Sons, 2005.
4. Rappaport, Alfred. *Creating Shareholder Value*. The Free Press, 2000. See Chapter 8.

SELF-TEST PROBLEMS

12.1 THE PRICE-TO-EARNINGS RATIO.

Explain, without using mathematical formulas, why growth and risk are the main factors that determine the price-to-earnings ratio.

12.2 ALTERNATIVE VALUATION METHODS AND VALUE-CREATING ACQUISITIONS.

Explain why each of the following statements is generally incorrect:

a. "A company's liquidating value acts as a ceiling on its market value, whereas its replacement value acts as a floor."
b. "Because accounting rules differ across countries, price-earnings ratios are better than price-to-cash-flow ratios when making international valuation comparisons."
c. "Different valuation methods, if properly applied, will generate estimates of firm values that are practically identical."

12.3 VALUATION BY COMPARABLES.

The Light Motors Company (LMC) is privately held. Its owners are thinking of listing at least 45 percent of their company's equity on the local stock exchange. Thus, they wish to estimate the value of their company using financial data drawn from the Rapid Engine Corporation (REC), a company listed on the local stock market and comparable to LMC in assets and financial structures. Based on the data given below, provide three estimates of LMC's value. Why do they differ from each other?

	LMC	REC
Earnings before interest, tax, depreciation, and amortization	$125 million	$250 million
Earnings after tax	$ 46 million	$ 90 million
Debt	$420 million	$800 million
Cash	$ 4 million	$ 10 million
Book value of equity	$270 million	$590 million
Number of shares outstanding	Not available	40 million
Share price	Unlisted	$ 30

12.4 EQUITY VALUATION.

Ralph Anders, single owner of Baltek Inc., a distribution company, wonders how much his equity in Baltek is worth. He expects that its cash flow from assets will be $1 million for the current year, with a growth rate of around 3 percent a year for the foreseeable future. He thinks that a return of 8 percent a year from investments in businesses as risky as Baltek is reasonable. Baltek has no debt.

a. What is the discounted cash-flow value of Baltek's assets?
b. What is the value of Baltek's equity?

12.5 DISCOUNTED CASH-FLOW VALUATION.

Using the discounted cash-flow method and the following assumptions, provide an estimate of Light Engines Company's (LEC) equity value.

- Sales, currently at $620 million, will grow by 8 percent for the next two years, by 6 percent during the following two years, and then by 4 percent in perpetuity
- Pre-tax operating margin will remain at 20 percent
- Capital expenditure will be equal to annual depreciation expense
- The working capital requirement will remain at 20 percent of sales
- LEC has $280 million of debt outstanding at 6 percent and is expected to pay a 40 percent corporate tax rate
- National Engines Corporation—a comparable firm that is listed on the local stock exchange—has a ratio of equity-to-total capital of 80 percent at *market* value, and an equity beta of 1.20
- Both the risk-free rate and the market risk premium are 5 percent

REVIEW PROBLEMS

1. **Valuation issues.**
   Explain why each of the following statements is generally incorrect:

   a. "Price-earnings ratios should increase when the yield on government securities rises."
   b. "A company's discounted cash-flow value is usually dominated by the magnitude of its expected cash-flow stream during the future five to ten years, whereas its terminal value usually has a negligible effect on its DCF value."
   c. "The use of high debt ratios to finance leveraged buyouts is essentially a device to capture the tax savings generated by the deductibility of interest expenses."

2. **Some issues in mergers and acquisitions.**
   Comment on the following statements:

   a. "Only synergistic mergers have the potential to create value."
   b. "If a merger cannot generate synergistic gains through cost reductions, it will not create value."
   c. "Conglomerate mergers can create value through superior growth in earnings per share."
   d. "There is strong empirical evidence indicating that acquiring firms create value mostly through their superior ability to uncover target companies that are undervalued by the stock market."

3. **Leveraged buyout.**
   What are the potential sources of value creation and value destruction in a leveraged buyout when compared with an acquisition?

4. **Mergers and price-to-earnings ratios.**
   Maltonese Inc. has 5 million shares outstanding selling at $60 each, and its price-to-earnings ratio (P/E) is 10. Targeton Corp. has 1.5 million shares outstanding with a market price of $30 each, and its P/E ratio is 6. Maltonese is considering the

acquisition of Targeton because it expects that the merger will create $15 million of value.

a. What is the maximum price that Maltonese should pay for one share of Targeton?
b. What would be the P/E ratio of the merged firm if Maltonese issues new shares to finance the acquisition, with Targeton shareholders receiving one Maltonese share for two Targeton shares?

5. **Mergers and price-to-earnings ratios.**
Mergecandor Corp. is considering the acquisition of Tenderon Inc. Mergecandor has 2 million shares outstanding selling at $30, or 7.5 times its earnings per share, and Tenderon has 1 million shares outstanding selling at $15, or five times its earnings per share. Mergecandor would offer to exchange two shares of Tenderon for one share of Mergecandor.

a. If there would be no wealth created from the merger, what would be the earnings per share of the merged firm? Its price-to-earnings (P/E) ratio? Its share price? Would there be any wealth transfer between the shareholders of the two companies?
b. Suppose that, after the merger, the market would not adjust the P/E ratio of Mergecandor, which will stay at 7.5. What would be the new share price of the merged firm? Would there be any wealth transfer between the shareholders of the two companies?

6. **Net present value of an acquisition.**
Motoran Inc. is contemplating the acquisition of a competitor, Tortoran Corp., for $25 million. Motoran's market value is $40 million, whereas that of Tortoran is $20 million. Motoran expects that after the merger the administrative costs of the two companies will be reduced by $1 million forever. Motoran's cost of capital is 12.5 percent.

a. What would be the amount of wealth created by the merger?
b. What is the net present value of the acquisition?

7. **Discounted cash-flow valuation.**
Murlow Company is a privately held firm. David Murlow, its owner-manager, has been approached by Murson Inc. for a possible acquisition. The firm has no debt. What is the minimum price David Murlow should ask, given the following information about his firm?

- Sales, currently at $500 million, are expected to grow by 6 percent for the next three years, and then by 4 percent in perpetuity
- The operating margin before tax is expected to remain at 20 percent of sales
- Annual capital expenditure is expected to be equal to the depreciation expense of the year
- The working capital requirement would remain at 18 percent of sales

- The corporate tax rate is 40 percent
- David Murlow requires a return of at least 10 percent for his family investment in the firm

8. **Discounted cash-flow valuation.**
We wish to estimate the value of Portal Inc. under alternative assumptions about the firm's performance.

   a. Using the discounted cash-flow (DCF) approach to valuation and the following assumptions, provide an estimate of Portal's value.

   - This year sales are expected to be $750 million. They are expected to grow at a rate of 5 percent per year for the next four years, and then at 3 percent per year forever
   - The pre-tax operating margin currently at 15 percent will grow at a rate of 1 percent every year for four years and then stabilize at 20 percent forever
   - The working capital requirement to sales ratio will remain at its current level of 18 percent forever
   - Capital expenditure will be $50 million this year and will grow at the same rate as the sales
   - Annual depreciation expense for the current year will be $50 million and then grow at the same rate as the capital expenditure
   - Portal Inc. has $500 million of debt outstanding. It can borrow at 6 percent
   - Portal's income tax rate is 40 percent
   - Portal's beta is 1.05. The risk-free rate and the market risk premium are 5 percent
   - The debt-to-total-capital ratio of Portal, at market value, is 50 percent

   b. Assume that Portal's performance can be improved through the following:

   1. A half a percentage point increase in the growth rate in sales every year
   2. An improvement in operating margin after tax of 1 percent per year, every year
   3. A reduction of the ratio working capital requirement to sales from 18 percent to 16 percent immediately
   4. A recapitalization that could lower Portal's weighted average cost of capital by 30 basis points

   Show how each of these actions will change the firm's estimated DCF value. What will the change in value be if all actions are implemented simultaneously? Why is the sum of the changes in value resulting from each action smaller than the change in value resulting from their cumulative effects?

9. **Alternatives to cash acquisition.**
Osiris Inc. is considering the acquisition of a competitor, Polos Corp. Osiris expects that the purchase would add $800,000 to its annual cash flow from assets indefinitely. Both firms are fully equity financed and do not carry any debt. The current market value of Osiris is $50 million, and that of Polos is $30 million. Osiris's cost

of capital is 8 percent. Osiris hesitates between offering $20 million in cash and offering 25 percent of its shares to Polos's shareholders.

a. What is the value of the acquisition to Osiris?
b. What is the cost of Polos to Osiris under each alternative?
c. What is the net present value of the purchase to Osiris?

10. **Cash or stock offer?**
Mirandel Inc. is considering the acquisition of Tarantel Corp. Mirandel's earnings after tax are $2 million, it has 2 million shares outstanding, and its price-to-earnings (P/E) ratio is 20. Tarantel's earnings are $1.5 million, it has 0.5 million shares, and its P/E ratio is 15. Mirandel's earnings and dividends are expected to grow at a constant rate of 5 percent per year. With the acquisition of Tarantel, the growth rate is expected to increase to 8 percent.

a. If Mirandel's current dividend per share is $1.50, what is Mirandel's cost of equity capital if its dividend per share grows at a constant rate of 5 percent forever? (Hint: Mirandel's share price is the present value of a dividend per share growing at a constant rate forever. See Appendix 9.1.)
b. What is the value of Tarantel for Mirandel's shareholders?
c. What will the net present value of the acquisition be if Mirandel offers $50 in cash for each outstanding share of Tarantel? What if it offers 756,000 of its shares in exchange for all the outstanding shares of Tarantel? Should Mirandel make a cash or share exchange offer?

MANAGING RISK

CHAPTER 13

Firms are exposed to multiple sources of risk because they operate in an uncertain economic, political, and social environment. Risk cannot be dissociated from business activities—it is the essence of doing business. If managers did not take any risk, their firm would not earn more than the rate of return on riskless assets. Who, then, would invest in a riskless firm when a risk-free rate of return can be earned by simply holding government bonds that are safe and highly liquid?

The question a value-creating manager should ask is *not* how to eliminate risk; it is whether the return from the firm's investments is high enough to compensate for the risk the firm is taking. This risk is borne by the firm's owners, not the firm's managers. If management is unable to generate an adequate *risk-adjusted* return for the firm's owners, they should take immediate action to either increase the expected return to a level that properly compensates owners for the risk they bear or reduce the risk to a level commensurate with current expected return. This is a direct application of the fundamental finance principle presented in Chapter 1 that calls for managers to make decisions that create value for the firm's owners. This principle, however, assumes that managers are able to identify, measure, and control the various risks the firm faces. We present in this chapter a comprehensive risk management system that helps managers achieve this objective.

We have shown in the previous chapters that firms are exposed to at least two broad types of risk called *business risk* and *financial risk*. Business risk occurs because of the firm's inability to know for certain the outcome of its investment decisions. The best-laid plans may go wrong, and the firm's value will suffer. Financial risk occurs when the firm borrows. It is the risk that the firm may not be able to service its debt, meaning that it may not be able to pay the interest on the funds it has borrowed and repay its loans when they are due.

We review in this chapter why business and financial risks occur and show how these risks should be managed. We also examine two other sources of risk a firm faces: *financial investment risk* (the unexpected changes in the value of the *financial* investments the firm has made) and *currency risk* (the risk associated with doing business in a foreign currency). Some of these risks are unavoidable and must be borne by the firm and its owners (such as the business risk associated with the launch of a new product). Other risks can be transferred to an insurance company (by purchasing insurance contracts against, for example, the risk of damage caused by fire) or reduced—and, in some cases, eliminated—through the use of risk management instruments. We show, for example, how a firm with international activities can use forward, futures, and option contracts to reduce the currency risk associated with the selling or buying of a foreign currency whose rate fluctuates against the local currency.

After reading this chapter, you should understand the following:

- What is risk and why it should be managed
- Why firms should manage risk centrally
- The difference between project risk and corporate risk
- The process of managing a firm's exposure to risk
- The four different sources of risk a firm faces: business risk, financial risk, financial investment risk, and currency risk
- How to measure the impact of risk on the firm's value
- The techniques and instruments available to control risk such as forward, futures, and options contracts

WHAT IS RISK?

We have encountered and discussed different types of **risk** throughout the previous chapters. In this chapter, we review the various kinds of risk presented earlier, extend the list to additional risks the firm faces, clarify *what* risk means, explain *why* it should be managed, and finally show *how* to formulate and implement a risk management program.

Risk manifests itself in various ways. It could be an **event risk** or an **ongoing risk**. An event risk is an unexpected incident (such as an earthquake or a disruption in the firm's supply chain) that reduces the firm's value if and when it occurs. An ongoing risk is the continuous, unexpected change in the firm's environment that causes the firm's value to *rise* or *fall* unpredictably. An example is the effect of continuous changes in **foreign-exchange rates**. Consider the case of a U.S. firm that receives quarterly dividend payments from a number of subsidiaries located around the world. An unexpected *fall* in the value of the U.S. dollar against foreign currencies will *increase* the firm's dividend receipts when measured in U.S. dollars. (The firm will get more dollars in exchange for its dividends denominated in foreign currencies.) An unexpected *rise* in the value of the U.S. dollar will have the opposite effect—it will *decrease* the firm's dividend receipts when measured in U.S. dollars. If the firm is unable to control these recurrent and fluctuating cash inflows, its value will rise or fall continuously and unpredictably.

Note that an event risk is always "bad news," because it always reduces the firm's value if and when it happens, whereas an ongoing risk can be either "bad news" or "good news" because it manifests itself as a deviation from an expected outcome. Consider again the firm that receives cash dividends from abroad: "bad news" means that the firm's value declines when it receives lower-than-expected dollar-denominated dividend payments, while "good news" means that the firm's value rises when it receives higher-than-expected dollar-denominated dividend payments. In other words, ongoing risk is defined as *deviations from expectations*: it either manifests itself as an unexpected "upside gain" when the outcome exceeds expectation or an unexpected "downside loss" when the outcome falls short of expectation.

Risk, then, means *knowing* that something can happen that will affect the firm's future value but *not knowing* when it will happen and how it will affect the firm's value when it happens.[1] In the next sections, we draw a comprehensive list of the potential risks a firm faces and suggest a method to measure and manage the firm's exposure to these risks. Before we do this, we first explain *why* a firm should manage risk and then make the point that the risks a firm faces must be managed *centrally* at the corporate level.

WHY SHOULD FIRMS MANAGE RISK?

Should a firm manage the risks it faces? According to the fundamental finance principle, the answer depends on whether the firm's value will be higher with risk management than without it. Benefits as well as costs are associated with managing risks: if the benefits exceed the costs, risk management is a value-creating activity, and the firm should actively manage the risks it faces.

To better understand the conditions under which risk management is a value-creating activity, we first examine the conditions under which it is *irrelevant*, that is, the conditions under which managing risk does not change the firm's value. Understanding when risk management is irrelevant will help us identify the cases when it matters.

We show in Chapter 11 that in the ideal setting of "perfect markets," the firm's value does not change when the firm increases its financial risk through borrowing. Perfect markets are characterized by complete and costless information available to everyone (meaning that managers and investors know all about the firm's prospects) as well as no taxes, no transaction costs, no financial distress costs,[2] no bankruptcy costs (meaning that no costs are associated with reorganizing bankrupt firms), and no agency costs (meaning that managers always make decisions that benefit the firm's owners; see Chapter 11).

When markets are perfect and risk management instruments are correctly priced, then managing a firm's risk does not change its value; this is a generalization of the irrelevance of debt financing in perfect markets to all the risks a firm faces. Firms cannot add value through risk management because investors can do it themselves. For example, an oil company could not increase its value by using

---

[1]Risk is thus "known-unknowns." (We know something can happen, but we do not know when and how it will affect the firm's value.) "Unknown-unknowns" (*not* knowing that something can happen and, obviously, not knowing how it will affect the firm's value) are *unidentifiable* sources of risk: there is not much a firm can do in this case except to become more flexible and resilient in its operations.

[2]When a firm experiences financial difficulties resulting from excessive risk taking, it incurs financial distress costs (see Chapter 11). Examples of these costs include the loss of suppliers who no longer want to sell goods to the firm, the loss of customers who no longer want to buy the firm's goods, and the loss of key employees who no longer want to work for the firm because they all fear that the firm may go out of business.

risk management instruments to protect itself against fluctuations in the price of oil because the firm's investors, who know as much as the firm's managers about that risk exposure and its consequences, could protect themselves *directly* and at the *same* cost as the firm if they want to eliminate that risk.

Now that we know that risk management is irrelevant in perfect markets, we should expect it to be relevant when markets are not perfect. In other words, risk management can be a value-creating activity in a world in which there are taxes, transaction costs, financial distress costs, agency costs, and imperfect and costly information.

When markets are imperfect, corporate risk management can add value by reducing the firm's income tax payments over time, by protecting the firm against risks at a lower cost than if investors did it themselves, by lowering the firm's financial distress and agency costs, and by providing clearer information to investors about the firm's core activities. Furthermore, when information is imperfect, managers know more about their firm's prospects than do outside shareholders. In this case, managers can identify risk exposures and protect against them better than outside shareholders.

RISK MANAGEMENT CAN REDUCE CORPORATE INCOME TAX PAYMENTS

A firm that faces a *progressive* income tax schedule can lower its expected tax payments over time, and thus raise its value, by reducing the *volatility* of its taxable income through hedging, that is, through the use of risk management instruments.[3]

RISK MANAGEMENT CAN LOWER THE COST OF PROTECTION AGAINST RISK

When markets are not perfect, firms can buy protection against risk at a lower cost than the firm's shareholders because firms—particularly the larger ones that are frequent buyers of risk-protection tools—have access to the wholesale market for risk-protection instruments, an option that is not available to individual shareholders. In this case, corporate risk management creates value for the firm's shareholders.

RISK MANAGEMENT CAN LOWER FINANCIAL DISTRESS COSTS

By controlling the risks the firm faces, risk management can reduce the probability that the firm would experience financial distress, thus lowering the costs associated with financial distress (see footnote 2) and increasing the firm's value.

RISK MANAGEMENT CAN PROVIDE CLEARER INFORMATION TO INVESTORS ABOUT THE FIRM'S CORE ACTIVITIES

By protecting itself against risks that are unrelated to its core activities (for example, **foreign-exchange risk**), a firm can provide a clearer picture of its core activities to investors because they will be able to better distinguish between performance

[3]See Graham and Smith (1999), who show that a 5 percent reduction in the volatility of taxable income can generate average tax savings of about 5.4 percent of expected tax liabilities. In extreme cases, these savings could exceed 40 percent.

related to superior management (for example, the ability to effectively operate in foreign countries) and performance related to luck (for example, gains from unexpected movements in foreign-exchange rates). Clearer information about the firm's core activities should allow markets to value the firm more accurately, which should raise its value.

RISK MANAGEMENT CAN LOWER AGENCY COSTS

Following up on the previous point, to the extent that risk management allows shareholders to distinguish between superior performance resulting from managerial skill and superior performance resulting from luck, one can expect managers who are evaluated on their skill rather than luck to make investment decisions that are more aligned with shareholders' interest than their own interests. We return to this point later in the chapter.

CORPORATE RISK MANAGEMENT

Having explained *why* firms should manage the risk they face, we now turn to the issue of *how* firms should formulate and implement a risk management program. We present in Chapter 6 the standard method to deal with risk when making an investment decision. Let's briefly review this method. To decide whether to make an investment, management should estimate the investment's net present value (NPV) by discounting to the present the cash-flow stream the investment is expected to generate in the future and deducting from that present value the investment's initial costs.[4] If the NPV is positive, the investment creates value and should be undertaken. If it is negative, the investment destroys value and should be rejected. How do we adjust the NPV formula to account for the risk of the investment? We do it by adjusting the discount rate for the risk of the investment: the riskier the investment, the higher the discount rate and the lower its NPV. In other words, the riskier the investment, the less valuable it is, reflecting the *risk aversion* of the firm's owners and lenders who financed the investment.

This method deals only with risk at the *project* level. Project-specific risks are best managed by the individuals who are directly responsible for the project. Firms, however, are exposed to multiple sources of risk that are not directly associated with specific projects. Some examples of **corporate risk** include the risk that key employees may leave the company, the risk of a company-wide labor unrest, the risk of a change in tax liability, the risk of a lawsuit, and the risk of damage to facilities caused by fire, weather, or earthquakes. These examples highlight the need to manage corporate risks centrally because otherwise some sources of risk unrelated to specific projects, may be overlooked. Other reasons for wanting to manage risk centrally include (1) risk netting, (2) cost savings, (3) risk policy, and (4) risk learning.

---

[4]The discount rate is the weighted average of the costs of debt and equity used to finance the investment, called the weighted average cost of capital (WACC). See Chapter 11.

Risk Netting

A risk-netting opportunity occurs when some project-specific risks cancel one another. For example, consider Felton, Inc., a U.S.-based firm with two divisions that have international activities. Division A *buys* machinery parts in Germany and is thus exposed to the risk of having to purchase euros with U.S. dollars to pay for the parts at a future date at an unknown exchange rate. Division B *sells* equipment in France and is thus exposed to the *opposite* risk of having to buy U.S. dollars with the euros it will receive from selling the equipment at a future date at an unknown exchange rate. Each division carries a separate exposure to foreign-exchange risk, but what matters to the firm as a whole (and its owners) is the *net* exposure to the euro at the corporate level, which, in this case, is significantly lower than the individual risks borne by the two divisions.

Cost Savings

A cost-savings opportunity occurs when risk protection can be purchased centrally at a lower cost than if purchased at the division level. For example, buying centrally a fire insurance contract to protect all the firm's facilities around the world should be cheaper than the sum of all the individual contracts purchased locally to protect each facility separately.

Risk Policy

A corporate-wide risk policy should be formulated because firms are exposed to multiple sources of risk with different individuals usually responsible for managing different types of risk. Typically, the treasurer buys protection against unexpected changes in foreign exchange and interest rates, the risk manager purchases insurance coverage and chooses the level of deductible, and the procurement manager decides whether to protect against the fluctuations in the price of the commodities the firm buys as inputs to its production process. In principle, these individuals should coordinate their decisions, but in practice, often do not. Thus, it is essential to spell out how particular exposures to risk should be dealt with at the corporate as well as the divisional level.

Additionally, a governance system should be adopted that ensures that the policy is enforced. This aspect of risk management can be achieved only at the corporate level. If each division adopts its own risk policy and governance system, the aggregate impact at the corporate level is unlikely to be optimal. The risk policy should indicate which types of risk are acceptable for the company and which should be rejected, and whether some protection against risk must be purchased if a risk is taken. We return to this point later in the chapter.

Risk Learning

One final reason for wanting to manage risk at the corporate level is to develop a central expertise in risk management. In this case, the department responsible for managing risk centrally can specialize in this function, learn from multiple experiences, develop deeper knowledge of risk management techniques, and provide better advice to each division than if they had to do it on their own. This approach, of course, does not mean that risk learning should occur only at the center. Risk learning should take place throughout the organization, from project-level all the way to headquarters, because risk is everyone's business.

THE RISK MANAGEMENT PROCESS

Firms may be exposed to risks they have not yet identified as well as risks they have identified but have not properly assessed, that is, risks they have either underestimated or overestimated. The consequences are obvious: (1) risks yet unidentified, against which the firm could have protected itself, can destroy value if they occur; (2) value-destroying investments are made because their risk has been underestimated; and (3) value-creating investments are turned down because their risk has been overestimated. To avoid these unfortunate consequences, firms must set up a comprehensive system to identify, measure, manage, and monitor the risks they face. The process required to set up such a system is described in Exhibit 13.1. It consists of the following five steps that are explained in the following sections:

Step 1: The identification of the potential risks the firm faces

Step 2: The measurement of these risks

Step 3: Their prioritization on a scale ranging from minor to major risks

Step 4: The formulation and enforcement of a company-wide risk policy that spells out how to deal with risk

Step 5: The continuous monitoring and improvement of the process over time

EXHIBIT 13.1 THE RISK MANAGEMENT PROCESS.

Step 1	Step 2	Step 3	Step 4	Step 5
Risk Identification	**Risk Measurement**	**Risk Prioritization**	**Risk Policy**	**Risk Monitoring**
Identifying and understanding the various sources of risk that can adversely affect the firm's cash-flows and value	Measuring the impact of each risk on the firm's value by assessing the probability that the risk will occur[1] and estimating the resulting reduction in the firm's value	Classifying the risks according to their intensity by assigning them to categories ranging from minor risks to major risks	Formulating a policy to help decide which risks should be rejected and which should be accepted (either without or with protection) Stating who in the organization has the responsibility to make these decisions	Putting in place an internal audit and control system to continuously monitor the risk management process Reviewing periodically the previous four steps and modifying them in light of any learning experience

[1]The probability of occurrence is assessed within a given period of time, typically equal to the firm's planning horizon.

EXHIBIT 13.2 TYPES AND LEVELS OF CORPORATE RISKS.

Level 1 Risks	Level 2 Risks	Level 3 Risks
1. Business risk	1.1 Macro risk	Economic risk Political risk Social risk
	1.2 Strategic risk	Competition risk Technological risk Other strategic risks
	1.3 Operational risk	Business process risk Commodity price risk Credit risk Fiscal risk Human capital risk Legal risk Property damage risk Reputational risk Other operational risks
2. Financial risk	2.1 Financial leverage risk 2.2 Financing cost risk 2.3 Refinancing risk	Financial distress risk
3. Financial investment risk	3.1 Liquidity risk 3.2 Price risk	
4. Currency risk	4.1 Exchange-rate risk 4.2 Exchange-control risk	Country risk Country risk

STEP 1: RISK IDENTIFICATION

The first step of any risk management system is to identify and understand the circumstances and events that give rise to a risk that may reduce the firm's value if it occurs. These circumstances and events are the source of risk—we say that they create a risk *exposure* for the firm. Of course, the number of such risks is large, and the purpose of the exercise is to come up with the list of those that are the most relevant to the firm. To facilitate this exercise, a checklist of potential risks is provided in Exhibit 13.2.

The first column in Exhibit 13.2 identifies the four distinct and main sources of risk faced by a typical firm and referred to as first-level risks or *level-1 risks*. These are (1) **business risk**; (2) **financial risk**; (3) **financial investment risk**; and (4) **currency risk**. Exhibit 13.3 shows where these four sources of risk originate on the firm's balance sheet. They are reviewed below.

BUSINESS RISK

Business risk is the most fundamental risk a firm faces. It is the direct consequence of conducting business in a constantly changing economic, political, and social

EXHIBIT 13.3 IDENTIFYING THE SOURCES OF FIRM RISK.

ORIGINATING FROM ITS BALANCE SHEET

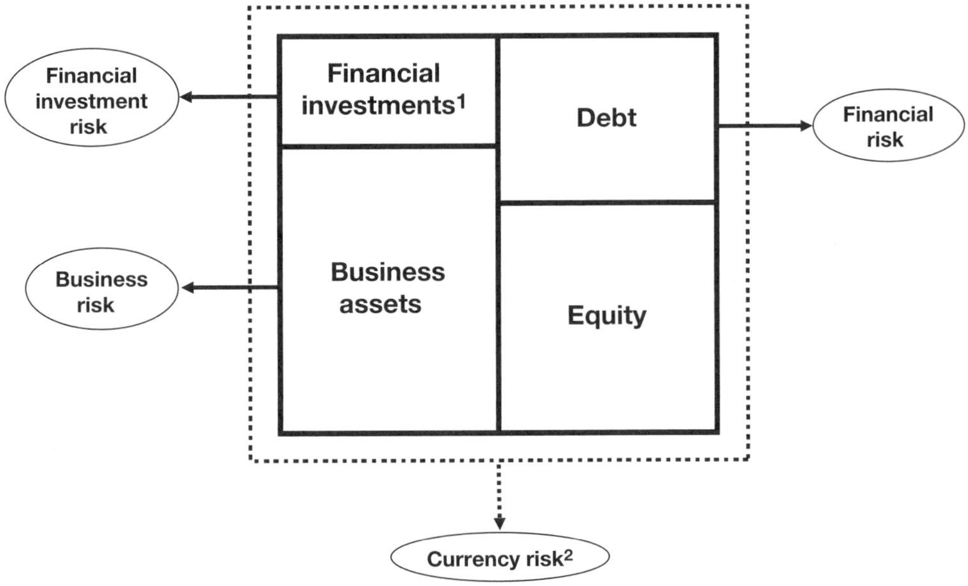

[1]Financial investments include cash, marketable securities, and long-term financial assets such as bonds and shares of other companies.
[2]Currency risk occurs when some of the firm's business assets, financial investments, or borrowing (debt) is denominated in a foreign currency. If a firm exports some of its products or services abroad, it will have accounts receivable denominated in foreign currencies; if it imports goods or services from abroad, it will have accounts payable denominated in foreign currencies.

environment while competing within an industry that is continuously evolving. Sources of business risk are unanticipated events and situations that can affect the firm's market value when they occur. As shown in Exhibits 13.2 and 13.4, this risk can be broken down into three nonoverlapping second-level risks or *level-2 risks*, called **macro risk, strategic risk**, and **operational risk**, discussed below.

A large number of future events and situations can create business risk. How can the firm's management identify them? The standard method is to interview employees and consult experts. Conducting in-depth interviews with experienced employees who are familiar with the various aspects of the firm's operations quickly will reveal a multitude of business risks. Of course, some of those risks may not be important at the corporate level even if they matter to a particular area of the firm, but the exercise must first be exhaustive before the list can be eventually narrowed down.

Macro Risk Macro risk originates in the broad economic, political, and social environments in which the firm operates. It can thus be broken down into three separate categories based on the three "environments" that affect the firm's performance. They are listed as *level-3 risks* in the last column of Exhibit 13.2 and referred to as **economic risk, political risk**, and **social** or **societal risk**.

EXHIBIT 13.4 SOURCES OF BUSINESS AND FINANCIAL RISKS.

Business Risk Events that affect the firm's expected cash flow from assets			Financial Risk Additional risks resulting from debt financing		
Macro Risk	**Strategic Risk**	**Operational Risk**	**Financial Leverage Risk**	**Financing Cost Risk**	**Refinancing Risk**
Unanticipated "macro" events (over which the firm has little control) that may reduce expected revenues and/or raise expected costs	Unanticipated industry events (over which the firm has little control) that may reduce expected revenues and/or raise expected costs	Unanticipated events that occur when the firm implements its strategy that may reduce its expected revenues and/or raise its expected operating costs	When a firm borrows, the variability of its net profits increases, thus making the firm more risky to its owners	Unexpected changes in market interest rates that increase the firm's cost of debt	Inability to renew a loan
<u>Examples</u>: ***<u>Economic risk</u>*** A steeper-than-expected slowdown in economic activity ***<u>Political risk</u>*** Unexpected government regulations that constrain the firm's ability to generate profits ***<u>Social risk</u>*** Unanticipated changes in employees' and consumers' behavior	<u>Examples</u>: ***<u>Competition risk</u>*** More competition in the product market that lowers product prices, or less competition in the input market that raises input prices ***<u>Technological risk</u>*** New technology that makes existing products obsolete	<u>Examples</u>: ***<u>Business process risk</u>*** Disruptions in the supply chain, IT system, etc.; delays in the delivery of plants and equipment; labor unrests; and/or frauds and thefts ***<u>Commodity price risk</u>*** ***<u>Property damage risk</u>*** Damage to property due to fire, accidents, natural disasters, etc. ***<u>Reputational risk</u>*** Withdrawal of defective products	<u>Example</u>: See the case of the Hologram Light Company (HLC) in Exhibit 13.5. If the firm does not borrow, its profits vary between minus and plus 26 percent (see EBIT); with borrowing its profits vary between minus and plus 31 percent (see EAT)	<u>Example</u>: The firm has taken a one-year loan at 7 percent to finance a two-year investment. At the end of the year, market interest rates go up as a result of a "tighter" monetary policy. The firm can only renew its one-year loan at 9 percent	<u>Example</u>: The firm has taken a one-year loan to finance a two-year investment. At the end of the year, the firm's bank refuses to renew the loan for an additional year. The firm is facing a major funding risk

An example of economic risk is a steeper-than-expected slowdown in economic activity that would reduce the firm's future cash flow from assets and thus its current market value. An example of political risk is *regulatory risk*, the risk of a change in government regulation that would restrict the firm's ability to raise the price of some of its goods and services; another example of political risk is *country risk*, the risk that a foreign government may prohibit a firm from transferring cash out of the foreign country in which it is doing business. Regulatory and country risks can be referred to as *level-4 risks*. This does not mean, however, that they are less important than higher-level risks. *For some firms, a level-4 risk, such as regulatory or country risk, may be the major source of business risk.*

Social risk is generated by unanticipated changes in people's attitude toward work and consumption. Examples include changes in the behavior of a younger generation of employees that may require firms to modify the way work is organized (more freedom, more creative challenges) or changes in consumer behavior that may affect the type of products and services they want to buy. Firms may not correctly anticipate these behavioral changes. This, in turn, could adversely affect their market value because of their failure to adapt to a new type of workforce or to adjust to new consumer tastes.

Strategic Risk Strategic risk is associated with unanticipated changes in the dynamics of a firm's *industry* that may have a negative impact on the firm's market value. Some of these risks are listed as *level-3* risks in the last column of Exhibit 13.2 and described on the left side of Exhibit 13.4. The major sources of strategic risk are actions taken by competitors and key suppliers that would reduce the firm's market value. They include competition risk and technological risk.

Examples of *competition risk* include an unexpected price reduction by a competitor on a product similar to the one offered by the firm that may force the firm to respond by cutting the price of its own product, which will reduce its future cash flow from assets and hence its current market value; the launch by a competitor of a new product or service that would erode the sales of the firm's similar offerings; and the decision of a supplier to raise the price of a key input for which no substitute is immediately available.

Other types of strategic risk include *technological risk*—that is, the risk that the firm may not be able to adopt as rapidly as its competitors an emerging technology that will render the existing one obsolete. A classic example of this phenomenon is digital photography that eventually wiped out chemical photographic films.

Operational Risk The third and last source of business risk is operational risk. Operational risk occurs when the firm implements its strategy. These risks are associated with the "execution" of the firm's strategy. Examples of this type of risk include unexpected disruptions and delays in the firm's supply chain and information technology (IT) systems, possible labor unrests, unforeseen delays in the delivery of new plants and equipment, and the risk of fraud and theft. We group these sources of operational risks under the heading of *business process risk*.

Other types of operational risk include *commodity price risk* (the unexpected changes in the price of commodities the firm uses as inputs in its production processes), **credit risk** (the risk that some customers may not pay on time for the goods and services they purchased and possibly default on their payments to the firm),[5] *fiscal risk* (the risk of a change in the amount of taxes a firm has to pay, either because of a tax audit that ends up raising the amount of tax payment or because of a change in the tax laws), *human capital risk* (the inability to replace key employees who may leave the firm), *legal risk* (the risk of a lawsuit that may create a significant legal liability for the firm), *property damage risk* (the risk caused by events that damage the firm's plants, equipment, and facilities such as fire, accidents, floods, and earthquakes), and *reputational risk*. Reputational risk occurs, for example, when the firm has sold a product that is harmful to consumers or defective, causing the firm to withdraw the unsafe product from the market or recall the product with defective parts. The risk is that the firm's reputation may be damaged, which may reduce the firm's value temporarily or permanently.

Commodity price risk has been classified as operational because firms can protect against it (for example, an airline company can hedge against unexpected changes in the price of fuel). Credit risk has been classified as operational because it arises from the business practice of letting customers pay their bills at a later date, which is essentially an operating decision. Reputational risk has been classified as operational because it occurs as a consequence of poor execution, not because of a flawed strategy. In other words, the firm may have the right strategy but has failed to put in place a rigorous enough quality control system to detect unsafe or defective products. (For example, it is a sound strategy for Toyota to build cars in the United States, but its reputation was sullied when some of its U.S.-built cars had defective parts.)

Changes in commodity prices, uncollectible accounts receivable, the departure of a key employee, supply disruptions, labor unrests, delivery delays, damages to property, higher-than-expected taxes, and defective products are not strategic risks. They are adverse events that occur in the process of carrying out the firm's strategy. The firm has some control over these *level-3* risks—indeed, hedging commodity prices, asking high-risk customers to pay their bills immediately in cash, introducing a more effective employee retention program, and enforcing more efficient management processes and policies can reduce these risks significantly.

FINANCIAL RISK

The second main source of risk a firm faces is financial risk. As pointed out in the introduction, this risk occurs when the firm borrows, as shown on the right side of the firm's balance sheet in Exhibit 13.3. If the firm is all-equity financed (that is, if it is 100 percent financed with equity capital), it does not carry any financial risk.

Financial risk is broken down into three nonoverlapping *level-2* risks that are the direct consequence of borrowing: **financial leverage risk, financing cost risk,** and **refinancing risk**. These risks are listed in the second column of Exhibit 13.2 and described in the right side of Exhibit 13.4.

Financial Leverage Risk We show in Chapter 11 that the risk borne by the firm's owners increases when the firm borrows. This risk, called financial leverage risk, is

[5] To protect against this risk, firms make allowances for doubtful customers' accounts, that is, they reduce the reported value of their accounts receivable to reflect the potential losses (see Chapter 2).

the most important manifestation of financial risk. When a firm borrows, it increases the *volatility* of its net profits, making the firm more risky for its shareholders. This phenomenon is illustrated in Exhibit 13.5 with the case of the Hologram Lighting Company (HLC), a firm we first encountered in Chapter 1. Its projected income statement, one year from now, shows expected sales of $1,000 million and expected operating expenses of $760 million (one half of operating expenses is variable, and the other is fixed). The resulting expected operating profit is $240 million (earnings before interest and tax, or EBIT). Deducting $40 million of *fixed* interest expenses gives a taxable profit of $200 million (earnings before tax, or EBT). Finally, deducting $100 million of tax expenses leaves an expected net profit of $100 million (earnings after tax, or EAT).

Consider now an unexpected drop or rise in sales of 10 percent. How does the variability of sales affect operating profit (EBIT) and net profit (EAT)? Look at the data in Exhibit 13.5. When sales vary between minus 10 percent and plus 10 percent, EBIT varies between minus 26 percent and plus 26 percent, and EAT between minus 31 percent and plus 31 percent. Clearly, the presence of *fixed* operating expenses has magnified the variability of EBIT. Likewise, the presence of *fixed* interest expenses has magnified the variability of EAT.

Had HLC not borrowed, its pre-tax net profit would be equal to EBIT (no interest expenses will be deducted in this case), and the risk borne by HLC's owners would be captured by the 26 percent volatility that is all business risk (there is no financial risk because there is no borrowing). With borrowing, HLC's pre-tax net profit is equal to EBT and the risk borne by HLC's owners has been magnified to 31 percent because of the financial risk created by the presence of *fixed* interest expenses. Conclusion: without borrowing, HLC's owners bear only business risk; with borrowing, they bear both business risk and financial risk.

What is the effect of financial leverage on the firm's value? We show in Chapter 11 that in the presence of taxes and costly financial distress (see footnote 2), the firm's value

EXHIBIT 13.5 UNDERSTANDING BUSINESS AND FINANCIAL RISKS: EFFECT ON EBIT, EBT, AND EAT OF A 10% DROP OR RISE IN SALES.

FIGURES IN MILLIONS

	Expected[1]	Sales Down 10%		Sales Up 10%	
Sales	**$1,000**	**$900**	**−10%**	**$1,100**	**+10%**
Less variable operating expenses	(380)	(342)	−10%	(418)	+10%
Less fixed operating expenses	(380)	(380)	0%	(380)	0%
EBIT (earnings before interest and tax)	**$240**	**$178**	**−26%**	**$302**	**+26%**
Less fixed interest expenses	(40)	(40)	0%	(40)	0%
EBT (earnings before tax)	**$200**	**$138**	**−31%**	**$262**	**+31%**
Less variable tax expenses (50% tax rate)	(100)	(69)	−31%	(131)	+31%
EAT (earnings after tax)	**$100**	**$69**	**−31%**	**$131**	**+31%**

[1]Note that the expected scenario is the same as the one shown in Exhibit 1.8 in Chapter 1.

is affected by financial leverage: there is an optimal level of borrowing for which the value of the firm's assets is maximized. Lower or higher levels of debt will reduce the value of the firm's assets below its optimal value.

Financing Cost Risk Financing cost risk, first introduced in Chapter 3, is the risk of not knowing the cost of the debt used to finance an investment. Why would a firm not know its cost of debt when it decides to make an investment? To illustrate, suppose that HLC borrows $1 million at 7 percent for *one* year to buy a new piece of equipment that it will operate over a period of *two* years. The firm's intention is to renew the one-year loan at the end of the first year for one more year. Assume further that HLC could have borrowed initially for two years at the same rate of 7 percent, but because it expected the one-year interest rate to drop below 7 percent next year, it decided to finance the investment with two consecutive one-year loans (instead of a single two-year loan at 7 percent). If next year's rate drops below 7 percent, the average cost of debt over the two-year investment will obviously be less than 7 percent. If it rises above 7 percent, the average cost of debt will be more than 7 percent. HLC is clearly taking a risk. More precisely, it is *speculating* that next year's interest rate will drop. It could have avoided that risk if it had borrowed for two years. Is that risk worth taking? Probably not, because the nature of HLC's business is not to make money speculating on the direction of interest rates. If HLC's owners wanted to speculate on the direction of interest rates, they would do it directly or invest in a financial firm that specializes in this type of activity.

Refinancing Risk Continuing with the same example, if HLC borrows for one year to finance the two-year investment, it is incurring an additional risk called refinancing risk, first discussed in Chapter 3. Suppose that in one year the economic outlook deteriorates and that HLC's bank responds to this new environment by restricting credit to HLC, turning down the firm's request to renew the loan for one year. What would happen in this case? HLC may have to terminate the project and sell the piece of equipment it bought last year to repay the loan. Most likely, it will sell it for less than $1 million and may thus find itself in a precarious situation if it is unable to repay the bank loan. HLC could have avoided this risk if it had borrowed for two years. Again, is that risk worth taking? Certainly not, because the consequences for the firm if it is not able to renew its loan are significantly more important than the potential gain from a possible drop in interest rate next year.

Financial Investment Risk

Although firms are generally net borrowers (their debt exceeds their cash holding), they also act as lenders to other firms and often hold shares in other companies. They thus carry risks associated with *financial* investments, which we call *financial* investment risk. This risk is shown on the left side of the firm's balance sheet in Exhibit 13.3. This risk is, in turn, broken down into two nonoverlapping *level-2* risks called **liquidity risk** and **price risk** (see Exhibit 13.2).

Consider HLC again. Assume it holds marketable securities such as commercial paper (see Chapter 9) as well as shares in a company called ALPAC. ALPAC was a division of HLC. Two years ago, HLC decided to list it on the stock market as a separate company through an initial public offering. HLC, however, still holds 10 percent of ALPAC shares. Both the marketable securities and the ALPAC shares that HLC holds carry a specific financial investment risk discussed below.

Liquidity Risk Even though the marketable securities HLC holds are liquid—meaning that HLC should be able to convert them into cash rapidly and without significant loss of value—they nevertheless carry a liquidity risk. This is the risk that HLC may have an unexpected need for cash and may end up selling some of these short-term securities at a loss if market conditions are unstable.[6]

Price Risk ALPAC shares carry a price risk—that is, the risk that their price may fall below the price HLC received when it listed them. The ALPAC share price moves up and down as the market updates its assessment of ALPAC's business prospects. Over time, ALPAC may underperform and its share price may drop below its original price. As a result, the value of HLC will decline to reflect the loss on the ALPAC shares it owns.

Currency Risk

Broadly speaking, currency risk occurs because of unexpected changes in the exchange rate between the home currency and the currency of a foreign country in which a firm is doing business. We can distinguish between two forms of *level-2* currency risk: **exchange-rate risk** and **exchange-control risk**. The former is caused by the market fluctuations in the exchange rates between two currencies in a regime of free-floating rates. The latter is caused by unexpected changes in the *fixed* exchange rate between two currencies in a regime of managed float or exchange control.[7] A *level-3* currency risk includes **country risk**, such as the restrictions imposed by a foreign government on the flow of funds between the home country and the rest of the world. Currency risk is examined in detail later in this chapter, and its effect on the firm's decision to invest abroad is examined in Chapter 14.

Step 2: Risk Measurement

Having identified the potential risks the firm is facing, management must now measure these risks and rank them. Identifying them is only the first step in the risk management process. If these risks cannot be measured, the firm will not be able

[6]We have argued earlier that firms should manage the risk of their *net* exposure; in this case, their *net* debt position (debt *net* of cash and marketable securities). However, two firms with the same amount of net debt might face a different risk exposure if they hold marketable securities with different liquidity risk. Furthermore, net debt is also affected by the risk associated with maturity mismatch (debt has typically longer maturities than cash and cash equivalents). We, therefore, recommend that firms manage the risk of their cash-equivalent position independently from their borrowing risk.

[7]In a managed float regime, a government allows its currency to fluctuate within a narrow band in relation to a foreign currency (usually the U.S. dollar) and intervenes in the foreign exchange market to buy or sell its currency to maintain it within the chosen band. In a fixed exchange rate regime, a government will intervene in the market to maintain a *fixed* rate between the home currency and a foreign currency (usually the U.S. dollar).

to manage them (you cannot manage what you cannot measure). What would then be the appropriate measure of a risk a firm is facing? Because what matters in the end is whether that risk has a negative impact on the firm's *value*, the appropriate measure of a risk is the *expected reduction in the firm's value if that risk occurs.* We call it **market value at risk** (**MVR**) and calculate it as follows:

$$\text{MVR} = \left[\begin{array}{c}\textbf{Reduction in the}\\ \textbf{firm's value if}\\ \textbf{the risk occurs}\end{array}\right] \times \left[\begin{array}{c}\textbf{Probability that}\\ \textbf{the risk will occur}\end{array}\right] \qquad (13.1)$$

To illustrate, let's consider the simplified case of the No Growth Company (NGC). It generates an annual perpetual cash flow from assets of $100 million, and its cost of capital is 10 percent. NGC's enterprise value is thus $1,000 million ($100 million of perpetual cash flow divided by a 10 percent cost of capital; see Chapter 12). Suppose that NGC is exposed to the four risks listed in the first column in Exhibit 13.6.

Risk A is a strategic risk. NGC's management believes that there is a 50 percent chance that a competing firm will launch a new product within the next 12 months that will reduce NGC's annual cash flow from assets by $20 million forever. The present value, at the cost of capital of 10 percent, of this annual perpetual reduction in cash flow is $200 million (see the third column in Exhibit 13.6). With a 50 percent chance of occurrence, the impact of this risk on NGC's enterprise value is $100 million (50 percent of $200 million). The $100 million is the measure of NGC's strategic risk exposure we call MVR.

Referring to Exhibit 13.6 and using the same approach, NGC's management estimates that the firm is exposed to a currency risk (Risk B) with an MVR of $20 million, a financing cost risk (Risk C) with an MVR of $10 million, and a business process risk related to potential disruptions in the supply chain (Risk D) with an MVR of $1 million (refer to the answer to Self-Test Problem 13.3 that shows how these risk measures are estimated).

EXHIBIT 13.6 RISK MEASUREMENT.

Type of Risk[1]	Probability of Occurrence[2]	Impact on the Firm's Market Value[3]	Market Value at Risk (MVR)		Ability to Control the Risk[4]
(1)	(2)	(3)	(4) = (2) × (3)	Rating	(5)
Strategic risk (A)	50%	$200 million	$100 million	High	Low
Currency risk (B)	10%	$200 million	$ 20 million	Moderate	High
Financing cost risk (C)	50%	$ 20 million	$ 10 million	Moderate	Moderate
Business process risk (D)	10%	$ 10 million	$ 1 million	Low	Moderate

[1]See Exhibit 13.2.
[2]Within the next 12 months.
[3]Estimation of the reduction in the firm's market value if the corresponding risk materializes.
[4]The firm's ability to take action to reduce the risk.

Note in the fifth column of Exhibit 13.6 the relative rating of the four risks. Risk A has the largest MVR ($100 million), but why is it rated "a high risk"? Recall that NGC's enterprise value is $1,000 million; thus the MVR of Risk A is equal to 10 percent of NGC's enterprise value, which represents a significant risk exposure. The MVR of Risk B is 2 percent of enterprise value and that of Risk C is 1 percent. Both are rated "moderate." The MVR of Risk D is 0.1 percent of enterprise value and is rated "low." In general, a risk with an MVR of 10 percent or more of a firm's enterprise value would be rated high and a risk with an MVR of 0.1 percent or less of a firm's enterprise value would be rated low. There is, of course, no rigid risk-rating rule—each firm should adjust the scale according to its owners' tolerance for risk.

STEP 3: RISK PRIORITIZATION

A firm does not have to bear all the risk exposures it faces. It can protect itself against some of them. For example, the currency risk NGC faces (Risk B) can be eliminated over the next twelve months using a technique we present later in this chapter. It is thus rated "highly controllable" in the last column of Exhibit 13.6, meaning that it is possible for NGC to eliminate this type of risk over the next twelve months at a reasonable cost.

Contrary to the case of currency risk, the ability of NGC to control Risk A is low because NGC cannot do much during the next twelve months to prevent the competitor's new product from eroding NGC's sales. NGC should have anticipated this move earlier. (Is NGC investing enough time and resources to find out what the competition is doing?) It could have launched a new product, but at this point, NGC can do little to mitigate that risk. The financing cost risk (Risk C) and the risk of disruptions in the supply chain (Risk D) are both rated "moderate." NGC could use risk-control instruments to reduce the financing cost risk it faces, but these instruments are not as reliable and inexpensive as those used to control currency risk. The supply-disruption risk was rated "moderate" because NGC has the ability to switch rapidly and inexpensively to another supplier if disruptions occur with its current supplier.

We can now put each risk in one of the nine boxes shown in the graph in Exhibit 13.7. The MVR is on the vertical axis, going from low to high MVR. The firm's ability to control risk is shown on the horizontal axis, going from high to low control. The graph has nine possible combinations: three are labeled "major risk," two are labeled "important risk," and four are labeled "minor risk." These three different labels (major, important, and minor risks) are a measure of **risk severity**. For example, Risk A (strategic risk) is a "major risk" because it has a high impact on NGC's value, but the firm's ability to control it is low. Risk C (financing cost risk) is an "important risk" because it has a moderate impact on NGC's value and the firm's ability to control it is moderate. Both Risk B and Risk D are minor risks.

A risk with a high MVR (meaning that its impact on the firm's value is high if it occurs) is not necessarily a major risk if it is highly controllable (see the upper-left-side box in Exhibit 13.7). Likewise, a risk with a moderate MVR can be a major risk if the firm's ability to control it is low (see the middle-right-side box in Exhibit 13.7). In other words, risk severity (major, important, or minor) depends on the impact the risk has on the firm's value *adjusted* by the firm's ability to control that risk.

EXHIBIT 13.7 MAPPING FIRM RISKS ACCORDING TO THEIR SEVERITY.[1]

Impact of risk on the firm's market value \ Ability to control risk	High	Moderate	Low
High	Important risk	Major risk	Major risk *(Risk A in Exhibit 13.6)*
Moderate	Minor risk *(Risk B in Exhibit 13.6)*	Important risk *(Risk C in Exhibit 13.6)*	Major risk
Low	Minor risk	Minor risk *(Risk D in Exhibit 13.6)*	Minor risk

[1]There are three levels of risk severity: minor risks, important risks, and major risks.

STEP 4: RISK POLICY

Having identified, measured, and mapped the risks the firm is facing, management must now formulate a policy to deal with these exposures. Specifically, faced with a risk exposure, management can do one of three things:

1. *Reject the risk altogether*, that is, decide not to undertake the activity that generates the risk (or abandon an ongoing activity whose risk has gone up)
2. *Accept the risk without protecting the firm against it (partially or totally)*, that is, decide to go ahead with the activity (or maintain it if it is ongoing) and cover any losses that may occur using the firm's own resources
3. *Accept the risk and protect the firm against it*, that is, go ahead with the activity and take action to protect the firm against the risk exposure through one of three methods: *insurance*, *diversification*, or *hedging*

The issue then is to formulate a corporate-wide risk policy that will help managers decide which options to select when confronted with a risky decision. Before examining these options, we first review some of the most important characteristics that a firm's risk policy should display.

GOVERNANCE

Who should formulate the firm's risk policy? It is the role of senior management to design the firm's risk policy and submit it to the board of directors for approval. The firm may then appoint a chief risk officer to oversee and coordinate the implementation of the policy, reporting to the firm's chief executive. If the firm is not large enough to justify the creation of the position of chief risk officer, the firm's chief financial officer or the senior executive in charge of strategy usually takes on the responsibility.

Who should make the decision to reject or accept the major and important risks the firm faces? That decision is often made by a *risk management committee* co-chaired by the firm's chief executive and the chief risk officer. In other words, risk management is the domain of the most senior executives. This does not mean, however, that the rest of the organization is not concerned; on the contrary, as we pointed out earlier, senior management should foster a culture of "risk-is-everyone's-business" throughout the firm.

VALUE CREATION

The guiding principle for making risk management decisions is still the fundamental finance principle stated in Chapter 1 and reviewed earlier in this chapter: management must manage the firm's resources with the ultimate objective of creating value. This value-creation objective is achieved only when the firm accepts new risky investments (or retains existing risky investments) that have a positive NPV *after adjusting the NPV for all the risks associated with the investment.*

CORPORATE RISK

The firm is not only exposed to project-specific risks but also to sources of corporate risk that are not captured by its individual projects. The firm's risk policy must provide guidance on how to deal with these risks. For example, the risk management committee, with the help of the firm's human resources department, should formulate a personnel-retention policy to reduce the loss of key employees, an important source of corporate risk. Other examples include the formulation of policies that minimize the risks of lawsuits, fiscal audits, product recalls, IT system failures, and so on.

ALIGNING THE INTERESTS OF MANAGERS WITH THOSE OF OWNERS

Managers may have a different tolerance for risk than that of the firm's owners. In general, one would expect them to be more conservative than shareholders because their salaries, employment prospect, and retirement income may be endangered if the firm makes risky investments that could threaten its survival. Shareholders are usually more diversified than managers (because they hold shares in many companies) and are thus willing to accept more risk than managers to achieve higher expected returns.[8]

---

[8]In some cases, the firm's managers are *more* diversified than the firm's owners and thus ready to invest in riskier projects than owners would have liked. This would be the case of a firm that belongs to undiversified owners who invested all their wealth in the firm while managers' wealth is diversified. In this case, some managers, particularly those with a bonus related to a high profit, would be ready to invest in risky projects that produce high profits (they get the bonus) or high losses (they lose the bonus, but their portfolio is not affected).

The firm's risk policy must align the interests of managers with those of shareholders by encouraging managers to accept value-creating projects even if these projects have more risk than they wish to accept as individuals.

Performance Evaluation

Consider a U.S.-based firm that exports some of its products to Japan. Manager A has bought protection against changes in the exchange rate between the U.S. dollar and the Japanese yen, and his division generated a year-end operating profit of $15 million ($16 million less $1 million of foreign-exchange protection) on $100 million of invested capital, that is, a return on invested capital (ROIC) of 15 percent (16 percent less the 1 percent cost of protection). Manager B did not protect her profit against foreign-exchange risk. A year later, the U.S. dollar weakened and her division, which also employs $100 million of capital, reported $20 million of operating profits of which $5 million were foreign-exchange gains resulting from the weakening of the U.S. dollar relative to the Japanese yen. Manager B's ROIC is thus 20 percent, including 5 percent of foreign-exchange gains. How should we judge the performance of the two managers?

If the firm's risk policy requires that foreign-exchange risk be systematically covered, then Manager A should *not* be penalized for covering his division's foreign-exchange risk and missing the opportunity to make a currency gain. His reward should be based on whether his 15 percent performance exceeds a minimum required rate of return for the division. Under the same policy, Manager B should *not* be rewarded for reporting a 5 percent extra operating profit through currency gains and *should* be blamed for not covering her division's foreign-exchange risk. Her reward should be based on whether her 15 percent performance exceeds a minimum required rate of return for the division.

Coordination with the Firm's Strategic Management Process

A firm's risk management process cannot take place separately from the firm's strategic decision-making process. The two processes must be coordinated. It is not possible to formulate a sound strategy independently of the risk exposures that the strategy creates. Likewise, it is not possible to devise a corporate-wide risk policy independently of the strategies that generate those risks. Clearly, the decisions of the risk management committee must be coordinated with those of the firm's strategy committee with the single objective of making risk-adjusted value-creating decisions.

Having presented a number of issues a firm's risk policy should address, we now return to the three options open to management when faced with an identified and measured risk. As you recall, there are three courses of action: (1) reject the risk and the investment that generates it; (2) accept the risk without protecting the firm against it; and (3) accept the risk and protect the firm against it. It is the role of the risk management committee to provide guidance on which alternative to choose when facing a particular risk.

The Decision to Reject the Risk

The firm's management may decide that some major risks are not acceptable either as a matter of principle (for example, the firm does not invest in developing countries with poor human rights records) or because management has concluded that the investment could not generate an expected return high enough to justify the risk (for example, the firm does not invest in countries where it believes political risk is too high even if the expected return is also high).

The Decision to Accept the Risk without Protection

In this case, the firm decides to undertake an activity that carries an important or major risk without trying to reduce that risk. Why would a firm undertake an activity without risk protection? One reason may be that the risk protection is unavailable or that it is prohibitively expensive and thus unjustified. But the most important reason to accept a risk without protection is that risk taking is the essence of business activities. As we said in the introduction, if the firm does not accept some risk, it would not be able to generate a return that would attract equity capital.

Accepting the risk without protection does not mean that the firm should not take any measure to reduce the risk. For example, if fire insurance is not available on some of the firm's facilities, strict measures should be enforced to prevent fires from occurring.

The Decision to Accept the Risk and Protect against It

As pointed out earlier, a firm can use three methods to protect itself against a risk exposure: insurance, diversification, or hedging.

Insurance In this case, the firm buys the protection (if available) by paying an **insurance premium** to an insurance company. (The premium is the amount of money the firm must pay to be insured against a risk during a specific period of time.)[9] Only certain types of risk can be insured; they are usually event risks, that is, risks that occur infrequently and that reduce the firm's value significantly if they occur.[10] An example of such "catastrophic" risk is the destruction of property caused by fire and natural disasters.

Firms usually do not purchase full insurance coverage; they may buy insurance for damages above a certain amount (called a deductible) to reduce the premia paid. The objective for the firm is to purchase an optimal insurance coverage at the least possible overall cost.

Diversification The risk-reduction property of diversification is explained in Chapter 10. As long as the firm combines investments whose expected returns are not perfectly positively correlated, the firm's owners will benefit from diversification because losses on some of the investments will be offset by gains on other investments in the firm's portfolio.

---

[9]The insurance company diversifies the risks it has taken by selling a large number of policies. A few facilities will be damaged by fires, and a large number will not. For the insurance company, it does not matter which firm falls into which category. To be profitable, the insurance company will set the premium so that the total money collected exceeds the expected payment to the firms whose facilities will be damaged.

[10]Some risks, for example, credit risks, can be controlled either through the purchase of an insurance contract or through hedging with a risk management instrument, such as a credit default swap (see the section on hedging). In this case, risk protection via insurance and hedging is quite similar.

The question to ask is whether this risk management policy creates value. We show in Chapter 12 that Company A cannot create value by buying Company B for the only purpose of reducing the risk of the combination (that is, the combined companies would *not* have a higher value than the sum of their separate values). The reason is straightforward: shareholders can achieve the same risk diversification by buying shares of the two companies, so why would they pay a premium to buy the merged companies? One way for a firm to create value and achieve risk diversification is to acquire assets that are *unavailable* to its shareholders and take action to increase their expected returns through better management. This could be achieved, for example, by buying assets in a foreign market that are not accessible to other firms and improving their performance.

Hedging Hedging is a risk management technique whose objective is to reduce or eliminate a risk exposure by taking an offsetting position. The offsetting position can be taken by buying or selling (1) a **forward contract**; (2) a **futures contract**; or (3) an **option contract**. These three types of hedging instrument are described in the next section in which we show how they can be used to **hedge currency risk** and compare their respective merits. The same principles and similar techniques exist to hedge financing cost risk as well as commodity price risk.

STEP 5: RISK MONITORING

The final step in the process recognizes the dynamic nature of risk management. Once the process has been initiated, it is the responsibility of the senior executive in charge of risk management to ensure that the system in place is monitored and audited on a continuous basis. The risk management committee that was established to formulate and enforce the firm's risk policy could also be tasked with reviewing the system periodically and, if required, modifying it to make it more efficient, that is, less costly, more integrated with the firm's strategic decisions, and more focused on value creation. Over time, management learns from its experience in dealing with risk and that learning should be used to improve the firm's risk management system.

A CLOSER LOOK AT CURRENCY RISK

We now turn to the examination of foreign-exchange risk. It is the risk caused by changes in the exchange rate between the home country currency and the currency of the foreign country in which the firm is doing business. Any firm with some international activities would be exposed to this type of risk: its cash flow from operating, investing, and financing activities would be directly affected by changes in the rate of exchange between the home country currency and the currencies of the foreign countries in which it is doing business, not only through export and import but also through investment in foreign subsidiaries, the payment of interest on loans contracted in a foreign currency, and the collection of dividends from foreign subsidiaries. Clearly, currency risk is broader than business risk because it affects both the firm's cash flow from assets (which is business risk) and its cash flow from financing activities (which is financial risk). This is why we classified currency risk separately from both business risk and financial risk in Exhibits 13.2 and 13.3.

A firm with international operations needs to buy and sell foreign currencies. It also needs to hedge its foreign-exchange exposure. It is through the foreign-exchange market that it can carry out these transactions. The next sections describe that market and examine how firms can hedge their foreign-exchange exposure using hedging instruments. The next chapter examines how firms should deal with currency risk when deciding to invest abroad.

THE FOREIGN-EXCHANGE MARKET

The **foreign-exchange market** is the world's largest financial market. In a survey conducted in 2007, the Bank for International Settlement (BIS) estimated that the average *daily* transactions in that market reached $3,200 billion. This market exists to handle the buying and selling of currencies. Any firm or individual can buy or sell a currency in this market at an **exchange rate** (or **currency rate**) that is determined by the constant interactions of those who are buying and selling currencies. The quoted exchange rate is the price that has to be paid in one country's currency to buy one unit of another country's currency. For example, if the exchange rate between the U.S. dollar (USD) and the euro (EUR) is quoted as €0.8000 per $1 (EUR/USD 0.8000), then $1 must be paid to buy €0.8000.[11]

Unlike most stock markets, the foreign-exchange market has no central location. It is a network of banks, dealers, brokers, and multinational corporations communicating with each other via computer terminals, telephone lines, and fax machines. Major participants are large commercial banks operating through the **interbank market**. Working in rooms specially designed for currency trading, traders are surrounded by telephones and display monitors connected to trading rooms around the world. If a trader in Chicago wants to exchange U.S. dollars for euros, up-to-date communication equipment helps her find, nearly instantly, a trader from another bank in the interbank market who is willing to trade euros for U.S. dollars. Over the phone or directly through the computer monitors, the two traders agree on price and quantity. Each trader then enters the transaction in his or her own bank recording system. The entire procedure lasts no more than a few seconds. Later, the two banks send each other written confirmations of the trade, which may take up to two business days to settle.

A typical interbank foreign-exchange quotation mentions two rates. The **bid price** is the price at which a trader in the market is willing to buy. The **ask, or offer, price** is the price at which a trader is willing to sell. The prices are given in units of one currency per unit of the other currency with the currencies usually identified by three letters. For example, suppose the exchange rate between the euro and the U.S. dollar is quoted at EUR/USD 0.7998–0.8002. This means that some banks are willing to buy U.S. dollars at €0.7998 per $1 (the bid price) and sell them at €0.8002 per $1 (the ask price).

---

[11]The exchange rate can also be expressed as USD/EUR 1.2500 (the price of €1 in U.S. dollars) instead of EUR/USD 0.8000 (the price of $1 in euros, which is the inverse of the price of €1 in U.S. dollars). However, the convention is to express the exchange rate in units of foreign currency per one U.S. dollar.

The difference between the bid price and the ask price is the banks' compensation for making the transaction, which is the reason why they do not charge commission fees. For widely traded currencies, the size of the **bid-ask spread** is usually a few **basis points** (a basis point is one-hundredth of 1 percent). Its size varies from one currency to another. For a given currency, the spread depends on the level of competition among traders in that currency, the currency's volatility, and the average volume of daily trade.

It is a common practice among traders to quote all currencies in reference to the U.S. dollar. The exchange rate between two currencies when neither is a dollar is calculated from their respective U.S. dollar values. For example, if the euro is quoted at EUR/USD 0.8013 and the Japanese yen at JPY/USD 100.06,[12] then the JPY/EUR exchange rate is the JPY/USD rate divided by the EUR/USD rate:

$$\frac{\text{JPY/USD } 100.06}{\text{EUR/USD } 0.8013} = \text{JPY/EUR } 124.87$$

Rates between currencies computed as above are called **cross rates**. Quotations of cross rates are provided daily by financial publications and are available in real time on the Web. Exhibit 13.8 reports cross rates for six currencies.

SPOT TRANSACTIONS VERSUS FORWARD CONTRACTS

A **spot transaction** is a trade between two parties in which both agree to a currency exchange at a rate fixed *now* with the delivery of the currencies taking place at a **settlement date**, usually two business days later. Individuals can trade currencies for immediate delivery at the nearest bank. However, the spread is usually quite large.

A forward contract is an agreement between two parties, generally a bank and a customer, for the delivery of currencies on a specified date in the *future* but at an exchange rate fixed *today*. The contract specifies the *currencies* to be exchanged, the *fixed date* in the future when the delivery will actually take place, the *amount of currency* to be exchanged, and the *fixed rate* of exchange. For major currencies, contracts traded in the interbank forward market usually have a maturity of one, three, six, and twelve months. However, the delivery date can be tailor-made to accommodate a customer's particular need, usually at a less favorable rate.

Spot rates and **forward rates** are provided daily by major international newspapers and in real time with currency converters on the Web sites. Exhibit 13.9 reports forward rates for up to one year for four major currencies.

HEDGING CONTRACTUAL EXPOSURE TO CURRENCY RISK

Consider the case of a U.S. wine distributor who has just signed a contract with a French company for the delivery of 400 cases of champagne. The contract calls for the payment of €100,000 when delivery takes place in three months. As soon as the contract is signed, the U.S. distributor is exposed to a foreign-exchange risk

[12] These rates are bid-ask midpoints. For example, EUR/USD 0.8013 is at the midpoint between the bid price of EUR/USD 0.8011 and the ask price of EUR/USD 0.8015.

Exhibit 13.8 Currency Cross Rates on January 20, 2010.

Key Currency Cross Rates: Snapshot of Foreign Exchange Cross Rates at 4 p.m. Eastern Time, January 20, 2010

	US Dollar (USD)	Euro (EUR)	British Pound (GBP)	Swiss Franc (CHF)	Mexican Peso (MXP)	Japanese Yen (JPY)
Japan	91.233	128.67	148.58	87.383	7.1517	–
Mexico	12.757	17.992	20.776	12.218	–	0.1398
Switzerland	1.0441	1.4725	1.7004	–	0.0818	0.0114
United Kingdom	0.6140	0.8660	–	0.5881	0.0481	0.0067
Euro-zone	0.7090	–	1.1547	0.6791	0.0556	0.0078
United States	–	1.4104	1.6286	0.9578	0.0784	0.0110

Souce: *The Wall Street Journal*, Market Data, The Key Currency Cross Rates, January 20, 2010.

because he does not know the rate at which he will have to buy euros in three months to pay for the champagne.

The distributor can hedge this exchange-rate risk in many ways, that is, protect himself against currency fluctuations. He can choose among several hedging techniques commonly used to reduce or eliminate the exchange-rate risk associated with the purchase of raw materials, the sale of goods, the purchase of assets, or the issuance of debt when they are denominated in a foreign currency. These techniques use instruments available in the financial markets, such as forward, futures, and option contracts discussed below.

Hedging with Forward Contracts

The **forward hedge**, which is the hedging technique most widely used by corporations, can completely eliminate the exchange-rate risk associated with foreign transactions. The distributor can arrange a forward hedge simply by entering into a forward contract with a bank to buy from that bank €100,000 with U.S. dollars in three months. In other words, the distributor can fix *today* the rate at which he will buy €100,000 from the bank in three months. The bank will most likely require the importer to establish a **foreign-exchange line of credit** to guarantee his ability to deliver U.S. dollars in three months.

What is the *net* result of the two transactions: (1) the purchase of champagne and (2) the purchase of euros forward? If today's three-month *forward rate* is EUR/USD 0.80, the distributor will have to pay the bank $125,000 (€100,000 divided by EUR/USD 0.80) in three months to get the €100,000. Regardless of how the USD/EUR exchange rate changes between the purchase date and the delivery date, the dollar value of the purchase will not change. It will remain equal to $125,000. The exchange-rate risk has been eliminated. By entering into a forward contract, the distributor has "locked in" an exchange rate of EUR/USD 0.80. Note that this rate is the forward rate quoted today and *not* the spot rate, which may be higher or lower than the forward rate.

EXHIBIT 13.9 INTERBANK FORWARD RATES ON JANUARY 20, 2010.

	US Dollar (USD)		Euro (EUR)		British Pound (GBP)	
	Closing Mid	Day's Change	Closing Mid	Day's Change	Closing Mid	Day's Change
United States						
Spot	–	–	1.4116	−0.0166	1.6277	−0.0095
One month	–	–	1.4115	–	1.6273	0.0000
Three months	–	–	1.4112	–	1.6266	–
One year	–	–	1.4084	0.0000	1.6220	0.0001
Euro-zone						
Spot	1.4116	−0.0166	–	–	1.1532	0.0068
One month	1.4115	–	–	–	1.1530	–
Three months	1.4112	–	–	–	1.1527	0.0000
One year	1.4084	0.0000	–	–	1.1517	0.0001
United Kingdom						
Spot	1.6277	−0.0095	0.8672	−0.0051	–	–
One month	1.6273	0.0000	0.8673	–	–	–
Three months	1.6266	–	0.8676	0.0000	–	–
One year	1.6220	0.0001	0.8683	−0.0001	–	–
Japan						
Spot	91.2100	0.0200	128.748	−1.4855	148.463	−0.8338
One month	91.1985	0.0008	128.723	0.0018	148.410	0.0018
Three months	91.1725	0.0028	128.663	0.0044	148.305	0.0059
One year	90.8185	0.0089	127.909	0.0214	147.306	0.0307

Souce: *Financial Times*, January 20, 2010.

What will happen if the cases of champagne are not delivered on the agreed-upon date and, consequently, the €100,000 payment to the French exporter is delayed? The distributor will still have to buy the €100,000 from his bank for $125,000 at the date fixed by the forward contract. He would then have the choice of keeping the €100,000 until the champagne is delivered or exchanging them for U.S. dollars at the prevailing spot rate.[13] If the distributor exchanges the euros into U.S. dollars at the settlement of the forward contract, he will again need €100,000 to pay the French exporter when the champagne is finally delivered. In other words, he will again be exposed to exchange-rate risk. However, he can hedge this risk as before by entering into a new €100,000 forward contract with

[13]In this scenario, the money will certainly be kept in a euro-denominated money market account at the bank and earn some interest.

the bank. This strategy is known as **rolling over the forward contract**. An alternative to a rollover would be for the distributor to enter a **forward window contract** at the beginning. This contract is the same as a standard forward contract except that the transaction does not have to be settled on a fixed date. It can be settled on any day during an agreed-upon period of time known as the *window*. The importer would have to pay an additional fee for this flexibility, but it may be cheaper than rolling over the original contract.

What if the distributor wants to get out of the forward contract before its expiration date? In this situation, he would have to *sell* €100,000 forward by entering a forward contract that has the same expiration date as the first contract. The cash settlement for both contracts will take place at their common expiration date. The distributor would gain or lose, depending on whether the forward rate on the second contract is lower or higher than the rate on the first contract (EUR/USD 0.80). For example, suppose the forward rate on the second contract is EUR/USD 0.78. In this case, he will receive $128,205 from this contract (€100,000 divided by EUR/USD 0.78) and pay $125,000 on the first contract. His gain will be $3,205 ($128,205 less $125,000). If the forward rate of the second contract is EUR/USD 0.82, he will lose $3,049, the difference between the $121,951 from the sale of euros (€100,000 divided by EUR/USD 0.82) and the $125,000 on the first contract.

HEDGING WITH FUTURES CONTRACTS

As an alternative to forward contracts, the U.S. distributor of French champagne can use currency futures contracts. **Currency futures contracts**, or simply **currency futures**, are similar to forward contracts, except that they have a standard contract size and a standard delivery date. Currency futures are traded every day on organized **futures markets**, such as the Chicago Mercantile Exchange (CME), the London International Financial Futures and Options Exchange (LIFFE), and ICE Futures U.S. (formerly the New York Board of Trade, or NYBOT).

TRADING IN CURRENCY FUTURES CONTRACTS

Like currency forward contracts, currency futures contracts are promises to deliver a given number of currency units at a specified price. However, trading in futures contracts differs considerably from trading in forward contracts.

First, the contracts between the purchasers and the sellers of the currency are made through a clearing corporation or clearinghouse. For example, a contract between seller A and purchaser B is, in fact, a sale by A to the clearing corporation and, simultaneously, a sale by the clearing corporation to B. The clearing corporation provides insurance against default by one of the parties. If A cannot deliver the amount of currency he promised, B will still receive what he purchased, unless, of course, the clearing corporation goes bankrupt. (To cover its losses from default, the clearing corporation charges a small tax on futures transactions.)

Second, currency futures have standard sizes and fixed maturity dates. For example, contracts denominated in Japanese yen have a size of ¥12.5 million, those in British pounds sterling have a size of £62,500, and those in euros have a size of €125,000. Maturity dates are typically at the end of March, June, September, and December. The standardization of the contracts' size and delivery date greatly improves the liquidity of the futures markets compared with what would be the case if any amount and any delivery date were possible.

Third, futures exchanges require traders to deposit collateral to ensure that they can make good on any losses. An **initial margin** must be deposited with the broker who will execute the trade. The size of the initial margin depends on the volatility of the underlying currency.

Fourth, currency futures are **marked-to-market** daily. This means that at the end of each trading day, any profit or loss from the previous trading day is immediately settled by the clearinghouse at the **settlement price** (the quote of the last trade of the day). For example, suppose you bought a €125,000 futures contract at $0.81 per €1 yesterday, and the price is $0.82 at the close of the market today. You have just made a profit of $1,250 (€125,000 multiplied by the difference of $0.01 between the settlement price and the purchase price). The clearing corporation will immediately pay you $1,250, close your previous position, and open a new one at the new futures price of $0.82. The system limits the default risk for the clearing corporation to only one day's loss. Furthermore, if a loss causes the margin to fall below a preset level, the trader is asked to post additional margin, known as a **margin call**. The margin deposits and daily settlements considerably reduce the risk borne by the clearing corporation. As a result, no recognized credit standing is required to trade in the futures market.

Finally, the two parties in the futures contract can exit the contract at any time during the life of the contract. The party that *bought* contracts just has to *sell* an offsetting number of the same contract (at the futures price prevailing on the day of the sale); the party that *sold* contracts just has to *buy* an offsetting number of the same contract.

Like forward rates, futures prices are reported in the financial press and in real time on the Web. Exhibit 13.10 reports the futures prices of some major currencies with information on the market in which they are traded, the size of the contract, the expiration month, and the number of contracts traded.

THE CURRENCY FUTURES HEDGE

If our champagne distributor wants to use currency futures contracts to hedge his exposure to euros, he will have to buy three-month futures contracts worth €100,000. Because currency futures contracts and forward contracts are similar instruments, the **futures hedge** should have the same overall effect as the forward hedge. However, there will be some differences.

First, the other party in the futures contract is not a bank, but is instead the clearing corporation. The distributor, through his broker, will have to *buy* euros futures and then *sell* them later. If, in the meantime, the euro appreciates (depreciates) relative to the U.S. dollar, the distributor will make a profit (loss) from his futures trade. But, if the euro appreciates (depreciates) relative to the dollar, he will also have to disburse more (fewer) dollars to buy, in the spot market, the €100,000 needed to pay his supplier. The profit (loss) made in the futures market will compensate for the increase (decrease) in the amount of dollars needed to buy the €100,000 in the spot market.

Second, because the size and the maturity of the futures contracts are standardized, it is not always possible to *perfectly* hedge transaction exposure using a futures contract. For example, if the distributor decides to buy euros futures contracts at the

Exhibit 13.10 Currency Futures on January 20, 2010.

(1) Jan. 20, 2010	(2) Market	(3) Size	(4) Exp.	(5) Open	(6) Sett	(7) Change	(8) High	(9) Low	(10) Est. vol.	(11) Open int.
€-Sterling	NYBOT	€100,000	Mar	0.8712	0.8662	-0.0080	0.8712	0.8662	2	2,151
€-Yen	NYBOT	€100,000	Mar	129.0800	128.6000	-1.5500	129.08	128.68	6	3,280
$-Canadian $	CME	C$100,000	Mar	0.9698	0.9548	-0.0149	0.9698	0.9531	98,653	117,476
$-Euro	CME	€125,000	Mar	1.4288	1.4105	-0.0185	1.4288	1.4078	331,302	162,547
$-Euro	CME	€125,000	Jun	1.4269	1.4101	-0.0185	1.4282	1.4073	503	1,277
$-Swiss franc	CME	SFr125,000	Mar	0.9687	0.9584	-0.0106	0.9688	0.9555	58,100	37,586
$-Yen	CME	¥12.5m ($ per ¥100)	Mar	1.0975	1.0967	-0.0013	1.1018	1.0935	99,858	121,595
$-Yen	CME	¥12.5m ($ per ¥100)	Jun	1.0975	1.0973	-0.0014	1.1022	1.0942	75	552
$-Sterling	CME	£62,500	Jun	1.6300	1.6271	-0.0074	1.6347	1.6228	103	911
$-Australian $	CME	A$100,000	Mar	0.9182	0.9028	-0.0160	0.9186	0.9019	115,948	128,713
$-Mexican peso	CME	Peso 500,000	Apr	–	77625	-625.00	–	–	–	–

(1) Currencies, (2) market, (3) contract size, (4) expiration month, (5) opening prices of the day, (6) closing prices of the day, (7) change from previous day's closing price, (8) highest price of the day, (9) lowest price of the day, (10) number of contracts traded, and (11) number of contracts not yet closed by an offsetting trade.
Source: *Financial Times*, January 20, 2010.

CME, he will have to buy contracts with a unit size of €125,000. If he buys one contract for €125,000, he will "overhedge" his exposure by €25,000. Moreover, the distributor will have to decide on the maturity date of the futures contract. The only four expiration dates for a futures contract are the third Wednesday of March, June, September, and December. Suppose the champagne supplier wants to be paid by the end of May? The distributor will buy June futures contracts because their expiration date is closest to the end of May. Then he will *sell* the futures contracts at the end of May. However, he will still be exposed to exchange-rate risk because he cannot know at the time the contract is bought what the price of the June futures contracts will be at the end of May. Suppose the supplier agrees to wait until July 1 to be paid and the distributor chooses to hedge with June futures? In this case, the distributor will be exposed to the USD/EUR exchange-rate volatility between the last Wednesday of June (when the June futures contracts expire) and July 1.

Finally, the distributor will have to place a margin with a broker. Also, the daily marking-to-market may trigger margin calls if the USD/EUR futures exchange rate goes down. In this situation, the distributor would have to make additional cash payments until the futures contracts expire.

A futures hedge has some disadvantages that are not present in a forward hedge. A futures hedge is more complicated, it does not completely eliminate exchange-rate risk, and it requires intermediary cash payments. These drawbacks are particularly significant for the champagne distributor, who may rightly prefer to hedge his contractual exposure with forward contracts. However, there is a feature of the futures market that makes this market appealing to small firms that do not have an established reputation or to firms that do not enjoy a high credit standing: no credit check is required before trading in the futures market.

HEDGING WITH OPTION CONTRACTS

Suppose our distributor hedges his exposure to the euros by buying euros forward at EUR/USD 0.80. Regardless of whether the euro appreciates or depreciates during the hedging period, the U.S. dollar cost of the champagne will be $125,000 (€100,000 divided by EUR/USD 0.80). If the euro appreciates, the hedge will have accomplished its purpose, that is, it will have protected the distributor against an increase in the value of the euro. But if the euro depreciates, the distributor would have been better off if he had not hedged with forwards because he would then have benefited from the decrease in the value of the euro. Indeed, it is always the case that a forward hedge protects a firm from unfavorable exchange-rate movements but prevents it from benefiting from favorable changes in the exchange rate. Does a hedging technique exist that insulates the distributor from an appreciation of the euro but allows him to benefit from its depreciation? The answer is yes, and the technique is the **currency option hedge**.

CURRENCY OPTION CONTRACTS

A currency option contract is available from either banks or organized exchanges. If you buy a currency **call option**, you have the right to *buy* a stated amount of currency at an agreed-upon exchange rate (the **exercise** or the **strike price**) from the seller, or **writer**, of the option. If you buy a currency **put option**, you have the right to *sell* the stated amount of currency at the exercise rate of the option to the writer of the option. The **expiration date** (also called **maturity date**) of an option is the date after which the option can no longer be exercised. For a **European option**, the exercise of the right can take place only at the maturity date; for an **American option**, the option can be exercised at any time before the maturity date.

Banks usually write over-the-counter (OTC) options. As for forward contracts, banks can tailor the currency, size, and expiration date of foreign-exchange options to the specific needs of their clients.

Exchange traded options have standard sizes and maturity dates, usually similar to those of futures contracts, with, again, a clearing corporation guaranteeing that the trade will eventually take place.[14] As in the futures market, trades are marked-to-market daily and the clearing corporation imposes stringent margin requirements. However, only the option writer is required to deposit collateral. The owner of the option does not have to deposit collateral because he is not obligated to purchase the underlying currency after the option is purchased.

An option is valuable for its owner because it gives him the right, *but not the obligation,* to buy or sell a currency at a predetermined exchange rate. The price of this right, also called the **option premium**, is determined in the option market.

The Currency Option Hedge

If the champagne distributor decides to hedge his euro exposure with options, he will buy a three-month euro *call* option. This will give him the right to buy euros at a predetermined exchange rate (the exercise rate). He is not obligated to exercise the option, and he will not do so if the exchange rate is unfavorable. For example, if the spot rate of the euro in three months is lower than the exercise rate of the option, the distributor will not exercise his option and, instead, will buy the needed euros in the spot market. On the other hand, if the spot rate is higher than the exercise rate, he will exercise his option to get the euros at a lower rate. The option hedge provides a flexibility that is absent in a forward or futures hedge. However, this flexibility comes with a price, which is the price of the option.[15]

To illustrate, suppose the distributor can buy from his bank a three-month European call option at $0.04 per €1, with an exercise rate of $1.25 per €1. This means (1) the distributor must now pay the bank $0.04 per €1, or $4,000 for €100,000 ($0.04 multiplied by €100,000)[16] and (2) in three months, the distributor can buy €100,000 from the bank at $1.25 per €1 for a total of $125,000 ($1.25 multiplied by €100,000). Whether or not the distributor will exercise the option in three months depends on the USD/EUR spot exchange rate prevailing at that time. Exhibit 13.11 examines four cases corresponding to the following exchange rates in three months: EUR/USD 0.77, 0.79, 0.80, and 0.82.

[14]Today, most exchanges trade in currency options for which the underlying asset is a currency *futures* contract. When such an option is exercised, one receives a futures contract on the specified currency instead of the currency.

[15]Note the similarity between an option contract purchased at a price called an option premium and an insurance contract purchased at a price called an insurance premium. Both provide protection when the unfavorable outcome occurs but do not generate a loss if the favorable outcome occurs except, of course, the loss of the option premium and the insurance premium.

[16]The bank will set the price of the option based on the option exercise price, the spot exchange rate, the time to maturity, the volatility of the exchange rate, and the level of interest rate.

EXHIBIT 13.11 COMPARISON OF CURRENCY OPTION COSTS FOR FOUR EXCHANGE RATES.

Spot Rate in Three Months' Time EUR/USD	Spot Rate in Three Months' Time USD/EUR	Exercise Rate USD/EUR	Will the Option Be Exercised?	Dollar Amount Paid for €100,000	Cost of Option	Total Cost
0.77	1.30	1.25	Yes	$125,000	$4,000	$129,000
0.79	1.27	1.25	Yes	$125,000	$4,000	$129,000
0.80	**1.25**	**1.25**	**No**	**$125,000**	**$4,000**	**$129,000**
0.82	1.22	1.25	No	$121,951	$4,000	$125,951

If the exchange rate is EUR/USD 0.77 (USD/EUR 1.30), the distributor will exercise his option because he will be able to buy for $1.25 what is worth $1.30. He will get the €100,000 for $125,000 ($1.25 multiplied by €100,000) from the bank (the seller of the option) and pay his supplier of champagne. However, the option costs $4,000, so the total cost of the champagne will be $129,000 ($125,000 plus $4,000). If the exchange rate is EUR/USD 0.79 (USD/EUR 1.27), he will also exercise his option and the total cost of the champagne will remain at $129,000. If the exchange rate is EUR/USD 0.80 (USD/EUR 1.25), that is, if it is equal to the exercise rate, the distributor no longer has any incentive to exercise the option because he can get the €100,000 in the spot market at the same exchange rate. For any USD/EUR exchange rate higher than the exercise rate of $1.25 per €1 (or for any EUR/USD exchange rate lower than $0.80 per €1), the distributor will exercise his option, and the total cost of the champagne will be $129,000.

If the exchange rate is EUR/USD 0.82 (USD/EUR 1.22), the distributor will not exercise his option to buy at $1.25 what is worth only $1.22. He will buy the €100,000 in the spot market at EUR/USD 0.82 for a total cost of $121,951 (€100,000 divided by EUR/USD 0.82) and pay his supplier. However, because he paid $4,000 for the option, the total cost of the champagne will be $125,951 ($121,951 plus $4,000). For any USD/EUR spot rate lower than the exercise rate of $1.25 per €1 (or for any EUR/USD exchange rate higher than EUR/USD 0.80), the distributor will let the option expire without exercising it and exchange dollars for euros at the spot rate. And the lower the USD/EUR exchange rate, the lower the dollar cost of the champagne.

Exhibit 13.12 shows the net result of the option hedge for the distributor for a wide range of spot rates in three months. The hedge accomplishes the dual goal of (1) protecting the distributor from an appreciation of the euro by setting an upper limit to the dollar amount he will have to pay for the champagne ($129,000) and (2) allowing him to benefit from a depreciation of the euro. If the euro rises above the exercise rate (the EUR/USD rate drops below 0.80), the distributor will exercise his right to buy euros at that rate, thus limiting his dollar cost of the €100,000 to $129,000 (the amount he will pay the bank ($125,000) when exercising the option plus the cost of the option ($4,000)). However, if the euro falls below the exercise rate (the EUR/USD rate rises above 0.80), the distributor

EXHIBIT 13.12 THE OPTION HEDGE FOR THE U.S. CHAMPAGNE DISTRIBUTOR.

CONTRACTUAL EXPOSURE: €100,000 TO BE PAID IN THREE MONTHS' TIME
THREE-MONTH CALL OPTION PRICE: USD/EUR 0.04
EXERCISE PRICE: $1.25 PER EURO OR EUR/USD 0.80

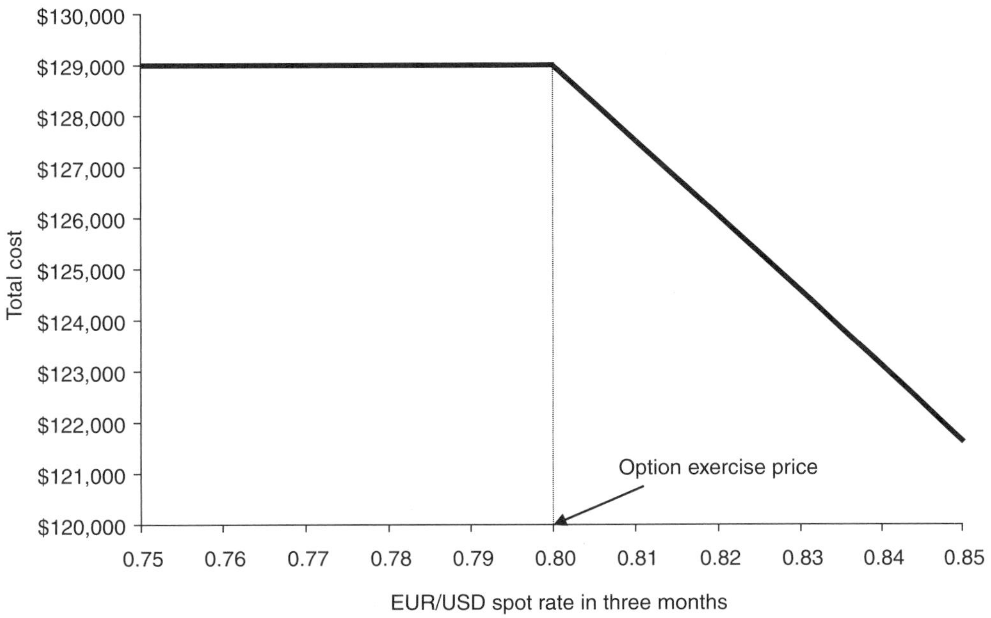

will not exercise his option. The dollar cost of the €100,000 will be equal to €100,000 multiplied by the spot rate in three months plus the $4,000 cost of the option.

SELECTING A HEDGING TECHNIQUE

Before deciding which technique to use to hedge a currency exposure created by a particular transaction, a manager must first decide whether a hedge is needed at all. The hedge is not needed if another business unit belonging to the firm has a currency exposure that is the opposite of the one created by the transaction. However, a business unit manager is not usually informed of the size and timing of the currency exposure of other business units. As pointed out earlier, this is the reason why large firms engaging in foreign trade have a centralized foreign currency management group that constantly monitors the firm's *net exposure* on a currency-by-currency basis and makes the required hedging decisions. Having all the business units' currency exposures consolidated and managed by a central unit prevents the multiplication of unnecessary and costly hedges.

Currency risk exposure can be further reduced using a procedure known as **leading and lagging.** This process consists of timing the cash inflows and outflows from the different foreign business units to reduce the firm's *overall* exposure to exchange-rate risk. For example, if a U.S. company has to make a payment in

Japanese yen, it can ask its Japanese subsidiary—assuming it has one—for an early payment of the same amount of yen on any of the subsidiary's outstanding debt to the parent company. This procedure is known as *leading*. If the parent company is owed money denominated in yen, it can delay the payment of some of its debt to the subsidiary until that money is received. This procedure is called *lagging*.

Which hedging technique should our champagne distributor use? We have shown that a forward hedge is preferable to a futures hedge for eliminating his €100,000 exposure. What about an option hedge? Exhibit 13.13 shows the net dollar cost of hedging the €100,000 exposure when using either the forward hedge or the option hedge for different spot rates in three months. The difference in the outcomes of the two hedging techniques is clear. With a forward hedge, the net cost is $125,000 (€100,000 multiplied by USD/EUR 1.25) regardless of the prevailing spot rate in three months. Furthermore, the distributor knows that cost when he enters the contract. With an option hedge, the net cost depends on the spot rate in three months, with the cost limited to $129,000 (€100,000 multiplied by USD/

EXHIBIT 13.13 THE FORWARD AND OPTION HEDGES FOR THE U.S. CHAMPAGNE DISTRIBUTOR.

CONTRACTUAL EXPOSURE: €100,000 TO BE PAID IN THREE MONTHS' TIME
THREE-MONTH FORWARD RATE: EUR/USD 0.80
THREE-MONTH CALL OPTION PRICE: USD/EUR 0.04
EXERCISE PRICE: $1.25 PER EURO OR EUR/USD 0.80

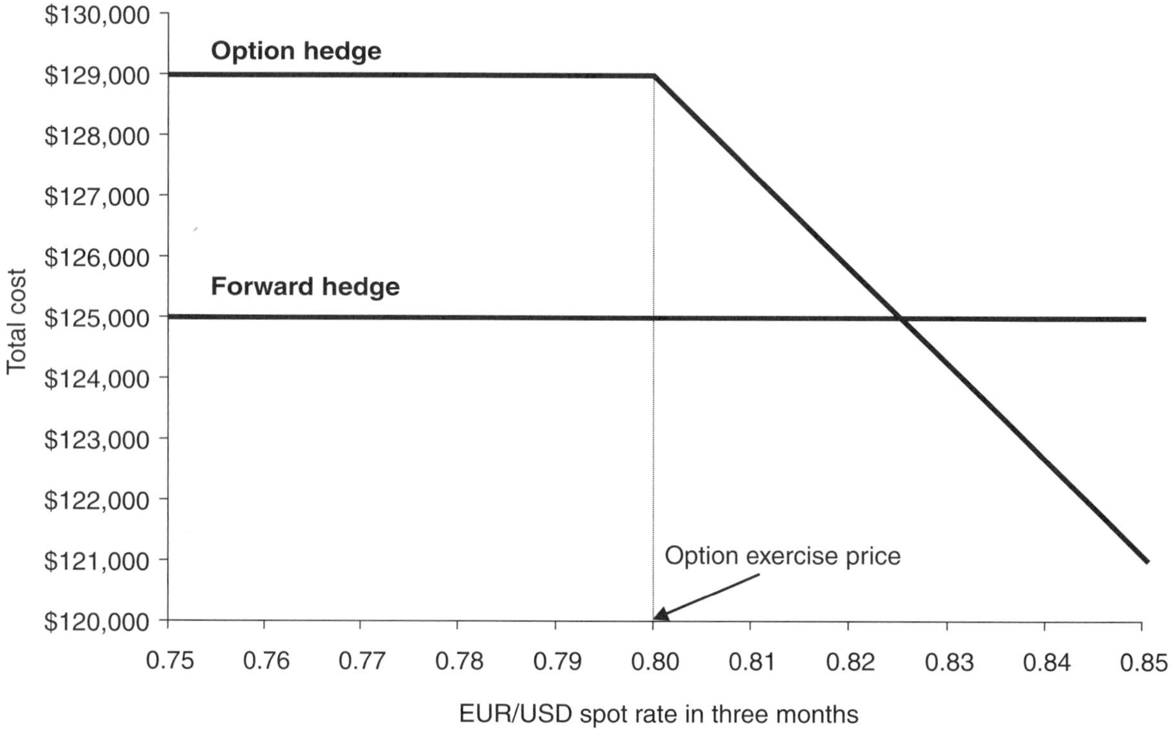

EUR 1.25, plus $4,000). Thus, the choice depends on the distributor's opinion of future changes in the USD/EUR spot rate. If he strongly believes the euro will depreciate in the following three months, he may consider that the extra cost of the option hedge (if it turns out the euro appreciates) is not large enough to dissuade him from taking a chance. However, if he has no strong opinion about future currency movements, he may prefer the certainty of the forward hedge to the uncertain outcome of the costlier option alternative.

In practice, the currency forward contract is the favorite hedging tool, followed by the currency option and futures contracts. Exchange traded instruments, such as traded options or futures contracts, are not used very often, which may imply that corporations prefer instruments tailored to their particular needs as opposed to those that are more liquid, but standardized.

HEDGING LONG-TERM CONTRACTUAL EXPOSURE TO CURRENCY RISK WITH SWAPS

Although currency forward, futures, and option contracts can be designed for any duration, in practice, they are most often used to hedge short-term exposure to currency risk. A banker may be willing to offer a customized currency forward or option contract for more than a year's maturity, but the risk premium would be high because the longer the contract, the higher the risk that unanticipated events may affect the firm's ability to honor the contract. In addition, the choice for futures or traded options is limited to the contracts available in the market, which typically have less than a year's maturity.

To hedge long-term contractual exposure to currency risk, a firm may prefer to enter a **currency swap contract** with its bank. The swap contract requires that the firm delivers a set of future cash flows denominated in the currency to be hedged in exchange for a set of cash flows denominated in the currency of its choice.

As an illustration, suppose a U.S. company has arranged a five-year, $10 million loan from an American bank to finance its operations in Singapore. The coupon rate, payable annually, is 7 percent or $700,000. The firm's finance officer decided against borrowing Singapore dollars (SGD) from a Singapore bank because she could not get the same attractive credit terms in Singapore dollars as she did on U.S. dollars borrowed in the United States. However, the firm is now exposed to exchange-rate risk because Singapore dollars (the currency of the firm's income from its operations in Singapore) will need to be exchanged for U.S. dollars to make annual interest payments of $700,000 and repay the $10 million principal on the U.S. dollar loan. But the firm did not need to take this risk. The finance officer could have simply entered a U.S. dollars to Singapore dollars swap agreement with a bank dealing in swaps at the same time she arranged the loan. Under this agreement, the bank would pay the company the U.S. dollars needed to service the $10 million loan, and in exchange, the company would make simultaneous payments in Singapore dollars to the bank. In addition, there would also be an initial and final exchange of the principals. For example, the agreement could result in the cash flows for the company shown in Exhibit 13.14.

From the U.S. dollar loan, the company would receive $10 million in exchange for paying $700,000 of interest every year for five years and repaying the

EXHIBIT 13.14 CASH FLOWS FOR $10 MILLION SWAP AGREEMENT.

FIGURES IN MILLIONS

	Initial Cash Flows		Cash Flows: Years 1–4		Cash Flows: Year 5	
	USD	SGD	USD	SGD	USD	SGD
1. U.S. dollar loan	+10		–0.70		–10.70	
2. Swap agreement	–10	+15	+0.70	–0.75	+10.70	–15.75
3. Net cash flow	**0**	**15**	**0**	**–0.75**	**0**	**–15.75**

$10 million at the end of the fifth year (line 1). From the swap agreement, these U.S. dollar cash flows would be exchanged for Singapore dollars (line 2). The net result would be a series of cash flows, all denominated in Singapore dollars. The initial cash inflow of SGD15 million would be followed by five annual payments of SGD750,000 and a final payment of SGD15 million at the end of the fifth year (line 3).[17] In other words, the swap agreement would transform the U.S. dollar loan into a Singapore dollar loan, thus eliminating the currency risk exposure generated by the U.S. dollar debt.

This illustration is one of the simplest forms of a currency swap. A more complex one is the swap of a floating coupon rate debt for a fixed coupon rate debt. This type of swap is particularly suited to the needs of most corporate borrowers who prefer fixed financing costs to variable financing costs but who have better access to the floating-rate bond market than to the fixed-rate bond market. By entering a fixed-for-floating currency swap, they can easily, and cheaply, transform their variable financial obligations into fixed ones and, at the same time, reduce their exposure to exchange-rate risk.

SUMMARY

A firm cannot create value if it does not take on some risk. The challenge then is to manage the firm's various risk exposures with the objective of maximizing value creation. To achieve this objective, management needs to put in place a comprehensive risk management process. This process, outlined in the chapter, requires the identification and understanding of the risks the firm faces, the measurement and prioritization of these risks, and the formulation of a policy to decide which risks the firm should reject and which risks it should accept. A firm may decide to take on a risk without protection and cover any potential losses with its own resources. Alternatively, it may decide to take on the risk and protect itself using three possible methods: insurance, hedging, and diversification.

[17]The notional principal of SGD15 million is determined by the prevailing spot rate of 1.50 Singapore dollars per U.S. dollar. The implicit interest rate on the Singapore dollar loan is 5 percent (SGD750,000 divided by SGD15 million).

The second part of the chapter examines currency risk. The currencies of various countries are traded in the foreign-exchange market, the world's largest financial market, which is a network of banks, dealers, brokers, and multinational corporations communicating with each other by telephone and through computer terminals. Two basic types of transactions take place in this market, spot and forward transactions. A spot transaction is an agreement to exchange currencies at a rate fixed today, with the delivery taking place usually within two business days. A forward transaction is also an agreement to exchange currencies at a rate fixed today, with the delivery taking place at some specific date several months in the future.

The chapter concludes with a survey and description of the financial instruments a firm can use to hedge its exposure to currency risk. These are forwards, futures, options, and swaps contracts. Similar instruments exist to hedge a firm's exposure to financing cost risk (the risk of unexpected changes in the level of market interest rates) as well as the commodity risk (the risk of unexpected changes in the price of commodities such as grains, metals, oil, and electricity).

FURTHER READING

1. Brealey, Richard, Stewart Myers, and Franklin Allen. *Principles of Corporate Finance*, 9th ed. McGraw-Hill, 2008. See Chapter 27.
2. Damodaran, Aswath. *Corporate Finance: Theory and Practice*, 2nd ed. John Wiley & Sons, 2001. See Chapter 26.
3. Eun, Cheol, and Bruce Resnick. *International Financial Management*, 4th ed. McGraw-Hill, 2007.
4. Graham, John, and Clifford Smith. "Tax Incentives to Hedge." *Journal of Finance* 54 (December 1999).
5. Koller, Tim, Marc Goedhart, and David Wessels. *Valuation: Measuring and Managing the Value of Companies*, 4th ed. John Wiley & Sons, 2005. See Chapters 17, 18, and 19.
6. Servaes, Henri, Ane Tamayo, and Peter Tufano. "The Theory and Practice of Corporate Risk Management." *Journal of Applied Corporate Finance* 21, no. 4 (Fall 2009).

SELF-TEST PROBLEMS

13.1 RISK MANAGEMENT.

Provide five reasons that would justify why a firm should manage its risk centrally, and briefly explain each reason.

13.2 RISK IDENTIFICATION.

Consider the following situations and events that are sources of firm risk. Say whether the situation or event is a source of business risk (which type?), financial risk (which type?), financial investment risk (which type?), or currency risk (which type?), and indicate what the firm could do to protect itself against the resulting risk exposure.

1. The General Media Company holds 10 percent of the shares of Fastcom, a telecom company over which it has no control
2. A European firm receives cash dividends for a subsidiary based in the United States
3. A Japanese firm has plants located in an island that is often hit by severe storms
4. The central bank is expected to announce a more restrictive monetary policy
5. A single supplier provides the firm with an important piece of equipment
6. The firm sells on credit to a government-sponsored agency
7. The firm finances an asset with a four-year useful life using a two-year loan
8. A firm manufactures old-fashioned baby dolls

13.3 RISK MEASUREMENT.

The No Growth Company (NGC) generates an expected annual perpetual cash flow from assets of $100 million and has a cost of capital of 10 percent. It is exposed to the four risks listed in the first column of Exhibit 13.6.

a. What is the market value at risk (MVR) of the strategic risk if the effect of this risk is to reduce NGC's expected cash flow from assets by $20 million if the risk occurs?
b. What is the MVR of the currency risk if the effect of this risk is to reduce NGC's expected cash flow from assets by $20 million if the risk occurs?
c. What is the MVR of the financing cost risk if the effect of this risk is to raise NGC's cost of capital to 10.2 percent if the risk occurs?
d. What is the MVR of the business process risk if the effect of this risk is to reduce NGC's expected cash flow from assets by $1 million if the risk occurs?

13.4 COMPARING ALTERNATIVE HEDGING TECHNIQUES.

Briefly describe how to hedge contractual exposure with forward, futures, and option contracts. What are the main advantages and disadvantages of these four hedging techniques? A firm with foreign-exchange exposure knows with certainty the cash flow that is affected by the currency exposure; which hedging instrument will provide the most reliable protection against the exchange-rate risk? What should the firm do if it wants to protect itself against the downside risk but remain exposed to the potential gains from a favorable change in the exchange rate?

13.5 SWAP AGREEMENT.

A Japanese company would like to increase its presence in Europe. It issued bonds in the Japanese market and received ¥3 billion. The bonds carry a 5 percent annual coupon and mature in five years. The company plans to use the proceeds from the bond issuance for its expansion in Europe and use its revenues from the expansion to pay both coupons and principal. At the same time, a German company wants to enter into the Japanese market by acquiring a Japanese company. It will need €23 million for this acquisition, which was borrowed in the local market by issuing five-year bonds at par to yield 5 percent annually.

Suppose the two companies have more or less the same credit risk. To mitigate the exchange-rate risk, they agree to swap the initial investments, the coupon payments over the five-year period, and the final principal payments. Assume that the exchange rate applied to the swap of the initial investments is ¥130.44 per €1 and that over the next five years, the JPY/EUR exchange rates are expected to be ¥125, ¥127, ¥130, ¥135, and ¥138 per €1, respectively. Ignoring transaction costs, show how much each company will profit or lose (in euros) from the swap.

REVIEW PROBLEMS

1. **Various types of risk.**
   Explain the difference between the risks that make up the following pairs:

   a. Business risk versus financial risk
   b. Diversifiable risk versus undiversifiable risk
   c. Systematic risk versus unsystematic risk
   d. Insurable risk versus uninsurable risk
   e. Project risk versus corporate risk
   f. Foreign-exchange risk versus currency risk
   g. Financial investment risk versus financial risk
   h. Financial risk versus credit risk
   i. Liquidity risk versus refinancing risk
   j. Financing cost risk versus refinancing risk

2. **Systematic risk.**
   A firm has no financial investments, and all its activities are in the domestic market where it faces no foreign competition. It has a debt-to-equity ratio of 1 and is the subject of a 40 percent tax rate. Its beta coefficient is 1.20.

   a. What are the risks the firm faces? Explain your answer.
   b. What is the percentage of its systematic risk that is financial?

3. **Risk policy.**
   What are the major issues that a firm risk policy must address? Indicate what a firm could do to resolve these issues.

4. **Measuring risk exposure.**
   The General Construction Company (GCC) is expecting next year a cash flow from assets of €50 million that is expected to grow forever at 3 percent. Its cost of capital is 11 percent. The firm is exposed to the following three risks:

   - There is a 10 percent chance that its cost of capital increases to 11.5 percent
   - There is a 60 percent chance that its growth rate drops to 1 percent
   - There is a 40 percent chance that its cash flow declines to €45 million

   a. What is the market value at risk of each one of the events listed above?
   b. Indicate if they are high, moderate, or low risk.

5. **Inventory value and the risk of obsolescence.**
HDM, a computer manufacturing company, holds computer parts in its inventory whose prices fall rapidly because suppliers can produce them faster, more efficiently, and in large quantities just a few months after they were first introduced on the market. HDM also uses a standard machine to assemble its computers. Over the last five years, the company that sells this machine has come up with a new, better performing piece of equipment every two years, rendering somewhat obsolete the assembler HDM bought earlier. What are the two types of risk HDM is exposed to, and what could it do to protect itself against these two sources of risk?

6. **Exposure to interest rate and currency risk.**
Consider the case of a firm that borrows abroad.
   a. What are the two major risks the firm is exposed to?
   b. Show how the firm can hedge these two risks using swap contracts.

7. **Swaption contracts.**
A swaption contract is a hedging instrument that combines the features of a swap contract and an option contract. Describe briefly how such a hedging instrument would work. What would be the advantage for a firm to use a swaption instead of a standard swap contract?

8. **Hedging imports with forwards, futures, and options.**
MPC imports computer equipment from Japan for sale in the U.S. market. Monthly imports have averaged ¥250 million to ¥275 million over the past year. A similar volume is expected for the coming year. Because of the volatility of the exchange rate between the Japanese yen and the U.S. dollar, MPC's management believes that it must hedge these imports. Using the "typical" exposure of ¥250 million for a ninety-day period, how should the company manage its current position? Current market data for various instruments appear as follows:
   - Spot JPY/USD = 108.09
   - Ninety-day forward JPY/USD = 106.42
   - September futures = $0.95 per ¥100 (¥12.5 million per contract); delivery date: September 17
   - Ninety-day yen call over-the-counter (OTC) option = $0.021 per ¥100 (¥108/$1 strike price)

9. **Currency risk management.**
Charles has a problem. His boss thinks that options are a form of gambling. The company he works for exports to European markets, which require euro invoicing. The market is cutthroat, and sales are made on the basis of competitive bidding. The average-size bid is €2.5 million. Firm offers (which means that if the bid is accepted, the company must deliver) are made each month. Normally, winning bids are announced one month after the offer is made. Delivery is made one month after acceptance of the offer. Payment terms are one month after shipment. This means that payment on successful bids normally is ninety days after the bid is submitted. The company's experience has been that two out of three bids are successful.

Charles recommended that the company buy one-month or three-month put options on the euro from its bank at the time a bid was made. However, his boss thought they should sell euros forward to hedge the exposure. Besides taking the view that options are speculative, Charles's boss disliked the idea of paying up front for something they might never need. Finally, he considered them much more expensive than a forward contract.

The current spot rate is $0.8870 per €1. The three-month forward rate is $0.8855 per €1. A one-month put option on the euro with the strike price set at $0.8850 would cost $0.0095 per €1; a three-month put option on the euro with a strike price set at $0.8850 per €1 would cost $0.0210 per €1.

Using the average-size bid of €2.5 million to illustrate, how should Charles's company hedge its euro risk? Prepare some arguments to support his recommendation, unless you believe him to be mistaken. In the latter case, indicate why.

10. **Long-term currency risk management.**
You have been given the task of evaluating the hedging policy used by a Singapore company that manufactures mobile telephones under contract for a major company in Europe. The management has a relatively new policy of taking long-term forward hedges on the planned sales revenue. They use a three-year rolling plan, and on the basis of the sales figures that were projected, hedge these amounts. This means that they have locked in the euro value of the plant's sales for each of the next three years. When the policy was first put into place, the planned sales for the first year were hedged with a one-year forward contract, the sales for the second year with a two-year forward contract, and the sales for the third year with a three-year forward contract. The idea was to update this at least once each year. When the new sales forecasts were made under the rolling plan, sales planned for three years ahead were hedged with a new three-year forward contract. At the same time, small adjustments might be made to the existing hedges to reflect changes in sales volume and forecasts. The plant manager in Singapore argued, "My margins are quite satisfactory doing this, and I can devote all of my attention to running the plant without worrying about something I can't control." Some data suggest that the Singapore dollar's current worth is about 10 percent overvalued compared with its major trading partners.

Evaluate the currency risk management policy described above. What are its main underlying assumptions? What are its major risks? What are possible operating strategies that the firm could use to manage this exposure?

Making International Business Decisions

CHAPTER 14

Firms do not operate exclusively in a domestic environment. Many companies have significant foreign operations that provide managers with new opportunities and constraints that do not exist in a purely domestic environment. New factors, such as fluctuations in exchange rates, differences in interest rates, accounting rules, tax systems, and the risk of doing business abroad, have to be taken into account. Of course, the fundamental principle of corporate finance still holds: a firm's resources must be managed with the ultimate goal of increasing the firm's market value. Foreign investment projects, like domestic ones, should be undertaken only if they provide a return in excess of that required by investors. The decision criteria in previous chapters, such as the net present value (NPV) rule, are still valid, but they are usually more complicated to apply because more than one currency is involved and because specific risks are attached to cross-border investments.

This chapter examines the effect of (1) currency risk (the risk resulting from exchange-rate fluctuations) and (2) country risk (the risk resulting from having operations in a country with an unstable political system or regulatory environment) on management decisions in an international environment.

A firm faces two types of risk when exchange rates fluctuate. One is accounting (or translation) exposure, which is the effect of changes in exchange rates on the firm's balance sheet and income statement. The other is economic exposure, which is the effect of exchange-rate fluctuations on the firm's future cash flows. We explain in Chapter 13 how managers can use financial instruments such as forward, futures, option, and swap contracts to reduce their firm's economic exposure to currency risk.

In this chapter, we examine the relationships between exchange rates, inflation rates, and interest rates that should prevail between two countries that have different currencies. Understanding these basic relationships allows you to make better international business decisions. We then show how to apply the NPV rule to two cross-border investments, one in a low-risk country and the other in a high-risk country. Finally, we propose a number of techniques and mechanisms to actively manage country risk. After reading this chapter, you should understand the following:

- The difference between accounting exposure and economic exposure to exchange-rate fluctuations
- Why interest rates (the cost of debt) usually are not the same in countries with different currencies
- The relationship between the interest rates prevailing in two countries with different currencies and how it affects changes in exchange rates
- Why inflation rates usually are not the same in countries with different currencies
- The relationship between the inflation rates prevailing in two countries with different currencies and how it affects changes in exchange rates
- How to apply the NPV rule to investment projects with cash flows denominated in foreign currencies and to projects in a politically or regulatory unstable environment
- How to actively manage country risk

THE FIRM'S RISK EXPOSURE FROM FOREIGN OPERATIONS

When a firm operates in a foreign environment, it is subject to a number of risks. **Foreign-exchange risk**, discussed in Chapter 13, is associated with the volatility of foreign-exchange rates. If the firm has assets and liabilities, revenues and expenses, and cash flows denominated in a foreign currency, changes in exchange rates will affect their values denominated in the domestic currency. **Accounting** (or **translation**) **exposure** is the effect of changes in exchange rates on the firm's balance sheet and income statement; **economic exposure** is the effect on the value of the firm's future cash flows. There is also the risk of operating in an environment that may not be as economically and politically stable as the domestic one. This risk, called **country risk**, takes many forms. It extends from the relatively milder risk originating from the imposition of exchange controls to the risk of expropriation of the firm's foreign assets without compensation.

ACCOUNTING, OR TRANSLATION, EXPOSURE

Accounting exposure arises from the need to translate the financial statements of the foreign business unit into the parent company's currency to prepare consolidated financial statements. A variety of approaches can be taken to translate balance sheet and income statement accounts. Most of these approaches are variations of the **monetary/nonmonetary method** and the **current method**, which are presented in Appendix 14.1. The objective of these methods is to show how changes in exchange rates affect *reported* earnings and *book* equity values. How important are the translated accounting data to the firm's owners? The data provide some useful starting points for a financial analysis of the foreign operations, but they are of limited use for the firm's shareholders because they are not *market* values. Economic exposure is much more relevant to the firm's owners.

ECONOMIC EXPOSURE

Economic exposure focuses on the effect of unexpected changes in exchange rates on the value of the firm's future cash flows. Economic exposure is classified as (1) **contractual** (or **transaction**) **exposure** or (2) **operating exposure.** Contractual exposure refers to the effect of exchange-rate volatility on the expected (future) cash flows from *past* transactions denominated in foreign currencies that are still outstanding. Operating exposure is also concerned with expected (future) cash flows, but from *future*, not past, transactions. In other words, although both types of exposure examine the effect of exchange-rate volatility on future cash flows, contractual exposure focuses on cash flows whose values in foreign currency are *certain*, while operating exposure is concerned with cash flows whose values are *uncertain* even when denominated in a foreign currency. The example in the following sections illustrates the distinction.

CONTRACTUAL, OR TRANSACTION, EXPOSURE

Let's go back to the case of the U.S. champagne distributor we first encountered in Chapter 13. Recall that he had just signed a contract with a French wine-producing company for the delivery of 400 cases of champagne. The contract calls for the payment of 100,000 euros (written as EUR or €) when delivery takes place in three months. As soon as the contract is signed, the distributor is exposed to exchange-rate risk because the dollar cost of the champagne will not be known until the distributor buys €100,000 to pay the French company. That purchase will be paid in dollars at the exchange rate that will prevail in three months. We say that the distributor's contractual exposure is €100,000.

In general, contractual exposure arises from the purchase or the sale of goods and services whose prices are denominated in a foreign currency. It can also arise from financial activities, such as borrowing and lending in a nondomestic currency. For most companies involved in cross-border transactions, the number of outstanding foreign contracts can be very large, typically with different maturity dates and different currency denominations. For these firms, the contractual exposure to a particular currency at a particular date is simply the *net* sum of the contractual (future) cash inflows and cash outflows in that currency measured at that date.

A firm with large and uncovered transaction exposure may find itself in a difficult financial situation resulting from adverse exchange-rate movements. The situation is similar to a firm borrowing too much debt and experiencing difficulty meeting its repayment schedule. Chapter 11 describes this situation as "financial distress" and shows that it adversely affects the value of the firm. For example, with too much exposure to exchange-rate risk, the firm may have to pass up valuable investment projects, customers may worry about the firm's ability to deliver goods and services and switch to competitors, and suppliers may be reluctant to provide trade credit. All these indirect costs will have a negative effect on the firm's value. Fortunately, this type of exposure can be controlled using financial instruments such as forward, futures, and option contracts, as shown in Chapter 13.

OPERATING EXPOSURE

Each time the U.S. distributor places an order for champagne with a French company, he enters a contract to deliver euros to the French champagne exporter and is immediately exposed to foreign-exchange risk. If the distributor's business is to sell French champagne, his exposure to foreign-exchange risk is not limited to the *outstanding* contracts with his French suppliers. Future purchases of champagne (not yet made) will generate continuous exposure to the volatility of the exchange rate between the U.S. dollar and the euro. This exposure to future exchange-rate changes is an example of an operating exposure.

It should also be pointed out that importers (or exporters) of goods and services are not the only firms subject to operating exposure. A firm that has only *domestic* operations also can be exposed to changes in exchange rates. Consider a U.S. distributor of American-made champagne. If the value of the euro decreases relative to the U.S. dollar (you get more euros for a dollar), the U.S. distributor of the French-produced champagne can keep the same margin by selling his champagne at a lower price and, in the process, take a market share from the distributor of U.S.-made champagne. A similar situation occurs when domestic firms that buy, produce, and sell domestic goods are faced with competition from abroad.

Clearly, operating exposure is more difficult to manage than contractual exposure. It requires a good understanding of the economic and competitive environment in which the firm operates. Although it is nearly impossible to quantify, it needs to be controlled. The firm must anticipate future developments in the foreign-exchange market and take measures to reduce the probability of experiencing financial distress from excessive exposure to exchange-rate movements. This can be achieved by diversifying operations and financing sources. On the operations side, the firm can diversify its sources of raw materials, the locations of its production facilities, and the regions around the world where it sells. On the financing side, diversification can be achieved by raising funds in more than one currency. As shown in Chapter 13, the firm can also use instruments available in financial markets to hedge against changes in exchange rates. But the difficulty of forecasting future cash flows, far beyond those arising from outstanding contracts, makes the estimation of operating exposure less precise than the estimation of contractual exposure. As a result, using financial instruments is less efficient in controlling operating exposure than in controlling transaction exposure.

Country Risk

A firm is exposed to country risk when unforeseen economic, political, and social events in a country affect the value of the firm's investments in that country. Changes in the host country's political environment may bring about changes in government regulations or add new regulations to existing ones, resulting in restrictions or penalties for foreign operations in the country. Examples of regulations that can adversely affect a foreign subsidiary include (1) imposing ceilings or discriminatory taxation on dividends or royalties paid to the parent company; (2) imposing unfavorable exchange rates for foreign currency transactions; (3) requiring that goods produced contain a certain percentage of local content; (4) requiring that nationals hold top management positions; (5) requiring that a portion of the profits be reinvested locally; (6) allowing only joint ventures with less than 50 percent ownership by the foreign parent; (7) imposing price controls; and (8) expropriating the subsidiary without adequate compensation.

We show in Chapter 13 that financial instruments, such as forward, futures, or option contracts, can considerably reduce a firm's exposure to contractual risk. They are, however, of no use to protect against country risk. How, then, could firms that invest in a politically unstable foreign country reduce their exposure to country risk? We show later in this chapter how that type of risk exposure can be reduced by following some simple rules.

FACTORS AFFECTING CHANGES IN EXCHANGE RATES

To understand how international investment decisions should be made, we should first identify and understand the factors that determine changes in the exchange rate between the currencies of two countries. Intuition tells us that if inflation in country A is expected to be higher than inflation in country B, we can expect country A's currency to weaken relative to country's B currency. At the same time, we would also expect interest rates in country A to be higher than interest rates in country B because country A has a higher inflation rate. In the following sections, we examine the **parity relations** that link the spot exchange rate (the exchange rate prevailing *today*), the forward exchange rate (the exchange rate at a specified *future* date fixed *today* contractually), and the interest rates and the inflation rates prevailing in the two countries. Appendix 14.2 provides a detailed analysis of each of these relationships and shows how the rates are linked to one another.

HOW DIFFERENCES IN INFLATION RATES AFFECT EXCHANGE RATES: THE PURCHASING POWER PARITY RELATION

The **purchasing power parity (PPP) relation** says that exchange rates should adjust so that the same basket of goods will cost the same in different countries. It is based on the following principle: if the price of goods increases faster in one country than in another because the inflation rate is higher in the first country than in the second, then the exchange rate between the two countries should move to offset the difference in inflation rates and, consequently, the difference in prices. More formally, according to the PPP relation:

$$\text{Expected future spot rate} = \text{Current spot rate} \times \frac{1 + \text{Expected inflation rate in the home country}}{1 + \text{Expected inflation rate in the foreign country}}$$

If $S^0_{h/f}$ is the current spot rate and $E(S^1_{h/f})$ is the expected future spot rate in one year (both expressed as the number of units of the *home* currency needed to buy one unit of the *foreign* currency), and if $E(i_h)$ and $E(i_f)$ are the expected inflation rates for next year in the home and the foreign countries, respectively, then we can write the following:

$$E(S^1_{h/f}) = S^0_{h/f} \times \frac{1 + E(i_h)}{1 + E(i_f)} \tag{14.1}$$

To illustrate this relationship, suppose that next year's expected inflation rate is 2 percent in the United States and 4 percent in the Euro-zone. Furthermore, suppose that the current spot rate is USD/EUR 1.25 ($1.25 buys one euro).[1] We have

---

[1]Note that the euro to U.S. dollar exchange rate is the *inverse* of the U.S. dollar to euro exchange rate. If the U.S. dollar to euro exchange rate is 1.25 ($1.25 buys one euro), then the euro to U.S. dollar exchange rate is $\frac{1}{1.25}$ = 0.80 (€0.80 buys $1).

$E(i_h) \equiv E(i_{US}) = 0.02, E(i_f) \equiv E(i_{EUR}) = 0.04$, and $S^0_{h/f} \equiv S^0_{USD/EUR}$ = USD/EUR 1.25. Substituting these values in equation 14.1, we get next year's expected USD/EUR spot rate:

$$E(S^1_{USD/EUR}) = [USD/EUR\ 1.2500] \times \left[\frac{1 + 0.02}{1 + 0.04}\right] = USD/EUR\ 1.2260$$

The value of one euro expressed in U.S. dollars is expected to *drop* from USD/EUR 1.2500 to USD/EUR 1.2260. In other words, the U.S. dollar is expected to **appreciate** relative to the euro. (It is expected to get "stronger" in relation to the euro because it will take \$1.2260, instead of \$1.2500, to buy €1; it also means that the euro will be "cheaper" to buy when paying in dollars.) Conversely, the euro is expected to **depreciate** relative to the U.S. dollar. (It is expected to get "weaker" in relation to the dollar because it will take €0.8157 [the inverse of \$1.2260], instead of €0.8000 [the inverse of \$1.2500], to buy one dollar; it also means that the dollar will be more "expensive" to buy when paying in euros.) In our example, the expected appreciation of the U.S. dollar relative to the euro, expressed as a percent, is as follows:

$$\frac{1.2500 - 1.2260}{1.2500} = 0.0192 = 1.92\%$$

Appendix 14.2 shows that when the expected inflation rate of the foreign country is small enough (less than 5 percent), equation 14.1 can be written as follows:

$$\frac{E(S^1_{h/f}) - S^0_{h/f}}{S^0_{h/f}} = E(i_h) - E(i_f) \qquad (14.2)$$

Equation 14.2 is a simpler version of the PPP relation. It says that the expected percentage change in the spot rate (in units of the home currency per unit of the foreign currency) is equal to the expected difference in the inflation rates between the home country and the foreign country. Using the expected inflation rates from the above example, the difference between the rates in the Euro-zone and United States is 2 percent (4 percent in the Euro-zone minus 2 percent in the United States). Thus, according to the simpler version of the PPP relation, the expected appreciation of the U.S. dollar relative to the euro should be 2 percent, which is close to the 1.92 percent predicted by the PPP relation given in equation 14.1.

The empirical evidence for the PPP relation is mixed. Many studies show that the relation usually does a poor job of forecasting spot rates in the near future (especially when differences in inflation rates are small). Also, the PPP relation requires a long-term forecast of inflation rates. However, if we need to forecast long-term exchange rates, such as in converting cash flows from a foreign currency to a home currency in the valuation of a cross-border long-term investment project, no other known forecast appears to be superior to the PPP relation.

THE RELATIONSHIP BETWEEN INFLATION RATES AND INTEREST RATES: THE FISHER EFFECT

Suppose that today you decide to invest \$100 in a one-year bank deposit carrying an interest rate of 7.12 percent. This rate, which is the one the bank will pay you in one year, is called the **nominal interest rate**. Alternatively, with the same amount of money, you could buy 100 bottles of mineral water at your local supermarket.

Suppose, too, that the inflation rate in the United States is expected to be 4 percent during the coming year and that inflation will affect all goods and services equally. In other words, you expect your local supermarket to charge you \$104 for 100 bottles of water at the end of the year.

In a year, the bank deposit will be worth \$107.12 [\$100 × (1 + 7.12 percent)]. With this cash, you can expect to increase the amount of bottles you can buy from 100 bottles to 103 bottles (\$107.12 divided by \$1.04 per bottle), that is, by 3 percent. In other words, your bank deposit, which offers you a nominal rate of 7.12 percent, allows you to increase your future purchasing power by only 3 percent because of price inflation. This 3 percent rate is referred to as the **real interest rate**. It is the interest rate adjusted for the cost of living. The difference between the real interest rate and the nominal interest rate reflects, obviously, the expected rate of inflation.

We would expect lenders to be willing to make loans only if they are compensated for the effect of expected inflation. For example, suppose the real interest rate is 3 percent. If the expected inflation rate is zero, no compensation is needed and the real and nominal interest rates are both equal to 3 percent. However, if the expected inflation rate is 5 percent, the *nominal* rate of interest must be such that one dollar invested now at this rate will grow at the 3 percent *real* rate of interest to become \$103 [\$100 × (1 + 3 percent)] and will also grow at the 5 percent expected inflation rate to become \$108.15 [\$103 × (1 + 5 percent)]. To generalize, we have the following:

1 + Nominal interest rate = (1 + Real interest rate) × (1 + Expected inflation rate)

If r denotes the *nominal* rate of interest, r_r denotes the real rate of interest, and $E(i)$ denotes the expected inflation rate, then we can write the following:

$$1 + r = (1 + r_r) \times (1 + E(i)) \qquad (14.3)$$

Solving for r, we get the following:

$$r = r_r + E(i) + (r_r \times E(i)) \qquad (14.4)$$

If the expected inflation rate, $E(i)$, is small enough, the term $r_r \times E(i)$ becomes insignificant and we can write the following:

$$r = r_r + E(i) \qquad (14.5)$$

In this case, the nominal interest rate is simply the sum of the real interest rate and the expected inflation rate. Equations 14.4 and 14.5 indicate that any change in the expected inflation rate is reflected in the nominal interest rate. This effect is known as the **Fisher effect**.

If real interest rates are different between two countries, we would expect capital to flow from the country with the lower rate to the country with the higher rate until the rates are equalized. Appendix 14.2 shows that the Fisher effect then implies the following relationship between interest rates and expected inflation rates in the home and foreign countries:

$$\frac{1 + r_h}{1 + r_f} = \frac{1 + E(i_h)}{1 + E(i_f)} \qquad (14.6)$$

A reasonable approximation of equation 14.6 is as follows:

$$r_h - r_f = E(i_h) - E(i_f) \qquad (14.7)$$

Equation 14.7 shows clearly that the difference in interest rates between two countries reflects the difference in their expected inflation rates. This effect is known as the **international Fisher effect**. Most empirical evidence supports the international Fisher effect, especially between countries with open financial markets.

HOW DIFFERENCES IN INTEREST RATES AFFECT EXCHANGE RATES: THE INTEREST-RATE PARITY RELATION

The **interest-rate parity (IRP) relation** describes how the difference in interest rates between two countries is related to the difference between their forward and spot exchange rates. Recall that the forward exchange rate, defined in Chapter 13, is the exchange rate agreed *today* at which two currencies will be exchanged at a specified *future* date. More precisely, if $F^0_{h/f}$ is the forward rate (in units of home currency per unit of foreign currency), $S^0_{h/f}$ is the spot rate, and r_h and r_f are the nominal rates of interest in the home country and the foreign country, respectively, we have the following:

$$\frac{F^0_{h/f} - S^0_{h/f}}{S^0_{h/f}} = \frac{r_h - r_f}{1 + r_f} \qquad (14.8)$$

Appendix 14.2 shows that IRP should hold because of the actions of interbank traders who try to take advantage of any deviation from the parity relation.

The IRP relation is better known under the following simplified version, which assumes that r_f is small compared with one:

$$\frac{F^0_{h/f} - S^0_{h/f}}{S^0_{h/f}} = r_h - r_f \qquad (14.9)$$

Equation 14.9 says that the percentage difference between the forward and the spot rates is equal to the difference in interest rates between the home country and the foreign country.

Ample evidence shows that the IRP relation holds in the real world, at least for short-term interest rates. Indeed, when no active market exists for a forward rate, banks often quote their clients a rate computed from the IRP relation.

THE RELATION BETWEEN FORWARD RATES AND FUTURE SPOT RATES

Suppose the one-year forward rate between the U.S. dollar and the euro is USD/EUR 1.30. (This means that you have a contract that guarantees you that rate in one year.) Would anyone be willing to *buy* euros forward if the *spot* rate in one year is expected to be USD/EUR 1.20? No, because no one would enter into a contract that says that, at some future date, an asset (euros, in our case) must be bought at a *higher* price (the USD/EUR forward rate of 1.30) than the market price expected to prevail on that date (the USD/EUR future spot rate of 1.20). Would anyone be willing to *sell* euros forward at USD/EUR 1.30 if the *spot* rate in one year is expected to be USD/EUR 1.35? Again, no, because no one would enter into a contract that says that, at some future date, an asset must be sold at a *lower* price (the USD/EUR forward rate of 1.30) than the market price expected to prevail on that date (the USD/EUR future spot rate of 1.35). Thus, in equilibrium, the *expected* future spot rate must be equal to USD/EUR 1.30. In other words, the forward rate must be equal to the *expected* future spot rate.

If $E(S^1_{h/f})$ is the expected value of the spot rate one year from now and $F^0_{h/f}$ is the current one-year forward rate (both expressed as the number of units of the home currency needed to buy one unit of foreign currency), the following relation must hold:

$$F^0_{h/f} = E(S^1_{h/f}) \tag{14.10}$$

Dividing both sides of this equation by $S^0_{h/f}$ and then subtracting 1 from both sides, we get the following:

$$\frac{F^0_{h/f} - S^0_{h/f}}{S^0_{h/f}} = \frac{E(S^1_{h/f}) - S^0_{h/f}}{S^0_{h/f}} \tag{14.11}$$

The empirical evidence for this relation is not clear-cut because risk was not taken into consideration when deriving it. The expected spot rate is only a forecast of what the spot rate will be in the future. The actual rate, which will be revealed only in one year, could be higher or lower. When you enter into a forward contract, you fix the price at which you will sell (or purchase) euros (see Chapter 13). In effect, you eliminate the currency risk. To eliminate the risk, you are willing to sell (buy) euros forward at a lower (higher) price than the expected spot price. Despite their failure to properly account for risk, equations 14.10 and 14.11 tend to hold *on average*.

PUTTING IT ALL TOGETHER

Exchange rates fluctuate constantly. The relationships we have presented show how these fluctuations are linked to changes in fundamental economic variables, such as inflation rates and interest rates. These relationships are summarized in Exhibit 14.1. The links among the parity relations are caused by the actions of **arbitrageurs**, the traders in the financial markets who try to make a riskless profit from price discrepancies, mostly in exchange rates (spot and forward) and interest rates across countries. We should expect that the lower the barriers to the free movement of capital flows, the swifter the action of arbitrageurs and the more likely that the parity relations will hold.

When a firm engages in cross-border activities, these relations have some important managerial implications. For example, the PPP relation can be used to forecast future exchange rates in the analysis of cross-border investment projects. Furthermore, these relations help to avoid classic mistakes, such as trying to increase profit from operations by buying currencies when they go down and selling them when they go up. If you borrow to accomplish these transactions, what you may gain on the foreign-exchange transaction, you would lose in interest income. The only time you could gain is when the change in the rate is higher than the difference

EXHIBIT 14.1 THE FUNDAMENTAL RELATIONSHIPS AMONG SPOT EXCHANGE RATES, FORWARD EXCHANGE RATES, INFLATION RATES, AND INTEREST RATES.

The Relation	What Does It Say?	The Simplified Version of the Relation
Purchasing power parity (PPP)	Spot exchange rates adjust to keep the cost of living the same across countries. As a consequence, the expected percentage change in the spot rate is equal to the expected difference in the inflation rates between the two countries.	$\frac{E(S^1_{h/f}) - S^0_{h/f}}{S^0_{h/f}} = E(i_h) - E(i_f)$ Equation 14.2
International Fisher effect	The difference in inflation rates between two countries is reflected in the difference in their interest rates.	$r_h - r_f = E(i_h) - E(i_f)$ Equation 14.7
Interest rate parity	The percentage difference between the forward and spot exchange rates is equal to the difference in the interest rates between the two countries.	$\frac{F^0_{h/f} - S^0_{h/f}}{S^0_{h/f}} = r_h - r_f$ Equation 14.9
Expected spot rate and forward rate	The percentage difference between the forward rate and the spot rate is equal to the percentage difference between the expected spot rate and the current spot rate.	$\frac{F^0_{h/f} - S^0_{h/f}}{S^0_{h/f}} = \frac{E(S^1_{h/f}) - S^0_{h/f}}{S^0_{h/f}}$ Equation 14.11

$E(S^1_{h/f})$ = expected spot rate one year from now expressed in units of home currency per unit of foreign currency.
$S^0_{h/f}$ = current spot rate expressed in units of home currency per unit of foreign currency.
$E(i_h)$ = expected inflation rate in the home country during the next year.
$E(i_f)$ = expected inflation rate in the foreign country during the next year.
r_h = one-year interest rate in the home country.
r_f = one-year interest rate in the foreign country.
$F^0_{h/f}$ = forward rate now in units of home currency per unit of foreign currency.

between the interest rates. Another example is the classic illusion of trying to lower the firm's cost of borrowing by taking advantage of foreign interest rates that are lower than domestic rates: on average, the net cost of borrowing abroad may not be much different from the domestic cost after accounting for the expected changes in exchange rates.

ANALYZING AN INTERNATIONAL INVESTMENT PROJECT

Chapter 6 shows how to use the NPV rule to select investment projects that create value and reject those that destroy value. The objective of value maximization applies to any management decision, so the NPV rule is also applicable to the decision to invest in a foreign country. However, two new factors must be taken into account. First, the project's future cash flows are usually denominated in a foreign currency with an exchange rate that may fluctuate; second, the cash flows may be affected by changes in local regulations governing foreign investments, a risk we refer to as country risk. These complications make the NPV rule more difficult to apply.

After a brief review of the NPV rule, we consider the case of Surf and Zap (SAZ), a U.S. manufacturer of a small remote-control device called Zap Scan, which can automatically show selected programs on a television set at regular and brief intervals of time. After a successful entry in the U.S. market, the firm wants to export the device to Europe and has to decide where to locate its regional distribution center. The choice is between Switzerland and the hypothetical nation of Zaragu, two countries with significantly different country risks.

THE NET PRESENT VALUE RULE: A BRIEF REVIEW

The NPV rule is the subject of Chapter 6. Here we review the NPV rule and its implications for investment decisions. Let CF_0 be the investment's initial cash outlay, that is, the amount of cash that has to be invested today to launch the project, and CF_1, CF_2, CF_3, ... , CF_N, the sequence of future cash flows that the project is *expected* to generate over its useful life. The last cash flow, CF_N, includes the receipts from the sale of the investment. Let k be the project's cost of capital, that is, the return that investors require from investments that have the same risk characteristics as the project. The NPV of the investment is defined as follows:

$$\text{NPV} = -CF_0 + \left[\frac{CF_1}{1+k} + \frac{CF_2}{(1+k)^2} + \frac{CF_3}{(1+k)^3} + \cdots + \frac{CF_N}{(1+k)^N}\right]$$

where the sum in brackets is the present value, or the value today, of the expected future cash-flow stream. Notice that the more distant the cash flows, the lower their contribution to the project's present value because the discount factor $\frac{1}{(1+k)^t}$ decreases with time. Note also that the higher the project's risk, the higher the rate of return (k) required by investors, the lower the discount factors, and the lower the present value of the expected cash-flow stream. In other words, everything else the same, the riskier a project, the less desirable it is, and the lower its NPV.

According to the NPV rule, a project must be accepted when its NPV is positive and rejected when its NPV is negative. The rule simply means that if the present value of the benefits generated by the project (the present value of the future expected cash flows) is larger than the cost of undertaking the investment (the initial cash outlay, CF_0), then the project will create value for the firm's owners and, consequently, must be undertaken. Otherwise, it must be rejected because it will destroy value. The NPV indicates how much richer (or poorer) the firm's investors will be if they put their money in the project rather than in an alternative investment with the same risk characteristics. Note, finally, that an NPV equal to zero does not mean that the project has a zero return. It simply means that the project will not change the wealth of investors if undertaken.

SURF AND ZAP CROSS-BORDER ALTERNATIVE INVESTMENT PROJECTS

To export Zap Scan to Europe, SAZ needs to set up a European distribution center. After an extensive search for the most convenient location, the choice was reduced to two countries, Switzerland and Zaragu. Both countries are in the center of Europe and from a logistical point of view neither one appears superior to the other. However, whereas investing in Switzerland would not carry any country risk, Zaragu

EXHIBIT 14.2 THE ZAP SCAN PROJECT.

CASH FLOWS IN MILLIONS

	Switzerland Alternative in Swiss Francs (CHF)	Zaragu Alternative in Zaragupas (ZGU)
Initial cash outlay	25.0	230
Annual cash flows		
Year 1	4.5	50
Year 2	5.0	60
Year 3	5.2	65
Year 4	5.4	70
Year 5	5.6	75
Liquidation value in Year 5	20.0	250
Current annual inflation rate	2%	10%
Current spot exchange rate	CHF/USD 1.3	ZGU/USD 10

has recently been the subject of unfavorable articles in the press. Analysts are concerned that the country's monetary situation may deteriorate in the future and that the earnings from the subsidiaries of foreign companies in Zaragu may soon be subject to a foreign tax in addition to the regular corporate tax. The local currency is the Swiss franc (CHF) in Switzerland and the zaragupa (ZGU) in Zaragu. Financial data on the alternative projects' cash flows are presented in Exhibit 14.2.

The cost of acquiring and refurbishing a building plus the project's startup costs are estimated at CHF 25 million for the Swiss alternative and at ZGU 230 million for the Zaragu alternative. It is expected that the investment will last five years, at which time digital television sets with incorporated zapping devices will make Zap Scan obsolete. The annual cash flows in Exhibit 14.2 are *net of all local and U.S. taxes*. It is estimated that the Swiss building can be sold for CHF 20 million and the Zaragu building can be sold for ZGU 250 million at the end of the fifth year.

The inflation rate in Switzerland has been remarkably stable in the past, at about 2 percent a year, and is not expected to behave differently during the next few years. In Zaragu, the inflation rate has continuously increased during the recent past. It is now at 10 percent a year and is expected to stay at this level for the foreseeable future. In the United States, the inflation rate is expected to average 3 percent a year for the next five years.

The current spot exchange rates are CHF/USD 1.3 and ZGU/USD 10. Finally, the rate of return required by SAZ from its distribution centers in the United States is 10 percent. Furthermore, SAZ requires that the NPV for all projects be estimated in U.S. dollars.

THE NPV OF THE SWISS ALTERNATIVE

To compute the NPV of the Swiss alternative of the Zap Scan project, we need to estimate both the project's expected cash flows and its cost of capital in U.S.

EXHIBIT 14.3 THE ZAP SCAN PROJECT'S EXPECTED CASH FLOWS FROM THE SWISS ALTERNATIVE.

	A	B	C	D	E	F	G
1		Now	End-of-Year 1	End-of-Year 2	End-of-Year 3	End-of-Year 4	End-of-Year 5
2							
3	**Expected cash flows in millions of Swiss francs (CHF)**						
4	Annual cash flow	(25.0)	4.5	5.0	5.2	5.4	5.6
5	Cash flow from liquidation						20.0
6	Total cash flow	(25.0)	4.5	5.0	5.2	5.4	25.6
7							
8	**Expected USD/CHF spot rate using PPP** (equation 14.1)						
9	Swiss expected inflation rate		2.0%	2.0%	2.0%	2.0%	2.0%
10	United States expected inflation rate		3.0%	3.0%	3.0%	3.0%	3.0%
11	Current spot rate CHF/USD	1.3000					
12	Current spot rate USD/CHF	0.7692					
13	Expected future spot rate USD/CHF	0.7692	0.7768	0.7844	0.7921	0.7998	0.8077
14							
15	**Expected cash flows in millions of U.S. dollars (USD)**	**($19.2)**	**$3.5**	**$3.9**	**$4.1**	**$4.3**	**$20.7**
16							
17	**Cost of capital**	**10.0%**					
18							
19	**Net present value**	**$6.071 million**					
20							
21	*Rows 4, 5, 9, 10, 11, and 17 are data.*						
22	*Formula in cell B6 is =B4+B5. Then copy formula in cell B6 to next cells in row 6.*						
23	*Formula in cell B12 is =1/B11.*						
24	*Formula in cell C13 is =B13*(1+C10)/(1+C9). Then copy formula in cell C13 to next cells in row 13.*						
25	*Formula in cell B15 is =B6*B13. Then copy formula in cell B15 to next cells in row 15.*						
26	*Formula in cell B19 is =B15+NPV(B17,C15:G15).*						
27							

dollars. This is done using the spreadsheet shown in Exhibit 14.3. The project's cash flows, taken from Exhibit 14.2, are shown in row 4 in Exhibit 14.3. To convert these Swiss franc cash flows into their U.S. dollar equivalents, we need to forecast the year-end USD/CHF spot rate for the next five years. We can use the PPP relation to predict these future spot rates.

As shown in equation 14.1, the PPP relation relates the expected changes in the spot exchange rates to the expected inflation rates in the home country and the foreign country. The inflation rates in the United States and in Switzerland are expected to be 3 percent and 2 percent, respectively, in the near future, so we can use these values for the expected inflation rates $E(i_h)$ and $E(i_f)$ in equation 14.1. To find the expected value of the year-end USD/CHF spot exchange rate for Years 1 to 5, we start with the current spot exchange rate of CHF/USD 1.3000 (row 11). This rate is converted into USD/CHF 0.7692 (row 12). We then solve equation 14.1 successively for each year, using the expected spot rate from the previous year (row 13).

The expected U.S. dollar value of the project's cash flows is obtained by multiplying the Swiss franc cash flows by the expected exchange rates (row 15).

To compute the project's NPV we need to estimate the cost of capital. SAZ requires a return of 10 percent from its distribution centers in the United States. Should the firm use the same cost of capital for the Swiss alternative or should it use a higher one to account for exchange-rate risk, that is, for the probability that the future USD/CHF exchange rate may be different from the expected one? Recall from Chapter 10 that the risk that matters to investors is not the *total* risk of the investment but rather the portion of the risk that cannot be reduced or eliminated by diversification. If we assume the portfolios of SAZ shareholders include either shares of foreign companies or shares of U.S. firms with international business activity, we can assume the shareholders have already eliminated the portion of the Zap Scan project risk associated with USD/CHF exchange-rate volatility. In this case, no premium should be added to the domestic (U.S.) cost of capital to account for the exchange-rate risk. What if SAZ shareholders are not diversified internationally? In this case, one can argue that the Swiss project gives them the opportunity to become diversified, albeit indirectly. As a consequence, the risk of their portfolio of assets would be *reduced*, which would imply a *lower* required rate of return for the project.

Taking a cost of capital of 10 percent and the project's expected cash flows in row 15 of Exhibit 14.3, we use the spreadsheet NPV formula to find the project's NPV (row 19):

$$\text{NPV}_{\text{Switzerland}} = \text{USD } 6.071 \text{ million}$$

The NPV is positive, so the Swiss project would create value for SAZ investors. But one question remains: would the Zaragu project create more value?

THE NPV OF THE ZARAGU ALTERNATIVE

The procedure to estimate the expected value of the Zaragu project's cash flows is the same as the one we used for the Swiss alternative. We estimate the U.S. dollar value of the project's expected future cash flows and then discount these cash flows at the project's cost of capital. The PPP relation is again used to estimate the year-end USD/ZGU spot rates for the next five years, using the expected inflation rates in the United States and Zaragu. The cash flows in zaragupas are converted into their U.S. dollar equivalents using the predicted spot rates. The procedure and the results of our estimation are shown in Exhibit 14.4.

If we assume for a moment that there is no country risk associated with the Zaragu alternative, there is no need to adjust the project cost of capital for exchange-rate risk. Thus, *in the absence of country risk,* the project cost of capital in the Zaragu alternative is 10 percent, the same as the rate used for similar projects

EXHIBIT 14.4 THE ZAP SCAN PROJECT'S EXPECTED CASH FLOWS FROM THE ZARAGU ALTERNATIVE WITHOUT COUNTRY RISK.

	A	B	C	D	E	F	G
1		Now	End-of-Year 1	End-of-Year 2	End-of-Year 3	End-of-Year 4	End-of-Year 5
2							
3	**Expected cash flows in millions of Zaragupas (ZGU)**						
4	Annual cash flow	(230.0)	50.0	60.0	65.0	70.0	75.0
5	Cash flow from liquidation						250.0
6	Total cash flow	(230.0)	50.0	60.0	65.0	70.0	325.0
7							
8	**Expected USD/ZGU spot rate using PPP (equation 14.1)**						
9	Zaragu expected inflation rate		10.0%	10.0%	10.0%	10.0%	10.0%
10	United States expected inflation rate		3.0%	3.0%	3.0%	3.0%	3.0%
11	Current spot rate ZGU/USD	10.000					
12	Current spot rate USD/ZGU	0.1000					
13	Expected future spot rate USD/ZGU	0.1000	0.0936	0.0877	0.0821	0.0769	0.0720
14							
15	**Expected cash flows in millions of U.S. dollars (USD)**	**($23.0)**	**$4.7**	**$5.3**	**$5.3**	**$5.4**	**$23.4**
16							
17	**Cost of capital**	**10.0%**					
18							
19	**Net present value**	**$7.814 million**					
20							
21	*Rows 4, 5, 9, 10, 11, and 17 are data.*						
22	*Formula in cell B6 is =B4+B5. Then copy formula in cell B6 to next cells in row 6.*						
23	*Formula in cell B12 is =1/B11.*						
24	*Formula in cell C13 is =B13*(1+C10)/(1+C9). Then copy formula in cell C13 to next cells in row 13.*						
25	*Formula in cell B15 is =B6*B13. Then copy formula in cell B15 to next cells in row 15.*						
26	*Formula in cell B19 is =B15+NPV(B17,C15:G15).*						
27							

in the United States or Switzerland. Using the U.S. dollar denominated cash flows from Exhibit 14.4, the NPV of the Zaragu alternative is as follows:

$$NPV_{\text{Zaragu}}^{\text{No country risk}} = \text{USD } 7.814 \text{ million}$$

However, as mentioned earlier, the project will be exposed to country risk because the authorities in Zaragu may impose a "foreign" tax on the project's earnings. To account for this risk, most firms systematically add a risk premium to their domestic cost of capital. We disagree with this procedure for three reasons. First, if we assume that shareholders have already eliminated the country risk by holding a well-diversified portfolio of assets, we do not need to make any adjustment at all. Second, there is no rational way to estimate the size of the risk premium for the particular risk that needs to be taken into account. For example, in the Zaragu alternative, should it be 1 percent, 2 percent, 10 percent, or another figure? No one knows. Third, simply adding an arbitrary "fudge" factor to the domestic cost of capital may lead to complacency and prevent managers from thoroughly assessing the effect of country risk on the project.

We suggest that any adjustment for country risk should be made on the project's *expected cash flows* rather than on the cost of capital. An expected cash flow is just a weighted average of the values that the cash flow can take in the future, where the weights are the probability that the cash flow will actually take these values. Thus, we can adjust these cash flows to reflect the likelihood of any form of country risk. If this is done, there is no need to adjust the cost of capital. Furthermore, the estimation of the expected cash flows forces managers to make a thorough analysis of country risk over time and its effect on the project.

Suppose that after a careful analysis of economic trends in Zaragu, we estimate a 20 percent probability that a monetary crisis will occur at some time during the project's life. Should such a crisis erupt, we can expect the project's earnings to be subjected to a foreign tax. When such a tax was imposed in the past, the tax rate was always 25 percent. There is no reason to expect that the rate will be different during the next monetary crisis, so we can apply the same rate to the project. To avoid cumbersome computations, we also assume that the project's *profits,* which will be subjected to the foreign tax, represent, each year, 90 percent of the project's operating cash flows in the absence of foreign tax.[2]

Exhibit 14.5 presents the detailed computation of the project's expected cash flows in a spreadsheet format, taking into account the risk that the foreign tax will be imposed on the project. The first section of the exhibit shows the cash flows in the absence of tax taken from Exhibit 14.4. The next section presents the computation of the operating cash flows net of the foreign tax if the tax is imposed. The third section shows the computation of the project's expected cash flows, taking into account the probability that the project will be subjected to the tax. If the probability of taxation is 20 percent during the life of the project, the project's *expected* cash flows are the cash flows net of the "foreign" tax multiplied by 20 percent plus the cash flows without the tax multiplied by 80 percent, because there is a 20 percent chance that the first outcome will occur and an 80 percent chance that the second will occur. The last part of the exhibit shows the dollar value of the expected cash flows, using the same expected future exchange rates as in Exhibit 14.4. The NPV of the project, obtained by discounting the cash flows at the 10 percent cost of capital, is as follows:

$$\text{NPV}_{\text{Zaragu}}^{\text{With country risk}} = \text{USD } 6.931 \text{ million}$$

---

[2]Recall that taxes are paid on profits, not cash flows. See Chapters 4 and 8 for the conversion of cash flows into profits for the purpose of estimating the amount of tax payment.

EXHIBIT 14.5 THE ZAP SCAN PROJECT'S EXPECTED CASH FLOWS FROM THE ZARAGU ALTERNATIVE WITH COUNTRY RISK.

	A	B	C	D	E	F	G
1		Now	End-of-Year 1	End-of-Year 2	End-of-Year 3	End-of-Year 4	End-of-Year 5
2							
3	**Expected cash flows in the absence of a foreign tax on the project's earnings**						
4	Millions of Zaragupas (ZGU)						
5	Annual cash flow	(230.0)	50.0	60.0	65.0	70.0	75.0
6	Cash flow from liquidation						250.0
7							
8	**Expected operating cash flows in the presence of a foreign tax on the project's earnings**						
9	Millions of Zaragupas (ZGU)						
10	Project's earnings as percent of annual cash flow		90.0%	90.0%	90.0%	90.0%	90.0%
11	Project's earnings		45.0	54.0	58.5	63.0	67.5
12	Foreign tax rate		25.0%	25.0%	25.0%	25.0%	25.0%
13	Foreign tax		11.3	13.5	14.6	15.8	16.9
14	Annual operating cash flow net of tax		38.8	46.5	50.4	54.3	58.1
15							
16	**Expected cash flows in zaragupas**						
17	Millions of Zaragupas						
18	Probability that the earnings will be taxed		20.0%	20.0%	20.0%	20.0%	20.0%
19	Annual operating cash flow		47.8	57.3	62.1	66.9	71.6
20	Total cash flow	(230.0)	47.8	57.3	62.1	66.9	321.6
21							
22	**Expected USD/ZGU spot rate using PPP** (equation 14.1)						
23	Zaragu expected inflation rate		10.0%	10.0%	10.0%	10.0%	10.0%
24	United States expected inflation rate		3.0%	3.0%	3.0%	3.0%	3.0%
25	Current exchange rate USD/ZGU	0.1000					
26	Expected future USD/ZGU	0.1000	0.0936	0.0877	0.0821	0.0769	0.0720
27							
28	**Expected cash flows in millions of U.S. dollars (USD)**	**($23.0)**	**$4.5**	**$5.0**	**$5.1**	**$5.1**	**$23.2**
29							
30	**Cost of capital**	10.0%					
31							
32	**Net present value**	**$6.931 million**					
33							

34 *Rows 5, 6, 10, 12, 18, 23, 24, 25, and 30 are data.*
35 *Formula in cell C11 is =C10*C5. Then copy formula in cell C11 to next cells in row 11.*
36 *Formula in cell C13 is =C12*C11. Then copy formula in cell C13 to next cells in row 13.*
37 *Formula in cell C14 is =C5–C13. Then copy formula in cell C14 to next cells in row 14.*
38 *Formula in cell C19 is =C18*C14+(1–C18)*C5. Then copy formula in cell C19 to next cells in row 19.*
39 *Formula in cell B20 is =B5. Formula in cells C20… F20 is =C19… =F19. Formula in cell G20 is =G19+G6.*
40 *Formula in cell C26 is =B26*(1+C24)/(1+C23). Then copy formula in cell C26 to next cells in row 26.*
41 *Formula in cell B28 is =B20*B26. Then copy formula in cell B28 to next cells in row 28.*
42 *Formula in cell B32 is =B28+NPV(B30,C28:G28).*

Not surprisingly, the NPV of the Zaragu alternative with country risk ($6.931 million) is lower than without country risk ($7.814 million). More to the point, however, is the finding that the NPV of the Zaragu alternative with country risk ($6.931 million) is *higher* than that of the Swiss alternative ($6.071 million). Can SAZ management therefore conclude that the distribution center should be located in Zaragu? The answer depends on how confident managers are in the assumptions they used to reach their conclusion.

In analyzing the alternatives, SAZ made two critical assumptions that could have a significant effect on the resulting NPVs. The first is that the purchasing power parity relation holds between the U.S. dollar and the two foreign currencies. The second is that the probability assessment of the imposition of a foreign tax on the project is reliable. More generally, the second assumption refers to the probability that a portion or all of a project's cash flows accruing to the parent will be expropriated and to the form this expropriation will take. The only realistic way to improve the confidence in the outcome of the NPV analysis of the Zaragu alternative is to do a *sensitivity analysis* that will show how responsive the project's NPV is to changes in the assumptions. For example, scenarios can be developed using percentage deviations from the purchasing power parity combined with different forms of expropriation that can be expected in Zaragu. Only then can a decision be made that fully accounts for the project's risk.

In the relatively simple case of the Zap Scan project, the sensitivity analysis can be aimed at the responsiveness of the project's NPV to changes in the probability of having the project subject to a foreign tax. Repeating the same computations as in Exhibit 14.5, we estimated the project's NPV with a range of probabilities from 0 to 50 percent. The results are reported in Exhibit 14.6. The probability for which the NPV of the Zaragu project is the same as the NPV of the Swiss project (USD 6.071 million) is approximately 40 percent. This probability is twice the expected probability of 20 percent. The difference is large enough to decide that, despite the presence of some country risk, the Zap Scan project should be located in Zaragu rather than in Switzerland.

MANAGING COUNTRY RISK

The previous section analyzes the effect on a cross-border investment's NPV if a foreign tax is imposed on the cash flows expected from the investment. As indicated earlier in the chapter, the possibility of a special tax being levied on foreign investments is only one aspect of the country risk that firms confront when

EXHIBIT 14.6 THE ZAP SCAN PROJECT'S NET PRESENT VALUE (NPV) FOR THE ZARAGU ALTERNATIVE AS A FUNCTION OF THE PROBABILITY OF THE PROJECT BEING SUBJECTED TO THE "FOREIGN" TAX.

Probability that the project will be subjected to the "foreign" tax	0%	10%	20%	30%	40%	50%
Project NPV in USD millions	7.814	7.373	6.931	6.489	6.047	5.605

investing abroad. The purpose of country risk management is to limit the exposure of the parent company to these direct or indirect impediments to the transfer of funds from its foreign investments. The following sections discuss a few actions that can help a manager design a proactive strategy for managing country risk.

INVEST IN PROJECTS WITH UNIQUE FEATURES

Projects that depend on input or output markets that are controlled by the parent company are less likely to be expropriated by a local government than projects that use raw materials or sell products and services that are readily available worldwide. Projects that require an expertise unique to the parent company are also less likely to be expropriated. For example, if a plant can be operated only by foreign nationals, the local government may not impose discriminatory regulations on the foreign affiliate for fear of having the plant shut down.

USE LOCAL SOURCING

Buying goods and services locally can reduce country risk because it increases local production and local employment. However, the benefits need to be weighed against the risk of having lower-quality products or services, unreliable delivery schedules, or high local prices.

CHOOSE A LOW-RISK FINANCIAL STRATEGY

Country risk can be substantially reduced if an agency of the host-country government or a powerful international institutional investor is included as a minority shareholder or lender in the cross-border project. The host government is less likely to impose restrictions on dividends or interest payments made by a firm in which either it or an international investor such as the World Bank or the International Finance Corporation is one of the firm's shareholders or bondholders. Furthermore, because dividends to the parent are usually the first remittance from the subsidiary to be limited, blocked, or taxed, it is usually preferable to finance a cross-border investment with as little equity as possible.

DESIGN A REMITTANCE STRATEGY

Dividends or interest payments are not the only way for a parent company to be compensated for its investments in a foreign country. Royalties, management fees, transfer prices, and technical assistance fees are other forms of remittances that can complement financial transfers. Because these transfers of funds are payments for goods and services, they are usually the last on the list of transfer payments to be restricted. However, a manager should not wait for the imposition of controls on dividends or interest payments to set a new funds transfer policy because the move will undoubtedly be seen by the host government as a means to circumvent the new regulation. Any remittance strategy must be implemented long before the imposition of restrictions on transfer payments.

CONSIDER BUYING INSURANCE AGAINST COUNTRY RISK

In many industrial countries, government-sponsored institutions provide insurance against country risk. Firms should consider buying such insurance for investments made in high-risk countries if alternative measures are difficult or costly to implement. Even if the insurance is not purchased, the insurance premium can be used to estimate the effect of country risk on the NPV of the cross-border investment. If we assume that the insurance policy eliminates the effect of any expropriation of the investment's cash flows, the present value of the insurance premium payments during the useful life of the project represents the amount by which the project's NPV should be reduced to account for country risk. This approach, contrary to sensitivity analysis, does not rely on the subjective assessment of the consequences of the country risk on the project's expected cash flows.

However, the present value of the insurance premium payments may underestimate the true cost of country risk because most insurance policies cover only the accounting value of the cross-border investment, which can be lower than the true value of the damages suffered by the parent company. Also, the insurance is provided by institutions that are generally set up by governments for the purpose of encouraging firms to invest in high-risk countries. Thus, the premium may be somewhat subsidized and be lower than the premium that would have been required by the private insurance market to cover the same level of risk.

SUMMARY

The fundamental principle of financial management still holds in an international environment. Foreign operations must be managed with the objective of creating shareholder value. However, the need to deal with more than one currency raises a number of issues that are specific to the management of foreign operations.

A firm is confronted with several risks when operating in a foreign environment. Changes in exchange rates affect the firm's financial statements. To address this accounting, or translation, exposure, regulators have established rules that firms should use to translate the financial statements of a foreign business unit into home currency units. The two most commonly used translation methods are the monetary/nonmonetary method and the current rate method.

Movements in the exchange rate also affect the value of the cash flows from the foreign business unit, an effect usually called economic exposure. Economic exposure is classified into two categories: (1) contractual, or transaction, exposure, which refers to the effect of exchange-rate volatility on the future cash flows from *past* transactions and (2) operating exposure, which is also concerned with future cash flows, but from *future* transactions that have not yet occurred. Finally, firms with foreign operations may also be subject to country risk arising from an unstable economic, political, and social environment.

Differences in expected inflation rates and interest rates between countries are the major factors governing the fluctuations in exchange rates. Three fundamental relations, known as the parity relations, link these variables. The purchasing power parity (PPP) relation links exchange rates and inflation rates. The interest-rate parity (IRP) relation links exchange rates to interest rates. Finally, the forward-spot relation provides the link between the forward exchange rate and the future spot rate.

The chapter presents a detailed analysis of a decision to invest in a foreign country. A cross-border investment project, like a domestic one, creates value only if its net present value (NPV) is positive. It is, however, more complicated to estimate the NPV of a foreign investment than that of a domestic one. First, most of the cash flows from an investment in a foreign country are denominated in the foreign currency, and, second, these cash flows may be subject to country risk. To convert cash flows denominated in a foreign currency into cash flows denominated in the domestic currency, we recommend using the PPP relation. The converted cash flows will have some exchange-rate risk attached to them because of the probability that future exchange rates may differ from those estimated by the parity relation. In principle, the cost of capital needs to be adjusted to account for this extra risk. In practice, however, no adjustment is necessary because most shareholders own diversified portfolios in which the exchange-rate risk has already been eliminated. To account for the effect of country risk on the NPV of a cross-border investment, we recommend adjusting the expected cash flows for the specific actions that the host government may take to reduce the parent company's claims on the project, rather than adding a "fudge" factor to the project's cost of capital. We also recommend that a sensitivity analysis be performed to show how responsive the project's NPV is to different assumptions about the form and the extent of possible expropriation measures.

Finally, country risk can be managed using techniques and mechanisms that can reduce the parent company's exposure to the expropriation of its foreign investments or to restrictions on the transfer of funds from its foreign subsidiaries.

Translating Financial Statements with the Monetary/Nonmonetary Method and the Current Method

APPENDIX 14

THE MONETARY/NONMONETARY METHOD

In the monetary/nonmonetary method, monetary assets, such as cash and accounts receivable, and monetary liabilities, such as accounts payable, accrued expenses, and short-term and long-term debts, are translated at the exchange rate prevailing on the date of the balance sheet. The nonmonetary items, such as inventories and fixed assets, are estimated using the rate prevailing at the date they were entered in the balance sheet, that is, the historic rate. The logic of this approach is that monetary assets and monetary liabilities are contracted amounts that would be redeemed at a rate that is likely to be closer to the rate prevailing on the date of the balance sheet than to the historical rate. The average exchange rate of the reporting period is used to translate the income statement accounts, except for those accounts related to the nonmonetary items, such as depreciation expenses, which are translated at the same rate as the corresponding balance sheet item. Any gain or loss from translating balance sheet accounts is reflected in the income statement and, as a result, affects reported earnings.

The top part of Exhibit A14.1.1 shows how the year-end balance sheet accounts of the French subsidiary of Uncle Sam's Bagel are translated into U.S. dollars according to the monetary/nonmonetary method. Two possible values are shown for the exchange rate, USD/EUR 1.24 and USD/EUR 1.26. The dollar values of cash, trade receivables, trade payables, and financial debt are obtained by multiplying their euro value by the year-end exchange rate. The dollar value of inventories and fixed assets is the same regardless of the year-end exchange rate because, as nonmonetary assets, their value is determined by the exchange rate on the date when they were recorded in the balance sheet, not on the date of the balance sheet. The dollar value of the subsidiary's owners' equity, which is the difference between the dollar value of its assets and that of its liabilities, depends on the exchange rate at the end of the year. It will be \$50 million if the exchange rate is USD/EUR 1.24 and \$45 million if the exchange rate is USD/EUR 1.26. The difference, \$5 million, is equal to the difference between the change in the value of the monetary liabilities and the change in the value of the monetary assets (\$8 million less \$3 million). Note, however, that owners' equity changes in the opposite direction of the change in the exchange rate: it *decreases* when the exchange rate

EXHIBIT A14.1.1 MONETARY/NONMONETARY METHOD[1] APPLIED TO THE BALANCE SHEET OF THE FRENCH SUBSIDIARY OF UNCLE SAM'S BAGEL AT YEAR-END.

FIGURES IN THOUSANDS

Monetary/Nonmonetary Method					
	Euros (EUR)		U.S. dollars (USD) End-of-year exchange rate USD/EUR 1.24	U.S. dollars (USD) End-of-year exchange rate USD/EUR 1.26	Change
Assets					
Cash	50,000		50,000 × 1.24 = 62,000	50,000 × 1.26 = 63,000	+1,000
Accounts receivable	100,000		100,000 × 1.24 = 124,000	100,000 × 1.26 = 126,000	+2,000
Total monetary assets		*150,000*	*186,000*	*189,000*	*+3,000*
Inventories	100,000		90,000	90,000	—
Property, plant, and equipment	250,000		270,000	270,000	—
Total nonmonetary assets		*350,000*	*360,000*	*360,000*	—
Total		500,000	546,000	549,000	+3,000
Liabilities and owners' equity					
Short-term debt	75,000		75,000 × 1.24 = 93,000	75,000 × 1.26 = 94,500	+1,500
Accounts payable	75,000		75,000 × 1.24 = 93,000	75,000 × 1.26 = 94,500	+1,500
Long-term debt	250,000		250,000 × 1.24 = 310,000	250,000 × 1.26 = 315,000	+5,000
Total monetary liabilities		*400,000*	*496,000*	*504,000*	*+8,000*
Owners' equity (Assets – Liabilities)		***100,000***	***50,000***	***45,000***	***–5,000***
Total		500,000	546,000	549,000	+3,000

[1]In the monetary/nonmonetary method, monetary assets and liabilities are translated at the exchange rate on the date of the balance sheet, and the nonmonetary assets are valued at the rate when they were entered in the balance sheet.

increases from USD/EUR 1.24 to USD/EUR 1.26. This is not surprising because, as long as monetary liabilities are larger than monetary assets, an *appreciation* of the foreign currency (the U.S. dollar cost of one euro increases) will increase the dollar value of the firm's liabilities relative to that of its assets, thus reducing the dollar value of its owners' equity. For most firms, the value of monetary liabilities is greater than the value of monetary assets, so an *appreciation* of the foreign currency will usually result in a *translation loss* when using the monetary/nonmonetary method. A *depreciation* of the foreign currency will result in a *translation gain.*

THE CURRENT METHOD

In the **current method**, known as FASB (Financial Accounting Standards Board) 52, *all* the balance sheet assets and liabilities are translated at the exchange rate on the balance sheet date. The income statement accounts can be translated either at the exchange rate at the date when the revenues and expenses are incurred or at the average exchange rate of the period. To avoid large variations in reported earnings, which may be caused by large fluctuations in the exchange rate, translation gains or losses are reported in a separate equity account of the parent balance sheet. The logic behind the current method is that it does not distort the structure of the balance sheet as the monetary/nonmonetary method does because all the assets and liabilities are affected proportionally by changes in exchange rates.

Exhibit A14.1.2 shows how the balance sheet accounts of the French subsidiary of Uncle Sam's Bagel are translated according to the current method, using the same data as in Exhibit A14.1.1 in which the monetary/nonmonetary method is

EXHIBIT A14.1.2 CURRENT TRANSLATION METHOD[1] APPLIED TO THE BALANCE SHEET OF THE FRENCH SUBSIDIARY OF UNCLE SAM'S BAGEL AT YEAR-END.

FIGURES IN THOUSANDS

Current Method					
	Euros (EUR)		U.S. dollars (USD) End-of-year exchange rate USD/EUR 1.24	USD/EUR 1.26	Change
Assets					
Cash	50,000		50,000 × 1.24 = 62,000	50,000 × 1.26 = 63,000	+1,000
Accounts receivable	100,000		100,000 × 1.24 = 124,000	100,000 × 1.26 = 126,000	+2,000
Inventories	100,000		100,000 × 1.24 = 124,000	100,000 × 1.26 = 126,000	+2,000
Property, plant, and equipment	250,000		250,000 × 1.24 = 310,000	250,000 × 1.26 = 315,000	+5,000
Total		500,000	620,000	630,000	**+10,000**
Liabilities and owners' equity					
Short-term debt	75,000		75,000 × 1.24 = 93,000	75,000 × 1.26 = 94,500	+1,500
Accounts payable	75,000		75,000 × 1.24 = 93,000	75,000 × 1.26 = 94,500	+1,500
Long-term debt	250,000		250,000 × 1.24 = 310,000	250,000 × 1.26 = 315,000	+5,000
Total monetary liabilities		*400,000*	*496,000*	*504,000*	*+8,000*
Owners' equity (Assets – Liabilities)		***100,000***	***124,000***	***126,000***	***+2,000***
Total		500,000	620,000	630,000	**+10,000**

[1]In the current method, all assets and all liabilities are translated at the exchange rate on the date of the balance sheet.

applied to these accounts. When the exchange rate increases from USD/EUR 1.24 to USD/EUR 1.26, the dollar value of *all* the French subsidiary's assets and liabilities increases by the same proportion as the exchange rate (1.61 percent). As a result, owners' equity also increases by the same proportion, from $124 million to $126 million. Contrary to the previous method, the current method always shows a *translation gain* when the foreign currency *appreciates* and a *translation loss* when the foreign currency *depreciates*.

WHICH METHOD IS BETTER?

The difference between the monetary/nonmonetary method and the current method comes from a different valuation of the nonmonetary assets. The first method values them at the historic exchange rate and the second at the current exchange rate. Which is the right approach? Neither approach is right because managing for value creation implies that the relevant value of a firm's assets is their *market* value, not their accounting value.

Which method do most companies use? Most companies use the current rate method, simply because it is recommended by most accounting regulatory bodies worldwide. We believe that regulators favor the current method because it is easier to understand and easier to apply. Most managers prefer the current method because of the difference in the treatment of gains and losses from translation adjustments: the monetary/nonmonetary method includes them in the computation of reported income, but the current method does not. Because managers' performance is often based on accounting figures, it may make sense to account for the effect of changes in exchange rates (over which managers have little control) separately from other sources of gain or loss.

The Parity Relations

APPENDIX 14

THE LAW OF ONE PRICE

Suppose there are no transaction costs (such as transportation costs or taxes) when buying gold in one country, say the United States, and selling it in another, say France. Also, assume the following:

1. The current spot rate is USD/EUR 1.25 ($1.25 per €1)
2. Gold can be bought for $800 an ounce in New York
3. Gold can be sold at €644 an ounce in Paris

At USD/EUR 1.25, the price of gold in euros in New York is €640 ($800 divided by 1.25). Under these conditions, buying gold in New York at €640 (where it is relatively cheaper) and selling it in Paris for €644 (where it is relatively more expensive) provides a €4 riskless profit. A trader can buy one ounce of gold in New York at $800, send it to Paris, and sell it there for €644. The €644 can be exchanged for $805 (€644 multiplied by USD/EUR 1.25) for a net profit of $5 ($805 less $800).

As you have guessed, the possibility of making such a riskless arbitrage profit will not remain unnoticed for long. Arbitrageurs will act and their actions will quickly move prices and exchange rates until the price of gold in New York and Paris is the same whether the currency is denominated in the U.S. dollar or euro.

Extending this market mechanism to any traded good, we obtain the **law of one price (LOP)**, according to which any traded good will sell for the same price regardless of the country where it is sold. The LOP can be written as follows:

$$P_h = P_f \times S^0_{h/f}$$

where P_h is the price of a good in the home country (the price of gold in the United States in our case), P_f is the price of the same good in a foreign country (the price of gold in France), and $S^0_{h/f}$ is the current spot exchange rate expressed in the number of units of the home currency needed to buy one unit of the foreign currency ($1.25 to buy €1 in our case). Applied to the case of gold, we have P_h = €644 × USD/EUR 1.25 = $805.

For the LOP to be true, some assumptions are necessary. For example, transaction costs must be zero, tax systems must be identical all over the world, and regulations (both real and hidden) must not prevent cross-country exchanges. The real world of international trade does not operate in such a frictionless fashion. In the case of the gold example discussed above, if these costs are at least \$5, arbitrage would be a worthless activity.

THE PURCHASING POWER PARITY RELATION

The purchasing power parity (PPP) relation is a version of the LOP with less stringent assumptions. It says that the *general cost of living* should be the same across countries, not the cost of any individual good as the LOP requires. Suppose the USD/EUR exchange rate is 1.25 (\$1.25 per €1) and the inflation rate next year is expected to be 2 percent in the United States and 4 percent in France. A basket of goods that currently costs \$1.25 in the United States will cost \$1.275 next year [\$1.25 × (1 + 2 percent)], and a similar basket of goods that currently costs €1 in France will cost €1.04 next year. The PPP relation implies that the spot rate must change so that next year one U.S. dollar exchanged into euros would still buy the same basket of goods. In other words, according to the PPP relation, the spot rate *expected* to prevail next year must be USD/EUR 1.275 divided by €1.04 or USD/EUR 1.226.

According to the PPP relation, we can write the following:

$$E(S^1_{h/f}) = S^0_{h/f} \times \frac{1 + E(i_h)}{1 + E(i_f)}$$

where $S^0_{h/f}$ is the current exchange rate, measured as the number of units of the home currency needed to buy one unit of the foreign currency; $E(S^1_{h/f})$ is the expected exchange rate in one year's time; and $E(i_h)$ and $E(i_f)$ are the expected inflation rates for next year at home and in the foreign country, respectively. This is equation 14.1 in the chapter.

Dividing both sides of the equation by $(S^0_{h/f})$, we get the following:

$$\frac{E(S^1_{h/f})}{S^0_{h/f}} = \frac{1 + E(i_h)}{1 + E(i_f)}$$

Subtracting one from both sides of this equation gives the following:

$$\frac{E(S^1_{h/f})}{S^0_{h/f}} - 1 = \frac{1 + E(i_h)}{1 + E(i_f)} - 1$$

or

$$\frac{E(S^1_{h/f}) - S^0_{h/f}}{S^0_{h/f}} = \frac{E(i_h) - E(i_f)}{1 + E(i_f)}$$

When the expected inflation rate in the foreign country is small enough, the term $1 + E(i_f)$ is not significantly different from one, yielding the simpler version of the PPP in equation 14.2 in the chapter:

$$\frac{E(S^1_{h/f}) - S^0_{h/f}}{S^0_{h/f}} = E(i_h) - E(i_f)$$

THE INTERNATIONAL FISHER EFFECT

Real and nominal interest rates are related through equation 14.3 in the chapter, also known as the Fisher effect. This equation is as follows:

$$1 + r = (1 + r_r) \times (1 + E(i))$$

where r is the nominal interest rate, r_r is the real interest rate, and $E(i)$ is the expected inflation rate. We can rearrange the terms of the equation to express the real rate of interest (r_r) as a function of the nominal rate of interest (r) and the expected inflation rate, $E(i)$:

$$1 + r_r = \frac{1 + r}{1 + E(i)}$$

or

$$r_r = \frac{1 + r}{1 + E(i)} - 1$$

If *real* interest rates are different from one country to another, capital will flow from the countries with the lowest rate to the countries with the highest rate until rates are equalized. In equilibrium, when the real interest rates are the same in all countries, the right side of the above equation must be the same in all countries, in particular in the home country and in the foreign country. Thus, if r_h and r_f are the nominal interest rates in the home and foreign countries and $E(i_h)$ and $E(i_f)$ are the expected inflation rates in the home and foreign countries, we must have the following:

$$\frac{1 + r_h}{1 + E(i_h)} = \frac{1 + r_f}{1 + E(i_f)}$$

or

$$\frac{1 + r_h}{1 + r_f} = \frac{1 + E(i_h)}{1 + E(i_f)}$$

This is equation 14.6 in the chapter. As indicated in the chapter, a reasonable approximation of that equation is as follows:

$$r_h - r_f = E(i_h) - E(i_f)$$

which is equation 14.7 in the chapter. The relation between interest rates and expected inflation rates as expressed by equation 14.6 or 14.7 is known as the **international Fisher effect.**

THE INTEREST-RATE PARITY RELATION

Suppose you have $1 million to invest and you observe the following data for the euro and the U.S. dollar:

- Spot exchange rate: USD/EUR 1.25
- Twelve-month forward rate: USD/EUR 1.27
- One-year euro interest rate: 5 percent
- One-year U.S. dollar interest rate: 6 percent

EXHIBIT A14.2.1 INVESTING IN USD VERSUS INVESTING IN EUR.

Strategy 1: Invest in Dollars ($)	Strategy 2: Invest in Euros (€)
Now: Invest $1,000,000 at 6 percent	*Now:* 1. Convert $1,000,000 at the current spot rate: $\frac{\text{USD } 1{,}000{,}000}{\text{USD/EUR } 1.25} = €800{,}000$ 2. Invest €800,000 at 5 percent. 3. Sell forward €800,000 × (1 + 0.05) = €840,000 at USD/EUR 1.27
In one year: Cash in your dollar investment. You get $1,000,000 × (1 + 0.06) = $1,060,000	*In one year:* 1. Cash in your euro investment. You get €800,000 × (1 + 0.05) = €840,000 2. Settle your forward contract and deliver €840,000. In exchange, you receive: €840,000 × USD/EUR 1.27 = $1,066,800
$1,060,000	**$1,066,800**

STRATEGY 1: INVESTMENT IN U.S. DOLLARS

It appears that you will be better off next year if you invest in U.S. dollars rather than euros because 6 percent is higher than 5 percent. Is this assumption warranted? No, because you cannot compare two interest rates expressed in different currencies. The correct comparison should be between the two investments *expressed in the same currency*. To invest in euros, you will have to change your dollars into euros and, after cashing your investment in one year, convert the euros you receive back into dollars. By selling these euros forward, you will know precisely the dollar amount you will get in one year. If the forward rate is advantageous, it may compensate for a lower interest rate. The two investment strategies are shown in Exhibit A14.2.1.

STRATEGY 2: INVESTMENT IN EUROS

Investment in euros produces $6,800 more than investment in U.S. dollars. The gain from buying spot euros at USD/EUR 1.25 and selling them forward at USD/EUR 1.27 is higher than the 1 percent interest rate foregone from lending at 5 percent instead of 6 percent.

To earn the extra $6,800, you do not need to own $1 million. You can just borrow this amount at 6 percent, implement Strategy 2, and repay your debt (interest included) in one year. You will still earn a riskless net profit of $6,800. In the competitive world of the foreign-exchange market, such "free lunches" will be short-lived. Interbank traders, acting as arbitrageurs, are quick to identify possible **arbitrage transactions** and immediately trade to benefit from them. In the above example, their actions will result in a higher interest-rate differential and a lower spread between spot and forward exchange rates. The process, which is almost instantaneous, will end when the outcomes of Strategies 1 and 2 are identical. How do these arbitrage transactions affect the spot exchange rate, the forward exchange rate, and the interest rates?

Looking again at the two investment strategies, let r_h and r_f be the nominal rates of interest in the home country and the foreign country, respectively. With Strategy 1, for one unit of the home currency invested, you will receive $(1 + r_h)$ in home currency a year later. With Strategy 2, you will first have to exchange one unit of the home currency for $1/S^0_{h/f}$ units of the foreign currency, where $S^0_{h/f}$ is the spot exchange rate (in units of home currency per unit of foreign currency). One year later, you will receive $(1/S^0_{h/f}) \times (1+r_f)$ units of foreign currency that will be converted into $[(1/S^0_{h/f}) \times (1+r_f)] \times F^0_{h/f}$ units of the home currency, where $F^0_{h/f}$ is the forward rate (in units of home currency per unit of foreign currency). If the net outcomes of the two strategies are the same, we can write the following:

$$1 + r_h = \frac{1 + r_f}{S^0_{h/f}} F^0_{h/f}$$

The terms of this equation can be rearranged to obtain the following:

$$\frac{F^0_{h/f}}{S^0_{h/f}} = \frac{1 + r_h}{1 + r_f}$$

Subtracting one from both sides of the equation gives the following:

$$\frac{F^0_{h/f}}{S^0_{h/f}} - 1 = \frac{1 + r_h}{1 + r_f} - 1$$

or

$$\frac{F^0_{h/f} - S^0_{h/f}}{S^0_{h/f}} = \frac{r_h - r_f}{1 + r_f}$$

The above equation is equation 14.8 in the chapter. It is called the interest-rate parity (IRP) relation. This relation is better known under its following simplified version, which assumes that r_f is small compared with one:

$$\frac{F^0_{h/f} - S^0_{h/f}}{S^0_{h/f}} = r_h - r_f$$

The above equation is equation 14.9 in the chapter. It says that the percentage difference between the forward and the spot rates is equal to the difference in interest rates.

FURTHER READING

1. Brealey, Richard, Stewart Myers, and Franklin Allen. *Principles of Corporate Finance*, 9th ed. McGraw-Hill, 2008. See Chapter 28.
2. Copeland, Tom, Tim Koller, and Jack Murrin. *Valuation, Measuring and Managing the Value of Companies*, 3rd ed. John Wiley, 2000. See Chapters 17 to 19.

3. Damodaran, Aswath. *Corporate Finance: Theory and Practice*, 2nd ed. John Wiley & Sons, 2001. See Chapter 26.
4. Eun, Cheol, and Bruce Resnick. *International Financial Management*, 4th ed. McGraw-Hill, 2007.
5. Ross, Stephen, Randolph Westerfield, and Jeffrey Jaffe. *Corporate Finance*, 8th ed. McGraw-Hill Irwin, 2008. See Chapter 31.

SELF-TEST PROBLEMS

14.1 ACCOUNTING VERSUS ECONOMIC EXPOSURE.

What is the difference among accounting, translation, economic, transaction, contractual, and operating exposure? Why is economic exposure more relevant than accounting exposure to shareholders?

14.2 PARITY RELATIONS.

Indicate in one sentence what the purchasing power parity relation says.

14.3 COUNTRY RISK AND THE COST OF CAPITAL.

The best way to account for country risk is to add a risk premium to the project cost of capital. True or false?

14.4 INTERNATIONAL CAPITAL BUDGETING (1).

A leading U.S. sport equipment company is considering setting up a sport shoe–manufacturing plant in Thailand. The investment will require an initial capital of Thai baht (THB) 50 million. The investment life is five years. Based on the information provided below, should the company set up the manufacturing plant in Thailand?

1. Sales, currently at THB 20 million, will grow at the annual rate of 5 percent over the next five years
2. Earnings before interest and tax, currently at THB 15 million, will grow at the same rate as sales
3. The inflation rate in Thailand is 3 percent, and it is 4 percent in the United States. These rates are expected to remain constant during the next five years
4. The corporate tax rate in Thailand is 35 percent
5. Annual capital expenditure is equal to annual depreciation expense
6. Working capital requirement equals 10 percent of sales
7. The terminal value of the plant at the end of the fifth year is expected to be THB 15 million
8. Spot exchange rate is THB 40 per USD 1
9. The company cost of capital is 12 percent

14.5 INTERNATIONAL CAPITAL BUDGETING (2).

The Kampton Company, an American firm, considers once again investing in Germany. The investment will cost €103 million and is expected to generate, after taxes, €25 million a year during the next five years. The project would be liquidated at the end of the fifth year, and its terminal value is estimated at €25 million. The cost of capital used by Kampton for its investments in the European Union is 7 percent above the yield on U.S. government bonds, whereas it is 5 percent for investments in the United States. Currently, the rate on U.S. government bonds is 6 percent and the exchange rate, which is not expected to vary much from its current value over the next five years, is EUR/USD 0.80.

1. Calculate the net present value of the project in U.S. dollars.
2. What would be the net present value if Kampton was using the same risk premium for its investments in Europe as in the United States?
3. Should Kampton use a higher-risk premium in Europe than in the United States?

REVIEW PROBLEMS

1. **Exposure.**
   A U.S.-based multinational corporation has a wholly owned subsidiary in the Philippines that manufactures electronics products to be sold in the North American market. The equity of the Philippines subsidiary is peso 2,500 million (from the latest balance sheet data). Because of recent political uncertainties in the Philippines, the multinational's head office in San Jose, California, is concerned that the peso could depreciate by as much as 20 percent against the dollar from its present level of 50 pesos per $1. The chief executive officer (CEO) believes that this exposure should be hedged with a forward contract. The three-month forward exchange rate is 53 pesos per $1. The U.S. company uses the current method (Financial Accounting Standards Board [FASB] 52) to translate foreign currency financial statements into dollars.

   Do you agree with the CEO? What are the arguments for and against hedging this exposure? For simplicity, assume that the subsidiary does not pay any tax.

2. **Parity relations.**
   Indicate in one sentence what the following parity relation says:

   a. Purchasing power parity relation
   b. International Fisher effect
   c. Interest-rate parity relation
   d. The relation between forward rates and future spot rates

3. **Interest-rate parity relation.**
   As a trader, you can trade based on the following data:

   1. Spot rate: $S^0_{USD/EUR} = 1.25$
   2. Forward rate: $F^0_{USD/EUR} = 1.248$
   3. U.S. one-year deposit rate: $r_{USD} = 3$ percent
   4. Euro-zone one-year deposit rate: $r_{EUR} = 3.15$ percent

      a. What is the return on one U.S. dollar deposit?
      b. What is the return in U.S. dollars on a dollar-covered euro lending?
      c. Can the given information provide an arbitrage opportunity?

4. **Arbitrage activity.**
You are a currency arbitrager for a Japanese bank. The spot rate this morning is JPY/USD 111.22, and early indications are that short-term interest rates in the United States (ninety-day rates) are about to rise from their current level of 3.125 percent. The Federal Reserve is worried about rising inflation and has announced that it is considering increasing short-term interest rates by twenty-five basis points (0.25 percent). The ninety-day forward rate quoted this morning to you by local banks are all about the same, JPY/USD 111.14. The current ninety-day yen deposit rate of interest is 2.156 percent. You have ¥250 million to invest.
   a. How can you make a profit through an interest arbitrage transaction as described in Appendix 14.2? How much profit in yen can you hope to make in ninety days, given the above data?
   b. If future spot exchange rates are determined by interest-rate differentials (that is, if the forward rate provided a good forecast of future spot rates), what would you expect the spot rate to be in ninety days if the Federal Reserve were to increase interest rates by twenty-five basis points?

5. **International Fisher effect.**
Suppose one country has a fixed exchange-rate regime. Prices in that country are rising faster than U.S. prices. Is the money of this country appreciating or depreciating in real terms? Explain.

6. **Real versus nominal cash-flow valuation.**
What are the pros and cons of real versus nominal cash-flow valuation?

7. **The purchasing power parity relation.**
   a. The finance manager of a U.S. pharmaceutical company has $10 million to invest for six months. The annual interest rate in the United States is 3 percent. The annual interest rate in the United Kingdom is 1 percent. The spot rate of exchange is $1.60 per £1 and the six-month forward rate is $1.65 per £1. In which country would the finance manager want to invest the money? (You can ignore transaction costs.)
   b. The spot rate between the U.S. dollar and the pound sterling is $1.70 per £1. If the interest rate in the United States is 4 percent and 2 percent in the United Kingdom, what would you expect the one-year forward rate to be if no immediate arbitrage opportunities existed?

8. **International capital budgeting (1).**
The Brankton Company, an American firm, considers investing in Spain. The investment will cost €125 million and is expected to generate, after taxes, €30 million a year during the next five years in real terms, that is, before inflation. The project would be liquidated at the end of the fifth year, and its terminal value is estimated at €30 million. The annual rate of inflation is expected to be 3 percent in the Euro-zone and 4 percent in the United States. The cost of capital used by Brankton for its investments in the Euro-zone is 7 percent above the yield on government bonds. Currently, the rate on U.S. government bonds is 5 percent and

the exchange rate is EUR/USD 0.80. Calculate the net present value of the project in U.S. dollars.

9. **International capital budgeting (2).**
Chateau Cheval Noir is one of the leading premium wine producers of France, with its fifty-acre vineyard at St. Julien in the Bordeaux region. The owners have wanted to expand their production, but the scarcity and astronomical prices asked for vineyards adjacent to the existing property have led them to explore the possibility of buying a top winery outside of France. They identified both Australia and California as regions that could produce wines of a quality approaching those from their own vineyards. In March 2010, during a trip to the Barossa Valley of South Australia, the owners found an eighty-acre vineyard that promised to meet all of their requirements: soil, exposure, microclimate, age and condition of the vines, condition of the wine-making facilities, and brand image. After a preliminary study, the French owners estimate that the Australian vineyard would have the following attributes:

    1. Annual sales of A$16 million, in real (March 2010) terms
    2. Earnings before interest and tax of A$14 million, in real (March 2010) terms
    3. Annual capital expenditure is equal to annual depreciation expense
    4. Working capital requirement equal to 10 percent of sales
    5. The economic life of the vineyard, for purposes of the analysis, is five years
    6. The value in Australian dollars of the vineyard at the end of five years is estimated as a growing annuity based on the level of cash flow after tax attained in the following year. No growth in real terms is expected after the end of the economic life of the project

    Other available information relevant to the investment:

    1. Annual expected inflation rates: Australia, 5 percent; Euro-zone, 2 percent
    2. Spot rate: A$1.75 per €1
    3. Required rate of return on investment: 10 percent in euros and 12 percent in Australian dollars
    4. Corporate tax rate in Australia: 30 percent; no additional taxes would be paid in France on repatriated income
    5. Risk-free rate in euros: 5.5 percent
    6. Country risk (penalty taxes imposed by Australia): very low to none

        a. What would be the maximum price in Australian dollars and in euros that the owners of Chateau Cheval Noir could pay for the Australian vineyard?
        b. Why is there a higher discount rate in Australian dollars than in euros?

10. **International capital budgeting (3).**
A major U.S. clothes manufacturing and distributing company plans to expand in Asia. To reduce its transportation costs, it wants to set up its own manufacturing plant in Asia. Two countries are under consideration: China and Indonesia. The

expected cash flows from the manufacturing plants in the two countries are as follows:

	Now	Year 1	Year 2	Year 3	Year 4	Year 5
Plant in China (millions of yuan)	–14	3	3	5	6	6
Plant in Indonesia (millions of rupiah)	-20,000	5,000	5,000	6,000	7,000	7,000

a. In which country should the U.S. company invest? The spot rate for Chinese yuans and Indonesian rupiahs are CNY 6.82 per USD 1 and IDR 9,699.78 per USD 1, respectively. The inflation rate in China and the United States is expected to be 4 percent and in Indonesia 6 percent during the next five years. The cost of capital of the U.S. company is 10 percent.

b. Suppose that the net present values of both projects are positive and equal. What are other possible factors that could help the U.S. company make a choice between the two projects?

Managing for Value Creation CHAPTER 15

Managing for value creation is more than a business slogan. It is a comprehensive approach to management based on the principle that managers at all levels of the organization must manage their firm's resources with the ultimate objective of increasing the firm's market value. Managing with the goal of creating value provides the basis for a comprehensive and integrated *valued-based management* system that helps managers formulate relevant business plans, make sound business decisions, evaluate actual business performance, and design effective management compensation packages.

This chapter reviews the financial principles underlying a value-based management system, examines the advantages and implications of this approach to management, and explains how the system can be implemented. We first show how to measure the value that a firm has created or destroyed. We then identify the key factors that drive the process of value creation and show how firms can align the interests of managers with those of owners by tying managers' performance and reward to these drivers of value creation. Finally, we summarize the value-based management approach using a framework we call the *financial strategy matrix*. This matrix is a convenient business diagnostic tool that can be used to make value-based strategic and financing decisions and to evaluate the resulting performance.

Managing to create value for the firm's owners is not incompatible with a dedicated workforce, a loyal customer base, and a cooperative group of suppliers. Increasing a firm's market value does not mean creating wealth for the firm's owners at the expense of employees, customers, or suppliers. On the contrary, no firm can expect to generate value for its owners if it does not also provide value to its employees, customers, and suppliers. Motivated employees, delighted customers, and efficient suppliers are an integral part of a successful recipe for enhancing the firm's value. As mentioned in Chapter 1, companies that achieve the largest increase in their stock market value are also the most admired for their ability to attract and retain better employees and loyal customers. After reading this chapter, you should understand the following:

- The meaning of managing for value creation
- How to measure value creation at the firm level using the concept of market value added (MVA)
- Why maximizing MVA is consistent with maximizing shareholder value
- When and why growth may *not* lead to value creation
- How to implement a management system based on a value-creation objective
- How to measure a firm's capacity to create value using the concept of economic value added (EVA)
- How to design management compensation schemes that induce managers to make value-creating decisions

MEASURING VALUE CREATION

To find out whether management has created or destroyed value at a particular point in time, we compare the *market value* of the firm's total capital (both equity and debt capital) with the amount of capital that equity holders and debt holders have invested in the firm (this is what we called the firm's **capital employed**). The difference between these amounts is the firm's **market value added** or, simply, **MVA:**

Market value added (MVA) = Market value of capital − Capital employed (15.1)

If MVA is positive, value has been created because the market value of the firm's capital (the market value of its equity and debt) is worth more than the amount of capital that has been invested in the firm (this is the term "capital employed" in equation 15.1). If MVA is negative, then value has been destroyed.

Consider InfoSoft, a software company created in 2000. On December 31, 2010, the firm's owners had a cumulative investment of \$280 million of equity capital in the firm and debt holders had lent the firm \$100 million. The total amount of capital available to InfoSoft was thus \$380 million. Suppose that the *market* value of that capital (equity plus debt) was \$500 million on that date (we show in the next section how to calculate this value). To summarize: at year-end 2010, InfoSoft employed \$380 million of capital whose market value was worth \$500 million. Deducting the amount of capital employed (\$380 million) from InfoSoft's market value (\$500 million) provides a measure of the amount of value InfoSoft has created as of December 31, 2010:

$$\text{InfoSoft's MVA}_{12/31/2010} = \$500 \text{ million} - \$380 \text{ million} = \$120 \text{ million}$$

MVA is a positive \$120 million, indicating that InfoSoft has created \$120 million of value as of December 31, 2010.

Suppose the market value of InfoSoft's equity and debt capital was \$300 million instead of \$500 million. In this case, InfoSoft would have *destroyed* \$80 million of value as of December 31, 2010, because the \$380 million of capital would be worth only \$300 million on that date.

MVA measures value creation or destruction at a *particular point in time.* To measure the value created or destroyed *during a period of time,* look at the *change* in MVA during that period. For example, if InfoSoft's MVA was $140 million a year earlier (December 31, 2009), the firm's management would have destroyed $20 million of value during 2010 ($120 million less $140 million).

ESTIMATING MARKET VALUE ADDED

To estimate a firm's MVA with equation 15.1, we need to know (1) the market value of the firm's equity and debt capital and (2) the amount of capital that shareholders and debt holders have invested in the firm. We now examine how these items can be estimated.

ESTIMATING THE MARKET VALUE OF CAPITAL

The **market value of capital** can be obtained from the financial markets, at least for firms whose equity and debt capital are publicly traded in the form of securities. If the firm is not publicly traded, its market value is unobservable and its MVA cannot be calculated. If someone makes an offer to buy the firm, however, we could then estimate the firm's MVA based on that offer price.

On December 31, 2010, InfoSoft had debt with a market value of $110 million: long-term bonds with a market value of $50 million and nontraded bank borrowing reported at $60 million in its balance sheet.[1] The firm had 3.9 million shares outstanding that were trading at $100 a share. The market value of its equity (its **market capitalization**) was thus $390 million ($100 multiplied by 3.9 million shares), and the total market value of its capital was $500 million ($110 million of debt plus $390 million of equity). This is the figure we used to estimate InfoSoft's MVA on December 31, 2010.

ESTIMATING THE AMOUNT OF CAPITAL EMPLOYED

The other input needed to measure a firm's MVA is the estimate of the amount of capital employed by the firm. This figure can be extracted from the firm's balance sheet and associated notes. Debt capital includes short-term and long-term borrowings as well as sources of capital that are equivalent to debt obligations—items such as lease obligations and provisions for the retirement and pension plans of employees. Estimating the amount of equity capital is more complicated. We must add to the book value of equity reported in the balance sheet a number of items that standard accounting conventions *exclude* from the figure shown in the balance sheet.

Exhibit 15.1 presents two versions of InfoSoft's balance sheets on December 31, 2009 and 2010, reported in their managerial format (see Chapter 3). A managerial balance sheet shows the firm's invested capital (cash, working capital

[1]We assume that the value of the bank debt is equal to its book value, that is, that the interest rates on these loans have not changed since InfoSoft has borrowed the funds.

EXHIBIT 15.1 INFOSOFT'S MANAGERIAL BALANCE SHEETS ON DECEMBER 31, 2009 AND 2010.

FIGURES IN MILLIONS

Unadjusted Managerial Balance Sheet	December 31, 2009			December 31, 2010		
Invested Capital						
Cash			$ 5			$ 10
Working capital requirement[1] (net)			100			100
Gross value	*$105*			*$110*		
Accumulated bad debt allowance	*(5)*			*(10)*		
Net fixed assets			185			190
Property, plant, and equipment (net)		95			110	
Goodwill[2] (net)		90			80	
Total			$290			$300
Capital Employed						
Short-term debt			$40			$20
Long-term financing			40			40
Lease obligations			40			40
Owners' equity			170			200
Total			$290			$300

Adjusted Managerial Balance Sheet	December 31, 2009		December 31, 2010	
Invested Capital				
Cash		$ 5		$ 10
Gross working capital requirement[1]		105		110
Net fixed assets		235		260
Property, plant, and equipment (net)	$ 95		$110	
Gross goodwill	100		100	
Capitalized R&D	40		50	
Total		$345		$380
Capital Employed				
Total debt capital		$120		$100
Short-term debt	$ 40		$ 20	
Long-term financing	40		40	
Lease obligations	40		40	
Adjusted owners' equity		225		280
Book value of equity	170		200	
Accumulated bad debt allowance	5		10	
Accumulated goodwill impairment	10		20	
Capitalized R&D	40		50	
Total		$345		$380

[1]WCR = (Accounts receivable + Inventories + Prepaid expenses) – (Accounts payable + Accrued expenses).
[2]Gross value was $100 million at year-end 2009 and year-end 2010.

requirement,[2] and net fixed assets) and the capital the firm employs (equity plus debt) to fund these investments.

The unadjusted balance sheets report invested capital and capital employed according to standard accounting conventions; the adjusted balance sheets add to invested capital and the book value of equity a number of items that accounting conventions exclude. The amount of debt capital at year-end 2010 ($100 million) is the same in both types of balance sheets and is equal to the figure we used to estimate InfoSoft's MVA.

What items should be added to the book value of equity to get the $280 million of adjusted owners' equity reported in the 2010 adjusted balance sheet in Exhibit 15.1? These are items—such as **allowance for bad debt**, the impairment of **goodwill**, and research and development (R&D) expenses—that, according to accounting conventions, are arbitrarily classified as expenses and reported in the income statement as a deduction from revenues. The effect of these deductions is to lower both reported profits and retained earnings. With less earnings retained, the equity account in the balance sheet is *understated*.

Invested capital in the 2010 unadjusted balance sheet in Exhibit 15.1 includes $10 million of accumulated bad debt allowance and $20 million of accumulated goodwill impairment. These two items, as well as $50 million of R&D expenses, are added to the $200 million of unadjusted book value of equity in 2010 to obtain the $280 million figure shown in the 2010 adjusted balance sheet.

Appendix 15.1 shows why and how these adjustments are made. Notice that their effects on the magnitude of InfoSoft's MVA are significant. Ignoring them would overstate InfoSoft's MVA by $80 million.

INTERPRETING MARKET VALUE ADDED

We can make several noteworthy observations about the definition and interpretation of value creation given by equation 15.1. We examine the most significant ones in this section.

MAXIMIZING MVA IS CONSISTENT WITH MAXIMIZING SHAREHOLDER VALUE

Strictly speaking, shareholder value creation should be measured by the difference between the market value of the firm's *equity* and the amount of *equity* capital shareholders have invested in the firm. The former represents the financial market estimation of shareholders' investment in their firm, and the latter the actual amount of money they invested in it. But MVA in equation 15.1 is the difference between the market value of *total* capital (equity and debt) and *total* capital employed. We can reconcile the two definitions by noting that MVA in equation 15.1 is the sum of (1) an *equity MVA,* defined as the difference between the market value of equity and its adjusted book value, and (2) a *debt MVA,* defined as the

[2]Working capital requirement is the difference between the firm's operating assets (Accounts receivable + Inventories + Prepaid expenses) and operating liabilities (Accounts payable + Accrued expenses). See Chapter 3 for details.

difference between the market value of debt and its reported book value. Thus, the definition of MVA in equation 15.1 can be restated as follows:

$$\textbf{MVA = Equity MVA + Debt MVA} \qquad (15.2)$$

For InfoSoft, equity MVA is $110 million (equity market value of $390 million less adjusted equity capital of $280 million) and debt MVA is $10 million (debt market value of $110 million less debt capital of $100 million). These amounts yield a total MVA of $120 million.

If we assume that debt MVA is different from zero *only because of changes in the level of interest rates,*[3] then, *for a given level of interest rates*, maximizing MVA is equivalent to maximizing shareholder value (equity MVA). The general level of interest rates is determined by macroeconomic variables over which managers do not have any control, so using MVA as a measure of management performance is problematic. To isolate the change in MVA attributable to management decisions, we should first neutralize the part that is caused by broader market conditions. One corrective measure would be to deduct an estimate of the change in MVA that arises from those broader market conditions.

MAXIMIZING THE MARKET VALUE OF THE FIRM'S CAPITAL DOES NOT NECESSARILY IMPLY VALUE CREATION

Suppose InfoSoft's management retains $15 million of profit and borrows $5 million to invest in a $20 million project. Assume that, as a consequence of the investment decision, InfoSoft's market value increases by $16 million (from $500 million to $516 million). Can we conclude that InfoSoft created $16 million of value? The answer is no. It has actually *destroyed* $4 million of value. To see why, calculate the firm's MVA after the project's announcement. It is $116 million ($516 million of market value less $400 million of capital employed—the original $380 million plus the $20 million investment). MVA is now $4 million *less* than it was before the project was announced ($116 million versus $120 million). This is because the company invested $20 million in a project that led to an increase in its market value of only $16 million.

Consider another example that shows why managers should maximize MVA rather than market value. Suppose we compare InfoSoft's market value with the $1 billion market value of TransTech. Although TransTech's market value is twice that of InfoSoft's, we cannot infer that TransTech has created twice as much value as InfoSoft. Before we can draw any conclusions, we need to know how much capital TransTech is employing. Its adjusted balance sheet (not provided here) indicates that it employs $940 million of capital. Its MVA is thus $60 million ($1 billion less $940 million), half of InfoSoft's $120 million MVA. Although the market value of TransTech is twice that of InfoSoft, its management has created half the value created by InfoSoft.

[3]In the case of InfoSoft, interest rates have gone down and the market value of its long-term debt has gone up. See Chapter 9 for an explanation of the inverse relationship between changes in interest rates and market values.

MVA INCREASES WHEN THE FIRM UNDERTAKES POSITIVE NET PRESENT VALUE PROJECTS

Recall the definition of a project's net present value (NPV) given in Chapter 6. It is the present value of the stream of cash flows the project is expected to generate less the amount of capital spent on it. In the MVA definition given by equation 15.1, capital employed is the same as the total amount of capital the firm has invested in its *past* and *current* investment projects. And the present value of the stream of cash flows these investments are expected to generate in the future is the market value of the firm's capital. MVA is thus the equivalent of the sum of the NPVs of all the projects the firm has undertaken. In other words, *saying that a firm has raised (or reduced) its MVA is the same as saying that it has invested in positive (or negative) NPV projects.* Later in the chapter, we show that the contribution of an investment project to a firm's MVA is indeed equal to the project's NPV.

A LOOK AT THE EVIDENCE

Consider the 500 U.S. companies that constitute the Standard & Poor's stock market index. Exhibit 15.2 shows the ten companies that achieved the highest MVA and the ten companies that produced the lowest MVA based on a 2009 ranking compiled by EVA Dimensions using 2008 data.[4] The first column provides the market value of the companies' total capital (equity and debt), and the second column shows the corresponding amount of capital employed (adjusted for accounting distortions). The difference is the companies' estimated MVA reported in the third column. We can make several noteworthy observations about the companies and their MVA.

First, the top-ten companies created slightly more than $1,000 billion of value, an amount that exceeds the gross national product (GNP) of most countries.

Second, as pointed out earlier, when we compare two companies, the one with the highest market value of capital is not necessarily the one that has created the most value. For example, Wal-Mart Stores (a retailer) has a higher market value of capital ($247.5 billion) than Microsoft ($187.8 billion), but it has created less value for its owners because its MVA is $123.7 billion compared to $162.3 billion for Microsoft.

Third, value creation is measured in *absolute* terms. Compare, for example, the performance of Exxon Mobil (an integrated oil company) with that of Oracle (a software producer). Exxon Mobil was the highest *absolute* value creator with an estimated MVA of $171 billion, whereas Oracle was ranked ninth, with a lower estimated MVA of $84.6 billion. But if value created is measured *per dollar of capital employed,* Oracle outperformed Exxon Mobil. It created $3.24 of value per dollar of capital employed ($84.6 billion divided by $26.1 billion) compared with $0.74 for Exxon Mobil ($171 billion divided by $230 billion). This occurs because Oracle is less capital intensive than Exxon Mobil.

Fourth, four of the ten companies with the highest MVA were in the computer and computer-related industries: Microsoft (software), Apple (hardware and software),

---

[4]For more information on data provided by EVA Dimensions, go to www.evadimensions.com.

EXHIBIT 15.2 TOP VALUE CREATORS AND DESTROYERS IN THE UNITED STATES: 2009 RANKING.[1]

RANKING BY MARKET VALUE ADDED (2004 RANKING IN PARENTHESES).[2] FIGURES IN BILLIONS

Top Ten Value Creators by MVA	Market Value of Capital	Capital Employed	Value Created (MVA[3])
1. Exxon Mobil Corp. (7)	$401.0	$230.0	+$171.0
2. Microsoft Corp. (3)	187.8	25.5	+162.3
3. Wal-Mart Stores Inc. (2)	247.5	123.8	+123.7
4. Google Inc.	118.0	16.6	+101.4
5. Apple Inc. (274)	103.5	3.1	+100.4
6. International Business Machines Corp. (12)	172.9	83.2	+89.7
7. Coca-Cola Co. (10)	122.0	33.2	+88.8
8. Procter & Gamble Co. (9)	214.9	129.6	+85.3
9. Oracle Corp. (21)	110.7	26.1	+84.6
10. Philip Morris International (18)	99.7	23.3	+76.4

Bottom Ten Value Destroyers by MVA	Market Value of Capital	Capital Employed	Value Destroyers (MVA)
491. Verizon Communications Inc. (469)	$194.3	$225.1	–$30.8
492. JPMorgan Chase & Co. (64)	138.1	175.1	–37.0
493. Sprint Nextel Corp. (681)	50.5	88.5	–38.0
494. JDS Uniphase Corp. (1000)	21.1	60.1	–39.0
495. AT&T Inc. (174)	271.9	321.3	–49.4
496. Time Warner Inc. (998)	71.4	123.8	–52.4
497. General Motors Corp.[4] (994)	–19.1	39.5	–58.6
498. Citigroup Inc. (4)	21.1	111.1	–90.0
499. Pfizer Inc. (14)	91.6	193.0	–101.4
500. Bank of America Corp. (22)	108.4	233.7	–125.3

[1]The data is compiled by EVA Dimensions LLC (www.evadimensions.com) for the 500 companies that constitute the Standard & Poor's Composite Index (S&P 500) based on data for fiscal year 2008. Used by permission.
[2]The 2004 ranking is for 1,000 companies based on data for fiscal year 2003.
[3]MVA = Market value of capital *less* Capital employed.
[4]Capital and market-value figures include "net pension debt," which is the cumulative service cost less cash contributions, after tax. In the case of GM, cash contributions exceeded cumulative service cost, hence a negative net pension debt, and from that, a negative market value.

IBM (hardware and software), and Oracle (software). The other six companies represented a diversity of industries: food and staples retailing (Wal-Mart Stores); Internet services (Google); food, beverage, and tobacco (Coca-Cola and Philip Morris); and household and personal products (Procter & Gamble). Note the absence of value-creating companies from the financial services industry. This is due to the financial crisis of 2007–2009 that reduced significantly the value of these firms, putting many of them among the bottom-ten companies with the lowest MVA (see JPMorgan Chase, Citigroup, and Bank of America).

Fifth, although five of the top-ten value creators were also ranked among the top-ten companies five years earlier, the rankings are not immutable. Some dramatic changes can occur such as Apple, which rose from number 274 to number 5, and Citigroup, which fell from number 4 to number 498. There are also newcomers such as Google, which was not listed in the 2004 ranking but was ranked fourth in 2009.

Sixth, value creators and value destroyers can be found in the same industry, no matter how well or how badly the industry is performing. For example, despite the severe crisis that hit the financial services industry in 2008–2009, there were value-creating companies in that sector such as Wells Fargo, which ranked 37 with an MVA of $21.4 billion, and Goldman Sachs, which ranked 40 with an MVA of $18.4 billion. Thus, management inability to create value cannot be blamed on industry factors alone.

The next section identifies the factors that drive value creation and explains why some companies are value creators and others are value destroyers.

IDENTIFYING THE DRIVERS OF VALUE CREATION

A firm's capacity to create value is essentially driven by a combination of three key factors:

1. The firm's operating profitability, measured by its after-tax return on invested capital (ROIC)
2. The firm's cost of capital, measured by its weighted average cost of capital (WACC)
3. The firm's ability to grow

The after-tax ROIC is defined here as the firm's **net operating profit after tax (NOPAT)** divided by its invested capital measured at the *beginning* of the accounting period:[5]

$$\text{ROIC} = \frac{\text{EBIT} \times (1 - \text{Tax rate})}{\text{Invested capital}} = \frac{\text{NOPAT}}{\text{Invested capital}}$$

where EBIT is earnings before interest and tax, NOPAT is after-tax EBIT, and invested capital is the sum of cash, WCR, and net fixed assets (see Exhibit 15.1).

The WACC (see Chapters 1 and 10) is as follows:

$$\begin{aligned}\text{WACC} = &\ (\text{After-tax cost of debt} \times \text{Percentage of debt capital}) \\ &+ (\text{Cost of equity} \times \text{Percentage of equity capital})\end{aligned}$$

[5] According to the managerial balance sheet (see Exhibit 15.1), invested capital is the same as capital employed. Thus, return on invested capital (ROIC) is the same as return on capital employed (ROCE). We can use the two ratios interchangeably.

To illustrate, we return to the case of InfoSoft. Let's assume it earned \$64.5 million before interest and tax in 2010. Its cost of debt is 6.7 percent, its estimated cost of equity is 12 percent (see Chapter 10 for how to estimate the cost of equity), and it is subject to a 36 percent corporate tax rate. Its adjusted invested capital at the beginning of 2010 (same as the end of 2009) is \$345 million, as shown in the adjusted balance sheet in Exhibit 15.1. Based on these figures, InfoSoft's after-tax ROIC is as follows:

$$\text{ROIC} = \frac{\$64.5 \text{ million} \times (1 - 0.36)}{\$345 \text{ million}} = \frac{\$41.28 \text{ million}}{\$345 \text{ million}} = 11.97\% \text{ rounded up to } 12\%$$

The WACC should be calculated with *market* value weights (see Chapter 11). Recall that the market value of InfoSoft's equity is \$390 million (3.9 million shares worth \$100 a share) and that of its debt is \$110 million. Thus, the WACC can be written as follows:

$$\text{WACC} = \left[6.7\% \times (1 - 0.36) \times \frac{\$110 \text{ million}}{\$500 \text{ million}}\right] + \left[12\% \times \frac{\$390 \text{ million}}{\$500 \text{ million}}\right]$$

$$\text{WACC} = [4.29\% \times 0.22] + [12\% \times 0.78] = 10.3\%$$

Let's see how we can link a firm's capacity to create value to these two rates (ROIC and WACC) and to the firm's rate of growth.

LINKING VALUE CREATION TO OPERATING PROFITABILITY, THE COST OF CAPITAL, AND GROWTH OPPORTUNITIES

To help us understand how ROIC, WACC, and the expected rate of growth interact to create value, we examine the particular case—without any loss of generality—of a firm that is expected to grow *forever* at a *constant* annual rate. Appendix 15.2 shows that in this case the firm's MVA is given by the following valuation formula:

$$\textbf{Market value added} = \frac{\textbf{(ROIC – WACC)} \times \textbf{Invested capital}}{\textbf{WACC – Constant growth rate}} \qquad (15.3)$$

The following sections discuss two important and general conclusions that can be drawn from equation 15.3.

TO CREATE VALUE, EXPECTED ROIC MUST EXCEED THE FIRM'S WACC

The valuation formula (equation 15.3) indicates that a firm creates value only if the return it *expects* to earn on its invested capital (ROIC) is higher than the cost of financing its investments (WACC). As long as the firm's expected ROIC exceeds its estimated WACC, the numerator of the valuation formula is positive and so is its MVA, indicating that the firm creates value. Conversely, if the firm's expected ROIC is lower than its estimated WACC, MVA is negative and the firm destroys value. As an illustration of this point, consider InfoSoft. InfoSoft's MVA is \$120 million, the difference between its market value of \$500 million and its invested capital of \$380 million. What is driving InfoSoft's capacity to create value? *Simply put, it is the market expectation that InfoSoft's managers will be able to earn a ROIC that exceeds the firm's estimated WACC of 10.3 percent.*[6]

Let's call the difference between ROIC and WACC the firm's **return spread:**

$$\textbf{Return spread} = \textbf{ROIC} - \textbf{WACC} \tag{15.4}$$

We can now restate the condition for value creation as follows: *positive expected return spreads are the source of value creation, and negative expected return spreads are the source of value destruction.* When the return spread is zero, the firm neither creates nor destroys value. This does not mean that the firm is unable to remunerate its suppliers of capital. When the return spread is zero, ROIC is equal to the WACC, which means that the firm generates enough profit from operations to provide debt holders and equity holders the exact return they expect and no more. To create value, the firm must deliver to its equity holders *more* than what they expect to receive, which is true only when ROIC exceeds the WACC. It is important to keep in mind that it is the entire *future* stream of *expected* return spreads, and not *past* or *historical* return spreads, that drives the process of value creation or destruction.

Thus, the objective of managers should not be the maximization of their firm's operating profitability (ROIC) but rather the maximization of the firm's *return spread*. This means that rewarding a manager's performance on the basis of ROIC may lead to a behavior that is inconsistent with value creation. For example, suppose one of InfoSoft's divisions has an average ROIC of 14 percent and that its manager must decide whether to make a single-year investment whose expected ROIC is 12 percent. The investment's ROIC is expected to exceed the firm's WACC of 10.3 percent, so it should be undertaken. However, the manager whose reward is related to his division's average ROIC may *reject* the investment because accepting the investment would *lower* the division's *average* performance (it has an expected ROIC of 12 percent that is lower than the division's ROIC of 14 percent) and would reduce his remuneration. Designing a reward linked to the *return spread* should avoid this problem.

Do we have any evidence indicating that companies with an ROIC greater (lower) than their WACC are value creators (destroyers)? This question is difficult to answer because a firm's MVA is related to its *future stream* of return spreads, not to its *past* return spreads. Unfortunately, future return spreads are not observable. But we can examine the relationship between a firm's MVA and its most recent ROIC and WACC, reported in Exhibit 15.3. Note that the top-ten value creators have an ROIC that exceeds their WACC, while the bottom-ten value destroyers have an ROIC that is lower than their WACC.

---

[6]If we assume that InfoSoft's growth rate is constant, perpetual, and equal to 5.4 percent, then, according to equation 15.3, InfoSoft's MVA is equal to the following:

$$\text{MVA} = \frac{(0.120 - 0.103) \times \$345\text{ million}}{0.103 - 0.054} = \frac{\$5.87\text{ million}}{0.049} = \$120\text{ million}$$

EXHIBIT 15.3 ECONOMIC VALUE ADDED (EVA) OF THE TOP VALUE CREATORS AND VALUE DESTROYERS IN THE UNITED STATES: 2009 RANKING.[1]

RANKING BY MARKET VALUE ADDED AS IN EXHIBIT 15.2. FIGURES IN BILLIONS

Top Ten Value Creators by MVA	Return on Invested Capital[2]	Cost of Capital	EVA[3]
1. Exxon Mobil Corp.	20.2%	6.0%	+$32.6
2. Microsoft Corp.	60.5%	10.8%	+12.7
3. Wal-Mart Stores Inc.	11.4%	5.5%	+7.4
4. Google Inc.	30.8%	12.3%	+3.1
5. Apple Inc.	347.5%	10.5%	+4.6
6. International Business Machines Corp.	12.0%	10.6%	+1.1
7. Coca-Cola Co.	14.7%	5.8%	+3.0
8. Procter & Gamble Co.	9.1%	6.6%	+3.3
9. Oracle Corp.	24.6%	10.4%	+3.5
10. Philip Morris International	25.1%	5.3%	+4.8

Bottom Ten Value Destroyers by MVA	Return on Invested Capital[2]	Cost of Capital	EVA[3]
491. Verizon Communications Inc.	4.5%	8.5%	–$7.7
492. JPMorgan Chase & Co.	6.0%	7.8%	–2.7
493. Sprint Nextel Corp.	0.3%	8.2%	–7.3
494. JDS Uniphase Corp.	–0.8%	10.6%	–6.8
495. AT&T Inc.	4.9%	8.6%	–11.9
496. Time Warner Inc.	4.5%	7.3%	–4.7
497. General Motors Corp.	–47.1%	6.7%	–20.9
498. Citigroup Inc.	–12.1%	7.8%	–18.6
499. Pfizer Inc.	6.6%	7.4%	–1.6
500. Bank of America Corp.	7.5%	7.8%	–0.5

[1]The data is compiled by EVA Dimensions LLC (www.evadimensions.com) for the 500 companies that constitute the Standard & Poor's Composite Index (S&P 500) based on data for fiscal year 2008. Used by permission.
[2]Measured as return on *average* capital employed over the preceding 4 quarters.
[3]EVA = [(Return on invested capital) less (Cost of capital)] × [Average capital employed].

ONLY VALUE-CREATING GROWTH MATTERS

Another general implication of the valuation formula (equation 15.3) is that growth alone does not necessarily create value. It is the *sign* of the return spread that drives value creation, *irrespective* of the firm's growth rate. Some high-growth firms are value destroyers, and some low-growth firms are value creators. Only growth that is accompanied by a *positive* return spread can generate value.

EXHIBIT 15.4 COMPARISON OF VALUE CREATION FOR TWO FIRMS WITH DIFFERENT GROWTH RATES.

FIGURES IN MILLIONS

Firm	Expected Growth Rate	Expected ROIC	Estimated WACC	Expected Return Spread	Invested Capital	Market Value Added According to Equation 15.3	Is Value Created?
A	7%	10%	13%	−3%	\$100	$\frac{-3\% \times \$100}{13\% - 7\%} = \frac{-\$3}{0.06} = -\$50$	No
B	4%	13%	10%	+3%	\$100	$\frac{+3\% \times \$100}{10\% - 4\%} = \frac{+\$3}{0.06} = +\$50$	Yes

As an illustration, we compare the performance of firm A with that of firm B, whose characteristics are given in Exhibit 15.4. Both firms have \$100 million of invested capital. Firm A is anticipated to grow at 7 percent, has an expected ROIC of 10 percent, and an estimated WACC of 13 percent. Its return spread is negative (−3 percent). According to equation 15.3, the firm has destroyed \$50 million of value (see calculations in Exhibit 15.4). Note that it does not matter if firm A grows faster or slower than at 7 percent. It will not create value unless its managers are able to change its negative return spread to positive by raising its expected ROIC above its estimated WACC. Now, consider firm B. It is expected to grow at the slower rate of 4 percent. But its 13 percent anticipated ROIC is higher than its estimated WACC of 10 percent, so firm B has a positive return spread. According to equation 15.3, even though firm B is growing at a slower rate than firm A, it is creating \$50 million of value (see calculations in Exhibit 15.4).

LINKING VALUE CREATION TO ITS FUNDAMENTAL DETERMINANTS

We can identify more basic drivers of value creation by breaking down the firm's expected ROIC into its fundamental components (see Chapter 5). Recall that pretax ROIC can be broken down into operating profit margin (the ratio of EBIT to sales) and capital turnover (the ratio of sales to invested capital). Taking the corporate tax into account, we can write *after-tax* ROIC as follows:

$$\text{ROIC} = \frac{\text{EBIT}}{\text{Sales}} \times \frac{\text{Sales}}{\text{Invested Capital}} \times (1 - \text{Tax rate})$$

$$= \text{Operating profit margin} \times \text{Capital turnover} \times (1 - \text{Tax rate})$$

Thus, management can increase the firm's ROIC through a combination of the following actions:

1. *An improvement of operating profit margin,* achieved by generating higher operating profit per dollar of sales

2. *An increase in capital turnover,* achieved by generating the same or higher sales with less capital (this can be done through faster collection of receivables, speedier inventory turns, and fewer fixed assets while keeping sales the same or, better yet, while sales are increasing)
3. *A reduction of the effective tax rate,* achieved, for example, by taking advantage of various tax breaks and subsidies

The various drivers of value creation are summarized in Exhibit 15.5. In addition to the two operating drivers, the exhibit also reports the components of the cost of capital. Together, they determine the sign and the size of the future stream of expected return spreads, which, in turn, determine the firm's MVA. If MVA is positive, the faster the firm grows, the more value it creates. The ability of managers to grow their business over a sustained period of time is driven by the economic, political, and social environments in which the firm evolves; the structure and dynamics of the particular sector in which it operates; and the competitive advantages and core competencies the firm has developed over time.

EXHIBIT 15.5 THE DRIVERS OF VALUE CREATION.

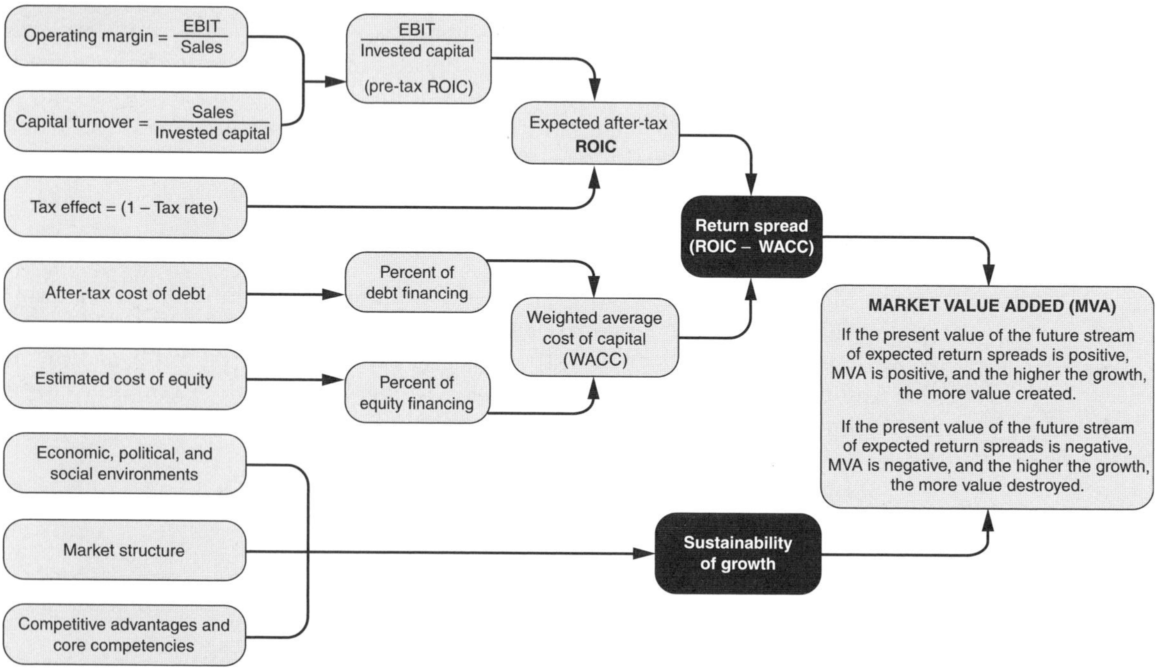

EBIT = Earnings before interest and tax (operating profit before tax)
Invested capital = Cash + Working capital requirement + Net fixed assets
WACC = (% Debt)(After-tax cost of debt) + (% Equity)(Cost of equity)

LINKING OPERATING PERFORMANCE AND REMUNERATION TO VALUE CREATION

In this section, we use a short case study to explain how a manager's operating performance, his remuneration package, and his ability to create value can be linked.

MR. THOMAS HIRES A GENERAL MANAGER

It is early 2011. Mr. Thomas, the sole owner of a toy distribution company called Kiddy Wonder World (KWW), is concerned about his firm's recent lackluster performance. During 2009, sales and profits grew at 5 percent while leading competitors achieved significantly higher average growth rates. The firm's financial statements for 2009 and 2010 are reported in Exhibit 15.6. They have been

EXHIBIT 15.6 FINANCIAL STATEMENTS FOR KIDDY WONDER WORLD.

FIGURES IN MILLIONS

Balance Sheets	December 31, 2009	December 31, 2010
Invested Capital		
Cash	$ 100	$ 60
Working capital requirement[1]	600	780
Net fixed assets	300	360
Total	$1,000	$1,200
Capital Employed		
Short-term debt	$ 200	$ 300
Long-term financing	300	300
Owners' equity	500	600
Total	$1,000	$1,200

Income Statements	2009	2010
Sales	$ 2,000	$ 2,200
less operating expenses	(1,850)	(2,000)
less depreciation expense	(20)	(50)
Earnings before interest and tax (EBIT)	$ 130	$ 150
less interest expense	(50)	(60)
Earnings before tax (EBT)	$ 80	$ 90
less tax expenses (40% of EBT)	(32)	(36)
Earnings after tax (net profit)	$ 48	$ 54

[1]WCR = (Accounts receivable + Inventories + Prepaid expenses) − (Accounts payable + Accrued expenses).

adjusted for the accounting conventions that could distort the value of invested capital and reported profits.

In November 2009, when the preliminary results for the year confirmed Mr. Thomas's prediction of poor performance, he decided to step back from day-to-day managerial duties and hired Mr. Bobson as general manager to run the company. Bobson was a successful business manager working for a competitor. The challenge to improve KWW's performance, as well as a higher salary supplemented by a bonus linked to the firm's profits, enticed him to join KWW in December 2009.

After getting acquainted with the company's operations, Mr. Bobson submitted his business plan for 2010 to Mr. Thomas. The plan was based on two major objectives: (1) increase sales by 10 percent through more aggressive marketing of existing products and the introduction of a new line of toys and (2) tightly control operating expenses to improve operating margin and enhance the firm's profitability. Mr. Thomas approved the plan and gave Mr. Bobson full authority to implement it as he wished.

In early 2011, Mr. Thomas received a copy of the company's financial statements for 2010, reported in the last column of Exhibit 15.6. Using these figures, Mr. Thomas wanted to assess the effectiveness of his general manager and evaluate his firm's 2010 performance compared with that of the previous year and against the performance of the leading firms in the sector. He also wondered whether the equity capital he and his family had invested in the company was adequately remunerated for the business and financial risks associated with the toy manufacturing and distribution business. He was recently contacted by a friend with a proposal to invest in an enterprise whose risk profile was similar to that of the toy distribution business and from which he could expect a return of 14 percent.

To carry out his analysis, Mr. Thomas needed financial information about leading firms in the sector. This information, which was provided by a consulting company specializing in the toy manufacturing and distribution business, is reported on the last column of Exhibit 15.7. In addition to information about competitors' performance, Exhibit 15.7 provides figures for KWW's 2010 performance (which reflect the outcome of Mr. Bobson's decisions) compared with the 2009 performance (before Bobson was hired). Based on all this information, Mr. Thomas had to determine whether Mr. Bobson achieved his dual objectives of faster growth in sales and earnings.

HAS THE GENERAL MANAGER ACHIEVED HIS OBJECTIVES?

Exhibit 15.7 indicates that in 2010 sales grew by 10 percent and earnings grew by 12.5 percent, both exceeding the previous year's results and the corresponding figures for the leading competitors in the sector. Operating expenses grew at a slower rate than sales (8.1 percent versus 10 percent), which explains why net profit grew faster than sales (12.5 percent versus 10 percent). It seems that Mr. Bobson has achieved his two objectives. How did he do it?

A closer look at the figures reported in Exhibit 15.7 reveals another aspect of Mr. Bobson's performance. The company's invested capital grew by 20 percent, much faster than during the previous year (4.2 percent) and much faster than the leading competitors (10 percent). This growth in invested capital was mostly the

EXHIBIT 15.7 COMPARATIVE PERFORMANCE OF KIDDY WONDER WORLD (KWW).

FIGURES IN MILLIONS

Performance Indicator	KWW Performance in 2009 (Before Mr. Bobson)[1]	KWW Performance in 2010 (With Mr. Bobson)[2]	Performance of Leading Competitors
Growth in sales			
% change from previous year	5%	10%	9%
Growth in earnings (net profits)			
% change from previous year	5%	12.5%	10%
Growth in operating expenses			
% change from previous year	6%	8.1%	8.8%
Growth in invested capital			
% change from previous year	4.2%	20%	10%
Growth in WCR			
% change from previous year	8%	30%	25%
Liquidity position			
$\frac{\text{Short-term borrowing}}{\text{WCR}}$	$\frac{\$200}{\$600} = 33.3\%$	$\frac{\$300}{\$780} = 38.5\%$	25%
Operating profitability			
$\text{ROIC} = \frac{\text{After-tax EBIT}}{\text{Average invested capital}}$	$\frac{\$130(1 - 0.40)}{\$980} = 8\%$	$\frac{\$150(1 - 0.40)}{\$1{,}100} = 8.2\%$	10%

[1]Previous year's figures are not provided. Invested capital was $960 million in 2008.
[2]Percentage changes are calculated with data from the financial statements in Exhibit 15.6.

outcome of a high growth in WCR (30 percent). A consequence of the high growth in WCR is the deterioration of the company's liquidity position. As shown in Exhibit 15.6, this growth, which is largely permanent in nature, was financed through a reduction in cash holding (from $100 million to $60 million) and a 50 percent increase in short-term borrowings (from $200 million to $300 million), resulting in a higher percentage of WCR that is financed with short-term debt, as shown in Exhibit 15.7.[7]

Finally, the firm's operating profitability, measured by ROIC, improved slightly from 8 percent to 8.2 percent, but is less than the average of 10 percent achieved by leading competitors. However, the reported improvement in ROIC is explained by the fact that invested capital is measured at its average value. If ROIC was measured with year-end values, it would have indicated a deterioration.

Mr. Bobson has increased sales and profits, but has he created value? We can find out by looking at the firm's return spread. The firm's latest ROIC is

[7]Chapter 3 shows that reliance on short-term debt to finance a long-term commitment (such as the permanent increase in WCR) is a sign of a deteriorating liquidity position.

8.2 percent. To know whether value was created, we compare this return on investment with the average cost of the capital that was required to achieve it. To estimate the firm's WACC, we need to know the proportions of equity and debt financing used to fund the firm's investments, the after-tax cost of debt, and the cost of equity.

The balance sheets in Exhibit 15.6 indicate that KWW's invested capital is financed with an equal amount of equity and debt capital.[8] The company can borrow at an average rate of 6.7 percent and the tax rate is 40 percent. Its average *after-tax* cost of debt is thus 4.02 percent. What is the estimated cost of equity? It is the 14 percent expected return that the firm's owner, Mr. Thomas, could earn if he invested his equity capital in a venture with the same risk profile as KWW.[9] We now have all the required inputs we need to estimate KWW's WACC:

$$\text{WACC} = (4.02\% \times 0.50) + (14\% \times 0.50) = 9.01\% \text{ rounded down to } 9\%$$

The firm's WACC of 9 percent is higher than its ROIC of 8.2 percent. The *historical* return spread is thus negative, indicating that the firm is unable to create value at a 9 percent cost of capital even though Mr. Bobson has raised both sales and earnings.[10] Mr. Bobson has invested too much capital at a cost (9 percent) that exceeds the return on that capital (8.2 percent). And, as mentioned earlier, the main reason for the growth of the firm's capital is the growth in the firm's WCR (30 percent higher than the previous year).

ECONOMIC PROFITS VERSUS ACCOUNTING PROFITS

The conclusion from our analysis of KWW is that Mr. Bobson was successful in increasing sales and profits but grew the company's WCR much faster than sales and profits. The result was an operating profitability that fell short of the firm's WACC and an inability to create value. In a way, the growth in WCR has provided the general manager with the resources (inventories and receivables) he needed to achieve his sales and profits objectives. In other words, the growth in WCR is not accidental; it was required to increase sales and profits. One question remains: why is Mr. Bobson pushing sales and boosting profits, and neglecting the management of working capital? Perhaps we should look at the way Mr. Bobson's remuneration package was designed. Recall that Mr. Bobson's compensation includes a bonus related to *profits*. Not surprisingly, profits are up. Because the growth of working capital does not affect his bonus, Mr. Bobson may be overinvesting in working capital to raise profits and increase his bonus.

---

[8]Chapter 10 explains that the proportions of equity and debt in the WACC should be estimated from the *market* values of equity and debt. However, KWW is not a traded company, so we used book values as proxies for market values. An alternative would be to use the market value ratios of a similar company.

[9]The cost of equity is, in this case, the owner's opportunity cost of capital. For a more specific estimation of the cost of equity, see Chapter 10.

[10]We are using the historical return spread to diagnose Mr. Bobson's ability to create value. We know, however, that value creation is determined by the future expected return spreads. The implicit assumption is that future return spreads are unlikely to become positive with the current growth strategy.

This behavior could have been prevented if Mr. Bobson had been penalized for his overinvestment in working capital and the increase in the capital required to finance it. One way to penalize Bobson for his overinvestment in working capital would have been to deduct from his NOPAT a "charge" for the capital he consumed to achieve those profits. This capital charge is determined by multiplying the firm's WACC by the amount of invested capital (cash plus WCR plus net fixed assets). We define **economic profit** or **economic value added (EVA)** as NOPAT less this capital charge:

$$\textbf{Economic value added (EVA)} = \textbf{NOPAT} - (\textbf{WACC} \times \textbf{Invested capital}) \quad (15.5)$$

where NOPAT is EBIT × (1 − Tax rate). For KWW, EBIT was $130 million in 2009 and $150 million in 2010. The WACC is 9 percent. Average invested capital was $980 million in 2009 and $1,100 million in 2010 (see Exhibit 15.7). Thus, we can write the following:

$$EVA_{2009} = [\$130 \text{ million} \times (1 - 0.40)] - [0.09 \times \$980 \text{ million}] = -\$10.2 \text{ million}$$

$$EVA_{2010} = [\$150 \text{ million} \times (1 - 0.40)] - [0.09 \times \$1{,}100 \text{ million}] = -\$9 \text{ million}$$

Although KWW is "profitable" when profits are measured according to *accounting* conventions (NOPAT and net profit are positive), it is not profitable when performance is measured with *economic* profits (EVA is negative). *Linking Mr. Bobson's performance and bonus to EVA rather than accounting profits would have induced him to pay more attention to the growth of WCR.*

There is another way to express the failure of Mr. Bobson's actions to create value. To see this, we factor out the term "invested capital" in the definition of EVA in equation 15.5:

$$EVA = \left(\frac{\text{NOPAT}}{\text{Invested capital}} - \text{WACC}\right) \times \text{Invested capital}$$

$$\textbf{EVA} = (\textbf{ROIC} - \textbf{WACC}) \times \textbf{Invested capital} \quad (15.6)$$

Equation 15.6 clearly shows that a positive return spread implies a positive EVA, which, in turn, implies value creation. Again, Mr. Thomas, KWW's owner, should have linked Mr. Bobson's bonus to EVA rather than to accounting profits. This would have motivated his general manager to pay closer attention to invested capital and to restrict the growth of the firm's assets, particularly the growth of WCR that was used to fund the growth in sales. The next section outlines the key features of an EVA-related compensation plan.

Let's return to Exhibit 15.3. The last column of the exhibit shows the EVA for the top value creators and destroyers estimated according to equation 15.6. Note that companies with a positive return spread have a positive EVA and those with a negative return spread have a negative EVA. As discussed earlier, a positive (negative) *historical* return spread or EVA does not imply that the company is necessarily a value creator (a value destroyer). Recall that it is the magnitude and the sign of the firm's *future* stream of *expected* EVA that determine whether a firm is a value creator or destroyer, not its *past* EVA.

DESIGNING COMPENSATION PLANS THAT INDUCE MANAGERS TO BEHAVE LIKE OWNERS

We have argued throughout this book that value creation should be a manager's ultimate objective. But the KWW case study clearly shows that managers do not always behave according to this principle. The challenge, then, is to create a compensation plan that induces them to make value-creating decisions rather than follow other objectives. One obvious solution is to turn managers into owners by remunerating them with equity ownership as opposed to a share of profits. Owners, however, do not always wish to transfer a significant portion of their equity investment to managers.

A possible alternative is to partly remunerate managers with a bonus linked to their ability to *increase* EVA, as mentioned in the previous section. A higher EVA is the key to value creation. Rewarding managers for their ability to improve EVA should motivate them to take actions consistent with the value-creation objective. For this type of compensation system to be effective, however, a number of conditions must be met.

First, managerial decisions made today (such as capital expenditure decisions) will most likely affect EVA for a number of subsequent years. Thus, the bonus should be related to the manager's ability to generate higher EVA for a period of several years, for example, from three to five years, not just for a single year.

Second, after the compensation plan has been established and accepted, it should not be modified and the reward should not be capped. Exceptional performance should be handsomely rewarded. But poor performance should be penalized. One way to do this is to allow managers to cash in only a *fraction* of their EVA bonus in a given year, say 25 percent, with the balance remaining on "deposit" with the firm. If EVA declines in subsequent years, the "deposit" will be reduced by an amount that is related to the magnitude of the decline in EVA. After three to five years, managers can withdraw the balance in their EVA deposit (assuming it is positive).

Third, to have a significant motivational effect on managers' behavior, the reward related to superior EVA performance must represent a relatively large portion of their total remuneration. For example, a remuneration plan in which EVA-related bonuses consist of 5 percent of total compensation, with the remaining 95 percent in the form of a guaranteed salary, is unlikely to be as effective as one in which EVA-related bonuses represent up to 50 percent of the total.

Fourth, as many managers as possible should be on the EVA-related bonus plan. The point is to focus the entire organization on generating economic profits and value. This objective is difficult to achieve if only a few senior managers are on this type of plan and the rest of the organization is on another type, such as a profit- or sales-related bonus plan, or on no bonus plan at all.

Fifth, if an EVA bonus plan is adopted, the book value of capital and the operating profit used to estimate EVA must be restated to adjust for the distortions caused by accounting conventions, as shown in Appendix 15.1. The adjustments should be limited to a few that are relevant and meaningful to managers. Too many adjustments may unnecessarily complicate a system whose major attraction is its simplicity and ease of understanding.

Finally, an EVA bonus plan must be consistent with the company's capital budgeting process, which is the key to making value-creating investment decisions (see Chapter 6). In other words, inducing managers to maximize EVA over the life of an investment must be consistent with the NPV rule we have advocated when making capital expenditure decisions. We demonstrate in the next section that this is indeed the case.

LINKING THE CAPITAL BUDGETING PROCESS TO VALUE CREATION

Chapter 6 describes how firms should make investment decisions and how they should organize their capital budgeting process. The objective is to make investment decisions that have the potential to increase the firm's market value. In this context, the NPV rule and the internal rate of return (IRR) rule both play a key role. A firm should accept only investment proposals that have a positive NPV or, equivalently, have an IRR higher than the project's WACC. Recall that we can calculate the NPV of an investment proposal by discounting to the present the cash flows the investment is expected to generate in the future and then deducting from that present value the initial cash outlay required to launch the project. Chapter 10 shows that the relevant discount rate needed to find the present value of the expected cash-flow stream is the WACC that reflects the risk of the investment. The investment's IRR is simply the discount rate for which the NPV of the investment is equal to zero.

The NPV rule, which is at the heart of the capital budgeting process, is based on cash flows, but the financial management framework described in this chapter is based on MVA and EVA. Earlier in this chapter, ROIC, WACC, and growth were linked to MVA, and operating performance and remuneration were linked to EVA. We now need to link EVA to MVA and to link the cash-flow-based NPV rule to both EVA and MVA. By connecting the measures of performance that are the concerns of the corporate finance function, we can provide a comprehensive financial management system that integrates the value-creation objective with the firm's value, its operating performance, and its remuneration and incentive plans, as well as its capital budgeting process.

THE PRESENT VALUE OF AN INVESTMENT'S FUTURE EVA IS EQUAL TO ITS MVA

We first examine the link between MVA and EVA. The previous section shows that the correct measure of a manager's ability to create value is the economic profit, or EVA, she is able to generate during a period of time, usually one year. Most managerial decisions, however, generate benefits over a number of years, not immediately. Thus, we need to measure the value *today* of the entire stream of *future* economic profits a business decision is expected to produce, not the economic profit generated during a single year. In other words, we need to measure the present value of the entire stream of future expected EVA. This present value is the measure of the potential value the business decision will create. The potential value created by a business decision is the MVA of the decision, which is shown in equation 15.3. The definition of EVA is given in equation 15.6. The numerator of equation 15.3 is the same as the EVA defined in equation 15.6. We can thus write equation 15.3 as follows:

$$\text{MVA} = \frac{\textbf{EVA}}{\textbf{WACC} - \textbf{Constant growth rate}} \tag{15.7}$$

where the stream of future EVA is, in this case, expected to grow forever at a constant annual rate. This valuation formula shows that the present value of the future stream of EVA that a business proposal is expected to generate is the MVA of that proposal. In other words, *management should maximize the entire stream of future EVA that their firm's invested capital is expected to generate to maximize their firm's MVA and create shareholder value.*

MAXIMIZING MVA IS THE SAME AS MAXIMIZING NPV

We have just shown that the value-creating manager runs her business with the goal of maximizing its MVA. In Chapter 6, we show that the value-creating manager makes decisions that maximize NPV. We now want to see whether these two decision rules are consistent with each other. We use the example reported in Exhibit 15.8 as an illustration. The exhibit is shown in a spreadsheet format.

The Investment A firm is considering investing in a piece of equipment. Data relevant to the investment are presented in the first part of Exhibit 15.8. The equipment, which would cost $1 million to acquire, has an expected useful life of two years and a residual value of zero. The equipment would be depreciated over the next two years, providing equal annual depreciation expense of $500,000. The investment is expected to generate sales of $2 million the first year and $4 million the second year. At the *beginning* of every year, the firm would have to increase its investment in working capital to support the sales that will be generated that year. The ratio of WCR to next year's sales is 10 percent and the ratio of operating expenses (*excluding* depreciation) to sales is 70 percent. The corporate tax rate is 40 percent, and the firm uses a cost of capital (the WACC) of 10 percent for this type of investment.

Net Operating Profit after Tax from the Investment Expected net operating profits are shown in part 2 of Exhibit 15.8. Operating profit is 30 percent of sales (because operating expenses are 70 percent of sales) less depreciation expense (because they are not included in operating expenses). Taxes are 40 percent of operating profit. The result is a NOPAT of $60,000 at the end of the first year and $420,000 at the end of the second year (row 17).

Cash Flows from the Investment Cash flows from the investment are calculated in part 3 of the exhibit. They are equal to the investment's NOPAT plus depreciation expense less net investment. Net investment includes the purchase of the piece of equipment ($1 million) and changes in the WCR over the lifetime of the investment. The firm would have to invest $200,000 of working capital at the investment date (10 percent of Year 1 sales), and another $200,000 a year later, for a total of $400,000 at the end of Year 2. Note that the $400,000 would be recovered at the end of Year 2 when the investment terminates. This calculation produces an initial cash outflow of $1.2 million to launch the project, followed by net cash inflows of $360,000 at the end of the first year and $1.32 million at the end of the second year (row 22).

EXHIBIT 15.8 EQUIVALENCE OF NET PRESENT VALUE MEASURED WITH CASH FLOWS AND NET PRESENT VALUE MEASURED WITH ECONOMIC VALUE ADDED.

FIGURES IN THOUSANDS

	A	B	C	D	E
1		Now	End-of-Year 1	End-of-Year 2	
2					
3					
4	**1. Investment data**				
5	Equipment cost	($1,000)			
6	Residual value of equipment			$ 0	
7	Depreciation expense		($ 500)	(500)	
8	Sales		2,000	4,000	
9	Working capital requirement/next year sales	10%	10%		
10	Operating expenses/sales		70%	70%	
11	Corporate tax rate		40%	40%	
12	Cost of capital	10%			
13					
14	**2. Expected net operating profit after tax (NOPAT)**				
15	Expected operating profit		$ 100	$ 700	
16	Taxes on operating profit		40	280	
17	Expected net operating profit after tax (NOPAT)		**$ 60**	**$ 420**	
18					
19	**3. Expected cash flow from the investment and net present value (NPV)**				
20	Working capital requirement	$ 200	$ 400	$ 0	
21	Change in working capital requirement	(200)	(200)	400	
22	**Expected cash flow from the investment**	**($ 1,200)**	**$ 360**	**$ 1,320**	
23	**Net present value**	**$ 218.2**			
24	**Internal rate of return**	**21%**			
25					
26	**4. Economic value added (EVA) and market value added (MVA)**				
27	Accumulated depreciation of the equipment		($ 500)	($ 1,000)	
28	Net book value of the equipment	$ 1,000	500	0	
29	Invested capital	1,200	900	0	
30	Capital charge		–120	–90	
31	**Economic value added (EVA)**		($ 60)	$ 330	
32	**MVA = present value of EVAs**	**$ 218.2**			
33					
34	*Rows 5 to 12 are data.*				
35	*Formula in C15 is =C8*(1–C10)+C7. Then copy formula in cell C15 to next cell in row 15.*				
36	*Formula in C16 is =C11*C15. Then copy formula in cell C16 to next cell in row 16.*				
37	*Formula in cell B20 is =B9*C8. Then copy formula in cell B20 to next cells in row 20.*				
38	*Formula in cell B21 is =–B20. Formula in cell C21 is =–(C20–B20). Then copy formula in cell C21 to next cell in row 21.*				
39	*Formula in cell B22 is =B5+B17–B7+B21. Then copy formula in cell B22 to next cells in row 22.*				
40	*Formula in cell B23 is =B22+NPV(B12,C22:D22).*				
41	*Formula in cell B24 is =IRR(B22:D22).*				
42	*Formula in cell C27 is =C7. Formula in cell D7 is =C27+D7.*				
43	*Formula in cell B28 is =–$B$5+B27. Then copy formula in cell B28 to next cells in row 28.*				
44	*Formula in cell B29 is =B28+B20. Then copy formula in cell B29 to next cells in row 29.*				
45	*Formula in cell C30 is =–$B$12*B29. Then copy formula in cell C30 to next cell in row 30.*				
46	*Formula in cell C31 is =C17+C30. Then copy formula in cell C31 to next cell in row 31.*				
47	*Formula in cell B32 is =NPV(B12,C31:D31).*				
48					

Net Present Value and Internal Rate of Return Using a cost of capital of 10 percent, the NPV of the expected cash-flow stream from the investment is $218,200 (row 23) and its IRR is 21 percent (row 24). The investment's NPV is positive and its IRR exceeds its WACC. Thus, the investment is a value-creating proposition and should be undertaken.

Economic Value Added and Market Value Added The capacity of an investment to create value can also be estimated by calculating its future stream of expected EVA and discounting EVA at the cost of capital (the WACC) to provide the investment's MVA. If MVA is positive, value is created; if it is negative, value is destroyed. The procedure is shown in part 4 of Exhibit 15.8. Expected EVA is computed by deducting from NOPAT a charge for capital equal to 10 percent of the invested capital at the *beginning* of the year. For the first year, NOPAT is $60,000 (row 17), invested capital at the beginning of the year is $1.2 million (row 29), and the charge for capital is $120,000 (row 30). The expected EVA is –$60,000 (row 31). For the second year, NOPAT is $420,000, the capital charge is $90,000, and EVA is $330,000.

The investment's MVA is equal to the present value of the expected future stream of EVA discounted at the WACC of 10 percent. This MVA, shown in row 32, is equal to $218,200. The MVA is positive, so the investment is a value-creating proposition and should be undertaken *even though the first-year EVA is negative*. Note that the investment's MVA in row 32 is *exactly the same* as its NPV in row 23.

Although the two methods are equivalent, management must be careful when using the MVA approach to value an investment decision, particularly when estimating the charge for capital consumption (invested capital multiplied by the WACC). The relevant figure is the amount of invested capital at the *beginning* of the period, not at the end of the period.

The major advantage of the NPV approach is that it takes into account any nonfinancial transactions related to the project that either reduce or add to the firm's cash holding. Thus, when using the NPV method, managers can ignore the amount of invested capital at the beginning of each period and worry only about the cash flows generated by the project. Recall that the project in Exhibit 15.8 has a *negative* first-year EVA but a *positive* first-year cash flow, an indication that although no value is created the first year, the investment does generate cash. The major advantage of the MVA approach, of course, is its direct relation to EVA, which is based on *accounting* data with which managers are familiar.

PUTTING IT ALL TOGETHER: THE FINANCIAL STRATEGY MATRIX

Exhibit 15.9 summarizes the key elements of a firm's financial management system and shows their managerial implications within a single framework that we call the firm's **financial strategy matrix**. The firm may have one or several divisions or businesses.

The vertical axis measures the capacity of a particular business to create value. This capacity is indicated by the sign and magnitude of the firm's return spread (its expected ROIC less its WACC). When the business's return spread is positive (the upper half of the matrix), there is value creation (EVA is positive). When the return

EXHIBIT 15.9 THE FINANCIAL STRATEGY MATRIX.

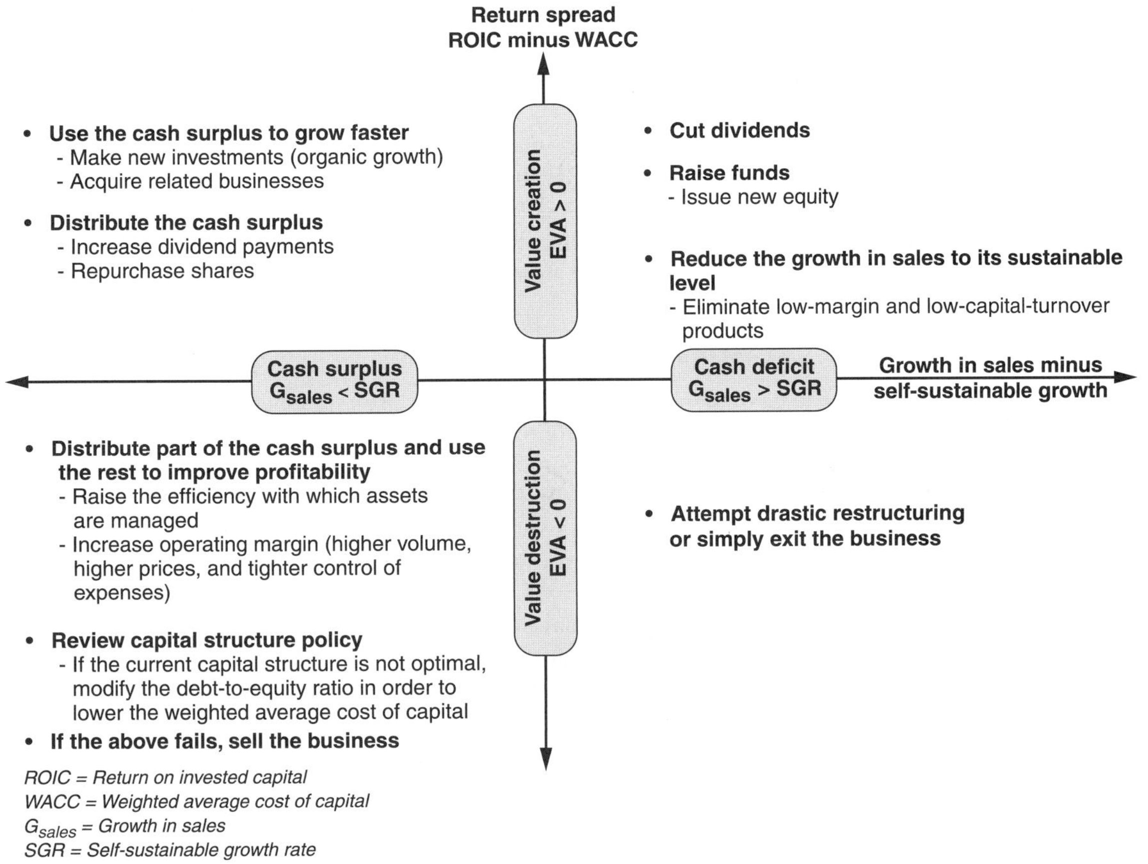
Return spread
ROIC minus WACC
• Use the cash surplus to grow faster
- Make new investments (organic growth)
- Acquire related businesses
• Distribute the cash surplus
- Increase dividend payments
- Repurchase shares
Value creation
EVA > 0
• Cut dividends
• Raise funds
- Issue new equity
• Reduce the growth in sales to its sustainable level
- Eliminate low-margin and low-capital-turnover products
Cash surplus
Gsales < SGR
Cash deficit
Gsales > SGR
Growth in sales minus
self-sustainable growth
• Distribute part of the cash surplus and use the rest to improve profitability
- Raise the efficiency with which assets are managed
- Increase operating margin (higher volume, higher prices, and tighter control of expenses)
• Review capital structure policy
- If the current capital structure is not optimal, modify the debt-to-equity ratio in order to lower the weighted average cost of capital
• If the above fails, sell the business
Value destruction
EVA < 0
• Attempt drastic restructuring or simply exit the business
ROIC = Return on invested capital
WACC = Weighted average cost of capital
Gsales = Growth in sales
SGR = Self-sustainable growth rate

spread is negative (the lower half of the matrix), there is value destruction (EVA is negative).

The horizontal axis measures the capacity of a business to self-finance its growth in sales. This capacity is measured by the difference between the expected growth in sales rate and the self-sustainable growth rate presented in Chapter 5. The **self-sustainable growth rate** is the maximum rate of growth in sales a business can achieve *without* changing its financing policy (same debt-to-equity ratio, same dividend payout ratio, and no new issue of equity or share repurchase) or modifying its operating policy (same operating profit margin and same capital turnover). We show in Chapter 5 that the self-sustainable growth rate of a business is equal to its profit retention rate multiplied by its return on equity (ROE).

A business will experience a cash shortage if its growth rate in sales is *higher* than its self-sustainable growth rate (the right half of the matrix). It will generate a cash surplus if its growth rate in sales is *lower* than its self-sustainable growth rate (the left half of the matrix).

What are the managerial implications of the matrix in Exhibit 15.9? A business can face four possible situations: (1) the business has the capacity to create value but is short of cash (the upper-right quadrant); (2) the business has the capacity to create value and generate a cash surplus (the upper-left quadrant); (3) the business is a value destroyer but generates excess cash (the lower-left quadrant); and (4) the business is a value destroyer and suffers from a shortage of cash (lower-right quadrant).

A firm with a single business will fall into one of these four quadrants. A firm with many different businesses will have to allocate them to their respective quadrant. After this diagnostic stage is completed, management will have to decide what to do with each business according to its position in the financial strategy matrix. We now examine the options available to management in each of the four cases.

THE BUSINESS IS A VALUE CREATOR BUT IS SHORT OF CASH

Management has two obvious options if the business creates value but is short of cash. One option is to reduce or eliminate any dividend payments if the business is paying a dividend to its parent company and, possibly, to other shareholders. The other option is for the parent company to inject fresh equity capital into the business. If the business is listed on a stock exchange as a separate entity, it can raise equity by issuing new shares to the public. With this additional equity capital, the business can borrow additional funds to maintain its capital structure at its optimal level. (For example, if the optimal structure is a debt-to-equity ratio of one, new equity can be matched with an equal amount of borrowing.)

If additional capital is not available, management would be facing a situation in which it is unable to fund a business that is creating value. In this case, management may have to scale back some of its operations and reduce the business overall rate of growth to its sustainable level. This can be achieved by eliminating low-margin, low-capital-turnover products and services. This strategy should enhance the value-creating capacity of the remaining activities by allowing the business to compete in a narrower market segment. The danger is that a cash-rich competitor may decide to enter the business and put pressure on margins.

THE BUSINESS IS A VALUE CREATOR WITH A CASH SURPLUS

The preferred situation is for a business to be a value creator with a cash surplus. Management can do one of two things in this case. The first is to use the cash surplus to accelerate the growth of the business. This can be accomplished by increasing internal investment or by acquiring similar and related businesses. What if organic growth opportunities or related acquisitions are not available? The temptation, of course, would be to use the cash surplus to diversify into *unrelated* businesses that may appear profitable. As shown in Chapter 12, however, this strategy is rarely successful and generally should be avoided.

If the cash surplus cannot be invested at an expected return that exceeds the cost of capital, it should be returned to the firm's owners. They could then invest it in a value-creating venture of their choice. This cash distribution can be achieved through a special dividend payment or through a **share buyback**, or repurchase, program.

THE BUSINESS IS A VALUE DESTROYER WITH A CASH SURPLUS

A value-destroying business with a cash surplus should be fixed rapidly, before the cash surplus runs out. Part of the excess cash could be returned to shareholders and the rest should be used to restructure the business as rapidly as possible, with the objective of raising its ROIC above its cost of capital.

As shown earlier in this chapter, ROIC can be increased through (1) an improved operating margin via a combination of higher volume, higher prices, and control of operating expenses and (2) a more efficient management of assets, particularly WCR, that is, with faster collection of trade receivables and higher inventory turns. (See Chapters 3 and 5.)

Management should also review the business's capital structure with the objective of lowering its WACC if it is not at its optimal level (see Chapters 10 and 11). The danger here is sinking too much cash into a business that has little or no chance of being turned around. The trick is to know when to seriously consider the sale of the business to someone who might manage it better.

THE BUSINESS IS A VALUE DESTROYER THAT IS SHORT OF CASH

A value-destroying business that is short of cash is the worst situation and one that requires management's immediate attention and swift action. If the business cannot be quickly and drastically restructured, it should be sold as soon as possible. By drastic restructuring, we mean the rapid sale of some of the assets to raise cash immediately and the scaling down of remaining activities to allow short-term survival with the objective of turning these remaining activities into a value-creating business. If a quick and successful turnaround is impossible, the business must be sold immediately before it affects the long-term survival of the rest of the company. The temptation to fund the business with the cash surplus generated by other businesses that have excess cash should be resisted at all costs.

SUMMARY

The greatest benefit of a management system that emphasizes value creation as opposed to earnings growth is that it induces managers throughout the organization to pay closer attention to expense control, to make a more effective use of the firm's assets, and to become more aware of the need to earn higher returns on the firm's invested capital. Good management can be many things—that is, superior marketing skill, great leadership, and a mastery of manufacturing. But, essentially, good *financial* management is only one thing—that is, good *capital* management, or *the art of deploying scarce capital skillfully.*

How can managers make capital allocation decisions that enhance value? A firm should allocate its existing capital and, if required, raise new capital, *only* if the return it expects to earn on the capital exceeds its estimated cost. Otherwise, capital should be returned to shareholders through dividend payments or a share buyback program. And, of course, there is no point in growing a business that does not earn its cost of capital. If a business cannot be restructured to generate a return in excess of its appropriate risk-adjusted cost of capital, it should be sold. A company creates value only if its market value added (MVA)—defined as the difference between the market value of its capital and the amount of capital invested in it by shareholders and debt holders—is positive. In other words, a company creates value only when the firm's capital is worth more than its reported (adjusted) book value.

One way to implement a management system that is consistent with and conducive to a value-creation objective is to link the firm's operating performance, investment decisions, and remuneration system to economic profit or economic value added (EVA), defined as the difference between net operating profit after tax and the dollar cost of the capital used to generate that profit. Managers who make decisions that maximize expected future EVA will increase MVA and create value. Also, this objective is consistent with the net present value and the internal rate of return rules used in capital budgeting.

The key drivers of a financial management system can be summarized into a financial strategy matrix that can help managers make value-creating strategic decisions. This matrix considers businesses that show positive EVA or negative EVA and that have cash surpluses or cash shortages.

We conclude this book with one of the clearest and shortest statements a chief executive has made about the nature of his business and the way it is managed. This is how a former chairman of the Coca-Cola Company defined his business and management approach: "We raise capital to make concentrate [syrup], and sell it at an operating profit. Then we pay the cost of that capital. Shareholders pocket the difference."[11] If you can think of your own business in those terms, we have achieved our goal of making you a true value manager.

[11]Roberto Goizueta in *Fortune* (September 20, 1993), p. 24.

Adjusting Book Values to Estimate the Amount of Invested Equity Capital and Operating Profit

APPENDIX 15.1

As an illustration of the adjustments needed to correct for the distortions generated by accounting conventions, this appendix shows how we estimated InfoSoft's $380 million of invested equity capital on December 31, 2010, and $80 million of earnings before interest and tax (EBIT) in 2010. These are the figures we used to estimate the firm's market value added (MVA), return on invested capital (ROIC), and economic value added (EVA) in 2010. Keep in mind, however, that more than 100 accounting adjustments have been identified. Obviously, the objective is to pick those few that make sense for analyzing a company's performance without adding undue complexity.

ADJUSTING THE BOOK VALUE OF EQUITY CAPITAL

Look at the asset side of InfoSoft's unadjusted 2010 balance sheet in Exhibit 15.1 at the beginning of the chapter: a $10 million accumulated bad debt allowance was deducted from the gross value of working capital requirement, and $20 million of accumulated goodwill impairment was removed from its net fixed assets. Accounting rules usually require that these **provisions** be charged to (deducted from) both the firm's assets and its profit. In monetary terms, the bad debt allowance represents the percentage of outstanding invoices on December 31, 2010, that InfoSoft did not expect to collect. Goodwill results from the acquisition of a company two years ago for $100 million *above* its **fair market value** (its value under normal market conditions). The $100 million payment in excess of fair value is goodwill. After examining the value of the goodwill in 2009 and 2010, the company's auditors concluded that it has been impaired (has lost some value) by an amount equal to $10 million during each one of the two years.

During the two years up to December 31, 2010, the bad debt allowance and the impairment of goodwill have reduced the amount of reported profit by $30 million ($10 million of bad debt allowances and $20 million of impaired goodwill). As a result, the accumulated amount of retained earnings and, consequently, the book value of InfoSoft's equity capital were also reduced by $30 million. Because the capital actually invested by its shareholders was not affected by these accounting adjustments, the book value of InfoSoft's equity capital on December 31, 2010, must be adjusted upward by $30 million, as shown on the right side of the 2010 adjusted balance sheet in Exhibit 15.1.

The next section shows that on December 31, 2010, InfoSoft reported a net profit of $30 million and retained the entire amount (it did not pay any dividends). Thus, the book value of its equity increased by $30 million in 2010. We will see that this profit figure came after the deduction of a $5 million allowance for bad debt, $10 million of goodwill impairment, and $30 million of research and development (R&D) expenses. We can adjust equity capital for the distortions caused by the way bad debt allowances and goodwill impairment are accounted for in reported profit. Is it necessary to also adjust for the way R&D expenses have been charged to the 2010 profit?

To answer this question, we need to know why $30 million was spent on R&D during 2010. If these expenses were incurred to increase profits only in 2010, it makes sense to account for them fully in that year. But if, as it would certainly be the case in most instances, the $30 million of R&D was disbursed to boost InfoSoft's profits for several years, allocating the full $30 million only to 2010 does not make much sense, although accounting conventions may require doing so.

If we assume that the $30 million spent on R&D will improve profits for a five-year period, each of these five years of profits should account for a portion of the $30 million "consumed" to generate that year's profit and, consequently, that year's increase in invested equity capital. In other words, the R&D expenses, like fixed assets, must be treated as an investment made in 2010 that needs to be amortized over a five-year period rather than fully expensed that year. For example, if the $30 million were amortized according to the straight-line method, only $6 million of R&D expenses ($30 million divided by five) should be charged to 2010 profit to estimate the invested equity capital at the end of that year. Furthermore, the **capitalization** of the R&D expenses (their conversion to assets) should not be limited to 2010. It should also apply to all the R&D expenses incurred by InfoSoft since its inception in 2000. How can this be done?

First, we add all the R&D annual expenses incurred since 2000, including the $30 million spent in 2010. Then, we apply an amortization schedule to each of these annual expenses, add all the annual amortization expenses up to December 31, 2010, and, finally, subtract the accumulated amortization expenses on R&D from the amount actually spent since 2000. Assuming that the result would be a capitalized value of $50 million on December 31, 2010, we can estimate that the firm's reported pre-tax profit since 2000 has been underestimated by $50 million. It follows that the firm's equity capital as of December 31, 2010, must be adjusted upward by the same amount, as shown on the right side of the 2010 adjusted balance sheet in Exhibit 15.1.

In total, InfoSoft's book value of equity capital on December 31, 2010, should be increased by $80 million to adjust for the accounting treatment of bad debt allowances ($10 million), goodwill impairment ($20 million), and capitalized R&D costs ($50 million). As a result, InfoSoft's estimated invested capital is $380 million, the sum of its reported book value of $300 million and the $80 million of adjustments.

As it is often the case, InfoSoft's reported invested capital ($300 million) underestimates the actual invested capital ($380 million) and, consequently, the total capital contributed by investors. In general, the extent of the underestimation depends on the number and size of the adjustments that must be made to reported profit. These adjustments, in addition to those related to bad debt allowances, goodwill impairment, and R&D expenses, include the consequences of any accounting convention that would affect reported profit without affecting the capital invested by shareholders and debt holders, such as charges associated with restructuring.

ADJUSTING EARNINGS BEFORE INTEREST AND TAX

Exhibit A15.1.1 shows both the unadjusted and adjusted income statements for InfoSoft in 2010. InfoSoft reported $55 million of earnings before interest and tax that year. This figure must first be adjusted upward by the $5 million increase in bad debt allowance, the $10 million impairment of goodwill, and the $30 million of R&D expenses. It must then be adjusted downward by the amortization of the R&D costs for 2010 that results from the application of the amortization schedule used when estimating the R&D capitalized expenses. If we *assume* an R&D amortization expense of $20 million, InfoSoft's EBIT should be increased by a total of $25 million (from $55 million to $80 million)—$5 million for bad debts plus $10 million of goodwill plus $30 million of R&D expenses less $20 million for the amortization of R&D costs. As a final adjustment to InfoSoft's 2010 income statement, we deduct the $8 million of interest expense (as given in the income statement) and the $17 million of tax expense (36 percent of the $47 million of pre-tax profit) from the adjusted EBIT to get an adjusted earnings after tax of $55 million. Because we assumed that InfoSoft did not pay any dividend in 2010, this $55 million of adjusted net profit is also the firm's adjusted 2010 retained earnings. Exhibit 15.1 shows that the firm's adjusted owners' equity went up by exactly $55 million, from $225 million at the end of 2009 to $280 million at the end of 2010.

EXHIBIT A15.1.1 INFOSOFT'S INCOME STATEMENT FOR 2010.

FIGURES IN MILLIONS

Income Statement 2010			
Unadjusted		**Adjusted**	
Sales	**$1,000**	**Sales**	**$1,000**
Cost of goods sold	500	Cost of goods sold	500
SG&A expenses	382	SG&A expenses	382
Lease expense	3	Lease expense	3
Depreciation expense	15	Depreciation expense	15
R&D expenses	30	Amortization of R&D expenses	20
Bad debt provision	5		
Goodwill impairment	10		
Earnings before interest and tax	$ 55	**Earnings before interest and tax**	$ 80
Interest expense	8	Interest expense	8
Tax expense (36% of pre-tax profit)	17	Tax expense	17
Earnings after tax (net profit)	$ 30	**Earnings after tax (net profit)**	$ 55

Estimating Market Value Added (MVA) when Future Cash Flows Are Expected to Grow at a Constant Rate in Perpetuity

APPENDIX 15

Chapter 12 shows that the discounted cash-flow value of assets—if we assume these assets will generate a cash-flow stream that is expected to grow at a constant annual rate forever—is given by the following:

$$\textbf{Value of assets} = \frac{\textbf{CFA}}{\textbf{WACC} - \textbf{Growth rate}} \qquad \text{(A15.2.1)}$$

where CFA is next year's cash flow from assets and WACC is the weighted average cost of the capital employed to finance the assets. CFA is given by

$$\text{CFA} = \text{EBIT}(1 - T_C) + \text{Depreciation expense} - \Delta\text{WCR} - \text{Capital expenditure}$$

where EBIT is earnings before interest and tax, EBIT(1 – tax rate) is net operating profit after tax or NOPAT, and ΔWCR is the change in working capital requirement. We can rearrange the terms of CFA to the following:

$$\text{CFA} = \text{NOPAT} - (\Delta\text{WCR} + \text{Capital expenditure} - \text{Depreciation expense})$$

Capital expenditure less depreciation expense is equal to the *change* in the firm's *net* fixed assets during the year. When added to the *change* in WCR, the sum represents the *change* in the book value of the firm's invested capital during the year (we assume no change in cash position). Thus, we can write the following:

$$\text{CFA} = \text{NOPAT} - \Delta\text{Invested capital}$$

Substituting this expression for next year's CFA in the numerator of the valuation formula (equation A15.2.1) and deducting the term "invested capital" from both sides of the equation, we get the following:

$$\text{Value of assets} - \text{Invested capital} = \frac{\text{NOPAT} - \Delta\text{Invested capital}}{\text{WACC} - \text{Growth rate}} - \text{Invested capital}$$

where the left side of the equation is the market value added or MVA. This equation can be written as follows:

$$\text{MVA} = \frac{\text{NOPAT} - \Delta\text{Invested capital} - (\text{Invested capital} \times [\text{WACC} - \text{Growth rate}])}{\text{WACC} - \text{Growth rate}}$$

Factoring out the term "invested capital" in the numerator, we have the following:

$$\text{MVA} = \frac{\left(\dfrac{\text{NOPAT}}{\text{Invested capital}} - \dfrac{\Delta\text{Invested capital}}{\text{Invested capital}} - \text{WACC} + \text{Growth rate}\right) \times \text{Invested capital}}{\text{WACC} - \text{Growth rate}}$$

The first term in the numerator is the ROIC, and the second term is the growth rate in invested capital, which is the same as the growth rate in cash flows because the growth rate is constant. Thus, we can write the following:

$$\text{MVA} = \frac{(\text{ROIC} - \text{Growth rate} - \text{WACC} + \text{Growth rate}) \times \text{Invested capital}}{\text{WACC} - \text{Growth rate}}$$

$$\text{MVA} = \frac{(\text{ROIC} - \text{WACC}) \times \text{Invested capital}}{\text{WACC} - \text{Growth rate}}$$

This equation is the valuation formula expressed in equation 15.3 in the chapter.

When MVA is positive, the ratio of market value to adjusted book value is greater than one. The factors that explain the sign of MVA are thus similar to those that explain the magnitude of the ratio of a firm's price per share to its book value per share. The price-to-book value ratio was presented in Chapter 12, where we said that the factors that explain its magnitude would be discussed in Chapter 15. The valuation formula (equation 15.3) indicates that these factors are as follows:

1. Return on equity (the equivalent of ROIC because we now deal with equity rather than total capital)
2. The cost of equity (the equivalent of WACC because we now deal with equity rather than total capital)
3. The firm's growth rate

Thus, when return on equity is higher (lower) than the cost of equity, the price-to-book value ratio will be higher (or lower) than one.

FURTHER READING

1. Ehrbar, Al. *EVA: The Real Key to Creating Wealth*. John Wiley & Sons, 1998.
2. Madden, Bartley. *Maximizing Shareholder Value and the Greater Good*. LearningWhatWorks, 2005.
3. Martin, John, and William Petty. *Value Based Management*. Harvard Business School Press, 2000.
4. Rappaport, Alfred. *Creating Shareholder Value*. The Free Press, 1998. See Chapter 1.
5. Stern, Joel, John Shiely, and Irwin Ross. *The EVA Challenge. Implementing Value Added Change in An Organization*. John Wiley & Sons, 2001.
6. Young, S. David, and Stephan F. O'Byrne. *EVA and Value Based Management: A Practical Guide to Implementation*. McGraw-Hill, 2001. See Chapters 1 and 2.

SELF-TEST PROBLEMS

15.1 UNDERSTANDING MVA AND EVA.

Explain why each of the following statements is generally incorrect:

a. "Management creates value by maximizing the market value of its firm."
b. "If a firm's market value added (MVA) is positive, then its current economic value added (EVA) must also be positive."
c. "EVA should be measured on the basis of net profits (the bottom line) and not on the basis of *operating* profit."
d. "One weakness of EVA as a performance measure is that it does not take risk into account."
e. "Giving managers a bonus related to their ability to increase the profit of their business unit is one way to enhance shareholder value."

15.2 ADJUSTING ACCOUNTING DATA TO ESTIMATE ECONOMIC VALUE ADDED.

The financial statements of the Advance Devices Corporation (ADC) are shown below with balance sheets reported in their managerial form. ADC has an estimated weighted average cost of capital of 11 percent. ADC had an estimated $55 million of research and development (R&D) expenses that should have been capitalized in 2009 and $70 million that should have been capitalized in 2010. Amortization of R&D expenses in 2010 is $30 million. Using this information, provide an estimate of ADC's economic value added in 2010 based on initial invested capital and average invested capital.

Income Statement 2010 (in millions)	
Net sales	$1,400
Cost of sales	780
Selling, general, and administrative expenses	330
Depreciation and lease expenses	45
R&D expenses	100
Bad debt provision	6
Goodwill impairment	25
Interest expense	14
Income tax expense	40
Net profit	$ 60

Managerial Balance Sheets (in millions)							
Invested Capital	**December 31, 2009**		**December 31, 2010**		**Capital Employed**	**December 31, 2009**	**December 31, 2010**
Cash		$ 10		$ 15	Short-term debt	$ 30	$ 10
Working capital (net)		140		160			
Gross value	*147*		*173*		Long-term debt	80	80
Accumulated bad debt allowance	*7*		*13*				
Net fixed assets		210		225	Lease obligations	50	50
Tangible (net)	110		150				
Goodwill (net)	100		75		Owners' equity	200	260
Gross value	*120*		*120*				
Accumulated impairment	*20*		*45*				
Total		$360		$400	Total	$360	$400

15.3 MARKET VALUE ADDED ANALYSIS.

The International Logistics Company (ILC) is considering buying an inventory control software program that will cost $140,000, delivered and installed (including personnel training). The program will allow the company to reduce its inventory by $100,000. The cost of the software will be expensed the year it is bought. ILC is subject to a 40 percent corporate tax rate, and its weighted average cost of capital is 10 percent. Should ILC buy the software program? Answer the question using economic value added and market value added analysis.

15.4 MARKET VALUE ADDED ANALYSIS OF THE DESIGNER DESK-LAMP PROJECT.

Refer to Chapter 8 for a description of the designer desk-lamp project. Exhibit 8.3 reports the cash flows the project is expected to generate. Use the information in the exhibit to estimate the project's economic value added and its market value added. The latter, if measured correctly, must be equal to the project's net present value of $415,083. The weighted average cost of capital is 7.6 percent.

15.5 THE FINANCIAL STRATEGY MATRIX.

Amalgamated Industries (AI) has four distinct business divisions that are run as separate companies and are listed on a stock market. AI has a majority ownership in the four companies for which the following financial data have been collected:

Company	Transportation	Restaurants	Beverages	Food
Sales growth rate	8%	15%	7%	4%
Return on invested capital	8%	15%	8%	13%
Return on equity	12%	20%	12%	15%
Weighted average cost of capital	10%	12%	9%	11%
Dividend payout ratio	50%	40%	25%	60%

a. Position the four companies on the financial strategy matrix.
b. What actions should AI take regarding each of these businesses?

REVIEW PROBLEMS

1. **Understanding market value added and economic value added.**
Explain why each of the following statements is generally incorrect:

    a. "The firm with the highest market value is the one that has created the most value for its shareholders."
    b. "If a firm's market value added (MVA) is positive, then its current return on invested capital (ROIC) must exceed its weighted average cost of capital (WACC)."
    c. "Growth is the key to increasing a firm's MVA."
    d. "This year's economic value added (EVA) is positive, so the firm's market value added must also be positive."
    e. "Giving managers a bonus related to their ability to increase the profitability (ROIC) of their business unit is one way to enhance shareholder value."

2. **Value drivers.**
Identify at least three value drivers related to the management of operations and three strategic value drivers that directly affect economic value added (EVA). Show how these drivers might increase or decrease EVA.

3. **Adjusting accounting data to estimate a firm's economic value added.**
Following are the balance sheets at year-end 2009 and 2010 followed by the 2010 income statement of Sactor Inc. The annual report for year 2010 provides the following supplemental information:

    1. The restructuring charge of $43 million, amounted to $28 million after tax
    2. Accumulated goodwill impairment was $98 million at the end of 2009 and $93 million at the end of 2010. Goodwill impairment was $22 million in 2010, or $14 million after tax
    3. The accounts receivable are net of bad debt allowance. At the end of 2009, the accumulated bad debt allowance was $26 million; at the end of 2010, it was $30 million
    4. In 2009, the firm had a nonoperating extraordinary loss of $35 million after tax

    a. Compute the unadjusted invested capital of Sactor Inc. at year-end 2009 and year-end 2010. Compute also the firm's net operating profit after tax (NOPAT).
    b. Adjust the amounts of invested capital and NOPAT for accounting distortions.
    c. Assuming a weighted average cost of capital of 10 percent, what was Sactor's economic value added in 2010?

Balance Sheets (in millions)				
	December 31, 2009		December 31, 2010	
Assets				
Cash		$ 239		$ 37
Accounts receivable, net		500		668
Inventories		416		547
Prepaid expenses		58		159
Net fixed assets		827		1,279
Property, plant, and equipment, net	$488		$634	
Goodwill, net	148		513	
Other assets	191		132	
Total		$2,040		$2,690
Liabilities and Owners' Equity				
Short-term debt		$23		$50
Accounts payable		264		346
Accrued expenses		437		681
Long-term liabilities		668		846
Owners' equity		648		767
Total		$2,040		$2,690

Income Statement (in millions)	
	2010
Net sales	$2,888
Cost of goods sold	2,167
Selling, general, and administrative expenses	434
Restructuring charge	43
Earnings before interest and tax	$ 244
Interest expense	62
Earnings before tax	$ 182
Income tax expense	64
Earnings after tax	$ 118

4. **Economic value added analysis.**
The Southern Communication Corporation (SCC) has $1 billion of capital invested in several telecommunication projects that are expected to generate a pre-tax operating profit of $170 million next year. SCC has an estimated pre-tax cost of capital of 15 percent.

a. What is the pre-tax economic value added (EVA) that SCC is expected to generate next year? Calculate EVA first based on pre-tax operating profit and then based on expected return on invested capital.

b. SCC is considering five possible actions that should improve its expected pre-tax EVA. These are as follows:

1. A $10 million reduction in operating expenses that should not affect revenues
2. A $60 million reduction in invested capital that should not affect operating profit
3. A reexamination of its capital structure (debt-to-equity ratio) that could lower its pre-tax cost of capital to 14 percent
4. The sale of assets at their book value of $100 million. These assets are expected to generate a pre-tax operating profit of $10 million next year
5. The acquisition of assets worth $100 million. These assets are expected to generate a pre-tax operating profit of $20 million next year

Show how each of these decisions would improve SCC's expected pre-tax economic value added.

5. **The relationship between a firm's market value, its market value added, and its economic value added.**

a. Equation 15.7 shows that market value added (MVA) of an investment project is the present value of the stream of the future economic value added (EVA) of the project. Because a firm can be viewed as a basket of investment projects, the MVA of a firm is simply the present value of the stream of future EVA generated by the firm from these projects. Show that the market value of a firm's capital is equal to the present value (PV) of the stream of future EVA expected from the firm plus its invested capital:

$$\text{Market value of capital} = \text{PV of expected future EVA} + \text{Invested capital}$$

b. Consider Value Inc. The firm's invested capital is $150 million, and the market value of its capital is also $150 million, so its MVA is equal to zero. Suppose that the firm announces a $50 million investment in a project from which it expects a return on invested capital of 14 percent for the next four years. Value Inc.'s weighted average cost of capital is 8 percent. By how much should the market value and the MVA of the firm increase at the announcement of the project?

6. **The effect of the management of the operating cycle on the firm's economic value added.**

Below are the last three years' financial statements of Sentec Inc., a distributor of electrical fixtures.

Income Statements (in thousands)	2008	2009	2010
Net sales	$22,100	$24,300	$31,600
Cost of goods sold	17,600	19,300	25,100
Selling, general, and administrative expenses	3,750	4,000	5,000
Depreciation expense	100	100	150
Earnings before interest and tax	650	900	1,350
Net interest expense	110	130	260
Earnings before tax	540	770	1,090
Income tax expense	220	310	430
Earnings after tax	$ 320	$ 460	$ 660
Dividends	$ 180	$ 200	$ 200

Balance Sheets (in thousands)	December 31, 2008	December 31, 2009	December 31, 2010
Cash	$ 600	$ 350	$ 300
Accounts receivable	2,730	3,100	4,200
Inventories	2,800	3,200	4,300
Net fixed assets	1,200	1,300	1,450
Total assets	$7,330	$7,950	$10,250
Short-term debt	$ 300	$ 500	$ 1,900
Accounts payable	1,400	1,600	2,050
Accrued expenses	200	260	350
Long-term debt	1,300	1,200	1,100
Owners' equity	4,130	4,390	4,850
Total liabilities and owners' equity	$7,330	$7,950	$10,250

a. Compute Sentec's working capital requirement (WCR) on December 31, 2008, 2009, and 2010.
b. Prepare Sentec Inc.'s managerial balance sheets on December 31, 2008, 2009, and 2010.
c. Sentec's weighted average cost of capital was stable at 11 percent over the three-year period from 2008 to 2010. How much value was created or destroyed by Sentec in each one of the three years?
d. What are the likely causes of value creation and destruction at Sentec?
e. In 2010, firms in the same business sector as Sentec Inc. have an average collection period of thirty days, an average payment period of thirty-three days, and an inventory turnover of eight times. Suppose that Sentec Inc. had managed its operating cycle like the average firm in the sector. On December 31,

2010, what would its WCR have been? Its managerial balance sheet? How much more value would Sentec have created?

7. **Return on invested capital versus economic value added–based bonus systems.** Fiona Berling's division of McSystems generates a net operating profit after tax, or NOPAT, of $1 million on an invested capital base of $1 million. The weighted average cost of capital of Ms. Berling's division is 20 percent. The division has been asked to launch a new investment project that would return $500,000 for an investment of $1 million.

   a. If bonuses at McSystems were based on return on invested capital achieved by its divisions, would Ms. Berling find the new project acceptable?
   b. What if the bonuses were based on economic value added achieved by its divisions?
   c. What bonus system would you favor? Why?

8. **Economic value added–based bonus system.** Astra Co. is considering introducing a bonus system based on economic value added (EVA) and has short-listed two bonus formulas. The first one would simply compute the bonus as a percentage of EVA, such that

$$\textbf{Bonus} = x \textbf{ percent of EVA} = x\% \times \text{EVA} \tag{1}$$

   The second bonus formula will make the bonus dependent also on the improvement in EVA from one year to another so that

$$\begin{aligned}\textbf{Bonus} &= y \textbf{ percent of EVA} + z \textbf{ percent of } \Delta\textbf{EVA}\\ &= y\% \times \text{EVA} + z\% \times \Delta\text{EVA}\end{aligned} \tag{2}$$

   a. Suppose that the firm anticipates that its EVA will be $16 million this year, $20 million next year, and $24 million the year after. If the bonus formula (1) is chosen, x would be equal to 2 percent. If the bonus formula (2) is preferred, y would be equal to 1 percent and z to 7.5 percent. What would be the three years' cumulative bonus for each of the two formulas?
   b. Suppose now that the expected EVA will be –$24 million this year, –$20 million next year, and –$16 million the year after. With the same value of x, y, and z as in the previous question, what would be the three years' cumulative bonus for each of the two formulas?
   c. Which formula would you advise Astra to use?

9. **Economic value added, market value added, and net present value.** Alvinstar Co. is considering investing in a new animal feed project. The product will be a soup for cats to be sold in cans. Alvinstar plans to sell 100,000 cans a year for four years at a price of $4 per can. Fixed costs will include rent on the production facility at $50,000 a year, plus annual depreciation expense of $50,000 on production equipment that will cost $200,000 installed. After taking into account the cost of removing the equipment, the net receipt of selling the equipment after four years is expected to be zero. Variable costs will amount to $2 per can. The project will require an investment in the operating cycle, or

working capital requirement of $40,000. The tax rate is 40 percent. Alvinstar's weighted average cost of capital is 10 percent.

a. Compute the project's net present value.
b. Compute the project's expected annual economic value added.
c. Compute the project's market value added.
d. What is the necessary condition for the project's net present value to be equal to the present value of its future expected economic value added and to its market value added?

10. **Comparison of investment analysis based on cash flows and economic value added.**
The Electronics Machines Corporation (EMC) is considering buying a $300,000 piece of equipment that could raise EMC's sales revenues by $1 million the first year, $2 million the second year, and $1.8 million the third year. The cost of the piece of equipment can be fully depreciated over the three-year investment according to the straight-line method with no residual value. Incremental operating expenses are estimated at 90 percent of sales, excluding depreciation expense. Working capital required to support the project's sales should be 10 percent of sales with working capital investment assumed to occur at the beginning of the year. EMC can borrow at 6 percent, is subject to a 30 percent corporate tax rate, and finances 60 percent of its activities with borrowed funds. The firm uses an estimated cost of equity of 12 percent.

a. What are the project's net present value and internal rate of return? Should the piece of equipment be purchased?
b. What is the project's market value added? Explain why the piece of equipment should be purchased even though its first-year economic value added is negative.
c. What is the key assumption used in the estimation of the project's cash flows and economic value added that makes the project's net present value equal to its market value added?

Answers to Self-Test Problems

2.1 Constructing Income Statements and Balance Sheets.

a. 2010 income statement:

In Thousands of Dollars	2010	
Net sales (see items 3, 19)		$ 320,000
Cost of goods sold		(260,000)
Material cost[1] (see item 5)	$224,000	
Labor expenses (see item 17)	36,000	
Gross profit		60,000
SG&A expenses (see item 12)	18,000	
Licensing fee (see item 13)	4,000	
Depreciation expenses (see item 9)	9,000	
Operating profit		29,000
Special items (see item 27)		(2,000)
Earnings before interest and tax		**$ 27,000**
Net interest expenses (see items 6, 15, 26)		(3,000)
Earnings before tax		24,000
Income tax expense[2] (see item 2)		(9,600)
Earnings after tax		**$ 14,400**
Dividends (see item 21)	*$ 9,360*	
Addition to retained earnings	***$ 5,040***	

[1]You could also infer the cost of material *sold* during the year by noting the following:
Purchases (item 11) = Cost of material sold + Change in inventories (item 19), where the change in inventories represents the cost of the material purchased but not yet sold.
We can thus write: Cost of material sold = Purchases – Changes in inventories = $228,000,000 – ($32,000,000 – $28,000,000) = $224,000,000.

[2]The tax paid in advance on December 15, 2010 (item 25) was exactly equal to the tax due for 2010.
The information in item 14 is irrelevant for the construction of the 2010 income statement.

b. 2009 and 2010 balance sheets:

In Thousands of Dollars	2009	2010
Cash[1] (see item 24)	$ 7,500	$ 3,515
Accounts receivable (see items 7, 1)	32,000	38,400
Inventories (see item 19)	28,000	32,000
Prepaid expenses (see item 28)	1,500	2,085
Net fixed assets (see items 4, 9, 20)	76,000	81,000
Total assets	**$145,000**	**$157,000**
Owed to banks (see item 26)	$ 3,000	$ 5,000
Current portion of long-term debt (see item 18)	4,000	4,000
Accounts payable (see items 8, 22, 11)	30,000	35,150
Accrued expenses[2] (see item 10)	4,000	1,810
Long-term debt[3] (see items 15, 18, 20)	23,000	25,000
Owners' equity[4] (see items 23, 16)	81,000	86,040
Total liabilities and owners' equity	**$145,000**	**$157,000**

[1]You should first identify accounts payable.
[2]Wages payable.
[3]Net long-term debt (2009) = $27 million (total amount) – $4 million (due this year). See item 15.
Net long-term debt (2010) = Long-term debt (item 15) – Debt repayment (item 18) + New debt (item 20)
= $23 million – $4 million + $6 million = $25 million.
[4]Owners' equity (2010) = Owners' equity (2009) + Addition to retained earnings ($5,040,000; see income statement).

2.2 FORECASTING INCOME STATEMENTS AND BALANCE SHEETS.

a. Pro forma income statement for 2011:
The reference item is for the determination of the 2011 pro forma statement.

In Thousands of Dollars	2010: Actual		2011: Pro Forma	
Net sales (see item 1)		*$320,000*		$352,000
Cost of goods sold (see item 2)		*(260,000)*		(286,000)
Material cost (see item 2)	$224,000		$246,400	
Labor expenses (see item 2)	36,000		39,600	
Gross profit (see item 2)		*60,000*		66,000
SG&A expenses (see item 3)	*18,000*		22,280	
Licensing fee (see item 4)	*4,000*		4,000	
Depreciation expenses (item 4)	*9,000*		9,000	
Operating profit		*29,000*		30,720
Extraordinary item		*(2,000)*		0
Earnings before interest and tax		*27,000*		30,720
Net interest expenses (see item 4)		*(3,000)*		(3,000)
Earnings before tax		*24,000*		27,720
Income tax expense (see item 4)		*(9,600)*		*(11,088)*
Earnings after tax		*$ 14,400*		$ 16,632
Dividends[1] (item 9)	*$ 9,360*		*$ 8,922*	
Addition to retained earnings	*$ 5,040*		*$ 7,710*	

[1]To determine the dividend payment, you should first find out how much retained earnings are necessary to "balance" the pro forma 2011 balance sheet. The expected dividend payment will then be the difference between the expected net profit and the anticipated addition to retained earnings (see following page).

b. Pro forma balance sheet for 2011:
The reference item is for the determination of the 2011 pro forma statement.

In Thousands of Dollars	December 31, 2010: Actual	December 31, 2011: Pro Forma
Cash (see item 9)	*$ 3,515*	$ 3,515
Accounts receivable (see item 5)	*38,400*	42,240
Inventories (see item 5)	*32,000*	35,200
Prepaid expenses (see item 6)	*2,085*	2,085
Net fixed assets[1] (see items 4, 7)	*81,000*	81,000
Total assets	***$157,000***	**$164,040**
Owed to banks (see item 8)	*$ 5,000*	$ 5,000
Current portion of long-term debt[2] (see item 8)	*4,000*	4,000
Accounts payable[3] (see item 5)	*35,150*	38,480
Accrued expenses (see item 6)	*1,810*	1,810
Long-term debt[4] (see item 8)	*25,000*	21,000
Owners' equity[5]	*86,040*	93,750
Total liabilities and owners' equity	***$157,000***	**$164,040**

[1] Net fixed assets (2011) = Net fixed assets (2010) – Depreciation expenses (2011) + New assets (2011)
= $81 million – $9 million + $9 million.
[2] Long-term debt is repaid at an annual rate of $4 million (item 18 in problem 2.1).
[3] Payables are 1.85 months of purchases.
Purchases = Material cost + Change in inventories = $246,400,000 + $3,200,000 = $249,600,000.
[4] Long-term debt (2011) = Long-term debt (2010) – Repayment + New borrowings = $25 million – $4 million = $21 million.
[5] To "balance" the balance sheet, owners' equity should rise by $7,710,000. Because there is no plan to issue new shares, this is the expected amount of addition to retained earnings.

3.1 EVALUATING MANAGERIAL PERFORMANCE.

a. Yes, in 2010 sales grew by 18.5 percent compared to a growth rate of 12.5 percent in 2009.
b. The restructured balance sheets in their managerial form, in millions of dollars, are as follows:

	Year-end 2008		Year-end 2009		Year-end 2010	
Cash	$100	14.9%	$ 90	13.2%	$ 50	6.5%
Working capital requirement	180	26.9%	205	29.9%	355	46.1%
Net fixed assets	390	58.2%	390	56.9%	365	47.4%
Invested capital	**$670**	**100.0%**	**$685**	**100.0%**	**$770**	**100.0%**
Short-term debt	$ 80	11.9%	$ 90	13.2%	$135	17.5%
Long-term debt	140	20.9%	120	17.5%	100	13.0%
Owners' equity	450	67.2%	475	69.3%	535	69.5%
Capital employed	**$670**	**100.0%**	**$685**	**100.0%**	**$770**	**100.0%**

where working capital requirement or WCR is equal to trade receivables plus inventories plus prepaid expenses less trade payables less accrued expenses. WCR is a measure of the investment required to support the firm's operating activities. It is mostly a *long-term* investment because ACC, a clothing manufacturer, should have little seasonality in its sales, meaning that its working capital requirement is essentially *permanent* in nature.

c. The structure of invested capital has changed between 2008 and 2010: the proportions of cash and net fixed assets have gone down and the proportion of working capital has gone up. The structure of capital employed has also changed, particularly the composition of debt capital: the proportion of short-term debt has risen, while that of long-term debt has declined.

d. In 2008, ACC financed its long-term investments (permanent working capital requirement and net fixed assets) with long-term funds, and its short-term investments (cash and cash-equivalents) with short-term debt, indicating a "matched," if not conservative, balance sheet. In 2010, a significant portion of long-term investments were financed with short-term debt, indicating a "mismatched" balance sheet.

e. Operational efficiency ratios:

	Year-end 2008	Year-end 2009	Year-end 2010
WCR/sales	15.0%	15.2%	22.2%
Average collection period	61 days	62 days	66 days
Inventory turnover	5.4 times	5.7 times	3.9 times
Average payment period	72 days	68 days	69 days

There is a significant deterioration of the efficiency with which the firm's operating cycle is managed. This is clearly indicated by the rise in the ratio of WCR over sales. It is confirmed by the lengthening of the collection period and the slowdown in inventory turnover.

f. Liquidity ratios:

	Year-end 2008	Year-end 2009	Year-end 2010
NLF/WCR	111%	100%	76%
Current ratio	1.69	1.65	1.67
Quick ratio	1.03	1.02	0.84

where NLF is net long-term financing, which is equal to long-term debt plus owners' equity less net fixed assets. The ratio of NLF to WCR, called the liquidity ratio, shows a clear deterioration: the percentage of WCR financed with long-term funds went from over 100 percent in 2008 to 76 percent in 2010. Note that the current ratio does not seem to pick up the deterioration in liquidity, although the quick ratio does.

g. The marketing objective was achieved in terms of growth in sales, but this accomplishment was accompanied by a deterioration in the firm's operational efficiency and the quality of its balance sheet.

3.2 WORKING CAPITAL MANAGEMENT FOR A RETAILER.

a. Operating assets include trade receivables and inventories; operating liabilities include trade payables and accrued expenses related to operations. Working capital requirement (WCR) is thus (data in millions of euros):

$$WCR = \text{Receivables} + \text{Inventories} - \text{Payables} - \text{Accrued expenses}$$
$$WCR_{(12/31/07)} = €863 + €6{,}867 - €17{,}077 - €2{,}848 = -€12{,}195$$
$$WCR_{(12/31/08)} = €779 + €6{,}891 - €17{,}276 - €2{,}947 = -€12{,}553$$

WCR is negative and thus represents a source of capital (cash) instead of an investment that needs to be financed. Note the magnitude of WCR; it amounts to close to 13 billion euros at the end of 2008.

b. Working capital requirement-to-sales ratios are as follows (data in millions of euros):

December 31, 2007	WCR = –€12,195	Sales = €82,149	WCR/Sales = –14.84%
December 31, 2008	WCR = –€12,553	Sales = €86,967	WCR/Sales = –14.43%

The negative value of WCR is due to significantly longer payment terms than average, coupled with a very short collection period (retailing is essentially a cash business) and a fast inventory turnover. The faster the company grows, the larger its (negative) WCR. Carrefour, or any other company with a negative WCR, usually has a relatively stronger liquidity position than firms with a positive WCR.

c. Operational efficiency ratios (data in millions of euros):

	Year-end 2007	Year-end 2008
Average collection period	= €863/(€82,149/365) = 3.8 days	= €779/(€86,967/365) = 3.3 days
Inventory turnover	= €64,609/€6,867 = 9.4 times	= €68,709/€6,891 = 10 times
Average payment period[1]		= €17,276/((€68,709 + €6,891 – €6,867)/365) = 91.7 days

[1]Purchases are estimated as the sum of the cost of goods sold plus the change in inventories. Because inventories at year-end 2006 were not available, we could not compute the purchases in year 2007.

d. Liquidity ratios (data in millions of euros):

	Current Ratio	Quick Ratio
December 31, 2007	= €18,125/€28,038 = 0.65	= €5,027/€28,038 = 0.18
December 31, 2008	= €19,177/€27,732 = 0.69	= €6,096/€27,732 = 0.22

The rule of thumb is for the current ratio to be close to two and the quick ratio close to one. But these standards apply to firms with positive WCR. Firms with a negative WCR can afford significantly lower ratios without experiencing a deterioration in their liquidity position.

4.1 CONSTRUCTING AND INTERPRETING CASH-FLOW STATEMENTS.

a. Cash-flow statement:

In Millions of Dollars	Year 2		Year 3	
Cash flow from operating activities				
Net sales	$1,350		$1,600	
less costs of goods sold	(970)		(1,160)	
less selling, general, and administrative expenses	(165)		(200)	
less change in working capital requirement	(25)		(150)	
less tax expense	(45)		(50)	
A. equals net operating cash flow		*$145*		*$40*
Cash flow from investing activities				
Sales of fixed assets	0		0	
less capital expenditure[1]	(50)		(30)	
B. equals net cash flow from investing activities		*($50)*		*($30)*
Cash flow from financing activities				
Increase in short-term borrowings	10		45	
Decrease in long-term borrowings	(20)		(20)	
less interest payments	(20)		(25)	
less dividend payments	(75)		(50)	
C. equals net cash flow from financing activities		*($105)*		*($50)*
Total net cash flow = (A) + (B) + (C)		($10)		($40)
plus opening cash balance		$100		$90
equals closing cash balance		$ 90		$50

[1]Capex = Change in net fixed asset + Depreciation expense
Capex Year 2 = ($390 − $390) + $50 = $50
Capex Year 3 = ($365 − $390) + $55 = $30.

In both years cash flow from operations was positive, and cash flows from investment and financing activities were negative. This is the expected pattern for a firm experiencing steady growth. The area of concern is the weakening of the cash flow from operations in Year 2 compared with the previous year. This deterioration is essentially because of the growth in working capital requirement, itself the outcome of the deterioration in the firm's operational efficiency, as shown in the answer to problem 3.1(e).

b. Net operating cash flow (NOCF) using earnings before interest and tax (EBIT):

In Millions of Dollars	Year 2	Year 3
Earnings before interest and tax (EBIT)	$165	$185
plus depreciation expenses	50	55
less change in working capital requirement (WCR)	(25)	(150)
less tax payments	(45)	(50)
equals net operating cash flow (NOCF)	$145	$ 40

The above approach starts with a measure of profit that includes depreciation expense, a non-cash item that must be removed. This is done by adding depreciation expense to profits. The approach in the previous question starts with sales and simply ignores depreciation expense.

c. Net operating cash flow (NOCF) using earnings before interest, tax, depreciation, and amortization (EBITDA):

In Millions of Dollars	Year 2	Year 3
Earnings before interest, tax, depreciation, and amortization (EBITDA)	$215	$240
less change in working capital requirement (WCR)	(25)	(150)
less tax payments	(45)	(50)
equals net operating cash flow (NOCF)	$145	$ 40

The above approach is essentially the same as the one in the previous question, because EBITDA is, by definition, equal to EBIT plus depreciation expenses.

d. Net operating cash flow (NOCF) using cash inflows and cash outflows from operations:

In Millions of Dollars	Year 2		Year 3	
Cash inflow from operations				
Sales	$1,350		$1,600	
less change in trade receivables	(30)		(60)	
A. equals cash inflows from operations		$1,320		$1,540
Cash outflows from operations				
Cost of goods sold	970		1,160	
plus selling, general, and administrative expenses	165		200	
plus change in inventories	10		130	
plus change in prepaid expenses	0		5	
less change in trade payables	(10)		(40)	
less change in accrued expenses	(5)		(5)	
plus tax expenses	45		50	
B. equals cash outflows from operations		$1,175		$1,500
Net operating cash flow = (A) – (B)		$ 145		$ 40

e. Cash flow from assets:

In Millions of Dollars	Year 2	Year 3
Cash flow from operations (NOCF)	$145	$40
plus cash flow from investments	(50)	(30)
equals cash flow from assets	$ 95	$10

Cash flow from assets is the sum of the net cash flow generated by *existing* assets—which is net operating cash flow—and the net cash flow generated by net capital expenditures during the year (acquisitions, net of disposals). It is the firm's net cash flow, *excluding* any cash movements related to financing activities.

f. Separation of margin and investment components in NOCF:

In Millions of Dollars	Year 2		Year 3	
EBITDA	$215		$240	
less tax expenses	(45)		(50)	
A. equals margin component		**$170**		**$190**
change in working capital requirement	25		150	
B. equals investment component		**$ 25**		**$150**
Net operating cash flow = (A) – (B)		**$145**		**$ 40**

Clearly, the growth of the investment component in Year 2 has dwarfed the improvement in the margin component, resulting in a sharp drop in net operating cash flow.

g. "The statement of cash flows" (FASB 95):

In Millions of Dollars	Year 2		Year 3	
A. Cash flow from operating activities		**$125**		**$15**
Earnings after tax	$100		$110	
plus depreciation expenses	50		55	
less change in working capital requirement	(25)		(150)	
B. Cash flow from investment activities		**($50)**		**($30)**
C. Cash flow from financing activities		**($85)**		**($25)**
increase in short-term debt	10		45	
decrease in long-term debt	(20)		(20)	
less dividend payment	(75)		(50)	
Total net cash flow = (A) + (B) + (C)		**($10)**		**($40)**

The above statement puts interest expenses into operating cash flow (it is taken into account in earnings after tax). As a consequence, interest expenses are no longer part of cash flow from financing activities.

4.2 EXAMINING THE OPERATING CASH FLOW OF A RETAILER.

a. Cash-flow statement:

In Millions of Euros	Year 2008	
Cash flow from operating activities		
Earnings before interest and tax (EBIT)	€3,300	
plus depreciation expense	1,861	
less change in working capital requirement	358	
less tax expense	(743)	
equals net operating cash flow		**€4,776**

b. Separation of margin and investment components in NOCF:

In Millions of Euros		Year 2008
Earnings before interest and tax (EBIT)	€3,300	
plus depreciation expenses	1,861	
less tax expenses	(743)	
A. equals margin component		€4,418
change in working capital requirement	358	
B. equals investment component		(€358)
Net operating cash flow = (A) – (B)		€4,776

Because the change in working capital requirement is *negative* (–€12,553 less –€12,195), the investment component of net operating cash flow is negative and thus is a source of funds that is *added,* rather than deducted, from the margin component. To put it differently, the *faster* Carrefour grows, the *larger* its negative working capital requirement and the *stronger* its cash flow from operations that can then be invested to sustain further growth.

5.1 PROFITABILITY ANALYSIS.

a. The restructured balance sheets in their managerial form are as follows:

In Millions of Dollars	Year-end 2008		Year-end 2009		Year-end 2010	
Cash	$100	14.9%	$ 90	13.2%	$ 50	6.5%
Working capital requirement	180	26.9%	205	29.9%	355	46.1%
Net fixed assets	390	58.2%	390	56.9%	365	47.4%
Invested capital	$670	100.0%	$685	100.0%	$770	100.0%
Short-term debt	$ 80	11.9%	$ 90	13.2%	$135	17.5%
Long-term debt	140	20.9%	120	17.5%	100	13.0%
Owners' equity	450	67.2%	475	69.3%	535	69.5%
Capital employed	$670	100.0%	$685	100.0%	$770	100.0%

where working capital requirement is trade receivables plus inventories plus prepaid expenses less trade payables less accrued expenses.

b. Return on equity (based on year-end data):

In Millions of Dollars	Year 2008	Year 2009	Year 2010
Pre-tax ROE	28.89%	30.53%	29.91%
After-tax ROE	20.00%	21.05%	20.56%

c. Alternative measures of pre-tax operating profitability (based on year-end data):

In Millions of Dollars	Year 2008	Year 2009	Year 2010
$ROIC_{BT}$ = EBIT/Invested capital	22.39%	24.09%	24.03%
ROTA = EBIT/Total assets	17.05%	18.13%	17.79%
ROBA = EBIT/Business assets	26.32%	27.73%	25.69%
ROA = EAT/Total assets	10.23%	10.99%	10.58%

where business assets are working capital requirement plus net fixed assets. The first three measures have the same numerator, and because total assets are generally larger than invested capital, which is itself usually larger than business assets, it follows that ROBA is higher than $ROIC_{BT}$ and $ROIC_{BT}$ is higher than ROTA. ROA is lower than the first three measures of profitability because net profit (EAT) is smaller than pre-tax operating profit (EBIT).

d. Return on capital employed before tax ($ROCE_{BT}$) is identical to return on invested capital before tax ($ROIC_{BT}$) because, according to the managerial balance sheet, invested capital is identical to capital employed. See the managerial balance sheets in the answer to question a.

e. Return on invested capital before tax (and generally speaking any measure of operating profitability) is driven by operating margin (EBIT/Sales) and capital turnover (Sales/Invested capital). It is equal to the product of these two ratios:

In Millions of Dollars	2008	2009	2010
Operating margin	12.50%	12.22%	11.56%
× Capital turnover	1.79	1.97	2.08
= Return on invested capital before tax	22.39%	24.09%	24.03%

Operating profitability has improved, and the improvement is due to a higher capital turnover (more efficient use of capital), whereas operating margin has actually deteriorated.

f. Pre-tax ROE is higher than $ROIC_{BT}$ because the firm finances its investments with borrowed funds (financial debt). This is what we called financial leverage or gearing. If the firm had not used any borrowing, its ROE would have been identical to its $ROIC_{BT}$.

g. No. Financial leverage can be unfavorable to shareholders, that is, borrowing may result in an ROE that is lower rather than higher than $ROIC_{BT}$. This will happen if $ROIC_{BT}$ turns out to be lower than the cost of borrowing.

h. Measures of financial leverage:

In Millions of Dollars	2008	2009	2010
Financial cost ratio (EBT/EBIT)	0.87	0.88	0.86
Times interest earned (EBIT/Interest)	7.50	8.25	7.40
Financial structure ratio (Invested capital/Equity)	1.49	1.44	1.44
Debt-to-equity ratio	0.49	0.44	0.44
Debt-to-invested-capital ratio	0.33	0.31	0.31

The first two ratios measure the effect of borrowing on the income statement (the effect of interest payments on profitability), and the other three ratios measure the effect of borrowing on the balance sheet (the effect of the *amount* borrowed on profitability). All ratios indicate a slight reduction in financial leverage over the three-year period.

i. ROE Structure

In Millions of Dollars	2008	2009	2010
Operating margin (EBIT/Sales)	12.50%	12.22%	11.56%
× Capital turnover (Sales/Invested capital)	1.79	1.97	2.08
= $ROIC_{BT}$ (EBIT/Invested capital)	22.38%	24.08%	24.04%
× Financial structure (Invested capital/Equity)	1.49	1.44	1.44
× Financial cost (EBT/EBIT)	0.87	0.88	0.86
= Pre-tax ROE	29.00%	30.51%	29.78%
× Tax effect (EAT/EBT)	0.69	0.69	0.69
= After-tax ROE	20.00%	21.05%	20.54%

Operating profitability improves slightly, mostly because of higher capital turnover (indeed, operating margin declined over the period). ROE, however, did not reflect the slight improvement in operating profitability because of the offsetting effect of a reduction in financial leverage.

j. Valuation ratios

In Millions of Dollars	2008	2009	2010
Earnings per share (EAT/number shares)	$ 1.80	$ 2.00	$ 2.20
Price-earnings ratio (Price/EPS)	11.1	12.0	13.6
Market-to-book ratio (Price/Equity per share)	2.2	2.5	2.8

The price-earnings ratio and the market-to-book ratio indicate a rise in the relative value of ACC over the three-year period, reflecting the growth of its earnings per share.

5.2 ROE STRUCTURE ACROSS INDUSTRIES.

Company A is **Boeing:** It has relatively high inventories, high advances from clients (clients make a deposit when they order planes), and high leverage.

Company B is **Cathay Pacific:** It has relatively high fixed assets (the plane fleet) and low inventories.

Company C is **Microsoft:** It has strong operating profitability, high cash holdings, and no debt.

5.3 SUSTAINABLE GROWTH ANALYSIS.

a. Growth in sales in 2010 is 18.5 percent ((\$1,600 – \$1,350)/\$1,350).

Sustainable growth rate = SGR = (Retention rate) × (ROE on beginning equity)

SGR = (\$60/\$110) × (\$110/\$475) = 54.5% × 23.2% = 12.6%

ACC has grown faster than its capacity to finance its activities *without* modifying its operating and financing policies. If it continues to grow much faster than 12.6 percent and does not improve its operating profitability significantly, ACC will most likely experience an increase in financial leverage and a reduction in its capacity to pay dividends, unless it decides to issue new equity.

b.1. If ACC expects to grow its sales by 25 percent in 2011 and does not modify its financing and operating policies, it will need 25 percent more equity in 2011 than in 2010, that is, \$134 million (25 percent of its 2010 equity of \$535 million). This equity capital can come from two sources: addition to retained earnings or a new issue of equity.

b.2. ACC will have to rely increasingly on debt financing, and thus its debt-to-equity ratio would rise.

b.3. ACC will have to rely increasingly on retained profits, and thus its retention rate should rise. By how much? ACC's profits in 2011 are expected to be 25 percent higher than in 2010, that is, \$137.5 million (\$110 million × 1.25). We know that ACC needs \$134 million of new equity. The implication is clear: ACC will have to retain most of its 2011 profits, precisely 97.5 percent (\$134 million/\$137.5 million). The question, of course, is whether its shareholders will accept a reduction in dividend of this magnitude.

b.4. The sustainable growth rate will have to rise to 25 percent, only through an improvement in return on invested capital before tax ($ROIC_{BT}$). The retention rate should remain at 54.5 percent (same as in 2010), and the financial leverage multiplier should remain at 1.24 (refer to the 2010 ROE structure in the answer to problem 5.1, where we found a financial structure ratio of 1.44 and a financial cost ratio of 0.86; multiplying these two ratios, we find a financial leverage multiplier of 1.24). Because *after-tax* ROE is equal to *after-tax* ROIC multiplied by the financial leverage multiplier, we can write

$$\text{SGR} = (54.5\%) - (\text{After-tax ROIC}) \times (1.24) = 25\%$$

from which we get an expected after-tax ROIC of 37 percent (25%/[54.5% × 1.24]). With an effective tax rate of 31 percent, this implies a $ROIC_{BT}$ of 53.6 percent, more than double the 2010 figure of 24.04 percent (see problem 5.1). It is doubtful that ACC could achieve such a dramatic improvement in operating profitability. It will then have to issue new equity unless it reduces its rate of growth in sales.

c.1. In this case ACC will grow at a slower rate than its capacity to fund its activities, because the sustainable growth rate will exceed the rate of growth in sales. As a consequence, ACC will generate extra cash.

c.2. ACC can use the extra cash to make acquisitions, repay debt, increase dividend payments, or repurchase shares. Unless acquisitions are value-creating propositions, they should be avoided. In this case, the extra cash should be returned to shareholders and debt holders through share buy-backs and debt repayment.

6.1 PRESENT VALUES AND THE COST OF CAPITAL.

a. We mean that if these cash flows could be traded (bought and sold) in a market for investment projects, the estimated *value* at which they would trade is \$20 million. This value takes into account the following two factors: (1) the time value of money (the further into the future the cash flows are, the less value they have) and (2) the risk attached to these cash flows, that is, the probability that they will actually differ from their expected values (the riskier they are, the less value they have). The present value of the cash flows is obtained by discounting them to the present at the project cost of capital.

b. We mean that we expect the market value of the firm's equity to increase by $10 million if the firm decides to go ahead with the project. It is the difference between the present value of the cash flows expected from the project and the initial cash outlay required to launch the project.

c. We mean that investors can get a return of 10 percent on a comparable or alternative investment. Thus, if they invest in the project under consideration they will have to give up a return of 10 percent. A comparable investment is one that exhibits the same risk characteristics as the project under consideration.

6.2 MANAGERIAL OPTIONS.
Managerial options refer to project-specific features that provide managers with opportunities to make alterations in reaction to changing circumstances regarding the project. Examples include options to switch technologies and options to abandon the project, as well as options to expand, retract, or defer the project.

6.3 NET PRESENT VALUE.

a. Present value (PV) of the project's expected cash-flow stream at 12 percent:

Part I Using a calculator

$$PV = \frac{\$50{,}000}{1 + 0.12} + \frac{\$50{,}000}{(1 + 0.12)^2} + \frac{\$50{,}000}{(1 + 0.12)^3}$$
$$= (\$50{,}000 \times 0.89286) + (\$50{,}000 \times 0.79719) + (\$50{,}000 \times 0.71178)$$
$$= \$120{,}092$$

Part II Using a spreadsheet

	A	B	C	D	E
1		0	1	2	3
2	Cash flows	–$100,000	$50,000	$50,000	$50,000
3	Cost of capital	12.00%			
4	Present value of cash flows	$120,092			
5	Net present value	$ 20,092			
6					
7	*The formula in cell B4 is =NPV(B3,C2:E2).*				
8	*The formula in cell B5 is =B2+NPV(B3,C2:E2).*				

b. Net present value = –$100,000 + $120,092 = $20,092.

c. $\text{Profitability index} = \frac{\text{Present value of expected cash flows}}{\text{Initial cash outlay}} = \frac{\$120{,}095}{\$100{,}000} = 1.20$

d. The project should be undertaken, because it is expected to increase the value of the firm's equity by $20,095 or, equivalently, because it returns more than one dollar per dollar spent (20 percent more).

6.4 CHOOSING BETWEEN TWO INVESTMENTS WITH UNEQUAL COSTS AND LIFE SPANS.

a.

Part I Using a calculator

$$\text{Present value of printer X costs} = -\$50{,}000 - \frac{\$5{,}000}{1 + 0.10} - \frac{\$5{,}000}{(1 + 0.10)^2} = -\$58{,}678.$$

$$\text{Present value of printer Y costs} = -\$60{,}000 - \frac{\$7{,}000}{1 + 0.10} - \frac{\$7{,}000}{(1 + 0.10)^2} - \frac{\$7{,}000}{(1 + 0.10)^3} = -\$77{,}408.$$

Part II Using a spreadsheet

	A	B	C	D	E
1		0	1	2	3
2	Printer X				
3	Cash flows	–$50,000	–$5,000	–$5,000	
4	Cost of capital	10.00%			
5	Present value of cash flows	–$58,678			
6					
7	Printer Y				
8	Cash flows	–$60,000	–$7,000	–$7,000	–$7,000
9	Cost of capital	10.00%			
10	Present value of cash flows	–$77,408			
11					
12	*The formula in cell B5 is =B3+NPV(B4,C3:D3).*				
13	*The formula in cell B10 is =B8+NPV(B9,C8:E8).*				

b. The two present values are not comparable because printer X will provide two years of service, whereas printer Y could be used one more year.

c. The annual-equivalent cost of a printer is the cost per year of operating the printer that has the *same* present value as the present value of the total cost. In the case of printer X, we have to find a two-year annuity (that is, two *equal* annual payments) with a present value of $58,678. And in the case of printer Y, we have to find a three-year annuity (that is, three *equal* annual payments) with a present value of $77,408.
To compute these annuities, we use formula A6.1.4 given in Appendix 6.1:

$$\text{Constant annual-equivalent cash flow} = \frac{\text{Present value of original cash flow}}{\text{Annuity discount factor}}$$

For printer X, the two-year discount factor is $\frac{1}{(1+10)^2} = 0.8264$, the annuity discount factor is $\frac{1 - 0.8264}{0.10} = 1.7355$, and the annual-equivalent cost is thus $\frac{-\$58{,}678}{1.7355} = -\$33{,}810$. For printer Y, the three-year discount factor is $\frac{1}{(1+10)^3} = 0.7513$, the annuity discount factor is $\frac{1 - 0.7513}{0.10} = 2.4870$, and the annual-equivalent cost is thus $\frac{-\$77{,}408}{2.4870} = -\$31{,}125$.

d. PCC should purchase printer Y because its effective annual cost of $31,125 is lower than the $33,810 equivalent cost of printer X. Although printer Y is more expensive than printer X to buy and operate, its longer useful life more than offsets the difference in costs.

6.5 REPLACING AN EXISTING MACHINE WITH A NEW ONE.

a. The present value of the expected cash flows from the new machine is as follows:

Part I Using a calculator

$$-\$150{,}000 + \frac{\$75{,}000}{1 + 0.10} + \frac{\$75{,}000}{(1 + 0.10)^2} + \frac{\$75{,}000}{(1 + 0.10)^3} = \$36{,}514$$

Part II Using a spreadsheet

	A	B	C	D	E
1		0	1	2	3
2	Cash flows	–$150,000	$75,000	$75,000	$75,000
3	Cost of capital	10.00%			
4	Net present value	–$36,514			
5					
6	*The formula in cell B4 is =B2+NPV(B3,C2:E2).*				

Use formula A6.5 in Appendix 6.1 to calculate the annual-equivalent cash flow. The three-year discount factor is $\frac{1}{(1 + 10)^3} = 0.7513$, the annuity discount factor is $\frac{1 - 0.7513}{0.10} = 2.4870$, and the annual-equivalent cash flow is thus $\frac{-\$36{,}514}{2.4870} = -\$14{,}682$.

b. Why replace a machine that produces an annual cash flow of $20,000 with a new one that will generate only $14,682 a year? The management of Pasta Uno should keep the old machine.

7.1 SHORTCOMINGS OF THE PAYBACK PERIOD.

The payback period rule ignores the time value of money and the risk of the project (unless you use the discounted payback period); it also ignores the cash flows beyond the cutoff period and, more generally, tends to favor short-term investments. Firms still compute the payback period because it is simple to calculate and easy to interpret: it provides an indication of the speed of the recovery of the initial investment.

7.2 IRR VERSUS COST OF CAPITAL.

The cost of capital is the rate of return that investors require from investments with the same risk as the project, whereas the project's internal rate of return (IRR) is the discount rate for which the net present value of the project is equal to zero. Put another way, the project's cost of capital is what the firm *should earn* from the project, whereas the project's internal rate of return is what the firm *can expect to earn* from it.

7.3 IRR VERSUS ROIC.
Both the return on invested capital (ROIC) and the internal rate of return (IRR) are measures of operating profitability, but there are several important differences between them:

	Return on Invested Capital	Internal Rate of Return
Measured with	*Accounting* data	*Cash-flow* data
Measurement period	*Single* period	*Multiple* periods
Typically used for analyzing	*Historical* profitability of *firms*	*Expected* profitability of *projects*

7.4 SHORTCOMINGS OF THE IRR AND PROFITABILITY INDEX RULES.
Internal rate of return: when the choice is between two mutually exclusive investments. In the case where the cash-flow streams of the two investments differ widely, the project with the cash flows concentrated mostly in the earliest years may have a higher internal rate of return than the project with the cash flows concentrated mostly in later years, although the second project may have a higher net present value, meaning that it will contribute the most to the firm's value.
Profitability index: when the size of the two investments are very different. In this case, the profitability index of the smaller project may be higher than that of the *bigger* project, although its net present value may be *smaller*.

7.5 EVALUATING TWO PROJECTS USING ALTERNATIVE DECISION RULES.
In what follows, all figures are in thousands of dollars.

a. **Net present values**

Part I Using a calculator

Net present value (project A) = –$2,000 + $2,451 = $451
Net present value (project B) = –$2,000 + $2,400 = $400

Part II Using a spreadsheet

	A	B	C	D	E
1		0	1	2	3
2	Project A				
3	Cash flows	–$2,000	$ 200	$1,200	$1,700
4	Cost of capital	10.00%			
5	Present value of cash flows	$ 451			
6					
7	Project B				
8	Cash flows	–$2,000	$1,400	$1,000	$ 400
9	Cost of capital	10.00%			
10	Present value of cash flows	$ 400			
11					
12	*The formula in cell B5 is =B3+NPV(B4,C3:E3).*				
13	*The formula in cell B10 is =B8+NPV(B10,C8:E8).*				

If the projects are independent, *both* should be accepted, because they both create value ($451 for project A and $400 for project B). If they are mutually exclusive, project A should be preferred because it creates *more* value.

b. **Payback periods**

Part I Using a calculator

To get the payback periods of the two projects, you need first to compute their cumulative cash flows:

	Project A		Project B	
Year	Cash Flows	Cumulative Cash Flows	Cash Flows	Cumulative Cash Flows
Now	–$2,000	–$2,000	–$2,000	–$2,000
1	200	–1,800	1,400	–600
2	1,200	–600	1,000	400
3	1,700	1,100	400	800

The payback period of project A is between two and three years, because the cumulative cash flows become positive between these years. The payback period of project B is between one and two years. We can write the following:

$$\text{Payback period project A} = 2 + \frac{\$600}{\$1{,}700} = 2.35 \text{ years}$$

$$\text{Payback period project B} = 1 + \frac{\$600}{\$1{,}000} = 1.60 \text{ years}$$

Part II Using a spreadsheet

	A	B	C	D	E
1		0	1	2	3
2	Project A				
3	Cash flows	–$2,000	$200	$1,200	$1,700
4	Accumulated cash inflows		$200	$1,400	$3,100
5					
6	Payback period		—	—	2.35
7					
8	*The formula in cell C4 is =C3. The formula in cell D4 is =C4+D3. Then copy formula in cell D4 to next cells in row 4.*				
9	*The formula in C6 is =IF(OR(C4<=–$B$3,B4>–$B$3),"–",B1+(–$B$3–B4)/C3). Then copy formula in cell C6 to next cells in row 6.*				
10					

Part II Using a spreadsheet (continued)

	A	B	C	D	E
11	<u>Project B</u>				
12	Cash flows	–$2,000	$1,400	$1,000	$ 400
13					
14	Accumulated cash inflows		$1,400	$2,400	$2,800
15					
16	Payback period		—	1.60	—
17					
18	*The formula in cell C14 is =C12. The formula in cell D14 is =C14+D12. Then copy formula in cell D14 to next cells in row 14.*				
19	*The formula in cell C16 is =IF(OR(C14<=–$B$12,B14>–$B$12),"–",B1+(–$B$12–B14)/C12). Then copy formula in cell C16 to next cells in row 16.*				

Discounted payback period

Part I Using a calculator

To get the discounted payback period, you need to compute the cumulative present value of the two projects' cash-flow streams. Using a discount rate of 10 percent, we have the following:

	Project A			Project B		
Year	Cash Flows	Present Value of Cash Flows	Cumulative Present Value of Cash Flows	Cash Flows	Present Value of Cash Flows	Cumulative Present Value of Cash Flows
Now	–$2,000	–$2,000	–$2,000	–$2,000	–$2,000	–$2,000
1	200	181.82	–1,800	1,400	1,272.73	–727.27
2	1,200	991.74	–826.44	1,000	826.45	99.18
3	1,700	1,277.23	450.79	400	300.53	399.71

The discounted payback period is between two and three years for project A and between one and two years for project B. However, because discounting reduces the value of the cash flows, the discounted payback periods are longer than the straight payback periods. We have

$$\text{Discounted payback period project A} = 2 + \frac{\$826.44}{\$1{,}277.23} = 2.65 \text{ years}$$

$$\text{Discounted payback period project B} = 2 + \frac{\$727.27}{\$826.45} = 1.88 \text{ years}$$

Part I Using a calculator

	A	B	C	D	E
1		0	1	2	3
2	Project A				
3	Cash flows	–$2,000	$200	$1,200	$1,700
4					
5	Cost of capital	10%			
6					
7	Discounted cash inflows		$181.82	$ 991.74	$1,277.23
8	Accumulated discounted cash flows		$181.82	$1,173.55	$2,450.79
9					
10	Discounted payback period		—	—	2.65
11					
12	*The formula in cell C7 is =C3/(1+$B$5)^C1. Then copy formula in cell C7 to next cells in row 7.*				
13	*The formula in cell C8 is =C7. The formula in cell D8 is =C8+D7. Then copy formula in cell D8 to next cells in row 8.*				
14	*The formula in cell C10 is =IF(OR(C8<=–$B$3,B8>–$B$3),"–",B1+(–$B$3–B8)/C7). Then copy formula in cell C10 to next cells in row 10.*				
15					
16	Project B				
17	Cash flows	–$2,000	$1,400	$1,000	$ 400
18					
19	Cost of capital	10%			
20					
21	Discounted cash inflows		$1,272.73	$ 826.45	$ 300.53
22	Accumulated discounted cash flows		$1,272.73	$2,099.17	$2,399.70
23					
24	Discounted payback period		—	1.88	—
25					
26	*The formula in cell C21 is =C17/(1+$B$19)^C1. Then copy formula in cell C21 to next cells in row 21.*				
27	*The formula in cell C22 is =C21. The formula in cell D22 is =C22+D21. Then copy formula in cell D22 to next cells in row 22.*				
28	*The formula in cell C24 is =IF(OR(C22<=–$B$17,B22>–$B$17),"–",B1+(–$B$17–B22)/C21). Then copy formula in cell C24 to next cells in row 24.*				

If the two projects are mutually exclusive, the initial investment of $2,000 (which is the same for both projects) will be recovered earlier from project B than from project A. However, this does not mean that you should choose project B, because the payback period does not tell you which project will create more value. We know from the answer to the previous question that project A creates more value than project B. Thus project A should be chosen over project B.

c. The internal rate of return (IRR) of the projects is the discount rates for which the net present value of the projects is equal to zero:

$$\text{Net present value (project A)} = 0 = -\$2{,}000 + \frac{\$200}{1 + \text{IRR}} + \frac{\$1{,}200}{(1 + \text{IRR})^2} + \frac{\$1{,}700}{(1 + \text{IRR})^3}$$

$$\text{Net present value (project B)} = 0 = -\$2{,}000 + \frac{\$1{,}400}{1 + \text{IRR}} + \frac{\$1{,}000}{(1 + \text{IRR})^2} + \frac{\$400}{(1 + \text{IRR})^3}$$

Using a spreadsheet

	A	B	C	D	E
1		0	1	2	3
2	Project A				
3	Cash flows	–$2,000	$ 200	$1,200	$1,700
4					
5	Internal rate of return	19.60%			
6					
7	*The formula in cell B5 is =IRR(B3:E3,.1) where .1 or 10 percent is a guess value for IRR.*				
8					
9	Project B				
10	Cash flows	–$2,000	$1,400	$1,000	$ 400
11					
12	Internal rate of return	23.56%			
13					
14	*The formula in cell B12 is =IRR(B10:E10,.1) where .1 or 10 percent is a guess value for IRR.*				

If the projects are independent, both should be accepted because their internal rate of return is higher than the 10 percent cost of capital. If the projects are mutually exclusive, intuition would suggest that project B, which has the higher internal rate of return, should be preferred to project A. However, this would be true only if project B was creating more value than project A, which we know is not the case. Thus project A should be preferred, although it has a lower internal rate of return. This will always be true as long as the projects' cost of capital is lower than the break-even discount rate of 12.9 percent. It is only when the cost of capital is higher than 12.9 percent that the ranking of the two projects is the same, using the net present value or the internal rate of return.

d.

Part I Using a calculator

Present value of project A future cash flows at 10% = $2,451
Present value of project B future cash flows at 10% = $2,400

$$\text{Profitability index A} = \frac{\text{Present value cash flows (A)}}{\text{Initial cash outlay (A)}} = \frac{\$2{,}451}{\$2{,}000} = 1.23$$

$$\text{Profitability index B} = \frac{\text{Present value cash flows (B)}}{\text{Initial cash outlay (B)}} = \frac{\$2{,}400}{\$2{,}000} = 1.20$$

Part II Using a spreadsheet

	A	B	C	D	E
1		0	1	2	3
2	Project A				
3	Cash flows	–$2,000	$ 200	$1,200	$1,700
4					
5	Cost of capital	10%			
6					
7	Profitability index	1.23			
8					
9	*The formula in cell B7 is =NPV(B5,C3:E3)/–B3.*				
10					
11	Project B				
12	Cash flows	–$2,000	$1,400	$1,000	$ 400
13					
14	Cost of capital	10%			
15					
16	Profitability index	1.20			
17					
18	*The formula in cell B16 is =NPV(B14,C12:E12)/–B12.*				

Both projects have a profitability index greater than one, which means that they both return more than one dollar for one dollar invested ($1.23 for project A and $1.20 for project B). Thus both projects would create value. They should both be accepted if they are independent. If they are mutually exclusive, project A should be accepted, because it generates more dollars for each dollar invested. Note that both the net present value rule and the profitability index rule lead to the same decisions: accept both projects if they are independent, and choose project A over project B if the two projects are mutually exclusive. As shown in the chapter, however, this may not always be the case, especially when both projects differ widely in size.

e. As long as the objective is to accept projects that create value, the only criterion that will always work is the net present value rule. Thus, because both projects have a positive net present value, they should be both accepted if they are independent. If they are mutually exclusive, project A is preferred to project B because it has a higher net present value.

8.1 INTEREST PAYMENTS AND PROJECT'S CASH FLOW.

Interest payments are cash flows *to* creditors, not cash flows *from* the project. They are claims on the cash flows generated by the project and do not affect these cash flows. Interest payments and, more generally, the costs of financing a project are taken into account in the project's cost of capital.

8.2 UNDERSTANDING THE STRUCTURE OF THE CASH-FLOW FORMULA.

The term EBIT(1 – Tax) is equal to EBIT – EBIT × Tax, so that the formula can be rewritten as follows:

$$\text{Cash flow} = \text{EBIT} + \text{Depreciation} - \text{EBIT} \times \text{Tax} - \Delta\text{WCR} - \text{Capex}$$

Note that by adding depreciation to EBIT, the effect of depreciation on the cash flow is washed out because EBIT includes depreciation as an expense. Furthermore, because EBIT × Tax is the amount of tax to be paid on the operating profit generated by the project, it clearly needs to be accounted for in the cash flow from the project. Finally, by deducting the increase in working capital requirement, the formula takes into account any lead or lag between the accounting revenues and expenses in EBIT and their corresponding cash inflows or cash outflows (see Chapter 4).

8.3 ALTERNATIVE FORMULA TO ESTIMATE A PROJECT'S CASH FLOW.

We can write EBIT = EBITDA – Depreciation
so that the first formula can be rewritten as follows:

$$\begin{aligned}\text{Cash flow} &= (\text{EBITDA} - \text{Depreciation})(1 - \text{Tax}) + \text{Depreciation} - \Delta\text{WCR} - \text{Capex}\\ &= \text{EBITDA}(1 - \text{Tax}) - \text{Depreciation} + \text{Tax} \times \text{Depreciation} + \text{Depreciation} - \Delta\text{WCR} - \text{Capex}\\ &= \text{EBITDA}(1 - \text{Tax}) + \text{Tax} \times \text{Depreciation} - \Delta\text{WCR} - \text{Capex}\end{aligned}$$

which is the second formula. Note that in the second formula, the term EBITDA (1 – Tax) overestimates the tax bill because it ignores the deduction of the allowable depreciation expenses. To compensate for this, the tax that would be shielded by the depreciation expense, which is captured by the term Tax × Depreciation, is added back.

8.4 IDENTIFYING A PROJECT'S RELEVANT CASH FLOWS.

Capital expenditures:

1. Is there any opportunity cost associated with the use of the parking lot? Where will company employees park their cars? Will Printers Inc. need to rent parking spaces? If this is the case, the project should be charged for the rent.
2. A residual value should be included at the end of Year 5.

Revenue: The sale price is assumed to be constant, that is, unaffected by competition, which is unreasonable.
Depreciation: Would the tax office accept an accelerated depreciation scheme that will save taxes earlier?
Research and development costs: These are sunk costs (they were spent earlier). They should therefore be ignored.

Overhead costs: The overhead costs charged to the project are not incremental costs—they are accounting allocations. The relevant amount of overhead costs is the increase in the company overhead charges that would result from the adoption of the project, if any.
Operating costs: The direct and indirect costs are assumed to be only variable costs, which is unreasonable.

Inventories:

1. Investment in inventories is supposed to stay constant, although sales are multiplied by a factor of 4 during the life of the project. This is also unreasonable.
2. The recovery of the investment in the inventories at the end of the project is ignored.
3. What about receivables? Payables? Working capital requirement?

Financing costs:

1. Financing costs are cash flows to those who invested in the project and not cash flows *from* the project. Therefore, they are irrelevant.
2. Furthermore, they are accounting allocations, not incremental costs, which is incorrect.

Discount rate: The discount rate is the project's cost of capital. It should reflect the risk characteristics of the project as well as the proportion of debt capital and equity capital that is relevant for the project. It is *not* Printers Inc.'s borrowing rate.
Other: Inflation is ignored.

8.5 ESTIMATING A PROJECT'S RELEVANT CASH FLOWS AND NET PRESENT VALUE (IN THOUSANDS OF DOLLARS).

Part I Using a calculator

	Now	Year 1	Year 2	Year 3	Year 4	Year 5
I. Revenues						
1. Expected unit sales in thousands		5,000	10,000	20,000	20,000	20,000
2. Price per unit		$ .8	$ .7	$ .6	$ .6	$ .6
3. *Sales revenues (line 1 × line 2)*		*$4,000*	*$7,000*	*$12,000*	*$12,000*	*$12,000*
II. Operating expenses						
4. Inflation rate		3%	3%	3%	3%	3%
5. Compounded (1 + Inflation rate)		1.030	1.061	1.093	1.126	1.159
6. Fixed costs (now)		$ 800	$ 800	$ 800	$ 800	$ 800
7. Fixed costs (line 6 × line 5)		$ 824	$ 849	$ 874	$ 900	$927
8. Variable costs per unit (now)		$ .400	$ .400	$ .400	$ .400	$ .400
9. Variable costs per unit (line 8 × line 5)		$ .412	$ .424	$ .437	$ .450	$ .464
10. Total variable cost (line 9 × line 1)		$2,060	$4,240	$ 8,740	$ 9,000	$ 9,280
11. Depreciation expenses ($6,000,000/10)		$ 600	$ 600	$ 600	$ 600	$ 600
12. Rental of parking spaces		$ 50	$ 50	$ 50	$ 50	$ 50
13. *Total operating expenses (lines 7 + 10 + 11 + 12)*		*$3,534*	*$5,739*	*$10,264*	*$10,566*	*$10,857*

Part I Using a calculator (continued)

	Now	Year 1	Year 2	Year 3	Year 4	Year 5
III. Operating profit						
14. EBIT (line 3 – line 13)		$ 466	$1,257	$1,734	$1,446	$1,148
15. less tax at 40%		($ 186)	($503)	($ 694)	($ 578)	($ 460)
16. *After-tax operating profit (line 14 + line 15)*		*$ 280*	*$ 755*	*$1,040*	*$ 867*	*$ 689*
IV. Cash flow generated by the project						
17. After-tax operating profit (line 16)		$ 280	$ 755	$1,040	$ 867	$ 689
18. Depreciation expenses (line 11)		$ 600	$ 600	$ 600	$ 600	$ 600
19. Working capital requirement (30% of year-end sales)	$1,200	$2,100	$3,600	$3,600	$3,600	$ 0
20. Change in working capital requirement	$1,200	$ 900	$1,500	$ 0	$ 0	($3,600)
21. Capital expenditure	$6,000					
22. After-tax resale of equipment[1]						$3,000
23. **Cash flow from the project (lines 17 + 18 – 20 – 21 + 22)**	**($7,200)**	**($ 20)**	**($ 145)**	**$1,640**	**$1,467**	**$7,889**
24. Cost of capital	12%					
25. **Net present value**	($ 758)					

[1]Salvage value = $3 million
Book value (original cost less accumulated depreciation) = $6 million – $3 million = $3 million
Capital gain = $0
Tax on capital gain = $0
After-tax cash receipt = $3 million

Part II Using a spreadsheet[1]

	A	B	C	D	E	F	G
1	In thousands of dollars	Now	Year 1	Year 2	Year 3	Year 4	Year 5
2							
3	**I. Revenues**						
4	Expected unit sales in thousands		5,000	10,000	20,000	20,000	20,000
5	Price per unit		$ 0.80	$ 0.70	$ 0.60	$ 0.60	$ 0.60
6	*Sales revenues*		*$4,000*	*$ 7,000*	*$12,000*	*$12,000*	*$12,000*
7							
8	*Values in rows 4 and 5 are data.*						
9	*The formula in cell C6 is =C4*C5. Then copy formula in cell C6 to next cells in row 6.*						
10							

[1]Some figures in the spreadsheet might be different from the figures in Part I due to rounding.

Part II Using a spreadsheet (continued)

	A	B	C	D	E	F	G
11	**II. Operating expenses**						
12	Inflation rate		3.0%	3.0%	3.0%	3.0%	3.0%
13	Compounded inflation rate		1.030	1.061	1.093	1.126	1.159
14	Fixed costs (now)		$ 800	$ 800	$ 800	$ 800	$ 800
15	Fixed costs		$ 824	$ 849	$ 874	$ 900	$ 927
16	Variable costs per unit (now)		$0.400	$0.400	$ 0.400	$ 0.400	$ 0.400
17	Variable costs per unit		$0.412	$0.424	$ 0.437	$ 0.450	$ 0.464
18	Total variable costs		$2,060	$4,244	$ 8,742	$ 9,004	$ 9,274
19	Depreciation expenses		$ 600	$ 600	$ 600	$ 600	$ 600
20	Rental of parking spaces		$ 50	$ 50	$ 50	$ 50	$ 50
21	***Total operating expenses***		***$3,534***	***$5,742***	***$10,266***	***$10,554***	***$10,852***
22							
23	*Values in rows 12, 14, 16, and 20 are data.*						
24	*Formula in cell C13 is =1*(1+C12). Formula in cell D13 is =C13*(1+D12). Then copy formula in cell D13 to next cells in row 13.*						
25	*Formula in cell C15 is =C14*C13. Then copy formula in cell C15 to next cells in row 15.*						
26	*Formula in cell C17 is =C16*C13. Then copy formula in cell C17 to next cells in row 17.*						
27	*Formula in cell C18 is =C4*C17. Then copy formula in cell C18 to next cells in row 18.*						
28	*Formula in cells C19 to G19 is =SLN(6000,10) where 6,000 is the investment and 10 the depreciation period.*						
29							
30	**III. Operating profit**						
31	EBIT		$466	$1,258	$1,734	$1,446	$1,148
32	less tax at 40%		($280)	($755)	($1,040)	($867)	($689)
33	***After-tax operating profit***		***$280***	***$755***	***$1,040***	***$867***	***$689***
34							
35	*Formula in cell C31 is =C6–C21. Then copy formula in cell C31 to next cells in row 31.*						
36	*Formula in cell C32 is =C31*(1–.4). Then copy formula in cell C32 to next cells in row 32.*						
37	*Formula in cell C33 is =C31–C32. Then copy formula in cell C33 to next cells in row 33.*						
38							
39	**IV. Cash flow generated by the project**						
40	Working capital requirement/ Year-end sales		30%	30%	30%	30%	30%
41	Working capital requirement	$1,200	$2,100	$3,600	$3,600	$3,600	$ 0
42	Change in working capital requirement	$1,200	$ 900	$1,500	$ 0	$ 0	($3,600)
43	Capital expenditure	$6,000	$ 0	$ 0	$ 0	$ 0	$ 0
44	After-tax resale value of equipment						$3,000

Part II Using a spreadsheet (continued)

	A	B	C	D	E	F	G
45	*Cash flow from the project*	*($7,200)*	*($20)*	*($145)*	*$1,640*	*$1,467*	*$7,889*
46							
47	*Values in row 40, 43, and 44 are data.*						
48	*Formula in cell B41 is =C40*C6. Then copy formula in cell B41 to next cells in row 41.*						
49	*Formula in cell B42 is =B41. Formula in cell C42 is =C41–B41. Then copy formula in cell C42 to next cells in row 42.*						
50	*Formula in cell B45 is =B31+B19–B42–B43+B44. Then copy formula in cell B45 to next cells in row 45.*						
51							
52	Cost of capital	12%					
53							
54	**Net present value**	($758)					

The project's net present value is negative after taking into account the relevant cash flows from the project and discounting them at the cost of capital of 12 percent. The proposal would destroy value if undertaken, and should therefore be rejected.

9.1 STRUCTURE AND CHARACTERISTICS OF FINANCIAL MARKETS.

a. "Direct financing" refers to raising capital directly from ultimate savers (households with a cash surplus), whereas "indirect financing" refers to raising capital from financial intermediaries (such as banks and pension funds) in which ultimate savers have invested their savings.

b. Primary markets refer to markets where securities are sold to investors for the first time, whereas secondary markets are markets where the securities that have already been issued are bought and sold. Note that the former provide fresh capital to the issuing firm, whereas the latter do not involve the firm.

c. Organized markets are regulated markets where only companies that can meet stringent conditions can list their shares, whereas over-the-counter markets have less stringent listing and reporting requirements.

d. Domestic securities are securities issued by firms in their local markets, whereas international securities are issued in the international markets, markets that are outside the direct control and jurisdiction of the issuer's country of origin.

e. Domestic securities are securities issued by firms in their local markets, whereas foreign securities are securities issued by firms in the domestic markets of other countries.

f. In a private placement, securities are sold to qualified investors and are not listed or traded in the financial markets, whereas in a public offering, securities are sold to financial market participants who can trade them without restrictions.

9.2 ESTIMATING EXTERNAL FUNDING NEEDS.

a. Total funding needs in 2011 = ΔCash + ΔWCR + Capex
= zero + $7.7 million + $10 million = $17.7 million

b. Internally generated funds = Addition to retained earnings + Depreciation
= \$7.7 million + (\$8 million + \$1 million) = \$16.7 million
c. External funding needs = \$17.7 million – \$16.7 million = \$1 million
d. The million-dollar gap should be borrowed. It is too small to justify an issue of new equity.

9.3 LEASING.

a. **True**
A buyer with a low effective tax rate would receive little tax credit from interest and depreciation deductions. A lessor with a high tax bracket will benefit more from the same deductions. Thus a market for leasing can emerge, with some of the tax benefit received by the lessor transfered to the lessee through low lease payments.

b. **True**
The lessee does not own the leased equipment when the lease expires. It is given back to the lessor. In fixing the lease payments, the lessor must estimate what the residual value of the equipment at expiration of the lease will be. Thus, the uncertainty in the valuation of the residual value is entirely borne by the lessor. The lessee would have to bear this uncertainty if the equipment were purchased.

c. **True**
Leased assets do not appear in the balance sheet for an operating lease, nor the corresponding liability to the lessor. However, it is unlikely that financial analysts would be fooled by the accounting treatment of operating leases. The balance sheet is typically adjusted by the amount of the lease liability.

9.4 SEMI ANNUAL COUPON BONDS.

a. Bond price

Using a spreadsheet

	A	B	C	D	E	F
1	Number of periodic payments	20				
2						
3	Coupon payment	\$ 40				
4						
5	Principal repayment	\$ 1,000				
6						
7	Market rate	4.5%				
8						
9	Bond price	\$934.96				
10						
11	*The formula in cell B9 is =–PV(B7,B1,B3,B5).*					
12						

b. Because the yield on the bond is 4.5 percent every six months, one dollar invested in the bond is expected to return 4.5 cents after six months, which invested again at 4.5 percent will return $(1 + 0.045)^2$ at the end of the year, so that the effective yield is $(1 + 0.045)^2 - 1 = 9.203$ percent.

9.5 VALUATION OF COMMON STOCKS.

a. To estimate the value of the common stock, you must first identify the stream of dividends NEC is expected to pay in the future and then discount it at the required rate of return of 12 percent. The expected stream of dividend payments is as follows:

	Now	Year 1	Year 2	Year 3	Year 4
Expected growth rate		8%	8%	8%	4% (forever)
Expected dividend	$2.00	$2.16	$2.33	$2.52	$2.62

The Year-4 dividend will grow at a constant rate of 4 percent in perpetuity. The value at the end of *Year 3* of that dividend stream is given by the valuation formula in equation 9.7:

$$\text{Value of dividend stream beyond Year 3} = \frac{\$2.62 \text{ (Year-4 dividend)}}{0.12 \text{ (Required return)} - 0.04 \text{ (Growth rate)}} = \frac{\$2.62}{0.08} = \$32.75$$

and the estimated share value is thus the present value of the entire dividend stream at 12 percent:

$$\text{Estimated share value} = \frac{\$2.16}{1+0.12} + \frac{\$2.33}{(1+0.12)^2} + \frac{\$2.52}{(1+0.12)^3} + \frac{\$2.62 + \$32.75}{(1+0.12)^4} = \$28.06$$

Using a spreadsheet

	A	B	C	D	E	F
1				End		
2		Now	Year 1	Year 2	Year 3	Year 4
3	Expected growth rate		8%	8%	8%	4%
4	Expected dividend	$ 2.00	$2.16	$2.33	$2.52	$ 2.62
5	Share price end Year 4					$32.75
6	Expected cash flows		$2.16	$2.33	$2.52	$35.37
7	Expected return	12%				
8						
9	Share price	$28.06				
10						
11	*Formula in cell C4 is =B4*(1+C3). Formula in cell D4 is =C4*(1+D3). Then copy formula in D4 to next cells in row 4.*					
12	*Formula in cell F5 is =F4/(B7–0.04).*					
13	*Formula in cell C6 is =C4+C5. Then copy formula in C6 to next cells in row 6.*					
14	*Formula in cell B9 is =NPV(B7,C6:F6).*					

b. The observed market price of $29.12 is 3.7 percent higher than the estimated value of $28.06. This can be interpreted as follows. If we assume that the estimated value is "correct," then the shares are overpriced and should be sold. If we assume that the price is "correct" then the model and the assumptions we have used to estimate the value of a share are incorrect and should be revised.

10.1 COST OF DEBT VERSUS COST OF EQUITY.

We mean that the amount of equity capital invested in the firm, the division, or the project is *expected* to return 10 percent to the equity holders, whereas the amount invested as debt capital is *expected* to return 8 percent to the debt holders. These returns are those that the investors can get from investing in firms having the same risk as that of the firm, the division, or the project. The cost of debt is lower than the cost of equity because debt holders have a priority claim over the equity holders on the cash flows generated by the firm, the division, or the project. As a consequence, debt is less risky than equity and the cost of debt is thus lower than the cost of equity.

10.2 CASH FLOWS FROM BONDS AND STOCKS.

The cash flows associated with a bond are the coupon payments and the principal repayment, whereas the cash flows associated with a share of stock are the dividends paid to the shareholders. The market value of a bond or a stock is the present value of their respective expected cash-flow streams (see equations 10.1 and 10.4). In the case of a bond, the coupon payments and principal repayment are discounted at the bondholders' expected return, whereas in the case of a share of stock, the dividends are discounted at the shareholders' expected return. Both returns depend on the risk associated with holding the securities.

10.3 THE CAPITAL ASSET PRICING MODEL.

1. The higher the risk of a security or an asset, the higher its expected return.
2. The only relevant risk of a security is that portion of the security risk that cannot be diversified away. This risk, called systematic, undiversifiable, or market risk, is measured by the security beta coefficient. A beta coefficient of one indicates that the security has the same risk as that of a well-diversified portfolio, also called the market portfolio. A beta coefficient higher (lower) than one indicates a higher (lower) risk than that of the market portfolio.
3. The expected return on a security is the sum of the risk-free rate (the rate of return of the safest security, for example the yield on government bonds held to maturity) plus a risk premium. This risk premium is the reward for bearing the systematic risk of the security. It is equal to the security beta coefficient multiplied by the market risk premium (the difference between the return expected from holding the market portfolio and the risk-free rate).

10.4 THE COST OF CAPITAL OF A FIRM.

a. From equation 10.11, Vanhoff's cost of equity, k_E, is

$$k_{E,Vanhoff} = R_F + (R_M - R_F) \times ß_{equity},$$

where R_F = 5 percent is the risk-free rate, R_M = 10 percent is the market portfolio expected rate of return, and $ß_{equity}$ = 1.16 is Vanhoff's equity beta coefficient. As a result,

$$k_{E,Vanhoff} = 5\% + (10\% - 5\%) \times 1.16 = 10.8\%$$

b. The relevant cost of capital of Vanhoff is the weighted average cost of its various sources of capital, that is, the weighted average cost of capital or WACC. To determine that cost, we apply equation 10.12:

$$\text{WACC} = k_D(1 - T_C) \times \frac{D}{E + D} + k_E \times \frac{E}{E + D}$$

where k_D = 6 percent is Vanhoff's before-tax cost of debt, T_C = 40 percent is the corporate tax rate, k_E = 10.8 percent is Vanhoff's cost of equity, $\frac{D}{E + D}$ the proportion of debt financing, and $\frac{E}{E + D}$ the proportion of equity financing.

Because Vanhoff Lines finances its activities with as much debt as equity, $\frac{D}{E + D} = 0.5$ and $\frac{E}{E + D} = 0.5$.

Putting all together, we get the following:

$$\text{WACC} = (6\% \times (1 - 0.40) \times 0.5) + (10.8\% \times 0.5) = 7.20\%$$

10.5 ESTIMATION OF THE COST OF CAPITAL OF A DIVISION.
There are two observations to make:

1. The weighted average cost of capital of 8 percent is the cost of capital of PacificCom, that is, the average of the costs of capital of its two divisions. If the risk, and more precisely the betas, of the two divisions are different, the cost of capital that is needed to evaluate each division's investment proposals cannot be equal to 8 percent.
2. The amounts of debt and equity capital that the consultant has used to compute the financing ratios $D/(E + D)$ and $E/(E + D)$ are taken from PacificCom's balance sheet. In other words, they are accounting values, whereas a proper WACC should be calculated with market values.

11.1 EFFECT OF BORROWING ON SHARE PRICE.

1. In the absence of tax and financial distress costs, the share price should not necessarily decrease, because, as the firm's debt goes up, the increase of the *expected* earnings per share will offset the negative effect of the increase in its volatility. Indeed, according to Modigliani and Miller, the compensation will be perfect, and the share price should not be affected at all.
2. In the presence of tax, the firm's tax bill decreases in proportion to its indebtedness because interest payments are tax deductible. The firm's share price will go up to reflect the present value of the tax savings that goes to the shareholders.
3. As the firm borrows more and more to take advantage of the interest tax shield, the probability of financial distress increases. If there are costs associated with financial distress, at some point the present value of these costs will be higher than the present value of the interest tax shield and the firm's share price will begin to decrease.

11.2 RISK OF DEBT AND EQUITY, AND RISK OF THE FIRM.
False. When debt is increased, more of the cash flows generated by the firm's assets are simply going to the debt holders than to the shareholders. The volatility of the cash flows from the firm's assets is not affected. Therefore, the risk of the firm as a whole will not increase.

11.3 FACTORS AFFECTING THE OPTIMAL DEBT-TO-EQUITY RATIO.

a. *Increase* the debt-to-equity ratio to take advantage of the increase in the interest tax shield
b. *Increase* the debt-to-equity ratio because a higher personal capital gain tax will increase the spread between the tax rate on equity income and the tax rate on interest income. See equation 11.8

c. *Increase* the debt-to-equity ratio because acquiring the building will increase the firm's tangible assets, and, as a result, the probability of financial distress should decrease.
d. If the ratio is optimal when measured on the basis of the current market value of the firm's equity, it is too high when measured on the basis of the fair value of its equity, because the firm's shares are undervalued. The firm should issue debt and buy shares with the proceeds, thus providing a strong signal that its shares are undervalued. The process should last until the share price reaches its fair value and the debt-to-equity ratio reverts to its current value.
e. *Do not change* the debt-to-equity ratio, because a decrease in the working capital requirement does not usually affect the probability of financial distress.
f. As long as Alternative Solutions Inc. and the acquirer are publicly held firms with well-diversified shareholders, the ratio should not change, because, in that case, the optimal debt-to-equity ratio is not determined by the identity of the owners of the firm's assets. Note that if Alternative Solutions Inc. were a private company and its new owners were not well-diversified investors, the ratio may have to change to reflect the new owners' optimal debt-to-equity ratio.

11.4 EBIT-EPS ANALYSIS.

a.

	Low Debt Plan			High Debt Plan		
1. EBIT	$ 90,000	$130,000	$170,000	$ 90,000	$130,000	$170,000
2. Number of shares before recapitalization	10,000	10,000	10,000	10,000	10,000	10,000
3. Share price before recapitalization	$ 100	$ 100	$ 100	$ 100	$ 100	$ 100
4. Amount borrowed	$200,000	$200,000	$200,000	$400,000	$400,000	$400,000
5. Interest rate	10%	10%	10%	10%	10%	10%
6. Number of shares after recapitalization [(2) – (4)/(3)]	8,000	8,000	8,000	6,000	6,000	6,000
7. Net earnings [(1) – (4) × (5)]	$ 70,000	$110,000	$150,000	$ 50,000	$ 90,000	$130,000
8. EPS [(7)/(6)]	$ 8.75	$ 13.75	$ 18.75	$ 8.33	$ 15	$ 21.67

b.

	Low Debt Plan	High Debt Plan
1. EBIT	$100,000	$100,000
2. Number of shares before recapitalization	10,000	10,000
3. Share price before recapitalization	$ 100	$ 100
4. Amount borrowed	$200,000	$400,000
5. Interest rate	10%	10%
6. Number of shares after recapitalization [(2) – (4)/(3)]	8,000	6,000
7. Net earnings [(1) – (4) × (5)]	$ 80,000	$ 60,000
8. EPS [(7)/(6)]	$ 10	$ 10

First, note that the value of the firm's assets is \$1,000,000, because Albine does not have any debt and its equity value is \$1,000,000 (10,000 shares at \$100 a share).

EPS is the same under the two plans, or any other recapitalization plan, because at that level of EBIT, the return on assets is 10 percent (\$100,000 divided by \$1,000,000 of assets), the same as the interest rate. At \$100,000 of EBIT, the cost of borrowing will exactly offset the benefit of distributing the net earnings to more (less) shares, when the amount of debt relative to the amount of equity increases (decreases).

11.5 THE VALUE OF THE INTEREST TAX SHIELD.
After the debt issue, the value of Ilbane Corp. will increase by the present value of the interest tax shield. As shown in the text, if we assume that the tax shield is forever, its present value, PV_{ITS}, is as follows:

$$PV_{ITS} = \frac{\text{Annual interest tax shield}}{\text{Cost of debt}}$$

a.

$$PV_{ITS} = \frac{\text{Tax rate} \times \text{Interest rate} \times \text{Debt issue}}{\text{Interest rate}} = \text{Tax rate} \times \text{Debt issue}$$

$$= 0.35 \times \$20 \text{ million} = \$7 \text{ million}$$

The value of Ilbane should increase by \$7 million after the debt issue.

b. The same formula would give a value of \$28 million for the interest tax shield (0.35 × \$80 million). However, with a debt-to-equity ratio of 4, the financial risk of Ilbane would increase significantly. Investors will have lower expectations regarding the value of the interest tax shield, a sentiment that will be reflected in Ilbane's share price. The share price will increase less than it would have if the financial risk would not increase significantly. As a result, the value of Ilbane Corp. will increase less than \$28 million.

12.1 THE PRICE-TO-EARNINGS RATIO.
Companies A and B are identical, including same current earnings per share and same share price volatility. However, the earnings after tax of A are expected to grow faster than that of B, making A shares more valuable than B shares. Therefore, the financial market will price A's current earnings more than B's earnings.
Companies A and B are identical, including same current earnings per share and same earnings growth expectations. However, the share price of A is more volatile than the share price of B, making A shares less valuable than B shares. Thus, the financial market will price A's current earnings less than B's.

12.2 ALTERNATIVE VALUATION METHODS AND VALUE-CREATING ACQUISITIONS.

a. A firm's liquidating value should be its *minimum* value and thus its *floor* (not ceiling) value. And its replacement value should be its *maximum* value and thus its *ceiling* (not floor) value.
b. No, price-to-cash-flow ratios should be better, because firms' cash flows are significantly less sensitive to accounting rules and conventions than are firms' reported earnings (profits).
c. Different valuation methods are expected to generate different estimated values because of conceptual differences among alternative valuation models. Furthermore, different models use different inputs (data) that do not have the same quality or reliability.

12.3 VALUATION BY COMPARABLES.

- Apply the following three-step method for the equity multiples:

  Step 1: *Convert the comparable firm's (REC) data on a per-share basis.*

1. Earnings per share ($90 million divided by 40 million shares)	$2.25
2. Book value per share ($590 million divided by 40 million shares)	$14.75

  Step 2: *Calculate the comparable firm's (REC) corresponding multiples.*

1. Price-to-earnings ratio ($30 divided by $2.25)	13.33
2. Price-to-book ratio ($30 divided by $14.75)	2.03

  Step 3: *Estimate LMC's equity value using REC's multiples.*

1. Price-to-earnings ratio:	$46 million × 13.33 = $613 million
2. Price-to-book value ratio:	$270 million × 2.03 = $548 million

- Apply the following four-step method for the asset multiple:

  Step 1: *Calculate REC's enterprise value (EV).*

$$\begin{aligned} \text{EV(REC)} &= \text{Market value of equity} + \text{Debt} - \text{Cash} \\ &= (\$40 \times 40 \text{ million}) + \$800 \text{ million} - \$10 \text{ million} = \$1{,}990 \text{ million} \end{aligned}$$

  Step 2: *Calculate REC's ratio of EV to EBITDA.*

  EV-to-EBITDA ratio ($1,990 million divided by $250 million) = 7.96

  Step 3: *Estimate LEC's enterprise value using REC's multiple.*

  $125 million × 7.96 = $995 million

  Step 4: *Add LMC's cash and deduct its debt to get LMC's equity value.*

  $995 million + $4 million − $420 million = $579 million

The estimated values of LMC's equity are not expected to be the same because they are based on different multiples drawn from the Rapid Engine Corporation. As long as the highest estimate is about 20 percent higher than the lowest estimate, the range of estimated values is acceptable. In our case, the highest estimate ($613 million) is 12 percent higher than the lowest estimate ($548 million).

12.4 EQUITY VALUATION.

a. From equation 12.1, we can write the following:

$$DCF_{\text{Baltek}} = \frac{\text{Next year's cash flow}}{0.08 - 0.03} = \frac{\$1 \text{ million} \times (1 + 0.03)}{0.05} = \frac{\$1.03 \text{ million}}{0.05} = \$20.6 \text{ million}$$

b. The value of Baltek's equity is the same as the value of its assets since the company has no debt.

12.5 DISCOUNTED CASH-FLOW VALUATION.
Apply the following three-step method:

Step 1: *Provide a formula to estimate the cash flows from assets (CFA) that LEC is expected to generate in the next five years.*

From equation 12.6, we can write

$$CFA = EBIT(1 - \text{Tax rate}) + \text{Depreciation} - \Delta WCR - \text{Capital expenditures}$$

where EBIT is earnings before interest and tax, or pre-tax operating profit, and ΔWCR is the change in working capital requirement. But because annual capital expenditures will be equal to annual depreciation expenses,

$$CFA_{LEC} = EBIT(1 - \text{Tax rate}) - \Delta WCR$$

Step 2: *Estimate LEC's weighted average cost of capital (WACC).*

1. Cost of equity according to the capital asset pricing model (CAPM) = 5% + 1.2 × 5% = 11%
2. Percentage of equity financing = 80%
3. After-tax cost of debt = 6% × (1 – 0.40) = 3.6%
4. Percentage of debt financing = 100% – 80% = 20%

$$WACC = (0.80 \times 11\%) + (0.20 \times 3.6\%) = 9.52\%$$

Step 3: *Using a spreadsheet, estimate the DCF value of LEC's equity as in Exhibit 12.5 from the forecasting assumptions:*

	A	B	C	D	E	F	G
1	Data in million of dollars			**End-of-Year Forecast**			
2							
3		Current	Year 1	Year 2	Year 3	Year 4	Year 5
4							
5	Sales growth rate		8.00%	8.00%	6.00%	6.00%	4.00%
6	Operating margin as percent of sales		20.00%	20.00%	20.00%	20.00%	20.00%
7	WCR in percent of sales	20.00%	20.00%	20.00%	20.00%	20.00%	20.00%
8	Sales	$620.0	$669.6	$723.2	$766.6	$812.6	$845.1
9	EBIT		133.9	144.6	153.3	162.5	169.0
10	EBIT × (1 – Tax rate of 40%)		80.4	86.8	92.0	97.5	101.4
11	WCR at year-end	124.0	133.9	144.6	153.3	162.5	169.0
12	less ΔWCR		–9.9	–10.7	–8.7	–9.2	–6.5
13							
14	**equals cash flow from assets**		**$ 70.4**	**$ 76.1**	**$ 83.3**	**$ 88.3**	**$ 94.9**
15							
16	Residual value end of Year 4[1]					$1,719.3	
17							
18							

[1]The residual value in Year 4 is given by the perpetual, constant-growth, valuation formula (see valuation formula 12.1). In step 2 we show that LEC's weighted average cost of capital (WACC) is 9.52 percent. The residual value is thus

$$\text{Residual value} = \frac{\text{Cash flow from assets}_{\text{year 5}}}{\text{WACC} - \text{Growth rate}} = \frac{\$94.9}{0.0952 - 0.04} = \frac{\$94}{0.052} = \$1719.3$$

and LEC's equity value is $1.168 million.

	A	B	C	D	E	F	G
19	Beginning Year 1						
20							
21	WACC	9.52%					
22	DCF value of assets	$1,448					
23	*less book value of debt*	*$ 280*					
24	**equals DCF value of equity**	**$1,168**					
25							
26	*Rows 5 to 7, 23, and plus cell B8 are data.*						
27	*Formula in cell C8 is =B8*(1+C5). Then copy cell C8 to next cells in row 8.*						
28	*Formula in cell C9 is =C6*C8. Then copy cell C9 to next cells in row 9.*						
29	*Formula in cell C10 is =C9*(1–.4). Then copy cell C10 to next cells in row 10.*						
30	*Formula in cell B11 is =B7*B8. Then copy cell B11 to next cells in row 11.*						
31	*Formula in cell C12 is =B11–B12. Then copy cell C12 to next cells in row 12.*						
32	*Formula in cell C15 is =C10+C12. Then copy cell C15 to next cells in row 15.*						
33	*Formula in cell F16 is =G14/(B21–G5).*						
34	*Formula in cell B22 is =NPV(C22,C14:F14)+F16/(1+B22)^4.*						
35	*Formula in cell B24 is =B22–B23.*						

13.1 RISK MANAGEMENT.

A firm should manage risk centrally because (1) there are risks at the corporate level that projects do not capture; (2) different risk exposures can be netted out at the corporate level; (3) the cost of risk protection can be reduced if managed centrally; (4) a consistent risk policy can be formulated and implemented across all the firm's divisions; and (5) the firm could learn to better manage risk if a dedicated staff oversees the process centrally.

13.2 RISK IDENTIFICATION.

Situation Event	Level-1 Risk	Level-2 Risk	Possible Protection
1	Financial investment risk	Price risk	Buy an option to protect against the drop in Fastcom share price
2	Currency risk	Exchange rate risk	Hedge against changes in currency rates
3	Business risk	Operational risk	Buy insurance against weather storms
4	Financial risk	Financial cost risk	Hedge against changes in interest rate
5	Business risk	Operational risk	Diversify the firm's sources of supply
6	Business risk	Operational risk	Require compensation if payment is not received after an agreed upon time period
7	Financial risk	Financing cost and refinancing risks	Finance the asset with a matching loan of 4-year maturity
8	Business risk	Strategic risk	Launch a new, more modern line of dolls

13.3 RISK MEASUREMENT.

a. Because the expected cash flow is a "perpetuity," the value of NGC is equal to its expected cash flow divided by its cost of capital (10 percent). If its expected cash flow is reduced by $20 million, its value will be reduced by $200 million ($20 million divided by 10 percent). If the probability that this event occurs is 50 percent, then MVR is $100 million.
b. As in the previous case, the value of NGC is reduced by $200 million. If the probability that this event occurs is 10 percent, then MVR is $20 million.
c. With a cost of capital of 10.2 percent, NGC's value is $980 million ($100 million divided by 0.102) and the reduction in value is $20 million ($1,000 million less $980 million). If the probability that this event occurs is 50 percent, then MVR is $10 million.
d. If the expected cash flow is reduced by $1 million, NGC's value will be reduced by $10 million ($1 million divided by 10 percent). If the probability that this event occurs is 10 percent, then MVR is $1 million.

13.4 COMPARING ALTERNATIVE HEDGING TECHNIQUES.

	What Is It?	Advantages	Disadvantages
Forward hedging	Buying (selling) forward an amount of foreign currency equal to the value of the underlying exposed cash outflow (inflow) denominated in the same currency and for the same delivery date.	It is a tailor-made hedge that provides a perfect hedge for transactions of a known amount and known delivery dates.	1. It requires a credit check 2. It often happens that the effective delivery date is not exactly the anticipated date 3. The bid-ask spread on forward contracts can be large for infrequently traded currencies 4. Getting out of a forward contract requires entering into an offsetting forward contract with the same delivery date as the original one
Futures hedging	Buying (selling) futures contracts in the same currency as the underlying exposed cash outflow (inflow). The number of contracts to buy (sell) and the delivery date should match those of the amount of cash flow exposed and its delivery date.	1. No credit check is needed 2. Transaction costs are low 3. Default risk is low because of marking-to-market 4. It is easy to get out of a position, and the cash settlement is immediate	1. One can trade only standard-size contracts with fixed maturity dates 2. Margin must be deposited 3. Trades are marked-to-market daily

	What Is It?	Advantages	Disadvantages
Options hedging	Buying options on the same currency as the underlying exposed cash outflow (inflow). The holder of the option has the right, but not the obligation, to buy (sell) foreign currencies over a specified period. In the case of over-the-counter options, the exercise price and the expiration date are contractually defined. In the case of traded options, the number of contracts to buy (sell) and the delivery date should match those of the amount of cash flow exposed and its delivery date.	1. It is an insurance against unfavorable exchange rate movements 2. Contrary to other hedging techniques, there is no obligation to buy (sell) the foreign currency 3. Transaction costs and default risk of traded options are lower than over-the-counter options 4. Options can be sold anytime before the expiration date	1. The firm has to pay a premium to get an option (the price of the option) 2. In the case of a traded option, one can trade only standard-size contracts with fixed maturity dates 3. Margin must be deposited
Swap hedging	Exchanging interest and principal payments in one currency for interest and principal payments in another currency.	1. It is a low-cost exchange of cash flows denominated in different currencies 2. The swap market is dominated by banks, which reduces the counterparty risk	1. Its use is most often limited to long-term exposures 2. There is potentially some counterparty risk

13.5 SWAP AGREEMENT.

The loss of the Japanese company from swap transactions is simply the profit of the German company from the same transactions. This is shown below, where the amounts are in millions.

	A	B	C	D	E	F	G	H
1			Now	Year 1	Year 2	Year 3	Year 4	Year 5
2	Exchange rate JPY/EUR		130.44	125.00	127.00	130.00	135.00	138.00
3								
4	The Japanese company							
5	*With swap transactions*							
6	Initial investment (EUR)	23.00						
7	Annual coupon	5.00%						
8	Cash flow (EUR)		23.00	−1.15	−1.15	−1.15	−1.15	−24.15
9								
10	*Without swap*							
11	Initial investment (JPY)	3,000.00						
12	Annual coupon	5.00%						
13	Cash flow (JPY)		3,000.00	−150.00	−150.00	−150.00	−150.00	−3,150.00

	A	B	C	D	E	F	G	H
14	Cash flow (EUR)		23.00	–1.20	–1.18	–1.15	–1.11	–22.83
15								
16	Profit (loss) (EUR)		0.00	0.05	0.03	0.00	–0.04	–1.32
17	Total profit (loss) (EUR)		–1.28					
18								
19	<u>The German company</u>							
20	***With swap transactions***							
21	Initial investment (JPY)	3,000.00						
22	Annual coupon	5.00%						
23	Cash flow (JPY)		3,000.00	–150.00	–150.00	–150.00	–150.00	–3,150.00
24								
25	***Without swap***							
26	Initial investment (EUR)	23.00						
27	Annual coupon	5.00%						
28	Cash flow (EUR)		23.00	–1.15	–1.15	–1.15	–1.15	–24.15
29	Cash flow (JPY)		3,000.01	–143.75	–146.05	–149.50	–155.25	–3,332.70
30								
31	Profit (loss) (JPY)		–0.01	–6.25	–3.95	–0.50	5.25	182.70
32	Profit (loss) (EUR)		0.00	–0.05	–0.03	0.00	0.04	1.32
33	Total profit (loss) (EUR)		1.28					
34								
35	*Rows 2, 6, 7, 11, 12, 21, 22, 26, and 27 are data.*							
36	*The data in cell C8 is =B6. The formula in cell D8 is =$B$6*$B$7. Then copy the formula from cell D8 to cells E8, F8, and G8. The formula in cell H8 is =$B$6*$B$7–B6.*							
37	*The data in cell C13 is =B11. The formula in cell D13 is =$B$11*$B$12. Then copy the formula from cell D13 to cells E13, F13, and G13. The formula in cell H13 is =$B$11*$B$12–B11.*							
38	*The formula in cell C14 is =C13/C2. Then copy the formula from cell C14 to cells D14, E14, F14, G14, and H14.*							
39	*The formula in cell C16 is =C8–C14. Then copy the formula from cell C16 to cells D16, E16, F16, G16, and H16.*							
40	*The formula in cell C17 is =sum(C16:H16).*							
41	*The data in cell C23 is =B21. The formula in cell D23 is =$B$21*$B$22. Then copy the formula from cell D23 to cells E23, F23, and G23. The formula in cell H23 is =$B$21*$B$22–B21.*							
42	*The data in cell C28 is =B26. The formula in cell D28 is =$B$26*$B$27. Then copy the formula from cell D28 to cells E28, F28, and G28. The formula in cell H28 is =$B$26*$B$27–B26.*							
43	*The formula in cell C29 is =C28*C2. Then copy the formula from cell C29 to cells D29, E29, F29, G29, and H29.*							
44	*The formula in cell C31 is =C23–C29. Then copy the formula from cell C31 to cells D31, E31, F31, G31, and H31.*							
45	*The formula in cell C32 is =C31/C2. Then copy the formula from cell C32 to cells D32, E32, F32, G32, and H32.*							
46	*The formula in cell C33 is =sum(C32:H32).*							
47								

14.1 ACCOUNTING VERSUS ECONOMIC EXPOSURE.

Accounting and translation exposures are the same thing. Both refer to the effect of exchange-rate changes on the value of the firm's financial statements' accounts. Economic exposure refers to the effect of exchange-rate changes on the value of the firm's *future* cash flows. Transaction, contractual, and operating exposures are subsets of economic exposure. Transaction and contractual exposures are synonymous. Both have to do with the effect of the exchange-rate volatility on the future cash flows expected from past transactions denominated in foreign currencies, and operating exposure is concerned with the effect on future uncertain transactions. In the following table, we indicate why economic exposure is more relevant than accounting exposure to shareholders:

Economic Exposure	Accounting Exposure
1. It is forward looking because it is concerned with *future* cash flows	1. It is backward looking because it is concerned with *past* transactions
2. It focuses on *cash flows* that are directly related to value creation	2. It focuses on *accounting values* that are only remotely related to value creation
3. It affects firms with foreign subsidiaries, export/import firms, as well as those that are subject to foreign competition in the input and output markets	3. It affects only a subset of firms that are subject to accounting exposure, that is, those firms that *record* transactions denominated in a foreign currency
4. Because it focuses on cash flows, it does not depend on the firm's accounting rules	4. It is affected by the accounting rules chosen by the firm

14.2 PARITY RELATIONS.

Purchasing power parity says that changes in the exchange rate between two countries' currencies are determined by the difference in the expected inflation rates between the two countries.

14.3 COUNTRY RISK AND THE COST OF CAPITAL.

False. Although it is often the case that firms mark up their domestic cost of capital when analyzing a foreign investment, the practice fails to properly account for country risk. A better way is to reduce the *expected* cash flows of the cross-border project according to the expected consequences of the country risk associated with the country in which the investment would be made. An added advantage of adjusting the cash flows instead of the cost of capital is that it forces management to clearly identify the risks taken. It also allows for sensitivity analysis.

14.4 INTERNATIONAL CAPITAL BUDGETING (1).

Answer: Since the project's NPV is positive, the company would invest in the project.

	A	B	C	D	E	F	G
1		Now	Year 1	Year 2	Year 3	Year 4	Year 5
2	Initial investment	-50,000,000					
3	Terminal value						15,000,000
4	Sales	20,000,000	21,000,000	21,630,000	22,278,900	22,947,267	23,635,685
5	Sales growth		5%	5%	5%	5%	5%
6	Inflation rate in Thailand		3%	3%	3%	3%	3%

	A	B	C	D	E	F	G
7	Inflation rate in the U.S.		4%	4%	4%	4%	4%
8	EBIT	15,000,000	15,750,000	16,537,500	17,364,375	18,232,594	19,144,223
9	Tax rate		35%	35%	35%	35%	35%
10	EBIT(1–Tax rate)		10,237,500	10,749,375	11,286,844	11,851,186	12,443,745
11	WCR as percent of sales	10%	10%	10%	10%	10%	10%
12	WCR	2,000,000	2,100,000	2,163,000	2,227,890	2,294,727	2,363,569
13	Change in WCR		–100,000	–63,000	–64,890	–66,837	–68,842
14	Investment cash flow in THB	–50,000,000	10,137,500	10,686,375	11,221,954	11,784,349	27,374,903
15	THB/USD	40					
16	USD/THB	0.02500000	0.02524272	0.02548779	0.02573525	0.02598510	0.02623739
17	Investment cash flow in USD	–1,250,000	255,898	272,372	288,800	306,217	718,246
18							
19	Cost of capital	12%					
20	NPV	3,335					
21							
22							
23	*Rows 2, 3, 5, 6, 7, 9, 11, 15, 19, cell B4, and cell B8 are data.*						
24	*The formula in cell C4 is =B4*(1+C5). Then copy formula in cell C4 to the next cells in row 4.*						
25	*The formula in cell C8 is =B8*(1+C5). Then copy formula in cell C8 to the next cells in row 8.*						
26	*The formula in cell C10 is =C8*(1–C9). Then copy formula in cell C10 to the next cells in row 10.*						
27	*The formula in cell B12 is =B4*B11. Then copy formula in cell B12 to the next cells in row 12.*						
28	*The formula in cell C13 is =B13–C13. Then copy formula in cell C13 to the next cells in row 13.*						
29	*The formula in cell B14 is =B2+B3+B10+B13. Then copy formula in cell B14 to the next cells in row 14.*						
30	*The formula in cell B16 is =1/B15. The formula in cell C16 is =B16*(1+C7)/(1+C6). Then copy formula in cell C16 to the next cells in row 16.*						
31	*The formula in cell B17 is =B14*B16. Then copy formula in cell B17 to the next cells in row 17.*						
32	*The formula in cell B20 is =B17+NPV(B19;C17:G17).*						

14.5 INTERNATIONAL CAPITAL BUDGETING (2).

a. The project cost of capital is 13 percent, the sum of the 6 percent U.S. government bond rate and the 7 percent risk premium.

Using a spreadsheet

	A	B	C	D	E	F	G
1		0	1	2	3	4	5
2	Expected cash flows in euros	–€103,000,000	€25,000,000	€25,000,000	€25,000,000	€25,000,000	€50,000,000
3	Expected exchange rate EUR/USD	0.80	0.80	0.80	0.80	0.80	0.80
4	Expected cash flows in U.S. dollars	–$128,750,000	$31,250,000	$31,250,000	$31,250,000	$31,250,000	$62,500,000
5	Cost of capital	13%					
6	Net present value	–$1,875,275					
7							
8	*Rows 2, 3, and 5 are data.*						
9	*The formula in cell B6 is =B4+NPV(B5,C4:G4).*						

According to this analysis, Kampton should not undertake the project, because its net present value is negative.

b. Using the same spreadsheet with a cost of capital equal to 11 percent (6 percent government bond rate plus 5 percent risk premium) gives a positive net present value of **$5,292,136.**

c. If we can assume that the shareholders of the Kampton Company hold internationally diversified portfolios, there is no rationale for adding an extra risk premium for European projects to the 5 percent premium used when estimating the net present value of projects in the United States.

15.1 UNDERSTANDING MVA AND EVA.

a. Value is created by maximizing the *difference* between the market value of capital and the amount of capital employed to produce that value, that is, the firm's market value added, not its absolute market value.

b. Market value added is determined by the stream of EVAs the firm is expected to generate in the *future*. If the present value of that future stream is positive, MVA is positive, even though *current* EVA can be negative.

c. Net profit is calculated by deducting interest expenses from operating profit, which means that net profit is adjusted for the cost of debt. If we then deduct a capital charge based on the WACC, we would be counting the cost of debt twice, once in net profit and again in the WACC.

d. EVA takes risk into account via the WACC. The riskier an entity's operating profit, the higher its WACC and the lower its EVA.

e. Higher profits are only half the story. If the charge for capital employed exceeds (operating) profit, value is destroyed.

15.2 ADJUSTING ACCOUNTING DATA TO ESTIMATE ECONOMIC VALUE ADDED.

$$\text{EVA} = \text{NOPAT} - \text{Charge for capital employed}$$

where: NOPAT = Net operating profit after tax = EBIT × (1 – Tax rate)
Charge for capital employed = WACC × Capital employed (same as invested capital)
To estimate EVA, apply the following procedure:

Step 1: *Estimate earnings before interest and tax (EBIT).*

Sales	$1,400 million
Cost of sales	(780 million)
Selling, general, and administrative expenses	(330 million)
Depreciation and lease expenses	(45 million)
Amortization of R&D expenses	(30 million)
EBIT	$ 215 million

Step 2: *Estimate the tax rate (data in millions of dollars).*

Tax rate = Tax expenses divided by ***pre-tax*** profit = $40/($60 + $40) = $40/$100 = 40%

Step 3: *Calculate NOPAT.*

NOPAT = EBIT × (1 – Tax rate) = ($215 million) × (1 – 0.40) = $129 million

Step 4: *Estimate the amount of capital employed (in millions of dollars).*

Capital Employed		December 31, 2009		December 31, 2010
Total debt capital		$160		$140
Adjusted equity capital		282		388
Book value of equity	$200		$260	
Accumulated bad debt allowance	7		13	
Accumulated goodwill impairment	20		45	
Capitalized R&D	55		70	
Total capital employed		$442		$528

Step 5: *Calculate EVA given that ADC has an estimated weighted average cost of capital (WACC) of 11 percent (data in millions of dollars).*

EVA(Beginning capital employed) = $129 – 11%[$442] = $129 – $48.6 = $80.4

EVA(Average capital employed) = $129 – 11%[($442 + $528)/2] = $129 – $53.4 = $75.6

15.3 MARKET VALUE ADDED ANALYSIS.

Acquiring the inventory-control software program costing $140,000 will immediately cut *after-tax* operating profit by $140,000 × (1 – 40%), that is, $84,000, and reduce EVA by the same amount. But *all* future EVAs will rise by $10,000 because invested capital will decrease permanently by $100,000 × 10%, that is, $10,000, because of the permanent reduction in inventories. To determine the net effect on ILC's value, we must get the present value of the entire stream of

EVAs. This present value is a measure of the effect of the decision to buy the software program on ILC's market value. In other words, it is the decision's market value added (MVA). Because that MVA is positive (+\$16,000), the software acquisition is a value-creating proposition:

$$\text{MVA(Software)} = -\$84{,}000 + \frac{\$10{,}000}{0.10} = -\$84{,}000 + \$100{,}000 = +\$16{,}000$$

Note: Because the future stream of EVAs is a constant perpetuity, its present value is that constant amount divided by the cost of capital (see the valuation formula 14.7; the growth rate in EVAs is zero in our case).

15.4 MVA ANALYSIS OF THE DESIGNER DESK-LAMP PROJECT.
The estimation of the future stream of economic value added (EVAs) that the designer desk-lamp project is expected to generate is given below. It is based on data taken from Exhibit 8.3 in Chapter 8. The project's market value added (MVA) is found by discounting the stream of EVAs at 7.6 percent, the project's WACC. The solution is presented in a spreadsheet format (the lines referred to are from Exhibit 8.3).

	A	B	C	D	E	F	G
1	In thousands of dollars	Now	End Year 1	End Year 2	End Year 3	End Year 4	End Year 5
2							
3	**I. After-tax operating profit**						
4	After-tax operating profit (line 15)		\$402	\$347	\$212	\$69	–\$84
5	Exceptional gain (line 21)						60
6	**Net operating profit after tax (NOPAT)**		**\$402**	**\$347**	**\$212**	**\$69**	**–\$24**
7							
8	**II. Invested capital at the beginning of the year**						
9	Working capital requirement (line 18)	\$360	\$330	\$255	\$175	\$90	\$0
10	Net book value of fixed assets	2000	1600	1200	800	400	0
11	Total invested capital	\$2,360	\$1,930	\$1,455	\$975	\$490	\$0
12							
13	**III. Capital charge**						
14	Cost of capital	7.6%					
15	Capital charge		–\$179.36	–\$146.68	–\$110.58	–\$74.10	–\$37.24
16							
17	**IV Economic value added (EVA) and market value added (MVA)**						
18	**EVA**		**\$223**	**\$200**	**\$101**	**–\$5**	**–\$61**
19	**MVA**	**\$415.083**					
20							
21	*Rows 4, 5, 9, and 14 are data.*						
22	*Formula in cell C6 is =C4+C5. Then copy formula in cell C6 to next cells in row 6.*						

	A	B	C	D	E	F	G
23	*Formulas in cells of row 10 is initial investment less accumulated depreciation at a rate of $400 a year.*						
24	*Formula in cell B11 is =B9+B10. Then copy formula in cell B11 to next cells in row 11.*						
25	*Formula in cell C15 is =$B$14*B11. Then copy formula in cell C15 to next cells in row 15.*						
26	*Formula in cell C18 is =C6–C15. Then copy formula in cell C18 to next cells in row 18.*						
27	*Formula in cell B19 is =NPV(B14,C18:G18).*						
28							

The project's MVA of $415,083 is exactly equal to its NPV as computed in Chapter 8.

15.5 THE FINANCIAL STRATEGY MATRIX.

a. To position the four companies in the financial strategy matrix, apply the following two-step procedure.

Step 1: *Estimate each company's return spread to determine its capacity to create value.*
The return spread is the difference between a company's return on invested capital (ROIC) and its weighted average cost of capital (WACC). If the return spread is positive, so is the economic value added (EVA), and the company has created value during the period under analysis. If the return spread and EVA are negative, value has been destroyed over the diagnostic period.

Step 2: *Estimate each company's self-sustainable growth rate to determine its capacity to finance its growth through earnings retention.*
The self-sustainable growth rate (SGR) is equal to the retention rate *(b)* multiplied by return on equity (ROE). Compare each company's SGR with its growth in sales. If the growth rate in sales is higher than the SGR, the company is experiencing a cash shortage or deficit. If the growth rate in sales is lower than the SGR, the company is experiencing a cash surplus.

We have the following:

Company	ROIC – WACC	*b* × ROE = SGR	Growth in sales – SGR
A. Transportation	8% – 10% = –2%	0.50 × 12% = 6%	8% – 6% = +2%
B. Restaurants	15% – 12% = +3%	0.60 × 20% = 12%	15% – 12% = +3%
C. Beverages	8% – 9% = –1%	0.75 × 12% = 9%	7% – 9% = –2%
D. Food	13% – 11% = +2%	0.40 × 15% = 6%	4% – 6% = –2%

The transportation company destroys value and is short of cash (point A). The restaurant company creates value and is short of cash (point B). The beverages company is destroying value but generating a cash surplus (point C). The food company is creating value and generating a cash surplus (point D).

b. Refer to Exhibit 15.9 and the corresponding text in the chapter, where you will find a summary of the decisions/actions that Amalgamated Industries should take regarding each one of the four companies.

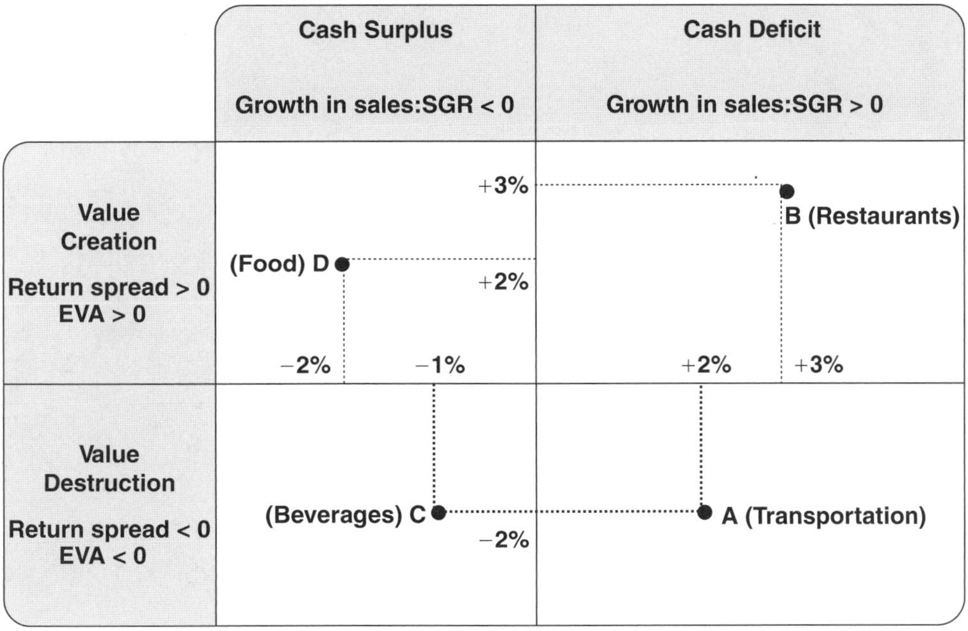
Cash Surplus
Growth in sales:SGR < 0
Cash Deficit
Growth in sales:SGR > 0
Value Creation
Return spread > 0
EVA > 0
Value Destruction
Return spread < 0
EVA < 0
+3%
B (Restaurants)
(Food) D
+2%
−2%
−1%
+2%
+3%
(Beverages) C
A (Transportation)
−2%

GLOSSARY

Terms are followed by the chapter number in which they appear.
Bold terms in a definition are defined elsewhere in the glossary.

AAR (7) *See* average accounting return.

Accelerated depreciation method (2) **Depreciation** method according to which annual **depreciation expenses** are higher in the early years of an **asset's** life and lower in the later years. *See* **straight-line depreciation method.**

Accounting exposure (14) Effect of changes in **exchange rates** on **balance sheet** and **income statement** accounts. Same as **translation exposure.**

Accounting life (8) Number of years over which an **asset** is depreciated. *See* **economic life.**

Accounting period (2) Time period covered by a **financial statement,** usually one year but sometimes shorter.

Accounting principles (2) Rules governing the systematic collection, organization, and presentation of financial information. Same as **accounting standards.**

Accounting standards (2) *See* **accounting principles.**

Accounts payable (1, 2) Cash owed by a firm to its suppliers for purchases made on credit and not yet paid; reported in the firm's **balance sheet** as a **current liability.** Same as **payables, trade payables,** and **trade creditors.**

Accounts receivable (1, 2) Cash owed to a firm by its customers for sales made on credit and not yet paid; reported in the firm's **balance sheet** as a **current asset.** Same as **receivables, trade receivables,** and **trade debtors.**

Accrual accounting (2) Accounting system with reporting based on the **realization principle** and the **matching principle.**

Accrued expenses (2) **Liabilities** other than **accounts payable** that arise from the lag between the date at which these expenses have been incurred and the date at which they are paid.

Accumulated depreciation (1, 2) The sum of the periodic **depreciation expenses** deducted from the **gross value** of a **fixed asset** to obtain its **net book value.** *See* Exhibit 2.3 and **acquisition cost principle.**

Acid test (3) *See* **quick ratio.**

Acquisition cost principle (2) Asset valuation principle according to which the **net book value** of a **fixed asset** is equal to its purchase price less the **accumulated depreciation** since that **asset** was bought. Same as **historical cost principle.**

Actual cash-flow principle (8) A capital budgeting principle according to which the **cash outflows** and **cash inflows** associated with an investment decision must be estimated at the time they actually occur.

ADF (6) *See* annuity discount factor.

Adjusted present value (APV) (12) A valuation method according to which the value of a firm's **assets** is equal to the sum of (1) their value assuming that they are financed only with **equity capital (unlevered asset value),** and (2) the **present value** of the tax savings provided by the portion of the **assets** financed with debt.

After-tax cost of debt (1, 10) (Pre-tax **cost of debt**) times (1 minus the marginal corporate tax rate). *See* equation 10.3.

Agency cost of debt financing (11) Costs associated with debt financing (and borne by **shareholders**) arising when lenders impose **restrictive covenants** that limit the firm's flexibility (for example, the **dividend** the firm can pay or the **assets** it can sell). *See* **bonding costs** and **monitoring costs.**

Agency cost of equity financing (11) Costs associated with **equity capital** (and borne by **shareholders**) arising when a firm's managers (acting as agents of **shareholders**) make decisions that benefit them at the expense of **shareholders.**

Agency problem (11) Problem arising from the separation of ownership and **control** of a firm.

Aggressive (financing) strategy (3) A firm's financing strategy that uses short-term funds to finance a portion of the firm's long-term investments. *See* **matching strategy** and **conservative strategy.**

Allowance for bad debts (15) **Provision** for the possible uncollectibility of **accounts receivable.**

Allowance for doubtful accounts (2) Accounts arising when it is expected that some customers will not meet their payment obligations toward the firm. *See* **allowance for bad debts.**

Alternative investment (6) An investment used as a benchmark for evaluating a project. The **alternative investment** must have the same **risk,** tax, **liquidity,** and other characteristics as the project. *See* **proxies** and **pure-plays.**

American option (13) An **option** that can be exercised at any time before the option's **maturity date.** *See* **European option.**

Amortization (2) The process of converting the cost of an **intangible asset,** such as **goodwill,** into periodic expenses reported in the firm's **income statement.** When the **asset** is **tangible,** the same process is called **depreciation.**

Annual report (2) Public report that is prepared by a firm annually and that contains the year's **financial statements.**

Annuity (6, 9) A cash-flow stream that is composed of a sequence of equal and uninterrupted periodic cash flows.

Annuity discount factor (ADF) (6) A **discount factor** that gives the **present value** of an **annuity.** *See* Appendix 6.1.

Appreciation (currency) (14) Increase in the value of one currency expressed in terms of another currency.

APV (12) *See* adjusted present value.

Arbitrage transaction (14) Transaction that attempts to take advantage of discrepancies between **asset** prices.

Arbitrageurs (14) Parties involved in an **arbitrage transaction.**

Arrearage (9) Refers to unpaid dividends for **preferred stock.** *See* Exhibit 9.12.

As-is value (1, 12) *See* **stand-alone value.**

Ask price (13) The price at which a trader in the market is willing to sell. Same as **offer price.** *See* **bid price.**

Asset (1, 2) An economic resource that is expected to generate a profit in the future. In financial accounting, assets refer to what **shareholders** collectively own on the date of the **balance sheet.**

Asset-based borrowing (9) Loans extended with **tangible assets** pledged as **collateral** or guarantee.

Asset beta (10, 12) The **beta** of a firm's stock if the firm is all-equity financed. Same as **unlevered beta.** *See* equation 10.7 and **equity beta.**

Asset multiple (12) A firm's asset value (usually its **enterprise value**) divided by a measure of its operating profit (usually its **EBITDA**). *See* **EBIDA multiple.**

Asset turnover (5) Sales divided by assets.

Asymmetric information (11) A situation that arises when managers (as insiders to the firm) know more about the firm's current performance and future prospects than do outsiders.

Average age of accounts receivable (3) *See* **average collection period.**

Average accounting return (of a project) (7) Average **earnings after tax** expected from a project divided by the project's average **book value.**

Average collection period (3) **Accounts receivable** at the end of the period divided by the average daily sales during that period. A measure of operating efficiency. *See* equation 3.8.

Average cost method (2) Inventory valuation method that assigns to all units in **inventory** the average cost of the units purchased. *See* **first-in, first-out (FIFO)** and **last-in, first-out (LIFO) methods.**

Average payment period (3) **Accounts payable** at the end of the period divided by the average daily **purchases** during that period. *See* equation 3.9.

Avoidable costs (8) Costs that can be saved if an investment is not undertaken.

Balance sheet (1, 2) **Financial statement** reporting, at a given date, the total amount of **assets** held by a firm and the **liabilities** and **owners' equity** that finance these **assets.** *See* equations 2.1 and 2.2, Exhibit 2.1, and **managerial balance sheet.**

Bank prime rate (9) The rate **banks** charge their most creditworthy customers.

Bankruptcy (11) A legal procedure through which the ownership of a firm's **assets** is transferred to **debt holders.**

Basis point (9, 13) One-hundredth of 1 percent. For example, 0.12 percent is equal to 12 basis points.

Bearer bonds/securities (9) **Bonds/securities** that do not indicate the holder's name. *See* **registered securities.**

Benchmark rate (9) Rate to which the **coupon rate** of a **floating rate bond** is linked.

Best efforts basis (9) A method of distributing **securities** whereby an **investment bank** undertakes to do its best to sell on behalf of the firm the **securities** the firm has issued.

Beta (coefficient) (10, 12) A measure of risk based on the sensitivity of an individual stock's returns to changes in the returns of a broad **stock market** index. Same as **systematic risk, market risk,** and **undiversifiable risk.**

Bid-ask spread (13) The difference between the **bid price** and the **ask price.**

Bidder (12) A firm that wants to acquire all or a portion of another firm's shares. *See* **takeover.**

Bid price (13) Price at which a trader in a market is willing to buy. *See* **ask price.**

Bond (1, 9) A debt **security** acknowledging a **creditor** relationship with the issuing firm and stipulating the conditions and terms under which the money is borrowed and repaid. *See* **century-, convertible-, Eurodollar-, floating-rate-, foreign-, perpetual-, Samurai-, Shogun-, Yankee-, zero-coupon bonds** and **Eurobonds.**

Bonding costs (11) Costs (borne by **shareholders**) resulting from lenders placing restrictions on managerial flexibility. *See* **covenants** and **monitoring costs.**

Bond market (9) Market where **bonds** are issued and traded.

Bond rating (9) Rating assigned by an agency (such as Standard & Poor's or Moody's Investors Service) that provides an assessment of the **bond's credit risk.**

Bond value (9) **Present value** of a **bond's** expected cash-flow stream discounted at a rate that reflects the risk of that cash-flow stream. *See* equation 9.4 and Appendix 9.1.

Bond value of a convertible bond (9) Value of a **convertible bond** if it did not have a **conversion option.**

Book runner (9) *See* **originating house** and **lead manager.**

Book value multiple (12) Share price divided by **book-value-of- equity** per share. Same as **price-to-book ratio.** Used to value a firm. *See* **valuation by comparables.**

Book value (of asset) (2) Value at which the **asset** is shown in the firm's **balance sheet.** Same as accounting value.

Book value of equity (1, 2) *See* **owners' equity.**

Bottom line (1, 2) *See* **earnings after tax.**

Brokers (9) Individuals or institutions that trade **securities** on behalf of a third party and do not own the **securities.**

Business assets (5, 12) **Working capital requirement** plus **net fixed assets.** *See* **enterprise value.**

Business cycle (of a firm) (1) Sequence of events starting with the acquisition of **assets** to generate sales, produce profits, pay **dividends**, retain earnings, build up **equity capital**, raise new debt, and grow the business via **asset** acquisition, which starts the cycle again. *See* Exhibit 1.4.

Business risk (1, 5, 10, 11, 13) The cumulative effect of **macro risk**, **strategic risk**, and **operational risk**, stemming from the firm's inability to know for certain the outcome of its current investing and operating activities and decisions. *See* Exhibits 1.10, 13.2, and 13.4.

Callable bond (9) A **bond** that gives the issuer the **option** to redeem (repay) the **bond** before it reaches its **maturity date.**

Call option (9, 13) A contract that gives the holder the right (with no obligation) to buy a fixed number of shares or a certain amount of currency at a fixed price during the life of the option (**American option**) or on its **expiration date (European option)**. *See* **put option.**

Call provision (9) **Option** available to a **bond** issuer to repay the **bond** before it reaches its **maturity date.** This provision can be immediate or **deferred.** *See* **call value** and **callable bond.**

Call value (9) The price at which the issuer can buy a **callable bond** from its holder.

CAPEX (1) *See* capital expenditure.

CAPM (10) *See* capital asset pricing model.

Capital asset(s) (2) *See* **noncurrent assets.**

Capital asset pricing model (CAPM) (10) A formula according to which a **security's** expected return is equal to the **risk-free rate** plus a **risk premium.** It can be used to estimate the **cost of equity** of a firm or a project. *See* equations 10.10 and 10.11.

Capital budgeting decision (1, 6) *See* **capital investment decision.**

Capital employed (1, 3, 5, 15) The sum of **owners' equity** and all borrowed funds (short and long term). Equal to **invested capital.** *See* **managerial balance sheet** and Exhibit 3.2.

Capital expenditure (CAPEX) (1) New investment in **fixed assets.**

Capital expenditure decision (1, 6) *See* **capital investment decision.**

Capital investment decision (6) The decision to spend cash now to acquire long-lived **assets** that will be a source of cash flows in the future. *See* **diversification, expansion, replacement,** and **required investments.**

Capitalization (of research and development [R&D]) (15) Conversion of R&D expenses into **assets** reported in the **balance sheet.**

Capital rationing (6) Limit on the amount of capital that can be used to finance investment projects.

Capital structure (1, 5) The amount of debt relative to **equity capital** a firm should adopt to finance its assets. Same as **financial structure decision.** *See* **target capital structure** and **optimal capital structure.**

Capital turnover (5, 15) Sales divided by **invested capital.** A measure of the efficiency with which **invested capital** is managed. *See* equation 5.4.

Captive finance subsidiary (9) A finance subsidiary owned by a firm.

Carry back (8, 10) Tax rule that allows a firm to deduct current interest expenses from *past* profits.

Carry forward (8, 10) Tax rule that allows a firm to deduct current interest expenses from *future* profits.

Cash and cash-equivalent (1, 2, 3) Cash in hand, cash on deposit with banks, and short-term liquid investments with less than a year's **maturity (marketable securities).**

Cash conversion period or cycle (3) *See* **cash-to-cash period.**

Cash dividend (1, 2, 10) The portion of a firm's **net profit** distributed to **shareholders** in cash. *See* **dividend.**

Cash flow from (business) assets (CFA) (4, 12) **Net cash flow** generated by a firm's **business assets.** Often referred to as **free cash flow.** *See* equations 4.5 and 12.5.

Cash-flow statement (4) **Financial statement** reporting how a firm's cash position has changed during a particular period of time. *See* **statement of cash flows.**

Cash inflow (4) Amount of cash or money that comes into a firm during a given period of time.

Cash outflow (4) Amount of cash or money that goes out of a firm during a given period of time.

Cash-to-cash period or cycle (3) Period between the date a firm pays its suppliers and the date it collects its invoices from customers. Same as **cash conversion period** or **cycle.**

CD (2, 9) *See* certificate of deposit.

Century bonds (9) **Bonds** with a 100-year **maturity.**

Certificates of deposit (CDs) (2, 9) Short-term **securities** sold by banks in the **money markets** to raise cash.

Certification role (9) Role played by **underwriters** with respect to guaranteeing the quality of the underwritten **securities.**

CFA (4, 12) *See* cash flow from assets.

Characteristic line (10) A line whose slope measures the sensitivity of a stock's returns to changes in the returns of a market index. *See* **beta coefficient.**

Cleanup clause (9) Loan clause that requires the firm to be completely out of debt to the bank for at least one month during the year.

COGS (2) *See* cost of goods sold.

Coinsurance effect (12) Describes a situation in which merged firms are perceived by their **creditors** to be less likely to fail as a combination than as separate entities.

Collateral (9, 12) Any **assets** pledged as guarantee to a lender in case the borrower defaults.

Commercial bank(s) (1, 9) **Financial intermediaries** that take deposits, make payments, and extend loans.

Commercial paper (CP) (1, 2, 9) **Unsecured security** issued by firms to raise short-term funds in the **money market.**

Common stock (2, 9) Certificate issued by a firm to raise **equity capital** that represents a specified share of total equity funds. *See* **stock certificate** and Exhibit 9.12.

Common stock (account) (2) Balance sheet account indicating the number of shares the firm has issued since its creation multiplied by the **par** or **stated value** of the shares. *See* Exhibit 2.5.

Comparables (12) *See* **valuation by comparables.**

Compensating balances (3) Deposits that banks may require their corporate clients to maintain with them in exchange for services they provide to the firm.

Compounded value (6) **Future value** of an amount of money growing at a particular compound (or growth) rate for a given number of years.

Compound factor (6) **Future value** of one dollar growing at a particular compound (or growth) rate for a given number of years.

Compounding (6) The process of finding the **future value** given the **present value.** The reverse of **discounting.**

Conglomerate merger (1, 12) Combination of unrelated businesses for which there are no obvious **synergies.**

Conservatism principle (2) States that **assets** and **liabilities** should be reported in **financial statements** at a value that would be least likely to overstate **assets** or to understate **liabilities.**

Conservative (financing) strategy (3) The use of long-term funds to finance both long-term investments and a portion of short-term investments. *See* **aggressive strategy** and **matching strategy.**

Constant annual equivalent cash flow (6) An equivalent stream of equal annual cash flows with the same **present value** as another stream with variable annual cash flows. *See* Appendix 6.1 and equation A6.4.

Constant growth dividend discount model (9) Formula that gives the value of a firm's equity as the **present value** of its expected future **dividend** stream discounted at a rate that reflects the risk of that **dividend** stream, when the **dividends** are assumed to grow forever at a constant rate. *See* equation 9.7 and Appendix 9.1. Also known as the Gordon Model.

Contingent value rights (CVR) (9) **Put options** sold by a firm that give the holder the right to sell a fixed number of shares to the issuing firm at a fixed priced during the life of the right.

Contingent voting rights (9) Right given to holders of **preferred stock** to elect members to the board of directors if the company has skipped **dividend** payments for a specified number of quarters.

Contractual exposure (14) Effect of changes in **exchange rates** on the firm's cash flows generated by *past* (contractual) transactions denominated in foreign currency and still outstanding. Same as **transaction exposure.** *See* **economic exposure.**

Control (retention of) (11) Refers to the policies adopted by current owners or management to prevent any outsiders from sharing or influencing the firm's operation and strategy. *See* Exhibit 11.17.

Conversion premium (9) Difference between the **conversion price** of a **convertible bond** and the current price of the **stock,** if the former is higher, divided by the current stock price.

Conversion price (9) Price at which the holder of a **convertible bond** has the right to buy one share of the firm's **common stock.**

Conversion ratio (9) The number of shares into which each **convertible bond** can be converted.

Conversion value (9) The current price of the **stock** multiplied by the number of shares to which the **convertible bond** can be converted.

Convertible bond (9) A **bond** that the holder can convert into the firm's **common stock.** *See* **conversion premium, conversion price, conversion ratio,** and **conversion value.**

Corporate bond (9) Debt **securities** issued by firms that usually have a **maturity** exceeding ten years and trade in the **bond market.** *See* **primary** and **secondary markets.**

Corporate note (9) Debt **securities** issued by firms that usually have a **maturity** between one and ten years.

Corporate risk (13) A risk not captured by a project, but that affects the firm.

Cost of capital (1, 6, 10) The return expected by investors for the **capital** they supply to firms. Also, the highest return on an **alternative investment** with the same risk as the investment under consideration. *See* **firm's cost of capital** and **project's cost of capital.**

Cost of debt (1, 10) The cost of borrowing new funds. *See* equations 10.2 and 10.3.

Cost of equity (1, 10) Rate of return required by the firm's owners on their **equity capital** used to finance the firm's **assets** or a particular project. Can be estimated with the **constant growth dividend discount model** (*see* equation 10.5) or the **capital asset pricing model** (*see* equation 10.11).

Cost of goods sold (COGS) (2) The cost of the goods the firm has sold during the accounting period; reported in the **income statement** as expenses.

Cost of sales (2) *See* **cost of goods sold.**

Cost synergy (12) Cost reductions resulting from combining the operations of two or more firms. *See* **market synergies.**

Country risk (14) The risk that the cash flows from a project may be affected by changes in local regulations governing foreign investments. A form of **political risk.**

Coupon payment (9) The periodic (contractual) interest payment paid to bondholders over the life of a **bond.**

Coupon rate (9) **Coupon payment** divided by the **face value** of a **bond.**

Covenants (restrictive) (9, 11) Conditions imposed by lenders and stipulated in a bond **indenture** that require managers to achieve certain financial targets or refrain from certain actions that may be detrimental to lenders' interests.

CP (1, 2, 9) *See* commercial paper.

Credit line (2, 3, 9) A nonbinding arrangement in which a **bank** lends a firm a stated maximum amount of money over a fixed but renewable period of time, usually one year. In general, no fee is charged but a **compensating balance** is required. Same as **line of credit.**

Credit market (9) Market in which debt **securities** are issued and traded.

Creditors (1) Parties to whom a firm owes money, including lenders and suppliers.

Credit rating (9, 11) Rating that provides an overall assessment of a borrower's **credit risk.** *See* **credit rating agency.**

Credit rating agency (11) An agency, such as Standard & Poor's or Moody's Investment Service, that provides **credit ratings.**

Credit risk (9, 13) The risk that a borrower will be unable to service its debt. *See* **debt service.**

Cross rates (13) **Foreign exchange rates** between two currencies computed from their exchange rate with a third currency.

Credit spread (9) *See* yield spread.

Currency futures contract (13) Standardized **forward currency contracts** traded in **futures markets**.

Currency option hedge (13) **Hedging** with currency options.

Currency rate (13) *See* **foreign-exchange rate.**

Currency risk (1, 9, 13) Risk arising from unexpected changes in the **exchange rate** between two currencies. *See* **foreign-exchange risk.**

Currency swap (contract) (13) Agreement with a bank to exchange a set of future cash flows denominated in one currency for another set denominated in another currency.

Current assets (2) **Assets** that are expected to be turned into cash within one year. Same as **short-term assets.** Reported in the **balance sheet.**

Current liabilities (2) Obligations of a firm that must be paid within one year. Same as **short-term liabilities.** Reported in the **balance sheet.**

Current maturity (9) At any point in time, the time remaining until a **bond** is redeemed (repaid).

Current method (of translation) (14) A method of translating the **financial statements** of a foreign business unit. **Balance sheets** accounts are translated at the **exchange rate** prevailing at the date of the balance sheet. **Revenues** and **expenses** in the **income statement** are translated at the rate when they occur or at the average rate during the period covered by the statement. *See* Appendix 14.1.

Current ratio (3) **Current assets** divided by **current liabilities.** A measure of **liquidity.** *See* equation 3.13 and **quick ratio.**

Current yield (9) A **bond's coupon payment** divided by its price.

Cutoff period (7) In **capital budgeting,** the period (usually in years) below which a project's **payback period** must fall in order to accept the project.

Days of sales outstanding (DSO) (3) *See* **average collection period.**

DCF (6, 12) *See* discounted cash flow.

Dealers (9) Individuals or institutions that trade securities that they own. *See* **brokers.**

Debentures (9) **Bonds** supported by the general credit standing of the issuing firm (U.S. definition).

Debt capacity (11) The ability to quickly raise debt in the future if a need for funds arises unexpectedly.

Debt capital (1) **Capital** provided by borrowed funds.

Debt holders (1, 9) Holders of loans, leasing agreements, **corporate bonds,** and similar **liabilities** issued by firms to raise **debt capital.**

Debt ratio (5) A measure of **financial leverage.** Usually identified as the **debt-to-invested capital ratio** or the **debt-to-equity ratio.**

Debt-to-equity ratio (1, 5, 11) Total interest-bearing debt divided by **owners' equity.** A measure of **financial leverage.**

Debt-to-invested capital ratio (5) Debt divided by the sum of debt and equity.

Default risk (9) *See* **credit risk.**

Deferred call provision (9) Provision that allows the issuer of a **callable bond** to repay (or call) the bond only after a specified date (first date of call).

Deferred tax (liability) (2) Taxes owed to the tax authority originating from the difference between the amount of tax due on the firm's reported pretax profit and the amount of tax claimed by the tax authorities.

Depreciation (accounting) (2) The process of periodic and systematic value-reduction of the **gross value of fixed assets** over their **accounting life.**

Depreciation (currency) (14) Reduction in the value of one currency expressed in terms of another currency.

Depreciation charge (2) *See* **depreciation expense.**

Depreciation expense(s) (1, 2) The portion of the cost of a **fixed asset** that is expensed during the accounting period and reported in the **income statement.** Same as **depreciation charge.**

DF (1, 4) *See* discount factor.

Differential cash flows (8) *See* **incremental cash flows.**

Dilution (9, 11) Reduction in the fraction of a firm's equity held by its existing **shareholders** after the firm sells **common stock** to new investors.

Direct costs of financial distress (11) The actual costs the firm will incur if it becomes legally bankrupt, such as payments to lawyers and other third parties. *See* **indirect costs of financial distress.**

Direct financing (9) When firms raise funds by issuing **securities** that are held by ultimate savers (**household sector**) instead of **financial intermediaries.** *See* **indirect financing.**

Direct lease (9) A **financial lease** involving a straight contract between the owner of an **asset** (the **lessor**) and the user of that **asset** (the **lessee**).

Discounted cash-flow (DCF) value/valuation (6, 12) The value today of an expected future cash-flow stream discounted at a rate that reflects its **risk.** The **DCF value** of a firm's equity equals the **DCF value** of its **business assets** minus the value of its debt. Same as **present value.** *See* **discounting.**

Discounted payback period (7) **Capital budgeting** method that measures a project's **payback period** with cash flows that have been discounted to the present at the project's **cost of capital.** *See* **discounted payback period rule.**

Discounted payback period rule (7) Accept (reject) the project if its discounted payback period is shorter (longer) than a given **cutoff period.**

Discount (from par value) (9) The difference between the price of a **bond** and its **face value,** if the former is lower.

Discount factor (DF) (6) **Present value,** at a particular **discount rate,** of one dollar to be received after a specified number of years.

Discounting (1, 6) The process used to convert future cash flows into their equivalent value today.

Discount rate (1, 6) Rate at which future cash flows are discounted to the present. *See* **discounting.**

Discretionary cash flow (4) Cash flow available to the firm for strategic investment and financing decisions after all of the firm's financial obligations are met.

Diversifiable risk (10) Risk that can be eliminated through portfolio diversification. Same as **unsystematic risk** or company-specific risk.

Diversification investments (6) Investments in areas unrelated to the existing activities of the firm.

Dividend (2) The portion of a firm's **net profit** paid out to its owners in cash.

See Exhibit 2.2 and **cash dividend, dividend payout ratio, dividend policy,** and **dividend yield.**

Dividend discount model (DDM) (9, 10) A formula that values a firm's equity as the present value of the entire stream of cash dividends the firm is expected to generate in the future. *See* Appendix 9.1 and **constant growth dividend discount model.**

Dividend payout ratio (1, 5) **Dividends** divided by **net profit.** *See* **dividend policy.**

Dividend policy (11) The decision regarding the portion of a year's profit that should be paid out in the form of cash dividends to the firm's **shareholders.** *See* **stable dividend policy.**

Dividend yield (10, 11) **Dividend** per share divided by share price. *See* equation 10.5.

Doubtful accounts (2) *See* **allowance for doubtful accounts.**

Earnings after tax (EAT) (1, 2) **Revenues** minus all **expenses,** including interest and tax expenses. Same as **net income, net profit,** and **bottom line.**

Earnings before interest and tax (EBIT) (1, 2) Difference between the firm's **operating profit** and any **extraordinary items** reported in its **income statement.**

Earnings before interest, tax, depreciation, and amortization (EBITDA) (4, 12) **Revenues** minus all **operating expenses** excluding **depreciation** and **amortization.**

Earnings before tax (EBT) (1, 2) **Earnings before interest and tax** minus net interest expenses.

Earnings multiple (5, 12) Share price divided by the firm's **earnings per share.** Same as **price-to-earnings ratio.** Used to value a firm. *See* **valuation by comparables.**

Earnings per share (EPS) (5) **Earnings after tax** divided by the total number of shares **outstanding.** *See* equation 5.13.

EAT (1, 2) *See* earnings after tax;

EBIT (1, 2) *See* earnings before interest and tax

EBITDA (4, 12) *See* earnings before interest, tax, depreciation, and amortization

EBITDA multiple (12) **Enterprise value** divided by **EBITDA;** used to estimate a firm's enterprise value. *See* **valuation by comparables.**

EBT (1, 2) *See* earnings before tax.

Economic exposure (14) Effect of changes in **exchange rates** on the value of the firm's *future* cash flows generated either by *past* and *known* transactions (**contractual or transaction exposure**) or by *future* and *uncertain* transactions (**operating exposure**).

Economic life (8) Number of years over which a project adds value to a firm, as opposed to the number of years over which it is depreciated (**accounting life**).

Economic payback period (7) *See* **discounted payback period.**

Economic profit (15) *See* **economic value added.**

Economic risk (13) Risk arising from unexpected sales fluctuations because of the uncertain economic environment in which firms operate. *See* **business risk** and Exhibit 13.4.

Economic value added (EVA) (15) **Net operating profit after tax (NOPAT)** minus a charge for the **capital** consumed to achieve that profit. *See* equations 15.5 and 15.6. Same as **economic profit.** *See* **market value added.**

Economies of scale (12) The ability of a firm to reduce its average costs of production and distribution because of size. A motivation to acquire other companies. *See* **cost** and **market synergies.**

Effective (corporate) tax rate (5) The tax rate at which a firm actually pays its taxes, which may differ from the **statutory corporate tax rate** if some of the firm's earnings are taxed at a different rate.

Efficient (securities) markets (1, 9) Markets in which security (share) prices adjust to new and relevant information as soon as it becomes available to market participants.

Enterprise value (12) A firm's market value of equity plus its market value of debt less its holding of cash and other financial assets. It is the value of the firm's **business assets.** *See* equation 12.1, Exhibit 12.5, and **EBITDA multiple.**

Entry barriers (1) Barriers that are costly enough to discourage potential competitors from entering a particular market.

EPS (12) *See* earnings per share

Equipment financing loan (9) A medium- to long-term loan backed by a piece of machinery. *See* **collateral.**

Equity beta (10) The **beta** of a firm's **common stock.** Same as **levered beta** and **market beta.**

Equity capital (1, 3) Funds contributed by **shareholders** that are equal to the difference, at a particular date, between what a firm's **shareholders** collectively own, called **assets,** and what they owe, called **liabilities.** Same as **equity funding, owners' equity, shareholders' equity or funds,** or **net asset value.**

Equity funding (1) *See* **equity capital.**

Equity kicker (9) The **conversion option** of a **convertible bond.**

Equity multiples (12) Ratios used to value a firm based on **valuation by comparables.** Same as **market multiples.**

Equity valuation models (12) Valuation models that provide a direct estimation of a firm's equity value. *See* Appendix 12.1.

Equity multiplier (5) **Invested capital** divided by **owners' equity.** A measure of **financial leverage.**

Eurobonds (9) **Bonds** issued in the **Euromarket.**

Eurocommercial paper (EuroCP) (9) **Commercial paper** issued in the **Euromarket.**

Eurodollar bonds (9) **Bonds** denominated in U.S. dollars that are sold simultaneously to investors in several countries via the **Euromarket.**

Euroequity (9) Equity issued in the **Euromarket.**

Euromarket (9) A market that is outside the direct control and jurisdiction of the issuer's country of origin.

European option (13) An **option** that can be only exercised on the **maturity date** of the **option.** *See* **American option.**

Euroyen bonds (9) Eurobonds sold by firms denominated in Japanese yen.

EV (12) *See* enterprise value.

EVA (15) *See* economic value added.

Event risk (13) Unexpected incident that reduces the firm's value if and when it occurs.

Excess cash (3) Amount of cash held by a firm in excess of the cash needed to support its operating activities.

Exchange control risk (13) Unexpected changes in the *fixed* exchange rate between two currencies. *See* Exhibit 13.2.

Exchange rate (13) The price one has to pay in one country's currency to buy one unit of another country's currency. Same as **foreign-exchange rate** or **currency rate.**

Exchange-rate risk (13) Risk borne by firms with foreign operations that originates from unexpected changes in the **exchange rate** between two currencies.

Exercise price (currency option) (13) The fixed **exchange rate** at which a currency can be bought or sold in an **option contract.** Same as **strike price.**

Exercise price (warrant) (9) The fixed price at which the holder of a **warrant** has the right to buy shares. Same as **strike price.**

Exit barriers (5) Barriers, such as high capital investment, that significantly reduce a firm's ability to leave an industry by selling its **assets** rapidly and easily.

Exit strategy (12) The way **leveraged buyout (LBO)** investors cash in on their investment by selling some (or all) of their shares after a period of time to other investors or through an **initial price offering (IPO).**

Expansion investments (6) Projects that result in additional sales revenues, margins, and **working capital requirement.**

Expected multiple (12) **Multiples** calculated using a forecast of future financial data; used to value a firm. *See* **historical multiples** and **valuation by comparables.**

Expense (1, 2) A firm's activity that results in a decrease in the value of **owners' equity.**

Expiration date (option) (13) The fixed **settlement date** of an **option** contract. Same as **maturity date.**

Ex-rights shares (9) Shares for which **rights** were issued but that are no longer traded with their **rights** attached. *See* **right, rights-on shares,** and equations 9.2 and 9.3.

External funds need (9) **Internally generated funds** less **funding needs.** *See* equation 9.1.

Face value (9) The fixed amount that has to be paid back to bondholders at the **maturity date** of a **bond.** Same as **principal, par value,** or **redemption value.**

Fair market value (2, 15) An estimate of the amount that could be received on the sale of an **asset** under normal market conditions (as opposed to an emergency or liquidating sale).

Fair price (9) Best estimate of the unobservable value of a firm's **assets** and **securities.**

FASB (4) *See* financial accounting standards board.

FCF (4, 12) *See* free cash flows.

FIFO (2) *See* first-in, first-out method.

Financial Accounting Standards Board (FASB) (2) The accounting body responsible for setting accounting standards in the United States.

Financial balance (5) Achieved when the firm can finance its growth without modifying its operating and financing policies and without issuing new equity. *See* **self-sustainable growth rate.**

Financial cost effect (5) The negative effect of an increase in debt financing on **return on equity (ROE)**—more debt means larger interest payments, which reduces **earnings after tax** (EAT) and lowers ROE. *See* **financial structure effect.**

Financial cost ratio (5) **Earnings before tax (EBT)** divided by **earnings before interest and tax (EBIT).** A measure of **financial leverage** based on **income statement** data. *See* **financial structure ratio** and **financial leverage multiplier.**

Financial cost risk (3, 13) Risk arising from unexpected changes in the level of interest rates that affect the firm's future cost of debt financing. *See* **refinancing risk** and Exhibit 13.4.

Financial distress (11) Situation arising when a firm finds it increasingly difficult to service its debt. *See* **debt service** and **financial distress costs.**

Financial distress costs (11) Direct and indirect costs borne by a firm, which has excessive borrowing and difficulties servicing its debt, and that reduce the firm's value. *See* **debt service** and **direct** and **indirect costs of financial distress.**

Financial distress risk (1, 12) The risk that the firm will experience **financial distress costs** as its use of debt financing rises. *See* Exhibit 13.2.

Financial flexibility (11) Having a buildup of cash that allows for immediate investment and that increases the firm's **debt capacity.** *See* Exhibit 11.17.

Financial intermediaries (9) Institutions that act as middlemen between the ultimate recipients of **capital** (firms) and the ultimate suppliers of **capital (household sector).** *See* Exhibit 9.4.

Financial investment risk (13) The risks associated with the firm's holding of financial investments such as shares and bonds of other companies as well as **cash** and **marketable securities.** *See* Exhibit 13.4 as well as **price risk** and **liquidity risk.**

Financial lease (9) A long-term lease that extends over most of the **useful life** of the **asset.**

Financial leverage (5, 11) The use of debt financing to complement equity financing. Same as **gearing.**

Financial leverage multiplier (5) The **financial cost ratio** multiplied by the **financial structure ratio.** *See* equation 5.10.

Financial leverage risk (13) Increase in the volatility of operating earnings because of borrowing and fixed interest payments. *See* Exhibit 13.4.

Financial markets (1) Markets in which financial assets are traded. Same as **securities markets.** *See* **financial system.**

Financial risk (1, 5, 10, 11, 13) All the risks that result from borrowing: **financial leverage risk, financial cost risk,** and **refinancing risk.** *See* Exhibits 1.10, 13.2, and 13.4.

Financial slack (11) Cash surplus that firms may build up during good times. *See* **financial flexibility.**

Financial statements (1, 2) Formal documents issued by firms to provide financial information about their business and financial transactions. *See* **income statement** and **balance sheet.**

Financial strategy matrix (15) A diagnostic and managerial tool that compares the capacity of a particular business to create value versus its capacity to finance the growth of its sales. *See* Exhibit 15.9.

Financial structure decision (11) *See* **capital structure decision** and **target capital structure.**

Financial structure effect (5) The positive effect of an increase in debt financing on **return on equity (ROE)**—more debt means less **equity capital** and thus higher ROE. *See* **financial cost effect.**

Financial structure ratio (5) **Invested capital** divided by **owners' equity.** A measure of **financial leverage** based on **balance sheet** data. *See* **financial cost ratio** and **financial leverage multiplier.**

Financial system (9) The institutions and practices that allow the cash surplus of savers to be channeled to firms with a cash shortage.

Finished goods inventory (2) The cost of completed units not yet sold at the date of the **balance sheet.**

Firm's cost of capital (10) The return expected by investors for the **capital** they supply to fund *all* the **assets** acquired and managed by the firm.

First-in, first-out (FIFO) method (2) Inventory valuation method that assigns to all units in inventory the cost of the unit purchased first. *See* **last-in, first-out (LIFO) method** and **average cost method.**

Fisher effect (14) States that the **nominal interest rate** is the sum of the **real interest rate** and the expected inflation rate.

Fisher's intersection (7) The point at which the **net present value (NPV) profiles** of two investments intersect. *See* Exhibit 7.15.

Fixed asset (2) *See* **noncurrent asset.**

Fixed asset turnover ratio (5) Sales divided by **fixed assets.** A measure of the efficiency of **fixed assets** management. Same as **fixed asset rotation.**

Floating rate bond or **floater** (9) A **bond** whose rate is linked to another rate that is revised periodically.

Flotation costs (9, 11) Costs incurred when issuing **securities.** Same as **issuance** or **issue costs.**

Foreign bonds (9) **Bonds** issued in the domestic **bond market** of another country.

Foreign-exchange line of credit (13) A **credit line** demanded by a bank to guarantee a firm's ability to deliver on its **foreign-exchange** obligations.

Foreign-exchange market (13) Market in which currencies are bought and s old. Same as currency market.

Foreign-exchange rate (13, 14) *See* **exchange rate.**

Foreign-exchange risk (9, 13, 14) Risk arising from unexpected changes in the **exchange rate** between two currencies. *See* **currency risk.**

Foreign securities (9) **Securities** issued in the domestic market of another country.

Forward contract (currency) (13) Agreement between two parties specifying the fixed price at which two currencies will be exchanged at a specified future date **(settlement date).**

Forward hedge (13) **Hedging** with **forward contracts.**

Forward rate (13) The fixed rate at which a **forward contract** is settled.

Forward window contract (13) Similar to a standard **forward contract** except that the transaction can be settled over a period of time (the window) instead of on a fixed date.

Free cash flow (4, 12) The cash flow generated by a firm's **assets.** *See* equation 4.5. Same as **cash flow from (business) assets.**

Fundamental finance principle (1) States that a business proposal will raise the firm's value only if the **present value** of the future stream of net cash benefits the proposal is expected to generate exceeds the initial cash outlay required to undertake the proposal. Same as the **net present value (NPV) rule.**

Funding needs (9) Funds needed to finance the growth of the firm's **invested capital.** *See* **internally-generated funds** and **external funds need.**

Futures (contract) (13) A **forward contract** that has a standardized contract size and a standardized delivery date; traded on **futures markets.**

Futures hedge (13) **Hedging** with a **futures contract.**

Futures markets (13) **Organized exchanges** in which **futures contracts** are traded.

Future value (6) The value at a future date of an amount deposited today that grows at a given compound, or growth, rate.

Gearing (5, 11) Same as **financial leverage.**

General cash offering (9) The issuance and sale of a firm's **securities** to any investor, including current **shareholders.** Same as **public offering.** *See* Exhibit 9.7 and **rights offering.**

Generally Accepted Accounting Principles (GAAP) (2) Accounting standards and rules that firms use to prepare their financial statements.

Going concern (12) An assumption according to which a firm will operate forever.

Goodwill (2, 15) The difference between the (higher) price at which a firm has been acquired and either its reported **net book value** or its estimated **fair value.**

Government bills (2) Short-term **marketable securities** issued by governments.

Gross profit (2) The difference between the firm's net sales and its **cost of goods sold.**

Gross value (of fixed assets) (2) The purchase price of **fixed assets** reported in the **balance sheet.** Same as **historical price.** *See* **net fixed assets.**

Ground floor financing (12) **Equity capital** financing in a **leveraged buyout (LBO).**

Hedge (currency) (13) The process of protecting the value of an **asset** or a **liability** from **currency** fluctuations.

Historical cost (principle) (2) *See* **acquisition cost principle.**

Historical multiples (12) **Multiples** calculated using past financial data. Same as **trailing multiples.** *See* **expected** or **prospective multiples.** Used to value a firm. *See* **valuation by comparables.**

Homemade diversification (12) The **diversification** investors can achieve themselves by combining shares of different companies in their personal portfolios.

Homemade leverage (11) Personal **financial leverage** as opposed to corporate **financial leverage.**

Horizontal merger (12) Two firms in the same sector pooling their resources.

Household sector (9) The sector of the economy composed of individuals and families.

Hurdle rate (7, 10) An investment's **cost of capital** (*see* **weighted average cost of capital**) when used in comparison with the investment's **internal rate of return.** Same as **minimum required rate of return.**

IASB (2) *See* international accounting standards board.

IFRS (2) *See* international financial reporting standards.

Impairment loss (2) The difference between the carrying amount of an asset in a balance sheet and its recoverable amount if the latter is smaller.

Impairment test (2) A check to find whether the carrying amount of an asset in a balance sheet exceeds its recoverable amount.

Income statement (1, 2) **Financial statement** reporting information about the firm's activities that resulted in changes in the value of **owners' equity** during a period of time, obtained by deducting from **revenues** the corresponding **expenses** incurred during that period of time.

Incremental cash flows (8) The difference between the firm's expected cash flows if the investment is made and its expected cash flows if the investment is not undertaken. Same as **differential cash flows.**

Indenture (bonds) (9) Formal contract between a **bond** issuing firm and its lenders.

Indirect costs of financial distress (11) Costs created by the increasing probability that a firm may become bankrupt, thus preventing it from operating at maximum efficiency. Includes loss of customers, departure of key employees, and the inability to obtain credit from suppliers. *See* **direct costs of financial distress.**

Indirect financing (9) When firms raise funds by issuing **securities** that are held by **financial intermediaries** instead of ultimate "savers." *See* **direct financing.**

Indirect method (4) Method of estimating **the net operating cash flow** that starts with **earnings after tax** and adjusts them for noncash items and transactions that are not related to the firm's operating activities.

Indirect securities (9) **Securities** issued by banks (checking and savings accounts) and other **financial intermediaries** (such as insurance policies and retirement plans).

Inefficient management (hypothesis) (12) Refers to a rationale for **takeover** whereby the **target firm** is not currently managed at its optimal level and the **acquiring firm's** managers believe that they can do a better job if they buy the target firm and run it themselves.

Initial margin (13) A requirement to deposit a portion of the initial investment when trading in a **securities** or **futures market.**

Initial public offering (IPO) (9) When a firm sells equity to the public for the first time. *See* **seasoned new issue.**

Institutional investors (9) Any **financial intermediaries** that invest in the **financial markets.**

Insurance premium (13) The amount of money that must be paid to an insurance company to insure against a risk during a specific period of time.

Intangible assets (2) **Assets** such as **goodwill**, patents, trademarks, and copyrights.

Interbank (currency) market (13) The **foreign exchange market** whose major participants are large banks.

Interest coverage ratio (5) *See* **times-interest-earned ratio.**

Interest-rate parity (IRP) relation (14) States that the percentage difference between the **forward** and **spot rates** is equal to the difference in interest rates between the home and foreign markets. *See* Exhibit 14.1, equation 14.9, and Appendix 14.2.

Interest rate risk (9) Risk arising from unexpected changes in the level of interest rates that affect bond prices. *See* **market risk** and **price risk.**

Interest tax shield (11) The annual and recurrent tax saving resulting from debt financing. *See* equations 11.3 and 11.10.

Internal equity financing (1) Refers to **retained earnings,** the part of a firm's profit that the firm's owners decide to invest back into their company.

Internally generated funds (9) The sum of **retained earnings** and **depreciation expenses.** *See* equation 9.1.

Internal rate of return (IRR) (1, 7) The **discount rate** that makes the **net present value** of a project equal to zero.

Internal rate of return (IRR) rule (1, 7) Accept (reject) a proposal if its **internal rate of return (IRR)** is higher (lower) than its **weighted average cost of capital (WACC).**

International Accounting Standards Board (IASB) (2) An international accounting body responsible for setting accounting standards.

International Financial Reporting Standards (IFRS) (2) Accounting standards and rules formulated by the **International Accounting Standards Board.**

International Fisher effect (14) States that the difference in interest rates between two countries reflects the difference in their expected inflation rates. *See* equation 14.7, Exhibit 14.1, and Appendix 14.2.

In the black (2) A firm with positive **earnings after tax.** *See* **in the red.**

In the red (2) A firm with negative **earnings after tax.** *See* **in the black.**

Inventory (1, 2) Raw materials, work in process, and finished goods not yet sold, reported in the **balance sheet** as **current assets.** *See* **first-in, first-out (FIFO); last-in, first-out (LIFO);** and **average cost methods.**

Inventory turn or **turnover** (3) **Cost of goods sold** divided by ending **inventories.** *See* equation 3.7 and Exhibit 3.10. A measure of the efficiency of inventory management.

Invested capital (1, 3) The sum of **cash** and **marketable securities, working capital requirement,** and **net fixed assets.** Equal to **capital employed.** *See* equation 3.1 and the **managerial balance sheet.**

Investment banks (1, 9) **Financial intermediaries** that act as "middlemen" between firms wanting to issue **securities** to raise funds and the suppliers of **capital.** *See* **book runner, lead manager, originating house, merchant bankers,** and **underwriters.**

Investment-grade bonds (9) Highly rated **bonds** (BBB and above) that can be purchased by pension funds and other **institutional investors.** *See* **speculative grade bonds** and **bond ratings.**

IPO (9) *See* initial public offering.

IRR (1, 7) *See* internal rate of return.

Irrelevant costs (8) Costs (past or future) that the firm must bear even if the investment project is not undertaken. *See* **unavoidable costs** and **sunk costs.**

Issuance or **issue costs** (9, 11) Costs incurred when issuing **securities.** Same as **flotation costs.**

ITS (11) *See* interest tax shield.

Junior bond/debt/loan (9, 12) *See* **subordinated bond/debt/loan.**

Junk bond/debt (9) *See* **speculative grade bond/debt.**

Last-in, first-out (LIFO) method (2) Inventory valuation method that assigns to all units in inventory the cost of the unit purchased last. *See* **first-in, first-out (FIFO) method** and **average cost method.**

Law of one price (LOP) (14) States that any traded good should sell for the same price (when expressed in the same currency) regardless of the country where it is sold. *See* Appendix 14.2.

LBO (12) *See* leveraged buyout.

Leading and lagging (14) Timing the **cash inflows** and **cash outflows** from different foreign business units to reduce the firm's overall exposure to **exchange-rate risk.**

Lead manager (9) Same as **originating house** and **bookrunner.**

Lease financing (9) *See* **direct lease, financial lease, leveraged lease, operating lease,** and **sale and lease-back lease.**

Lessee (9) The user of the **asset** that is leased.

Lessor (9) The owner of the **asset** that is leased.

Leverage (11) *See* **financial leverage.**

Leveraged buyout (LBO) (12) Transaction in which a group of investors purchase a firm by borrowing an unusually large amount of debt relative to **equity capital.**

Leveraged lease (9) A **financial lease** in which the leasing company finances the purchase of the **asset** with a substantial level of debt, using the lease contract as **collateral.**

Levered assets (12) **Assets** financed with some **debt capital.**

Levered beta (10) The **beta** of a stock when the firm is indebted. Same as **equity** or **market beta.**

Liabilities (1, 2) What a firm's **shareholders** collectively owe on the date of the **balance sheet.**

LIBOR (9) *See* London interbank offering rate.

LIFO (2) *See* last-in, first-out method.

Line of credit (2, 9) Same as **credit line.**

Liquid assets (3) *See* **cash** and **cash equivalents.**

Liquidation value (12) Amount of cash that can be raised if the various items that make up a firm's **assets** are sold separately. Usually the minimum value of **assets.**

Liquidity (of a firm) (3) The ability of a firm to meet short-term recurrent cash obligations. *See* **solvency.**

Liquidity (of a market) (9) Characterizes a market in which buyers and sellers can quickly trade their **securities** at the quoted price and settle their transactions at a relatively low cost.

Liquidity (of an asset/a security) (2, 3, 9) The speed with which an asset or a **security** can be turned into cash without significant loss of value.

Liquidity ratio (3) **Net long-term financing (NLF)** divided by **working capital requirement (WCR).** A measure of a firm's **liquidity** position. *See* equation 3.6.

Liquidity risk (13) A deterioration in **money market** conditions that would prevent a firm from selling rapidly and without loss of value the **marketable securities** it holds. *See* Exhibit 13.2.

Listed securities (9) **Securities** of firms that meet a number of stringent conditions that allow them to be traded in **organized stock exchanges.** *See* **over-the-counter (OTC) market.**

London Interbank Offering Rate (LIBOR) (9) The interest rate at which international banks lend U.S. dollars to one another.

Long-term debt/liabilities (2) **Debt/liabilities** due after a period longer than one year.

Long-term financing (3) **Equity** plus **long-term debt.**

Lower-of-cost-or-market (2) Reporting method according to which **inventories** are shown in the **balance sheet** at their lowest value (their cost or their **liquidation value** if the latter is the lowest).

Macro risk (13) Economic, political, and social risk; it is a component of **business risk.** *See* Exhibit 13.2.

Managerial balance sheet (1, 3) Restructured **balance sheet** that shows **invested capital (Cash + Working capital requirement + Net fixed assets)** on one side and **capital employed (Debt + Equity capital)** on the other side. *See* Exhibit 3.2.

Managerial options (6) Options that can be exercised to alter a project during its useful life, including the options to abandon, expand, or defer a project.

Margin call (13) Call for additional deposit when the margin account has dropped below a preset level. *See* **initial margin.**

Marked-to-market (13) **Futures contracts** are marked-to-market when daily profits or losses are settled at the end of each trading day.

Marketable securities (2) Short-term, **liquid assets investments** with less than one year's **maturity** held by a firm as a cash-equivalent **asset.**

Market beta (10) **Beta** of a **stock** when the firm is indebted. Same as **equity** or **levered beta.**

Market capitalization (1, 12, 15) Market value of a firm's **equity.** Equal to its quoted price per share multiplied by the total number of shares the company has issued. Also referred to as market cap.

Market multiples (12) Ratios used to value a firm. Same as **equity multiples.** *See* **valuation by comparables.**

Market portfolio (10) A benchmark portfolio containing all the **assets** in a particular market.

Market power hypothesis (12) **Takeover** rationale according to which the acquiring firm has a larger market share after the acquisition that may enable it to raise the price of its products.

Market risk (of a bond) (9) Sensitivity of a **bond price** to changes in interest rates. *See* **interest rate risk** and **price risk.**

Market risk premium (10) The difference between the expected return on a portfolio of all existing securities and the **risk-free rate**. *See* **capital asset pricing model.**

Market synergies (12) Increased **revenues**, beyond pre-merger levels, resulting from combining the operations of two or more firms.

Market-to-book ratio (5) Share price divided by **book-value-of-equity** per share. Used to value firms. *See* **valuation by comparables.**

Market value added (MVA) of a firm (15) The difference between the **market value of a firm's capital** (equity and debt) and the amount of **capital** that **shareholders** and **debt holders** have invested in the firm.

Market value added (MVA) of an investment (15) The **present value** (at the **project's cost of capital**) of the future stream of annual **economic value added** that the project is expected to generate in the future.

Market value of capital (15) The market value of the firm's total **capital**, that is, the sum of its **market capitalization** and the market value of its **debt capital.**

Market value at risk (MVR) (13) The expected reduction in a firm's market value if a **risk** occurs. *See* equation 13.1.

Market yield (of a bond) (9, 10) The rate that makes the **bond price** equal to the **present value** of the **bond's** future cash-flow stream.

Matching principle (2) Accounting principle according to which **expenses** are recognized in the **income statement** not when they are paid but during the period when they effectively contribute to the firm's **revenues**. *See* **accrual accounting.**

Matching strategy (3) The financing of long-term investments with long-term funds, and short-term investments with short-term funds to minimize **financing cost risk** and **refinancing risk**. *See* **aggressive strategy** and **conservative strategy.**

Maturity (2, 9) A measure of the time before a **liability** is due.

Maturity date (9, 13) The date on which the **face value** of a **bond** must be repaid. The date on which an **option contract** must be settled. For an **option contract**, the **maturity date** is the same as the **expiration date.**

Members of the exchange (9) **Dealers** and **brokers** who have the right to trade in a **stock exchange.**

Mezzanine financing (12) **Junior unsecured debt** in a **leveraged buyout (LBO).**

Minimum required rate of return (7) An investment's **cost of capital** (*see* **weighted average cost of capital**) when used in comparison with the investment's **internal rate of return.** Same as **hurdle rate.**

MM theory of capital structure (11) The Modigliani and Miller theory of how changes in debt financing affect the value of a firm and its cost of capital.

Monetary/nonmonetary (translation) method (14) A method of translating the **financial statements** of a foreign business unit. Monetary **assets** (**cash** and **receivables**) and monetary **liabilities** (**payables, short-term,** and **long-term debt**) are translated at the **exchange rate** prevailing at the date of the financial statements, and nonmonetary **assets** (**inventories** and **fixed assets**) are translated at the rate that prevailed when they were purchased. *See* Appendix 14.1.

Money market (1, 9) Market in which firms raise short-term funds and **money market instruments** are issued and traded.

Money market funds (2) **Financial intermediaries** that invest in the **money market.**

Money market instruments (9) **Debt securities** with **maturity** not exceeding one year.

Monitoring costs (11) Costs resulting from lenders placing restrictions on the use of the funds they lend to companies. These costs are borne by **shareholders.**

Mortgage bond/loan (9) A mediums long-term **bond**/loan backed by real estate. *See* **collateral.**

Multiples (12) Ratios used to value firms. *See* **historical multiples, expected multiples, equity multiples, market multiples,** and **valuation by comparables.**

Mutually exclusive (investments) (6, 7) If one is chosen, the other(s) must be turned down.

MVA (15) *See* market value added.

MVR (13) *See* market value at risk.

NAL (9) *See* net advantage to leasing.

Negotiable (certificates of deposit) (9) Short-term **securities** sold by banks in the **money markets** to raise **capital.**

Negotiable (security) (9) A **security** that can be traded (exchanged among investors) in the **securities markets.**

Net advantage to leasing (NAL) (9) The **net present value** of the difference in cash flows between leasing and buying an **asset**. If **NAL** is positive, the **asset** should be leased.

Net asset value (2) The difference, at a particular date, between what a firm's **shareholders** collectively own, called **assets**, and what they owe, called **liabilities**. Same as **net worth, owners' equity, shareholders' equity,** and **shareholders' funds.**

Net book value (2) The value at which a **fixed asset** is reported in the **balance sheet.**

Net capital expenditure (12) **Capital expenditure** less cash raised from the sales of existing **assets.**

Net cash flow (2) The difference between the firm's **cash inflows** and **outflows** during an **accounting period.**

Net cash flow from financing activities (4) The net cash flow from the firm's financing activities during an **accounting period.**

Net cash flow from investing activities (4) The net cash flow from the firm's investing activities during an **accounting period.**

Net earnings (2) Same as **earnings after tax, net profit,** and **net income.** Also called the **bottom line.**

Net fixed assets (1) Long-term **assets**, such as equipment, machinery, and buildings, from which **accumulated depreciation** expenses have been deducted. *See* Exhibit 1.6 and **fixed assets** and **gross value of fixed assets.**

Net income (2) *See* **earnings after tax.**

Net interest expenses (2) The difference between the interest expenses and interest income during an **accounting period.**

Net long-term financing (NLF) (3) **Long-term financing** less **net fixed assets**. *See* equation 3.4 and **liquidity ratio.**

Net loss (1) A negative change in the book value of equity over a period of time.

Net operating cash flow (NOCF) (4) The net cash flow originating from the firm's operating activities during the period under consideration (**cash inflows** from operations minus **cash outflows** from operations). *See* equations 4.1 and 4.3 and Appendix 4.1.

Net operating profit after tax (NOPAT) (4, 15) **Earnings before interest and tax** × (1 – Tax rate). *See* **economic value added.**

Net Operating Profit Less Adjusted Taxes (4) (NOPLAT). Same as **NOPAT**.

Net present value (NPV) (1, 6, 7) The **discounted value** (at the **weighted average cost of capital**) of an investment's future stream of cash flows (**net operating cash flows** less **net capital expenditures**) less the initial cash outlay required to launch the investment. *See* **fundamental finance principle** and **net present value (NPV) rule.**

Net present value (NPV) profile (7) A graphical representation of the changes in the **net present value** of an investment as the **discount rate** varies.

Net present value (NPV) rule (6) If a business proposal has a positive **net present value (NPV)**, it should be carried out because it will increase the firm's value by an amount equal to the proposal's NPV. If a proposal's NPV is negative, it should be rejected.

Net profit (1, 2) A positive change in the book value of equity over a period of time. *See* **earnings after tax.**

Net sales (2) The **revenues** of the accounting period net of any discounts and allowances for defective merchandise and returned items.

Net short-term financing (NSF) (3) Short-term debt less cash. Equals **working capital requirement (WCR)** less **net long-term financing.** Same as the portion of WCR financed with **short-term debt.** *See* equation 3.5.

Net working capital (NWC) (3) **Current assets** less **current liabilities.** *See* equation 3.12.

Net worth (2) *See* **owners' equity.**

NLF (3) *See* net long-term financing.

NOCF (4) *See* net operating cash flow.

Nominal cash flows (8) Cash flows measured in nominal terms, that is, including inflation.

Nominal interest rate (14) The interest rate that a borrower will actually pay, including a premium for the rate of inflation.

Nominal value (of a bond) (9) *See* **face value.**

Noncurrent assets (2) Long-lived **assets** that are not expected to be turned into cash within a year. Same as **long-term financial assets, fixed assets,** or **capital assets.** Can be **tangible** or **intangible assets** as well as financial **assets.**

Noncurrent liabilities (2) Obligations of a firm that are payable after more than one year.

Nondiscretionary cash flows (4) **Cash outflows** that the firm is legally obliged to meet.

NOPAT (4) *See* net operating profit after tax.

NOPLAT (4) *See* net operating profit less adjusted taxes.

Notes payable (2) Bank **overdrafts,** drawings on **lines of credit,** short-term **promissory notes,** and the portion of **long-term debt** due within a year.

NPV (1, 6) *See* net present value.

NSF (3) *See* net short-term financing.

Offer price (13) *See* **ask price.**

Ongoing risk (13) The continuous, unexpected change in the firm's environment that causes its value to rise or fall unpredictably.

Operating activities (3) The activities related to the management of a firm's existing investments to generate sales, profit, and cash.

Operating assets (3) **Assets** related to a firm's **operating cycle,** that is, **trade receivables, inventories,** and the portion of **prepaid expenses** associated with **operating activities.**

Operating cash (3) Amount of cash held by a firm and needed to support its ongoing operations.

Operating cycle (3) The sequence of **operating activities** that begins with the acquisition of raw materials and ends with the collection of cash for the sale of final goods. *See* Exhibit 3.3.

Operating expenses (1) Expenses related to **operating activities,** that is, **cost of goods sold, selling, general, and administrative expenses,** and **depreciation expenses. Operating expenses** *exclude* interest expenses, which are related to financing activities.

Operating exposure (14) Effect of changes in **exchange rates** on the firm's cash flows generated by *future* and *uncertain* transactions. *See* **economic exposure.**

Operating lease (9) A short-term lease for which the length of the contract is shorter than the **useful life** of the **asset** leased.

Operating liabilities (3) **Liabilities** related to a firm's **operating cycle,** that is, **trade payables** and the portion of **accrued expenses** associated with **operating activities.**

Operating profit (2) **Net sales** less **operating expenses.**

Operating profitability (1, 5) The profitability of a firm's operations, which excludes all costs related to financing the firm's activities. *See* **return on invested capital.**

Operating profit margin (5) **Earnings before interest and tax (EBIT)** divided by sales. A measure of profitability.

Operating working capital (1, 3) Same as **working capital requirement.**

Operational risk(s) (13) The risks that arise in the course of implementing a firm's strategy; includes business process risk, commodity price risk, credit risk, legal risk, fiscal risk, and reputational risk. *See* Exhibit 13.2.

Opportunity cost (8) Loss of **revenues** that results from giving up an activity to carry out an alternative one.

Optimal capital structure (1, 11) The **debt-to-equity ratio** that maximizes the market value of the firm's **assets.** *See* **target capital structure.**

Option (contracts) (13) A contract that gives the holder the right (with no obligation) to buy (**call option**) or sell (**put option**) a fixed number of **securities** or a stated amount of currency, at a specified price before (**American option**) or on the **expiration date** (**European option**) of the option.

Option premium (13) The market price of an **option.**

Organized stock exchanges (9) Regulated markets in which **securities** must meet a number of stringent conditions to be listed and traded. *See* **over-the-counter (OTC) markets.**

Original maturity (9) The time between the day a **bond** is issued and the day it is **redeemed** (repaid).

Original price discount (9) The difference between the issuing price of a **bond** and its **face value** when the former is lower.

Originating house (9) The **investment bank** that has initiated and carried out the issuance of **securities** for a firm. Same as **lead manager** or **book runner**. *See* **underwriting syndicate.**

OTC (9) *See* over the counter market.

Outstanding securities (1) **Securities** that have been issued already.

Overdraft (2) A drawing of money against a previously established **line of credit.**

Overhead (expenses) (2) *See* **selling, general, and administrative expenses.**

Over-the-counter (OTC) markets (9) Markets that do not require companies to meet the listing requirements of **organized exchanges.** Stocks are traded through dealers connected by a network of telephones and computers.

Owners' equity (1, 2) The difference, at a particular date, between what a firm's **shareholders** collectively own, called **assets,** and what they owe, called **liabilities.** Same as **net asset value, net worth, shareholders' equity, equity capital,** and **shareholders' funds.**

P&L (1, 2) *See* profit and loss statement.

P/B (12) *See* price-to-book ratio.

P/E (12) *See* price-to-earnings ratio.

Paid-in capital in excess of par (2) The difference between the cumulative amount of cash that the firm received from shares issued up to the date of the **balance sheet** and the cash it would have received if those shares had been issued at **par value.**

Parity relations (14) Relationships linking the **spot exchange rates,** the **forward exchange rates,** the interest rates, and the inflation rates prevailing in two countries. *See* Exhibit 14.1 and Appendix 14.2.

Par value (2, 9) For a share of **stock,** an arbitrary fixed value set when shares are issued. For a **bond,** the fixed amount (**face value**) that has to be paid back to bondholders at the **maturity date** of the **bond.**

Payables (2) *See* **accounts payable.**

Payback period (7) The number of periods (usually years) required for the sum of the project's expected cash flows to equal its initial cash outlay. *See* **payback period rule, cutoff period,** and **discounted payback period.**

Payback period rule (7) Accept (reject) the project if its **payback period** is shorter (longer) than a given **cutoff period.** *See* **discounted payback rule.**

Pecking order (11) Refers to the order in which firms raise **capital,** relying first on **retaining earnings** then issuing debt before finally raising new equity.

Pension liabilities (2) **Liabilities** owed to employees and paid to them when they retire.

Perpetual bond (9) A **bond** that never matures. *See* equation 9.5.

Perpetual cash-flow stream (12) A cash-flow stream with an infinite life.

Perpetuity (6, 9) An **annuity** with an infinite life. *See* Appendix 6.1.

PI (7) *See* profitability index.

Political risk (13) Unexpected government regulations and decisions that constrain the firm's ability to generate profits. *See* Exhibit 13.4.

Preferred stocks (9) A **security** that has a priority over **common stock** in the payment of **dividends** and a prior claim on the firm's **assets** in the event of liquidation, but that has no voting rights. *See* equation 9.6 and Exhibit 9.12.

Premium (from par value) (9) The difference between the price of a **bond** and its **face value,** if the former is higher.

Prepaid expenses (2) Payments made by a firm for goods or services it will receive after the date of the **balance sheet.**

Present value (PV) (1, 6) The value today of an expected future cash-flow stream discounted at a rate that reflects its **risk.** Same as **discounted value.** *See* **discounting.**

Pre-tax operating profit (1) *See* **earnings before interest and tax (EBIT)** and **pre-tax trading profit.**

Pre-tax trading profit (1) *See* **earnings before interest and tax (EBIT)** and **pre-tax operating profit.**

Price risk (9, 13) An unexpected drop in the price of financial assets or **securities (stocks and bonds).** Part of **financial investment risk.** *See* **market risk** Exhibit 13.2.

Price-to-book (P/B) ratio (12) Share price divided by **book value of equity** per share. Same as **market-to-book ratio** and **book value multiple;** used to value a firm. *See* **valuation by comparables.**

Price-to-earnings ratio (P/E ratio) (5, 12) Share price divided by the firm's **earnings per share.** Same as **earnings multiple.** Used to value a firm. *See* **valuation by comparables.**

Primary markets (1, 9) Financial markets in which newly issued **securities** are sold to the public. *See* **secondary markets** and **underwriting.**

Principal (9) *See* **face value.**

Private equity investors (12) Investors who acquire firms privately to improve their performance and resell them at a profit. *See* **leveraged buyouts.**

Private placement (9) The issuance and sale of a firm's **securities** directly to financial institutions and **qualified investors,** thus bypassing the financial markets. *See* **public offering.**

Profitability index (PI) (6, 7) The **present value** of an investment's expected cash-flow stream divided by the investment's initial cash outlay. *See* **profitability index rule.**

Profitability index (PI) rule (7) Accept (reject) the project if its **profitability index** is higher (lower) than one.

Profit and loss (P&L) statement (1, 2) *See* **income statement.**

Profit retention rate (1, 5) **Retained earnings** divided by **net profit.**

Pro forma (statements) (2, 12) **Financial statements** based on estimated, or projected, data.

Project's cost of capital (6, 10) The return expected by investors for the **capital** they supply to fund a specific project. Same as **project's opportunity cost of capital.**

Project's opportunity cost of capital (6) The highest return on an **alternative investment** that must be given up to undertake another investment with the same risk. *See* **project's cost of capital.**

Promissory note (2) A debt **security** acknowledging a **creditor** relationship with the issuing firm and stipulating the conditions and terms under which the money was borrowed.

Property, plant, and equipment (2) **Tangible assets** such as land, buildings, machines, and furniture reported in the firm's **balance sheet** as **fixed assets.**

Prospective multiples (12) *See* **expected multiples.**

Provisions (for bad debt) (15) Provision for possible uncollectibility of **accounts receivable.** Same as **allowance for bad debts.**

Proxies/proxy firms (10) Firms that exhibit the same risk characteristics as a project and that are used to estimate the **project's cost of capital.** Same as **pure-plays/pure-play firms.**

Public offering (9) The issuance and sale of a firm's **securities** not only to its existing **shareholders,** but also to the public at large. Same as **general cash offering.** *See* Exhibit 9.7 and **rights offering.**

Purchases (4) **Cost of goods sold** plus change in **inventories** minus production costs. *See* equations 3.10 and 3.11 and Appendix 4.1.

Purchasing power parity (PPP) relation (14) States that the general cost of living should be the same across countries. *See* equation 14.2, Exhibit 14.1, and Appendix 14.2.

Pure-plays/pure-play firms (10) *See* **proxies/proxy firms.**

Put option (9, 13) A contract that gives the holder the right (with no obligation) to sell a fixed number of shares or a certain amount of currency at a fixed price during the life of the **option** (**American option**) or at the **expiration date** of the **option** (**European option**). *See* **call option.**

PV (1, 6) *See* present value.

Qualified investors (9) Investors who meet some minimum standards set by regulatory authorities that allow them to buy **securities** directly from firms. *See* **private placement.**

Quick assets (3) The sum of cash and **accounts receivable.**

Quick ratio (3) **Cash** plus **accounts receivable** divided by **current liabilities.** Same as **acid test.** A measure of **liquidity.** *See* equation 3.14 and **current ratio.**

Raw materials inventory (2) The cost assigned to materials that have not yet entered the production process at the date of the **balance sheet.**

Real cash flows (8) Cash flows calculated with no adjustment for inflation.

Real interest rate (14) The interest rate adjusted for changes in the cost of living. *See* **nominal interest rate.**

Realization principle (2) The recognition of **revenue** (in an **income statement**) during the period when the transaction generating the **revenue** has taken place, not when the cash generated by the transaction is received.

Recapitalization (1, 5, 11) The substitution of **debt** for **equity,** leaving **assets** unchanged.

Receivables (2) *See* **accounts receivable.**

Redeeming the bond (9) Repaying a **bond's face value** or **call value.**

Redemption value (of a bond) (9) *See* **face value.**

Redemption yield (of a bond) (9) *See* **yield to maturity.**

Reference rate (9) The rate to which the **coupon rate** of a **floating rate bond** is linked.

Refinancing risk (3, 9, 13) Risk arising from the unwillingness of a lender to renew the loans made to finance **assets,** thus forcing the firm to sell part or all of these assets to repay the loan. *See* **financial cost risk** and Exhibit 13.2.

Registered bonds/securities (9) **Bonds/securities** that identify the holder's name. *See* **bearer securities.**

Relevant cash flows (8) Cash flows that are affected by an investment decision.

Relevant costs (8) Costs incurred only if the investment project is undertaken.

Replacement investments (6) Cost saving projects that do not generate extra **cash inflows.**

Replacement value (of an asset) (12) What it would cost today to replace a firm's **assets** with similar ones to start a new business with the same earning power.

Required investments (6) Investments a firm must make to comply with safety, health, and environmental regulations. *See* **replacement** and **expansion investments.**

Reserves (2) The accumulation of **retained earnings** since the creation of the firm.

Residual value (of an asset) (2, 8) The resale, or scrap, value of an **asset.** Same as **salvage value.**

Restrictive covenants (11) *See* **covenants.**

Restructuring plan (12) Changes in a firm's **assets** or financing structures to improve its performance.

Retained earnings (1, 2) The part of a firm's profit that owners decide to invest back into their company. *See* **retention rate.**

Retention rate (5) **Retained earnings** divided by **earnings after tax (EAT).**

Return on assets (ROA) (5) **Earnings after tax (EAT)** divided by **total assets.** A measure of profitability.

Return on business assets (ROBA) (5) **Earnings before interest and tax (EBIT)** divided by **business assets** (**working capital requirement** plus **net fixed assets**). A measure of operating profitability.

Return on capital employed (ROCE) (1) **Net operating profit after tax (NOPAT)** or (**earnings before interest and tax (EBIT)** × (1 – Tax rate)) divided by **capital employed** (equity plus **debt capital**). Equal to **return on invested capital (ROIC).**

Return on capital employed before tax ($ROCE_{BT}$) (5) Same as **return on capital employed** with **earnings before interest and tax** replacing **net operating profit after tax.** Equal to **return on invested capital before tax ($ROIC_{BT}$).**

Return on equity (ROE) (1, 5) **Earnings after tax (EAT)** divided by **owners' equity.** A measure of the firm's profitability to **shareholders.**

Return on invested capital (ROIC) (1, 5, 15) **Net operating profit after tax (NOPAT)** or (**earnings before interest and tax (EBIT)** × (1 – Tax rate)) divided by **invested capital** (**cash** plus **working capital requirement** plus **net fixed assets**). Equal to **return on capital employed (ROCE).**

Return on invested capital before tax ($ROIC_{BT}$) (5) Same as **return on invested capital,** with **earnings before interest and tax** replacing **net oper-**

ating profit after tax. Equal to **return on capital employed before tax** ($ROCE_{BT}$).

Return on investment (ROI) (5) A general measure of profitability that refers to the ratio of a measure of profit to a measure of the investment required to generate that profit.

Return on sales (ROS) (5) **Earnings after tax (EAT)** divided by sales. Same as **net profit margin**. A measure of profitability.

Return on total assets (ROTA) (5) **Earnings before interest and tax** divided by **total assets**. A measure of profitability.

Return spread (15) The difference between a firm's, or a project's, after-tax **return on invested capital (ROIC)** and its **weighted average cost of capital (WACC)**. *See* **economic value added.**

Revenues (1, 2) A firm's activities that result in increases in the value of **owners' equity.**

Revolving credit agreement (9) A legal agreement that a bank will lend a stated maximum amount of money over a fixed but renewable period of time. *See* **line of credit.**

Right (9) The privilege given to existing **shareholders** to buy shares of their firm at a fixed price during a specified period of time. *See* equation 9.3.

Rights offering (9) Offering of a firm's **common stocks** exclusively to its existing stockholders. *See* **subscription price, standby agreement, public offering,** and Exhibit 9.8.

Rights-on shares (9) Shares for which **rights** were issued and which are traded with their rights attached. *See* **ex-rights shares** and equations 9.2 and 9.3.

Risk (1, 6, 13) A term used to describe a situation in which a firm only knows the *expected value* of its future cash-flow stream. *See* **business risk, financial risk,** and Exhibits 13.2 and 13.4.

Risk-averse (investors) (1, 6) Investors who would buy shares of firms with riskier projects only if they expect to earn a higher return to compensate them for the higher **risk** they have to bear.

Risk class (6) A group of investments that exhibit the same risk characteristics.

Risk-free rate (10) The rate of return of a risk-free **asset,** usually government securities. *See* **capital asset pricing model.**

Risk severity (13) A measure of how intense is a risk: minor, important, or major. *See* Exhibit 13.7.

ROA (5) *See* return on assets.

ROBA (5) *See* return on business assets.

ROCE (1) *See* return on capital employed.

ROE (1, 5) *See* return on equity.

ROI (5) *See* return on investment.

ROIC (5) *See* return on invested capital.

$ROIC_{BT}$ (5) *See* return on invested capital before tax.

Rolling over the forward contract (13) Entering into a new **forward contract** after the first contract expires.

ROS (5) *See* return on sales.

ROTA (5) *See* return on total assets.

Sale and leaseback (lease) (9) A **financial lease** under which the **lessee** sells the **asset** to the leasing company which immediately leases it back to the **lessee.**

Salvage value (8, 9) The resale, or scrap, value of an **asset.** Same as **residual value.**

Samurai bonds (9) Yen-denominated **bonds** issued by non-Japanese firms to Japanese investors. *See* **Shogun bonds.**

Seasoned issue (9) When a firm returns to the market after an **initial public offering** for another issue of equity.

Secondary distribution (9) *See* **secondary public offering.**

Secondary market (1, 9) Financial market in which outstanding securities are traded. *See* **primary market.**

Secondary public offering (9) The first-time sale to the public of a relatively large block of equity held by an outside investor who acquired it earlier directly from the firm. Not to be confused with a **seasoned issue.**

Secured bond (9) A **bond** for which the issuer has provided **collateral** to the lender.

Securities and Exchange Commission (SEC) (9) U.S. government agency that approves the issuance and distribution of **securities** and regulates their subsequent trading on public markets.

Securities markets (9) Markets in which **securities** can be traded.

Security (1, 9) Certificate (or a book entry in the security holder's account) issued by a firm that specifies the conditions under which the firm has received the money. *See* **bonds** and **preferred** and **common stocks.**

Security market line (SML) (10) A straight line that relates the expected returns on risky investments to their corresponding risk measured by the **beta coefficient.** *See* Exhibits 10.5 and 10.10, and the **capital asset pricing model.**

Self-liquidating (loans) (9) Short-term bank loans to firms that need to finance the seasonal buildup in their working capital investment and that bankers expect the firm to repay with the cash that will be released by the subsequent reduction in working capital.

Self-sustainable growth rate (SGR) (1, 5, 15) The fastest growth rate a firm can achieve by retaining a constant percentage of its profit, keeping both its operating and financing policies unchanged, and not issuing new equity. Equal to the profit **retention rate** multiplied by **return on equity.** Same as **sustainable growth rate.** *See* equation 5.18.

Selling concession (9) The fee received by the **selling group** for its efforts to sell the **securities** allocated to them by the **underwriter** of an issue. *See* **selling group.**

Selling, general, and administrative expenses (SG&A) (2) Expenses incurred by the firm that relate to the sale of its products and the running of its operations during the **accounting period.**

Selling group (9) A group of **investment banks** that agree to sell for a fee the **securities** allocated to them by the **underwriter** of an issue. *See* **selling concession.**

Senior bond/debt/loan (9, 12) A **bond/**debt/loan that has a claim on the firm's **assets** (in the event of liquidation) that precedes the claim of **junior** or **subordinated debt.**

Settlement date (currency trading) (13) The date at which the delivery of the currencies takes place.

Settlement price (for currency futures contracts) (13) The quote of the last trade of the day for a **currency futures** that is **marked-to-market**.

SG&A (2) *See* selling, general, and administrative expenses.

SGR (5) *See* self-sustainable growth rate.

Share buyback program (15) The buying by a firm of its own shares for the purpose of reducing the number of shares outstanding. Same as **share repurchase program**. The opposite of a new issue of shares.

Shareholders (1, 2) Investors who have bought **common stocks** issued by a firm to raise **equity capital**. Shareholders are the owners of the firm.

Shareholders' equity (2) *See* **owners' equity**.

Shareholders' funds (2) *See* **owners' equity**.

Share repurchase program (12) *See* **share buyback program**.

Shogun bonds (9) **Bonds** issued by non-Japanese firms to Japanese investors and denominated in any currency other than yen. *See* **Samurai bonds**.

Short-term assets (2) *See* **current assets**.

Short-term borrowing/debt/financing (2, 3) Short-term interest-bearing debt that includes bank **overdrafts**, drawings on **lines of credit**, short-term **promissory notes**, and the portion of any long-term debt due within a year.

Short-term liabilities (2) *See* **current liabilities**.

Signaling effects (11) Market reactions to a firm's actions, such as a drop in the firm's share price when the firm skips a dividend payment—an action interpreted by the market as a signal of weakening corporate cash flow.

Sinking fund provision (9) Requires that a **bond** issuing firm set aside cash in a special account according to a regular schedule to allow the firm to redeem the **bond** at **maturity**.

SML (10) *See* security market line.

Social (or societal) risk (13) Unanticipated changes in the behavior and attitudes of employees and consumers that can affect the firm's value.

Solvency (3) A firm's ability to meet its long-term cash obligations. *See* footnote 4.

Special items (2) Extraordinary, exceptional, and nonrecurring losses or gains reported in the firm's **income statement**.

Speculative-grade bonds (9) Corporate **bonds** with ratings below BBB. Same as **junk bonds** or **high-yield bonds**. *See* **bond ratings**.

Spot rate (13) The rate at which a **spot transaction** is executed.

Spot transaction (13) A trade between two parties in which both agree to a currency exchange at a rate fixed now for immediate delivery. *See* **currency forward contract**.

Spread (in floating rate bonds) (9) The difference between the floating **coupon rate** and the **benchmark rate**.

Spread (in underwriting) (9) The difference between the price at which an issue is sold to the public and the price paid by the **underwriter** to the issuing firm.

Stable dividend policy (11) A dividend distribution policy that attempts to maintain a stable **dividend yield** over time.

Stakeholders approach (1) Managing a firm with the objective of balancing out the interests of all its stakeholders: its employees, customers, suppliers, owners, and the community where it is located.

Stand-alone value (1, 12) Estimated value of a **takeover target firm** before the acquiring firm factors in any performance improvements. Same as **as-is value**.

Standby agreement (9) An agreement between a firm and an **underwriting syndicate** of **investment banks** such that the syndicate agrees to buy any shares that have not been sold during the period that a **rights offering** is outstanding.

Standby fee (9) Fee received by **investment banks** for **underwriting** the unsold portion of a **rights issue**.

Stated value (2) An arbitrary fixed value attached to each share of **common stock** when it is issued.

Statement of cash flows (2, 4) **Financial statement**, such as **Financial Accounting Standards Board (FASB)** Standard 95, that provides information about the cash transactions between the firm and the outside world by separating these transactions into cash flows related to operating, investing, and financing activities. *See* **cash-flow statement**.

Statement of shareholders' equity (2) The statement that reports changes in owners' equity other than retained earnings, such as cash dividends, stock issued, and stock repurchased over the accounting period.

Statutory (corporate) tax rate (5) Tax rate on earnings imposed by the tax authority. *See* **effective corporate tax rate**.

Stock (certificate) (9) An equity **security** that recognizes an ownership position in the issuing firm, that provides holders with a claim on the firm's earnings and **assets**, and that entitles holders to vote at shareholder meetings.

Stock exchange (9) An **organized market** in which shares of companies are traded.

Stock markets (9) *See* **stock exchange**.

Straight-line depreciation method (2) **Depreciation** method according to which the firm's **tangible fixed assets** are depreciated by an equal amount each year. *See* **accelerated depreciation method**.

Strategic risk (13) Risk associated with unanticipated changes in the dynamics of a firm's *industry* that may have a negative impact on the firm's market value. *See* Exhibit 13.4.

Strike price (13) *See* **exercise price**.

Subordinated bond/debt/loan (9, 12) **Bond**/debt/loan that has a claim on the firm's **assets** (in the event of liquidation) that follows the claim of **senior debt holders**. Same as **junior bond/debt/loan**.

Subscription price (9) The price at which shares will be sold to existing **shareholders** during a **rights issue**.

Sunk costs (8) Money already spent that cannot be recovered irrespective of future decisions. Same as **irrelevant costs** and **unavoidable costs**.

Sustainable growth rate (1, 5, 15) *See* **self-sustainable growth rate**.

Sweetener (in a convertible bond) (9) The **conversion option** of a **convertible bond**.

Synergy (1, 12) *See* **cost synergies** and **market synergies**.

Systematic risk (10) **Risk** that remains despite the risk-reduction property of diversification. Measured with the **beta coefficient**. Same as **market risk** or **undiversifiable risk**. *See* **capital asset pricing model**.

Takeover premium (12) The difference between the acquisition price paid by the **bidder** and the current market value of the **target firm**.

Take-up fee (9) The discount on the price of the shares offered to the investment bankers engaged in a **standby agreement**.

Tangible assets (2) **Assets** such as land, buildings, machines, and furniture (collectively called property, plant, and equipment) and long-term financial **assets**.

Target capital structure (10, 11) The **debt-to-equity ratio** that maximizes the market value of the firm's **assets**. *See* **optimal capital structure**.

Target firm (12) The firm whose shares the bidder is trying to acquire in a **takeover**.

Tax-effect ratio (5) **Earnings after tax (EAT)** divided by **earnings before tax (EBT)**.

Taxes payable (2) The amount of taxes owed on the date of the **balance sheet**.

Tax shield (4, 11, 12) *See* **interest tax shield**.

Terminal cash flow (8) Cash flow that occurs in the last year of a project.

Terminal value (of a firm) (12) The estimated value that the firm will have at the end of a forecasting period, which is determined by the expected cash flows beyond the forecasting period.

Term loan(s) (9) Medium- to long-term loans extended by banks and insurance companies.

Times-interest-earned ratio (5) The ratio of **earnings before interest and tax (EBIT)** divided by interest expenses. Same as **interest coverage ratio**. A measure of financial leverage based on **income statement** data.

Time value of money (6) Time has value because a dollar received earlier is worth more than a dollar received later.

Top floor financing (12) **Senior collateralized debt** in a **leverage buyout (LBO)**.

Total net cash flow (4) The difference between the total amount of dollars received (**cash inflows**) and the total amount of dollars paid out (**cash outflows**) over a period of time.

Tracking stock (9) A special class of common stock carrying claims on the cash flows of a particular segment of a company, such as a subsidiary, division, or business unit.

Trade creditors (1, 2) *See* **accounts payable**.

Trade debtors (1, 2) *See* **accounts receivable**.

Trade-off model of capital structure (1, 11) **Optimal capital structure** reached by means of a trade-off between the **present value** of the **interest tax shield** and the present value of **financial distress costs**.

Trade payables (1, 2) *See* **accounts payable**.

Trade receivables (1, 2) *See* **accounts receivable**.

Trailing multiples (12) *See* **historical multiples**.

Transactions cost (9) Cost incurred when buying or selling an **asset** or a **security**.

Transaction exposure (14) *See* **contractual exposure**.

Transaction loan (9) A one-time loan used to finance a specific, nonrecurrent need.

Translation exposure (14) *See* **accounting exposure**.

Transparency (11) Providing complete information about a firm's operations and future prospects to its (outside) **shareholders**.

Treasury stock (2) The amount that a firm has spent to repurchase its own shares up to the date of the **balance sheet**.

Trust/trustee (9) A third party (usually a financial institution) that ensures that the issuer of a **bond** meets all the conditions and **provisions** reported in the bond's **indenture**.

Unavoidable costs (8) Costs incurred regardless of whether the investment is undertaken. Same as **irrelevant costs** or **sunk costs**.

Undervaluation hypothesis (12) **Takeover** rationale according to which the acquiring company has superior skills in finding undervalued **target firms** that can be bought cheaply.

Underwriter (9) **Investment bank** that buys the **securities** a firm wants to issue and then resells them to the public at a higher price.

Underwriting syndicate (9) A group of **investment banks** jointly **underwriting** an issue.

Undiversifiable risk (10) Same as **nondiversifiable risk**. *See* **systematic risk**.

Unlevered asset value (12) The estimated value of **assets** assuming they are financed only with **equity capital**. *See* **adjusted present value**.

Unlevered beta (10) *See* **asset beta**.

Unlevered cost of equity (12) The **cost of equity** of an all-equity financed firm. Can be estimated with the **capital asset pricing model** using the firm's **asset beta**.

Unlevered firm (5) A firm without borrowed funds, or an all-equity-financed firm.

Unlisted securities (9) **Securities** of firms that do not meet the listing requirements of **organized exchanges**.

Unsecured bond/debt/loan (9, 12) **Bond**/debt/loan supported only by the general credit standing of the issuing firm.

Unsystematic risk (10) Risk that can be eliminated through portfolio diversification. Same as **diversifiable risk** or company specific risk.

Useful life (8) *See* **economic life**.

Valuation by comparables (12) A valuation method that uses financial data for firms similar to the business or firm to be valued to estimate the market value of its equity or its **enterprise value**. For example, the estimated equity value of a firm is equal to its **earnings after tax (EAT)** multiplied by the **earnings multiple** (or **price-to-earnings [P/E] ratio**) of the comparable firm.

Value-based management (system) (1, 15) Managing a firm's resources with the goal of increasing the firm's market value.

Variable rate bond (9) A **bond** with a **coupon rate** that takes different (known) values during the **bond's** life.

Venture capital firm (9, 12) An investment firm specializing in the financing of small and new ventures.

Vertical merger (12) For example, the integration of a car manufacturer with its major supplier or its major distributor.

Volatility (of an asset) (10) Unpredictable fluctuations in the market price of an **asset**.

WACC (1, 10, 12) *See* weighted average cost of capital.

Wages payable (2) The amount of wages owed and not yet paid at the date of the **balance sheet**.

Warrants (9) **Call options** sold by a firm that give the holder the right (with no obligation) to buy a specific number of the firm's shares of **common stock** at a fixed price during the life of the **warrant**. *See* **contingent value rights**.

WCR (3) *See* working capital requirement.

Weighted average cost of capital (WACC) (1, 10, 12) The weighted average of the after-tax **cost of debt** and **cost of equity**. The minimum rate of return a project must generate in order to meet the return expectations of its suppliers of **capital** (lenders and **shareholders**). *See* equations 10.12 and 10.13, and **hurdle rate**.

With/without principle (8) States that the **cash flows** that are relevant to an investment decision are only those that increase or decrease the firm's overall cash position if the investment is undertaken.

Working capital requirement (WCR) (1, 3) The difference between **operating assets** (**trade receivables**, **inventories**, and **prepaid expenses**) and **operating liabilities** (**trade payables** and **accrued expenses**). WCR measures the firm's net investment in its **operating cycle**.

Work-in-process inventory (2) The cost of the raw materials that were used in the production of unfinished units plus labor costs and other costs allocated to these units.

Writer (of an option) (13) The party who sells the underlying **asset** in an **option contract**. Same as the seller of an **option**.

Yankee bonds (9) **Bonds** issued by foreign firms in the United States, denominated in U.S. dollars or other currencies.

Yield spread (9) The difference between the **market yield** on a nongovernment bond and the yield on a government **bond** with the same **maturity** and currency denomination.

Yield to maturity (9, 10) The rate that makes the **bond** price equal to the present value of the **bond's** future cash-flow stream.

Zero-coupon bond (9) A **bond** with no **coupon payments** that is sold at an original discount from face value. *See* equation 9.4.

INDEX

Present value of an annuity of $1 for *n* periods at discount rate *k*

Period (*n*)	Discount Rate (*k*) 1%	2%	3%	4%	5%	6%	7%	8%	9%	10%
1	0.99010	0.98039	0.97087	0.96154	0.95238	0.94340	0.93458	0.92593	0.91743	0.90909
2	1.97040	1.94156	1.91347	1.88609	1.85941	1.83339	1.80802	1.78326	1.75911	1.73554
3	2.94099	2.88388	2.82861	2.77509	2.72325	2.67301	2.62432	2.57710	2.53129	2.48685
4	3.90197	3.80773	3.71710	3.62990	3.54595	3.46511	3.38721	3.31213	3.23972	3.16987
5	4.85343	4.71346	4.57971	4.45182	4.32948	4.21236	4.10020	3.99271	3.88965	3.79079
6	5.79548	5.60143	5.41719	5.24214	5.07569	4.91732	4.76654	4.62288	4.48592	4.35526
7	6.72819	6.47199	6.23028	6.00205	5.78637	5.58238	5.38929	5.20637	5.03295	4.86842
8	7.65168	7.32548	7.01969	6.73274	6.46321	6.20979	5.97130	5.74664	5.53482	5.33493
9	8.56602	8.16224	7.78611	7.43533	7.10782	6.80169	6.51523	6.24689	5.99525	5.75902
10	9.47130	8.98259	8.53020	8.11090	7.72173	7.36009	7.02358	6.71008	6.41766	6.14457
11	10.36763	9.78685	9.25262	8.76048	8.30641	7.88687	7.49867	7.13896	6.80519	6.49506
12	11.25508	10.57534	9.95400	9.38507	8.86325	8.38384	7.94269	7.53608	7.16073	6.81369
13	12.13374	11.34837	10.63496	9.98565	9.39357	8.85268	8.35765	7.90378	7.48690	7.10336
14	13.00370	12.10625	11.29607	10.56312	9.89864	9.29498	8.74547	8.24424	7.78615	7.36669
15	13.86505	12.84926	11.93794	11.11839	10.37966	9.71225	9.10791	8.55948	8.06069	7.60608
16	14.71787	13.57771	12.56110	11.65230	10.83777	10.10590	9.44665	8.85137	8.31256	7.82371
17	15.56225	14.29187	13.16612	12.16567	11.27407	10.47726	9.76322	9.12164	8.54363	8.02155
18	16.39827	14.99203	13.75351	12.65930	11.68959	10.82760	10.05909	9.37189	8.75563	8.20141
19	17.22601	15.67846	14.32380	13.13394	12.08532	11.15812	10.33560	9.60360	8.95011	8.36492
20	18.04555	16.35143	14.87747	13.59033	12.46221	11.46992	10.59401	9.81815	9.12855	8.51356